JOHN XXIII

JOHN XXIII

The Official Biography

By Mario Benigni and Goffredo Zanchi

Translated by Elvira DiFabio
Professor of Romance Languages, Harvard University
with Julia Mary Darrenkamp, FSP

BOOKS & MEDIA

BOSTON

Library of Congress Cataloging-in-Publication Data

Benigni, Mario.
  [Giovanni XXIII. English]
  John XXIII / by Mario Benigni and Goffredo Zanchi ; translated by
Elvira Di Fabio.
     p. cm.
  Includes bibliographical references.
  ISBN 0-8198-3971-X
  1. John XXIII, Pope, 1881–1963. 2. Popes—Biography. I. Zanchi,
Goffredo. II. Title.

  BX1378.2 .B4313 2001
  282'.092—dc21
  [B]

                      2001001732

Cover design: Helen Rita Lane, FSP

Printed and published in the U.S.A. by Pauline Books & Media, 50 Saint Pauls Avenue, Boston MA 02130-3491.

www.pauline.org

Pauline Books & Media is the publishing house of the Daughters of St. Paul, an international congregation of women religious serving the Church with the communications media.

1 2 3 4 5 6 7 8 9 10   09 08 07 06 05 04 03 02 01

Contents

PART I

Bergamo
1881–1921

PART II

IN THE SERVICE OF THE HOLY SEE
1921–1953

FOREWORD BY
LORIS FRANCESCO CAPOVILLA

On September 3, 2000, Pope John Paul II beatified his predecessor, Pope John XXIII, who, on the threshold of his eightieth birthday, had written the following reflection on his life:

> Retreating into myself and reflecting on the various events in my humble life, I recognize that the Lord exempted me from the tribulations that make service to truth, justice, and charity so difficult and demanding for many people. I lived through my infancy and youth without noticing the poverty, without worrying about family, studies, or dangerous circumstances such as those I faced, for example, during my military service at the age of twenty, and during the Great War…. Little and humble as I acknowledge myself to be, I was always warmly welcomed wherever I went, from the seminary in Bergamo and later in Rome; through the ten years of my priestly life near my bishop in my native city; from 1921 until now, 1961, that is from Rome and back to Rome, as far as the Vatican. O good God, how do I thank you for the gracious manner in which I was received wherever I went in your name, always in pure obedience, not to do my own, but your will?[1]

This paragraph from his *Journal of a Soul* must be reflected on as the summary of John XXIII's life, his inherent religious spirit, the kindness showed him, and his willingness to do everything and risk everything so that God's will might be completely fulfilled in him. He attested to this, at the age of eighty, fully aware that his life had developed like a ball of yarn, under the signs of simplicity and purity.[2]

This should be kept in mind above all when one reads in the biography of his difficulties and misfortunes, which are part of everyone's daily life and are to be judged in the light of faith and of the necessary norms of Christian asceticism.

On November 18, 1965, Pope Paul VI communicated to the Council Fathers his approval for the opening of the cause for the beatification and canonization of John XXIII. That day, as prelate of the antechamber, I was next to the pope. I remember the look that he directed toward me; I can still hear the words he spoke to me, before and after, with such kindness and solemnity. While applause resounded throughout the Vatican hall, I asked the Prefect of the Pontifical House if I might absent myself from the assembly. Then I went down to the Vatican grottoes and poured out my feelings, recalling Paul VI's words a few hours after his election, "I accepted in order to continue the work begun by Pope John."

First from Rome, then from Abruzzo, from the Marches, and from Bergamo, I collaborated with the postulator of the case, the late Father Antonio Cairoli; then with Father Juan Folguera y Trapet, the postulator from 1989, also is also now deceased; and finally, with Father Luca De Rosa, who concluded the long canonical process.

I could not have imagined in 1965 that Providence would allow me to see the day — December 20, 1999 — when the decree of Pope John's heroic virtues was read, and the day — January 27, 2000 — when the decree of the authentic miracle obtained through the intercession of the venerable servant of God was made public. I lived these two events in the silence of Camaitino, Roncalli's old residence, a beloved sanctuary and a treasury of Pope John's memories.

When I was encouraged from all sides to express my sentiments, nothing else came to my lips but to give "thanks to God the Father at all times and for everything in the name of our Lord Jesus Christ" (Eph 5:20). I thank all of those who cooperated in placing the torch on the candelabrum (cf. 1 Mc 4:50). First of all Pius XII who, in raising Angelo Giuseppe Roncalli to the College of Cardinals and in making him Patriarch of Venice, gave him the opportunity to render great service to the Church. Then Paul VI and John Paul II, whose personal testimony seals and authenticates that of others. And also to the Roncalli family who impressed upon Angelo Giuseppe both human and Christian virtues, treasuring St. Augustine's thought, which was repeatedly cited by Pope John.

"Sacred Scripture teaches us that we must praise not only the life, but also the parents of great persons. In this way it can be said that, in those whom we wish to exalt, the purity which they inherited shines through." The venerated Pope John commented on these words on June 23, 1960: "What consolation it is for a clergyman, as a humble servant, to be able to pass on what he has received from his parents and from his family."

Gratitude also goes to the clergy and laity who accepted and understood him, who supported his religious and pastoral objectives in the spirit of the motto which he coined and honored: *Fedeltà e rinnovamento* (fidelity and renewal). Many names come to mind, especially that of Archbishop Angelo Dell'Acqua, deputy of the secretary of state, and Bishop Alfredo Cavagno, his confessor and confidant — both incomparable collaborators and loyal counselors.

As far as I am concerned, as the scribe and chronicler, I feel like the great St. John the Baptist, who said, "Now my joy is complete. He must increase, while I must decrease" (Jn 3:29–30).

There is nothing astonishing in Paul VI's decision to open John XXIII's cause. The book *Papa Giovanni nella mente e nel cuore del suo Successore* (Pope John in the mind and heart of his successors)[3] contains many statements of Paul VI that show how he interpreted the affection, devotion, and recognition bestowed on Pope John, which was demonstrated by both Christians and non-Christians alike, and by his trusted friends from every part of the world. In fact, despite some voices to the contrary, Paul VI immediately understood that "such a spontaneous current as the one manifested on Pentecost 1963 cannot be reversed."[4]

Unlike those who were timid and frightened, Montini seized the line that had been thrown to him by the captain who was in the act of bringing the boat to the open sea. He believed that "the moment had come to recognize the signs of the times, to seize the opportunities, and look high and wide" (May 24, 1963). It never crossed his mind to turn back, as some would have wanted. "The new pope had to respond to the previous pontificate with prudence and strength; above all on an essential point — the opening to the East. Before it was too late, the new pope had to continue what John XXIII had begun."[5]

With wise determination, Montini continued to navigate along the indicated course, which ultimately led to the great event of December 1, 1989 when, before the entire world and supported by the Orthodox

Church of Russia, Mikhail Gorbachev met with John Paul II. Both men desired to meet not for economic or political reasons, but in obedience to the God who works in the human conscience. They met with the conviction that they could begin a new course in human relations…in order to construct "a new order founded on the truth, built according to justice, enlivened and integrated by charity and placed into effect by freedom."[6]

Following the example of Jesus, even in anticipating the cross —not usually a part of our natural human makeup — Montini and Wojtyla decided to take the barque of Peter out to the open sea and go beyond, far beyond Roncalli's initiatives. So it was. Moreover, the events of the Jubilee Year of 2000 prove not so much that the prophet was inspired as that he was obedient:

> In taking his leave, he was able to affirm like his Master: "Peace I leave with you; peace, my peace I give to you. I do not give to you as the world gives" (Jn 14:27). But Pope John was leaving his peace to the modern world, to the world of Nietzsche and Marx, which has in fact not abandoned hope. He was the greatest of the six popes under whom I have lived, perhaps the holiest. Through him, the advancement of history has become the advancement of grace.[7]

For Paul VI, the crystal-clear example of Pope John's life was a signal not so much for our admiration as for our imitation. He said as much during the funeral celebration in the Duomo of Milan:

> Will we ever be able to abandon roads so skillfully traced, even for the future? That must never be thought! Faithfulness to the great directives of his pontificate will perpetuate his remembrance and his glory, and will make him seem ever more fatherly and closer to us.[8]

Popes differ from one another by nature, education, culture, experience, and personal charisms. Over the centuries, not all of them have shone brightly with holiness. The popes of the modern era carry with and within themselves the legacy of the reformers from the twelfth to the fifteenth centuries and the Council of Trent. In the nineteenth and twentieth centuries, the popes have responded with generosity to the "Follow me" (Jn 21:19) that Jesus directed to Peter; they followed him faithfully and traveled the path of holiness.

St. Thérèse of Lisieux, who earned the title of doctor of spiritual childhood, died three years before the Jubilee at the beginning of the twentieth century, which saw many pilgrims to the Eternal City, among them the 19-year-old Angelo Giuseppe Roncalli. Thérèse's arrival on the spiritual scene with her "little way" amazed Leo XIII and Pius X, moved the heart of Pius XI and inspired the writer, Georges Bernanos: "Saints and heroes are men (and women) who have never left childhood, but who, little by little, enlarged it to the measure of their destiny."[9]

This biography enables the reader to follow Roncalli's simple yet remarkable life, which was marked by docile obedience to God's will and a faithful following of the Gospel path identified with the "little way" of Thérèse of Lisieux.

At several points the reader may ask if Roncalli — the diocesan priest in Bergamo, papal representative in the East and West, papal nuncio in France, Patriarch of Venice, and finally, pope of the Universal Church — could possibly have taken upon himself more than he did; if he could have done more, or if he could have done it better. Of course the answer is yes, because even the just man is "subject to weakness" (Heb 5:2) and "falls seven times...[and] rises again" (Prov 24:16). Free will, even when sustained by divine grace, does not erase human limitations, natural defects, flaws of upbringing, and sensitivity. I found answers to my own questions about this in an excellent essay by Madeleine Delbrêl who interpreted the amazement of the first commentators on the election of a 77-year-old pope:

John XXIII, the teacher whom we did not expect, led us back to where we needed to return to: nursery school. He stretched out his arms to the whole world and drew it close to himself. He was everyone's neighbor and he left to Providence what he could not do for all classes of people, all races, and the masses. He embraced modern technology, which gave him a voice to be able to reach every person, to the four corners of the earth, because God is a father to everyone.

He was the humble, faithful, and resounding witness to the fatherly goodness of God. He belonged to God just as every living person does. He took his place, among all the people God created, as a real person. He made us understand that only our resistance can imprison Christ's mission. However, this mission is set free when the one who carries it within obeys the one who gave it.

He reminded us that if the Gospel of Christ is to be announced in human tongues, then it cannot be separated from the very language of Jesus Christ, which is the language of goodness. He reminded us that goodness — so undervalued in the world and even among ourselves — is the flesh of charity. After his first few weeks as pope, many of us began to realize how evangelically illiterate we were. He spoke to us of the works of mercy as if of a form of knowledge from nursery school. As for us, we no longer even knew its name. But when he practiced one of those works of mercy, non-believers in front of their television sets, in front of their radios, in front of their newspapers marveled as if they were before some unknown phenomenon.[10]

Benigni and Zanchi, both of Bergamo, priests formed like Roncalli, alumni of the same seminary, analyzed the archival documents and Roncalli's personal notebooks, especially the *Journal of a Soul*. They read and understood, interpreted and translated his thoughts and projects, and placed in perspective the often-misleading anecdotes. They read Pope John's life not as if under a microscope in a laboratory, but as the early monks would read their ancient manuscripts with faith and gladness. Benigni and Zanchi have revealed the transparency of Pope John's soul, the innocence and beauty of his eyes, and the purity of his great heart.

Last March 24, I received a phone call from a young Hindu Indian studying at the prestigious university of Harvard. He told me he had learned Italian just to be able to understand the core of the thought of Pope John — that man not confined within the space of the Mediterranean basin; a Christian who at the beginning of his pontificate declared with charming simplicity, "All the world is my family." This student also told me that to better prepare himself for his doctoral dissertation, he keeps in mind Pope John's final lesson:

For the benefit of the whole world we deal with matters of the greatest importance, taking our inspiration from the Lord's will. Now more than ever, and certainly more than in centuries past, we intend to serve man as he is, not just Catholics; to defend above all and everywhere the rights of all human beings, not only those of the Catholic Church. Contemporary circumstances, the needs of the last fifty years, doctrinal deepening, have placed a new reality before our eyes. As I said in my discourse at the opening of the Council, it is not the Gospel that has changed, it is we who begin to understand it better. One who has lived longer, who was alive at the beginning of the century faced with the new demands of social action that empowers every man; one who has been, as I was, in the East for twenty years and in France for eight and was able to compare diverse cultures and traditions, knows that the moment has arrived to recognize the signs of the times, to seize the opportunities, and to look far beyond (May 24, 1963).

Benigni and Zanchi help us to look at John XXIII with at least the same admiration of the young Indian student, a noble representative of an immense nation to which Roncalli turned his prophetic gaze:

> The great peoples of Central Asia and of the Far East, whose lights of civilization doubtless preserve the traces of the original Divine Revelation, will be called one day by Providence — I turned toward it as a hidden voice of the Spirit — to allow themselves to be penetrated by the light of the Gospel, which blazed from the shores of Galilee, opening a new era of history not to a people, or to a group of nations, but to all the world.[11]

John XXIII! He was a pope with open eyes and an open heart, a pope of a tradition far richer and more fruitful than we can imagine, a pope who reached considerable heights on the mount of the Beatitudes.

As his beatification drew near, I read again his notebook, containing "scattered notes," in which he had written:

> Eulogy for Pope St. Eugene (654–657) from the breviary of June 2:
> *He was a benevolent man, meek and approachable and, what matters most, renowned for holiness of life.* Wouldn't it be wonderful to get at least that far?

St. Eugene's service at the imperial court in Constantinople, his unique election to the papacy, his human and pastoral qualities, and his sufferings for Christ and for purity of doctrine certainly inspire the question, "Wouldn't it be wonderful to get at least that far?"

That question seals this biography and makes it precious. In it the reader will likely discover the key to reading ancient and recent texts, to a faith more solid than rock, to an invincible hope, to a charity without limits. In it the reader encounters the biblical breadth of Roncalli's copious discourses, writings, and activities to the point of feeling encouraged to emulate "the simplicity of speech and of heart"[12] that led Pope John "at least that far"; that is, to benevolence, to meekness, to holiness of life.

Sotto il Monte, May 15, 2000
Thirty-ninth anniversary of the encyclical *Mater et Magistra*

EDITOR'S NOTE TO THE ENGLISH EDITION

This volume is the official biography of Pope John XXIII inasmuch as it was written under the auspices and direction of the Diocese of Bergamo. As Pope John's home diocese, Bergamo introduced his cause for beatification and promoted its progress.

As their primary sources in preparing this work for publication, the authors consulted the mountains of data gathered for the cause of beatification and the unedited correspondence preserved in the archives of the seminary at Bergamo. The result is a work of extraordinary reliability and, because it closely follows the writings of Pope John, one that becomes a guide to his soul.

Editor's Note

The idea for this book was conceived by Monsignor Mario Benigni, vice-postulator of the cause for the beatification of John XXIII. Benigni died on May 12, 2000, after a long illness. When he had been diagnosed with his illness, he requested and obtained the help of Professor Goffredo Zanchi of the seminary of Bergamo. These two historians then divided their work: Benigni would treat the life of Roncalli up to the end of his nunciature in Paris (1881–1953), and Professor Zanchi would write of Roncalli's years as Patriarch of Venice and as pope (1954–1963). Professor Zanchi deserves much gratitude for having completed his part within the established timeframe. Benigni managed to finish the chapter on Roncalli's diplomatic mission in Bulgaria, but as his illness progressed, he was unable to complete his work. He obtained the assistance of Dr. Gilberto Gilberti and Dr. Marco Roncalli for chapters eleven and twelve.

Monsignor Benigni wanted his biography of Pope John to have the unique characteristic of a narrative, similar in style to Augustine's *Confessions,* since he had at his disposal the abundant autobiographical material used in Roncalli's *Journal of a Soul,* as well as letters from his vast correspondence.

It was unfortunate that Benigni, who knew Pope John's writings so well, could not complete his work, but the current volume is entirely due to his expertise. If the reader notes a kind of elusiveness, it is because the author could not reread the text. The originality of the work makes it unique within the panorama of publications dedicated to Pope John on the occasion of his beatification — yet another reason to express gratitude to Monsignor Benigni.

The present work owes much to the Diocese of Bergamo and its bishop, Roberto Amadei. Particular gratitude is also due to Monsignor Loris F. Capovilla, who was so generous in his direction and suggestions. Thanks to their support, this work is an invaluable contribution to the study of the life, the works, and the times of the new Blessed Pope John.

CHRONOLOGY

Main Events in the Life of Pope John XXIII

Youth and Seminarian

1881

- Angelo Giuseppe Roncalli is born at Sotto il Monte, Bergamo, November 25

1888

- Makes his first confession at the end of the year

1889

- Receives the Sacrament of Confirmation at Carvico from Bishop Gaetano Camillo Guindani, February 13
- Recieves First Communion at the Church of St. Mary in Brusicco, March 31

1892–1895

- Studies at the minor seminary of Bergamo

1895–1900

- Studies at the major seminary of Bergamo
- Receives clerical habit and first tonsure, June 24

1896

- Begins *Journal of a Soul*
- Receives minor orders of porter and lector, July 3
- Don Francesco Rebuzzini dies, September 25

1899

- Receives minor orders of exorcist and acolyte, June 25
- Makes Holy Year pilgrimage to Rome in September

1901

- Begins studies at the major Roman Seminary, January 4
- Receives degree in theology, June 25
- Wins an award for proficiency in the Hebrew language
- Enters military service in Bergamo, November 30

1902

- Receives military promotion to Sergeant, November 30
- Resumes studies at the Roman Seminary

1903

- Roncalli is ordained subdeacon at the Basilica of St. John Lateran by Cardinal Respighi, Vicar General to the Pope, April 11
- Ordained deacon at Basilica of St. John Lateran by Cardinal Respighi, December 18

1904

- Receives doctorate in sacred theology, July 13

Priest

1904

- Roncalli is ordained to the priesthood by Bishop Giuseppe Ceppetelli, August 10

1905

- Appointed secretary to Bishop Giacomo M. Radini Tedeschi, January 29
- Makes his first pastoral visit with Bishop Radini Tedeschi, December 8

1906

- Begins teaching Church history in the diocesan seminary, October 22 (later teaches apologetics and patrology as well)

1908

- Begins the historical research and account of the apostolic visit of St. Charles Borromeo to Bergamo

1909

- Becomes member of editorial staff of *La Vita Diocesana,* January

1910

- Named secretary for the thirty-third Synod of the diocese of Bergamo, April 26–28
- Named president of the fifth division of Catholic Action, October 20

1911

- Becomes a member of the Diocesan Congregation of the Priests of the Sacred Heart, November 6

1914
- Death of Bishop Radini Tedeschi, August 22

1915
- Begins conscripted service in the army, May 24

1916
- Roncalli publishes his volume: *In memoria di Msgr. Giacomo Radini Tedeschi, vescovo di Bergamo* (In memory of Msgr. Giacomo Radini Tedeschi, bishop of Bergamo), Società Editrice S. Alessandro, Bergamo, August 22

1918
- Roncalli completes his military service, December 10
- Becomes spiritual director at the seminary of Bergamo

1921
- Returns to Rome to begin work at the Sacred Congregation for the Propagation of the Faith, January 18

1924
- Made professor of patrology at the Lateran University, November

Bishop

1925
- Pius XI appoints Roncalli apostolic visitor in Bulgaria
- Roncalli is raised to the episcopate with the title of Archbishop of Areopolis, March 3
- Consecrated bishop by Cardinal Giovanni Tacci, March 19

1931

- Pius XI appoints Roncalli first apostolic delegate to Bulgaria, September 26

1934

- Appointed apostolic delegate to Turkey and Greece, November 24

1944

- Pius XII appoints Roncalli apostolic nuncio in France, December 22
- Roncalli arrives at Orly airport, Paris, December 30

1953

- Roncalli is made a cardinal, January 12
- Pius XII appoints Roncalli the Patriarch of Venice, March 15

Pope

1958

- Death of Pius XII, October 9
- Roncalli is elected pope and takes the name of John XXIII, October 28
- Solemn Coronation, November 4

1959

- Pope John XXIII announces the Synod for the Roman Diocese and a Council for the Universal Church at the Benedictine monastery of St. Paul, January 25
- The pope issues his first encyclical, *Ad Petri Cathedram,* June 29
- The pope issues the encyclical, *Sacerdotii Nostri Primordia,* for the centenary of the death of the saintly Curé d'Ars, August 1

- John XXIII issues the encyclical, *Grata Ricordatio,* on devotion to the Holy Rosary, September 26
- The pope issues the encyclical, *Princeps Pastorum,* for the fortieth anniversary of *Maximum illud* of Benedict XV, November 28

1961

- Pope John XXIII issues the encyclical, *Mater et Magistra,* for the seventieth anniversary of Leo XIII's encyclical *Rerum Novarum,* May 15
- The pope issues the encyclical, *Aeterna Dei Sapientia,* for the fifteenth centenary of the death of St. Leo the Great, November 11
- Promulgates the Apostolic Letter, *Humanae Salutis,* announcing the Second Vatican Ecumenical Council, December 25

1962

- Pope John issues the encyclical, *Paenitentiam Agere,* calling for fervent prayer and penance for the success of the Council, July 1
- Pope John manifests the first signs of his grave illness, September 23
- The Second Vatican Ecumenical Council opens, October 11
- John XXIII preaches a sermon in St. Peter's to close the first session of the Council, December 8

1963

- Pope John issues the encyclical, *Pacem in Terris,* April 11
- Pope John XXIII dies at 7:49 P.M., June 3

1999

- Decree of the heroic virtues of Pope John XXIII, December 20

2000

- Decree of an authentic miracle obtained through the intercession of the Venerable Servant of God, Pope John XXIII, January 2000
- Beatification of Pope John XXIII, September 3

2001

- The body of Blessed John XXIII is exhumed and found to be perfectly preserved, January 16
- Blessed John XXIII's incorrupt body is displayed in St. Peter's Square exactly 38 years after his death, June 3

PART I

BERGAMO
1881–1921

Mario Benigni

CHAPTER 1

THE RONCALLI FAMILY

"It certainly is of some interest to research just who the Roncallis were, from what family branch such a precious bud was to blossom."[1] So begins the autobiographical notes of John XXIII who wrote of himself in the third person. In 1959, he began a draft that went only as far as the year 1904. In 1964, these notes containing information about his ancestry were published as an appendix to the first edition of the celebrated *Journal of a Soul and Other Devotional Writings*. The accuracy of this information is confirmed by studies of the genealogy of the Roncalli family[2] and by recent unpublished research from the archives of Bergamo.[3] The family's story is therefore recounted as it came from the author's pen.

The family name of Roncalli is found in the oldest pages of Bergamasque history, especially in the Valle Imagna and particularly in the townships of Corna and Cepino. Each of these locations has a hamlet that is called a *roncaglia* (derived perhaps from the word *ronchi* — in the local dialect, *ruc* or *roncai* — a typical terrace cut into the mountainside to cultivate vineyards).

Each township has some documents about the *de Roncalli* or *de Ronchali* line, dating as far back as the beginning of the 1300s. From the line of the Roncaglis of Cepino in the fifteenth century, a certain Martino Roncalli, also known as Maitino, went to Sotto il Monte where he built his home at the foot of the hill.

Today, Sotto il Monte is more than just a town, but still a group of farms and villages spread out along the hills and the plains, sloping down from Canto Basso toward the Adda River. Each isolated dwelling and group of houses has a name. The one built by Martino Roncalli, *dictus Maytinus,* the newcomer to Sotto il Monte from the Valle Imagna, was immediately called *Camaitino,* and that name has remained.

A document dated August 26, 1418 that mentions Martino Roncalli *(Martinus dictus Maytinus filius quondam Tomasi de Roncallis)* appears among the acts of the notary Gualmino de Grecis, and is kept in the Episcopal archive of Bergamo. Other details are learned from the notarial documents of Giovanni da Corte dated September 8, 1429; Gianfranco Salvetti, March 22, 1429; and Gian Antonio Vavassori da Medolago, March 16, 1443.

Apparently, Martino had three children — Tonolo, Pedrino, and Giovanni. Historical sources show that the Roncalli family extended throughout Sotto il Monte and from there expanded into the surrounding area of Bergamo.

The family members, who separated from the original clan and dispersed throughout Bergamo and other parts of Italy, took various nicknames. Therefore, in addition to the Maytinis of Sotto il Monte, there were the Roncalli Bragini, the Piretti, the Parolini, the Frosio, and the Quadri clans, who settled in Bergamo, Brescia, Udine, Rovigo, Tuscany, Foligno, Rome, and Venice.

The first house built by Martino, or *Maytino* (the first Roncalli in Sotto il Monte, also called Berzio), still exists. Over the centuries, it has had various owners: the Roncalli, De Vecchi, Macassoli, Mangili, and Scotti families. The last owners rented the house to Monsignor Roncalli for more than thirty years, from 1925–1958, as a summer home.

When the prelate took up residence there, and the restoration process was underway, frescoes were discovered on a wall that was probably once the external facade of the original building. The images, dating from the fifteenth century, depict St. Bernardine; the great saint of that century, St. Anthony the Abbot; and a Madonna and Child. This was crowned by a family coat of arms in which appears a field tower with white and red bands — exactly like that of Maytini of Sotto il Monte. With few additions, the same crest became the coat of arms of the archbishop, patriarch, cardinal, and then Supreme Pontiff, Angelo Giuseppe Roncalli, who took the name John XXIII.

Quartered by St. Mark's coat of arms, this papal crest reflects the passion of a man who lovingly researched the history of his birthplace as a scholar rather than an opportunist desiring to lay claim to noble origins. What is evident here is the gusto of a person who loves to feel rooted to his native land and not one searching for heraldic glory. It is certain that the family of Pope Roncalli had honored and worthy origins that date back to the beginning of the fifteenth century and the first Roncalli of Sotto il Monte. The family can be traced back to a certain Bonadio in the middle of the thirteenth century, and then a Teubaldo who appears from 1257–1285. The family line descends uninterruptedly until 1616. At that point, the parochial archives note the names of Donato (1616), Donato (1637), Giovanni (1659), Bartolomeo (1682), Giovanni Battista (1714), Antonio (1735), Giuseppe (1768), Giovanni Battista (1797), Angelo (1826), and Giovanni Battista (1854), the father of Pope John XXIII.

Angelo Roncalli was always convinced of these facts. In 1929, the parish priest of Sotto il Monte asked Roncalli for his advice about new names for the districts of the town. Roncalli affirmed categorically, "Maitino was the first of the Roncalli ancestors to come to Sotto il Monte. There are 500-year-old documents which mention him. He is the progenitor of all the Roncalli family of Sotto il Monte and perhaps of all those of Isola.... No, let's not touch the poor, dear *Martinus Roncalli dictus Maytinus*. His district will end up being the most noble of the town."[4]

Sotto il Monte

Sotto il Monte, the land of San Marco of Manzoniona fame, borders the Adda River from Milan. Then, as today, its attraction lies in the tranquil beauty of the countryside.[5]

On the afternoon of August 16, 1881, about three months before the birth of the Roncalli's most renowned son, the town was celebrating. With the festive peals of the church bells, the blast of firecrackers, and the music of a band, the townspeople gathered to welcome "the most illustrious and most reverend Bishop of Bergamo, Gaetano Camillo Guindani."[6] The occasion was the new bishop's pastoral visit, in the diocese of Bergamo where he had resided for just over a year and a half. In August, he had visited the parishes of Val Taleggio and, perhaps as an interlude before tackling Val di Scalve, he decided to stop at the episcopal academy in Celana for a few days. From there he passed through Villa d'Adda and Carvico, arriving in Sotto il Monte on the afternoon of August 16.[7]

Guindani was a slender man of pale complexion, with a high broad forehead; lively, expressive, and benevolent eyes; and a calm, modest demeanor. His dignified smile expressed a profound goodness, and his penetrating gaze reflected an almost timid temperament. Preceded by the clergy and accompanied by the influential people of the town, the bishop walked under the traditional canopy. Smiling, he walked along the streets strewn with flowers and adorned with triumphal arches. He blessed the people who had gathered to welcome him. The people bowed in reverence, and parents pointed him out to their curious children while teaching them to bow and to make the sign of the cross.

When the procession reached the church, the bishop presided at solemn Vespers. Afterward, with the banner of the Blessed Virgin Mary held aloft, the procession moved on to the cemetery. That evening's sky was illuminated by beautiful fireworks. The next day the townspeople again filled the church to attend the bishop's Mass, where everyone present received Holy Communion. The festively decorated church, the children's singing, the people's devotion, and the investiture of the faithful, with uniforms and badges according to the respective congregations and associations, made it a moving ceremony. All the faithful lined up and genuflected in perfect order to receive the Bread of Angels from the hands of Guindani. This heartfelt and unanimous manifestation of faith must have been a great comfort to the parish priest of Sotto il Monte.

Don Francesco Rebuzzini[8] was recognized and venerated as a holy priest by everyone who knew him. A modest, humble man, he radiated incomparable piety, wisdom, and goodness.[9] He lived an exemplary priestly life and was conscientious about his parish.[10] At fifty-six, Rebuzzini had been a priest for thirty-two years.

In preparation for the bishop's visit, Rebuzzini had compiled an ample and accurate report on the state of the parish of St. John the Baptist. In it, the priest meticulously described the social and religious reality of the town. The parish territory extended toward the southeast for a traveling distance of one hour, toward the south for three-quarters of an hour, and toward the west and northwest for a half-hour. It bordered the parish of Fontanella to the north and to the east, Terno and Carvico to the south, and Carvico to the west. The parish was divided into twenty-eight hamlets situated at a considerable distance from the church, which presented obvious hardships for the poor parish priest.

The ancient and beautiful parish church established in this mountainous and isolated area was far from most homes. It had not been used for church services for nearly fifty-eight years (since 1823). Instead, the Oratory of St. Mary of the Assumption in the Brusicco district served as the parish church. Although a more convenient distance for most parishioners, it was insufficient for "holding all the people." The parish had 844 parishioners, 587 of them adults who were "admitted to Communion."

> The sacraments are very well attended by everyone for the major feasts of the year; by the majority for feasts of the Blessed Virgin and the first and the third Sundays of the month; and by the devout for all Sundays and still other days of the week. They gather for the homily and for the catechism. During the winter months, the homily is given at 9:30 in the morning, and during the summer months at 8:30. It is never omitted except on Easter and Christmas when the second celebration is held. Catechism class begins at 12 noon during the winter and at 12:30 during the summer. It is omitted for two or three holy days of obligation during the silkworm season, but the instruction is never omitted for the children and for those who need more help to understand. In addition to the Easter Season, confession is heard at other times, including Christmas, the triduum [of the dead], and the feast of the Assumption — always with previous instruction for the given day and with preparation directed by the parish priest.

In addition to the pastor, five priests ministered to the faithful in the other five territorial churches. St. Mary of the Assumption in Brusicco substituted temporarily for St. John the Baptist. Then there was the Oratory of the Presentation of the Blessed Virgin above the village of Corna, and the smaller Oratory of St. Rocco in the hamlet of Bercio. Finally, the noble Mangili family had annexed a private oratory, dedicated to the Passion of our Lord, to their home in the village of Camaitino.

Together with these sacred places, there also existed two small chapels, one of the Madonna and Child, and one erected in memory of the ancient cemetery on the hill and the new cemetery at the entrance to the town. Scattered as they were throughout the various hamlets, each sacred building embraced a community strong in Christian traditions. These good peasants lived obedient to God and by the hard work of their hands. Most of these peasants were sharecroppers of the Mangili family and of the Morlani brothers of Bergamo: Counts Ottavio, Guido Maria, and Don Giovanni.[11]

The economic and social situation of the town was similar to that of the neighboring towns of Isola. The peasant sharecroppers lived practically at a subsistence level. Thanks in part to the new bishop's initiative, the people were beginning to organize themselves into Catholic Workers' societies, insurance cooperatives, agricultural and people's banks for the protection of livestock and harvest, and groups of Catholic Action.[12] By the turn of the century, the greatest number of the region's Catholic organizations were located in Isola.[13]

A social club dependent on the Diocesan Committee for the Work of the Congresses was founded in Sotto il Monte. The sponsor, president, secretary, and treasurer of the committee — as was often the case in many of the neighboring towns — was the parish priest, Don Francesco Rebuzzini.[14]

The Roncallis of Sotto il Monte

On November 25, 1881 at 10:15 A.M., the household of Giovanni Battista Roncalli was gladdened by the birth, after three girls, of their fourth child — a boy.[15] Following the local custom, baptisms were performed immediately after birth, but the Roncalli family had to wait until later that day. Their parish priest had gone to the neighboring town of Terno d'Isola for a meeting of the vicariate. Finally, in the silence of the late evening when the wind and the rain had forced everyone indoors, the ceremony was celebrated in the nearby church of St. Mary. The newborn boy was named Angelo Giuseppe.

No sooner was the infant raised from the baptismal font than his godfather, old Uncle Zaverio, consecrated him to the Sacred Heart so that he would grow up a good Christian under the Lord's protection.[16]

Who were Angelo's parents? The town had no photographers at that time, but as an adult, Angelo skillfully sketched the spiritual features of his father, Giovanni Battista Roncalli, and his mother, Marianna Mazzola.

> How pleasant the memory, as it returns to me, of [my father's] faithfulness to his religious responsibilities: to the Mass every morning, to the lively interest that he took in all things concerning the Church, to his spirit of scrupulous honesty, to certain charming forms of his devotion to Mary Immaculate, to the Christ Child, all of which gladdened his life and served to edify his children and grandchildren.[17] The elderly said that he had inherited much from his ancestors who were a serious and profoundly Christian people. But he owed much to his poor mother who died when he was a little

boy, a Rizzi of the Ca' de Rizzis of Pontida.[18] Oh! Surely, we will all see one another in paradise if we remain faithful to the teachings that she, our dear mother, gave us. Simplicity and goodness, her most distinguished virtues, marked the rest of her long and blessed life. Going back in thought, remembering what Mamma Marianna dei Roncalli meant to us: what conscientiousness, faith, just and holy love for her dear ones, spirit of piety, generosity, and serenity of mind in everything. What swiftness in turning everything toward the Lord! Ah, it is truly moving. And what a heart! What a heart she had, poor soul, for everyone![19]

On January 25, 1877,[20] Giovanni Battista Roncalli, the second of seven children, had married Marianna Mazzola, a girl from the town who was the fifth of eight siblings. They were both 23 years old. After the church ceremony, they traveled fourteen kilometers round-trip on foot to Bergamo for their honeymoon. On February 12, they registered their marriage at the city hall.[21]

Three girls were born during the first three years of their marriage: Catherine, Maria Teresa, and Ancilla. After Angelo's birth another nine children would follow, one every year until 1896: Zaverio, Maria, Assunta, Domenico (who died after only a few months), Alfredo, Giovanni Fransceso, Enrica, Giuseppe, and Luigi (who also died as an infant).[22]

Both Giovanni and Marianna could read, write, and count, but Giovanni had more opportunities to use his knowledge because he associated with people outside the family. He dealt with the landlords, wrote out and signed rental contracts, receipts, and much more. He corresponded with the children whenever they traveled far. Above all, he continued the family tradition of actively participating in the public life of the parish. He served as the president of the parish council for a number of years, and at times exercised the role of councilor, assessor, and justice of the peace in the city hall.[23]

Marianna very quickly inserted herself into the large Roncalli family and, as most mothers of that time, was very busy with raising her children. Nevertheless, she participated in her husband's various activities.

Angelo's godfather and great-uncle, Zaverio Roncalli, was the oldest of Giovanni's seven uncles. Zaverio had never married and remained in his father's home. He was a very devout man who was well educated in the things of God and of the faith. He naturally assumed the task of transmitting the religious traditions of the people to his nephews and great-nephews.

This aged first son who remained unmarried died at the age of 88. As much as possible, and without trying to make him into a priest, he gave his godchild an edifying and effective religious instruction. It was a preparation worthy not of a simple priest, but of a bishop and of a pope whom Providence would then guide. Zaverio was familiar with the meditations of Don Luigi Da Ponte, and he would regularly read the *Salesian Bulletin* and the Catholic newspapers of Bergamo. In those days, Catholic Action in Bergamo was still beginning. From the moment the little boy no longer needed his mother's constant care, his great-uncle Zaverio took him entirely to himself and infused in him, by word and by example, the charisma of his religious spirit.[24]

All the Roncalli men ruled the family home, and Angelo's paternal grandfather, who died at the age of 89, lived under the same roof as did his four brothers who lived until the ages of 88, 87, 86, and 85.[25] Giovanni's cousin Luigi and his wife, Angelina Carissimi, as well as their fourteen children, also lived in the family house. The Roncalli household was the largest in the town. With thirty-plus mouths to feed three times a day, their daily fare was simple and never included bread, only a little corn meal; they had no wine for the children or young adults; they rarely ate meat and, at Christmas and Easter, they hardly had a slice of homemade dessert. The clothing and shoes worn for church services had to last for years.[26]

> But God took care of everything: the well-worked fields [five hectare of Count Morlani's property] provided the grain and the vine; the animals in the stable [six cows] provided milk and its products; and the fear of God, who maintained the order and serenity of a collective life pledged to good work done well with mutual and reciprocal respect, provided for a domestic and Christian peace that was never disturbed.[27]

Early Childhood

As with all infants of that era, very few records or historical testimony remain for the Roncalli children. But the little that does exist is sufficient to tame the imagination of those who look for the extraordinary. The things that stand out among the Roncalli family's memoirs are the first prayers Angelo learned from his godfather.

> I remember among the first prayers that I learned on the lap of that good soul, the lovely little prayer that today is so dear to me and

that I repeat: *Sweet Heart of my Jesus, may I love you more and more.* In the evening, every evening, it was old Uncle Zaverio, the head of the household, who would intone the rosary, and everyone would respond, forming sweet music, the memory of which after so many years still touches my heart.[28]

Angelo's first clear memory of his early childhood was an autumn morning in 1885. It was November 21, the liturgical memorial of the Presentation of Mary celebrated at the shrine of the Madonna of the *Càneve* (cellars), in Corna. To reach the small town one had to travel along a road that made its way through the cultivated fields, meadows, and vineyards of the Church of St. Mary in Brusicco. Angelo's recollection of that day, written seventy-seven years later when he was pope, reveals the profound emotion he experienced as a 4-year-old child:

> When I arrived in front of the little church, not being able to enter because it was overflowing with the faithful, my only chance of seeing the venerated image of the Madonna was through one of the two lateral windows of the main entrance, which were rather high and covered with an iron grating. Then my mother raised me in her arms saying, "Look, Angelo, look at how lovely the Madonna is — I consecrate you entirely to her."[29]

This was not the only Madonna the child became familiar with; Angelo often stopped to admire the image of Our Lady Help of Christians that hung above his godfather Zaverio's bed.[30] Then there was the Madonna of the Holy Rosary that stood above the marble altar in the church at Brusicco, dressed beautifully in gold-embroidered satin and placed on a throne of gilt wood for special processions. Two beautiful paintings were also arranged around the altar of the Madonna: the Sacred Heart of Jesus and the Sacred Heart of Mary.[31] There was also the Madonna in a painting in the little chapel of Badesco. And eight miles from the town stood the large statue of the Madonna of the Forest who smiled upon him, blessed his childhood,[32] and encouraged his priestly vocation.[33] According to his testimony, it was there that Angelo began to marvel at the grace of the Lord.[34]

Angelo treasured other childhood memories for the rest of his life. He was barely four and a half when, on the evening of June 5, 1886, news of Don Luigi Palazzolo's death reached the town. Luigi Palazzolo was the great priest of Bergamo who, some twenty years earlier, had founded the Congregation of the Sisters of the Poor to assist the sick, the orphaned, the poor, and abandoned girls.

Early December of 1888 became a lasting memory because Uncle Zaverio returned from his pilgrimage to Rome. He and 300 pilgrims from the Bergamo region had been received in audience by Pope Leo XIII. In the name of their diocese, they congratulated the pope on the fiftieth anniversary of his priestly ordination. One can only imagine the emotions that ran through the family as Zaverio gave his account of that legendary trip.[35]

The next year, Angelo's father, an active member of the Catholic Federal Society of Mutual Assistance of the Isola parishes, decided to take his son along to the second celebration of the Catholic Workers' Society of Bergamo in the nearby town of Ponte San Pietro.[36] Perhaps Roncalli thought his firstborn son was old enough to participate in a demonstration of Catholic laborers and farmers! The meetings included discussion of local problems such as wages. The members would also publicly affirm their faith in the pope and the Christian community, and make clear their opposition to liberal and socialist trends. Angelo was still very small, and his father lifted him carefully onto his shoulders so that he could admire the demonstration of Catholic faith and Berga-masque fervor.[37] Although it is common for a child to be hoisted onto an adult's shoulders, the occasion endured in his memory; after he was pope, he would recall it with great fondness as he was lifted up on the papal throne for the first time.

During the school vacation of his first or second year, Angelo visited Somasca. This small town was made famous by St. Jerome Emiliani who died there on February 8, 1537, after founding the Congregation of Regular Clerics of Somasco.

The town was about ten kilometers from Sotto il Monte in the nearby Val San Marino, above Vercurago. On July 20, Angelo visited Somasco with his parents, perhaps to celebrate the saint's feast day. He was deeply impressed. "The first and only time that I went there was with my good mother when I was a little lad of 6 or 7 years old, and I still remember my impressions as a child."[38] The area surrounding the shrine seemed intended to stir the imagination of a child his age. Immersed in that striking scenery of nature and popular art, the memory was still vivid thirty years later.

All of these selected incidents suggest that the boy grew up in a serene family environment, under his father's care and in a family dedicated to work and prayer. They trusted in God's Providence rather than human means. Both the family home and piety[39] were supported by the exemplary guidance of Uncle Zaverio, who was always the first to arrive at church in the morning and the last to leave in the evening.[40] Each day began with morning prayer and the Angelus and ended with evening prayer and the rosary. The family also read some passages from a simplified edition of the Bible, the writings of the Fathers of the Church, or from *Remembrances of the Martyrs* — a little book in which a very young hand had written the name of Angelo Roncalli.[41] Every Saturday of the year was dedicated to the Virgin Mary, and particular months were dedicated to specific devotions: January to the Child Jesus, March to St. Joseph, May to Mary Most Holy, June to the Sacred Heart, July to the Most Precious Blood, October to the Rosary, November to the holy souls.

Everyone participated in the feasts of the parish throughout the year, that numbered eleven in all. On June 24, the titular feast of the parish, the birth of St. John the Baptist, was celebrated. "We would climb up the blessed hill that rose above our houses, and there we would savor the fragrance of the spring in bloom and of the summer rich in its gifts."[42] On August 29, the parish celebrated the martyrdom of their patron saint. The finding of the True Cross, on May 3, was celebrated with a procession. September 14 marked the solemnity of the Exaltation of the Cross. The great feast of the Assumption of Mary into heaven on August 15 was a true celebration in the town with Mass, Vespers, a sermon, and a procession. "All received the Blessed Sacrament, and then, fireworks, illuminations, music, bands, procession: a beautiful sight, with a great number of people coming together even from other towns — and not a sour note."[43] Then there were the feasts of St. Anthony of Padua on June 13; the solemnity of the Sacred Heart of Jesus with sung Mass, vespers, sermon, and procession; the triduum for the deceased during the first days of November, with an instruction and a sermon on each of the three days; the Presentation of Mary in the little shrine at the *Càneve*, with Mass, vespers, and a sermon on November 21; the feast of St. Rocco on August 16; the first Sunday of May with the blessing of the countryside; and finally the feast of St. Luigi in June. And on the third Sunday of every month, the parish had Eucharistic procession.

The parish was truly a school of immeasurable and irreplaceable worth. It was the first school of religious and civic virtue, of humility and simplicity; a blessed sanctuary of the most cherished affections.[44] Experience also teaches us that there is nothing more beautiful than those things which are capable of gladdening the simple years of adolescence.

Such proved the gentleness of native landscapes, the places where we lived as the children of a holy and blessed tradition,[45] and the upbringing that left the most profound traces: "I have forgotten much of what I have read in books, but I still remember very well that which I learned from my parents and elders."[46]

Primary School

> During my first year of school I went to the house of Camaitino — the first house on the right-hand corner of the so-called *piazza*, on the way from the jail. On the other side was the store of Rosa Bonanomi and her invalid sister, Marianna. It must have been either 1886 or 1887. The year after, with the new town council at Bercio, a new school was opened and for two years I was among the first to attend it.[47]

So read the autobiographical notes concerning Angelo's primary education. However scanty, they are precious considering the lack of other documentation. Guided by facts from later events, it may be assumed that Angelo's scholastic training began sometime during October of 1887, when he was not quite 6 years old.

In the Sotto il Monte of 1887, classes were held in the basement of a small cabin in the area of Camaitino, directly in front of the villa of the Mangili noblemen. The school consisted of two classrooms for the multilevel classes — one for boys and one for girls. The following year classes were moved to a building that had been constructed to serve as the school and the offices of the public administration in the Bercio territory.

The names of four teachers appear in the written documents and on the memory of former students. Two teachers were assigned for the boys and two for the girls; a fifth remains anonymous — a teacher from the plains of the lower Lombard region, a "liberal," nicknamed *Orbi* (blind), because he was blind in one eye.[48]

The program for the first class — broken into beginning and advanced sections — consisted of verbal pronunciation, spelling, writing, and penmanship. Above all, the school required every student to learn Italian. "He [the instructor] must always use the national language while teaching and require the young people to do the same. He should correct with loving patience the imperfections deriving from the dialect of the province. This is to be done from the first day the children enter the first level; dialect may be used only to clarify Italian words which the pupils do not yet know."

In the second year, the advanced section of the first level, students began to use a reader, but it is impossible to establish which text the young Angelo Roncalli used. As pope, he remembered a few poetic verses to the Blessed Virgin, which he said he had learned from his first schoolbook:

"How gentle to the heart / is your name, Maria. / Every sweetness of mine / comes from your name. / What a beautiful idea of love / I acquired from your name, / what beautiful lighted desires / are awakening in my heart." These verses are the beginning of the first poem I learned as a child, and I learned it from the second book that was used then in the public school.[49]

After the 1870 reform of Minister Correnti, the law specified that whenever parents requested it, catechism was to be taught in the elementary schools under the supervision of the local parish priest. "The parts of the catechism that must be studied in each class — stated the *Istruzioni* (Instructions) — will be determined according to the various dioceses of the Kingdom by the provincial council over the schools. The curriculum will be such that in two or three years the children will have the time to study and learn well the most important parts of Christian doctrine."[50]

Therefore, we know that religious instruction was offered in Sotto il Monte. However, according to Don Rebuzzini, the teachers tended to have their students memorize the instruction with none of the necessary explanations. Thus, the parish priest or curate explained the catechism twice a week beginning usually at one o'clock in the afternoon after regular classes.

During his second year of school, Angelo Roncalli received the sacrament of Confirmation and then his First Holy Communion. Such important events in the life of this 7 or 8-year-old boy occurred over a brief period of less than two months at the end of the winter of 1889. In November the year before, during the triduum of the dead or at the latest on Christmas 1888, Angelo made his first Confession. In January 1889, he began to prepare for his Confirmation, which he received on February 13. Immediately after, on February 24, on Sextagesima Sunday [the second Sunday before Lent] as it was called then, he began to prepare for his First Communion.

On Wednesday, February 13, in the church of the neighboring town of Carvico, Angelo and fifty-four classmates from Sotto il Monte were confirmed by the bishop of Bergamo, Camillo Guindani: "He received Holy Confirmation at Carvico, from the venerated bishop Gaetano Camillo Guindani; it was his first glimpse of the stately and much loved bishop."[51] Angelo's narration of his First Communion is much richer in detail. He received Holy Communion from the parish priest in the church of Brusicco, on March 31, the fourth Sunday of Lent.

> He was admitted to First Communion when he was 8 years old, on a cold Lenten morning and without festivity in the Church of St. Mary of Brusicco.... Only the boys and girls were present with their parish priest, Rebuzzini, and the coadjutor, Bortolo Locatelli. He [Angelo Roncalli] always loved to remember the great simplicity of this ceremony, and the following detail that stayed in his heart. After the ceremony, the new communicants went off to the rectory to be registered, one by one, in the Association of the Apostleship of Prayer. The parish priest, Rebuzzini, entrusted Angelo with the honor of writing the list of the names and surnames of his classmates and of the girls.[52]

The winter of 1888/1889 was certainly an intense period in Angelo's spiritual life, and his Christian initiation was crowned by his enrollment in the Apostleship of Prayer. More than twenty years earlier, the French Jesuits had promoted the association in order to spread devotion to the Sacred Heart of Jesus. Already widespread in many parts of the world, the Apostleship of Prayer was immediately brought into the parish and "even now is present with moderate progress," as Don Rebuzzini affirmed.[53]

It is easy to imagine how Angelo's fervor, immediate and spontaneous interest in everything about the Church, and his calm, innocent manner attracted special attention. His classmates called him Angelino — meaning both *little Angelo* and *little angel* — and the "little priest."[54] Rebuzzini was so fond of him, perhaps because he had watched Angelo grow up to become such a devout altar server,[55] that he permitted him to receive his First Communion at a younger age than usual.

To the many memorized prayers he already recited daily, little Angelo added the self-offering of the members of the Apostleship of Prayer:

> Divine Heart of Jesus, I offer to you through the Immaculate Heart of Mary my prayers, actions, and sufferings of this day, in reparation for my offenses against you and the offenses of all people, especially for the blasphemies against your holy name, according to the intentions through which you continually sacrifice yourself on

our altars. I offer these to you especially for all the intentions of those enrolled in the Apostleship of Prayer this day and throughout the month.

In his Uncle Zaverio, known by the entire town as the "defender" of the Sacred Heart, Angelo had a special teacher in this devotion. "I still remember that every year on the fourth Sunday of September when the Feast of the Sacred Heart was celebrated, everyone in my parish called it the feast of my Uncle Zaverio. He prepared for it with a great deal of fervor and persuaded me to do the same, according to my age at the time."[56]

For Angelo the scholastic year of 1889/1890 would be the last of the usual three years of schooling, as Sotto il Monte did not offer the fourth and fifth years.

Like all the other children in the town, Angelo's formation was not limited to primary school training as important and serious as its aims were. In addition to school, the children attended catechism classes every Sunday afternoon from 12:00 to 1:00. In Sotto il Monte and throughout the diocese, catechetical instruction was organized according to the standards established by Bishop Luigi Speranza in 1858. These norms were reconfirmed in 1880 by his successor, Bishop Guindani. A booklet containing the norms was printed under the very lengthy title: *Ordini e regole per la scuola della dottrina cristiana della città e diocesi di Bergamo riprodotto per ordine di Monsignor Vescovo Pietro Luigi Speranza* (Orders and rules for the school of Christian doctrine for the city and diocese of Bergamo, published by order of Monsignor Bishop Pietro Luigi Speranza).[57] The booklet described in detail the duties of those responsible for the various grades, as well as the organization of the lessons, texts, and teaching materials.

The children always had their religious instruction even when, on very rare occasions, the homily and adult instruction were omitted. The catechism text that the teachers, priests, and children were obliged to use was the 1863 edition of *Breve esposizione della dottrina cristiana ossia piccolo catechismo per fanciulli ad uso delle chiese e scuole della città e diocesi di Bergamo* (A brief explanation of the Christian doctrine, or little catechism for children used by the church and schools in the city and diocese of Bergamo). In 1895, Bishop Guindani reluctantly agreed, for purposes of uniformity, to adopt the texts prescribed for the archdioceses of Milan and Turin and by extension the dioceses of Lombardy and Piedmont. The *Little Catechism* used by the teachers and children, and probably by Angelo Roncalli, was indeed a very small book. The fifty-two-page paperback had no illustrations or pictures and began with the Latin prayers that the children had to say, on their knees before the Blessed Sacrament, at the beginning of each school day. These prayers included the Our Father, the Hail Mary, the Creed, and Our Actions. They were followed by the Acts of Faith, Hope, Charity, and Contrition. After the prayers, the book presented thirteen lessons in a question-and-answer format. It ended with a prayer to be recited, with heads bowed and arms outstretched, before class was dismissed. The first lesson was on the sign of the cross, which distinguishes one as a Christian. The subsequent lessons covered the classical themes of religious education including God, our final end, the unity and trinity of God, the Incarnation, the passion and death of Jesus Christ, the Creed (recited and explained in both Latin and Italian), the Ten Commandments, the laws of the Church, the evangelical counsels, and the sacraments.

Preparation for the Seminary

After completing his lessons in the multilevel classes in the summer of 1890, Angelo "received his first more precise lessons in the Italian language from the coadjutor of Carvico, Don Luigi Bonardi. Angelo studied Latin under the parish priest, Pietro Bolis, a somewhat rigorous instructor who used older teaching methods. These were months of demanding study, especially for a 9-year-old boy."[58]

The decision to seek private tutoring (a common practice in the diocese for boys preparing for the seminary) must have matured in the hearts and minds of those responsible for the "little priest." It seems that Angelo's father and mother, Uncle Zaverio and Don Bolis all recognized the boy's serious intention to become a priest.

"During his childhood, Angelo, the first son, never showed any other inclination or desire than to become a priest. In the parish, his classmates had already been calling him Angelo the 'little priest.' The name stayed with him until he entered the seminary."[59]

The diocesan seminary required a precise knowledge of Italian and Latin, and someone had to teach Angelo. Two priests of Carvico, friends of Don Rebuzzini who were perhaps already teachers, took this matter to heart. Carvico was nearby, a safe, short walk through the fields. It was decided that Angelo would study with the two priests at least for a year, and then they would see about the next move.

Angelo was not totally devoid of a knowledge of Latin; it was used in his catechism classes and perhaps in the family prayers at home. Almost all Church services were in Latin, from the altar server's long prayers during Mass to the songs of the people and choir on solemn occasions. It is possible that Uncle Zaverio and Uncle Giuseppe used Latin expressions at home, which they had heard from the priests. Angelo's ears were certainly already accustomed to hearing Latin. Although it was probably pronounced badly, it was still Latin. Sensible, serious, and intelligent, Angelo must have understood many of the Latin prayers from the Mass, the celebration of the sacraments, the litanies, and the processions. It is also likely that his first exercises in reading Latin came from the prayer cards found in the sacristy and on the altar. But to master this difficult language systematically was something entirely different. Learning Italian had been easy for Angelo. He had excelled in this subject more than in any other because of his natural inclination and perhaps a good foundation.

Under the guidance of the two very good priests of Carvico, Angelo Roncalli's first exposure to classical studies seemed to have been judged well. After only a few months, an important decision was made. Angelo would go to the Bishop's Academy in Celana to complete his seminary preparation as a day student during the 1891–1892 scholastic year.

The village of Celana in the Caprino township consisted of a few homes spread across a verdant landscape, reminiscent of the Umbrian hills in the beautiful San Martino Valley. Celana lies about ten kilometers from Sotto il Monte in the direction of Lecco. In order to get there one had to travel along a cart-road that passed through Pontida in the La Cava territory, and from there, to the Caprino territory where one had to then hike through meadows and woods to reach Celana.

Fortunately, Angelo did not have to travel the entire distance every day — only on Monday mornings and on Saturday afternoons. Some relatives from his paternal grandmother's side lived in a small district of Pontida, and they offered him hospitality during the week.

The boarding school in Celana boasted of ancient and glorious beginnings under St. Charles Borromeo. The saint had established the school as one of the southern-most seminaries of his vast Milanese diocese, which, at the time, included the San Martino Valley. Various events, not always favorable, occur within the school's 350-year history. By the end of the 1800s, the Academy had become a preparatory and boarding school completely independent from the bishops of Bergamo who had once supported it in a thousand ways throughout its history.

Rectors were appointed by the bishop to supervise the school, which offered practical training as well as upper-level education prescribed by the laws of Italy's new Kingdom. The last rector, Francesco Benedetti,[60] held office from 1875 to 1912. Under the administration of this most worthy priest, the institution enjoyed a renewal of its facilities and inner life.[61]

Although Angelo only attended morning sessions, for a mere 10-year-old boy whose sum total of knowledge had been acquired at the small school of Carvico, the curriculum proved strenuous.

Andrea Castelli,[62] an older student who became a priest and voice teacher in the boarding school, offers a glimpse of Angelo's life during those initial months at the Academy:

> I met him for the first time during the thirty-minute recreation period before lunch. We were playing in the piazza in front of the church; he was leaning against a wall near the porter's lodge. I asked him who he was and where he was from, and it moved me to hear how far he had to travel and how much difficulty he was having in his studies. I remember that during the break he and I, both of us being day students, would each eat our five-cent sandwich without meat.[63]

For the four semesters, which ended on July 6, 1892, Angelo received grades that were decidedly poor. And, despite the professors' reputation for being generous in their grading, this was enough to dissuade him from attempting the final exams for promotion.

> Although owing to circumstances perhaps independent of my good will, I could not take advantage, except in a tenuous manner, of the few months of schooling that I had at the Academy when I was only 10 years old. Yet, the memories of Celana have remained indelible and most dear to my heart. I often return there in my thoughts to relive the simple and serene memories of my childhood.[64]

The experience at Celana must have been precious because of the excellent religious and disciplinary training in a social and civil life. There he also learned about St. Charles Borromeo, founder and patron of the institution. When he saw the sculpted image of St. Charles on the ancient door of the Academy for the first time, the simple and innocent young boy was deeply impressed. The saint became his light and inspiration for all that Providence prompted him to study and for imitating that great master of the episcopate of the Universal Church.[65]

CHAPTER 2

THE SEMINARY

Angelo returned to Sotto il Monte for the summer of 1892, but he spent his vacation studying. Like the other fifty seminary students at Bergamo hoping for admittance to the third level, he anxiously awaited the required exams scheduled for the first week of October.

Angelo's first real exam of his scholastic career lasted two days, October 5 and 6. The reported results only gave the final judgment, which is clear yet enigmatic: "admitted on a trial basis."[1] Angelo and his family had a few more weeks of vacation to prepare for Angelo's official entrance to the seminary at Bergamo.

Bergamo's seminary complex stood on the hill of San Giovanni where it had relocated more than a century earlier following the French Revolution. The storms of revolution that threatened to shatter even the most solid of institutions did not affect the seminary.[2] The beautiful and ancient church dedicated to the holy evangelist was surrounded by the complex of very old buildings and the newer ones that had been completed in 1834.[3]

When Angelo Roncalli arrived at the seminary, he was only one of many young men who aspired to a priestly vocation. The experience must have had a great impact on the young boy who had left behind the verdant pastures and thick woods of the country to suddenly encounter an overwhelming city environment.

Perhaps his first impression was that of having fallen into an enormous cage. The rigid regulations, the inflexible schedules, and the strict supervision of the superiors must have weighed heavily on him. It probably took months before the new group of thirty-five "fellow disciples," lost among the more than 500 students, grew accustomed to their new life. The desire for study and the satisfaction it gave them, the spontaneity of devotion and the initial trust in the institution gradually made their new life agreeable if not pleasant. Yet, their families were so far away, and their vacation would not be until Easter.

The dormitories were immense, interconnected rooms with a row of iron beds along each of the longer walls. Next to each bed stood a small iron bench and a single iron wall peg on which to hang clothes. Enormous closets with many compartments where the seminarians kept their personal belongings lined the entire width of the remaining walls. The nearby lavatories had great marble or stone tubs unlike the more familiar large basins used for personal hygiene at home. The building had no electricity, showers, or central heating.[4] The dormitories and the lavatories were ventilated by large windows that were opened after the wake-up call. They remained opened all day long, both in the summer and in the winter, until the boys returned to their rooms to recite evening prayer on their knees beside their beds. For this reason, especially during the winter, the seminarians went to bed almost fully clothed and it took quite some time to get warm. Often, the few secret tears welling up in the eyes of a homesick boy were added to the damp air of the room.

The seminarians spent most of their time in the classrooms, which also served as study halls and, in rainy weather, as recreation halls. The furnishing consisted of a podium, school benches, and a wood burning stove for the winter months. For outdoor recreation, they had small narrow courtyards where the boys could run and release their energy.

Within the seminarian community there were three distinct groups, which were divided according to studies: students of the humanities (five years), the primary level; students of philosophy (three years), the secondary level; and students of theology (four years). The standards of discipline were extremely high. The seminarians were expected to wear cassocks (beginning at age 13 or 14), to act in an appropriate manner, form healthy relationships, and to observe silence and punctuality. The day's activities were regulated by the ringing of a bell from the tower which, rising high above the rooftops, could be heard throughout the complex. It first tolled at 5:30 A.M. on weekdays and at 6:00 A.M. on Sundays and holidays. After a brief recreation following their supper, the evening bell signaled the beginning of the "great silence," which lasted until morning when the students gathered for breakfast in the large refectory. Silence was again observed during lunch and supper while a theology student read from the lives of the saints.

The students were nourished and strengthened in their faith and prayer. The philosophy and theology students prayed in a larger church. The structure's beauty, its brightness, and the ascending vertical beams raised the spirit spontaneously toward God. The younger students prayed in one of the small rooms where they lived, which had been converted into a chapel. The perennial darkness gave it a somber atmosphere.

These were some of the scenes Angelo Roncalli of Sotto il Monte saw when he arrived in Bergamo. He was in the company of new friends who came from various corners of the vast diocese.

Traveling on foot with his father from their hometown of Isola, Angelo arrived at the seminary on Monday, November 7, 1892.[5] His sketchy autobiographical notes only allow us to guess at the fear and emotion of that day and the first months.

Angelo certainly could not help being taken up in the excitement of his first days,[6] as he began to familiarize himself with his new environment, superiors, and classmates who were all two years his senior. He probably felt quite homesick as well, considering his very sensitive, introspective nature that made him more prone to keep to himself.

The first days at the seminary were somewhat relaxed for the students and the superiors. The recreations were longer and the students went on walks on the outskirts of the city. Then, little by little, school, study, and discipline took over.

Yes, discipline. In 1892, Bishop Guindani had published a new edition of the *Regole prescritte ai chierici del seminario di Bergamo* (Rules prescribed for the clerics of the seminary at Bergamo).[7] Each seminarian received a copy, and once a month the way of life that the community strove to follow was read aloud in the large refectory. These rules expressed the ideals of community life for the boys and young men preparing themselves with study and prayer to become priests of the diocese. Obviously, the ideal was not always achieved and therefore the rules had to be read often.

It is easy to imagine Angelo's intensity as he studied that book of rules, "well-known to our youth." [8] Aided by a good, reflective, and adaptable character — "the kind of stuff that allows itself to be shaped as one wills," as the vice-rector said of him years later — he was happy observing the rules and felt he had found his true way of life.

Most days were taken up with school and study: four hours a day for school (twenty hours a week), and at least as many for individual study. This made the days concentrated and shaped the boy, the adolescent, and the young man. The time spent at the seminary amounted to about ten months a year (from November to Easter, a few days at home and again from Easter to August 15), and the rigorous schedule had long-lasting effects. A less rigorous schedule was observed only on Sundays, religious holidays, and vacation days. But even on those days, the seminarians studied and fulfilled their religious practices. Actually, on those special days their time for prayer was greater; besides the usual morning Mass, they had a sung Mass and daytime chanting of the breviary when liturgical services were not held in the cathedral.

Angelo Roncalli: Seminarian and Cleric

Angelo Roncalli attended the seminary at Bergamo from November 1892 to November 1899, that is, from his eleventh to eighteenth year. He moved along as a student — first of humanities, then the three years of philosophy, and lastly of theology.[9]

The preparatory school or seminary of the little boys, as it was then called, was located in the Sozzi building, the sunniest of the entire complex. The bottom floor consisted of classrooms and a chapel; and the dormitories were on the top floors. Here Roncalli spent the school years of 1892–1893 and 1893–1894. He completed these terms with a final evaluation of "completely satisfactory" in the first year and "decidedly good" in the second.

In the summer of 1894, Angelo returned to his family for vacation in Sotto il Monte, but to the new and spacious home called *Colombera,* where the Roncalli family had moved with great-uncle Zaverio. The nearby "Palazzo" had become too small for the ever-growing Roncalli tribe, but they were still tenant farmers and sharecroppers of the Ottavio family of Bergamo.

According to Don Francesco Rebuzzini, "during the long autumn vacation"[10] Angelo's behavior was not just good, but edifying. He seemed inclined to sincere goodness by nature. He attended daily Mass without fail, made visits to the Blessed Sacrament, and prayed the rosary every evening in church. He regularly attended church services, and did not seek forms of entertainment. If he was not in church, he was at home with his family or at the pastor's residence. He was faithful to his daily practices of prayer and fulfilled them with devotion as he did at all holy functions. Rebuzzini wrote the seminary rector:

> From the general conduct that he has shown thus far, I think I can infer that the aforementioned young man has been called to the ecclesiastical state, and I do not doubt that he will achieve great things in the Church. Had I the least doubt that he was not called, I would certainly not have made as many sacrifices as I have to date, or continue to make, to keep him in the seminary, as he is very needy indeed.[11]

The poverty of the seminarian from Sotto il Monte is confirmed by the *Registri dei crediti o degli arretrati di pagamento* (The register of credit or of outstanding debts) and by the *Registri di grazia* (Register of grace), which dealt with the discounts on seminary fees. Such documentation indicates that his family was utterly poor. They could not even provide Angelo with books and clothes, and the little that they gave him — it is said — was due to the generosity of charitable people. This situation continued until the 1896–1897 school year when Monsignor Giovanni Morlani — one of the brothers who owned the land the Roncallis cultivated — paid the entire tuition for his protégé.[12]

In the school year of 1894–1895, Angelo moved from the boys' seminary to that of the young men, located in the larger section of the complex on the northern side of San Giovanni hill. This building housed the theology and all other higher-level students.

That year Angelo's grades were decidedly better and a standard was now set that would become the norm. His evaluation of 62/70, for which he received a third place scholastic prize, was quite high for one not quite 14 years old! But the young Roncalli also showed promise in other areas. In June of that year, he was allowed to wear the cassock. A few days later, on the eve of the feast of Saints Peter and Paul, he was admitted to the holy tonsure, the symbolic haircut that signified entrance into the clerical state. This early induction was "an exceptional rather than unique case at that time or any time," as he himself would comment in his autobiographical notes with apparent satisfaction.[13]

Both of these solemn rites were made all the more impressive by the young boy's age, and they had a truly profound effect on him.[14] He later wrote to another priest:

> I cannot forget that year of 1895 in which I received my first tonsure. The memory of your first tonsure made me recall one of the happiest days of my life — an evening in June 1895 when I, too, still a very young 13-year-old [actually 14!], said to Jesus more with my heart than with my head: *Dominus pars haereditatis meae et calicis mei* (the Lord is my portion and my cup). From then I began to savor *quam suavis est Dominus* (how sweet the Lord is), and I no longer felt the need to adhere to the sweetness of the world.[15]

The two ceremonies gave Angelo an even greater awareness of the priestly state. His classmates had called him the "little priest," something the people of Sotto il Monte probably continued to call him, and he truly wanted to prove himself "a little priest." During the summer of 1895, Angelo had an occasion to prove himself the model cleric his pastor had described.

On Sunday, July 21, the feast of the Sacred Heart, dressed in the sacred vestments, Angelo served the solemn sung Mass in the small parish of St. Gregory — his old haunt near the boarding school of Celana. He stayed for dinner, but managed to excuse himself early from the company of merrymakers and to pray in the church[16] until the afternoon's solemn vespers.[17]

In September, he joined the pilgrimage from Bergamo to participate in the Thirteenth National Eucharistic Congress, which took place in Milan. In 1903, he wrote that the Congress "taught me the magnificence of the Most Holy Sacrament."[18] He saw Cardinal Andrea Ferrari for the first time at the Congress — a man who would later play a major role in the life of the young priest. The scene of Cardinal Ferrari in the cathedral, his extraordinary Eucharistic devotion, and his ardent commentary on the words of the Gospel of John: *Manete in dilectione mea* — remain in my love (Jn 15:9)[19] — were deeply etched in Angelo's memory. Also in the crowd was a Roman bishop, Radini Tedeschi,[20] a well-known organizer of congresses who would become, only a few years later, Angelo's "lord and bishop." Perhaps the young cleric saw or met him there.

The Marian Sodality

After he had returned to the seminary from that "ever so long autumn vacation," cleric Roncalli began what was then called the second year of rhetoric. In his autobiographical notes, the elderly pope observed that the young cleric "seemed to take flight both in his study and in his spiritual formation."[21] Significant events in the spiritual formation of the young cleric occurred that year: his admission as a novice into the seminary's Marian Confraternity, and taking the habit as a Franciscan tertiary.

Angelo began copying by hand, in his characteristically miniscule script, certain passages of the "Rules of Life to Be Observed by Those Youth Who Wish to Make Progress in the Life of Devotion and in One's Studies." There was also the "Way of Life for a Young Man [Cleric] Who Wants to Progress Along the Road of Virtue." He wrote these out in small notebooks for his personal use and affixed personal notations specifying the nature of the guidelines:

> Little Orders and Company (Confidential Documents on the Spiritual Life of Select Students of the Seminary of Bergamo for the Use of the Seminarian Angelo Roncalli 1895–1900); and again: The Little Rules (Special and Confidential Guidelines for Select Seminarians) Bergamo, Seminary, 1895.[22]

These passages were taken from the *Manuale del Maestro de' Novizi* (Manual of the director of novices), a small manuscript dating back to 1840, that contained the collected teachings and practical guidelines communicated by the rector, the spiritual director, and other superiors of the seminary. The *Manual* was addressed to the students who were members of a private society that had been established 150 years earlier to promote spiritual formation and observance of the principal ideals of ecclesiastical life.[23] The task of recruiting new members was entrusted to the directors of the novices who had the duty of forming the novices of the Marian Sodality which had existed in the seminary — at least since the end of the eighteenth century, under the title *Annunciationis Beatæ Mariæ Virginis Immaculatæ*. Initially, membership in the sodality was reserved for the best students, but gradually it expanded to embrace almost all the students, and for all practical purposes, its rules and regulations directed the spiritual life of the entire institution. Before a definitive acceptance, the members lived a trial period of two years called the novitiate.

When the cleric Roncalli was admitted to the novitiate, he began copying one of the many editions of the *Manual* that circulated in the seminary at the time so that he could memorize the rules and orders.

The Rules of Life offered guidelines, virtues, and practices for every day, week, month, and year — in fact for every occasion. These were followed by other rules especially for the young men who were already wearing the cassock, a few devotional guidelines for the triduum dedicated to St. Francis Xavier, and for the four days dedicated to St. Francis de Sales. *The Rules* ended with two prayers; the first was a prayer to do the will of God from Book III, Chapter XV of the *Imitation of Christ*. The other prayer, of uncertain origins, was to Jesus Christ, and the novices prayed it in order to consecrate all their abilities to the glory of the Lord and of his bride, the Catholic Church.

The Way of Life almost repeated the guidelines for every day, week, month, year, and every occasion of the *Rules*. Added to these were the devotions for the month of May, guidelines for the particular examination of conscience, and at the end a way of life to be observed during vacations.[24]

The spirituality contained was influenced by the nineteenth-century Jesuits, but with preference for St. Francis de Sales, a model of gentleness, zeal, and surrender to God. The book also made constant and satisfied references to certain diocesan priests who had earned a reputation for their holiness of life. This seemed to confirm the validity of this particular tradition for training seminarians for the priestly life, and showed it as a valuable method consonant with daily practice.

If one accepts the principle that a priest must be holy because he is called by the Lord and entrusted with the task of leading others to holiness, the main objective of seminary training is formation to holiness.

Angelo Roncalli the adolescent must have taken these rules and guidelines very seriously. His spiritual director considered him worthy enough to belong to the group of seminarians willing to take up the challenge of a more ascetic way of life. Angelo made this the starting point of his internal work. Following the directives of the novice masters, and undoubtedly confirmed by his spiritual director,[25] during the spiritual exercises of February 1896 he began to write down in a small notebook the resolutions he would use for future examinations of conscience.[26]

> I was an innocent boy, a little shy. I wanted to love God at all costs and I did not think of anything other than becoming a priest at the

service of simple souls who were in need of patient and careful
care. But I still battled an enemy within: pride, which actually allowed itself to be disciplined. I grieved in feeling its traces and its
return; I fretted over distractions during prayer and imposed difficult sacrifices upon myself in order to free myself of this. I took
everything very seriously and my examinations of conscience were
exact and severe.[27]

Roncalli's fervor remained strong during his first year of novitiate.
He read and reread the biography of Luigi Palazzolo, a holy priest of
Bergamo, published a few months earlier.[28]

From those pages, how many impulses that youthful heart received
regarding the vocation of which the Lord had given him an early
indication. One read and reread, as if to familiarize the soul with
that lively piety and zeal with which our priesthood would vibrate
one day if one would truly give honor to Jesus Christ, to his Church,
or even — why leave it unsaid? — to the good tradition of the cleric
from Bergamo; a tradition of selflessness and sacrifice, of work and
faithfulness, not only to preserve, but to increase the blessed energies of a strong people, proud of the faith of its fathers.[29]

In that enthusiastic climate, and perhaps upon the strong advice of
his spiritual director, another important decision matured in Roncalli: to
become a member of the Franciscan Third Order. The ceremony, offici-
ated by Don Luigi Isacchi, took place in the seminary church. Angelo
was admitted into the Franciscan Order and received the habit of the
Third Order members.[30] As he said years later in an address:

Allow us to add a special word from the heart about how many of
those here present belong to the peace-loving army of lay tertiary of
St. Francis. "I am Joseph, your brother." With tenderness, we love
to tell you so. We have been so since being a young lad of barely 14.
On March 1, 1896, we were formally enrolled, by the priest Luigi
Isacchi, our spiritual father, when he was director of the seminary at
Bergamo. We love to bless the Lord for the grace he bestowed upon
us in blissful harmony with the act of initiation to the ecclesiastic
life through the holy tonsure that very same year. Oh! The serene
and innocent joy of that coincidence! Franciscan tertiary and
cleric on the way to the priesthood, received with the same cords
of simplicity — unconscious and happy — that would accompany us all the way to the blessed altar and would then give us
everything in life.[31]

Journal of a Soul

On Wednesday, December 8, 1897, Roncalli was officially enrolled in the Marian Sodality after almost two years of novitiate. For the occasion he tore out a page from his notebook and wrote a declaration of intentions and commitments concerning "the inestimable treasure of holy chastity."[32] With his spiritual director's approval he consecrated these resolutions to the Virgin of virgins through the hands of his special protectors: St. Louis Gonzaga, St. Stanislas Kostka, and St. John Berchmans.

What enthusiasm he experienced on that day when he consecrated himself entirely to the Virgin Mary!

> Long live Mary Immaculate! The one most unique, most beautiful, most holy, most dear to God of all creatures! O Mary, O Mary, you are so beautiful that, if I did not know that one must render the highest honors to God alone, I would adore you. You are beautiful. But who can say how good you are? A year has now passed since you showed me that mercy, which you know very well how little I deserved. Today you remind me of it with great insistence, recalling to my mind the sweet duties that accompanied it and which I had the honor of taking on.[33]

Those duties regarding chastity were: devotion and prayer to Mary, to St. Joseph, and to the three holy young saints who were invoked; mortification of the eyes in every circumstance; discretion in dealing with women, whether relatives or holy women; the greatest modesty in speech and in the treatment of one's own body; mortification even at table.

> When I am in an occasion that may offend holy chastity, then, more than ever, I will instantly turn to my guardian angel, to God, to Mary with the familiar prayer, "Mary Immaculate, help me!" Then I will think of the scourging of Jesus Christ and of the last things, mindful of what the Holy Spirit says: "In all you do, remember the end of your life, and then you will never sin"(Sir 7:36).[34]

Among his resolutions he lists particular practices that he would like to insert into his day, including devotion to St. Joseph, "the most chaste spouse of Mary, reciting twice a day the prayer: 'O guardian of the virgin....' At night before going to sleep, after placing the rosary of the Blessed Virgin around my neck, I will cross my arms over my chest, a position in which I will try to find myself in each morning."[35]

That year, he made his spiritual exercises at the end of February. As in previous years, he wrote down the thoughts and maxims he had drawn from his meditations.[36] Afterward, he began to draft annotations in small notebooks. First on a weekly and then on a daily basis, he would write about the state of his soul. He noted his spiritual progress and relapses, giving form to a true diary of the spirit, or a real "journal of a soul" as he would later call it. In minute detail, he wrote every movement of the spirit and the episodes that provoked it. It was a true chronicle of his soul, which he continued uninterruptedly for months.

He came out of his spiritual exercises with this conviction: "From me, cleric Angelo Roncalli, Jesus wants not just a mediocre, but the highest morality. He is not pleased until I at least try my utmost to become holy. Many and great are the graces that he has bestowed on me to that end."[37]

But Roncalli had many difficulties to overcome, especially in conquering his pride. His Easter vacation went fairly well, but the small family annoyances seemed to torment him. May had just begun and he had much hope in this month dedicated especially to Mary. If *she* helped him, he would certainly make some progress. In short, if Jesus and Mary blessed him, helped him, and gave him what he needed, including good will, he would surely become holy.[38]

He also had to reckon with his adult neighbors who not only remembered but continually referred to his last vacation when it seemed that he had become an arrogant upstart. He could only ponder his failings and cry. Cursed pride and cursed vacation! He had finally begun to open his eyes and learn something about his weakness; he learned his lesson!

Despite his limitations and youth, Roncalli became an assistant to the other seminary students, many of whom were older than he was. He urged his classmates to observe the rules and devotions, and he spoke to them with great passion about love of the Eucharistic Christ. He also had to admit that he still felt far behind, certainly further behind than his classmates, in attention at school, during classes, or at the liturgical ceremonies.

> Everyone laughed at me, and I deserved it. I carried the thurible during the solemn vespers for the first time, and I cut the figure that I deserved — I, who always criticize others — and on June 21, the feast of St. Luigi! Next time I will be more humble and watch myself better. [39]

The Summer of 1898

Sunday, July 10. After a long period of distraction, Angelo resumed writing in his "journal of a soul." He lamented his lack of fervor despite the grace he had received in the two minor orders of porter and lector.[40] In the ceremony that was held when the philosophy students had completed their studies, the bishop solemnly conferred on the new clerics certain faculties regarding the liturgy, which included caring for the church building and reading the sacred books in public worship.

Ten days after the ceremony, Roncalli went on a vacation to Sotto il Monte. This time he was faithful to his diary, adding entries every evening, which noted his progress, failures, intentions, and small lapses during the day.[41]

Roncalli could be found praying in church, studying in his room, or talking with his parents and siblings in the kitchen. Sometimes, he could be found at the home of the pastor or curate, or visiting a fellow seminarian entrusted to him as a vacation companion. He would visit the nearby monastery of Franciscan friars at Baccanello in the Calusco district for his weekly confession and a few hours of monthly spiritual retreat.

He noted every detail in the diary, from a toothache to the celebration of the feast of the Assumption, and from the gathering of priests to how the death of a parishioner impressed him. He wrote about his confession for the feast of the Pardon of Assisi, the prayers he recited with his siblings, and the inevitable burdens he experienced — perhaps with too much emotional distress — because of his family. The grave illness of his little brother Giovanni suddenly filled Angelo with a serious fear of his own death. He also wrote that no matter how much he tried to overcome his fallen nature, it would make itself felt in certain "hellish dreams" where he found himself ensnared unawares.[42] He dedicated more time to preparing for the solemn feasts for the sixteenth centenary of the martyrdom of St. Alexander, patron of the diocese, and for the episcopal jubilee of Bishop Guindani.

After the diary's digression on the topic of the celebrations for the feast of St. Alexander,[43] Angelo returned to that of his vacation. He recounted the beautiful devotions to the Virgin Mary, the prayers, novenas, rosaries, visits to country chapels, and his union in spirit with the Marian Congress being celebrated at Turin. He also wrote about how he studied so little and was often too sleepy when he did. He wrote of his presumptuous discussions with those who were older: the curate, the town doctor, and others. He lamented, with a good deal of irony, over the fact that he sometimes had a glib tongue — like a preacher.

In the summer of 1898, everyone was talking about the riots that had broken out in the larger cities because of the rising cost of bread. At the beginning of May, the anti-government demonstrations reached their peak. Martial law had been declared in Milan and other cities, and civil order was restored only after the violent clashes had resulted in several deaths. Many socialist supporters had been imprisoned, Prime Minister Di Rudini had been forced to resign, and General Luigi Pelloux had taken his place at the end of June. Law enforcement officials had clashed with the workers' socialist organizations that were revolting against government policies. The riots seemed limited to cities like Milan, but there was reason to fear — or hope — that the revolt would extend beyond Milan to the peasants.

The military authorities were concerned about the "subversive" activity of many Catholic diocesan and parochial committees. Their activities, though less explicitly opposed to the government, so frightened the authorities that drastic measures were adopted. The Catholic social organizations at the forefront of the association of Congresses were suppressed. Yet, this critical moment offered hope to Catholics. There was reason to believe that the hour of a direct involvement in government was approaching, if only through participation in the upcoming elections that would be united by means of Catholic political organizations.

In Bergamo the diocesan committee, the parochial committees, the interparochial committees and their regional sections had all been dissolved.[44] The headquarters had been searched and everything confiscated: documents, funds, registers, emblems, flags. Meetings were banned.[45] In Sotto il Monte the parochial committee of St. John the Baptist had been dissolved, the meeting hall closed, and the committee flag placed under lock and key.[46] Such events contributed to the lively polemics that took place at the curate's home, as well as to the heightened curiosity of the cleric Roncalli who only held it in check with great difficulty. By means of the strength of his uncommon ascetic efforts, he managed not to speak more than he should or read more than was allowed of those newspapers still prohibited in the seminary.[47] Roncalli was truly an ideal cleric of good character and praiseworthy conduct.

He spent his vacation days peacefully at home, in church, and with the pastor who took advantage of his presence to update the archival registers and the minutes of the Society of St. John the Baptist. Every day Angelo attended Mass and visited the Blessed Sacrament, receiving Communion several times a week. He went to confession once a week. He assisted at the liturgy, attended catechism, and, when his energies permitted, helped with teaching the children. He dedicated some time each day to meditation, spiritual reading, and study.[48] He added to his list of devotional books: *The Informed Youth of St. John Bosco, The Month of the Sacred Heart of Jesus, The Spiritual Combat of Scupoli, The Holy Rosary of Monsabrée* and the *Life and Teaching of Our Lord Jesus Christ of Avancino*.[49]

In the midst of his peaceful holiday, Angelo was unexpectedly shaken by the sudden death of the 73-year-old parish priest, Francesco Rebuzzini. Angelo deeply mourned this good father "who had done so much for me, who raised me, who directed me toward the priesthood."[50]

Very early on the morning of September 25 (Sacred Heart Sunday in Sotto il Monte), as Don Rebuzzini was preparing to go to the church to celebrate Mass, he collapsed on the floor of his bedroom. When *his* Angelo, as Rebuzzini called him, did not see the priest in church, he went to the house and knocked at the door. After there was no response, he opened the door and found the priest lying on the floor in a pool of blood. He was dead.

> I did not cry, I was so petrified. Seeing him like that on the floor, in that state, with his mouth open and red with blood, with his eyes closed, facing me — Oh! I will never forget that image — he looked like the dead Christ taken down from the cross. He no longer spoke, no longer saw. His position told me that he had knelt down and, no longer able to hold his balance, had fallen backward.[51]

Don Rebuzzini had carved a deep and lasting impression on the young cleric. As an aging pope rereading his notebooks in 1962, he added to the entry dated October 4, 1898 the title: "After the death of the pastor Rebuzzini, the holy guardian of my childhood and my vocation."[52] It was as if a new period of his life began on that day, one marked by the memory of the holy priest. Later, in 1959, Roncalli dictated his own special dedication for the first page of an edition of the *Speculum Asceticum*. In it he recalled how his old pastor had nourished himself as well as the young cleric with the knowledge contained in that golden book attributed to St. Bernard: "We, ever since childhood and mirroring ourselves in him, have admired the living image of this upright priest."[53]

Roncalli was happy to have obtained a remembrance of the beloved pastor in his old edition of the *Imitation of Christ:* "his à Kempis, the very one that he used every evening from the time he was a seminarian. To think that with this little book he had become holy. This will always be for me a most cherished book, one of the most precious gems I have!"[54]

Perhaps it was at this time that he began to copy into his diary, with the memorable quotes he had gleaned from one source or another, the exhortations from this most "cherished book." Among these was a passage that became the most assimilated and often cited quote of his entire life: the *quatuor magnam importantibus pacem* from the twenty-third chapter of the third book.

> Endeavor, my son, to do the will of others instead of your own; choose to always have less rather than more; always seek out the lowest place and to be subordinate to everyone; always wish and pray that God's will be entirely fulfilled in you. Thus may a man enter quiet peace.[55]

The First Two Theology Courses

Returning to the seminary in November for the 1898–1899 academic year, Angelo attended his first theology course. At 17, he was by far the youngest of his classmates. While there was only one new superior in the person of the vice-rector, all the scholastic subjects and the teachers were new. The teachers were young men who had earned their degrees in Rome at the Pontifical Seminary of St. Apolinarus. All of them had already published their writing, and they were destined to serve in the seminary for a long time, while playing important roles in the diocese.

In *Journal of a Soul* Roncalli does not go into much detail regarding his first theology course. However, he does accuse himself of a curious state of excessive merriment, although he adds: "it is always better to be happy than to be sad."[56] He also noted how his classmates considered him "too much of a simpleton, credulous of things that have no importance." At times, he was laughed at behind his back, but these occasions helped him to practice humility. Only a brief mention is made to school and study: "a few words during school time."[57]

But his final grades and his exercise in homiletics provide concrete evidence of his scholastic progress. He gave a sermon to his classmates during the novena for Pentecost (1899) on the theme, "Mary in the Cenacle."[58]

Mid-November brought another grievous sorrow. The recent death of Don Rebuzzini was followed by that of Don Luigi Isacchi, Angelo's spiritual director for four years. Three days later, still deeply impressed by the sudden death, wake, and solemn funeral in the cathedral, Angelo wrote in his notebook:

> Since the good Jesus has sent me another misfortune with the death of my good director, I will frequently recommend to the Lord that good soul together with my pastor, so that those two people, who knew my conscience and my shortcomings well, might recommend me to Jesus and Mary, and might implore for me humility, fervent love for Jesus, and for all the souls that have been redeemed by his most Precious Blood.[59]

On Sunday, June 25, 1899, at the end of the first year of theology, Roncalli and nineteen classmates received the last two minor orders of exorcist and acolyte in the seminary chapel.[60] Although these minor orders have now been either eliminated or reclassified, for the young seminarians of that time, they represented a closer step toward priestly ordination and to the bishop with whom they were becoming more familiar.

When he returned home for vacation, Roncalli met the new pastor, Luigi Battaglia.[61] He was a humble, amiable, and cultured priest and Roncalli would later describe him as "one of the last buds to blossom at the feet of that beautiful and fertile tree which Bishop Alessandro Valsecchi was for the Church of Bergamo, and he carried his stern and good spirit everywhere."[62] According to seminary rules, the cleric Roncalli could not participate in the installation of the new pastor except in spirit. With the improvisation of a poet, the seminarian sent the guest of honor a song of eleven verses: "To the new pastor of Sotto il Monte / The Most Revered Don Luigi Battaglia / who on this day / under the protection of the angelic St. Louis / solemnly inaugurates / his pastoral ministry."[63]

That particular vacation would remain in his memory above all because of his good fortune in meeting the parochial coadjutor of Ghiaie di Bonate Sopra at the home of Don Alessandro Locatelli. This distinguished prelate, Giacomo Radini Tedeschi, was a canon of the Vatican and a fellow townsman from Sotto il Monte.[64] Entrusted with the burdensome yet exciting task of organizing pilgrimages to Rome for the great Jubilee, Tedeschi had come to Ghiaie on the occasion of the consecration of the altar for the new church.[65]

Roncalli returned from vacation to begin his second year of theology. In *Journal of a Soul,* Angelo persistently makes note of what he considered a certain exaggerated delight in his study that was not always inspired by noble motives. He mentions an excessive desire to study and to move ahead. He hints that he used words and clever phrases out of a secret desire to flaunt his knowledge and to make known, whether directly or indirectly, that he had studied. At times, he tells himself not to take offense if others display little esteem for his knowledge.[66]

During the spiritual exercises he made in 1900, after the Mass celebrated by the bishop, he opened a new notebook in his *Journal of a Soul* to write his solemn promise to the Sacred Heart of Jesus.

> In the holy spiritual exercises of this year of grace 1900, the nineteenth year of my life, on this last day of the retreat (February 27), while sacramentally united to the Most Sacred Heart of Jesus through Holy Communion, in the presence of my most holy Mother, Mary Immaculate, her most chaste husband and my principal protector, St. Joseph, and all the other saints, my particular intercessors, my guardian angel, and the entire celestial court, I, the cleric Angelo Joseph, a sinner, to the very same Most Sacred Heart do promise, with all the solemnity and power this act may have, to remain always — today and forever — by the grace of God, pure and free from the slightest attachment to any voluntary venial sin. [67]

He again took up his old notebook in August after a lapse of six months, this time somewhat against the wishes of his spiritual director. The one event that marked his vacation was assuredly a painful misunderstanding with his mother.

An unfortunate event occurred this evening to disturb my peace. Although it was really nothing in itself, it still left a profound and painful impression on me. My mother became terribly offended by something I said to rebuke her curiosity (which, truthfully, I could have said more gently). She said some things to me that I would never have expected from my mother who, except for matters relating to heaven, I love with all my heart. To hear her say that I am always rude to her, without manners or good conduct, while it seems to me that I have never behaved in that way, hurt me deeply. If she felt distressed because of me, I was all the more so in seeing her sadness and, I must admit, her weakness. After so much tenderness, to hear her say that I cannot stand her and other such things that I dare not recall, was too much for the heart of a son, especially a son who feels the greatest affection. This thorn filled me with bitterness, and wounded the most intimate and delicate fibers of my heart. How could I not cry? O mother of mine, if you only knew how much I love you and how I wish you to be happy, you would not be able to contain your joy.[68]

Other events of a much greater scope characterized those agitated months and found a place in his *Journal of a Soul*. The political and social climate had become turbulent because of the fast approaching national commemoration of the thirtieth anniversary of the breach of Porta Pia and the capture of Rome. Already the coming celebration had stirred up malicious and evil insults against the great Pope Leo XIII.[69] The Seventeenth National Catholic Congress would be celebrated in Rome at the same time that September. The Congress would deal with the serious question of the organizational reform of the entire Institute of Congresses and its relationship with the new Christian Democratic Movement supported and headed by Don Romolo Murri. Nicolò Rezzara, an apostle of social initiatives in Bergamo, was the secretary general. The Congress paved the way in Italy for Catholic unions, and it demanded that the hierarchy accept permanent associations, which would promote the moral and juridical interests of the entire working class. Once confederated under the diocese, it was hoped that these associations would transform the already existing ones into professional leagues or actual unions.

Roncalli also went along with the priests, behaving somewhat like a professor of political science and speaking out, for right or wrong, on one topic or another, immersing himself in the fray in a way that was perhaps less than befitting for a young cleric.

The diocesan pilgrimage to Rome for the jubilee indulgence was planned for September. This pilgrimage, announced some months before, was warmly supported by the bishop and followed the two pilgrimages of April and June, which both had over a thousand participants.[70] The dates were set for September 11–19 so that the pilgrims would be able to leave Rome before the demonstrations began for the anniversary of Porta Pia. The trip had been advertised for some time in the daily Catholic paper, *L'Eco di Bergamo*. In fact, *L'Eco* was anxious to support the pilgrimage of the faithful from Bergamo because its success would be a providential victory over its rival newspaper, *La Gazzetta Provinciale di Bergamo*. On a number of occasions, *La Gazzetta* had described the pope as a small, weak-minded, and hot-tempered man. More recently, it referred to an article published in the *Corriere di Napoli* that had called him a decrepit old man.[71]

Roncalli certainly never dreamed of participating in the pilgrimage. The expense for the registration and third class train ticket alone would have cost him about thirty-two lire, not to mention food and lodging. However, at the last minute, an opportunity presented itself. The vice-pastor offered Roncalli twenty lire for the trip, more than half the cost.[72] Angelo must have worked very hard to cover the remainder of the expense, and he received free lodging at the Basilica of the Sacred Heart that was run by the Salesian brothers at Castro Pretorio.[73]

The 7,000 pilgrims from Bergamo — another true victory for the local church — finally arrived in Rome singing hymns of praise after twenty-nine hours of travel. On Thursday morning, they gathered at the Church of the Twelve Holy Apostles for a meeting that preceded the devotions for the Jubilee. The president of the international committee for the Holy Year, the Vatican canon Giacomo Maria Radini Tedeschi, greeted the pilgrims and acted as their guide through the basilicas, catacombs, and shrines.[74]

Sunday was set aside for a meeting with Leo XIII. The audience included pilgrims from six different dioceses, many bishops, religious associations, and 7,000 Daughters of Mary carrying banners and standards — 20,000 people in all. Along the entire course of the Basilica of St. Peter, both upon his arrival and upon his departure, the Holy Father received enthusiastic applause. An indescribable display of affection! According to news reports, the people commented on the healthy appearance and vigorous voice of the 90-year-old pope.[75]

The splendor of Papal Rome deeply impressed Roncalli. It opened a new horizon that would become familiar to him from that day forward.[76] He brought home a beautiful memento for himself and his family: the plenary indulgence "for the moment of death," which extended to relatives and blood relations three times removed, as stated the corresponding certificate.[77]

On his return journey, Roncalli passed through Assisi and Loreto where he experienced the only sad note of those joyous days.

At two o'clock in the afternoon, having received Holy Communion, we could then pour out our soul in prolonged and moving prayer. For a young seminarian what could be more delightful than to linger with our dear heavenly Mother? But oh my! The painful circumstances of those times that had diffused the air with subtle mockery regarding spiritual values, religion, and the holy Church turned that pilgrimage into bitterness as soon as we heard the petty, idle talk in the piazza. Madonna of Loreto, I love you very much, and I promise to be a good seminarian who is faithful to you — but you will never see me here again.[78]

CHAPTER 3

THE ROMAN SEMINARY

When Angelo Roncalli's vacation of 1900 was over, he did not return to the seminary of Bergamo for theology courses. Instead, he and two of his classmates were selected to continue their studies at the seminary in Rome. Roncalli recalls this episode in his autobiographical notes.

Thanks to the precious last will and testament — (dating from 1640, but only put into effect at the end of the eighteenth century) — of its illustrious prelate, Bishop Flaminio Cerasoli (†1640), the diocese of Bergamo obtained a college in Rome for the purpose of ecclesiastical studies. This college, Nobile Collegio Cerasola, was to be a resource for promising young men from Bergamo. They were chosen by the bishop and nominated by a special committee of the venerable Archconfraternity of the Bergamaschi nell'Urbe.[1] The muddled and painful events that occurred after September 20, 1870 caused some people to question the purpose of the Flaminio Cerasola Foundation and to want to have its funds redirected to lay students. The well-deserving ecclesiastic, however, had willed them exclusively in favor of clerics from Bergamo. While the matter was in court no clerics were sent to Rome for ten years, the time it took to conclude the civil trial. As one might expect, the court recognized Cerasola's last will and testament, and the bishop of Bergamo reclaimed full rights in the name of his diocese.[2] From 1900 on, young clerics from Bergamo were again sent to the Pontifical Roman Seminary. As a remarkable coincidence, the first to be chosen for this scholarship was Angelo Roncalli. With two fellow seminarians from Bergamo...he resumed the noble chain of the

Cerasolian students. This chain was already shining with the success of a series of distinguished ecclesiastics who greatly contributed to the work of the diocese of Bergamo and the Universal Church itself.[3]

The necessary civil and ecclesiastical documents were prepared in early December, including birth certificate, family status, immunizations and health condition, financial status, police records, and a certificate of tonsure. These required certification and had to be attached to the formal application, which was then sent to the Guardians of the Venerable Archconfraternity of Saints Bartholomew and Alexander, and to the Archconfraternity of the Bergamaschi nell'Urbe,[4] heir to the Cerasoli estate for the college in Rome.

Canon Giovanni Morlani, one of Angelo's benefactors from his earliest days in the seminary, took care to recommend him as a "young scholar with whom the superiors of the seminary are very satisfied."[5] He reported this to the future cardinal, Felice Cavagnis from Bergamo, the former rector of the Roman Seminary (1888–1893) and present secretary of the Vatican Congregation for Extraordinary Affairs. Morlani was certain Roncalli would do very well both in his studies and in his overall formation.

Along with other necessary documentation, the superiors of the seminary in Bergamo sent detailed information about the three prospective Cerasoli scholars: "They are three exceptional young men who will achieve complete success. Roncalli was also a prefect here at the seminary. He is like good clay ready to be shaped into the best form.... I believe I am not mistaken in my assessment of their characters. As soon as you get to know them, I think that your Lordship will agree with me. Certainly, you can accept them without hesitation."[6]

With this letter in hand, they prayed at the tomb of St. Charles in the Cathedral of Milan, and arrived in Rome on the morning of January 3, 1901[7] after a very long and tiring train ride. The next day, the three students were officially registered as auditors in the schools of the Pontifical Roman Seminary. The acolyte Angelo Roncalli, registered as number 1567, was admitted to the second class of theology and assigned to the St. Philip Neri dormitory.[8]

In truth, the ancient Palazzo dell'Apollinare was inadequate to house so many young men. The condition of the rooms, the absence of wide corridors, gardens, courtyards, recreation halls, and an infirmary, as well as the lack of adequate bathrooms left much to be desired.[9] However, Roncalli saw everything in a good light. After a week, he wrote to his parents to reassure them about his new life, which he could not imagine being any better.

The Lord could not have blessed me more than he did, nor could I imagine better fortune for myself. As for my health, I feel wonderful. Here, as you know, it is not like Sotto il Monte or Bergamo. Here we are treated as lords. Indeed, they tell me I have already changed, and grow fatter every day! So please be at peace and do not worry about me. I received the warmest welcome I could imagine, and the reverend superiors' love for me is really beyond any praise. I found excellent companions and we have already become so well acquainted with each other that I can consider myself an old member of the seminary. I was given a pleasant single room, with a nice bed — a bit too hard to be honest, but it will do me good. The room has every comfort: a chest of drawers, a little table, a high-backed chair, a bookshelf, a water basin, etc. I am not at all bothered by classes and study; indeed, I am enjoying myself. Even regarding piety, it is possible to do one's own practices very well. In our chapel, we venerate a most beautiful image of Our Lady of Confidence. I recommend you to her every morning and evening so that she may bless you, give you peace, and console you in all your trials and tribulations. Every day I go out for a walk, so I have the possibility of visiting many holy places and so pray for all of you and for me. I have already visited St. Peter's, the Church of the Gesù and the tombs of St. Louis and St. John Berchmans twice. Only today, I visited the tomb of St. Philip Neri in his beautiful church of Vallicella. It is impossible to mention all the wonders you can see here. The other night, for example, I sat in on a gathering at the college of *Propaganda Fide.* There I listened as forty clerics who had completed their studies presented their papers — in forty different languages — before returning to their own countries as missionaries. If only you could have seen it! There were people of every color: white, black, red.... Some had faces and hands as black as coal. And the pope? I was already able to see him on Sunday evening in St. Peter's, in the midst of a thousand splendors. I got close enough to get a good look at him and receive his blessing.[10]

As expected, rules and schedules governed life in the Roman Seminary.[11] Students were assigned a single room in dormitories supervised by a prefect. The typical daily schedule alternated between hours of prayer, study, and classes that were held from 8:00–11:00 A.M. and then from 1:00–3:00 P.M., followed by recreation. Silence was mandatory for long stretches of the day. The seminarians addressed one another in a formal fashion, and they had assigned seats in the chapel and dining hall. From time to time, the seats were changed, as was the companion for the daily walk for visits to the Blessed Sacrament in the surrounding churches with the seminarians forming a line and standing in twos.

Aside from a few details, Roncalli was able to re-establish the rhythm of the simple, serene life he had led in the seminary of Bergamo. He never needed much space, not even for recreation. He was content to spend free time inside or outside on the terrace. Even in his narrow room, number 15 in the St. Philip Neri dormitory, with its small grated window he did not suffer as others did from the lack of fresh air or from the poor lighting.[12] On the contrary, he remembered how he had an even smaller room at the Colombera College in Sotto il Monte.[13] He also remembered the *pax in cella* (peace in the room) of the much poorer room of his venerated pastor, Francesco Rebuzzini, the beloved *Speculum asceticum* (mirror of asceticism).

He continued his prayers and devotions that would always warm his spirit, especially his devotion to the Blessed Virgin Mary under the title Our Lady of Confidence, which probably dated back to the second half of the eighteenth century. A copy of the small painting that depicted the Madonna holding the Christ child in her arms hung in the Poor Clare monastery of Todi. There Roncalli would offer his heart to the Blessed Virgin Mary by writing: *"Ego Angelus Roncalli Deiparae Immaculatae cor meum obtuli."*[14] He had his May devotions: "O, how the lovely songs we used to sing in the evenings after the service keep coming back to mind, and in particular that little tune, 'Oh Virgin Mary, let me too honor you.'"[15] Its poetic tenderness still echoes in my heart."[16] He continued his devotion to the Sacred Heart and the novenas for Saints Peter and Paul, St. Charles, St. Louis, the triduum for St. Joseph, the holy martyrs Apollinarus, Fiorentino, Socio, and Vittorino. He discovered the joy of visiting the Seven Churches and satisfied his devotion to his favorite saints by visiting their tombs when he took his daily walks or by making special trips on their feast days.

Roncalli and the two other seminarians from Bergamo, Achille Ballini[17] and Guglielmo Carozzi,[18] joined their new classmates: Olinto Marella, Nicola Turchi, Luciano Geraci, Salvatore Ballo, Silvio Guidetti, Paolo Giobbe, Fortunato Esperto, Ernesto Buonaiuti, Ermanno Pozzi,

Vincenzo Misuraca, Mariano Gatto, and Giuseppe Rambelli, and the prefect was Costantino Aiuti. These names were tied to diverse destinies: Marella is now a Servant of God; Giobbe became a cardinal; Geraci, Aiuti, and Ballo became bishops; Buonaiuti became one of the major proponents of Modernism and was excommunicated; and for some time Turchi followed Modernist thought.

After a few days, Roncalli was given the seminary uniform. It was a purple garment similar to those worn by the pope's personal attendants. He had himself photographed while wearing it and sent the picture home to Sotto il Monte, along with *La vera Roma* for his great-uncle Zaverio. This weekly political-religious journal was published by the staunch Catholics of Rome, and Zaverio never wanted to miss an issue.[19]

As Roncalli promised, he wrote home every three weeks in his particularly vivid style. Once, upon returning from a visit to the catacombs of St. Callistus, he felt a great consolation. Later in his journal, he wrote a hymn to the many martyrs who made those places holy, the pontiffs, the many anonymous men, women, and children, Saints Tarcisius and Cecilia. "Why am I not as you were?" he wrote, invoking them to stir him to total self-denial and to overcome his self-love. "To finally obtain victory over the enemies of Christ, and with this victory the salvation of many souls who are far from the fold and the heart of the Supreme Shepherd, the blessed Jesus."[20] From what he wrote to his family, Angelo was filled with fervor for work, sacrifice, and even martyrdom.[21] He had no doubts that the Lord wanted him to be a priest so he could help the poor. It was for this reason that the Lord had overwhelmed him with so many gifts. He made it possible for him to go to Rome and live under the gaze of his Vicar the pope in the Holy City where so many illustrious martyrs and holy priests are buried.[22]

> In order to raise my spirit to stronger feelings of faith and charity, he led me to this blessed land under the shadow of his Vicar, at the source of Catholic truth, near the tombs of his apostles, where the soil is still red from the blood of his martyrs and the air carries the perfume of the holiness of his confessors.[23]

Given his fervent attitude during the first months in Rome, the appointment of Felice Cavagnis of Bergamo as cardinal and all the related celebrations[24] failed to impress Roncalli. He was deeply affected, however, by his indirect encounter with the pope.

On March 3, Roncalli and his fellow seminarians were in the Ducal Hall of the Apostolic Palace as Leo XIII passed through on his way to the Sistine Chapel. Roncalli greatly admired Leo XIII's intelligence and deep wisdom. He spoke enthusiastically about the pope, praising his dogmatic and social encyclicals, which he often reread and meditated on. When Roncalli spoke about Leo XIII, he would conclude by repeating in a solemn voice: "Pope Leo! Pope Leo!"[25] He wrote to Leo XIII to request an apostolic blessing for his studies, "assuring him of his indomitable affection." He also asked for a special blessing for himself, his relatives, benefactors, and friends. He later received a written confirmation under a large framed picture of the pope that was embellished with images of the apostles and the four major basilicas.[26]

Years later Roncalli said that the education he received at the seminary gave his "youth wings, opened up to them larger horizons, and at the same time restrained them from following the temptation of change and dangerous experimentation."[27] Study became the main part of his daily routine: three hours of class in the morning and two in the afternoon 140 days out of the year. The texts chosen were from among the most renowned authors: Ubaldi and Martinetti for Sacred Scriptures; Perrone for theology; Drouen, Billuart and Billot for sacramental theology; Ballerini for moral theology; and Bruk for Church history.[28] The teachers were all relatively young — the average age was 37 — and represented the generation educated in a climate of openness and new cultural definitions under Leo XIII.

Another factor contributing to the renewal at Apollinare was the emergence of the historical-critical method promoted by Leo XIII. The method was used especially in the disciplines of archaeology and Sacred Scripture, which benefited from the teaching of Hebrew and Oriental languages. More than simply opening students to culture and unknown problems, this method formed a demanding *habitus mentale* (way of thinking) regarding problems related to Scripture studies and the history of early Christianity.

A stimulus to study — if Roncalli needed it — came from living with so many men of remarkable talent and exceptional intelligence. One may imagine the topics of their discussions, their exchange of ideas, and their dialogues during daily walks or recreations. Without a doubt, there were comments and debates on the problems discussed in classes and the positions taken by their professors.

Military Service

Roncalli seemed to have found his place in the fatherly affection of his rector, the consolations of the Holy City, the cherished people, and the joys of seminary life.[29] Moreover, his superiors liked him in a special way: they had a high regard for him and praised his pleasant character and good behavior. They pointed to him as a model seminarian, outstanding in every aspect.[30]

He excelled in scholastic achievements and received second place in the course *locorum theologicorum,* third place in Church history, fourth place in Assyriology and Egyptology, and third place in sacred archaeology. He also received second prize in Hebrew. With his fellow students, Angelo, still the youngest among them, received a baccalaureate *in re theologica.*

However, as lightning is feared though foreseen, Roncalli was finally called into compulsory military service in place of his brother, Zaverio, who was needed to work in the fields. Angelo made the customary request to forego the draft by voluntarily signing up and thus his military service in Bergamo would be reduced from two years to one. He also had to pay 1,200 lire to file this request, a considerable sum that was paid by the diocese.[31]

All this happened between the beginning of July and the end of November 1901, the entire time of vacation Roncalli spent in Sotto il Monte. As his personal military record indicates, he was assigned to the Umberto I Barracks of Bergamo on November 30, matriculated as number 11331-42 of the Eighth Company of the seventy-third Infantry Regiment of the Royal Italian Army. He was described as being 1.66 meters tall, with straight black hair, chestnut eyes, a pale complexion, healthy teeth, high forehead, and an oval face. His epithet was *Acerrimus hostibus* — toughest against enemies.[32]

Like all the recruits, he spent the first weeks learning the military disciplines and rules governing everything from the morning rising to wardrobe maintenance, dress code and uniform, salutes, behavior toward superiors and fellow soldiers, meals, physical activity, and sleeping quarters. As a seminarian, he lived the whole experience as a real purgatory, a great sacrifice. He wrote:

> And yet, I feel the Lord and his Providence always close to me beyond every expectation. Sometimes I marvel over how I can gladly

endure this difficult and frightening situation. The only explanation I have is the thought of all my dear ones praying as they had promised; of Our Lady of Confidence, whose image I always carry on my chest; of the Sacred Heart of Jesus, the bright center of my every ideal as a young and fervent cleric who wants nothing but to do a little good every day....[33]

His excellent military superiors grew fond of Roncalli. The respected him and wanted him to be respected as a cleric, and they allowed him the freedom to carry out his practices of prayer. His comrades, mainly from Bergamo and Brescia and the south, rendered him little services that, if nothing else, saved him a lot of annoyance. Every night outside the barracks at his "old" seminary of Bergamo, he met the rector who welcomed him as only a father could. Roncalli found consolation in prayer, in study, and in support from his religious superiors who had great affection for him. He was even allowed to check out books from the library to read later in the barracks.[34] All in all, he still felt fresh and energetic and continued to be amazed over the circumstances which helped "that joyful unfolding" of a life otherwise empty and poor. He no longer understood why he had experienced such fears about military life.[35]

At the end of May, he was promoted to corporal and moved from the Eighth to the First Company of the same regiment. Along with his promotion, however, came other changes that were not all for the best. Indeed, "it was for me an unhappy change. Perhaps my being a cleric annoys my new captain who believes that because of this I love Italy and its institutions less."[36]

Finally, at the end of October, Roncalli announced that he would be leaving the barracks in twenty days, that he would wear again "the treasured and glorious habit of a cleric."[37] He eagerly took up his life with a series of spiritual exercises to wash away some of the "dust" that had accumulated from the military marches and maneuvers. Having "escaped by God's grace from the flames of this furnace," the overall outcome of his experience seemed positive.

I could have lost my vocation as many other unfortunate fellows did, yet I did not. I did not lose my purity, or the grace of God. The Lord did not allow that. I passed through the mire, and he preserved me from stain. I am still alive, healthy, and as robust as before, even more than before. I strongly believe that I gained advantages from the army: a deeper and more precise understanding of the great need for priests to work with holiness and knowledge for the good of souls. And a strong will to do all I can to achieve that ideal of a holy and learned priest, which the Church wishes and the times require.

On November 15, he left the barracks with an authorization for unlimited leave of absence pending official discharge. This was granted on November 30 with a certificate of good behavior and a promotion to the rank of sergeant. From Sotto il Monte he sent the news with uncontainable joy to his rector in Rome, who had been his secure point of reference throughout his year of exile.

> *Cantemus Domino, gloriose enim magnificatus est* — Let us sing to the Lord, for he has shown himself to be great and glorious. Just imagine...how much consolation floods my heart. At last, I have come back to being a cleric, this time forever, even in my habit. As soon as I left the barracks, I took off that awful military uniform, tearfully kissed my dear cassock, and returned among my superiors, friends, and relatives, worthier of their company. *Iam hiems transit, imber abiit et recessit* — Winter is over, the rain has stopped, it has gone away. Here, in my hometown, the winter has just begun with its fog and snow, yet for me the winter is gone, the spring flowers are blossoming, the flowers of Easter. I can hear their friendly voice calling me. Here I am again. *Resurrexi et adhuc sum tecum, alleluia!* — I have risen, and now I am with you, alleluia.[38]

Francesco Pitocchi: Spiritual Father

After a brief visit to the seminary in Bergamo to return the books he had borrowed and to meet the rector and the superiors from the diocese, Roncalli re-entered the Apollinare Seminary in Rome on his twenty-first birthday.

Fifteen days later, he began the spiritual exercises, which he called his "post-Babylonian captivity."[39] The retreat was preached by the spiritual director of the seminary, Canon Luigi Oreste Borgia.[40] The method and classical themes of St. Ignatius were used during the ten days. Roncalli began writing in a completely new notebook. For the first time, he used the title "Giornale dell'Anima" (Journal of a Soul) on its cover, to which he added: *"Soli Deo honor et gloria* (To God alone be glory and honor). *Il Giornale dell'Anima. 16 dicembre 1902.*" On the first page he wrote: "*Anno gratiae MCMII. Diario Spirituale. In Nomine Domini. Cor Jesu flagrans amore nostri, inflamma cor nostrum amore tui*" (Year of grace 1902. Spiritual Diary. In the name of the Lord. Heart of Jesus, burning with love for us, enflame our hearts with your love.)[41]

The night before he began the retreat, Roncalli met Don Francesco Pitocchi,[42] a Redemptorist priest who Monsignor Bugarini wanted as a confessor at the seminary.

> Providence sent him to me at the right moment. The first talk I had with him during the spiritual exercises of my "re-cleaning" was enough for me to feel in my soul a sense of security and great trust in what that man would ask me to do to follow the Lord's will. At the conclusion of our meeting, he left me with a motto to repeat calmly, but frequently: "*Dio è tutto, io sono nulla*" (God is all, I am nothing). For me, that motto was the key that opened my eyes to a new, unexplored horizon full of mystery and spiritual attraction. And I was happy! Finally, I had found what I had desired for so long: near or far, in all the events of my life, I would have a sure counselor and confidant, a staunch and gentle friend. Most of all, I found a father, a true father who by his nourished and nourishing word, both forms and makes Jesus Christ grow within so that the soul might be led toward the virility of the Christian and priestly life.[43]

Roncalli confided everything that was in his soul to Pitocchi. Then he felt assured, comforted, and full of hope for his spiritual growth. He wanted to be holy at any cost, even of his study.[44] His spiritual life would become his only concern. Through his devotion to the Sacred Heart, Roncalli wanted to reach a deep union with Jesus. Practically speaking, his spiritual father would be everything for him, and his particular devotions few but constant. "Cheerfulness always, peace, serenity, freedom of spirit in all things…. After a failure, an act of deep humility. Then I will begin anew, happy, always smiling as if Jesus had given me a hug and a kiss and lifted me up with his own hands; then I will move on secure, confident, blessed *in nomine Domini.*"[45]

Pitocchi was recognized as a great confessor by cardinals and prelates, a highly respected and well-loved educator of a whole generation of young priests.[46]

> He used to listen with great goodness, but he did not engage us in long conversations. Often, it was enough for him to present us with

a thought from Scripture; a little thing, certainly, but enough to establish and maintain that spiritual current which touched our heart and mind and was our life. One had the impression that this man of God took care of the soul of every person as if that were the only task the Lord had given him. He would be there in our moments of weakness and in our small efforts to improve; he supported us with paternal goodness.[47] He could read our eyes and our hearts, which seemed to open spontaneously for him. We told him everything, asked his advice even about the smallest things. Thus it happened that his word, his advice quietly and gently penetrated all the events and relationships of our lives.[48]

How charity, the *caritas Dei* (love of God) of St. Paul, would shine in his eyes, on his smiling lips, throughout the entire person of Don Francesco! To approach him, open one's heart and feel the heartfelt warmth of his fatherly tenderness, would take but an instant. His goodness was patience, *patientia Christi* (the patience of Christ), endlessly bearing the weight of our troubles and indiscretions. He was not sentimental, but possessed a simple and dignified gentleness, which tempered his corrections and made them easier to accept. Even when it happened that he had to speak a strong word — on joyous days as well as those days of uncertainty and pain — it was always with finesse and warmth. The memory still moves us.[49]

Soon it was Advent — the first Advent at the "school" of Pitocchi, the father and spiritual master who seemed to emanate the invigorating air of the spirit of his great patron and father, St. Alphonsus de Liguori.[50]

While keeping vigil in his small room on Christmas Eve, Roncalli lived a mystical experience that neither his drowsiness nor the noises of the city outside could interrupt: "He [Jesus] came in and consoled me; I was able to stay with him for a long time and to tell him all that I desired."[51]

From then on, the thoughts he expressed in his *Journal of a Soul* frequently took the form of a more intimate dialogue with Jesus. Roncalli begins to speak less about himself and more about Jesus and total confidence in his grace. Less and less are there expressions of fear of his shortcomings and nothingness; more and more, he refers to his confidence in God's action that had revealed his personal way to holiness. This too was a great discovery:

I shall take the substance of the saints' virtues, not the accidents. I am not St. Louis, so I should not try to become holy the way he did, but rather according to my own way of being, my own character, my own circumstances. I do not have to be the pale, dried-up reproduction of even the most perfect model. God wants us to follow the examples of the saints, assimilate the vital substance of their virtues, convert it into our own blood, and adapt it to our own unique habits and special circumstances.[52]

The "New Culture"

Once Roncalli had returned full time to the seminary community, he was appointed as an assistant in the infirmary. This duty continually offered him — as he says — ever-new occasions to humble himself, especially through acts of charity, kindness, and little sacrifices. It is easy to imagine the spiritual and corporal works of mercy he was called to perform for the young patients in that infirmary room notoriously inadequate for its purpose.[53]

He continued to love his studies, perhaps because of his quiet and reflective nature or because so many of his companions were especially gifted and enjoyed studying. His admiration for his teachers may have motivated him or it may have been his clear understanding of scholastic pursuits in an age so enamored of science. He may have felt the need to make up in some way for the time he had lost in the military. Whatever the reasons, he became more fascinated with study, so much so, in fact, that he considered it an obstacle to his spiritual progress.

> Oftentimes, because of study, I forget my good resolutions and lose my presence of mind. I find myself less attracted to prayer and feel the lack of the pure oxygen of a devout life. Woe is me; my study should be a continuous prayer and my prayer an uninterrupted study. Above all, I must be vigilant over superficiality, inconstancy, and an obsession for study, for new things, new books, new systems, and new persons. I must be careful and watch what I say about these things. Yes, I have to consider everything and follow with interest the ascending movement of Catholic culture, but within reasonable proportions: *Ne quid nimis* (moderation in everything).[54]
>
> Yesterday, my learned professor of Church history (Umberto Benigni) gave us excellent advice, especially useful for me. He said: "Read little, read well." What he said about reading I can apply to just about everything: little but well. How many books I did not read during my years of study, my vacations, my military life!...

I feel a craving to know everything, all the noted authors, all the recent scientific achievements in the various fields, and in fact, I read and devour books here and there, but in the meantime, I achieve very little.[55]

What could possibly create problems within a Catholic culture or seminary? Roncalli spoke of a mania to become men of science at the highest levels. He spoke of recent scientific achievements, about superficiality, frivolity, excesses in study, new things, books, systems, and people. The Roman Seminary did, indeed, provide young proponents of the new Italian Catholic culture the opportunity to meet one another and to become acquainted with students or professors.

The new culture and the new way of studying, researching, and teaching began right there at St. Apollinare. By admitting younger professors to the faculty, Pope Leo XIII chose the college as a training ground for a renewal in methods of study, above all Thomistic-philosophic studies, but also biblical exegesis, archaeology, history, and Oriental studies. The new methodology was to be positivistic and more critical compared to the older, which was strictly dogmatic and traditionalistic. According to its promoters, this new scientific method should be joined with the proper Roman tradition, under the guidance of the superiors.

However, many students and professors became so enamored of the extreme criticism the new method employed, which at times resulted in a dogmatic relativism, that they went so far as to say that the only true Christian faith was that of the learned. They held to this position despite the fact that it meant disobedience to the Church's directives. They aligned themselves with and even emulated the champions of the new religion: Giovanni Semeria in Italy and Alfred Loisy beyond the Alps. At the time, these men probably lived like the *Carbonari,* a secret political society that awaited the victory of a "New World" to allow them to come out of their "catacombs."

New doctrines circulated secretly at night in the seminary through pamphlets, magazines, newspapers, and books — all "extraneous" readings, as Roncalli would refer to them. He was well aware of the new currents of thought, which "seemed modern" — he wrote — "but were only an ugly copy of old errors in the history of the Church."[56]

Despite many conversations and endless discussions in a friend's room or on walks along the streets of Rome,[57] Roncalli, with the benevolent and simple smile of his younger years,[58] chose to listen to his spiritual director who had pointed out to him the maxim of Terentius: *"Ne quid nimis,"* that is, "nothing in excess,"[59] and recommended "the good and very learned author of the *Imitation of Christ.*"[60] In his *Journal of a Soul,* Roncalli continued to copy passages from that book as maxims to put into practice.

For two years at the beginning of the new century, Roncalli was able to take advantage of more frequent meetings with Don Pitocchi. These years were among the most difficult for all the young ecclesiastics who were the hope of the Church in Italy and elsewhere. Twenty-five years later, Roncalli wrote of Don Pitocchi:

> That wind of modernity was blowing everywhere, sometimes forcefully, sometimes gently; then it degenerated in part into so-called "modernism," which poisoned the breath and spirit of many. It was a temptation for everyone, especially in the beginning. The superiors of the seminary kept a firm hold on us, imposing punishment when needed, even at the cost of being considered narrow-minded and closed to new ideas, yet trusting that the future would vindicate them. And after a short time, the future did indeed prove them right, showing the foresight, prudence and good practical sense of their behavior.[61]

Major Orders

Although the early months of 1903 were marked by intense study, Roncalli involved himself in the ordinary activities of the Roman seminary. Along with his classes, he had many spiritual encounters and activities, which he diligently noted in his *Journal of a Soul.*

On Holy Saturday of that year, April 11, as all the bells of the world were greeting the Risen Christ, Roncalli was ordained a subdeacon in the great Basilica of St. John Lateran.[62] Cleric Roncalli was now Don Angelo Roncalli.

He had spent days in an exceptional state of spiritual fervor that left him exhausted and confused by the profusion of graces poured out on him. He relived the ceremony as a great feast of love, an event of purest joy, impossible to describe except with the inspired words of the Psalmist:

> So great was the sweetness of my ordination, that I cannot possibly express it. *O quam dilecta tabernacula tua, Domine virtutum:*

concupiscit et deficit anima mea in atria Domini (How lovely is your dwelling place, O Lord of hosts; my soul longs for your courts). Truly *cor meum et caro mea exultaverunt in Deum vivum* (my heart and my flesh exult in the living God). This morning's celebration in St. John Lateran was so solemn in itself, and even more solemn for me, that I will never forget it. Now I truly am a new man; I have made my decision. The most eminent vicar cardinal, in the name of the Holy Father and the Church, welcomed, blessed, and consecrated my renunciation of all the things of this world, my total, absolute, and indissoluble dedication to Jesus Christ. After the solemn prostration, I approached the altar, and the cardinal, while accepting my vow, vested me in a new and glorious tunic. I felt as if all the popes, confessors, and martyrs who were sleeping in the silent tombs of the basilica awakened to give me a fraternal embrace. I felt them rejoicing with me and uniting with the choir of the angels of the resurrection in a hymn to the glorious Jesus, who let a miserable creature like me ascend to such a height. No words could ever express all the tenderness of that moment, but its memory will last in my heart eternally. I will never cease to thank and praise my Lord's love, greatness, and glory.[63]

After that memorable day, he settled back into his daily routine of work in the infirmary and preparing for his upcoming examinations. Doubtless, these months were dedicated to intense study since he would have to present his dissertation in a solemn academic ceremony held on June 30. At that ceremony, Roncalli was declared *prolita in sacra teologia,* obtaining his degree in theology and receiving the diploma signed by the vicar cardinal.[64]

Roncalli was probably in St. Peter's Square on the morning of August 4 when the news of a new pope was announced. There is no doubt that he was present in St. Peter's the following Sunday to attend the solemn rite of coronation. Twenty-five years later in one of his homilies, he recalled the culminating moment of the blessing:

The new pope was standing beside the tomb of the Prince of the Apostles as his successor. He looked around at the huge crowd gathered there, resplendent with the sacred tiara they had just placed on his head. The moment the choir concluded the antiphon, *Corona aurea super caput eius* (a golden crown is placed on his head), the pope raised his arms and extended them as if to embrace and hold to his heart all people from all nations. Then, with a voice strong yet filled with emotion, he pronounced the blessing and sent it to the whole world: *urbi et orbi* (to the city and to the world). I

still preserve in my ears and in my heart the final echo of this blessing — *Et maneat semper* (and may [this blessing] remain with you
forever). These profound words echoed the excited applause of the
whole crowd — the most international one imaginable — enthusiastically expressing the sentiments of their hearts now inspired at
seeing the Holy Father. The whole crowd had tears in their eyes as
they made the sign of the cross and felt the blessing of the Lord
penetrate their souls.[65]

By mid-August, Roncalli had finished his exams and was finally
able to go on vacation to Roccantica with his companions. The Roman
Seminary owned a villa in the town of Sabina and this was the first time
Roncalli was able to join the other clerics. He had spent the past two
summers in Sotto il Monte, the first waiting for the call to arms and the
second in forced marches with his battalion in Bergamo. The vacation at
the villa would last until the end of October; the academic year would
resume on November 4.

In the cultural atmosphere of the seminary and the Church in general, the beginning of the new century introduced years when "the spirit
of faith was gradually disappearing under the so-called requirements of
the critical method in the breath and light of the new times."[66] In his
practical application of the virtue of faith, "a very important virtue in the
present day," Roncalli reaffirmed his resolve to be a priest with a living,
simple, and undivided faith. He would stand with and for the pope, even
in what was not defined and in the smallest ways of seeing and feeling.
He wanted to be like those good old priests from Bergamo who did not
see — and did not want to see — beyond what the pope, the bishops,
common sense, and the spirit of the Church viewed as legitimate and
proper. Roncalli had a high regard for scientific criticism and he eagerly
followed its most recent findings. He kept himself updated with new systems of thought and their continuous developments and studied their
tendencies. Criticism is light and truth, and truth is holy, and there is
only one truth — his rule was to listen to everything and to everyone, to
think and to study. He felt he should not be surprised by anything, because surprise is born chiefly from ignorance. Nevertheless, in all the
sacred sciences and in theological or biblical questions, he would first
study the traditional doctrine of the Church and make this the basis for
his judgment of the latest scientific data. "For the rest, even if faith is
nourished by those things from which my piety and popular sentiment
can draw spiritual advantage, even if they are not all confirmed by posi-

tive and certain data, can it not be equally refined to virile strength together with great tenderness and pleasant candor?"[67]

Roncalli received his degree on July 13, 1904, at the young age of 22. He would always remember that the assistant for the written doctoral exam was a young Roman priest, Don Eugenio Pacelli.[68]

Priestly Ordination

Roncalli was not yet 23 and had to obtain a dispensation to be ordained because of *super defectu aetatis* (insufficient age). On August 10, in the Church of Santa Maria di Monte Santo in Piazza del Popolo, he was ordained with thirteen other candidates from various dioceses. The ordaining bishop was Giuseppe Ceppetelli, vice-regent of Rome and Latin Titular Patriarch of Constantinople.[69]

The spiritual exercises to prepare for ordination began on August 1, at the Passionist Fathers of Saints John and Paul on the Caelian Hill. About ten men from various towns and colleges made the exercises and they were all directed by the same priests. The retreat house was a little paradise. From the window, one could contemplate the Coliseum, the Basilica of St. John Lateran, and the Appian Way. From the garden could be seen the Palatine Hill and the Caelian Hill crowned with its Christian monuments. The Basilica of Saints John and Paul were close by, and Roncalli went there every evening for the novena in honor of Our Lady of the Assumption. Under the basilica was the *Clivus Scauri,* the house of the martyrs. Roncalli's room was close to the one in which St. Paul of the Cross died; everything about the house conveyed the idea of holiness, generosity, and sacrifice.[70]

On Tuesday, August 9, 1904, the day before his ordination, Roncalli went with his retreat director to St. John Lateran to renew his act of faith. He ascended the *Scala Santa* (Holy Stairs) on his knees, and then he went to the Basilica of St. Paul Outside the Walls. "What did I tell the Lord that night, on the tomb of the Apostle of the Nations? *Secretum meum mihi.* A secret I keep to myself."[71]

At dawn on the feast of St. Lawrence, the vice-rector, Don Domenico Spolverini,[72] accompanied Roncalli from the monastery and they proceeded in silence through the city. The unforgettable ceremony of priestly ordination took place at Santa Maria in Monte Santo in the Piazza del Popolo.[73]

During the rite, Angelo Roncalli did not lift his eyes from the missal or the celebrant. He looked up at the end and only then did he notice that amid the lights and flowers was the image of the Virgin Mary. She seemed to smile at him, infusing "a sense of sweet spiritual tranquillity, generosity, and security, as though she were telling me how happy she was and that she would always protect me. She communicated to my spirit a wave of sweet peace that I will never forget."[74]

As soon as he returned to the seminary, he wrote a letter to Bishop Gaetano Guindani. "I told him in a few words what I had told the Lord at the feet of Bishop Ceppetelli: 'I renewed my *promitto oboedientiam et reverentiam* (promises of obedience and reverence).'"[75] Then Roncalli wrote to his parents and family to share with them the joy of his heart, inviting them to give thanks to God and to pray that the Lord would keep him faithful.[76]

That afternoon he remained alone — alone with his God who had raised him so high, alone with his thoughts, his resolutions, and the joy of his priesthood.[77] He went out later for a walk and was so absorbed in God that it seemed as if Rome were a deserted city. He visited his favorite churches, the altars of his familiar saints, the images of our Lady.

The next day, he went to St. Peter's in the company of the vice-rector to celebrate his first Mass.[78] "How many things that square told me while I crossed it! Often I had felt moved while walking there, but never like that morning...and inside the majestic temple, among the venerable memories of the history of the Church!... I went down to the crypt, near the tomb of the Apostle."[79]

Don Roncalli celebrated the votive Mass of Saints Peter and Paul:

Oh, the consolations of that Mass! Among all the feelings that overflowed from my heart, I remember one that dominated the others: a great love for the Church, for the cause of Christ, for the pope, a total dedication of myself to the service of Jesus and the Church, of an intention, a sacred vow of fidelity to the chair of St. Peter, of untiring work for souls.... As I said to the Lord on the tomb of St. Peter: "Lord, you know all things; you know that I love you!" (Jn 21:17) I left there lost in reverie. On that day, the marble and bronze pontiffs along the walls of the basilica seemed to look at me from their sepulchres with a new meaning, as if to instill in me courage and great confidence.[80]

A new joy awaited him later that day. He was granted an audience with Pope Pius X.

> As soon as the pope came to where I was, the vice-rector intro-duced me. The pope smiled and bent his head to hear me. I was kneeling before him, telling him I was happy to be humbly at his feet, telling him the feelings I experienced during my first Mass at the tomb of St. Peter. I told him briefly, as best as I could. Then the pope, still bending over me and putting his hand on my head, al-most speaking in my ear, said: "Well done, well done, son...I am happy to hear this. I will pray to the Lord to bless your good inten-tions, so that you may really be a priest according to his heart. I also bless all your other intentions, and all the persons who rejoice with you in these days." He blessed me and offered me his hand to kiss. Then he moved on and spoke with someone else, a Polish man, I believe. But right after, as if following his course of thought, he turned back to me and asked when I would be back home. I an-swered, "For the feast of the Assumption." He replied, "Oh, imag-ine what a great feast there will be up there, in your little town (he had asked me before what town I was from), and how those beauti-ful Bergamasque bells will ring out that day!"[81]

At last, on Monday August 15, the feast of the Assumption, Roncalli arrived in Sotto il Monte for one of the happiest days of his life — and not only for him but also for his relatives, his benefactors, for everyone! What happened on the feast of the Assumption in Sotto il Monte can only be imagined. It had been years since the town had celebrated a newly ordained priest. Though they were poor, the people prepared tri-umphal arches and scattered flowers along the streets for Don Angelo just as they would have for a bishop. After all, the young priest had come home to Sotto il Monte to celebrate one of his first Masses with them on the feast of the Assumption. An organ and other instruments accompanied the sung Mass celebrated in the church of Brusicco. Then dinner was prepared and served at the parish house where memo-ries, both happy and sad, were cradled in the serene, simple, and pleas-ant atmosphere. Seated between his blissful parents, Battista and Marianna, the new priest was the honored guest at the central place of the celebration.

CHAPTER 4

RADINI TEDESCHI: BISHOP OF BERGAMO

By mid-October, Angelo had returned to St. Apollinare in Rome and had registered to begin his studies in canon law. The three-year program was divided into two main topics. The first course in canon law covered the *jus pontificum universum*: the universal pontifical law and ecclesiastical public law treating the classic themes of the perfect society, the Church as the perfect society, and the relationships between Church and State. The second course was the *potestas indirecta in temporalibus,* the indirect power of the Church over material things. The professors were very young: Guglielmo Sebastianelli, prefect of studies; Massimo Massimi, instructor of civil institutions; Vincenzo La Puma, professor of canon law; and Michael Lega and Giacomo Sole, teachers of the canonical text.

Unfortunately, the academic year began with sad news. The 70-year-old Bishop Gaetano Camillo Guindani, whose profound goodness had captivated Roncalli, had died. Now Don Angelo felt content "to have always loved him as a son loves his father, that venerable, erudite, and most pious prelate, and to have grown up in the shadow of his pastoral guidance, the last flower, however small and modest, of his garden," and hoped to receive "his blessings which were the caresses and delight of his adolescence."[1]

The year also began with the solemn celebrations honoring the fiftieth anniversary of the proclamation of the dogma of Mary's Immaculate

Conception. Bishop Giacomo Maria Radini Tedeschi was the moving force behind the festivities, the exposition, and the International Marian Congress.[2]

Roncalli participated in the daily celebrations, which began with the inaugural address by Pietro Maffi, Archbishop of Pisa, in the Church of the Twelve Apostles and closed with the cantata by Lorenzo Perosi in Santa Maria Sopra Minerva. Angelo exulted with spiritual joy on December 8 in St. Peter's Basilica because of the papal choir. While blending in among the crowd of young seminarians, he was so close to the altar that he had an excellent view of almost the entire ceremony. For the young priests participating in that celebration with him, the experience marked the "first revival of Catholic vitality after the uncertainties of the past."[3]

Just one month later, news arrived of the appointment of the new bishop of Bergamo. The announcement in the newspaper *La Tribuna* appeared unofficially on January 8, at the end of the beatification ceremony of the Curé of Ars.[4] It was confirmed ten days later in *L'Osservatore Romano*. The new bishop was the Vatican canon, Giacomo Maria Radini Tedeschi of Piacenza, the great organizer of pilgrimages and the soul of the Jubilee celebrations and recent festivities honoring the Immaculate Conception. A professor of sociology at the Collegio Leoniano in Rome, he was one of the more influential organizers in the *Opera dei Congressi* (Working documents of the Congress).[5]

Roncalli had never forgotten the day in September 1899 when he had met the distinguished prelate at the house of his parish priest, Alessandro Locatelli. No doubt, Don Alessandro later spoke at length to Roncalli about the prelate. Locatelli had been dormitory prefect at the episcopal College of St. Alexander in Bergamo when the young Radini Tedeschi was a student there. His father had sent all his sons to complete their secondary school education at the college. Roncalli also remembered Radini Tedeschi as an exceptional guide on the pilgrimage to Rome for the Holy Year 1900; in particular, the young priest recalled his convincing words and fervent manner.

Because it was common knowledge, Angelo was aware of the new bishop's interest in Bergamo. As clerk for the secretary of state, Radini Tedeschi had participated in the *Opera dei Congressi*. A substantial amount of correspondence from 1890 linked him with Count Stanislao Medolago Albani of Bergamo,[6] president of the Christian economic section of the *Opera*. All of Rome, all of Italy in fact, and many important people from abroad knew Radini Tedeschi. Roncalli could only be enthusiastic about his new bishop.

> His tall, slender, noble figure, his distinguished piety, his vast and profound learning, his eloquent speech, his innumerable and worthy personal relationships and connections, his majestic and affable manner especially with little ones, and above all his apostolic zeal for all things good and beautiful, for the glory of God and for the Immaculate Conception, for the good of souls — a zeal that burns within his breast and shines forth from his eyes and from all his works — all these things have made Radini Tedeschi one of the most outstanding examples of the Roman prelature. As is generally stated, only the great esteem and affection of the Holy Father for our diocese explains the reason for his appointment to the diocese of Bergamo.[7]

Pius X had personally consecrated Radini Tedeschi as bishop, something that had not happened for many years — at least not during the twenty-five-year pontificate of Pope Leo XIII. The ceremony took place in the Sistine Chapel on Sunday, January 29, the feast of St. Francis de Sales. The concelebrants were Giovanni Battista Scalabrini,[8] Bishop of Piacenza, from Radini's home diocese, and Giacinto Arcangeli of Bergamo, Bishop of Asti. Don Roncalli and Don Carozzi assisted the new bishop elect.[9]

Don Roncalli recalled the most significant moment of the ceremony when he had "the great honor of holding the missal on his shoulders, while the hands of Pius X were raised for the preface of the *qui benedixerit* and the *qui maledixerit*[10] of the prayer of consecration." This prayer invoked the benediction or malediction of the Lord on whoever would bless or curse the new bishop. Surely, Don Angelo must have sensed in that prayer a program of veneration and love for the new bishop whose head, freshly anointed with the sacred chrism, remained devoutly covered with the book of Gospels.

Secretary to the Bishop

A few days after Radini Tedeschi's episcopal consecration, the rector asked Don Angelo to invite the new bishop, in his name and that of the students from Bergamo, to celebrate a solemn Pontifical Mass in the seminary church on February 13, feast of the Madonna del Portico or Queen of the Apostles. A dinner was held afterward in the bishop's honor and all the seminarians were present. Could the new bishop have already had Don Roncalli in mind and heart for his new secretary? Whether or not Radini Tedeschi had decided before the dinner, within a few days Roncalli would accept the position.[11]

In fact, the bishop has asked the seminary rector, Monsignor Bugarini, his opinion of this delicate choice that seemed almost natural since Roncalli was the "most Romanized" of the Bergamase priests. Radini Tedeschi preferred him even to Don Carozzi who could actually be considered more suitable for the position because he was older.[12] Roncalli's appointment not only interrupted his immediate preparation for the February exams, but the entire program of studies.

While he was still in Rome, Roncalli had the good fortune, on several occasions, to be presented to Pope Pius X as Radini Tedeschi's secretary. On March 18, the eve of the feast of St. Joseph, Radini Tedeschi left Rome and the pope to return to his diocese. Roncalli often recalled the pope's encouraging words to the bishop, "Go. Go to Bergamo, for however it can console a bishop, Bergamo is the first diocese of Italy."[13] Above all, he would always remember the pope's words to him: "Don Roncalli! *Fidelis servus et prudens! Et prudens!* (Faithful and prudent servant! And prudent!)"[14]

Before assuming his duties as secretary, Don Roncalli spent three days (March 19–21, 1905) on retreat at the Camaldolese hermitage in Frascati. Then he traveled directly to Bergamo with the bishop for the installation ceremony of Sunday, April 9. This was "a triumph and a solemn popular acclaim, unmatched by any other reception of its kind in the history of Bergamo. The memory of that indescribable demonstration will remain forever in whomever had the good fortune to be present."[15]

Naturally, Roncalli's first months as secretary were months of adjustment. The bishop was also adjusting to a new household, which included the house-steward, master of ceremonies, and service personnel. Don Roncalli kept account of the smaller daily expenses and then passed this along to the administrator.

Roncalli made a daily schedule that began in the evening. Before going to bed at 11:30 P.M., he prayed Matins and Lauds and then he spent a short time before the beautiful image of Our Lady of Confidence, which he had brought with him from Rome. After rising at 5:30 A.M., he would spend from a half-hour to fifteen minutes in meditation, celebrate Mass, and recite the Office. After breakfast, he would attend to his work.

Following his afternoon meal, he would read the newspapers, then make his spiritual exam, pray Vespers, and make a brief visit to the Blessed Sacrament. After the evening rosary that was prayed with the bishop's household, he would read a good book to uplift his spirit.[16]

As expected, Roncalli took his duties as the bishop's secretary seriously, and he carried them out with great sensitivity.

> I must always have the greatest reverence for the bishop in my mind, heart, and actions, both privately and publicly. I must offer him full obedience and remain united with him in spirit. I have the obligation to give good example and conduct myself as a priest should in every situation by showing charity and kindness in all circumstances. I must be attentive especially to my tongue: to speak little and well. Above all, to know when to be quiet without pretension...maintaining tranquillity of spirit and serenity with everyone, showing the greatest courtesy in my manners and words.[17]

Roncalli got along well, very well in fact, with the bishop.

> It is said that no one is great in the eyes of his household; however, no matter how close I am to him, in my eyes Bishop Radini Tedeschi never diminishes. He is always polite, always loving, even when I make a mistake, even when things do not go well. For me, being in his company is a true school from which I hope to learn a great deal.[18]

Tedeschi's appearance, as well as his spirit, made a great impression on Roncalli.

> Here he is, Bishop Radini Tedeschi, handsome and tall, an imposing figure, coming to meet us with his ever kind, expressive gaze, eyes ready to sparkle or grow dim with every shadow of the spirit. Nature was very generous with him also in those external qualities the world takes notice of and which make up what is commonly called a handsome man: *pulchra facie et decorus aspectu* (a beautiful face and appearance, cf. Gen 29:17). His open and serene countenance gives his face a delicate and fine line, enhanced by a vivid shade of red. His small, thin lips, his mouth composed in dignity, know nothing of flattery or falsehood. His lips are often parted in a smile that at times seems touched with irony by his kind but piercing eyes. His character, his gait, his whole person radiates vigor and energy, together with recollection and tranquillity. His appearance is solemn and yet peaceful, serious and yet affable, reserved and yet friendly. Above all else, his every gesture and word has an un-

equaled elegance, never belied, but always full of naturalness and grace. All this gives him an excellence that everyone immediately recognizes and respects.[19]

On April 29, twenty days after returning to Bergamo, Don Angelo departed for Lourdes on the national pilgrimage which Radini Tedeschi guided. The journey by train lasted several days and passed through several cities, stopping at Genoa, Marseilles, and Montpellier. On the return trip, they also stopped at Lyons for the celebration in honor of Joan of Arc, who had been declared Venerable. In the city of Ars they visited the tomb of the venerated Curé John Vianney who had been beatified on January 8 of that year. They also stopped at Paray-le-Monial and finally at Turin before returning to Bergamo on May 18.

For six full days, the pilgrims stayed in Lourdes where Roncalli found himself...in paradise.

> I have been here for only a few days and I find myself in paradise. Although the rain comes down in torrents, one feels so good here that it does not matter. The thought of Mary Immaculate totally absorbs me and keeps me in a heavenly atmosphere where I can only be silent, pray, and cry.... To my immense consolation, I was able to celebrate Mass at the grotto; it is impossible to describe the profound impressions one receives here. For the rest, everything at Lourdes seems to speak: when one comes here, one never wants to leave.[20]

Standing at the bishop's side, Roncalli listened to the ardent and moving words Radini Tedeschi spoke at the grotto in the Church of the Rosary during the nocturnal Eucharistic adoration and along the Way of the Cross.[21]

A few days after returning to Bergamo, Roncalli was again on the road with the bishop, this time to Rome for the International Eucharistic Congress. Roncalli participated in all of the ceremonies and, on his own initiative, sent the general pro-vicar two letters narrating the activities of the Congress. The pro-vicar used these to write articles about the great event for the daily paper, *L'Eco di Bergamo*.[22] With great enthusiasm, Roncalli described the various phases of the great Congress, the select and crowded gatherings, the ceremonies, the benedictions, the pontifical audiences, the final procession — everything that took place within the beautifully decorated basilicas. He rejoiced to be able to visit the Holy City again after only a brief absence.

First Historical Essay

The summer and fall passed quickly as Roncalli accompanied the bishop on his frequent trips to visit the parishes and religious communities of the diocese or in meetings with the Lombard bishops at Rho and at Milan. Roncalli wrote that he felt like a "suitcase forever in transit."[23]

Roncalli continued to be enthusiastic about the bishop despite some criticism by priests who would have preferred a less compromising bishop for Bishop Guindani's successor, perhaps one of the diocesan clergy. Roncalli was pleased when all the priests, young and old, eventually placed themselves at the disposition of the bishop and were ready to do anything asked of them. As admiration for the bishop grew, the spirit of criticism slowly dissipated.[24] In a short time, it became obvious that the diocese of Bergamo was permeated by fervor as no other diocese of the world. The bishop truly had a burning fire in his heart that did not diminish for even a moment. Roncalli, always at Radini Tedeschi's side, tried to match his fervor as much as possible.

> I know that the bishop is happy with my company. The strongest observation he offers me is: *homo pacis meae* (my peaceful man). But here in Bergamo, even the quickest are all a little like this, according to the bishop. So what about me? What does he expect? I have the weakness to believe that my peace, united with his fire and apostolic dynamism, is providential. It is important that I do not make myself unworthy of the extraordinary grace that the Lord has given me by placing me near a bishop so filled with the spirit of Jesus Christ.[25]

Among the many wonderful things being planned, Don Angelo was surely thinking about the bishop's initiative to restore the Congregation of the Priests of the Sacred Heart. In his position as an observer, Roncalli followed the evolution of this initiative very closely and noted his observation in the pages of his *Diary,* which he began on December 8.

A congregation of priests living the vowed life in common and at the complete disposition of the bishop already existed in the diocese at the end of the 1700s. Unfortunately, it now had very few members. Bishop Radini Tedeschi wanted to revitalize and restructure the congregation modeled after the Oblates of St. Charles Borromeo of Milan. While fervently attending to personal holiness, these priests would assist the bishop in a particular way through their total obedience. They would preach at parish missions or at retreats for the clergy, and provide spiritual direction for the seminarians, diocesan priests, and religious sisters. The priests would manage the episcopal colleges, but would also be present in the public schools and other educational facilities of the diocese. Besides educating leaders of Catholic associations, they would also act as administrators in vacant parishes, or as the bishop's delegates in matters of importance.

To promote this initiative, Roncalli was asked to do some historical research on the origins of the congregation. While his study served as a means for reorganizing existing information, as his first historical work, it also revealed marvelous examples of bishops and priests from the diocese of Bergamo in the last two centuries.[26] He did not fail to report his impressions:

> In reviewing the past, in gathering the few scattered pieces of information regarding its hidden history, one remains filled with wonder and moved when faced with the fact that, from the end of the eighteenth century to most recent times, the venerable priests of the diocese of Bergamo, best known for their virtue, doctrine, special talents, and dignity which brought splendor to our Church, were all members of the apostolic college. From the intimate communion of souls, by frequent gatherings, and by feeling bound to their special promises in the service of God, of souls, and of their own bishop, they drew ever fresh and generous energies to work and to sacrifice themselves to carry out their priestly ministry.[27]

Pastoral Visit

"Here begins the holy visit, which, because of the bishop's zeal, influence, and greatness, is a new triumph. For me, work increased tremendously. Besides all my other tasks, I had to carry out the pastoral ministry of preaching, hearing confessions, etc. Sympathize with me and understand if I write in haste, for it is just a few minutes to midnight."[28] Don Roncalli wrote these words on December 14, 1905, to his beloved rector in Rome.

Radini Tedeschi's first pastoral visit to the diocese had begun only six days before, and Roncalli was already so busy that he used the last minutes of a very long day for his correspondence. This would be the case for many months. From the day the visit began on December 8, Roncalli kept a personal diary with the intention of following both the religious and social developments of the event.[29] However, now only fragments of the diary exist. The first volume goes uninterruptedly from December 8 to January 12, and contains news items and annotations of the visit — even the days of rest — enlivened with Roncalli's wonderful description of people and situations.

Meanwhile, Roncalli had also been asked to preach at the beginning of the Christmas novena at the Church of St. Michael the Archangel, a short distance from the bishop's residence. It took more time to prepare than he had anticipated, and he did not get much sleep. The next morning he could not remember a single word of the homily he prepared the evening before! But things could not have gone too badly because the trial was followed by his being asked to preach the entire novena. He was even asked to preach for the feast of St. Francis de Sales on January 29, at the Church of St. Alexander in Colonna.

Confirmation of this well done, if long-suffered, experience remains in a note written by Roncalli as the pope, to the sculptor Giacomo Manzù. Manzù's father was the sacristan of St. Alexander in Colonna at the time the young Don Angelo preached. At the end of his first homily, Roncalli had given the sacristan one of the two lire he had received for his service. After all, the sacristan had accompanied the young preacher to the pulpit and had stayed nearby. Moreover, from time to time during the homily, he would furtively tug at the young priest's vestment to indicate that, despite Roncalli's nervousness, things were going quite well. The budding orator concluded his sermon "with much fear, but good results."[30]

Radini Tedeschi's pastoral visit continued throughout the 350 parishes of the diocese with surprising alacrity. By their solemn and moving demonstrations of faith and love, his people showed their devotion to him and made the heavy burdens of his ministry seem lighter.[31] Don Roncalli carried a heavy load as well. Outside the office, there was the intense work of the pastoral visit; and in the office, there were the other never-ending duties. He wrote jokingly to his classmate, Don Spolverini, of the many people who visited his office more than they had the vice-rector's at the seminary.[32] In the seven months since the pastoral visit had begun, Roncalli had not found even two hours of free time to visit his family.[33] As pro-chancellor or secretary of the visit, he followed the bishop and his collaborators and was called upon to serve and provide for them. He was away for 115 days, often for entire weeks at a time, traveling from one part of the diocese to another, even to places that were difficult to reach because of limited means of transportation. He managed to visit ninety-four parishes and was happy about it: "I live joyfully in the affection the bishop has for me. I am working full force for the pastoral visit, which multiplies the consolations and the proofs of love for the bishop on the part of his children. I feel the desire to do much more to cooperate with the great grace God gives me."[34]

Pilgrimage to the Holy Land

On September 12, Don Roncalli accompanied the bishop on another trip. After a two-day stopover at Piacenza, four days in Rome, and one in Naples, the third Italian national pilgrimage, with Bishop Radini Tedeschi as the director and guide and Roncalli as the special correspondent, set off for the Holy Land.

Don Roncalli described in detail the spiritual experience he lived. It was a true "being with Jesus" as on Mount Tabor because he was at the side of his spiritual director, Don Fachinetti, who had joined the pilgrimage. Roncalli had made a commitment to write something for the monthly review, *Il Giardinetto di Maria: Eco di Lourdes e di Palestina*, of which Radini Tedeschi was honorary director. Instead, the travel notes of Giuseppe Molteni, a correspondent for *L'Osservatore Cattolico* of Milan were preferred. Roncalli's notes were published as a series of articles in the October issues of *L'Eco di Bergamo*, with this byline: "our special correspondent."[35] One of the periodical's four-page summaries even appeared in the Catholic weekly *Pro Familia* under the title, "Jerusalem."[36]

On the morning of Tuesday, September 25, the group disembarked at Beirut and from there, they traveled through Lebanon by train all the way to Damascus, tracing the footsteps of St. John the Baptist, St. Paul, and St. John Damascene. They returned to Beirut and set sail for Haifa and then on to Carmel to reach Nazareth.

I will not soon forget the moment we arrived in Nazareth. We formed a procession toward the Basilica of the Annunciation, singing the litanies of the Madonna. Once inside the basilica, our reverend bishop immediately intoned the holy rosary and added other short prayers. However, contrary to his custom, he did not say another word. Under the altar of the crypt where the great mystery was fulfilled, we read these words: *Verbum caro hic factem est* (here the Word became flesh). It was the most beautiful sermon, and enough for us to recollect ourselves and to reawaken the dearest memories of our holy faith. Life in Nazareth is peaceful and tranquil. It seems that in this blessed town, Jesus left something of the serenity, peace, and sweet recollection in which he spent so many years of his life. The spirit finds rest in Nazareth; prayer comes spontaneously to the lips. The exercise of those virtues that cost us so much in life — humility, obedience, hiddenness, sacrifice — here become natural and easy. The soul feels itself to be better because it is closer to God.[37]

They traveled from Nazareth to Cana where Radini Tedeschi consecrated the new main altar of the parish church, and from Cana they went to the city of Tiberias and stood by its lake.

All the sentiments that I felt in the little church of my town as a boy when I listened to the Gospel account from the lips of my good pastor; all the holy sentiments I experienced later as a seminarian when I went about reading one passage or another from the little divine book for my spiritual comfort; or in school, reconstructing and placing all the facts and ideas about the life of Jesus in my mind; these things came to mind last night when I was visiting the enchanting Lake of Tiberias.[38]

But I will never be able to forget the charm of that lake and of that stretch of road (from Tiberias to Capernaum), the consolation, the spiritual delight that I felt this morning while passing over those waters.... I wanted to walk the pathway and accompany the sight of all these venerable places with the reading of the biblical passages that referred to them, but at a certain point, I could no longer do it. The divine book closed in my hands; my soul and the souls of everyone with me were amazed and overwhelmed by the wave of sweet memories that swept over us. Admiration changed into prayer. Jesus showed himself to us and we saw him. Despite our unworthiness, we went to meet him on the waters; our prayer was silent, yes, but spontaneous and meaningful.[39]

On their return along the road from Capernaum to Haifa, Don Roncalli climbed Mount Tabor.

When, after some amount of sweat, one has gained that summit made holy by the presence of Jesus, and rests mind and body in the memory of that great event, it is truly natural to say: *Bonum est nos hic esse* (It is good for us to be here, Mt 17:4). Our faith experienced stronger impulses on Tabor, and the cries of our souls rose more spontaneously to Christ, to him who, above the beech woods of the forest, allowed a ray of his divinity to appear. *Tu es Christus filius Dei vivi* (You are the Christ, the Son of the living God, Mt 16:16).[40]

The pilgrims traveled by sea from Haifa to Jaffa and from there to Jerusalem by train. Immediately upon their arrival, without taking rest or refreshment, Don Roncalli and the others hurried to the Holy Sepulcher — the goal of their long voyage.

> We knelt before the holy crypt. I do not remember what my soul was saying, or those of the pilgrims with me, at that moment before the triumphant Jesus. Then, one by one we passed into the holy crypt to place our lips on the glorious stone. I did not see the Greek monk who was standing in the small inner room waiting for the pilgrims' offerings. I cannot even say what the little cell looked like. I only remember the feeling of that mysterious and very tender first kiss on the cold marble, which I will remember as long as I live.[41]

They remained in Jerusalem about ten days, praying alone, in small groups, or all together for traditional devotions such as the *Via Crucis* through the streets of the city. They visited all the sites that are most dear to Christians, the interior of the city and even some of the outskirts, all the places our Redeemer sanctified during his life on earth. Roncalli wrote:

> We have been in the Holy City for eight days, fortunate for the spiritual consolations this beautiful journey gives us. From the first moment we came here and kissed the glorious stone until now we have enjoyed an uninterrupted succession of holy emotions. We have been confronted with the memories, at times joyful, at times mournful, of the people of Israel, of the life of Jesus, of the origins of Christianity, and of the entire life of the Church. I have always had a great desire to visit Jerusalem, but the sentiments, the joy, the spiritual comfort that I have experienced in these days surpassed all my expectations. I would like to remain here a long time to see, to admire, to study, because the more one knows Jerusalem, the more interest it awakens. The city exercises a strong, irresistible charm.... Jerusalem is always Jerusalem, the Holy City par excellence, even before Rome could call herself holy. No city in the world can compare itself to her memories, her religious monuments, and the light she radiates.... And to always keep our spirit immersed in this wave of sacred memories, to hear the voices that speak to us from the rocks, the streets, the monuments, the sanctuaries — this is our most blessed life these days.[42]

Sunday, October 14 came — the sad day of their departure. In the morning, Don Roncalli celebrated Mass at Gethsemane with a friend, then passed by the Holy Sepulcher to kiss the sacred tomb one more time. "Oh, the eloquence of that last goodbye and of that last kiss!"[43]

Once the pilgrimage ended, Don Roncalli no longer felt any interest in the trip. They returned by way of Alexandria and Cairo to Naples. He wrote that the accounts he sent to the newspaper were really nothing compared to all he had seen and what he *could* have said, or said better if there had been more time.

CHAPTER 5

PROFESSOR OF CHURCH HISTORY

On Saturday, November 10, at exactly 2:45 P.M., Roncalli taught his first class on Church history. His students were the clerics from the first three courses of theology who took the class as required by the regulations of the Lombard seminaries.

Roncalli was not yet 25 and had been ordained only two years when he was appointed a lecturer in Church history. Whether the appointment was a planned or spontaneous decision, it was the obvious result of Bishop Radini Tedeschi's marked presence in the internal life of the seminary and his growing esteem for Roncalli.

Radini Tedeschi wanted Roncalli not only to act on behalf of the bishop's office concerning the seminary, but also to take a personal interest in it. This is seen in the bishop's letter from Rome in November 1906 in which he entrusted the delicate twofold task to Don Roncalli. He was to be spokesperson for the seminarians on one hand, and on the other, for the members of the disciplinary commission. Radini Tedeschi was counting on the young priest's firmness to act toward reform. It is apparent from the letter's tone that the two had already discussed issues concerning the seminary in general and the faculty in particular, and that Roncalli had spoken with the seminarians named in the letter regarding these matters.[1]

But why a history teacher? Don Roncalli was certainly not an expert in the subject though he did hold a degree in theology from the Apollinare. Roncalli was assigned to substitute for a Don Pedrinelli who was at the Louvain to complete his studies. Roncalli's natural interest in Church history led him to enjoy reading it in his spare time, and to do research on the origins and evolution of the apostolic college. He had also done some work in the archdiocesan archives of Milan on documents relating to the apostolic visit of St. Charles to Bergamo. Given time, there would be no difficulty in transferring the teaching post to Roncalli.[2]

Don Roncalli set about his task, as he would later write to Cardinal Baronius, "reluctantly at first to narrate and then to write the history of the Church, motivated only by obedience, without even the slightest qualification for such an undertaking, but he obeyed."[3] The history curriculum was quite demanding. The course was developed around a three-year cycle and divided into three parts: the Church from its foundation to the end of the seventh century; from the eighth century to Luther's Reformation; from Luther's Reformation to the present.

One student later commented that Don Roncalli's method of teaching was rather monotonous. Unlike the teacher he would later become, expounding on the topic freely, Roncalli limited himself to merely reading the text,[4] an understandable and justifiable choice during one's first year of teaching. What text did he use? There is no documentation. Whether he used the Italian edition of the Bruck Manual as edited by the rector of the seminary, Don Castelletti, or Hergenrother's that he had acquired for his own study the year before, remains a question. It is as uncertain if he used the handouts of his "very gifted history teacher," Umberto Benigni, or those of his former fellow disciple, Ernesto Buonaiuti, who hurriedly sent all his notes to Don Angelo before the course began.[5]

Meanwhile, Don Angelo continued to carry out his duties as the bishop's secretary. Because he was so busy with school, Roncalli only occasionally accompanied the bishop on pastoral visits, and then only in the city parishes in the capacity of co-visitor.[6] He sought to accomplish his delicate and weighty duties as secretary with charity and tact in every circumstance,[7] with a kind and gentle spirit of patience and tranquility[8] — with *charm* — just as he accomplished his other duties.[9]

Roncalli's participation in the life of the diocese became more active and direct after the bishop entrusted him with various important duties. Little by little the priests and religious of the diocese began to know Roncalli, and they asked him to collaborate in activities related to preaching and apostolic work. He played a major role in several diocesan events and initiatives. At a young age, he had become a public personality in the diocese and he felt good about it. The many tasks sent his head and heart into ecstasy, though he was so overwhelmed that he did not know which saint to turn to for help. "Here at Bergamo everything is going rather smoothly. My humble life is evolving happily, although somewhat arduously amid a series of diverse and major tasks that never let up."[10]

During the summer of 1907, he took on the responsibility of temporary pastor of Santa Maria d'Oleno in the small parish of Sforzatica that had been left vacant by the death of the parish priest in early July.[11] In reality, the assignment was a way to prevent him from being recalled to military service for the summer as was customary.[12] Because Bishop Radini Tedeschi needed Don Roncalli's assistance, he filled the assignment only until a new pastor was appointed in November. He did not reside at the parish, but went there every Saturday and stayed until Sunday night or Monday morning. He would also go whenever he was needed. It was a period of ordinary administration because the nature of the assignment did not permit more. The parishioners grew fond of the young priest, who was so faithful to his duties, especially the brief explanation of Church doctrine on Sunday afternoons.[13] Roncalli later recalled that this time allowed him to experience being a simple priest among simple people from whom a pastor, with a little goodwill and kindness, could succeed in getting all the cooperation he needed.[14] His notes reflect a ray of priestly and evangelical poetry and express a certain tenderness: "August 11: gave 9.00 lire to the poor mother of the first baby I baptized."[15]

Teacher of Patrology and Apologetics

During that same summer of 1907, Don Roncalli was also occupied with the study of patrology and apologetics — subjects that would become, as he wrote, his future pastime.[16] When Don Pedrinelli returned from the Louvain, Roncalli left the history post to his friend and was immediately given a new assignment: to teach patrology to the theology students and apologetics to the philosophy students.

Roncalli spent the summer preparing for the new task. Staying with the bishop at Castel San Giovanni in the peaceful surroundings of the Apennines, he had the opportunity to read and reread *Pascendi,*[17] the encyclical that had been made public on September 8. Roncalli defined the work as admirable and said that he had been truly shaken by it, as he believed it must have shaken everyone a little and changed the minds of many.[18]

With that encyclical letter, Pius X condemned the unorthodox trend that had emerged among Catholics in recent decades. It was a trend that proposed to renew and interpret Church doctrine according to modern thought, and for this reason became known as "Modernism." Only two months after the promulgation of the encyclical, Roncalli began teaching his courses. He could not help thinking of the concerns the document had expressed, especially in reference to what was being taught in seminaries. "School is a great means for doing good to young clerics even when a professor simply remains within the limits of his own competencies. It is the truest demonstration of *gutta cavat lapidem*" (the drop of water that makes a hole in the stone).[19]

His students remember Roncalli entering the classroom, briefcase tucked under his arm and breathless from having climbed the many stairs of the old seminary. As soon as he reached his desk he would take out his notes and distribute handouts.[20] Available testimony, though inadequate, confirms his total dedication to magisterial teaching expressed in a calm freedom of judgment, a new way of treating the subject matter, and a new method of teaching.

> [He was] always calm, welcoming, and refined; clear, slow, and careful in his explanations; entrusting much to the open-mindedness and interaction of his students. To younger students who were just beginning their philosophical speculations, he would confidently open up new horizons on the subject matter and draw them to the sources: the Fathers of the Church, the classical texts of learned theologians and philosophers, and the most current reviews, especially those of French scholars.[21] Of all the seminary classes, his was the most popular. When he would test us, he did not require us to repeat the text verbatim, but allowed us to comment freely on the theme discussed in our own words and in detail.[22] He had a simple and total faith that manifested itself in a respectful adherence to the truth and the teachings of the Church.[23]

Cardinal Caesar Baronius

By the summer of 1907,[24] Don Angelo had also been assigned to prepare the official address for the opening of the new academic year.

The theme: Cardinal Caesar Baronius (1538–1607), the learned and holy Oratorian. On the advice of St. Philip Neri, Baronius had countered the polemical Protestant work, *Centuriae magdeburghesi,* with his far superior *Annales ecclesiastici.* Written between 1588 and 1598, these twelve volumes narrated the history of the Church from its apostolic origins to A.D. 1198. Since 1907 marked the third centenary of the scholarly cardinal's death, the occasion was ripe for celebrating the happy marriage between historical science and faith in the Church — one that Modernists seemed to deny.

Don Roncalli had read about the famous cardinal "some time before,"[25] and while in Rome he had visited Baronius' modest country home in Frascati sul Tuscolo. In his own study of history, Don Roncalli had probably come across the cardinal's name, but it was not until he received the assignment that he began to research bibliographical material. In particular, Roncalli used *The Life and Works of Cardinal Caesar Baronius,*[26] a recently published work by the Oratorian priest, Generoso Calenzio.

Roncalli gave an excellent talk. In fact, the next day the local paper, *L'Eco di Bergamo,* commended his presentation.

> Timely, concise, brilliant. That is the only way to describe the academic discourse on Cardinal Baronius, the great historian and father of Church history, chronicled by the priest, Dr. Angelo Roncalli. The cardinal's solid virtue and exacting scholarship, worldwide fame and profound humility, the dignity of his office and the simplicity of his life — the orator ably expounded upon all of these qualities for his audience that listened for almost an hour with great interest and delight, a rare occurrence for an academic talk. Those attending only complained that it was too short.[27]

Bishop Radini Tedeschi did not know how to praise his young secretary enough except to have the talk published in Milan's scholarly review, *La Scuola Cattolica.* It was printed in the first issue of 1908[28] and reprinted later that year in a thirty-six page, large-format brochure published in Monza.[29] Roncalli received compliments from all sides, but the most rewarding praise came from Cardinal Ferrari of Milan.[30]

Indeed, the essay, written in a captivating literary style, was lively, warm, and engaging. Following a dedication to his bishop, Don Roncalli treated the subject in a way that was professional and academic and yet at the same time succeeded in bringing to life the person, the character, and the works of Baronius. Roncalli did not avoid those details that could be applicable to the current state of the Church and its historical culture. Indeed, such points were made by an animated apologist. He did not shy away from a sincere expression of his feelings. In a quasi-auto-biographical way, he communicated the soul of Baronius by revealing his own — that of an educated priest who directed all his desires toward holiness. Cardinal Baronius was a holy man, and in reading the *Annali,* Don Roncalli discovered a person of principle, a tireless worker, a saint though not yet canonized. While studying Baronius' life, Roncalli's spirit was deeply stirred. He felt transported toward vast horizons illuminated by the light of truth and sanctity. How did the young priest define sanctity?

> Recent falsehoods have attempted to undermine the concept of holiness among us. They have distorted this concept, colored it in lively shades perhaps only tolerated in a novel, but which, practically speaking, are out of place in the real world. To know how to humble oneself constantly, destroying within and around oneself what others seek praise for from the world; to keep alive in one's own heart the flame of a most pure love for God, above and beyond weak, earthly affections; to give all, to sacrifice oneself for the good of others, with humility and love for God and one's neighbor; to follow faithfully the roads Providence indicates, which lead elected souls to fulfill their special mission. This is holiness.[31]

Baronius became a saint through his obedience. Baronius' brief, simple, and often repeated gesture of kissing the foot of the bronze statue of St. Peter in the Vatican as a declaration of his total obedience to the pope led Roncalli to meet the man in his entirety. "Those words of his, *pax et oboedientia,* have a great significance for me and, if I am not mistaken, they cast light upon and explain his life very well."[32] Roncalli often used the same words, but he transposed them as *oboedientia et pax.*[33] The motto would come to explain his behavior as a Catholic scholar in harmony with the new demands of the times and the claims of contemporary science amid a "whirlwind of deceptive ideas, which try to undermine the concept of that authority which both illuminates and guides the minds of Catholic scholars."[34] Roncalli's animated text borrowed words and at times entire phrases from the encyclical *Pascendi* to describe the strange movement of ideas that he claimed to witness.

> We Catholics are attacked on every side in the name of positive scholarship. The least they say about us is that we are obscurantists,

closed in the narrow-mindedness of old formulas devoid of meaning. We have also placed ourselves in the field of positive scholarship, steadfast in those sacred principles of the ancient wisdom of
the Fathers and of the illustrious scholastic doctors, whose stability
no attack can weaken. New times and new needs demand this of us,
if we are to walk the sure path and respond to the attacks of unbelievers. We will be more confident, however, if we do not lose faith
in our cause and in the victory of that truth which alone can liberate
us from the crisis that we face. It seems to me that abandoning these
strong faith convictions is one of the principal factors of that
strange movement of ideas, which, until recently, has disturbed
Catholic consciences and is a serious daily concern for them. Certain poor, deceived souls — I believe it right to call them so — have
judged the Church and Christianity according to the standards of
all-too-human criteria. Resulting from its criticism of the traditional
teachings of the Church, German theological rationalism made il-
logical and unjust applications, which seemed to tear down the
Church's perennial stability. Perhaps with the good intentions of
saving her, out of what I call fear, we resorted to other means.
These other means, by some strange irony, represent the destruction
of every true scientific process and the dreadful regression toward
the worst sort of subjectivism.[35]

The essay ended with a wish, almost an exhortation that "above
philosophical speculation, although drawn from the pure font of the
Aquinate [the thought of St. Thomas and Thomistic scholars], and from
positive inquiry, there is always faith — the supernatural habit that re-
moves all doubts and uncertainties, that makes us fear nothing, certain
that the victory of truth, however the truth manifests itself and from
wherever it may come, will always be a victory of the Church."[36]

"Diocesan Life"

Because the lecture was such a great success, Roncalli became
known as a devotee of history to an audience beyond the seminary. Perhaps this convinced him to undertake other projects, but this time on
local history such as the bishops of Bergamo. "In the bits of free time I
have left, I enjoy putting together the portraits of the former bishops of
Bergamo. Since I can find little information here, I am bothering people
outside of Bergamo."[37]

Actually, Roncalli was preparing articles on the bishops of Bergamo
for a new series to appear in the *Bulletin of the Secretariat for the Clergy*

of the Diocese of Bergamo. This monthly periodical was for the clergy of the diocese and had been commissioned by Bishop Radini Tedeschi in 1906. The bulletin of information was later expanded and enriched with articles that included "Succession of Bishops of Bergamo,"[38] "The Roman Breviary,"[39] and other historical studies. Although published as anonymous, all of the articles had been written by Roncalli with his friend, Guglielmo Carozzi. With the bishop's approval, the two priests were preparing to change the periodical's format.

In January 1909, the first issue of the new monthly appeared under the title: *Bulletin of the Secretariat for the Clergy — Diocesan Life — Official Periodical of the Bishop and of the Curia*. They based the idea on the monthly periodical, *Diocesan Life* of Malines, which had been commissioned by a friend of Bishop Radini Tedeschi, Cardinal Mercier. Like the Belgian publication, the *Bulletin* would contain the official acts of the Holy See and those of the bishop and his curia, but it would also publish articles for the continued education of the diocesan clergy.[40] The periodical had a modest but dignified presentation: thirty-six pages bound with a cover imprinted with the medieval seal of St. Alexander and the words: *"Beate Alexander, serva clerum ac plebem* (Blessed Alexander, protect the clergy and the people)."[41]

Don Roncalli was undoubtedly behind the new publication, and the notes dated May 11, 1960, written when he was pope, confirm this.

> The incentive for the first publication attempt in Italy had come from the *Acta Apostolicae Sedis,* which the Holy Father Pius X had initiated at that same time. At that time a "Diocesan Bulletin" containing the "Acts of the Curia" already existed in Bergamo. It was only a few pages of documents concerning ordinary administration. Milan also had a *Foglio ufficiale* [an official paper], as it was called, with little content. In January 1909, the priest Angelo Roncalli, secretary to Bishop Radini Tedeschi and a seminary professor — drawing inspiration from the monthly periodical "Diocesan Life" of Malines that Cardinal Mercier sent to his friend in Bergamo — proposed to the bishop that something similar be published for Bergamo. Bishop Radini Tedeschi approved his secretary's proposal and Roncalli personally saw to everything concerning the editing of the diocesan periodical, with Guglielmo Carozzi as managing editor.[42]

According to Roncalli's intentions, the monthly was to be for the priests:

...a good and discreet friend to be warmly welcomed, who while delivering the voice and the thought of the authorities, will also add practical juridical information and clear criteria of judgment regarding issues of theology, so important today. May it dwell, briefly and without tiring, on the beautiful history of our Church, and may it furnish all the news that pertains to the current activities of the diocese. May it be a source of support, of honest inquiry, and an introduction to broader scholarship in order to further an enlightened and generous priestly ministry. I hope that all this will be achieved with tact, tranquillity, and honesty, so that the bulletin will please everyone. May each one be united in the brotherhood of Christ *quae decet sanctos* [to which holiness is fitting].[43]

Don Angelo wrote all the regular columns including "Diocesan News," "Miscellaneous News," and "Bibliographical Notes, Ideas, and Works," as well as scholarly pieces on history, art, music, and short biographies of saints. He also wrote articles on the history of Bergamo, events in the diocese, and information concerning Catholic Action and selected points of Church scholarship. He contributed the most to the review, as he himself would confess very naturally to the Bergamasque cardinal, Antonio Agliardi. "It is a great pleasure to learn that Your Eminence follows our activity here in Bergamo, and that you read 'Diocesan Life.' In this humble publication Your Eminence has probably read my thoughts, since those few pages are put together almost exclusively by the humble undersigned."[44]

St. Charles Borromeo

In Bergamo they say that St. Charles is part of the family because so many of the churches, chapels, shrines, and schools are dedicated to him in remembrance of his presence and positive influence on the people's devotion and the clergy's pastoral attitude. For this reason, Bergamo had to participate in the solemn celebrations marking the third centenary of his canonization.

In early 1909, Bishop Radini Tedeschi established a commission of seminary professors to study and elucidate the various relationships between St. Charles and the diocese.[45] This included St. Charles' apostolic visit in 1575, and the consequent reform of the Church of Bergamo, as well as how the saint was represented in art and in worship. In November, the bishop wrote a special pastoral letter,[46] and in December, he appointed a second commission with the task of helping to spread devotion to St. Charles and to promote interparochial pilgrimages to the tomb of the great archbishop.[47]

Naturally, Don Roncalli was a member of both commissions since he had suggested the in-depth study of St. Charles' apostolic visit to Bergamo. A few years earlier while in Milan, Roncalli had discovered detailed manuscripts on that visit.

> In 1906 I came to know the *Carteggio della Visita Apostolica di San Charles Borromeo a Bergamo* when I accompanied Bishop Radini Tedeschi to Milan for the meetings of the preparatory commission for the eighth Provincial Council, held at the residence of the Most Eminent Metropolitan, Cardinal A. C. Ferrari. I had nothing interesting to do while I waited except to visit the large archdiocesan archives that house many yet unexplored historical treasures, and not just those of the Archdiocese of Milan. I was immediately taken with the collection of thirty-nine parchment volumes entitled *Archivio Spirituale: Bergamo.* I explored these and returned to see them on successive visits. What a pleasant surprise for me! To find all those interesting documents on the Church of Bergamo in one place, which at that time following Trent — the most intense period of fervor of the Catholic Counter-Reformation — was so noted for Church renewal. Because of my teaching, my experience in exploring archives, and my love of historical scholarship, I was familiar with this type of research. I wanted all the more to see such precious and long-forgotten material used to preserve the history of my homeland. At first, this desire seemed to be only a dream, but instead it became a concrete project in the spring of 1909. It was then that the idea took root in the mind of Bishop Radini Tedeschi, so cordial and open to worthwhile propositions and generous undertakings. He made the project his own, presenting it to the diocese as one of the most fitting ways to express the recognition and devotion of the citizens of Bergamo for St. Charles, on the third centenary of his canonization.[48]

Roncalli continued his contacts with Cardinal Ferrari,[49] the archdiocesan archives and the *Biblioteca Ambrosiana,* and its prefect, Monsignor Achille Ratti,[50] the future Pope Pius XI. Roncalli contacted anyone he knew who would have direct knowledge of the documents[51] or who could discover documents in yet unexplored archives such as those of the Vatican Congregations.[52] He kept the clergy informed on the project's progress, and asked for and collected documentary contributions from the various parishes and from the Cathedral Chapter.[53] He assumed the burden and responsibility for the undertaking. As so often happens, a project may begin with a committee, but the work inevitably rests almost entirely on the shoulders of one person.[54] Roncalli arranged for the printing of the volume containing the results of his research and collected the necessary funds to cover the cost of the publication.[55] To facilitate the whole operation, he registered with the Historical Society of Lombardy.[56]

The final goal was to publish a large work in two parts: the first would be a study of the most important documents, under the title: *Acts of the Apostolic Visit of St. Charles to Bergamo in 1575.* The second part was to be historical accounts of selected topics, such as the state of the diocese, the influence of the saint, St. Charles in worship and in art, etc.[57]

> Having conceived the design, we began its execution. We had the two fundamental volumes transcribed, the sixth and seventh on proceedings and visits, from photographs which Monsignor Ratti had so kindly obtained for us. I assembled my seminary students, instructed them on how to accurately decipher and reproduce ancient writing, and distributed the work among the best. Each one could work during vacation with serenity and dedication. The other thirty-seven volumes remained. I personally examined and highlighted all those pages, as an archeologist might search in the ruins for pieces of an ancient monument he wants to reconstruct. With the first reordering of the vast material, I researched whatever I could find on the great event in the public and private archives of Milan, Venice, and especially of Bergamo in the municipal archives of the Misericordia Maggiore and of the seminary. I had the favorable opportunity to consult the correspondence of St. Charles, preserved at the Ambrosiana in Milan, enabling me to take notes and make transcriptions under the eye of the prefect, Monsignor Ratti. Transcribing all the material in the Archdiocesan archives required a great deal of time. In his generosity, Cardinal Ferrari offered me the greatest hospitality, always in the archbishop's residence and in the seminary at Corso Venezia during vacation, for whomever I brought with me from Bergamo to help with the work. One time, for several days, ten seminarians from Bergamo accompanied me. They forged ahead on the first transcriptions until October 13, 1909, after which time I had to carry through with the endeavor almost exclusively on my own. I visited the archives often, transcribing or taking notes so that the printing proceeded and the documents were placed according to the pre-established outline.

The printing was entrusted to the workers in the shop of the Società Editrice St. Alessandro, but I was personally responsible for the first proofs, which had to conform to the publishing criteria of the Italian Historical Society. A distinct Elzevir font was selected and cast. Special paper was used that had a watermark bearing the *Humilitas* of St. Charles on one side and on the other the words: *Sancta Bergomensis Ecclesia MDLXXV–MCMX* [the years of the apostolic visit (1575), and centenary year of canonization (1910)]. The appendix of the first volume, *Storia della Compagnia di Gesù* by Don Tacchi Venturi, which was published toward the end of 1909, contained an excellent essay. It gave essential information on particular documents, which were numbered progressively with the date, title and, if the document was a letter, the author and addressee. This was followed by a brief summary of the document's content, its location in the archive, and then the full text. I took advantage of the essay's order and clarity. The printing began in 1910, and continued each year through 1914, progressing slowly since I had to oversee the work along with a number of teaching responsibilities, my priestly ministry, and my service to the bishop.[58]

Don Roncalli, however, used his research to publish several detailed articles in *Diocesan Life*[59] and *The Echo of Bergamo*.[60] Still others were published in the monthly review of the diocese of Milan, "St. Charles Borromeo on the Occasion of the Third Centenary of His Canonization."[61] He wrote an article for the review, *La Scuola Cattolica*,[62] and many others for *Bergamo a San Carlo Borromeo nel III centenario della canonizzazione (1610–1910),* which the second committee proposed to use for the planned festivities of September 1910.

Perhaps the results did not seem equal to the massive amount of time and work invested. However, it gave Roncalli his first opportunity to confront the strict demands of the historical critical method — to trace, examine, arrange, and select sources, as well as to study whatever had been written on the subject up to that point. Then he had to synthesize all the information correctly in a complete report, under the vast theme he had undertaken within the vaster historiography of Catholic reform. Roncalli also deepened his knowledge of the condition and potential of the diocese of Bergamo in the 1500s, and he learned how to make appropriate comparisons with the present times.

He began with the intriguing study of the religious history of Bergamo, a sweet relief from his other fatiguing duties. The study gave him great joy and soon led him to conceive of a more amplified and organic plan for research and publication.[63] Above all, the study drew him into the spirituality of St. Charles, the great reformer, and helped him to understand the characteristic traits of a good pastor.[64] Cardinal Ferrari had described these traits in a homily at the cathedral for the centenary feast,[65] when he had meditated on parts of a volume by Arvisenet,[66] who described St. Charles as an example of a good priest and pastor. These traits had been obscured by the dust that had settled on the historical memory of St. Charles. He was to become so familiar to Don Roncalli that he felt as if St. Charles were always with him; Roncalli even spoke with him as if he were alive. The young priest said that studying the saint's work enabled him to enter "the most intimate rapport with him." Roncalli depended greatly upon his intercession.[67] He wrote of this spiritual experience in a series of articles for *Diocesan Life* in view of the centenary celebrations.

> Perhaps we are accustomed to admiring the great archbishop too much from afar. The decisiveness of this true giant of pastoral holiness who seemed larger than life, the apparent rigidity that we associate with him because of his austere lifestyle, the energy and inflexibility with which he set out to accomplish his noble and holy goals — all of these engendered in us a respectful fear. That is only a mistaken first impression. *Prima frons decipit multos* (the first impression misleads many). Instead, it is well worth drawing near this great saint with confidence in order to study every attitude, movement, word that came forth from his mouth or from his pen, every fold of his garment. Studied in this way, St. Charles Borromeo is transformed before our eyes. His face radiates a gentle and attractive goodness. Above all, one feels he is close to a great heart. And St. Charles' heart explains a great deal about his life and always renders him good-natured, even when his actions seem to have been inspired by an excessive austerity.[68]

The lengthy and articulate lecture, "The Origins of the Seminary of Bergamo and St. Charles Borromeo," delivered to the students and faculty of the seminary at the beginning of the academic year 1910, was sure proof of the historical method acquired by Roncalli. The talk was published in *Diocesan Life* without critical notes and with an announcement that the next edition would appear in a separate volume.[69] His essay was well supported by the documentary material he had gathered regarding the church of Bergamo and St. Charles. Roncalli's sincere and enthusiastic affection for the great saint was apparent as he again underscored the zeal, prudence, pastoral concern, and administrative astuteness of St. Charles.

This speech was the foundation for a more extensive essay, complete with critical notes, published in 1938 in *Humilitas, Historical Miscellany of the Milanese Seminaries,* under the title, "The Origins of the Seminary at Bergamo and St. Charles Borromeo."[70] The following year, he used this material for a monograph with the same title.[71]

The Diocesan Synod

In the year of the centennial festivities for St. Charles, Bergamo's clergy experienced one of its most solemn moments: the diocesan synod. A synod had not been celebrated in Bergamo for almost 200 years.

In *Diocesan Life* Roncalli explained the reasons for this long wait and the goals of the new synod, the work of the bishop and pre-synodal commission, the decree of indiction, instructions for the people's participation before and after the event, logistical measures, and the great enthusiasm for the wonderful moment to be celebrated from April 26–28.[72]

Moreover, Roncalli participated in the event as a member of the preparatory commission,[73] as undersecretary of the synod with his friend Don Carozzi, and finally, as the official journalist — a role fulfilled a few weeks after the synod. "When the soul overflows with holy enthusiasm," he observed, "the tongue is silenced and even the pen trembles in one's hands." He composed his account as a history, and even called it *Historical Notes,* because for Roncalli the synod signaled the most beautiful page of the modern history of the Church in Bergamo.[74]

His entire description of the proceedings took on something of the splendid and was destined to impress its readers and above all to remain in the heart of its author. "When the strong impressions of Rome begin to disappear, as happens with everything left behind, and one's spirit is completely taken up with the life, the history, and the hopes of one's own diocese, as is happening to me now in view of such recent events, one experiences a spiritual exultation that finds no comparison."

After the opening prayers of the synod, the *Veni Creator* was intoned. "Who in the audience at that moment did not feel the breath of the Divine, vivifying Spirit settle on them as on the day of the first Christian Pentecost?"[75] The synod was now officially open. Roncalli and Carozzi, as pro-secretaries, called the authorities and the individual priests to convene. The roll call was impressive in its simplicity.

The most important event of the afternoon was the solemn profession of faith proclaimed by the bishop, using the formula of Pius IV. "There is nothing new in those words and in those truths that pass through your mind one after another. They are the truths that continually nourish the thoughts of the priest, truths which we speak about and live. Calling them to mind all together at that moment, and making a prompt and sincere act of adherence of the intellect, seems to grant these truths a special kind of light and clarity. To profess them in harmony with so many hearts instills in each of us a sense of great strength and great courage to uphold them. In preaching them, one feels as if our faith is truly our glory and our victory. *Haec est victoria quae vincit mundum fides nostra* [This is the victory that conquers the world, our faith]."[76]

The second day of the synod opened with a Mass celebrated for all the bishops and priests who had died since the synod of 1724. Then the meetings proceeded according to the agenda, with the bishop's homily and the reading of the various synodal decrees.

The third and final day of the synod began with the bishop's eloquent and powerful discourse on fraternal love among the priests and of sincere submission to the authority of the Church, especially to that of the Roman Pontiff.

When the work of the synod was complete, Roncalli read the last decree, *De dimissione Sinodi*. It concluded with a wish inspired by St. Paul: *ut certemus bonum certamen, cursum consummemus, fidem servemus* (that we may fight the good fight, run the race, and keep the faith).[77]

As pro-secretary, Roncalli's work included overseeing the printing of the more than 500-page volume containing the Acts. The many valuable appendices of *Bergomensis Ecclesiae Synodus XXXIII* were edited by Bishop Radini Tedeschi,[78] while Don Roncalli edited the commemorative compilation, *Numero Unico,* which, he acknowledged with satisfaction, everyone seemed to appreciate.[79]

CHAPTER 6

ASSISTANT TO THE UNION
OF CATHOLIC WOMEN

In the account of the synod's second day, Roncalli underlined the passage from Bishop Radini Tedeschi's talk on the official consecration of "the immense work of Christian social organizations that is the glory of the clergy and the Catholic laity of Bergamo."[1] The bishop recognized that the Catholic laity of Bergamo, organized into many associations, had been working zealously for many years. With a constant, single-minded devotion to the bishop and the pope, they had been assisting the clergy for the glory of God, out of respect for their faith and nation, but especially for the true good of the people. The bishop had hoped that the synod would be a powerful impetus to Catholic Action, through the unity, activity, and generosity of the clergy and laity. Each within their own sphere would work for the cause of the Church and the nation, the pope and the people, Christian society and Christ.[2]

Don Roncalli could not help becoming involved in the good being done by this vast sector of Bergamo. The training he had received from the time he was a young seminarian to his studies in Rome had prepared him for this. The people had shown their affectionate enthusiasm for Bishop Guindani, and still more for Pope Leo XIII and later Pius X — all of whom had been actively involved in social work. The same was true of Bishop Radini Tedeschi, who had championed Women's Catholic Action from the time he had directed *Opera dei Congressi*. He had wholeheartedly promoted social action since it emerged in the diocese.

Roncalli accompanied Radini Tedeschi to the annual celebrations of the Catholic associations, where he heard the bishop's impassioned voice and had transmitted his words into articles for *Diocesan Life*. Roncalli's position as the bishop's secretary gave him the opportunity to meet the two most important protagonists of the Catholic laity: Count Stanislao Medolago Albani and Nicolò Rezzara. Roncalli admired Albani's prudence, energy, faith, and obedience to the pope. He must have understood the crisis Albani faced as both his collaborators and the clergy doubted the sincerity of his intentions. Count Albani confided all of this to Radini Tedeschi who encouraged and supported him. Nicolò Rezzara was the apostle and ingenious organizer of social action in Bergamo.[3] Roncalli had heard both men speak at the new *Casa del Popolo* (House of the people), a large building right next to the train station that Rezzara had given Bergamo to make it a center for Catholic groups.

From November 1907, Don Angelo had been collaborating in an initiative of the Diocesan Council of Catholic Action: the Training or Public School of Religion for newly appointed women teachers. The school was established to further the religious education of the young women who attended the government-run teacher training schools, as well as any other women who wished to take advantage of the program. The school prepared the new teachers for a catechetical diploma allowing them to teach religion in the elementary schools. Over the years, the school expanded and opened new branches in different parts of the city, taking on more teachers for the number of religious subjects covered in a three-year cycle. Don Roncalli collaborated in the effort, and for several years was the only teacher. His good name sufficed as a recommendation for the initiative.

Actually, Roncalli's particular gift or inclination for this type of apostolic work was revealing itself. Perhaps that is why he accepted the request of Bergamo's Union of Catholic Women, in January 1910, to become their ecclesiastical assistant.[4]

This union was the last association born within the scope of Women's Catholic Action in Bergamo that embraced a number of organizations with the specific aims of worship and piety.

Bergamo's local chapter of the Union of Catholic Women of Italy had recently been established at the first assembly of the House of the People on January 8, 1910, by the women of the Catholic Society of

Mutual Aid. Don Roncalli explained that this organization would "bring together the scattered forces of Catholic women to increase them a hundred-fold, making them more effective in their social work, for the good of family, society, and country, especially in the field of education and publishing."[5]

Immediately following their second meeting in January, the group presented the bishop with its unanimous request to have Don Roncalli as their ecclesiastical assistant. The bishop agreed quite willingly and the board, according to the recorded minutes, was greatly satisfied with the appointment.[6]

As assistant, Roncalli was to participate in the weekly meeting of the board of directors and the monthly meeting of the members — always well attended because membership was steadily increasing. He was responsible for selecting the theme for these meetings and guest speakers — at times Bishop Radini Tedeschi or Rezzara — and for promoting the society in parishes by establishing a good rapport with the pastors. Roncalli organized the retreats in preparation for major feasts of the year, as well as the annual three-day spiritual exercises. He arranged for prayers and Masses to be offered for the deceased members of the Union, and he directed the weekly religion lessons for the teachers and aspiring teachers. The members of the Union also attended these classes, which they always found very interesting and from which they learned, as the book of minutes states, "with true satisfaction to the soul."[7]

Education was the greatest goal that the assistant Roncalli pointed out to the Union Board. He reminded the members as soon as possible of "the importance of works of education, which represent the most formidable battle against one of the worst enemies of the Church and of good — ignorance, the enemy that each of us carries within. Teaching, especially religious instruction, must go hand in hand with works of piety."[8] He soon became the promoter of a Women's Education Club. He saw its concrete system as a practical means to meet the need for education. He thought it would be an ideal "meeting place...to study current moral and social issues and exchange ideas" for the student teachers and studious young women.[9]

After a few attempts the club was born, and thereafter the group met every week in the halls of the House of the People, bringing together younger and older women from every social status for readings and lectures. With the ever-expanding library, and lecturers by the greatest experts in Italy, including Nicolò Rezzara and Roncalli himself, the club was becoming a sort of public university. Not satisfied with this, Roncalli also scheduled and taught Sunday courses for those women who worked in offices or other professional capacities and could not attend otherwise.

Classes were held in the afternoon and ranged from Italian grammar to accounting, from the study of French and German to economics, from current events to sociology and apologetics that were taught only by Don Roncalli. His words were "brief and simple, but good and straightforward, inspired by the principles of faith, presenting the principal points of Catholic doctrine and explaining them in a way adapted to the listeners. For their part, the members appreciate the excellent lessons on apologetics and get together periodically to compile summaries, transcribe them, and pass them out to the student teachers."[10]

On a wider scale of diocesan activity, Roncalli invited the associates to support the efforts of all Catholic Action and those of the bishop in blocking plans of the provincial board to ban religious instruction in the schools. The bishop felt that these plans were a true attempt to "de-Christianize society and take away from the young the most precious thing they have: their faith."[11] Roncalli's first initiative was to organize all the women from Bergamo-Alta to help with teaching after school,[12] in order to offer the students the catechism classes the state school denied them.[13]

In this same area, Don Roncalli placed himself as the leader of the federations of fathers and mothers who wanted to bring catechetical teaching back into the state schools. He asked members to follow him in the beginning and then to continue the activities and to keep constantly informed about the problem. He went so far as to bring his collaborators along to national catechetical congresses and conferences.[14]

After only one year, the diocesan leadership of Catholic Action officially recognized the work of the Union of Catholic Women and of its assistant, Don Roncalli, who was by now the president. He was elected a member of the Social Economic Section of the diocesan council and a member by right of the Diocesan Electoral Union.[15] This proved to be another burdensome task that required many hours of study to prepare for the administrative and political voting during those difficult years of Italian social life.

Added to all the other work he had as the bishop's secretary, Don Roncalli participated by right and by duty in the board meetings. He continued teaching in the seminary and overseeing the work that would constitute Bergamo's monument to St. Charles, *Gli Atti della visita apostolica del 1575.* Don Angelo wrote almost all the historical articles in *Diocesan Life,* and he researched and wrote about local religious history for various popular publications.

All of these activities made increasing demands on his time. "Sometimes I feel so overwhelmed by my duties that I am almost tempted to complain to God about it."[16] Feeling his strength diminishing he wrote, "I find myself with more work than my head and my poor shoulders can possibly bear."[17] He had to deal increasingly with the feverish activity that so contrasted with his own patient, calm attitude toward work. "The ever increasing number of small tasks I have to take care of, and for which I have had to turn my rather natural tranquil habits into perpetual motion, by now constitute my normal life. But I do not complain, because if I wish I have the opportunity to find God also in this circumstance and, therefore, peace and spiritual joy everywhere."[18]

Modernism in the Seminary?

Fatigue became Roncalli's constant companion. "I am well, but I'm a bit tired,"[19] he wrote his father cutting his letter short. Still, he knew that in the autumn he would again have to teach Church history.

He wrote, "For a while I have been suffering immensely," and this suffering was caused by a situation that had arisen in the seminary.[20] The pervading climate of tension and mistrust between the superiors and the professors at the seminary at Bergamo, as in many seminaries at the time, weighed on Roncalli. This tension was sometimes heightened whether intentionally or not by new teachers who were not openly modernist, but who imprudently exposed their students to innovations in the Catholic cultural world.[21] In fact, two young teachers, one of Church history and sociology and the other of introductory biblical studies that included biblical Hebrew and Greek, were dismissed from the school because of their erroneous teachings. Things only grew worse when people began to take sides during the months of inquiry and the small hearings the bishop thought appropriate.[22]

Although he did not show it, Roncalli suffered deeply over this episode. "The more costly life's pains and discomforts, and the heavier they become for those who suffer, the more these persons know how to hide them within the folds of Christian and priestly piety and humility."[23]

And Roncalli was one of these persons, for sadness enveloped his spirit. "Here, we are going through a sad hour, and oh, if you only knew how the lack of piety, obedience, humility, and faith just in oneself affects practical life!"[24] It was a time of sadness among friends who were separated from one another. This changed to quiet joy a few months later when Roncalli reported that things "are not going badly, [the two] have returned amiable and docile into the arms and heart of the bishop, who has done so much and suffered so much for them...."[25]

During Roncalli's retreat in October, the few notes he wrote were about modern errors. He described them clearly, along with a sad reflection on how many had fallen into error. He also decisively reaffirmed his faith, the simple and pure faith of his ancestors, and wrote about the attitude one should have toward the students.

> During these exercises, Jesus, my blessed Lord, was pleased to give me a special light to understand the necessity of keeping whole and most pure my *sensus fidei* [sense of the faith] and my *sentire cum Ecclesia* [being of one mind with the Church].... He also showed me, under a more splendid light, the wisdom, timeliness, and beauty of the measures taken by the pope to safeguard the clergy in particular from the infection of the modern errors (so-called Modernist errors) that in an underhanded and tempting way try to destroy the foundations of Catholic doctrine. The painful experiences of this year, noted here and there, the grave preoccupations of the Holy Father, and the voices of holy shepherds, persuade me, even without a desire to look elsewhere, that the wind of modernism blows strongly and more widely than it seemed at first. It easily strikes and bewilders even those who had only wanted to adopt the ancient truth of Christianity to modern needs. Many people, even good men, have fallen into error, perhaps unconsciously. They have let themselves be drawn into the field of error. The worst is that from mere ideas one quickly passes to the spirit of independence, of thinking one can judge everything and everyone. On my knees, I thank the Lord who preserved me in the midst of so much tumult and agitation of brains and tongues. But the experience of others, the fact that I was able to save myself until now, are a warning to me to keep watch over my impressions, thoughts, feelings, and words, over everything that in any way could be compromised by this devastating whirlwind. I must always remember that the Church contains within itself the eternal youth of the truth and of Christ, which is of all times. The Church transforms and saves the people and the times, not the other way around. The first treasure of my soul is my faith, the blessed, pure, and simple faith of my par-

ents and of my good ancestors. I will be cautious and strict with myself so that the purity of my faith will not suffer any harm. My grave responsibilities as a professor in the seminary, given me by my superiors, do not only oblige me to think of the purity of my own faith alone. I must also be sure that from everything I teach the young clerics in school, and from my words and my behavior, there emanates only a spirit of intimate union with the Church and with the pope. I must edify and educate them and bring them to think that way themselves. I will, therefore, be most discreet in all I say, taking care to imbue in the students that spirit of humility and of prayer in all their studies, which strengthens the intellect and ennobles the heart.[26]

Spiritual Director

In November 1910, Roncalli taught apologetics courses in the three secondary classes, basic theology in the first course of theology, and Church history in all three courses.

Roncalli's first biographer, having actually read some of his lessons from students' notebooks, said that he could only define them as prudent.

> They disclose a mature and measured knowledge, evident in his absolute respect for the Church's thought, as well as his efforts to evaluate the most modern theological concepts in the light of Church teachings. However, one could not define the lessons as timid. They do not raise the useless dust of doubts; rather they are just, serene, and honest. The professor apparently knew the points of heated discussion, and at times attempted to formulate the problems critically, leaving the door open, where possible, for more daring solutions even when he himself preferred those more within the boundaries of orthodoxy. He found a lot of material to teach even outside controversial issues! Church history, his field of experience, was especially rich with admirable content. That hard-fought and miraculous life was so suited to him, despite its entanglement in human affairs, suggesting the sensitivity of Providence — the mysterious fulfillment of God's designs![27]

Roncalli was not only the esteemed and charming secretary to Bishop Radini Tedeschi, the editor of *Diocesan Life,* assistant to the Union of Catholic Women, president of the fifth section of Catholic Action, member of the diocesan council, and councilor to various diocesan boards, he was also a recognized and authoritative spokesman for the seminary faculty. As such, he sat on the various committees for the com-

petitive examination of the young priests.[28] He was on the committee to
revise the diocesan proper of the breviary and charged with studying the
historical readings for the feasts of the saints of Bergamo.[29] He was also
on the bishop's committee, *Pro Catechismo,* for the promotion of
catechetical works in the city and in the diocese.[30] Moreover, as a popular speaker, he was often called on for official celebrations.

He often said that school, and not only at the seminary, gave him a
means to do good — it was an apostolic opportunity. As a young priest,
he dreamed of other work and other achievements. "I too have had my
plans and my visions; I have found and I still find them natural. If I were
to go back to relive these past ten years of my life, I believe I would do
the same. However, I have abandoned myself into the arms of obedience. For the most part my dreams and visions have disappeared. God
has disposed of me differently."[31] Don Roncalli did not renounce other
forms of ministry; he was happy, for example, to welcome the good
souls the Lord placed around him as their spiritual advisor.[32]

> Ah, how beautiful is the humble, silent, priestly ministry, which
> also has its worries. But these concerns always please the Lord be-
> cause they are directed toward the good of beautiful, generous, and
> hidden souls, who are also sensitive and anxious amid the dangers
> of life. But they are virtuous souls who also smell as sweet to the
> Lord as the little hyacinths outside your window, which blossomed
> with a kiss from the first rays of sunlight.[33]

To a friend for whom he was in a way a spiritual director, he wrote:

> I am anything but a spiritual director. But I know that the prin-
> ciples of my asceticism, which I seek to apply to myself and to
> those hidden but good souls whom the Lord has placed around me,
> are certainly true. I think that your present serenity is one of the
> most successful tests of these principles. Now I, who a few years
> ago (do you remember?) saw in you perhaps a bit of exaggerated
> sentimentalism, have become a poet like you. It is so beautiful to
> sing together the kindness of the One whom we love, the One for
> whom we work and belong to in life and in death! Often during the
> day, it is fitting that we say "no" to sentimentality, which naturally
> (because of our wounded nature) searches only for worldly, human
> beauty. What comfort we find in saying "no," which so pleases him
> who is all our love, and who rewards us with unspeakable spiritual
> joy amid our small daily sacrifices. Is it not true that the sweetness
> of our union with God gives us the most accurate concept of the
> value of life?[34]

One of the ascetical principles Don Roncalli suggested to his directee was to practice the spirit of piety.

If I may wish something for you, it is this: *exerce teipsum ad pietatem* (practice piety). I mean the spirit of piety. Those [priests] who are truly pious do a great deal of good. They find in piety the strength that gently disposes them to large and small sacrifices, the sweetness that refines and makes them and their works pleasing, and that holy poetry of the heart, which sustains their enthusiasm for doing good without going astray or deviating in any way.[35]

Roncalli nourished his own piety through hymns, the liturgy, the breviary, animated joy, and true spiritual pleasure. "As I glance through our prayer gathered from the delightful variety of psalms, it almost seems that a new harmony awakens around us."[36] "Amid all the concerns that occupy my day, piety — to which I am faithful at all costs — gives me endless comfort. Oh, may the grace of priestly piety to which, thank God, we were trained, embrace us both!"[37]

Humility was another of Don Roncalli's basic ascetical principles. Humility is the poetry of simplicity because even humiliation is a work of God.

The one who exalts us even before the world is God, and God alone. Every honor that comes to us should reflect God, or we must despise it. Does the Lord permit a small humiliation? So be it. Oh, if we only knew the great value of these humiliations! They have a very great influence on our entire spiritual life, and they leave very precious traces of good. Go before Jesus and tell him with sincere abandonment of spirit: O Jesus, I entrust myself to you. If you permit humiliations, I will be more than happy to find myself united to you, humiliated and scorned with you. When one is thrown to the ground in this manner, it is not possible to fall lower; one can only rise. The regard of the world then, *quatenus tale* (the world as such), is all the more vain and contemptible for us as priests to imagine.[38]

Truly, the touchstone for judging a mature vocation is *ama nesciri et pro nihilo reputari* (the desire to be unknown and to be esteemed as nothing regarding even the slightest matter).[39]

Thus must our life be: to examine ourselves, to humble ourselves always and to continue with new courage along the way the Lord has called us. This is how the lives and fruitful activities of the saints unfolded. We must be ready and willing to see our ego wounded. When we have allowed ourselves to be humbled, to be reduced to nothing in the hands of God, it is precisely then that the Lord uses us to confound the strong, to accomplish his wonderful works.[40]

One has to be a bit of a poet to recognize the wonderful works of the Lord.

It is expedient for you to breathe in the fragrance of Rome wherever you find it, however it presents itself: the fragrance of Catholic truth, the Church's discipline, of martyrdom, of sainthood, of the sciences, the arts, of nature itself. We who are young need to find healthy stimulation to elevate our spirit. We must be poets, provided we do not fall into weak and unproductive sentimentalism. Even poetry is useful, and blessed is the person who knows how to savor all the sweet and suggestive charm of the Church's mystic poetry and ecclesiastical life.[41]

Possessing these qualities, one can also be noble, though never lacking in the charity of the gospel. There are many examples of how humility, charity, and nobility have together made saints.

If your nobility gives you scruples sometimes, try to immerse your whole life — your thought, your works, your feelings — in a great bath of charity. Charity is the perfect democracy. Charity is everything and must shine through all our actions, as stars of dew shine on tender flowers at the first rays of the sun. Remember always the great figure of Cardinal Manning, an accomplished, noble man, yet he was one of the most democratic men of his century. Don Francesco [Pitocchi] will speak to you of St. Alphonsus de Liguori; I will take you as far as St. Francis de Sales, and with delight Borgoncini will lead you still higher, to the poor saint of Assisi. From the harmonious poetry of their souls, and the widespread charity of their hearts, all these men displayed great beauty, nobility, and dignity. They were democratic souls to the highest degree who felt the needs of their times, and accomplished immense good for humanity. These are our ideals. Let us follow them with energy and enthusiasm.[42]

Roncalli lived his ascetical principles and traveled along the road of total obedience, so much so that he did not feel the need to express his own reasons or desires. He had made his own Cardinal Baronius' program of life: *pax et oboedientia,* though significantly inverting the terms. He asked a friend, "The first time that you go to St. Peter's, kiss the foot of the famous statue for me, saying the words that Cardinal Baronius always said: *oboedientia et pax.* "[43]

Another principle of Don Roncalli's spirituality was a desire for heaven. "You point out certain sad reflections this painful case stirs up in you. The thoughts are sad, but the conclusions drawn from them are happy. Oh, it will truly be a beautiful day when we are united in heaven, bound in eternal friendships, faces smiling with the light and love of God!"[44] But in the meantime we must work "with joy on our faces and in our hearts, happy that God sees us and takes into account the only desire that moves us — his glory and his kingship over souls and over the world."[45]

Author and Publisher

While he continued to oversee the official monthly review of the diocese, Roncalli programmed and prepared other research projects on local Church history. He also began two other publishing initiatives: the collective letter of the Lombard bishops for the sixteenth centenary of the Edict of Milan, and the first book that was entirely his own work, the *Misericordia Maggiore* of Bergamo.

To commemorate 1,600 years of religious freedom, celebrations were planned for 1913. The Lombard bishops had decided to publish a collective letter calling attention to the restrictions currently placed on the Church, and in particular, those concerning the teaching and education of the young. The letter, dated September 21, 1912, was published in various diocesan bulletins of Lombard, in *Diocesan Life*,[46] and in a small, stylish booklet by the *Società Editrice Romana* under the title, *La libertà della Chiesa e l'insegnamento religioso* (The freedom of the Church and religious instruction). On the first page of his own copy, Roncalli noted, "Drafted by Don Roncalli of Bergamo, at the invitation of his bishop, Radini Tedeschi, and with the best wishes of Cardinal Ferrari, Archbishop of Milan, September 1912."[47]

The assignment to draft the letter was first entrusted to Bishop Radini Tedeschi, but it was passed on to his secretary with the approval of Cardinal Ferrari.[48] This type of responsibility was not new to Roncalli. Just the year before, Radini Tedeschi had given him the task to "assemble and discuss" the small work entitled *Atti collettivi e deliberazioni dell'Episcopato lombardo nelle annuali conferenze* (Collective acts and deliberations of the Lombard Episcopate at the annual conferences).[49] The critical issue of the freedom to teach religion in public schools had been deeply felt in Bergamo. The bishop had fought for this with conviction, even in his 1912 Lenten pastoral letter: *Della libertà e della religione nella scuola* (On freedom and religion in the schools), which would become the theme of his larger study, *Il problema scolastico odierno* (The problem with education today).[50] Don Roncalli supported Radini Tedeschi's efforts as a teacher and an influential member of numerous organizations and diocesan commissions.

Roncalli used Radini Tedeschi's works and those of Bishop Geremia Bonomelli for this latest assignment.[51] Once the first draft had been completed, the letter was sent to all the bishops of Lombard for comments, corrections, and additions. With a few modifications, it was sent to the Vatican secretary of state for definitive approval. The letter was published under the title, *Il XVI centenario dell'editto di Milano e la libertà della religione nelle scuole* (The sixteenth centenary of the edict of Milan and the freedom of religion in the schools), and later printed in pamphlet form.[52] All the Lombard bishops, except for Bonomelli, signed the letter. Bonomelli insisted that the text was flawed because of its allusion to the Italian government as a persecutor of the Christian people.[53] "And to think," Roncalli later recalled, "that I borrowed the idea from his own texts!"[54]

The letter began with an introduction recalling that "the anniversary gives us reason to rejoice, for we share with our mother and teacher, the Church, the pain and the joy of her life."[55] The faithful were invited to pray and hope, because "the Lord can turn to good the evil deeds of his enemies, transforming their wills so they turn from their erroneous ways."[56] The main body of the document recalled the history of the Edict of Milan that had been so decisive for the vitality of the Church, and it described "the modern conditions of religious freedom and especially of religion in schools."[57] It then confirmed the "legitimate and godly protests,"[58] responded to current objections, and concluded with a summary of the duties of Catholics in the present hour.[59]

Roncalli's second publishing initiative was the volume, *La Misericordia Maggiore di Bergamo e le altre istituzioni di beneficenza amministrate dalla Congregazione di Carità* (The Misericordia Maggiore of Bergamo and the other charitable institutions administered by the Congregation of Charity), a "small booklet that was growing in his hands during those months."[60] On December 30, Radini Tedeschi gave his *imprimatur* to the work that Roncalli had personally overseen in all its particulars: the format, the paper, the jacket, and the title page design with the words — tongue in cheek — "If the content is of little worth, at least the typographical work will be pleasing."[61]

The volume was much appreciated, not only for its pleasing design, but because it filled the historical gap concerning the notable institutions of the Church of Bergamo. The small publication was so popular that it was sold out in a month. The author was pleased and thought to continue his research — this time on the Dominican friar Pinamonte Brembati of Bergamo, founder of the *Misericordia Maggiore*. Of course, the project would be added to his ongoing research and secret projects — perhaps on the bishops of Bergamo — for which Roncalli gained the interest of his friends and those at the archives of the Roman Congregations.[62]

Roncalli gained a reputation as an outstanding historian, and in early 1913, he was given another burdensome task for the anniversary of the Edict of Milan. He was asked to give a series of ten lectures organized by the Popular University for the Catholic Youth Club in the House of the People on the theme, "The Church, Science, and School."[63] These lectures were publicized and later published in part by the local press.

Roncalli treated these extensive topics in light of the Church as a divine institution, but he also confronted the vehement, common objections regarding its history. The lectures were a great success and he was asked to give another series the following winter on the theme "The Church, Science, and Morals."[64] This time he had "an even more select and numerous audience. This shows that the historical lectures can and must be useful in some way, not only to satisfy idle curiosity but also to develop that religious culture we need so much. Above all, they can instruct those devoted to the Church and her enemies as well. Not in vain did Cicero write that history is the teacher of life."[65]

Time to Balance

On November 4, 1912, as Roncalli neared his thirty-second birthday, he joined four other priests in the small church of St. Joseph, and in the hands of the bishop, made the special promises of Priests of the Sacred Heart. Don Roncalli was to be an "extern" or non-resident member of the revitalized diocesan congregation. This caused some misunderstanding among his fellow clergy, but he had learned to disregard what others might think of him. "The esteem of the world is even more vain and contemptible for us priests than can be imagined";[66] "it would be a waste of time to seek comforts and rewards from the world, or anything else."[67]

He had conquered many difficulties that had almost weakened his good intention. He had conquered self-love so that he was happy to trample on the judgments of the world, including the ecclesiastical world. Assuring himself that his intention was right and pure, he was happy to run generously where he thought the Lord was calling him: to the Congregation of the Priests of the Sacred Heart. "Notwithstanding the smirks of many, today I took my vows and I have become a Priest of the Sacred Heart."[68]

In this way he placed an external seal on the intention he had carried from his first years as a cleric: to be "entirely and solely under obedience, in the hands of the bishop, even in little things." His promise was a declaration before the Church of his desire "to be reduced to nothing, to be scorned and rejected for the love of Jesus and the good of souls, to always live in poverty and detachment from all earthly interests and goods."

The older he became, the more Roncalli was convinced of the wisdom of the *Imitation of Christ*. His understanding of Book III, Chapter LVI, deepened: *"Fili, quantum a te vales exire, tantum in me poteris transire"* (Son, the more you can go out of yourself, the more you will be able to enter into me). This was the very touchstone of holiness: *l'ama nesciri et pro nihilo reputari* (the desire to be esteemed as nothing). This was the desire of saints like St. Francis Caracciolo, who vowed to flee all earthly honor and distinction, and Baronius, whose motto of *oboedientia et pax* Roncalli treasured because "you feel so good that way...almost outside of the world to enjoy all the sweetness of the priestly sacrifice."[69]

During the spiritual exercises of October of 1913, Roncalli took stock of his life and weighed his achievements in the balance. Perhaps his insistence on this spiritual work reflects something more than ascetical practice; he may have sensed something in his life was about to change. "Perhaps the seven years that have gone by [from the first spiritual exercises of 1906] only represent the abundance of God's gifts to me. Could it be that now begin the seven years of famine? I would deserve them, given my lack of correspondence to so many graces. Very well, let the purifying famine come, the bitterness, the humiliations, and the sorrows. I will accept them willingly as a token of the sincerity of my love for Jesus."[70]

Roncalli would not ask his superiors to lighten his workload a bit, although they probably would have granted such a request. "I had decided to ask that my workload be lightened somewhat, but in last month's exercises, and during this morning's Mass, considering the example of St. Charles, I decided instead to remain quiet."[71] He wished to follow his spiritual father and superior among the Priests of the Sacred Heart, who always loved to repeat, "Let us go…with our heads in the sack of Divine Providence."[72]

The older he grew and the more he lived his ministry, the more "his concept of the Lord's mercy expanded."[73] This awareness was sufficient for him to be able to live in joy, gentleness, and peace,[74] always modest and serious, with a spirit of goodness — of much goodness — patience and compassion for others,[75] and with poetry in his heart.

> They say that poetry fades with the years. I am experiencing, instead, that it is returning. My studies, the continuous preaching — not formally but familiarly to those who hear me — the effort to do some charitable works, the persons around me, and the things amid which I live: All these joined with the desire to do even more, to suffer something, keep my soul rejoicing.[76]

Roncalli's presentiment that something important and perhaps dramatic or something that would weigh on him during the tenth year of his priesthood, did not prepare him for the sudden breakdown in Radini Tedeschi's health. His bishop meant everything to him, "the Church, the Lord Jesus, God."[77] Nor could Roncalli have imagined that he would soon have to defend his credibility before a cardinal who under the circumstances represented the pope and the Church.[78]

Bishop Radini Tedeschi had been suffering from severe intestinal pains since June of the previous year.[79] When the pains grew more frequent, his doctors advised that getting away from the preoccupations and business of the city might be of some help.[80] Early in May Bishop Radini Tedeschi retired to his villa in Groppino in the upper Valle Seriana. Don Roncalli commuted to Bergamo to pick up mail, accompany priests and bishops on visits, or just to stay close by.

Ill or not, the bishop had to continue with some business that needed to be resolved. One question still under consideration was the building of a vacation house in Groppino for the seminarians. Although Radini Tedeschi wanted to do this, the opposition of several influential priests put a stop to the idea. The bishop decided to seek a reconfirmation of the backing of the Sacred Congregation for Seminaries. He assigned this delicate mission to the rector of the seminary and asked Roncalli to accompany him to Rome.

Roncalli had a number of meetings in Rome during the first three days of June, but the one with Cardinal Gaetano De Lai, Secretary of the Congregation for Seminaries, shook him to his very soul. De Lai considered himself a guardian of the most rigid orthodoxy of the Church and he believed this was being threatened by the latest fires of modernism. When De Lai spoke with Roncalli he recommended that the young seminary professor of Bergamo exercise extreme vigilance in his teaching, especially in the area of Sacred Scripture. In fact, he told Roncalli, news had already reached Rome that he was a compliant reader of Duchesne and "other questionable authors."[81] He also seemed "prone to that current of loose ideas that tend to upset the value of the traditions and the authority of the past."[82] He would definitely have to break with his "unhappy enchantment with certain books and certain authors."[83]

De Lai's accusations opened a wound in Roncalli's heart as deep as it was unexpected. He anguished over the suspicions that in his teaching he had lacked correctness of doctrine and methods. After his meeting with the cardinal, he prayed at length over the tomb of St. Ignatius in the Church of the Gesù. The next morning he prayed at the tomb of St. Peter in the Vatican, considering and reconsidering what he ought to do. He decided to write an aggrieved but firm letter of clarification to the cardinal.

> I was never responsible for teaching Sacred Scripture, but for apologetics, Church history, and patrology. The voice of my good conscience attests that I have never felt differently from the teachings and the spirit of the Church, whether in small matters or disputable questions. Rather, it seems to me that I have worked with great rectitude and with all my heart, according to my modest strength, by word, pen, and example, in public and in private, in the manifold exercise of my priestly ministry, to promote a joyous and confident spirit of docility and love for the Church, for the Holy See and its policies, both through doctrine and through lifestyle. This has formed one of the principal goals of my teaching and my activity among the seminarians and the laity.[84]

Several days later Roncalli received a letter of acceptance of the clarification from the cardinal. This seemed to end the matter,[85] and Don Roncalli felt somewhat relieved. Perhaps on the advice of Bishop Radini Tedeschi,[86] Roncalli wrote De Lai again, but this time he addressed the cardinal's charges and explained his conduct and teaching methods. He cited concrete and indisputable facts to support his integrity, which he was ready to confirm *cum iuramento* (on oath).

I never read more than fifteen or twenty pages, and even then, only skimming here and there, of the first volume of *Histoire ancienne de l'Eglise* of Duchesne. I never even saw the other two volumes.... Monsignor Spolverini can confirm what I read in the (Roman) seminary. From the time I left the seminary to become the secretary to Bishop Radini Tedeschi, I can give evidence that I never read a single book, pamphlet, or review tainted by modernism, with the exception of *The Saint* by Fogazzaro before it was placed on the Index.[87] I had leafed through it because of my ministry as confessor. Thanks to the Lord, by the intentions I renew every year in my spiritual exercises and meditation, I have always preferred to be uninformed, or at least to appear that way. I am content to learn of modern errors through the pages of their adversaries, to avoid the danger of being taken in by such falsehoods. I was never disposed to that current of broad ideas that, as Your Excellency states well, tend to upset the value of the traditions and the authority of the past. Rather, I have always borne witness in my teaching, brief writings, and in familiar conversations to the most orthodox modern historians, to the reasons for a calm and truly scientific historical criticism, with the deepest respect and heartfelt veneration even for popular traditions and for the authority of the past.[88]

Cardinal De Lai's second letter put a definitive end to the incident. "I am very happy that my words provoked such precise explanations, and the precious confession of your sentiments. I have no reason to doubt your word, so straightforward and clear, as a priest. There is nothing more but to congratulate you, and wish that you forever preserve such sentiments."[89] Don Roncalli felt completely at peace. That letter was dearer to him than all the gold in the world.[90] Now, the bishop's health became his major preoccupation.

CHAPTER 7

THE DEATH OF BISHOP RADINI TEDESCHI

The increased pain the bishop experienced, and the unexpected improvements followed by frequent relapses, kept Roncalli nearby. Radini Tedeschi nearly always needed some assistance.[1] The two spent all of June and July at the villa in Groppino, with diminishing hopes and increasing fears.[2] Finally, they had to admit that the relentless disease, an intestinal tumor, was rapidly taking its toll.[3]

On August 11, Roncalli took upon himself the sad duty of informing the bishop of the true state of his health because Roncalli had decided to take Radini Tedeschi back to Bergamo...to die.[4] During the trip back, Don Roncalli sat silently next to his bishop who had withdrawn in the mystery of his pain and approaching death. Soon after came the drama of August 20.

> About 3:30 in the morning, after I had obeyed the bishop's order and gone to rest, he called me back. As soon as I went to him, bent over to raise him a bit, I felt his arms and his head fall against my shoulders with such exhaustion and abandon that it took me by surprise. The bishop sobbed like a child. I had never seen him cry like that, and I said, "Take courage, bishop. Why are you so troubled? Are we not always in the hands of the Lord, who gives strength and life?" "Ah, my son," he replied, "I am troubled by the thought of my responsibilities. I am a bishop, I am a bishop!"[5]

But he composed himself and listened appreciatively to Don Roncalli's consoling words. Then Radini Tedeschi spoke calmly about his approaching death and his last will and testament. "He added with great humility and benevolence things about me in particular and the service I had rendered him for ten years. The memory of these last words will remain one of the sweetest comforts for my spirit for the rest of my life."[6]

In the morning, Radini Tedeschi underwent surgery in a last effort to save him. He received Viaticum and the Sacrament of the Sick. He spent that night peacefully. Some relatives and dignitaries came to visit the next day, and as secretary Don Roncalli had to welcome and entertain them while continually attending to the bishop's needs. Having regained his serenity, Radini Tedeschi "was as though on his throne during a Pontifical Mass, serene and self-possessed, without showing even a moment's weakness or anxiety."[7]

> For as long as he could, the bishop repeated the words of the prayers that I suggested to him. He repeated them word for word, in Latin and in Italian. At a certain point, he fell silent and it seemed he was not listening anymore. As soon as he noticed my own silence, he opened his eyes and whispered in my ear, "Courage, courage, Don Angelo. Everything is all right. Do continue. I understand everything, you know!" So I continued, "O Jesus Crucified, I willingly offer you the sacrifice of my life, in union with yours on the cross, in atonement for my sins and for the sins of my people, for the Church, the new pontiff, my priests, my seminary, my country." At this point he opened his eyes and fixed them, it seemed, on a distant vision, then with a strong, clear voice, he added, "And for peace, and for peace." I took up the rhythm once again, using his theme on peace, *Agnus Dei...dona nobis pacem* (Lamb of God, grant us peace). But he no longer heard me. While I was saying these last words, he looked at me. He just looked at me....[8]

A few minutes later he died, "gently, without the slightest spasm, as if he were about to fall asleep. Those of us who were present recited the first prayers for the repose of his soul as I closed his eyes and kissed his forehead. In the meantime, the great bell in the city hall sounded the hour — 11:30 in the evening of Saturday, August 22, 1914...."[9]

For Roncalli the bishop's death confirmed the truth of all he believed, hoped for, and loved. From that day forward, death became his companion, a glad and welcome companion.[10] The bishop's death suffused his soul with peace, satisfaction, and a sad but pure sweetness that he could not express.[11] A gentle yet generous acceptance transformed his grief into a renewed priestly fervor and zeal for the noble, divine cause for which he had been consecrated.[12] He was convinced he now had a protector in heaven who was surely looking down on him, hearing him, and consoling him.

With that gentle grief in his heart, Don Roncalli returned to his previous duties. After attending to some final details, he moved back to the seminary and took up a new life of intense study, reflection, and even some pastoral ministry.[13] "My new position is now based entirely in the seminary without neglecting my pastoral ministry. It will therefore be a life of greater calm and greater recollection, exactly what I have desired. So I will love my room and my seclusion, completely immersed in prayer and study."[14]

He resumed teaching apologetics and history at the seminary, where he occupied two small rooms above the upper church of St. John. He again participated in Catholic Action board meetings[15] and the assemblies of the Union of Catholic Women, continuing his role as assistant. He once more took charge of the Sunday and afternoon classes they had organized,[16] and remained the group's official diocesan representative.[17]

He resumed his research and writing projects for *Diocesan Life*. Aside from all of this, his brother priests thought that he must be more available now and made more requests of him. And Roncalli could only say yes.

These many and familiar responsibilities awakened happy memories for Don Angelo. Meanwhile, signs of esteem overflowed from every part of the diocese and beyond during the interim before the appointment of the new bishop elect of Bergamo. Luigi Marelli, bishop of Bobbio, was a 56-year-old Milanese and a member of the Oblate Priests of Rho. He had been chaplain and rector of the Madonna of the Woods shrine in Imbersago.

While awaiting Marelli's arrival, in the peaceful silence of his seminary room, Don Roncalli continued gathering documents and testimonies for the projected biography of Radini Tedeschi. For this initiative, he contacted eminent personalities mostly from outside the diocese. Among these were Augusto Grossi Gondi, an active promoter of the Roman Catholic lay movement who had collaborated with Bishop Radini Tedeschi in various undertakings; bishops from surrounding dioceses; Professor Giuseppe Toniolo, and Cardinal Andrea Ferrari.[18] These contacts gave Roncalli a more detached perspective from which to view the prolonged attempt by some people in Bergamo to forget, at least in part, Radini Tedeschi's episcopate. Thus, he preserved "discretion and absolute, sweet silence, without rancor," but not devoid of some measure of anguished bitterness.[19]

But even this became a very small matter as far more dramatic days were in store for Roncalli and for the world.

Military Chaplain

On April 26, the Italian government signed a secret treaty with England, France, and Russia obliging it to enter a war against Austria. On May 3, Italy denounced the treaty of the Triple Alliance. Demonstrations began, the mobilization of troops commenced, and war was officially declared against Austria on May 24.

Don Roncalli was not exempt and, like most priests, he was enlisted in the medical corps. He reported for duty in Milan at the Hospital Barracks of St. Ambrose.

On Sunday, May 23, the Feast of Pentecost, just as I was about to begin the celebration of Mass at St. Michael's, I was informed of the general mobilization that included my year. The immediate celebration of the Holy Sacrifice helped to put my soul at ease, abandoning my life into the hands and heart of God. I felt an immediate interior joy to be able to show in deed how I as a priest loved my country, for this love is nothing more than the law of charity justly applied. As soon as I returned to the seminary, I put my papers in order as best I could, adding a few things to my meager will, and entrusted it to the rector, Monsignor Re. In order to receive more information about where to report, I went to the district office. Then I went to the cathedral to hear the bishop's homily. In the afternoon, I dashed over to Sotto il Monte to say goodbye to my family, whom I found at peace and ready for anything. Early the next day I was in Milan at the hospital-barracks of St. Ambrose. By the afternoon, I had already been issued a military uniform. Where would they send me? I did not know and I was not too worried about it. Was not God supposed to think about that? And he did! From a low wall that cuts the arches of St. Ambrose and surrounds the monastery-barracks, a sergeant was shouting: "We need soldiers for Bergamo. Who wants to go to Bergamo?" (Bergamo had been chosen and declared a hospital city.) A dear seminary student of mine suddenly presented me, becoming a small arbiter of my military destiny. I was placed on the list for Bergamo without any effort whatsoever.

I then called to mind the "ask nothing and refuse nothing" of St. Francis de Sales, and found myself content in spite of all the assaults on my self-love. The Lord helped me silence those assaults so well that for several months he made me find it perfectly natural to be called sergeant, and nothing other than sergeant.

The two days I spent in Milan left different impressions on me. I remember the nuns running here and there making alterations on my uniform, which was too small for my large frame. I remember the concern and sadness I experienced when a silent battalion of Alpine infantrymen on the way to the front lines passed along the still deserted Via Meravigli. I recall the visit to St. Ambrose, to the tomb of St. Charles at the cathedral, to the cardinal archbishop, to other places and people. I remember the reunion of all the priest-soldiers on the evening of May 25 at the archbishop's residence, where His Eminence spoke so well. I would have liked to respond to him in the name of all the priests of Lombardy present that night, but I did not have the courage to say a single word. I remember, in the crush of all the drafted men waiting their turn to try on their uniform, I met a defrocked priest. I no longer remember his diocese in Romagno, but the poor man told me that I had inspired trust within him by my kind words of comfort. How sorry I am that I never met up with him again! Perhaps his soul would have been touched by grace to return to God and to his priestly duties.

Around noon the next day, as if I were the general in charge of Italy's army, I accompanied another twenty-five men. I left from the Milan train station for Bergamo and arrived at the garrison infirmary where Captain Volpi[20] informed me that I was destined for the military hospital at the seminary. That very night I was at my post, with different clothes, but living in the same room near the upper chapel where I had left with the thought of perhaps never seeing it again three days before. How true it is that *qui confidit in Domino non minorabitur* (whoever trusts in the Lord will never fail, Sir 32:24).

Three days earlier when I left the seminary, my colleagues and superiors consoled me — the only one enlisted at the time — and wished me good fortune. Now after such a short time, I was the only one who could once again occupy my small room. All the others had to give up theirs to make room for the soldiers.[21]

So began the military service of Sergeant Angelo Giuseppe Roncalli, age 34 years and 6 months, in the Third Medical Corp. For the most part the seminary had been transformed into a large hospital where Roncalli wore the requisitioned military uniform, hopefully for only a brief time while awaiting better organization.[22] Don Roncalli found himself serving in the same large dormitories he had occupied as a young seminarian.

The building was now a little better equipped with plumbing and electricity, but the rooms still had the same iron beds, iron stools, and other meager furnishings he had once used.

The health sergeant was at the complete service of the sick under the command of a field marshal and a lieutenant physician. He had to be ready to serve in all the minor and major necessities of the brief or extended illnesses: disinfecting, vaccinating, transporting the seriously ill to civilian hospitals, and doing the laundry and general cleaning of all the facilities. His day began very early and did not follow a fixed schedule. However, it did allow him some spare time and a certain amount of freedom, thanks also to the excellent rapport he quickly established with his superior officers.[23]

He continued to carry out his role as the assistant to the Union of Catholic Women, and he preached every Sunday at the convent of the Daughters of the Sacred Heart. He was able to accept the frequent invitations he received to preach on special occasions throughout the diocese. He managed to publish various commemorative articles on Bishop Radini Tedeschi in *Diocesan Life*,[24] although he left the editing work to his friend, Don Carozzi. Roncalli completed the biography of Bishop Radini Tedeschi in stages. He published the first mini-biography in the same diocesan review[25] toward the end of 1914, and prepared a second for August 1915,[26] which remained in draft form. In the latter half of January 1916,[27] he traveled to Rome to speak about this work with the new Pope Benedict XV, formerly Giacomo Della Chiesa, archbishop of Bologna. The pope had been a great friend and admirer of the late Bishop Radini Tedeschi and had promised Don Roncalli "a word" for the first page of the projected volume.[28]

Roncalli continued teaching the seminarians within the limits imposed by his new office and by the war. For several months, the seminary was the main military hospital,[29] and the students could not return to the seminary to settle in until early November. After seven months, in early January of 1916, the sick and injured soldiers were moved to *Ricovero Nuovo,* a home for the elderly, and the residents were transferred to the seminary hospital for the duration of the war.[30]

The military draft put the inner life of the seminary and its schools to a serious test. Within a few months most of the superiors and professors were drafted, along with a large number of the students — almost all the theologians and many philosophy students. Those who remained were, as Roncalli described them, truly *"rari nantes in gurgite vasto"* (scattered bodies swimming in a vast ocean),[31] citing the famous verse by Vergil *(Aeneid* I, 118).

Church history classes were suspended, but Don Roncalli continued to teach patristics and philosophy until 1917. These courses were reduced to a few semesters. Not all students could attend, and the war took them away one by one until no one was left. Roncalli distributed handouts of his notes for class, perhaps because he was not satisfied with the current textbooks or was unable to obtain others due to the economic restrictions imposed by the war. Unfortunately, the only trace of these handouts is found in one student's memory:

> With calm...Professor Roncalli always respectfully referred to the leading figures of the theories he discussed as "our adversaries." What seemed consistently outstanding in his method was the serene farsightedness of a person who is sure that in the end good sense will prevail, that the truth is one, and that certainly, indisputably, no truly scientific conclusion will conflict with the Word of God. In the case of an alleged conflict, it is certainly not that the Bible is wrong, but that we do not adequately understand its meaning. It is very important to show that the Bible does not contradict science. Scientific discoveries actually help biblical science, which makes progress in its own research.[32]

In March 1916, Sergeant Roncalli was transferred from the principal military hospital to the garrison infirmary, along with seventy sick men and twenty from the ranks. He was the only sergeant in the company. He felt a greater freedom and autonomy there, like the *dominus loci* (lord of the place).[33] Shortly afterward, while still involved in pastoral ministry at the garrison hospital, he received a long-awaited appointment as chaplain at the military reserve hospital at Bergamo.[34] The 150-bed facility was called the "Banco seta" (silk bench), because it was located in the old silk marketplace on the outskirts of the city.

The military chaplain ministered to the hospitalized soldiers, as well as to the nuns who served there, and promoted pastoral initiatives for the enlisted men and officers. After the war, Don Roncalli summarized his work as a chaplain:

> Oh, the long watchful nights among the cots of the noble and brave soldiers, welcoming their confessions and preparing them to receive the Bread of the strong the next morning! Oh, the beautiful songs to Mary intoned at the simple provisional altars! Oh, the sublime solemnity of the field Masses and the special feasts in the hospital

where the soldiers could relive a little of the Christmas, Easter, and May devotions of their own parish churches with tender memories of their mothers and their faraway spouses who anxiously wait for the war to end! Humble priests generously fulfilling their duty to their country, but better still, they were sons of a higher and more sacred duty to the Church and souls. So many times, we bent over the panting chests of our young dying brothers to listen to the labored breathing of a nation during its passion and agony. The simple and holy death of so many poor sons of our people, unpretentious workers of the fields from the Marches, Garfagnana, Abruzzo, the Calabrias who left this life with the Sacrament of Jesus in their hearts and the name of Mary on their lips, never cursing their harsh destiny, but pleased to offer the flower of their youth as a sacrifice to God for their brothers.[35]

Don Roncalli did not limit himself to hospital work, but played an active part in the initiatives of Catholic Action during the war. The general military enlistment persuaded the curia and the Catholic associations to call for volunteers among the faithful. The movement was directed by a central executive committee in charge of the diocesan board of Catholic Action, and the various local committees. Besides organizing prayers for peace and for the countries at war, they immediately dedicated themselves to providing all kinds of assistance to the soldiers, military priests (those from Bergamo alone were 360 in number[36]), the sick, and the wounded. They staffed relief posts at train stations for the wounded in transit, and assisted war orphans and the families of enlisted men. They offered protection to young women fleeing occupied countries, and distributed wool to girls' schools to make clothing for the soldiers at the front lines.[37] Finally, the House of the People set up a commission to provide religious services for the field soldiers and those in the infirmaries. Priests administered the last rites, offered prayers for the souls of the dead, and invited members of the associations to participate in funeral processions. They also helped the military priests to catechize soldiers.[38]

Don Roncalli successfully communicated the importance of providing religious assistance to all military personnel in the territory. In September 1915, the committee was already able to publish an account of its activity. To soldiers in combat and those of the city garrisons were distributed hundreds of images of St. Alexander with indulgenced prayers, hundreds of crucifixes, medals, rosaries, books of devotion, scapulars of Our Lady of Mount Carmel and the Sacred Heart, and thousands of religious flyers. The volunteers enabled the soldiers to write home by furnishing them with paper, envelopes, postcards, and even stamps. Funds were being collected to open a soldier's home, and small, mobile libraries had already been set up in the barracks. The committee introduced the practice of having a Mass celebrated every Sunday in the Church of St. Bernardino in Pignolo for the soldiers. During the week, two Masses were celebrated, one for those soldiers who had died in battle and one for those in the hospital.[39]

Roncalli completed the work he had most at heart during this time: the sizable volume in memory of his beloved Bishop Radini Tedeschi. He dedicated the 500-page book to Pope Benedict XV;[40] it was published in August under the title: *In memoria di Monsignor Giacomo Maria Radini Tedeschi, vescovo di Bergamo* (In memory of Monsignor Giacomo Maria Radini Tedeschi, bishop of Bergamo). The carefully designed cover bore the late bishop's coat of arms and motto, *"mit zei"* (with time). Below this appeared the words of Jesus, *hic magnus vocabitur in regno coelorum* (whoever does and teaches [my commands] will be called great in the kingdom of heaven, cf. Mt 5:19). A color portrait of the bishop dominated the back cover design.

The volume synthesized Radini Tedeschi's life and contained discourses and commemorations on the occasion of his death; it offered the testimonies of notable persons who had known the bishop and contained a collection of the bishop's writings. Each section of the book was preceded by a rich collection of photographs.

In his brief introduction, Don Roncalli excused himself for the limitations he recognized in his tribute, but it had not come to birth in the quiet of his study. Rather, it was written amid his varied responsibilities as a soldier and priest in the military, with the anguish of a terrible war raging in Europe that had cost so much blood and tears. He hoped that the book would pay homage to the memory of a great bishop, "a just tribute of veneration, of recognition, of love, to accomplish a work of truth and peace, as was so pleasing to him."[41]

The War

On various occasions in his letters, homilies, and a few pages of his diary, Don Roncalli assessed the First World War in its distinct phases. Above all, his assessment was based on faith; nothing could happen to him if not willed or permitted by God, as he expressed in several letters to his brother Zaverio, who was also in the military.

If the Lord is with us, who can be against us? We are not afraid of hunger, cold, malaria, Albania, the Germans, is it not so?[42] When we think, our life is always in the hands of God who can take it away even while we are at home. So we understand that no one can take it from us in war if the Lord does not permit it.[43]

In his diary he even noted the results of his medical exam: "Fit for the labors of war. Will I then leave for the front? I would leave willingly, happy to do some good even there. *Dominus defensor vitae meae, a quo trepidabo?*"[44] (The Lord is my light and my salvation, whom shall I fear? Ps 27:1).

The Lord did indeed permit many lives to be taken violently: a mystery of silence, sorrow, and love of both God and one's fellow man, reflected Don Roncalli. This was a mystery of humanity's participation in the sufferings of Christ for the just atonement and necessary reparation of the whole world without distinction of peoples or nations. Europe had endured great sorrows. So many young lives were sacrificed, so many individual, domestic, civil, national, and social interests compromised and ruined by the consequences of war, a scourge even for the victors, with the anguish, tears, and clash of arms and peoples that gushes forth in a river of blood. But there is an intimate union among those whose blood is shed upon battlefields, the tears and sorrows of desolate homes and the blood shed by the heart of Christ. To those who suffer, who cry, who fear, who fight, who die:

> Come now! Away with useless laments! We are strengthened by trials and sorrows. Our suffering has a great value as long as and because it is associated with those of Jesus. In this way, we participate more worthily in the great act of expiation that the war brings to completion. Our sorrows and shared misfortunes appear less grave and are more or less tolerable because it is sweet to cry with Jesus. We are better prepared by our own tears to penetrate and appreciate the mystery of love that the Sacred Heart of Jesus opened for us even in the events of this war.[45]

Don Roncalli was convinced that the sacrifice of thousands — even millions — of human lives on the battlefields of Europe had to be considered in the light of a collective expiation united to the redemptive suffering and death of Jesus Christ.

> Do we deeply grieve the incessant news about the death of so many fresh, flowering lives? Let us take comfort. At the cost of their blood the people are purified and prepare themselves to become

better. Let us all pray that the war might end and that truth, justice, and peace might finally reign over the world. Let us pray that the Lord might also grant to our purified Italy the strength to regain, in the light of the Church and of the pope, its way of genuine greatness and Christian civilization.[46]

The current agitation of the peoples signifies, at least in those who are the cause of it, the loss of the principles of the Christian faith. We drown again in naturalism. The triumph of the three concupiscences (desires of the flesh, desires of the eyes, and the pride of life) explains all wars, especially the current war. We rely on politics too much; we rekindle hatred and blood flows. Human devices fail, armies grow weak...and mothers cry. Let us learn how to see in our everyday happenings a little more of the hand of God. Through the present evils, he calls us to a new life, to a more just understanding of the values of life. He tells us that blessed will be those people who proclaim the Lord as their God.[47]

The Christian's attitude in all this is summarized by the word "charity," the supernatural virtue, the very charity of Jesus, to which can be grafted the love of one's country.

Like the first Christians who gathered in the crypts of Rome to honor the martyrs, confessors, and pontiffs while Caesar's legions ran through the Empire spilling blood and bringing destruction everywhere, we have gathered here to render homage and to affirm the triumph, not of material forces, but of an idea — the idea of the love of Christ. We are living in a time of change. Today's events are a preparation for the uncertainties and the work of tomorrow. Tomorrow we will have to rebuild a new people, (fruit) of the sacrifices of energy and blood that this terrible war is squeezing from our families and our nation, which we love according to the Lord's law of charity.[48] We do not discuss very much, nor do we chatter uselessly as do many idlers, is that not true? We know that love of country is none other than love of one's neighbor, and this merges with the love of God.[49] Unfortunately, when soldiers hear talk of "country," many shrug their shoulders, laugh, or even swear and curse. We do not. We fulfill our duty with eyes raised to heaven. The men who have governed us and who govern us now do not deserve our sacrifices, but our country, which is in danger today, is worthy of all our sacrifices. Men pass, but the nation remains. In sacrificing ourselves for the nation, we know we are sacrificing ourselves for God and for our brothers and sisters.[50]

The soldiers, so ill and worthy of every care and sacrifice, gave Don Roncalli great spiritual consolation and indescribable comfort.[51] On the first day of 1917, he consecrated his "poor soldiers" (as he loved to call them in his writings) to the Sacred Heart in a ceremony presided over by Bishop Marelli in the country church of the Holy Spirit.[52]

The soldiers wholeheartedly accepted their chaplain who was always so busy inside and outside the hospital. They loved him "too much," and he, "with a little gentleness and the grace of God, succeeded in obtaining everything from them."[53] With simplicity and the best of intentions, he was convinced that he did only what his heart suggested.[54] And he sacrificed very willingly for those boys who were so good.

> I am moved when I think of how easily a priest, if he wishes, can find his way into their hearts, and I experience the beauty of those young souls not yet spoiled by unhealthy contacts with a world of vice. *Confirma hoc, Deus, quod operatus es in nobis* (Strengthen, O God, what you have already accomplished in us).[55] On the other hand, one cannot help but love these young soldiers once you get to know them. They deserve every care and comfort. For myself, I confess that I would like to sacrifice myself for them even more than I already do.[56]

It is impossible to imagine what Roncalli felt in his heart. Alone in his room and on his knees he often found himself crying like a child. He could not contain his emotion over the simple and holy deaths of so many poor sons of Italy. From the spiritual contact he had with his soldiers, Don Roncalli formed the consoling conviction that Christian Italy was not dead. Like the little girl in the Gospel story before Jesus worked his miracle (cf. Mk 5:35 – 43), Italy was only sleeping, waiting for a new spring of moral ascent and greatness.[57]

Don Roncalli believed that military priests should forget themselves and show a total devotion to God.[58] He honestly recognized these qualities in himself, as his spirit was being gradually transformed. *Oboedientia et pax,* by now his enduring motto, was valid even in wartime.[59]

The first two years of the war were truly demanding. Yet he was filled with great peace and strengthened by a lively sense of the supernatural in all things, which by God's goodness kept his spirit joyful.[60] But he began to experience more frequently the toilsome days that filled him with a wide range of emotions.

> The anxiety for these dear soldiers, inside and outside the hospital; the sorrows expressed by so many souls who pour out their pains to me — so many reasons for grief! I am glad to work in this way for my Lord without many consolations for my self-love but with the

greatest spiritual comforts. *Superabundo gaudio* (I am overflowing with joy even in my tribulations).[61] In the midst of all this work, however, I am very content. I have no idea why the Lord loves me so much. *Caritas Christi urget nos* (the love of Christ urges us on) as it did St. Paul; when it fills the soul, little as it may be, it instills so much delight that one can desire nothing better on earth.[62]

Early on in his spiritual evolution, Roncalli had learned to deal with the bitterness of criticism from well-meaning brother priests by resolving to remain serene.

I confess that when it seems to me I really am following my heart's desire with simplicity and purity of intention, glad to give my post to whoever would want to fulfill it as well as or better than myself, even a hint of criticism from my brothers leaves me very bitter. I am wrong in being bitter and wonder why it disturbs me. Courage, my soul, this is only a bit of rain and snow. What will you say when a storm of criticism and opposition arrives? It is important to prepare myself for it. O Lord, *da mihi animas, cetera tolle* (give me souls, take away the rest). I will also accept opinions, good or dubious, that others have or spread about me.[63]

By 1918 Roncalli had already resumed writing his impressions and reflections on what was happening around him. He did this almost daily in the evenings, on intermittent pages of his diary.

He noted the consolations he experienced over his success in preaching to the soldiers or in the pastoral initiatives he had developed for them. With equal sadness, he noted the unkind judgments these initiatives sometimes evoked from his brother priests and, surprisingly enough, he even remarked on the mealtime discussions with his colleagues in the seminary. "These excellent and upright priests live at their desks and among their books; they see the war only from a distance.[64] Although good in themselves, in every sense they are completely ignorant of real life.[65] At that table which lacks nothing, where no one suffers a loss or injury from the war, they speak of nothing other than war.... The entire priestly spirit is turned to bitter complaints and sarcasm over the errors of the young soldiers and the nation. They never offer even one good word for the nation, never, ever. Everything is seen as ridiculous, suspicious, and blameworthy and is condemned, while even in the midst of the great evil of this war, Italy certainly also has much good."[66]

Filled with hope, Roncalli wrote of the many encounters he had with the very diverse people placed in his path by divine Providence: Protestants, evangelicals, atheists, Muslims, etc. He had resolved that when introducing himself he would not do so with a whip in hand. Rather, he would follow the example of Jesus and the saints who treated everyone with great kindness, tolerance, and respect.[67] He was convinced that the priest should be kind, patient, even-tempered, explaining the truth clearly, and responding to objections promptly. "Never mind thunderbolts from heaven! Charity, charity and simple, direct, loving truth!"[68]

In his reflections, Roncalli presented his own or another's outlook on the course of the war, on Catholic opposition, on international involvement or defeatism. He scrutinized government politics, particularly that of Italy and especially the relationship between Church and State. He always mentioned special anniversaries, such as his ordination to the priesthood or Bishop Radini Tedeschi's death and the lessons the event reawakened within him. He often alluded to his detachment from life, honors, and worldly riches, and wrote of his desire for the Lord and the apostolate. He wrote of the joy he felt over his meetings with Cardinal Ferrari in Milan, and his concerns about the new bishop, Marelli. "An apostolic man, but...he left me with the impression that he is growing old, very old, before his time."[69] These concerns did not cause Don Roncalli to hold back; rather they encouraged him to help the bishop as much as possible and as often as he was asked. "After prayer I drafted a circular letter for the bishop to sign outlining the practical policies pastors were to adopt concerning patriotic demonstrations. The bishop approved everything completely, showing his great satisfaction. To tell the truth, I too am very pleased, although I do not know if it is because I find my thoughts in harmony with those of the bishop, or vice versa."[70]

Finally, Don Roncalli expressed his position on the benefits of the long-awaited peace agreements: "Whether from a military or political standpoint, the war is still the useless slaughter that has been condemned by the papal 'Nota.' Is this not very true?"[71] About the festivities for the signing of the peace treaties he wrote: "Apparently the Lord has blessed us, despite the endless complaints of people including my confreres — albeit with good intentions, but not in the true spirit of Jesus — who expected, even for our homeland, lightning bolts and punishments from God and adulation for Germany and Austria."[72] He was pleased that "Catholics who have to atone for so much indifference and fear of accidentals that they neglected the substantial, thereby damaging the Church and its cause" were now involved in demonstrations.[73]

Roncalli's very spirit radiated from the pages of his diary, whether he was calm or preoccupied, happy or sad, critical and stern or hopeful and optimistic, trusting always in Providence and in human goodness. Without intending it, he had composed an assessment of the war and its influence on his way of seeing the world, people, and things.

It is a great grace that I understand that people's souls are indeed good. If they abandon the Church, a large part of the guilt belongs to us priests. If we are all holy and apostolic, the Italy of the future will truly again be ours in Christ. But courtesy, patience, and humility are needed. *Beati mites, quoniam possidebunt terram* (Blessed are the meek, for they shall inherit the earth).[74] The world is more evil than we think, but it is also better than we think. Instead of wasting long hours in continual whining and complaints that benefit no one, we priests have to work and seize the good wherever we find it, hold it up to the uncontaminated light of principles, and multiply it.[75] I maintain an incorrigibly optimistic outlook; and I do not know how to think otherwise. I never met a pessimist who accomplished any good. Since we are called to do good rather than to destroy evil, to build up rather than to tear down, I seem to find myself in the right place to continue always seeking the good without looking for different ways of understanding or judging life. Ah, the saints, the saints…. How they were practical, fervent, and good. Above all good![76]

Tuberculosis and the Spanish Influenza

On July 19, 1918, the feast of the great saint of charity, Vincent de Paul, Don Roncalli, still serving as military hospital chaplain, received an "offer" from the director of hospitals in Bergamo. Roncalli was asked to provide religious assistance and moral support to prisoners of war returning from Austria who were suffering from tuberculosis and would stay in the large *Ricovero Nuovo* complex. Roncalli accepted willingly and without hesitation. He confirmed his acceptance with a letter written that same night. He felt certain of the Lord's blessing on this good work, which he had not sought after in the least.

Don Roncalli was well aware of the fact that his new assignment placed him at risk of contracting the disease. When he was certain of his future transfer to the *Ricovero Nuovo* he wrote in his diary:

I do not know how to explain this fact even to myself: from the moment the Major assigned me here, no anxiety has troubled me, even though this duty brings the danger of contracting the illness and I must take every precaution. Am I assuming too much in saying that it is the Lord who helps me considerably, perhaps even as a reward for having taken the assignment with great simplicity and trust in him? What if I, too, contracted the illness and died from it? Let God's will be done. I do this work of charity willingly, offering my life in sacrifice to the Lord, to atone for my sins and negligence, and for the good of the Church and of my brethren.[77]

If in a little while you should hear that I became ill and died of tuberculosis, do not believe that I performed a heroic act. Everyone here realizes the danger to which I have exposed myself, everyone, that is, except me. I will likely enjoy the reward for simplicity and remain untouched by this danger. And if I should indeed die, what death would be more enviable than mine?[78]

Roncalli's transfer coincided with the arrival of the first trains carrying the sick soldiers and the outbreak of the terrible Spanish Influenza in Bergamo. At first the *Banco Seta* hospital recorded one death a day, then two, then those who succumbed grew in numbers until no one kept count. For fear of spreading the illness, the authorities closed the road that led to the cemetery — a daily trek for Don Roncalli. When a Lieutenant-chaplain and friend visited Roncalli, he told him about field hospitals along the front lines where ninety cases of influenza had been reported —with no survivors. The chaplain also became a victim of the illness after assisting his soldiers. Not even this shook Don Roncalli. "And if I, too, contracted the illness? Of my good nuns at the Nigrizia, four are in bed with a fever. Your will be done, O Lord! As long as you give me a beautiful heaven and let your glory triumph."[79]

He chose to spend that Christmas with the former prisoners of war, and New Year's in the hospital chapel deep in prayer.

It is midnight. While the old year goes out and the new year comes in, my spirit keeps watch near Jesus in the chapel of the *Ricovero Nuovo*, amid the labored breathing of so many poor men whom the war has struck down and who feel death drawing near. With a glance, I see all the events of the past year, the Lord's goodness to me, my many failings, the good works I have done, the ones begun. I entrust myself quietly to his most loving Heart in life and in death. I want to live a more fervent priestly-apostolic spirit, and I want to die a holy death. *Veni, Domine Jesu* (Come, Lord Jesus).[80]

As the end of the war approached, the number of sick soldiers in the *Ricovero Nuovo* gradually decreased. Don Roncalli spent less time ministering to them and the other military personnel under his care. First he stopped offering the Mass of the Soldier in the Church of the Holy Spirit, "in order to bring to an end," he wrote, "a stirring up of personal sympathies."[81] Finally, on February 28, his discharge papers arrived, freeing him from military service. With joy he removed from his uniform his little stars, the *signa servitutis* (signs of his servitude), as he called them. Then he made a course of spiritual exercises that the bishop wished all former military priests to make.

Don Roncalli made his retreat in the house of the Priests of the Sacred Heart. Once again he took up his *Journal of a Soul* and wrote with intensity of his gratitude to God for the good that had been accomplished during the war years from the perspective of a man poor in both goods and honors, and with the fervor that zeal proposed in favor of youth.

> In four years of war, spent in the midst of a world in turmoil, how many graces I received from the Lord, how much experience, how many occasions to do good for my brothers! My Jesus, I thank you and bless you. I recall the many souls of the young men whom I had come to know during this time, many of whom I accompanied to the threshold of the next life. I am still deeply moved, and the thought that they will pray for me comforts and encourages me.[82]

The House of Students

In February 1918, the bishop asked Don Roncalli to be the chaplain at an evening gathering place for students that was to open in the *Città Alta* (Upper City). The location was to be the old Marenzi home behind the bishop's house, in the little piazza of St. Salvatore. Roncalli said yes immediately.[83] This was the first idea for a *Casa degli studenti* (a house of students), something between a boarding school and a hostel.

He began at once to obtain furniture for the house, for the chapel, and for the personnel. His two sisters, Ancilla and Maria, would live there. Some of the clerics and young priests would help with the education of the boys residing there.

This undertaking, however, proved a test for his spirit that he wanted to keep free from any shadow of attachment to worldly things. It became a new and unexpected training ground for comparing his own pedagogical ideas with those of others, especially with the gentleman who had proposed the House of Students, Count Medolago Albani. He was a great benefactor to Don Roncalli, but the priest differed with him over methodology. "The count is a man of *unius verbi* (one word). I instead prefer *'loquebantur variis linguis magnalia Dei'* ('they were proclaiming God's greatness in various tongues')."[84] Soon Roncalli would have to confront his pedagogical ideas with the reality of the young people who were always unpredictable even if carefully selected.

The outcome, however, was positive.

> Who would ever have thought? In a few weeks I have become the founder (!), no less, and director of a House of Students with a hostel, a school of religion, a place to gather in the evenings and after school, etc. I have also become the noted driving force behind one of the largest programs to form and assist the young students of Bergamo. I hope my efforts will result in great good for the education of strong Catholic minds and men who will become future *men of action*. It seems to me that the Lord has helped me overcome the first test — that of the beginning. The enterprise has won general approval. The principals and professors of the public schools are following the project with favor and are sending their students to me. I still have worries, often profound, especially for the young people of the hostel. Although I chose them carefully from among the many who applied for admission, the objectionable behavior of one or two causes sorrow and pain that cannot be erased even by the satisfaction and contentment resulting from the others who do so well.... But in general I am very pleased. I hope that, even at the cost of a few sacrifices, the Lord will help me in the future. This work concerns his glory. I never imagined being called upon to carry out such an endeavor, which one fine day I felt placed upon my shoulders. Only complete trust in him sustains me.[85]

The House of Students opened its doors in early June 1918. The center began its first pastoral activities for the young people, which included Mass for the students, Sunday religious instruction for the young men of the hostel, and religious education for all. Don Roncalli was entirely absorbed in his new activity. He considered organizing three other student homes in the city based on the model of the first, and three hostels like the famous College of St. Alexander. Indeed, he had become an influential driving force in the diocese in the field of educational ministry to young people.

Given the task of preparing a basic document to re-launch his newest undertaking, the "Work of St. Alexander,"[86] Roncalli drafted his proposals.

I observed the national holiday of September 20 by preparing, in writing, the project for reconstituting the Work of St. Alexander, which would bring together all the energies directed to the apostolate among the young students of Bergamo.... So, while the eternal merrymakers celebrate the date of Italy's unification with the taking of Rome...we are preparing the building blocks of a new Italy in the young people of tomorrow who are called to reawaken the true and ancient splendors of the nation.[87]

CHAPTER 8

THE ASSOCIATION FOR
YOUNG CATHOLIC WOMEN

Over the years, Don Roncalli had established some select and valu-able friendships in Milan. Cardinal Ferrari considered him his spiritual son and one of his best priests. Don Roncalli wrote:

> He is always so good to me! Sometimes I would like to avoid meet-ing him, and simply send my regards. However, he is offended if I do not show up, and when he does receive me, he envelops me with so much kindness that it is almost embarrassing. Even this morning he greeted me with an embrace and we parted with one as he said to me: "Let us go, but let us part with an embrace, my dear Don Angelo!"[1]

Aside from his relationship of mutual esteem with Monsignor Cavezzali, Radini Tedeschi's collaborator in leading pilgrimages, Don Roncalli cultivated sincere and energizing friendships with Don Giovanni Rossi, secretary to Cardinal Ferrari, and Don Enrico Mauri,[2] secretary to Bishop Marelli. Roncalli never missed a chance to chat at length with them each time he went to Milan. Almost the same age and sharing many common interests, their mutual esteem and trust grew over the years. Besides the fact that all three men were secretaries to bishops, they were also assistants to Catholic women's organizations. Each in his respective diocese had helped to establish the new Association of Young Catholic Women, an offshoot of the Union of Catholic Women.

In his parish of St. Gregory in Milan, Mauri had conceived the idea of the new association in 1917. The following year, Rossi organized it with the blessing of the cardinal. Through the untiring support of the Servant of God Armida Barelli and the staunch patronage of Pope Benedict XV, the association extended to the national structure of Catholic Action in November of 1918.[3]

In early 1918, Don Roncalli had helped in some way to establish the association in Milan. He participated in the discussions with Don Rossi regarding its organization and statutes, and took part in the last of three organizing assemblies. At that meeting St. Agnes, St. Joan of Arc, and St. Catherine of Siena were chosen as the models and patrons of the movement. At the conclusion of the meeting, Roncalli gave a talk on "St. Catherine of Siena and Devotion to the Pope."[4]

In Bergamo, it was necessary to wait for the pontifical disposition of November 1918 before the women's union could officially take charge of the foundation of the Association of Young Catholic Women. However, the details had evidently been worked out some time before by Don Roncalli. The year before he had drafted a list of the names of twelve young women as the first group needed to begin and promote the work.[5] He even took upon himself, "as a kind of apostolic commissioner,"[6] all the work related to the preparation and promotion of the group in parishes.[7]

In January 1919 he succeeded in establishing the newsletter *Lilies and Roses* as an instrument of the women's youth movement.[8] Founded and directed by his friend and benefactor, Bishop Morlani, *Lilies and Roses* was a publication of the Diocesan Pious Union of the Daughters of Mary. There was an increase in the number of articles on women, social and political topics, woman's mission in light of the Gospel, and Catholic social doctrine, especially in reference to divorce, freedom of education, and the problems of workers.[9]

The first true step toward establishing the Association for Young Catholic Women came in February with the nomination of a temporary committee accepted by the bishop. The initiative continued in March with a lecture by Professor Maria Magnocavallo of the National Council of the House of the People. This lecture was preceded and followed up by two unsigned articles in the daily *L'Eco di Bergamo,* written by Don Roncalli. He introduced the speaker to the members of the Union of Catholic Women "with fitting words" and wanted to conclude the meeting by adding "a few practical thoughts on her well-received talk."[10]

Oil paintings of the parents of Pope John XXIII:
Giovanni Battista Roncalli and Marianna Mazzola.

Alfred and Joseph Roncalli, two of the Pope's brothers.

Roncalli as a seminarian, above in 1901, and below in 1902.

Angelo Roncalli, seated at the center,
with fellow students of the Roman Seminary in 1904.

A group photo with Bishop Radini Tedeschi.

Roncalli in 1914.

Roncalli, seated at center, with other members
of a medical unit during Word War I.

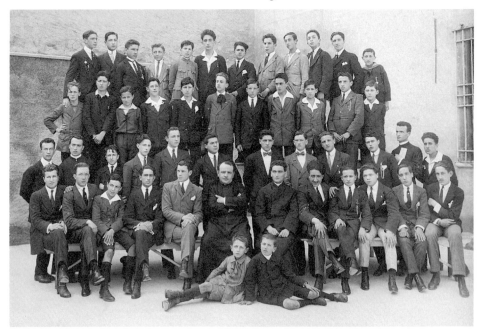

A group photo at the students' house.

Episcopal consecration of Roncalli.

Roncalli with his clergy of Istanbul.

The solemn entrance of Cardinal Roncalli into Venice.

At last, in May, at the College of St. Alexander, the official presentation of the association took place with all the parochial delegates and supporters in attendance. On the feast of Corpus Christi in June, the first two parish groups of the city were inaugurated. A morning ceremony was held at the cathedral parish in the *Città Alta,* and in the afternoon at the cathedral parish in *Città Bassa,* at the Sisters of Charity.

Between the summer and late autumn, a number of groups began in the city and throughout the diocese with very promising names: *Fede e azione* (Faith and action), *Oliva speciosa in campis* (An olive tree standing in the plain), *Stella alpina* (Alpine star), *Ut palma florebit* (It will flower like a palm tree).[11] The groups had been prepared, initiated, and followed by Don Roncalli who traveled to the various parishes, often with great sacrifice. On Sunday, November 9, in the Rubini Theater at the House of the People, overflowing with people attending the formal ceremony, the diocesan Association of Young Catholic Women was officially inaugurated. Talks were given by Armida Barelli, the General Vice-President (now Servant of God); Don Enrico Mauri, the national assistant; and Monsignor Giovanni Morlani, the diocesan assistant.

Don Roncalli recorded his great satisfaction and joy that evening in his diary.

> The women's conference which I prepared in the Rubini Theater was a splendid success and I bless the Lord from my heart. This ends my work of silent and almost hidden preparation, and opens the horizons to a vaster and more active apostolate. My new responsibility at the seminary prevents me from remaining the ecclesiastical assistant of women's works. However, I leave content to have accompanied the Women's Catholic Action during these ten years, until today's successful event, which is like the radiant morning of a more glorious day.[12]

In early summer, in the midst of those fervent pastoral initiatives, the bishop had proposed a new and more critical responsibility to Roncalli. The spiritual director of the major seminary had been named canonical penitentiary of the cathedral church and he had to be replaced. Marelli's request for Roncalli to take on the position no doubt proved the bishop's respect and trust in him. Roncalli accepted as a true act of obedience. However, he was simply replacing the spiritual director — who had held the position for twenty years. The spiritual formation of clerics is a sensitive and important task in itself and was very demanding. Most of the theology students and many philosophy students returned to the seminary after years of fighting in the war. They brought back with them the weight of their harsh experiences on the battlefields, and the death of fourteen of their confreres left a void. The spiritual director had to help the seminarians to clear away the emotional debris so that they could begin to rebuild their lives. Don Roncalli doubted his ability to fulfill the duty and hoped that the bishop would reconsider and choose someone else for the task. "Woe is me! What a responsibility! Let's hope they find a better candidate."[13]

The spiritual director had to be a father to the younger boys and the clerics. They returned from the war eager to resume their studies for the priesthood, but showing definite signs of fatigue. At 37, Don Roncalli was still rather young to be directing them. However, his experience of military service in peace and at wartime, and the fact that he had also been a witness to intense human misery, suffering, and death, would help him understand the seminarians' struggles. His brother priests respected him and were pleased with the choice. As a Priest of the Sacred Heart, Roncalli knew the seminary staff and current superiors very well; they had been his colleagues for ten years.

Unsuccessful in his attempts to decline the position and responsibility, Don Roncalli finally accepted with serenity. Although there was little about the work that appealed to him, he took on the full weight of the burden and entrusted himself entirely to the Lord. He found comfort in the bishop's trust and in the unanimous approval of the clergy. They were happy because "in this assignment many wanted to see an act of respect, not for my humble person, but to the memory of Bishop Radini Tedeschi."[14]

While the new appointment allowed him to remain the director of the House of Students, it required that he give up other responsibilities, but for the most part he was pleased to do so. In November he resigned as assistant to the Union of Catholic Women,[15] handed over the care of the Association for Young Catholic Women to Bishop Morlani,[16] and gave up his teaching position at the seminary.

One of the last obligations he felt compelled to honor was his participation in the Social Week for the Ecclesiastical Assistants held in Rome at the end of October. He accompanied Bishop Morlani and felt especially happy to visit Rome and his friends again. He had a special audience with Benedict XV, and in the bishop's name presented those initiatives underway in Bergamo for the benefit of young students.

The conference of the Ecclesiastical Assistants, however, did not satisfy him. It did refresh his spirit, but his heart was in Bergamo with the young people of the House of Students, whether he was in pleasant meetings at the new Lateran Seminary, or with his old friends who admired Radini Tedeschi — and himself. He had to confess that the older he became, the less attachment he felt for the Roman milieu. "Here I find myself at ease as a pilgrim, but at this point I would not like to live here permanently, even though I see an immense good to be done."[17]

While awaiting a meeting with the Holy Father, the time spent in Rome became burdensome, a true torment, but the impressions he brought back to the seminary were very dear. At noon on Thursday, November 6, Don Roncalli presented the pope with a written report of everything he was doing in Bergamo, and a request for a blessing.[18] The pope listened to Roncalli as he spoke of the work for young students, especially the *Casa di via San Salvator*. The Holy Father "approved by wholeheartedly blessing this work and the work that Don Roncalli was about to begin among the seminarians."[19]

Spiritual Director at the Seminary

Roncalli began his work among the seminarians and clerics by meeting with each of them every week for confession and for personal spiritual direction whenever they asked, and during the monthly retreat and spiritual exercises when the spiritual director is a true protagonist. "The seminarians are in my heart much more than the lay students. Many open their hearts to me and show how much they understand what I am trying to instill in them day after day in meditation and individual contacts. Oh, how necessary I find this discernment of spirits, this transfusion of fervor in the thought of this great mission!"[20]

The individual interviews were more frequent during the spiritual exercises and in the weeks preceding ordination. The seminary required that the clerics preparing for sacred orders receive, among other things, a declaration of admission from the spiritual director.

Despite the other demands placed upon him, Don Roncalli fulfilled all of his ordinary and extraordinary duties. Because the seminary and the House of Students were located in the same vicinity, Roncalli could more easily go from one house to the other on very active days. In any case, he desired to remain the spiritual director of the seminary, if not until his death,[21] at least for a while. If for no other reason, frequent changes in personnel in this type of ministry could prove damaging to the formation of seminarians.[22]

Roncalli's responsibilities were not limited to the seminary and the House of Students. He was undeniably one of the most visible and well-regarded priests among the diocesan clergy. "A true and holy minister of God, full of gentleness, awareness of the world, and great love for young people,"[23] as the Daughters of the Sacred Heart described him.

It was considered an honor to have his name on a list of committee members,[24] to have him preach on particular feast days, in religious institutes, or in city churches. Roncalli was asked to begin the meditations on "The Seven Last Words" for Good Friday of 1920 in the Basilica of St. Mary Major. The text was set to music selected from the work of Bergamo's greatest composer, Maestro Agostino Donini. Present for the occasion were the bishop and "the entire city, and the success was greater than anyone had anticipated."[25]

The superiors of the Roman Seminary invited Roncalli, the only priest among prelates and cardinals, to say a few words of thanksgiving on the feast of Our Lady of Confidence.[26] That same year, he was invited to give a few words of praise in the cathedral during the bishop's Pontifical Mass in honor of St. Alexander, the patron saint of the diocese. "I commented on the epistle of the Mass, applying it to the saint, 'Brothers, remain strong in the Lord and in the power of his strength.' I also took an appropriate thought from an ancient Ambrosian preface in honor of our martyr. May this annual solemnity be everlasting and ever new, and may we be worthy to share in the grace of holiness; and give to each of us through his intercession purity of heart and cleansing of our faults."[27]

Cardinal Gusmini asked Roncalli to guide a course of spiritual exercises in September for a group of laity in Bologna;[28] scholars considered it an honor to speak at Don Angelo's House of Students. For the opening of the academic year, the superiors asked Roncalli to resume the role of historian and commemorate the first centenary of the transfer of the seminary to the Hill of St. John.[29] Bergamo's Academy of Sciences, Letters, and Arts had made Roncalli a member the year before.[30] He had also been offered the honor of *cavaliere della corona d'Italia* (knight of the crown of Italy) for his achievements as a military chaplain. However, he refused this honor.

> I am very pleased by the good intentions of these people, although in the little good I was able to do, my goal was simply to fulfill my

duty as a military chaplain, obedient before God and mindful of his reward and not that of men. However, this decoration, which is wholly secular, does not suit me. At one time, a priest who was a *cavaliere* indicated that he was a liberal. This notion still partly endures. I do not want to be a liberal, nor in any way be seen as such.[31]

Don Roncalli was a member of the Governing Council of the Diocesan Committee to prepare for the Sixth National Eucharistic Congress of Bergamo. The commission in Milan chose Roncalli to represent the diocese of Bergamo on the organizing committee for the reconstruction of the seminary of Lombardy.[32] Perhaps Cardinal Ferrari, who never failed to show his paternal affection for Roncalli each time they met, recommended him for the position.[33]

The Labor Office

It was during this time that the diocese of Bergamo began to experience a critical period of events. Conflicts began to arise between some of the laity, priests, and the Labor Office, an organization of the central committee of Catholic Action. Even the bishop, the Vatican secretary of state, and Pope Benedict XV became involved in the dispute.

Bishop Radini Tedeschi had established the Labor Office in 1906, and it had always distinguished itself for the help it offered workers engaged in union disputes. However, internal dissension over management ended the organization. It resumed activities only later under the direction of Bishop Marelli who wanted the Church to be present among the working class.[34]

But there were problems. Ignoring the principles of the Gospel and the social doctrine of the Church, some of the people in charge of the office wanted to resolve labor disputes with strikes and class struggle. The matter grew more sensitive when the administration of the Office was entrusted to a team of priests and lay persons from Catholic Action.

Accusations against the Labor Office for subversive ideas and methods began to surface early in 1919. The diocesan board, parish priests, and Catholic businessmen voiced their complaints to the bishop. The daily Catholic paper publicly criticized the Office of Labor before an agitated assembly of the House of the People, which Don Roncalli attended. He left the meeting worried, especially over the threat to the bishop's authority and the unity of Catholics.

In September, Bishop Marelli published a declaration disclaiming the proponents of the Office of Labor who were spreading theories and social methods in open contradiction to the Church's authority.[35] People asked Roncalli to intervene with the bishop who, it was rumored, was planning to dismiss certain directors. Don Roncalli began to take a prudent interest in the matter.

The events surrounding the Labor Office were interwoven with the tensions disturbing the Popular Party's first year of existence in Bergamo. For a long time, priests had remained indifferent to the new party because of its non-sectarian policy, its social-political program, and their fear of mixing faith with politics and activism. These priests were the same who clashed with the Labor Office and challenged the social choices of Catholic Action itself.[36]

While Don Roncalli welcomed the new social-political party with a hopeful enthusiasm, he quickly understood the difficulties it encountered among the Catholics and the clergy of Bergamo. "Blessed people, who only know how to criticize and tear down, to place themselves even above the leaders, and in the meantime give our enemies reason to laugh at us and work for our destruction."[37]

The birth of the new party forced Catholics to take a clear political stand and, according to statements made by Pope Benedict XV, to separate political action from the works of Catholic Action. A demand for true social action was made of the Popular Union groups, and things proceeded along these lines in Bergamo. Don Roncalli was involved in forming the new Catholic social action, and he went so far as to suggest the group take its name from the first bishop of the city: St. Narno.

It was evident that the difficulties within the Office of Labor created a negative reputation for the Popular Party in the diocese. This was especially true among Catholic middle class liberals who could not detach themselves from the more secure and reassuring paternalistic vision of the working class. The elections were held in November 1919. The next day while Don Angelo waited for the results, he noted in his diary:

> For the first time the new Italian Popular Party, which is bringing together the best Christian forces of the nation, is taking on the electoral struggle. Naturally in Bergamo there also exists bitter opposition from liberals who are afraid of losing their hold on public matters, which they have enjoyed for over fifty years. The unfortunate circumstances that accompanied the composition of our register have distressed quite a few and estranged many. However, discipline

above all. I think that with the new voting system inaugurated today the Popular Party's crusade will have a remarkable victory. We are always taking new steps forward toward the re-vindication of the Christian spirit in the public arena. That is a great good, for which we must thank the Lord.[38]

This was an easy prediction, even with Roncalli's adjective, *"remarkable."* The results proved him correct: Sixty percent of the votes from Bergamo went to the Popularists, twenty percent to the Liberals, and fifteen percent to the Socialists. Roncalli commented with satisfaction: "Complete victory for the Popularists; five out of their six candidates were elected. An unexpected disaster for the Liberals. It is the same all over Italy, with strong support for Socialism. However, our party must have confidence; it expresses life and what is to come. With yesterday's elections, we took a gigantic step forward. Let us give thanks to God for this."[39]

At the beginning of the New Year, Roncalli noted that things at the Labor Office were getting worse. "A stubborn desire to uphold unacceptable supporters at any cost will compromise this good and beneficial movement. Today, I spoke at length with Count Medolago, and despite our differing opinions, I agreed with him on many things and cannot condemn his criteria. Let's hope that the organization does not suffer great damage and that above all the bishop's authority is respected."

Eventually, the secretary of state intervened to clarify the matter, and Pope Benedict XV sent a document to Bergamo, signed March 11, to support the bishop's actions. Beset from all sides, Roncalli continued to take an interest in the situation, but remained firmly united with the bishop in everything.

The episode ended with the dismissal of several lay leaders of the Labor Office, who later started a new organization, the Labor Union, which was recognized by the Catholic Italian Chamber of Labor.

The Sixth National Eucharistic Congress

In September 1920, the Sixth National Eucharistic Congress was held in Bergamo — a dream of Radini Tedeschi's that had been kept alive in Don Roncalli's heart. It had been the former bishop's desire for Bergamo to host that important ecclesial event since 1905. After only two months in Bergamo, Radini Tedeschi had such great hope that the people would respond to this initiative that he even referred to it in the closing assembly of the International Eucharistic Congress in Rome.

In January, Bishop Marelli announce the celebration of the Congress, and in February, he named the preparatory commissions and steering committee. Don Roncalli was among the twenty members of the third commission that was responsible for finding suitable accommodations for the cardinals, archbishops, bishops, prelates, priests, and the laity who would also attend.[40] In the months preceding the celebration, Roncalli always accepted occasions to speak to various groups to prepare them for the great event. This was the case with the well-received lecture held at St. Alexander's College that addressed the members of the Association for Young Catholic Women who had attended the Social Week of Eucharistic Culture.

The Congress opened with vespers on Wednesday, September 8, the feast of the Birth of the Blessed Virgin Mary, and closed on Sunday, September 12, the feast of the Holy Name of Jesus. The participants were divided into five sections. There were morning study sessions for each section and a general assembly every afternoon in the Rubini Theater of the House of the People. Because Don Roncalli was one of the vice-presidents of the Young Catholic Women section, it was his place to open the sessions and introduce the presiding bishop-president and the official speakers to the audience.

The official program listed that Tortona's Bishop Grassi would deliver the opening address.[41] However, circumstances prevented him from attending and the program officials quickly entrusted Don Roncalli with the theme: *The Eucharist and the Madonna: the Loves of the Christian.* Although it was only the night before the talk, Roncalli accepted.

The words of the improvised talk flowed out from the abundance of his love for the Eucharist and the Blessed Mother.[42] With simplicity and directness, his talk was a moving canticle interwoven with biblical citations, historical references, and personal experiences, including his pilgrimage to Lourdes and his ministry in the military hospitals. This was an exaltation of our forefathers' faith, those who knew how to produce masterpieces in honor of the two great loves of the Christian soul. They were spurred on by a faith that took expression in the even greater works of economic and social organizations of which their children could be justly proud.

In conclusion, Don Roncalli hoped that even the disquieting news during those months of unrest and social demands would resonate in their hearts. The malcontent he referred to was exemplified in the "red banners, symbols of violence and of oppression, [seen] waving ominously over the factories,"[43] which caused the people to fear they were on the eve of a social revolution. Instead, they were simply on the eve of administrative elections. Roncalli assured them that only through the continual nourishment of faith could they meet head-on the "economic problem, the terrible unknown of our time, a period so agitated amid the insatiable crowds that will never be satisfied."[44] "It is everyone's duty, each imposing renunciations and sacrifices on themselves, to contribute to a solution that is equitable and corresponds to the highest principles of Catholic doctrine, springing from the Gospel and from the clear and solemn teaching of the Church."[45]

The newspapers reported how often Roncalli's talk was interrupted by the spontaneous applause of the audience that literally squeezed into every corner of the otherwise spacious theater. At the end, Roncalli received a standing ovation.

The Call to Service at the Holy See

"Satis, Domine, satis [Enough, Lord, enough]. This was the cry of St. Francis Xavier, today's saint. The spiritual consolations that the Lord gives me for the little good that I do are truly greater than I deserve."[46] A week after Don Roncalli wrote this exclamation of priestly joy in his diary, Bishop Marelli summoned him. He had a letter from Cardinal Guglielmo van Rossum for Roncalli to read.[47] The Redemptorist prefect of the Roman Congregation *Propaganda Fide* requested that the bishop free Roncalli for service in Rome. He intended to put him in charge of the general administration of the Association for the Propagation of the Faith in Italy.

"I was dumbfounded," he wrote in his diary, "and my first reaction is that perhaps I am not suited to that office. On the one hand, Rome attracts me, and my self-love inclines me there. But I must — I want to — use my head above all else. I worry more about making a good place for myself in heaven than I do about honorary positions and a career on earth."[48]

Days of doubt and uncertainty, prayer and advice followed. As much as Roncalli always felt ready to do God's will, this unexpected assignment would change the circumstances of his life completely, and he was stunned.

> At first [I felt] a sense of deep aversion for the new office, because it seemed unsuited to my tendencies and habits. Then [I felt] an interior struggle between the meaning, which seems sincere, of the

adveniat regnum tuum, fiat voluntas tua (your kingdom come, your will be done) on the one hand, and self-love and reasons of the heart on the other. Lastly, [I felt] a flash of light holding me in balance and persuading me that it is for this particular ministry that the Lord is calling me.[49]

Three days later he wrote a clear, sincere letter to the bishop outlining the pros and cons of the proposal as it appeared to him: the beauty of the work on the one hand, his specific limitations on the other. He knew that he did not have that spirit of initiative and the organizational skills necessary for the success of the movement. He was afraid of being useless to the Holy See. The decision was then left up to the bishop and the superiors in Rome. Their decision would be the will of God.[50]

But was the proposal truly God's will? Roncalli wrote his friend, Don Giovanni Rossi, who was secretary to Cardinal Ferrari in Milan. He hoped that perhaps Rossi could learn the cardinal's opinion on the matter. Roncalli received a response signed by the cardinal himself. "God's will is more than manifest. Where God calls one goes, without hesitation, abandoning himself in all things to the Lord's loving Providence. In this way you will have profound peace."[51] While the response was a great spiritual comfort, not even Cardinal Ferrari could say *what* Roncalli was going to do in Rome. Would he be capable? And his heart? "How it bleeds!" he confessed. "For my heart it is a true sacrifice to detach myself from all that I love so much."[52]

Roncalli would only later learn the details of his appointment. He had been selected from among his friends in Rome and, as he suspected, the news of the "blows that had knocked him over for several days"[53] spread very quickly. A few months earlier Cardinal von Rossum had turned to Don Paolo Giobbe,[54] Roncalli's former classmate and rector of the *Collegio Urbaniano di Propaganda Fide* and president of the National Committee of the Propagation of the Faith in Italy. Rossum asked Giobbe to suggest some names for the reorganization of the committee to be separated from the Diocesan Commission of Rome. After seeking the advice of former classmates, Giobbe decided to place Roncalli's name at the top of the list. He spoke about him with the pope who "very willingly" agreed with the choice; as a close friend of Radini Tedeschi he already knew Roncalli. The position would involve reorganizing the Association for the Propagation of the Faith in Italy in order to create a national center with several diocesan committees. As head of the association, with the title of national president, Roncalli would be in charge of a council responsible for the administration of the office. He would reside in Rome and visit the various dioceses throughout Italy, not to ask for money, but to promote the formation and organization of the diocesan councils. He would be in contact with the bishops and those involved in missionary works already in existence. He would also have to add to the oral propagation of the faith that of the written word.[55]

Despite the explanations and clarifications of his new position, Don Roncalli spent the remainder of the year feeling uncertain if it was truly God's will for him. In any case, while waiting for a definitive answer from Rome, he familiarized himself with missionary literature to understand the situation better.[56] He was by no means ignorant of the material; his interest in the works of the propagation office began in 1912 when Bishop Radini Tedeschi had established a diocesan secretariat to coordinate assistance for missionaries and Catholic missions.[57] In the midst of World War I (1917), the Servant of God Don Paolo Manna of the Institute of Foreign Missions and founder of the Missionary Union of Clerics arrived in Bergamo with Blessed Guido Maria Conforti, the Bishop of Parma and first president of the union.

The following year, a diocesan branch of that union was founded in Bergamo. The year 1919 was an important one for the missionary organization of the diocese. Two memorable missionary days took place for the laity and for priests in July, and this gave rise to a network of parochial commissions that wanted, above all else, to involve youth groups.[58] In November, the Missionary Union for young women held an impressive conference in the Rubini Theater of the House of the People. Don Roncalli attended, and he wrote down his thoughts in his diary that same night:

> Though there is still much to do here, it is also good to lift our eyes to the vast world that still lives in darkness and the shadow of death. Recounting what the missionaries and the nuns do in those nations is a great encouragement to our work in this country.[59]

In January 1920, Bishop Marelli entrusted the diocesan secretary of the Missionary Union of Clerics, through its monthly bulletin *Missionary Life*,[60] with the task of organizing and directing three papal missionary works in the diocese.[61] Several conferences were planned throughout the diocese for 1921 in order to animate the young people even more. The activities would include a missionary week in June for the young women of Bergamo. Don Roncalli had just been invited to speak on the theme, "The Missions, a Continuation of the Work of the Apostles,"[62] when he was unexpectedly[63] called to Rome.

Separation from Bergamo

With the new year already begun, the wait for a final decision from Rome seemed endless to Don Roncalli who could only encourage himself to be patient.[64] He finally received word on January 14. Cardinal Ferrari had already assured him that in accepting this important office, he would completely fulfill the Lord's will.[65] "I wished nothing more than to know exactly the Lord's will. This is now clear to me. *Etiam si Hierosolimis tribulationes me manent* [Even if tribulations await me in Jerusalem, I care little]. *Dominus illuminatio mea et salus mea* [The Lord is my light and my salvation, Ps 27:1]."[66] Roncalli wrote to his new superior immediately, accepting the assignment and entrusting himself to the cardinal's paternal goodness. Knowing he lacked the passionate zeal of the Apostle Paul, Roncalli believed that the Lord would at least grant him the tranquil yet active spirit and constant zeal of Barnabas — a good man full of the Holy Spirit.[67]

During the first six months of his new assignment, Don Roncalli commuted between Bergamo and Rome in order to meet his superiors and collaborators and to discuss plans for the immediate work. He also looked for a location for a new office and a house for himself and his sisters, Ancilla and Maria, whom he planned to bring with him. On Easter Monday, Pope Benedict XV received Roncalli in a private audience. The "good, trusting and friendly" pope kept him for more than a half hour discussing not only the Association for the Propagation of the Faith, but also the recent political and social events in Bergamo. Don Roncalli was happy "to have answered everything with serenity and with a great deal of respect for everything and everyone."[68]

During the times he spent in Bergamo, Roncalli began to bring his activities to a closure. That meant offering and accepting the warm, heartbreaking farewells[69] of members of his beloved organization, his students, and the seminary faculty. He received several awards in recognition for his work in the diocese. On March 18, in a solemn and unexpected ceremony, he became an honorary canon of the Cathedral Chapter.[70] At one time, the bishop had opposed conferring this honor on Roncalli, though not with great vigor; he had merely wished to keep Don Roncalli for his seminary where, as he had written, "he does very well."

Now the bishop wanted to give Roncalli a sign of his great esteem and gratitude for all his services by making him a member.

The canons of the Chapter heartily approved the bishop's proposal "as a public testimony of the diocese to a very deserving priest for the offices he has fulfilled as secretary to the late Bishop Radini Tedeschi, as professor and then spiritual director at the major seminary, as founder and first director of the House of Students, and as a zealous cooperator in the many activities of the Catholic clubs and associations."[71] Don Roncalli was delighted with the honor. He considered it "a stronger motive to intensify that affection and reverence [for the bishop] which, with the Lord's help, I have always wanted to show him both in public and in private, also in order that it might be a lesson and example to the young clerics."[72]

The city of Sotto il Monte also congratulated its now illustrious citizen,[73] but the most solemn and memorable occasion was the official farewell from Bergamo. On the evening of Sunday, June 5, the first day of the Missionary Week,[74] in the prestigious Sala Piatti at the heart of Città Alta, and only a short distance from the House of Students, the city bid farewell to Don Angelo with a choral celebration. The Catholic daily reported:

> The ceremony held yesterday in honor of Canon Angelo Roncalli turned out to be a true celebration of the heart attended not only by students, but also by city officials and fellow citizens. In the *Sala Piatti*, which was kindly provided by the Congregation of Charity, there gathered not only the young students of the House of St. Salvatore and the St. Alexander club, but also the other students from the public schools who appreciate the talents and work of Monsignor Roncalli. When he entered the room wearing his official attire, he was welcomed by repeated applause and best wishes. Even before the magnificent musical program began, many of the students wanted to show Monsignor Roncalli their heartfelt gratitude for all the good he had done for the student body through his zealous efforts marked by wise Christian discernment. Monsignor Roncalli answered everything most nobly, with that dignified eloquence and delicate sentiment that is all his own. The guarantee that, even from afar, Bergamo would always hold him in its heart greatly pleased him, as it did all the people of Bergamo. Those who attended the festivities felt very satisfied to know that Roncalli would forever carry with him to Rome and elsewhere the remembrance of Bergamo as something dear to his heart.[75]

Roncalli was in fact leaving with Bergamo in his heart, with the entire diocese as his cathedral. Everything was sacred to him: the history, the relics, the ceremonies, the tombs.... And if he "happens, with calm and patience, to do a little bit of good even in Rome and elsewhere," he wrote, "it will be [in] the good tradition...of Bergamo, with illustrious names and resplendent honors."[76]

What did people think of this Professor Roncalli, not quite 40 years old, who was separating himself from his Bergamo in order to serve — he hoped worthily — the Holy See? In December 1920, he had a premonition that his fortieth year would be the last year of his life, but he quickly recovered and did not allow himself to be overcome by such notions, because *sive vivimus, sive morimur, Domini sumus* (both as we live and as we die, we are in the Lord).[77]

People thought of him as a hard worker, but he maintained that he was a man who did little. He would say that by nature he was actually slow in writing and easily distracted from his work. Even in the few good works he had done, he had only seized the opportunities to do the good that Providence had placed in his path day by day. He carried them out as they developed naturally and nothing more, as he confided to his bishop.[78] Of course, he was drawn by great desires of his mind and heart, but as far as fulfilling them, he felt he was ordinary in deed and weak in strength. True, he was always dedicated to his work, "but that happens by a mere strength of will that the Lord helps." He confessed frankly to the bishop that a life of intense activity was a burden for him, not an ideal. He thought of himself as a priest who preferred a life of prayer, meditation, and study with a desire for a direct ministry to souls, but a quiet one — without noise.

> Retreating into myself and reflecting on the various events in my humble life, I recognize that the Lord exempted me from the tribulations that make service to truth, justice, and charity so difficult and demanding for many people. I lived through my infancy and youth without noticing the poverty, without worrying about family, studies, or dangerous circumstances such as those I faced, for example, during my military service at the age of 20, and during the Great War.... Little and humble as I acknowledge myself to be, I was always warmly welcomed wherever I went, from the seminary in Bergamo and later in Rome; through the ten years of my priestly life near my bishop in my native city; from 1921 until now, 1961, that is from Rome and back to Rome, as far as the Vatican. O good God, how do I thank you for the gracious manner in which I was

received wherever I went in your name, always in pure obedience, not to do my own, but your will?[79]

Everything seemed to harmonize with his natural, peaceful temperament, a quality Roncalli recognized within himself, and a characteristic he saw as a pathway along the road that Providence had marked out for his holiness. "The particular aptitudes of my character, my experiences, and circumstances lead me to calm, peaceful work outside the battle-field, rather than into combative activity, polemics, struggle. Very well, then, I do not want to make myself holy by disfiguring a fairly good original in order to become an unfortunate copy of others who have a temperament different from mine."[80]

He had acquired his own style, made of great ideas and a great heart, of optimism in thought and in life, calmness, charity, and a simple, direct, loving truth. He felt a real joy at being able to live in the present times. He considered the direct care of souls to be the most beautiful honor he could desire for heaven and for this world, the glory of the Good Shepherd *qui animam suam dat* (who offers his life). He was truly sincere when he prayed, "My Lord, wrap me in the charm of this glorious characteristic, so that I may never be taken in by other things. Above all, I want to carry out a pastoral ministry. The rest counts for little or nothing here below." He often recalled the exclamation of St. John Bosco, "O Lord, give me souls, and take all the rest." Or he considered the classic assertion of St. Paul: "...As long as Christ be proclaimed, whether out of opportunism or through the truth, and in this I rejoice."[81]

The various forms of apostolate to which the Lord could call him seemed marvelous. "It will even happen to you, that which seems to me to be the sign of God's direct action in our life. That is, to seem to be called to one form of service and instead, after achieving the first steps, receive another assignment. It turns all our energies elsewhere, in order to succeed in new and unexpected tasks, and to succeed better than we ourselves would have expected."[82]

How many times this had already happened in the sixteen years of his priesthood, and in a more bewildering fashion: director of the House of Students, spiritual director in the seminary, the call to Rome. *Oboe-dientia et pax!* "The complete separation from oneself, the constant preoccupation to seek nothing but God in everything, his glory, his Church, is a great guarantee of success in our various ministries. I force myself to hold onto these principles and I know, with great pleasure, that the Lord helps and blesses me."[83]

PART II

IN THE SERVICE
OF THE HOLY SEE
1921–1953

Mario Benigni

CHAPTER 9

AT THE OFFICE FOR THE
PROPAGATION OF THE FAITH
1921–1925

Fifteen years after [ordination in 1904], the field of worldwide Catholic missions opened out to me. It came about unexpectedly as a matter of obedience and was always, before and after, agreeable and important to me. Although it disrupted my pastoral ministry directed to young people, it still seemed to me worthy of careful and fervent attention.... The Holy Father Benedict XV had me summoned from my Bergamo, and Pius XI encouraged me by word and example in this new form of apostolate.[1]

Don Angelo was referring here to his nomination as president of the Central Council of the Association for the Propagation of the Faith in Italy. He resided in Rome under the title of Domestic Prelate of His Holiness. He considered the demanding nature of these posts and their weight on his spiritual life. *"Etiam si Hierosolimis tribulationes me manent* (Even if tribulations await me in Jerusalem, I care little). *Dominus illuminatio mea et salus mea* (The Lord is my light and my salvation)."[2] As far as the pontifical title was concerned, he felt it a greater responsibility weighing on him than an honor: *Non jam nobis honor vestium, sed splendor animarum.* (What concerns us is not the dignity which clothing gives, but the splendor of souls won for Christ and his Church).[3]

149

After his first visit to Rome in mid-January 1921, he returned in March to stay for the entire month as a guest at the seminary. He would make several more visits before he could locate a site for his office and, after an even more painstaking search, a house for himself and his sisters. They lived on Via Volturno at first, a noisy and out-of-the-way street. Then they occupied several small rooms abutting the church of St. Mary on Via Lata, where he could offer hospitality to his old friend and beloved rector of the seminary, Monsignor Vincenzo Bugarini.

While he searched for appropriate housing, Roncalli also began to familiarize himself with his new work. Early in the year, he met with the managers of the Congregation for the Propagation of the Faith in Rome, on whom he would depend in the immediate future, and he corresponded frequently with Cardinal van Rossum. Don Roncalli set up informal meetings with Don Paolo Manna del Pime and Bishop Conforti[4] of Parma, founder of the Xaverian Missionaries. Don Manna del Pime was the soul and founder of the Missionary Union of the Clergy, and Bishop Conforti was its president. Both men worried that the new Congregation for the Propagation of the Faith would hinder their own initiatives, which were already doing so much good among the clergy. In his meetings with del Pime and Conforti, Roncalli established his personal approach with the motto: *"Flectar, non frangar"* (bend, do not break), that intentionally reversed the ancient axiom: *"Frangar, non flectar"* (break, do not bend).[5] Roncalli impressed the two priests as being a cultured and religious man with a direct and affable manner, and one who knew his business very well.[6]

By January 30, Roncalli had already written what would become the constitutive document of the Work of the Propagation of the Faith in Italy, approved by the pope with a few amendments proposed by Cardinal van Rossum.[7] In line with the encyclical on Catholic missions, *Maximum Illud,* the international character of the work was highlighted as was the nature of the Roman Catholic Church, mother of all people, respectful of every nationality without preference and a stranger to preoccupation, political dealings, and nationalism.[8] Roncalli's job was to coordinate, not supplant the existing missionary works and to foster harmonious and cordial relationships among them.

On March 1, a decree was issued instituting the Central Office for the Work of the Propagation of the Faith in Italy, which would promote, regulate, and manage the work in the dioceses. On March 12, Angelo Roncalli was named president.

On Pentecost, May 15, 1921, a letter announcing the new organization was prepared by Roncalli, signed, and sent to the bishops. A characteristic of spiritual renewal at that time was fervor for vocations to the foreign missions and the people's desire to cooperate in the spread of the Gospel. For this reason, a new Central Council was needed for the dioceses of Italy to organize the Work of the Propagation of the Faith. Roncalli's letter outlined the task of the new council, which would enkindle a true enthusiasm for its work throughout the dioceses, to establish direct rapport with the bishops, maintain frequent contact with the diocesan directors, visit the bishops and the various diocesan centers, publish a bulletin, and foster, follow, and direct the solicitation of offerings.

The summer and autumn months were occupied with organizing his new office in the rooms of the former Borgia Museum in the Piazza di Spagna. Roncalli also selected and appointed his closest collaborators: Don Giovanni Dieci of Reggio Emilia as secretary, and Don Carlo Rusticoni of Vercelli, both alumni of the Scuola Sociale of Bergamo.

In mid-December, Don Joseph Maria Drehmanns, special secretary to Cardinal van Rossum, accompanied Roncalli on an extended trip to France, Belgium, Holland, and Germany. Their intention was to inform the diocesan missionary offices about the new effort in Italy and to observe and study the best organizational methods. They also hoped to create "a smooth chain" of relationships between Rome and the local missionary organizations in view of the serious and perhaps painful transfer of the center for the Work for the Propagation of the Faith from Lyons to Rome.[9]

After visiting the missionary centers in Savoy, Lyons, and Paris, then Lieges and Brussels in Belgium, Roncalli and Drehmanns traveled to Holland where they spent Christmas in Wittem. Don Angelo and his companion then proceeded to Aachen and Cologne in Germany, and Munich in Bavaria.[10]

Observing things in all their complexity from outside, that trip convinced Roncalli that the Lord, through the recent tribulations of his people, was carrying out a great design of mercy for the whole world. He felt that the Church and the Roman pontificate were now more than ever "light and revelation to the people, glory of the people Israel!"[11]

Don Roncalli was asked[12] by the Holy See to draft the solemn act of the transfer of the central offices of the Propagation of the Faith to Rome. This decision of Pope Benedict XV was made known in the January 18 issue of *L'Osservatore Romano,* only four days before his death.

The new pope, Pius XI, reconfirmed the act in the conviction that nothing greater could be expected of the Vicar of Christ...than the extraordinary irradiation of evangelical doctrine on the world and the spirit of reconciliation.[13] The *Romanorum Pontificum,* as it was called, ordered the administration of the Propagation of the Faith to move from Lyons to Rome. The document was dated May 3, the one hundredth anniversary of the founding of the Congregation in Lyons in 1822.[14]

That centenary year was one of heavy commitments for Don Angelo, who willingly accepted invitations to speak to various groups and institutes. The most important and best conference he attended was held on May 3, the birthday of the Propagation of the Faith. The event, held at the Apostolic Chancery, was attended by many prelates and cardinals.[15]

Roncalli was forced to hasten the organization of a printing office, and he named Don Carlo Rusticoni as the director. The establishment of the office was hindered by operational difficulties and by the misunderstanding, fear, and jealousy of those in charge of the other missionary publications throughout Italy,[16] above all *The Catholic Mission* of the Missionary Union of the Clergy.

The first fruits of the office were a booklet on the *Propagation of the Faith,* entirely edited by Don Angelo, and a new monthly periodical, *The Propagation of the Faith in the World.* This bulletin would be a link between the dioceses and the Italian missionary organizations by summarizing the activity of the Central Council and reporting on the donations received. The first issue came out between December 1922 and January 1923, with 150,000 copies printed and diffused throughout the dioceses and parishes of Italy. In an editorial, Roncalli expressed his joy and enthusiasm for the missionary fervor that the publication represented more than for the periodical itself.

> The Orient glows in the dawn of a new day for Christian civilization. The worker hidden in the valley does not see it. But those who pray on the mountain have accompanied it.... What are you doing, men of little faith, intent on crying because even among the peoples of Catholic tradition the evening twilight is descending and the night appears to be approaching? *Lift up your heads!* Behold, the Lord is always with us! He is returning to shine on the holy mountain where was announced: *Lux mundi* [light of the world].[17]

The Church was truly witnessing a new Pentecost, and Roncalli saw the fervent ideal of his work for the future as a contribution to the *apostolatus inter gentes* (apostolate to the nations).[18] For as long as the Lord gave him life he was ready to work for the triumph of Jesus and his Church, and to lead people to holiness "according to the ways most adapted to the circumstances and sustained by that mysterious spirit, gentle and confident, of a wholesome discipline that was the strength of the apostles."[19] Years later, he recalled with the same enthusiasm, "Ah, what memories! What affirmations! What prayers! Just then in the official rite of the Church a supplication was introduced: *Ut omnes errantes ad unitatem Ecclesiae revocare et infideles universos ad Evangelii lumen perducere digneris, Te rogamus, audis nos* (That all those in error will return to the unity of the Church, and those who have not yet heard the Gospel will come to its light, hear us, O Lord). Here is a prayer to the Lord; there is a wish for the Pope; there is hope for all!"[20]

As President of the National Council, Roncalli was asked to speak at missionary congresses throughout Italy. However, his frequent speeches aggravated what had been a minor ailment until now — a frequent and sudden dropping off of his voice. The doctors ordered a treatment of baths, inhalers, atomizers, and other special prescriptions together with a month of absolute silence — if he did not want to ruin his voice forever.[21] He underwent a month of intensive treatment in Salsomaggiore. This was followed by another month of absolute silence when he stayed at Rapallo in the villa of the Ursulines of the Sacred Heart, a guest of the superior, the sister of Bishop Radini Tedeschi.

At 40 years of age, Don Angelo initially accepted this first experience of a serious health problem as a simple mortification.[22] But then he considered it as a real illness, which involved the divine will. "I still do not have the courage to ask [God] to give me back my voice. His holy will, not mine; his pleasure and wish, not mine. That is what I repeated to him even this morning after Mass with much joy."[23]

Having completed the treatment and with his voice restored, Roncalli visited all the dioceses of Calabria. His plan was to sensitize the bishops, priests, and seminarians to the ideals and interests of the Propagation of the Faith and to cultivate an interest in the foreign missions.

In his diary, he recorded his impressions of his travels and his various meetings with a positive and hopeful assessment. To a friend he wrote, "Calabria is very interesting and also very beautiful. I am hoping that my visit will be fruitful, with the help of God. How many souls to save and to sanctify even there."[24]

During the winter, he was busy with his ordinary duties as president. He also preached courses of spiritual exercises, retreats, and parish Lenten services; he taught various groups, seminarians, and young students in and around Rome. Not only had his voice returned, but there was an ever growing esteem for the young monsignor from Bergamo. Soon after Easter (1923), he resumed his promotional trips throughout Italy.

In April 1924, he passed through Siena, Livorno, and Bergamo for the Diocesan Congress of the Missionary Union of the Clergy. Then he went on to Modena and Bologna. He visited all the larger cities in Sicily in May. He described Sicily as a beautiful garden and commented that the Sicilians were good, amiable, and hospitable people, the women modest and reserved.[25] Writing to a friend, he remarked that he brought back valuable experiences for his priesthood from all his trips.[26] He expressed true satisfaction and much hope that the many and sometimes difficult steps he had taken, the simple but innumerable words he had spoken, had been an instrument of blessing for the work of the Propagation office.[27]

In November he found an equally positive welcome on his next trip to the southern dioceses, all the while feeling the Lord's help and blessing. "I thank God and continue to entreat him *ut sit illuminatio mea, salus mea, et protectio vitae meae in quo speravi* [that the one in whom I hope may illuminate me, save me, and protect me]."[28]

The complex and new work continued to go well, but Roncalli wanted to expand his offices, which had been relocated to the building for the Propagation of the Faith in Piazza Mignanelli. He also wanted to add more personnel to the staff, preferring to employ men and women. He began to sense that his projects were becoming the target of pious envy. In fact, he began to realize the harmony that existed between his collaborators and himself and that the enduring calmness of working together daily, often into the night, "was an unusual occurrence, it seems, here in Rome."[29]

Meanwhile, enthusiastic preparations for another great event were underway: the Missionary Exposition for the Holy Year 1925. The exhibition was to be set up in the rooms of the Lateran Palace and inaugurated by the pope on December 21, the eve of the opening of the Holy

Door. Roncalli displayed the mission publications: missionary atlases, guides, postcards, albums, posters, and cards to be diffused throughout the world, and a large illustrated periodical published in several languages through the collaboration of experts from around the world.

Preparatory meetings for the exposition multiplied over the course of the year, but not everything that was said and proposed appealed to Don Angelo who vented his feelings to his friend, Monsignor Gustavo Testa. "The responsibility as President of the Publishing Commission for the Exposition makes me see some real conflicts every day. Oh, if you were only here a while, how many arguments we could have, but together at least we would have the chance to make certain comments!... Here everyone has his own patron saint. Imagine what patience it takes to keep them at bay and out of the arena."[30]

Overall, he felt that everything was a little too negative. "My good president does nothing but say 'no' and reject proposals."[31] This "good president" of the preparatory commission for the Exposition was Archbishop Francesco Marchetti Selvaggiani, secretary of the Congregation for the Propagation of the Faith. In his new assignment, Selvaggiani tended to show off. His typically innocent remarks and the hot and cold outbursts of a genuine Romanesque spirit helped maintain his collaborators' good humor. On occasion he showed the "stern aspect and agitated authority" that too often characterized his leadership.[32]

Cardinal van Rossum complained about the unsatisfactory results of the work, and Roncalli suspected that the cardinal's opinion had been conditioned by someone who did "not give him a good impression." It was true that one could not expect anything in Rome but illusions and bitterness. "I do not expect satisfaction and rewards except from God. But it is beautiful to work with this thought! It keeps me happy and serene, prepared for everything."[33] He felt that he had "suffered so little until then!" and could very well have thought that the Lord was preparing him for greater tribulations. "I tremble just to think of it. Yet, I feel it is good that these crosses come for the salvation of my soul, and that my priesthood is more conformed to that of Jesus. *Domine adiuva me!* (Lord, help me!)"[34]

He dedicated all — mind, heart, word, pen, prayer, labors, sacrifices, day and night, in Rome and beyond — for the Congregation for the Propagation of the Faith. He accepted other works of ministry as secondary and only if they, too, served his primary reason for being in

Rome.[35] Despite this, his responsibilities as a preacher multiplied. He spoke in almost all the churches and to the confraternities of Rome, not wanting to shirk this obligation. Although this indicated the esteem and respect his confreres had for him, together with his required visits to various cities, these responsibilities in some way distracted him from his principal occupations.

As if this were not enough, in November he was assigned as a professor of patrology at the Lateran Seminary. Apart from the supposed prestige of the assignment, the unexpected appointment pleased him because he was happy to be engaged again in study and research, which he had enjoyed for so many years. He hoped that teaching would bring him some rest and spiritual joy.[36] And it actually did. He would recall as pope that all the lessons were a surprising success and accompanied by the students' hearty applause.[37]

As the year came to a close, the Jubilee began. At the ceremony to open the Holy Door on the night of December 24, Don Angelo was among those named to hold a pole of the pope's canopy, an honor and a testimony of faith: "…a little tiring, but I did it as an act of devotion to the Holy Father. This peaceful triumph of the pope always reawakens in my heart the deepest emotions. Let's hope that this Holy Year will truly be a year of blessing for me, for the Propagation of the Faith, for the Church."[38]

"Holy Year — Year of the Missions" was the theme of the first circular letter of 1925 sent to the bishops and other diocesan leaders. "The Holy Church can no longer endure the indifferent. All those who want to be worthy of the name 'Catholic' must awaken. No one can escape the responsibility every Catholic has to collaborate in the proclamation of the Gospel to those who have not yet heard the good news."[39]

In the same circular, Roncalli reaffirmed the pre-eminence of the Propagation of the Faith over all the other missionary organizations, whose merits he enumerated. At their February board meeting, the Missionary Union of the Clergy invited Roncalli to explain his position and affirm the full autonomy of the Union.[40] Roncalli attended the meeting, and with his usual good-hearted, intelligent words that were faithful to his motto of "bend, don't break," seemed to satisfy everyone.

By now other important decisions were on the horizon, and his life was about to undergo a sudden change.[41] On February 17, he wrote in his diary:

This evening the most eminent Cardinal Gasparri, secretary of state to His Holiness, summoned me to the Vatican and informed me that it is the will of the Holy Father that I, with the episcopal rank of bishop, go first to Bulgaria to visit those religious congregations, and later, it seems, I am to go to Argentina as apostolic delegate. I asked if this was an obedience. His Eminence replied, "Yes, it is an obedience." He added that the proposal came from the Prefect of the Eastern Congregation and that the pope, as soon as he had heard it, said, "Yes, very well, he is the one that Providence sends."[42]

Four days later in an audience with the Holy Father, Don Angelo heard words that were of great comfort to him. "I am to go not among the Bulgarians who are already good religious people, but among the unbelievers. I feel tranquil and disposed for everything."[43] Roncalli found a successor for his work in Don Luigi Drago of Bergamo, a confrere of the Priests of the Sacred Heart. Leaving the students very disappointed, Don Angelo terminated his spontaneous, orderly, and down-to-earth patrology classes at the Lateran[44] and prepared himself for his episcopal consecration on March 19, the feast of St. Joseph.

He desired to be a sentinel of service, as he wrote in the bulletin of the Propagation of the Faith, but this service "sometimes changed according to obedience, in a spirit of silence, obedience, and peace."[45]

Just one year before, in January of 1924, he had written a few phrases from St. Ignatius in his retreat notes: "It is necessary to become indifferent to every created thing" and, "Everyone must consider that he will profit more in spiritual matters the more he detaches himself from self-love, from his own will, and from his own interests." He then concluded, "It is quite clear: to love God, not myself; to do God's will, not my own; to seek comfort for others, not for myself. And all of this always, everywhere, and with great joy."[46] He also commented on the biblical recommendation: "As an angel of the Lord, do not allow yourself to be swayed by either compliments or criticisms" (cf. 2 Sam 14:17). Then he added, "What a beautiful encouragement to despise the world for one who, by the name of Angelo, would like to be an angel even in deed!"[47]

As recorded in his notes, he often used the "Meditation on the Kingdom" from the Ignatian exercises, promising himself that every morning he would repeat the beautiful and powerful prayer that concludes the colloquy:

Eternal Lord of all things, I make my offering, with your favor and help, before your infinite goodness, and before your glorious Mother and all the saints of your Heavenly Court. Provided it be for your service and praise, it is my firm decision, which I want and desire, to imitate you in sustaining every insult and all scorn and every type of poverty, both real and spiritual, if your Most Holy Majesty wishes to elect me to that state of life.

CHAPTER 10

APOSTOLIC VISITOR AND
DELEGATE IN BULGARIA
1925–1934

Episcopal Appointment

I did not seek or desire this new ministry, but the Lord has chosen
me with such evident signs of his will that to refuse would be a
serious fault. Therefore, he is obliged to make up for my failings
and insufficiency. This comforts me and gives me tranquillity and
security.[1]

Roncalli wrote these words during the retreat before his episcopal
consecration. It was not so much the immediate transfer to Bulgaria that
dismayed him. Indeed, the apostolic visitation would last only a few
months and then he would be available to act as a pontifical representative for other nations. For him, the office of bishop was not an honor, but
a demanding ministry that he believed himself incapable of fulfilling.

When the will of the Holy Father was communicated to me, I was
dismayed from the very start. During the night, I shed many tears;
even now when I think about it again, all alone, and especially in
prayer, my eyes fill with tears. [But] by entrusting myself to Providence in everything, I take courage in making sacrifices and I offer
myself in obedience *tamquam agnus* [like a lamb].[2]

All in all a great honor for me, most unworthy and wretched, and no satisfaction to my self-love. Rather, spiritual misery, tempered only by the thought that I neither wanted nor desired any of these things.[3]

My friends see only the honor. I, instead, feel that responsibilities have become greater for me. By becoming a bishop, the good times are over for me. May God's will be done, however, in everything.[4]

As for myself, what was I to do when the Holy Father gave me this office? Say no because he is sending me far away? Say no so that I do not have to abandon my sisters? I know that I am most unworthy of the honor and the task the Church has imposed on me. But if this is truly the Lord's will for me, how can I be sure that I will have the Lord's blessing if I refuse to do his will only because it costs a little?... I never desired any of these honors, because I know by experience that they are terrible responsibilities.[5]

Perhaps Roncalli thought of the many tribulations that awaited him along the way. But with the Lord's help, he felt ready for everything;[6] he awaited a greater glory in heaven.[7] As a gift from God for overcoming his natural reluctance and for obeying,[8] Roncalli experienced heartfelt peace once again.[9]

On my coat of arms I insert the motto *oboedientia et pax,* the words Caesar Baronius used to say every day while kissing the Apostle's foot in St. Peter's. These words are a little like the story of my life. Oh, may they glorify my humble name throughout the centuries![10]

His episcopal consecration was presided over by Cardinal Giovanni Tacci of the Congregation for the Eastern Churches. It took place in the church of St. Charles al Corso in Rome on the feast of St. Joseph. The ceremony had a profound effect on Roncalli[11] and led him to make a habit of professing his love for the holy cross in words borrowed from St. John Eudes: *"Crux tua sit mihi gloria sempiterna"* (Your cross is my glory forever). [12] "I profess to place all my glory, my treasure, and my joy in your cross, in humiliations, privations, and sufferings, saying with St. Paul: *'Mihi autem absit gloriari nisi in cruce Domini nostri Jesu Christi,'"* (May I never boast except in the cross of our Lord Jesus Christ, Gal 6:14). To this he added, "As far as I am concerned, I want no other paradise in this world, if not the cross of my Lord Jesus Christ." This program of life was suggested, indeed imposed on him, by the words in the Roman Pontifical's rite of episcopal consecration, which he never reread without deep emotion: *"Sit sollicitudine impieger, neque eam umquam deserat, aut laude aut timore superatus"* (Let him be constant in his care and never abandon it, nor be overcome by praise or fear).[13]

Dignitaries, his parents, relatives, friends, and admirers from Bergamo and Rome crowded into St. Charles. According to the reports in *L'Osservatore Romano,* the deep emotion of the people was apparent as the new bishop, pale and tearful, went through the church imparting his first episcopal blessing.

Immediately following the ceremony, Roncalli's family and invited guests went to the seminary for dinner. The next day, his relatives and friends were with him as he celebrated Mass at the tomb of St. Peter — just as he had after his ordination to the priesthood. On Easter Sunday, the new bishop celebrated his first solemn Pontifical Mass in the cathedral of Bergamo. In his homily, Roncalli spoke of the faith, joy, and unity that Easter represented and recalled how he had thought of "the cross and death"[14] while his head was bowed under the hand of the cardinal during his consecration. From his seminary days, he explained, he had attended many episcopal consecrations and yet "all have passed, all have passed."

On the feast of the Annunciation, all the inhabitants of Sotto il Monte had the opportunity to honor their compatriot-bishop with grand festivities throughout the day. Roncalli remained in his hometown until April 22, when he left for his new assignment in Bulgaria.

The First Months

After a comfortable trip from Milan,[15] Roncalli arrived on April 25 in Sofia, the capital of Bulgaria. He found it in the aftermath of a state of siege.[16] The city was calm after the recent attack by agrarian communists that left 200 civilians dead and the Cathedral of St. Nedelia destroyed.[17] He went directly to the house built by Benedict XV and Pius XI at Rue Liouline 3, next to the new Catholic church. Roncalli was accompanied by his provisional secretary, the Benedictine monk Don Costantino Bosschaerts, and two local priests, the pro-administrator for Eastern Rite Catholics and his assistant.[18]

Roncalli spent his first days receiving visitors from the leaders of various Catholic communities of Sofia. They formed two basic groups: the Thracians, with about 100 members, and the Macedonians, with 300 members. He listened to all sides with great patience. "They are good people, but among themselves, oh, how heated they become! One would wish to have Solomon's ability to judge!"[19] It became obvious that a mere three or four days would not be enough for the visitation. It would take much longer for the hearts of these Easterners to trust him. Roncalli would allow them to have their say and then he would have to take more time to decide matters.

On Thursday, April 30, King Boris III received him in a very cordial meeting — the first of many encounters.[20] The bishop explained the scope of his visit and its essentially religious character, as well as his method of patience and gentleness. They discussed some particular problems, including the nomination of a Bulgarian bishop for the Bulgarian Catholics of the Byzantine-Slavic Rite, the presence and activity of the various congregations of men and women religious, the importance of the Catholic Church for Bulgaria, and the destabilizing influence of Bolshevist philosophy and revolutionary approach on everything in the Balkans.

On Sunday, May 3, after having assisted at the Eastern Orthodox Mass in one of their small churches, Roncalli celebrated Mass in the Capuchin church with a larger congregation that included the foreign delegation. He spoke with great simplicity and cordiality, and communicated the Holy Father's greetings, encouragement, and blessing.

A few days later, he visited Kalfoff, the Minister of Foreign Affairs and of Worship who was open to consider the advantages of a closer rapport with Rome. On his part, Roncalli spoke at length about his commitment to and respect for the religious freedom of the Bulgarians. He emphasized his high regard for their culture and stated that he intended to promote peace by making and unifying efforts among Catholics.

Roncalli knew that he handled these diplomatic encounters well with the Lord's help: "I always entrust myself to him, and I am not at all worried for myself. I worry only about making the Roman Church and the pope loved and respected."[21]

In the few days before he began his pastoral visits, Roncalli sought to establish relations with representatives from other countries: Italy, France, Hungary, Poland, Belgium, and Greece. He also tried to become better acquainted with the priests in order to determine who was best suited for the office of bishop so that he could present Rome with three names and his evaluation.

He had already met some Orthodox and Russian religious leaders "of great merit." For this reason, without falling into the deception of false expectations, he hoped Bulgaria would be the door on the eve of a great spiritual movement toward the union of the Churches. He desired, as did the Orthodox Synod and its Metropolitan Bishop Stephan, to neglect no occasion that might contribute to beginning this beautiful and grand initiative.[22]

It seemed that an ideal solution would be to establish a permanent group of Benedictine Fathers distinguished for doctrine, sincerity, and holiness, who were ready to clarify, counsel, and comfort. By becoming Bulgarian among the Bulgarians, they could engage in social works and undertake cultural projects in history, the arts, and religion. Roncalli believed his secretary, Don Costantino Bosschaerts, was the right man to guide the group as its abbot.

Roncalli knew, however, that he had precise instructions from the Congregation for the Eastern Churches. He had been given four goals to accomplish: to search out Eastern Rite Catholics who were refugees from Turkey and Macedonia and regroup them where possible, furnishing them with a priest, chapel, school, and whatever else was needed for their spiritual welfare; to provide names for the selection of a bishop, and then to help him organize the new eparchy based on the Byzantine model; to prepare a seminary for the formation of local clergy; and to take in hand the material and moral restoration of the Eucharistine Sisters, a new and entirely Bulgarian religious congregation, finding a new residence where the community could expand and develop. Aside from these tasks, he also had to organize the Eastern Rite Church, helping it reach out by good example and respect to the Orthodox Christians, and to reconcile the faithful and priests who had been separated from the Catholic Church.[23]

It seemed to Roncalli that the Lord had mysteriously disposed everything for his glory and for the benefit of the Church and its members, "asking of us poor men only the docility to obey, contrary to our inclinations and initial plans, claiming all for himself, even the choice of paths and the preparation of the circumstances, *ut sit ipse in omnibus* [that God may be all in all]."[24]

On his first apostolic trip (May 20–29),[25] he encountered the extraordinary beauty of Bulgaria's flourishing countryside and he became truly enchanted.[26] Everywhere he went he found great harmony among the priests and the faithful. It seemed truly possible to hope that the Lord was bringing the fruits of peace and holiness to maturity.

Roncalli was particularly struck by the poverty of the churches and the priests' residences.

> They are truly wretched. You have to see where they live, what they eat, how they live.... They live totally on some bartered offerings that the Catholics of the villages give.... The insecurity resulting from the almost total lack of funds causes worry, distracts them from the pursuit of spiritual goods, and renders everything a search for material sustenance.... Many must work the fields in order to live; then they have to sell their produce.... They even have to cook for themselves. And what about the dangers of solitude and discouragement that often come with such poverty?[27]

Roncalli also realized that all the Catholics lived in uncertainty as they anticipated the decision of the Sacred Congregation regarding the definitive structuring of the Eastern Church. He repeatedly wrote about this to his superiors. "I, too, feel I am on pins and needles from this waiting, even though by the grace of God I manage to conceal it. Every day of delay does nothing more than weaken my humble efforts."[28]

On June 8, he began a second apostolic trip, visiting the larger and smaller cities in the north and the east. The trip to the Turkish territory, the birthplace of the Unionist movement, proved more valuable for learning about the Bulgarian Church than reading large volumes of history. Many people had emigrated and the population was so sparse that it was largely abandoned. Terrible squalor was found everywhere.

As he traveled from Svilengrad to Pokrovani, he found a succession of marvelous landscapes among hazardous and deserted mountains. The entire village was Catholic and the small church was charming, but the residence of the parish priests was a corn granary with two beds in a corner. He rode to Atheren on horseback and traveled through heavy rain to the other villages in the area. They were all poor, with their houses and churches that were little more than sheds. For the return trip to Svilengrad, he acquired a meager oxcart. The last town he visited was Malko Turnovo, situated on the outskirts near the Black Sea. It was the Bulgarian Vendée because of Catholic resistance to the Turkish attempts to destroy the faith.

A warm reception awaited him wherever he went. Bells rang out from their towers as soon as he was sighted and the faithful of both Rites formed an honor guard for him to pass through as children threw flowers. Anyone who wished could approach him; Roncalli listened, encouraged, and advised. Don Stefano Kertev was Roncalli's chosen collaborator and companion on the visit. His was one of the three names that Roncalli recommended for bishop to the fifty thousand Bulgarian Catholics. In the meantime, Kertev had been nominated the apostolic pro-administrator.

The visits gave Roncalli a great deal of work, but also gave him a great deal of joy, comparable only to the joy of the humble and good people who welcomed him. He met and came to know each priest personally, and his general impressions were much better than he had anticipated.[29]

His assignment gave him a great deal of spiritual consolation, but he knew the end of his mission was soon approaching. He waited anxiously for Rome's directives on the important issues he had brought to the Vatican's attention: the appointment of a new bishop; religious to staff the minor seminary, the questions regarding mixed marriages, his authority, the irregular situation of certain priests, and finally the quasi-"nationalistic" activity of the Association Pro-East that had been formed and spearheaded by an Italian priest.

Although Roncalli rightly concluded that the Eastern Catholic Church in Bulgaria faced several sensitive issues, the field was very promising — the Holy Father's expectations concerning the return of the East to Catholicism were not mere illusions. Indeed, it was worth sending men, money, and sacrifice into the field in order to hasten the triumph of the "one flock and one shepherd," which would be the consolation and the glory of the century.[30]

Rome, however, was not ready to act. Roncalli expressed his frustration in a letter to his good friend, Don Gustavo Testa. He did not want to change his assignment, but to obey. He had come to Bulgaria willingly and he was disposed to remain for many years. It was enough for him to know what he had to do and the limits of his authority.[31] Intentionally avoiding concrete undertakings did not make a good impression.[32]

Instructions from Rome finally arrived at the end of August, but very little was said. The situation would remain as it was. No resolutions were forthcoming concerning the issues Roncalli considered most important, especially the formation of a group of men dedicated to work for unity in the Catholic Church of Bulgaria. Vatican directives stated that Roncalli should consider his powers "elastic," but not claim any competencies he did not have or at least did not have yet; he would have to unravel the tangle of affairs himself.[33] "The comfort that I now experience," he immediately wrote, "makes me forget my spirit's long torment in waiting.[34]

If suffering awaits me personally, *ego in flagella paratus sum* [I am prepared for scourgings], provided that even along this path I am able to converge with the 'good of souls' and the 'one flock.'"[35]

Life as Apostolic Non-Delegate

Roncalli returned to Italy in early October for vacation. On October 13, he had the joy of introducing the members of the second Bulgarian pilgrimage for the Holy Year to the pope. The Holy Father had received Roncalli in a private audience the day before and they had discussed many things. The pope gave him permission to purchase the house he had found as a residence for the future delegate. In the meantime, it would serve Roncalli's needs while he carried out the apostolic visitation that, according to the pope, would have to continue indefinitely.[36]

When all was said and done, it was clear that Pius XI preferred Roncalli for the role as representative in Bulgaria. Although he did not wear official attire, he had succeeded in becoming well aware of the situations and needs in a very short time. Perhaps another prelate would not have spent as much precious time getting to know the people and circumstances or setting out to do as much as Roncalli had already managed to do very well.

When Roncalli returned to his assignment, he had to face head-on the problems he had left behind. The matter of the work of the Benedictine Fathers had not been resolved, and he had to find a new secretary to replace Bosschaerts, who had returned to Belgium. He wondered how he would find someone willing to stay with the *omnium minimus* (least of all), the representatives of the Holy See, and to live a life of poverty in such unsuitable conditions.[37]

"His" Bulgaria, as Roncalli fondly called it, was not exactly the pearl of the Holy See's diplomatic missions — not even of the Catholic missions! Yet it was very precious to him simply because Providence had put him there.[38] Of that much Roncalli was certain. Although nothing had changed and he was returning to Bulgaria with the same title and competencies,[39] a new period of Roncalli's life was beginning.[40]

He was "alone as a sparrow, as the sparrows that fly over the snows," he wrote. "But I accept it. I do some good and I am content,[41] and while it snows outside I spend my life at the typewriter. I always have many things to write to Rome...!"[42]

Roncalli drafted long reports concerning difficulties caused by the Orthodox bishops of the Holy Synod.[43] What appeared to them as the encroachment of the Roman Church alarmed them,[44] especially after the success of the "pope's soup kitchens," a charitable work set up to feed poor refugee children exiled in the Messembria region,[45] which Roncalli had visited on several occasions.[46]

The need for two minor seminaries — one for the Eastern Rite and one for the Latin Rite — to be staffed by a religious congregation caused great concern.[47] There was the problem surrounding the selection and nomination of the new Eastern Rite bishop, Kertev.[48] The future of the Eucharistine Sisters,[49] entrusted by Roncalli with the supervision of the soup kitchens and to whom would be given the care of the future seminary, continued unresolved. And the prospect of having an apostolic delegate in Sofia rather than a mere visitor seemed to unsettle the Orthodox bishops.[50]

Roncalli sent Rome at least twenty detailed plans for construction and restoration projects of churches, homes for priests, and a house for the future delegate. The delegate's residence would be simple and modest, but suitable as the permanent property of the Holy See — and this was important since Bulgaria was almost completely Orthodox.[51]

He wrote of this and more to his friends in the Secretariat of State and in the various offices of the Curia. He recommended his official reports and bemoaned the amount of red tape and the silence of the various congregations that seemed to be testing his patience. "In the future, if God gives me life, I will remember the suffering the present state of affairs and the disorganization handed on to me have caused throughout this entire visit. I think I will have occasion to bless the Lord who wanted to subject me to a form of tribulation I had not yet experienced. Now I know just how serious it is and how worthy of being pitied in others."[52]

Roncalli cherished this cross and would never think of exchanging it. He had learned how to use suffering for his personal sanctification. Never had he taken so much pleasure from reading his "dear little book," the *Imitation of Christ,* or from studying the "simple but impressive and delightful" *St. Francis de Sales: Guide and Model of Devout Souls* than during the blessed solitude of that winter. In the *Imitation of Christ,* he found guidance to live by. He sought only to detach himself from a vain and deceitful world that brought nothing but bitterness.[53] "For my edification I often read the words of the *Imitation of Christ:*

Videbis quod omnia temporalia nulla sunt; sed valde incerta et gravantia quia numquam sine sollecitudine et timore possidentur. Non est hominis felicitas habere temporalia ad abundantiam; sed sufficit mediocritas [You will see that all temporal things are nothing but very uncertain and burdensome, because they are never possessed without anxiety and fear. Having an abundance of temporal goods makes no one happy, for having the essential suffices]."[54] From St. Francis de Sales he learned holy indifference, availability to the action of grace, and total abandonment to Providence. The indifferent heart is like a ball of wax in God's hands; it is completely disposed to follow God's will.[55] Roncalli could therefore affirm:

> The brief experience of these months as bishop convinces me that in life there is nothing better for me than to carry the cross exactly as the Lord places it on my shoulders and in my heart. I must consider myself as a man of the cross and love the cross God gives me without thinking of any other. Whatever is not for God's honor, the service of the Church, and the good of the faithful is secondary to me and of no importance.[56]

Roncalli wanted to be pleasant and optimistic at all times, concealing others' shortcomings and dismissing their failings unless a serious duty of conscience required him to speak.[57]

> It seems to me that the grace of this new status [as bishop], which should be the object of perfection, has reinforced my natural inclination to leniency, to know how to understand and to sympathize with people who are more easily won by kindness and patience than anything else. The exercise of my episcopal ministry as the pope's representative in this country — so mysterious and yet a field in which to accomplish great good — is so humble and at the same time so great that I could not succeed at anything if I did not hold on to a simple spirit. In talking to people, I see that nothing is more skillful and diplomatic than to always speak the truth without deception. There is nothing more valuable for confounding the worldly wise than sincerity, honest courtesy, and a humble manner.[58]

Roncalli knew there were many who sympathized with him for his difficult and dangerous mission that was marked by poverty and trials.

> All this must be somewhat true. The Lord, however, gives me the grace to overlook the austerity and the frustrations, and he gives me the peace of heart that comes from obedience and from letting go of any wish or plan for the future, except to satisfy the Lord himself

and to serve the Church and souls. *Sis, Jesus, nostrum gaudium qui es futurum praemium* [Jesus, our joy is in the future reward]. This is everything.[59]

Things were going ahead, however. The residence for the visitor and future delegate was almost completed, with funds finally arriving from Rome, albeit a little at a time. Roncalli was pleased with everything about the small but very beautiful house[60] where at last he could reserve the Blessed Sacrament in the chapel. The Eucharistine Sisters were busy both at Messembria with the refugee children and at the hospice in Kniajevo where they were doing a great deal of good. The city of Sofia had sold land to the Sisters so they could begin the construction of a novitiate, an orphanage, and a building for other social services.[61] Relations with the Eastern Orthodox Church improved somewhat, although the nomination of a new bishop for Bulgaria was still a source of resentment. The Bulgarian government, instead, viewed the nomination as something positive and recognized it as an expression of the Holy Father's kindness and personal concern for the country.[62] Bishop Kertev was consecrated on December 5 in the Basilica of St. Clement in Rome. Roncalli accompanied him to Italy and introduced him to the marvels and miseries of the capital of Catholicism. Together they made a course of spiritual exercises under the direction of Abbot Schuster at St. Paul Outside the Walls, and afterward Roncalli brought the new bishop to Sotto il Monte for the Christmas holidays. Sotto il Monte! During the twenty years of his priestly life, Roncalli had never desired the tranquility of a solitary life in the countryside so much — a curious phenomenon he noted. There among the good, simple peasants he truly found his kingdom.[63]

Roncalli left Rome for Sofia in early January 1927 with the Holy Father's blessing. The pope always showed him a goodness that truly comforted him.[64] Roncalli did not return directly to Sofia, but first traveled to Greece and Turkey where he felt he would learn more about the complex issues concerning the unity of the Eastern and Western Churches than from reading many books. His mind would be opened more from this trip than from deep meditations from afar.[65] Roncalli and Bishop Kertev were received everywhere with expressions of Christian fraternity that gave them a remarkable impression of unity of spirit.[66] Roncalli wrote how necessary it was to put aside whatever could divide in any way Catholics, and Catholics and Orthodox, and to take up those things that unite.[67]

Roncalli felt things were truly going well with the Orthodox Churches. He even thought they might be close to entering into full communion with the Roman Church, provided they received a bit more help from the Catholics.[68] "Here the law of mutual charity and gentleness is little deepened. If I could succeed by word and example to make it understood that this is the foundation and the spirit of Catholic life, my poor work would not be in vain, at least for the future."[69] He later added that "the world goes on and everything changes; we must look for the good everywhere and see how the Lord presents us with opportunities to do good."[70]

An opportunity did present itself in Constantinople. Roncalli visited there in March and April 1927 for the consecration of the archbishop of Athens, and he met with the Orthodox Patriarch Basil III. The patriarch expressed his pleasure on meeting a Catholic bishop and his desire to meet the pope in Rome in order to discuss joining efforts in the great work for unity among the Churches. The patriarch believed that this corresponded to one of humanity's greatest needs. Although others minimized the importance of the patriarch's willingness as merely the personal desire or action of one man, Roncalli could not neglect it. That man, after all, was the Patriarch of Constantinople and his actions could serve as a powerful example.[71]

Roncalli was also meeting quite regularly with the Orthodox Metropolitan, Stephan of Sofia, and found their conversations very useful, especially since it became easier for the Orthodox to let go of their hesitancy. In addition, Roncalli grew in his understanding of the Orthodox mentality that wished to be treated with patience, with charitable works and dedication more than with discussions and exhortations.[72]

Another opportunity presented itself in December when the Orthodox Metropolitans and the bishops of the Bulgarian Church gathered in Sofia for their plenary council. Roncalli did not let the occasion pass without an act of courtesy. He sent a humble and reverent message of religious respect and fraternity. From his heart he wished the Holy Spirit's grace upon their work so it would be fruitful in attaining a daily deepening of the kingdom of our Lord Jesus Christ, the peoples' growth in holiness, and the good of their dear country. In return the assembly sent Roncalli their warm thanks, and reciprocated with greetings for Christmas.[73]

He could never imagine succeeding on his own in this undertaking of the union of the Churches. He could not follow his own plans. He reminded himself and others that often the unknown and half-completed tasks are the earth from which the Lord mines the extravagance of his wisdom and love in governing the world.[74] Roncalli was well aware how long and arduous was the road to Rome and that the Catholic Church had a lot of work to do even among the most intelligent and upright people whose reluctance concerning unity was in good faith.[75]

Roncalli continued to lament Rome's persistent silence to his repeated appeals for material assistance, moral support, and greater sensitivity toward the problem of the union of the Churches. He brought this problem up repeatedly, especially in his long reports to the offices that directed his activities in Bulgaria: the secretary of state, the Congregation for the Eastern Churches, and the Propagation of the Faith.[76] The concerns he now had at heart were the same he had voiced after his first visitation: the appointment of an apostolic delegate while the new political situation favored it,[77] the founding of a minor seminary,[78] the Eucharistine Sisters,[79] the study for ecclesiastical legislation, and a practical means of dissemination such as the Catholic press.[80] He vented his feeling to an official from the Congregation for the Eastern Churches.

This mission of mine is evolving in a forest of thorns. At any cost, I want the spirit of charity to prevail, despite the difficult and obstinate nature of some of these good Bulgarians. This requires the exercise of great patience, forbearance, and prudence, which becomes toil and tension even for those who do not have to carry on this battle of nerves. There are also serious problems and painful worries concerning those of the Latin Rite in the north and south. I have to live among spies and amid the snares of hostile Orthodox, who try to compromise me in public on every possible occasion. I must pass under the lynx-eyes of the young Bulgarian Freemasons who, as King Boris says, watch my every move. On the other hand, all the Catholics look to the apostolic visitor, who for them — and for the Orthodox, for that matter — takes the pope's place in doing good and restoring everything according to the spirit and purpose of the Catholic Church. Every day all the complaints and discouragement of the bishop and the poor priests beat down on this poor man. They cannot understand why it is taking so long to address the practical measures that were proposed some time ago to resolve situations Rome has so often been made aware of and which endanger the good of souls.[81]

Later, a smiling Pope Pius XI referred to Roncalli's outburst as "the ire of the lamb."[82]

Roncalli confessed:

Such complex circumstances, if they continue month after month,
as is happening to me — not to mention finding myself completely
alone among a people of another race and language — can tempt
one to become discouraged, to distrust himself, and can break his
heart. I know very well that even in these fears it is possible to fall
into exaggeration and that the Lord's grace can scatter them. But in
short, *nec fortitudo lapidum fortitudo mea, nec caro mea aenea est*
[my fortitude is not the fortitude of a stone, neither is my flesh as
hard as bronze]. At certain moments, an outburst can offend charity
and justice. But the Lord may even permit things like this because it
might serve me as a more important and enduring interior discipline and as a healthy humiliation.[83]

In his daily life, Roncalli definitely had opportunities to grow in the
exercise of charity, patience, and forbearance. He had become accustomed to certain forms of suffering, and he hoped they would obtain for
him a beautiful paradise.[84]

He certainly could not say that he had done nothing for the faithful.
He was far too convinced that "doing the will of the Lord with the total
spirit of Jesus Christ is already an apostolate." In the "petitions of the
Our Father, 'your kingdom come' is linked immediately to 'your will be
done.'"[85] He often said he could not imagine being chosen to do anything outstanding in his life.

The Lord concerns himself with these matters; he chooses the
people and the circumstances and he does not want us to interfere
by what we do or think. Our greatness, our glory is found in our
serene daily efforts — without excesses — marked by profound
love for Jesus. In our daily effort to carry out the duty Providence
has assigned us, we should give more attention to doing the little
things well rather than trying to accomplish great works. Be especially careful to preserve humility, simplicity, and interior joy. In
your work, the Lord reserves the fulfillment to himself, and he indicates the time and the circumstance, sometimes disposing that we
remain in the dark. But he will fulfill.[86]

To the people closest to him, he repeated:

This is what the Lord wants from us: only to begin. Then it is his task
to carry it out with power and with calm, to multiply, to finish. The
measure of God's effective involvement in our works corresponds to
the spirit of simplicity and humility with which we begin them. We

must therefore make up our minds and begin with pure intentions, a simple and humble heart, and the utmost trust in the Lord. He in turn will assist us, even in unexpected and miraculous ways.[87]

Roncalli strengthened his spirit with his favorite devotional readings, and each morning after Mass he recited the prayer of St. Ignatius, confirming that he was "ready, if God gives me the grace, to suffer every insult, offense, and privation for the love of Jesus who was crucified and died for me."[88]

At night, he read one page of the Gospel and the *Imitation of Christ*,[89] either in Latin or Bulgarian,[90] "calmly, savoring every word." He confessed that his eyes would often fill with tears as his heart turned toward heaven. He was becoming accustomed to surrendering daily to the dispositions of Providence, in which he rested as secure as an infant in the arms of its mother.[91]

His life as apostolic visitor in the East was like that of the Holy Child lying in the hay: wherever he turned, he would be pricked. Everything seemed like Bethlehem. True, there were heavenly consolations and some earthly satisfaction from the many simple and good people, but in general, he met difficulties, suspicion, and sometimes even snares and threats. But the light of Bethlehem dispelled everything and renewed his courage to carry on the good and noble task that was obviously the design of Providence for his Church at that time.[92]

"Make me love your cross"
(1930–1931)

The year 1929 was marked by the ever-present hope that the seminary — perhaps the only tangible goal of his mission — would finally be realized. This would surely free his heart to sing the joyful thanksgiving hymn, the *Nunc dimittis* (Now you can dismiss your servant, Lord).

Throughout the year, Roncalli corresponded with the Holy See about the land for the seminary building, the sales contracts, the means of payment, the structural plans, and the qualities of the students, professors, and superiors. In private correspondence, he often expressed his conviction that the first stone would be in place by the spring of 1930, thus beginning "a new era for the triumph of Catholicism in Bulgaria."[93] If in that long apostolic visit he only succeeded in launching the foundation of the seminary, overcoming all the difficulties that seemed like bad dreams, he would be happy. From the perspective of personal satisfaction and the true good of the country, he believed that he could not do better,[94] because, as he said, "one can hope for nothing good if not by forming young people with a sound ecclesiastical education."[95]

When everything was finally arranged, the Holy See wired an order to postpone purchasing the land. Apparently, the Propagation of the Faith had found new objections concerning the juridical administration of the new seminary.[96] One can only imagine the frustration and embarrassment this must have caused Roncalli. He had already made a sizable down payment on the property and now had "to renege on the word given in the name of the Holy See with a legal contract, and all this in the face of the Orthodox."[97]

If the copious exchange of telegrams, letters, and dispatches that followed between Sofia and Rome did not lead to Bishop Roncalli's excommunication, it did bring a reprimand the likes of which he had never experienced in his entire life. What everyone in Sofia judged as obvious good sense, instead seemed to Rome an indication of the tendency to act before receiving directions. "I answered as a good son. Now I believe the Holy Father will be informed; that is enough for me." How could Roncalli know that someone in Rome was working to destroy the good opinion the Holy Father had always had of him?[98]

As a good son, then, Roncalli wrote to Rome and professed to accept "with the most devout reverence and submission whatever else [would come] from the Holy Father, as a reprimand and warning." He offered "humble apologies for his hastiness in dealing with this matter." The incident caused much suffering, but that meant less to Roncalli than his sincere desire to comply with the wishes of the Holy Father.[99] And the wish of Pius XI? To construct on the land an institute for the formation of the clergy of both Rites.[100] Oddly enough, Roncalli had also felt the need for this initiative. The project was later entrusted to the Jesuits whose presence in Bulgaria Roncalli had always hoped for.[101]

As much as Roncalli tried to minimize the incident, he admitted that he had suffered — though one suffers better when his conscience and his heart are at peace. He later received some kind words from the Holy Father, who benevolently followed his "modest work."[102] Roncalli acknowledged his fault: "The opposition which I received will serve to keep me always more humble and more intent on seeking God alone."[103] With the Lord's grace, he wrote, the wound would heal little by little. Applying the invocations of the *Stabat Mater* to himself, he confessed, *"Fac me plagis vulnerari* [make me feel your wounds]: we have arrived thus far. *Fac me cruce inebriari* [make me love your cross]: here we have not yet arrived, but at least I am not lacking in desire and intention."[104]

With the invocation, "make me love your cross," Roncalli began his reflections during the spiritual exercises made from April 28 to May 4, 1930, in a house of the Passionist Fathers in northern Bulgaria. Because he expected to gain great spiritual benefit and personal satisfaction from this retreat, he wrote with intensity.

> By divine grace I feel that I want to be truly indifferent to all that the Lord wishes of me regarding my future.... For some time now I have been reciting every morning after the holy Mass — and I believe I say it with my heart — the prayer St. Ignatius used to conclude his great meditation on the kingdom of Christ: *O aeterne Domine rerum omnium, ego facio meam oblationem* [O eternal Lord of all things, I offer myself as an oblation... *Spiritual Exercises*, n. 98]. Truly, I find it difficult to say this prayer. But since I want to keep myself totally absorbed in the holy will of God and in the spirit of Jesus crucified and scorned, from now on I will make even the following profession daily: "O eternal Lord of all things, O heavenly Father, grant to me, your unworthy servant, that I may always be faithful to this desire: if it is a matter of equal praise and glory to your divine majesty, and to better imitate Christ our Lord so that I may grow more like him, I want to choose actual poverty with the poor Christ, and not riches; reproach with Christ who was reproached, and not honors; and I desire to be considered worthless and foolish for Christ who was once scorned, rather than being considered wise and prudent in this world" (*Spiritual Exercises*, n. 167).
>
> The love of the Lord's cross attracts me all the more in these days.... I have found another beautiful prayer that corresponds very well with the circumstances of my situation, a prayer from St. John Eudes. I humbly make it mine as well, and I hope that is not too presumptuous of me. "O Jesus, my crucified love, I adore you in all your suffering. I ask your pardon for all the shortcomings I have committed until now in the afflictions you have been pleased to send me. I give myself to the spirit of your cross, and in this spirit, as in all love of heaven and earth, I embrace with all my heart, for your love, all the crosses of body and spirit that will come to me. And I promise to place all my glory, my treasure, and my happiness in your cross, that is, in humiliations, in privations and sufferings, saying with St. Paul: 'May I never boast of anything except the cross of our Lord Jesus Christ' (Gal 6:14). As far as I am concerned, I do not want any other paradise in this world, except for the cross of my Lord Jesus Christ."

It seems to me that everything is leading me to habitually make this solemn profession of love for the holy cross.... The Lord wants me all for himself, along the "royal road of the holy cross." And it is along this path and no other that I wish to follow him. I like to repeat the image that St. Francis de Sales used: *I am like a bird that sings in the thorny wood;* this must be a continual invitation for me.... The motto of my dear spiritual director during the first ten years of my priesthood returns to me: *Semper in cruce, oboedientia duce!* [always in the cross, under obedience].[105]

At the end of his retreat notes and reflections, he transcribed another meaningful prayer of Don Lintelo, an apostle of the Eucharist in Belgium during the late 1800s. "O my Jesus, grant me a life that is harsh, laborious, apostolic, crucified. Deign to increase in my soul a hunger and thirst for sacrifice, suffering, humiliation, and self-denial. I no longer want satisfaction, rest, consolation, or enjoyment. What I yearn for, O Jesus, and implore from your Sacred Heart, is to be always and ever more a victim, a sacrificial offering, an apostle, virgin, and martyr for your love."[106]

With peace, calm, and inner joy Roncalli resumed his daily life, which he described as a hidden work concerning matters of no apparent importance, but a work which he felt sure was preparing a good future for the Church in Bulgaria. This is what the Lord wanted of him, and Roncalli could only thank God. He would even be content if he were found one day alone and dead in a ditch of some remote area of the country,[107] happy for having filled some valley, whittled down some dry branches, and hewn out of some large rocks a path of truth and charity in that rough and ever mysterious Orient.[108]

Matters of No Apparent Importance

Among the many works Roncalli took upon himself was his attempt to organize Catholic Action out of the already existing groups named after Saints Cyril and Methodius. Roncalli was content to lay the foundations at a convention for the various groups, and then to allow the seed to germinate on its own and be cultivated by the local bishops.

Roncalli was convinced of the importance of having a Catholic press, and so he began with the already existing weekly leaflet, *Istina-Verità,* and then obtained financial assistance to keep it going. He suggested printing Bulgarian translations of the major papal documents, especially those concerning the social doctrine of the Church — *Rerum*

Novarum and *Quadragesimo Anno* in particular — as well as publishing the few, innovative works in the field of liturgy.

He wanted to introduce the Association for the Propagation of the Faith, but not to collect offerings from the Christians he knew were in need of assistance themselves. Instead, he desired to sensitize them to the catholicity of the Church. Through the Association, they sponsored religious leaflets, conferences, and study days for groups chosen from the various dioceses.

Roncalli never stopped hoping that a seminary — or at least something like a seminary — staffed by the Jesuits would be realized. He held on to the land purchased with the pope's approval, and kept alive the expectation of the bishops of the region. He helped schools to develop: the girls' secondary schools that already existed, the boys' secondary school that the Austrian Fathers of the Divine Word wanted to open in Sofia, and trade schools in the various agricultural centers, which he wanted to entrust to the Salesians.

Another matter of "no apparent importance" was a "small but especially bothersome thorn"[109] — the permanent residence for the papal representative. After presenting the Holy See with plans to enlarge the already existing residence, Roncalli was pleasantly surprised when the pope decided to acquire a new residence nearer the center of the city. The larger building was certainly more suitable, and Roncalli willingly interrupted his planned trip to France as the guide for the Bergamo diocesan pilgrimage to Lourdes in order to sign the contract. The new house was magnificent and had been found almost by chance near the principal Orthodox church, the most beautiful of the Balkans, and a short distance from the palace of the Holy Synod.[110] With typical roncallian style, he personally took care of the furnishings and had a new heating system installed. Accommodations were prepared for the service personnel, two Eucharistine Sisters, and the secretary he dreamed of having one day. Shortly before Christmas, Roncalli was able to move into his third residence since arriving in Bulgaria.

He immediately began to consider how best to use the former residence. Should he entrust it to a group of men or women religious? Rent it out after major renovations? Make it a social youth center for the Catholics of the city? This was not a priority, however, compared to his preoccupation with the tense situation in Bulgaria.

The majority of the population was Orthodox, and Catholics numbered slightly over 40,000 of the Latin Rite, and about 6,000 of the Eastern Rite. In

1883, the Eastern Rite had obtained the status of an ecclesiastical organization. Following the Balkan wars, serious difficulties had not only impeded the growth in membership, but also threatened to destroy the fruits already attained. The Holy See was concerned about the situation and did what it could to provide a remedy. Roncalli was sent as apostolic visitor, the Bulgarian Catholic Ordinariate was established, and the Holy See provided material assistance.

Bishop Roncalli viewed the Bulgarian Catholic community as being on the road to promising development. The ministry of the clergy and the devotion of the faithful were gaining the attention and admiration of the Orthodox. Although individuals including professionals, doctors, and lawyers were joining the Catholic community, economic problems remained an obstacle to the ministry of the Church. In general, Catholics were poor and could not support the clergy or teachers, could not pay for the construction of churches and chapels, and could not contribute to the development of charitable works. The generosity of the Holy Father and zealous efforts and sacrifices of the Bulgarian Catholic clergy filled positions that had never been occupied by Catholic priests or that had been abandoned because of the lack of financial resources. If changes were taking place so that money and sacrifices seemed well spent, in view of even greater hopes for success, the necessary nourishment to live and prosper could not be lacking.[111]

Roncalli was involved in the controversy over the marriage of King Boris III to Giovanna di Savoia. The Roman Catholic wedding was celebrated at Assisi on October 25, and the king gave his word beforehand that he would not have an Orthodox Catholic ceremony. He also promised to have their children baptized in the Catholic Church and see to their Catholic education. All of this was witnessed to by Borgoncini-Duca, the papal nuncio in Italy. Contrary to the agreements, however, upon the couple's return to Sofia the following week, a marriage ceremony was celebrated in the Orthodox Church. This provoked Pius XI's well-known protest in his Christmas Eve address when he announced the promulgation of the encyclical, *Casti Connubi* (On Christian Marriage), made more opportune and necessary by the recent royal wedding.[112]

Notwithstanding conflicting press reports, Bishop Roncalli and all the Bulgarian bishops declined the royal couple's invitation upon their return from Italy to attend a reception and the Orthodox wedding ceremony. Roncalli's attitude toward the royal couple was consistent, cordial, respectful, and clear. Shortly after the wedding, Roncalli suggested that the king issue a statement to downplay its significance; his advice was disregarded. "As far as I am concerned," Roncalli wrote, "I maintain my serenity, the true gift of the Lord in these circumstances."[113] "I continue to remain very calm, precisely because I have nothing on my conscience; I did everything that I believed was my duty."[114] "Personally I am enjoying great internal peace: the *gaudium de veritate* [joy of truth] of St. Augustine, knowing that the task I fulfilled was in complete accord with the Holy Father."[115] The entire affair left prolonged and painful effects on Catholic-Orthodox relations. Some Orthodox leaders wanted Roncalli removed and sent elsewhere — somewhere far away, like Afghanistan[116] — as they tried to compose themselves and ease the impact of the papal discourse.[117]

In the midst of this small storm, on November 25, 1930, Roncalli celebrated his birthday. He wanted to sanctify his passage into his fiftieth year with an extended time of solitary, nocturnal prayer. With praise, blessing, and thanksgiving to God he again offered his sacrifices in the land he so loved, and which he wanted to see "resplendent in the light of the Catholic Church, mother and teacher of civilization." He did not worry about the future; he repeated from his heart the invocation that had become his second motto: *Crux tua sit mihi gloria sempiterna* (your cross is my glory forever).[118]

Unwittingly, Roncalli was living a true religious "novitiate," inasmuch as he understood it to be a complete transformation of the soul that no longer recognizes itself, but rejoices in such an intimate union with Jesus Crucified that it is completely transfigured.[119]

> I also deem it characteristic for true servants of the Lord to feel themselves called to do one thing and instead to have to do another. In a way, that is what is happening [to me]. Could I not have been the good cathedral canon [of Bergamo], to do my best to help the young clerics of the seminary, to teach religion, to practice patience with humble souls who are content with little? That could have been my life. Instead, this is what I must do. I have an unmerited office of honor and the power to govern, which I cannot even exercise as a simple priest does. Rarely do I have an occasion to give a spiritual talk, and I never hear confessions. Often I spend the whole day in front of the typewriter or engaged in annoying conversations, discussing difficulties and problems with people who, while belonging to Jesus Christ and by right to the Catholic Church, have little *sensus Christi* [Christian sense], and even less *sensus Ecclesiae* [ecclesial sense]. I am always in contact with so-called important

people who are narrow-minded regarding spiritual things. I carefully prepare for events from which I expect a very good outcome and then I see the frailty of human hope.[120]

In October 1931, the papal representative in Bulgaria was elevated to the rank of apostolic delegate. This fulfilled the dream Roncalli nurtured since 1925 when he believed he was completing his visit. Roncalli was appointed as the first delegate, and he wholeheartedly thanked the Holy Father and the Sacred Congregation for "all their kindnesses." He stated that he would apply himself willingly "to develop opportune measures" so that the Catholic Church of Bulgaria might carry out to its fullest the divine ideal of the universal triumph of truth and love in union with Christ and his vicar.[121] He observed once again that a general principle of Providence at work in the history of the Church had been verified: things do not happen by chance; rather they are prepared with diligence, humility, patience, and attentive anticipation. At any given moment, almost unexpectedly, the old plan is carried out and promises are fulfilled. There is no time and it is not worth stopping to look at the long trodden path; everything is founded and built on the Lord's blessing.[122]

Roncalli marveled at the ease with which the negotiations for the new apostolic delegation took place, and without a single sour note from Sofia.

With this, seven years of patience and waiting have ended and a new era begins. We must trust the Lord. He makes us wait for him, but he always answers. Courage and joy always, therefore. *Caritas Dei et patientia Christi* (the love of God and the patience of Christ). How I love these words! They mean more to me than the thought of living for a long or short time in this place or elsewhere.[123]

The Challenges of a New Apostolic Delegate
(1932–1933)

For some time, Bishop Roncalli had needed a full-time, official secretary. The many tasks related to the work of an apostolic delegate multiplied and became more demanding. Don Metodio, the elderly Assumptionist who had been with Roncalli for five years, was wonderful in graciously welcoming the poor and visitors — important tasks in promoting good relations with the people. However, he did not know Italian and could not help Roncalli with correspondence. Because Don Metodio was often sick, Roncalli could not rely on him to carry out tasks that required any amount of physical stamina.

The erection of an apostolic delegation in Bulgaria earned greater respect and esteem for papal representation from influential circles: government, courts, and diplomatic officials on various levels. Consequently, he had to give attention to more serious matters, but the correspondence alone absorbed so much of his time that Roncalli had little left for studies or other works that required prolonged reflection — things he would have enjoyed doing.[124]

The papal representative was responsible for dealing with government and public figures, supporting Catholics in every way possible in their contacts with the Orthodox, upholding the right of Catholics to religious freedom and the Church's right to expand. Thankfully, this expansion seemed well underway, and had there been a corresponding movement among the small groups of Eastern Rite Catholics scattered throughout the country, the Catholic Church would have made progress beyond expectations.[125]

This time of hope inspired zealous Catholic bishops and priests of the Eastern Rite to turn to the apostolic delegate and remind him of their ongoing initiatives and their need for assistance. Roncalli did his best to convince them that the Holy See was doing everything possible to meet their demands. It was well aware of their good works and continued to show proof of its particular concern for Bulgaria in many ways. The Holy See had limited funds, however, and great need existed in other areas of the world — places where the growth of Catholicism was more promising. Roncalli told the bishops that they must learn how to wait and that help would arrive at the opportune moment to bring with it a blessing. "They quiet down for a few days," Roncalli wrote, "and then they start up again, offering me an opportunity to exercise a little patience compared to the great amount of patience which I think the Sacred Roman Congregation has to exercise."[126]

Fertile ground waited to be cultivated. The little already harvested was only a small indication of how much more could be reaped with the grace of God — and if the Holy See would only proceed seriously with the measures Roncalli had already proposed.

At the end of 1932, Roncalli at last had a new secretary — a young priest from the diocese of Bergamo, Giacomo Testa, a student of the Cerasoli College where he would later complete his *curriculum* in canon law. Roncalli was immediately impressed with the young man who seemed to be exactly what he was looking for: a good, humble, and simple priest, full of eagerness to do good. "He still has all the simplicity and liveliness of a young boy, which makes him dear to everyone, but above all he possesses those qualities of nature and grace which will gradually make him a precious instrument in the service of Holy Mother Church."[127] Roncalli and Testa shared the same ideals, lifestyle, and purpose. They both understood the importance of conquering evil with good, of being optimistic, and of stressing what unites rather than what divides people. They sought to bring grace for the well-being of everyone, especially in difficult and sad times, disposing hearts to embrace the best in every circumstance. "Even here in my ministry, among these good Orthodox people, I do not see how I could succeed more effectively than to follow the New Testament...."[128] New needs and circumstances imposed new forms of pastoral ministry, but the underlying spirit had to remain the same, the same intensity and priestly piety, the same enthusiasm in exercising zeal, patience, and charity.[129]

Roncalli and Testa believed that to present themselves with a spirit of national pride in Italian civilization, culture, art, Catholicism, holiness, courtesy, etc., while expecting the Orient to accept these gifts as a favor, was a terrible mistake. Instead, the approach had to be "inverted in the sense that the Church of Christ has brought these gifts to the world and to individual nations to the extent that they know how to benefit from them and are manifested through the characteristic genius of the individual nations. However, this external expression — let us call it Italian, French, or Spanish — is not the cause, but the effect. And it does not imply an apostolic mandate in relation to other nations of the world, except in the sense of the love of one's neighbor as stated in the Gospel. This is the foundation," Roncalli concluded, "this is the unadulterated truth, this is the doctrine of the Church and of the pope as expressed in the encyclicals *Maximum Illud* of Benedict XV and *Rerum Ecclesiae* of Pius XI."[130]

After years of silence, Roncalli finally had a kindred spirit with whom he could converse. Yet, he could not expect — in fact did not want — his secretary to submit absolutely to his way of life; as is said in the *Imitation of Christ* (Book III, Chapter XXXVII): *De pura et integra resignatione sui, ab obtinendam cordis livertatem. Nudus nudum Jesum sequere* (Forsake yourself, resign yourself and your heart will be free.... Thus stripped, follow Jesus).[131] In Testa, Roncalli found a companion in prayer and in his devotions during May and June when his chapel at the delegation was adorned with flowers from his garden. He could celebrate and assist at Mass, then pause afterward to repeat his usual prayers of offering and adoration composed by his spiritual guides: Augustine,[132] Ignatius, Thomas, Bernard, and Francis de Sales. Then at dinner or while walking in the garden, he would comment on their writings and ideas, while forming his own in Christian philosophy.

> Ah! Everything on earth passes: youth, health, riches, pleasures, and worldly grandeur. Only charity remains. Only charity is reserved for the final transformation in eternal glory and joy with the saints in paradise. The more one seeks the cross, the more one feels the sweetness flowing from it — a foretaste of heaven. I will say of the cross what an Eastern proverb says of patience: it is a tree with bitter roots, but sweet flowers and fruit.[133] Find sweetness in doing everything in the will of the Lord. I almost no longer know where I left my own will. Now it is somewhat like an amputated leg. It is no longer there, thanks be to God, but occasionally it makes itself felt due to changing temperatures or unpleasant weather.[134]

Roncalli managed to tolerate his frequent seasonal ailments. He often dismissed symptoms as the flu, and he continued to suffer from gastrointestinal problems. An attack of kidney stones forced him into the hospital for treatment, then to the springs of Bulgaria, and finally to his beloved Bergamo for recovery during his autumn vacation.[135] Though his health was generally good, his heart and stomach problems required attention. "I think I am headed toward sunset, and more than ever I am becoming familiar with the call to my celestial homeland."[136]

Roncalli was now able to handle more calmly the various daily difficulties he dealt with as the papal representative. In the midst of his bishops and in harmony with those of both Rites, Roncalli would illustrate their responsibility by repeating the words of St. Francis de Sales, which he liked to apply to himself, too. "The bishops are like public fountains from which everyone, men, women, and animals benefit; some drink, others dive in, others wash themselves, and still others receive a few splashes. Everyone enjoys the fresh water that gushes out, and everyone receives a blessing from it."[137]

The most persistent and futile difficulty Roncalli faced was the situation of the extradited, immigrant Macedonians who were associated with Freemasonry and Bolshevism; almost daily they were victims of cruel murders and the source of social disorder, insecurity, and discontent. The general attention of the country was focused on the emigrants of the

Agrarian party who, ten years after the coup d'ètat following Stam-
bolijski's death, had been granted amnesty and were re-entering the
country. The strength of the Bulgarian government at that point hinged
on the Agrarian party, a fact the papal representative was aware of.[138]

For a long time, politics in Bulgaria was almost exclusively occupied keeping over thirty members of the so-called worker's party from
entering the Chamber of Deputies. These political exiles from the communist party presented a serious threat to state security. While the coup
had been successful and allowed the government to purge the nation of
Bolshevism before it encircled the whole country in its grip, it was already too late. Every day new strongholds emerged in factories, schools,
barracks, and even among Orthodox monks and priests. Meanwhile, the
hostilities against the Macedonians continued, and gunshots could be
heard even around the apostolic delegation. Young people gambled with
their lives for the sake of a struggle among party leaders who were tear-
ing one another to pieces.[139]

Added to Roncalli's other burdens was the long and painful controversy involving King Boris III. On January 15, 1933, the royal family's
firstborn child, Princess Maria Luisa, was hastily baptized in the Orthodox Rite. While the Bulgarian constitution required that a male heir to
the throne be baptized in the Orthodox Church, no such demands applied
to the Princess. King Boris had willfully violated the solemn promise he
made at the time of his marriage. Bishop Roncalli acted as mediator and
took upon himself the painful duty of "telling the truth *coram regem et
presides* [before kings and rulers], and assuming the role of John the
Baptist rather than John the Evangelist. But this is what [the Lord]
wanted, and so he helped me in a way that was amazing even in my
eyes — I who am accustomed to feeling my insufficiency."[140]

> To play the role of John the Baptist is much more difficult than that
> of John the Evangelist. Still more difficult is to carry out one's duty
> at any cost with great charity and tact before the powerful of the
> world in order to preserve good relations and not burn any bridges
> for the future. But I love the Baptist very much, he who had the task
> of leveling the rough paths. I try to imitate as much as possible this
> glorious saint....[141]
>
> I certainly suffered throughout this painful incident, but the
> Lord gave me the grace of great calm and simplicity; everything
> seemed to resolve itself as if according to a well-ordered plan. I had
> the spontaneous and clear affirmation of the downtrodden rights of

the human and Christian conscience — even in the face of the government that wanted to assume all the responsibility and of the king who in fact was the sole author of the controversy. Certainly, no one knows the king's soul or the gravity of the situation as does the apostolic delegate. Therefore, although I cannot excuse him, I am willing to be understanding and lenient to a degree. Of course, the situation of the king is always serious, and on another occasion we will be back at the beginning again. Naturally, the gravity of the situation and my concern to salvage whatever I could led me to have several meetings with the queen. She is always delightful, full of goodness, spiritual beauty, and solid religious principles. Her intentions are good, but the environment, while strong from a moral perspective, is totally Orthodox. What can she do in this kind of atmosphere? She is queen of a people whom she must love, but by the fact that they are Orthodox are far from her own spirit. [142]

Undoubtedly, Bishop Roncalli did not find it easy to assume the role of a John the Baptist. He hardly had time to feel irritated or offended when already his peaceful consideration of the difficulties induced him to understanding and patience. With the passing of time, however, this seeming limitation actually proved to be a strength. Roncalli's patience and availability opened hearts and engendered trust and confidence, which is exemplified in his long relationship with the king and queen of Bulgaria. When Roncalli left Sofia, the king gave him a sixteenth-century cross, and his words on that occasion are quite enlightening. As he presented Roncalli with the gift, the king said to the queen, "What will we offer the bishop who is leaving us? We will give him this cross, so closely linked to our marriage that became for him the cause of such pain." [143]

That day the queen predicted that Roncalli would become pope, and she promised to go to Rome with her husband to pay homage to the new pontiff. Roncalli merely smiled, but noted in his diary: "Blessed women, dreamers, even the good Queen Giovanna who has predicted the papacy for me!" [144]

"Catholics and the Orthodox Are Brothers"

During the latter half of 1934, Roncalli was informed that he was to leave Bulgaria for Turkey. In his farewell address to the faithful on Christmas Day, he spoke of his sojourn in Bulgaria with characteristic diplomacy. "I tried to be among you, with the grace of the Lord, above all in unity and peace, without ever allowing myself to waver from my intention of great discretion and faithfulness in evaluating everything." [145]

This one declaration signaled the emergence of a new style, more than a theory, as expressed by Roncalli. It may be summarized as follows:

1. Obedience to the pope and to the curia did not prevent Roncalli from giving an account of the difficulties of the local Church. The tension between directives from Rome and his attention to the people in their concrete circumstances was often a cause of suffering. Roncalli responded by intensifying his spiritual life through the reading of the Gospel and the *Imitation of Christ,* which instilled in him a true mysticism of the cross. The verse of the *Stabat Mater, Fac me cruce inebriari,* seemed to him to be very much in keeping with his spiritual disposition, especially during the years 1929–1930.

2. In giving attention to concrete situations, the apostolic delegate had to deal with the problem of nationalism among the small group of Bulgarian Catholics. In pursuing a solution to the difficulty posed by a nationalistic spirit, Roncalli delved into his own spiritual life. He sought to deepen the concept of catholicity as the source of international solidarity, and of true universal brotherhood, and over the years to develop an attitude of courtesy and impartiality toward all.[146]

3. The care of the local Church in a situation similar to Bulgaria's — where Catholics were a minority — persuaded Roncalli to review and deepen the theology of Church unity, which he had studied in Rome. In a letter to Flessati, Roncalli posed the question he asked himself so often: How can we bring about union with Rome in a predominantly Orthodox environment? At the time, he was still influenced by the unionist theology he had learned in Rome. He understood, however, that his primary commitment was that of charity, brotherhood, and respect. In 1926, Roncalli wrote to a young seminarian, "Since you have given me the opportunity, allow me to invite you — as I have always done with the young Orthodox men I was fortunate enough to meet in Bulgaria — to benefit from the studies and the education you receive in the seminary at Sofia. Catholics and Orthodox are not enemies, but brothers."[147]

As an evident conclusion of his experience, we cannot speak yet of a vision cultivated by Roncalli that surpassed the traditional theology concerning the union of separated brethren with Rome. However, his tone and expressions seem to suggest that he felt urged toward another direction. As he stated in his address on December 25, 1934, "The respect that I have always professed in public and in private for each and every one...must have spoken of the sincerity in my heart."[148]

CHAPTER 11

APOSTOLIC DELEGATE IN TURKEY AND GREECE
1934–1944

A Painful Transfer

When a possible transfer to Istanbul was discussed in December 1933, despite his feelings of reluctance, Roncalli repeated his sincere commitment to obey, "even if they wanted to send me temporarily to hell."[1] He knew he would not be able to live fully his calling as a pastor in Turkey, a cross that had also been a source of grief during his years in Bulgaria.

By the autumn of 1934, the transfer was taken for granted. With typical serenity, Roncalli awaited the official news of the appointment. From Sotto il Monte he wrote: "Nothing new on Istanbul, which makes me think they have probably decided on someone else. If that were the case, I would continue to be just as tranquil as I have always been. We will spend our winter in Sofia, in peace."[2]

The following week in Rome, Roncalli felt sure that his appointment had been ruled out because Cardinal L. Sincero, prefect of the Congregation for the Eastern Churches, opposed it. Again, Roncalli was serene in his determination to follow God's will. "I...remain very happy and calm in my total indifference.... We live by the Gospel and require nothing more for our sanctification."[3]

A letter dated November 16 speaks of an audience with Pius XI, who was particularly gracious; they exchanged opinions that strengthened Roncalli's resolve to respect the traditions of the Eastern Churches.[4] The next day, by some unexpected turn of events, Cardinal Sincero announced Roncalli's appointment. Roncalli communicated his surprise to his secretary: "This morning, believe it or not, Cardinal Sincero left the Holy Father's office beaming, and announced to the Congregation my appointment to the position in Istanbul."[5] Moreover, Sincero went out of his way to be courteous and told Roncalli what the pope had said about his appointment: "…And then, we want to give Bishop Roncalli a special sign of esteem and trust because, by not asking anything for himself, he has enlightened us a great deal. Even in the last audience we did not succeed in drawing from his lips a single word expressing personal discomfort, complaint, or even a desire to be transferred after ten years of such a difficult life in that environment."[6]

Initially assigned as the delegate to Istanbul, Roncalli told his secretary a week later that he was also made the delegate to Greece. Roncalli did not consider this burdensome, but he had enough experience to know it was a sensitive mission. For that reason, he stayed in Rome a few more days to study the situation well.[7]

Relieved from the tension of uncertainty, Roncalli felt truly happy. But he soon received news from his family that caused him much grief: his nephew Angelino, the 13-year-old son of his brother Giovanni, had died of acute appendicitis. "In these past days my family has suffered great anxiety, and now they are in mourning. Dear Angelino has gone to heaven. What do you expect? Secretly and in silence, even I have shed some tears. I loved him very much."[8]

Time, however, was pressing. Roncalli had to return to Sofia before Christmas for the solemn festivities and to bid farewell to the people of Bulgaria so that he would arrive in Istanbul for the New Year to begin his new mission.

Turkey: Gate to the Orient

Roncalli had visited Turkey on various occasions and he knew that the country had undergone a radical transformation. The defeat in World War I brought Turkey from being the center of an empire to a republic with much less territory. The nation's political configuration had changed profoundly, especially in its relationship with the leaders of the various 1,000-year-old religions established in Turkey.

Rather than maintaining a policy of religious tolerance, the new republic of Kemal Atatürk was more vigilant. The situation grew worse for the many Christian churches as compared with the Islamic, which, if only for cultural reasons, progressively recovered its former active role in society. Being a true Turk now presupposed belonging to Islam.

Moreover, the demographic changes during and after the war, with the Armenian Holocaust and the relocation of the Greek community, left an insignificant minority of Christians. When Roncalli arrived as the new apostolic delegate and administrator of the Latin Catholics, they numbered about 30,000 with the population concentrated mainly in Istanbul. This community followed two rites: the Latin Rite for the Italians, French, Austrians, and other Europeans; and the Eastern Rite for the Armenians, Chaldeans, Syrians, Melchites, Georgians, and Greco-Byzantines.

Almost all these faithful were "Levantines," a word used to refer to foreigners living inside the Ottoman Empire who kept their own distinct economic and cultural life. They preserved the bond between their elective land and their respective European nation, feeling a deep attachment to the cultural, linguistic, and religious traditions. These people had developed their own lifestyle — apart and closed in their own world — and nurtured a sense of superiority over their Turkish hosts.

Roncalli encountered this situation when he and his secretary, Giacomo Testa, were welcomed by Bishop Dell'Acqua to Istanbul on January 5, 1934. The Catholics were still suffering from friction that had developed under the previous delegate, Bishop Carlo Margotti, which involved both the laity and the approximately 800 men and women religious. Apparently, Bishop Margotti had challenged the centuries-old right of autonomy that every national community jealously defended with the support of their respective national authorities both at home and in Turkey. More precisely, Margotti had tried to reduce a predominantly French presence to the advantage of the Italians. Thus, the French-Italian friction that Roncalli had already faced in Bulgaria was far worse in Turkey. He had to use his diplomatic skills in an attempt to reconcile these heated conflicts.

Turkey lacked the presence of native clergy, something Roncalli considered "one of the greatest errors committed [by his predecessors]." Again, he had experienced a similar situation in Bulgaria, so it seemed that the question of forming native clergy followed the apostolic delegate. In 1937, he wrote to Don Giovanni da Fivizzano, "Preparing a native clergy is an important matter. If they had thought of it earlier, we would find fewer difficulties today along our path."[9]

A closely related issue was that of using Turkish language in the liturgy. Although Roncalli believed the problem needed attention, the Catholic community seemed entirely unconcerned, but they did not even use the language in daily life! He wrote to Bishop Tisserant: "The fault of Catholics, priests included, is that there is not one among them, after so many years of being in Turkey, who can approach the Turkish authorities and handle these affairs in the language of the country. They have allowed the new situation to take them by surprise without developing enough resources to handle it."[10]

Keenly aware of all these problems, Roncalli decided to use Turkish in the Cathedral of the Holy Spirit at certain parts of the liturgy, such as the Divine Praises. Given the tense situation, the reaction of the Levantines was not surprising. Roncalli described it: "When the *Tanre Mubarek olsun* [blessed be God] was recited, many left the church in displeasure."[11] Roncalli, however, persisted in his resolve because, as he explained, "the Catholic Church respects everyone, whoever they may be. The apostolic delegate is a bishop for everyone, and he seeks to be faithful to the Gospel that does not prefer any nation, is not fossilized, and looks to the future."[12]

The historian Morozzo della Rocca commented:

> His diplomacy obviously had a religious goal. This was the ideal spirit of Vatican diplomacy, to which Roncalli was faithful in the best possible way.... It was very clear to him that the purpose of diplomatic work was the well-being of souls, though perhaps in a more indirect way when compared to ordinary pastoral ministry. Roncalli dedicated himself to diplomatic work with the professionalism required. There is a sense of the human in his approach that has sometimes been neglected.... [He] always keeps the pastoral goal of his diplomatic activity and natural tendencies aligned with the religious objectives of Vatican diplomacy.[13]

To define Roncalli's approach one might call it a "pastoral diplomacy." This is true of his diplomatic activity in general, but compared to his experience in Bulgaria, Roncalli's activity in Turkey and Greece acquired new aspects especially as the administrator of the Latin Rite Catholics: "For the first time he truly felt himself to be a bishop and pastor. Until then, he had been without a diocese.... [Now] he had his own cathedral, his own faithful."[14]

Certainly, Roncalli's diplomatic mission often overshadowed his pastoral ministry. Contacts with representatives of the Western powers in Istanbul took up a great deal of his time, especially the conflicts between the French and the Italians. Although the Italians were a larger community, the French enjoyed a longer history in Turkey and had, therefore, the presence of many more religious institutions.

Why were the two communities divided? First there was the issue of the "liturgical honors," for which Italians and French competed in Istanbul, Smyrna, Ankara, and elsewhere. Then there was the problem of the parishes in the new Turkish capital. Traditionally, the only parish in Ankara had been staffed by French priests. Then Bishop Margotti created a second parish and staffed it with Italian priests.

No less troublesome was the Episcopate of Smyrna that was under the administration of a temperamental Maltese monk. To resolve the continuous conflicts among the faithful there, Roncalli was forced to replace the monk and entrust the diocese to an Italian priest of French background. "In these different incidents Roncalli's conduct shows a rather clever diplomatic style, attentive to changing situations, and intent on preventing any of the conflicting parties from feeling that the apostolic delegate was against them."[15] In negotiating the opposing positions of the diplomats, "he adopted...a style marked by balance and ingenuity."[16]

At the end of his first year in Istanbul, Roncalli made his annual retreat, but the few lines from his journal are little more than a brief account of the activities of the previous months.

> Spiritual exercises. I made them here, at the apostolic delegation, with my dear priests of the cathedral.... We did the best we could, but I was not completely satisfied. One must get away from all business and from one's usual environment. It is just not possible to tend to one's responsibilities at home while at the same time trying to attend to one's soul. This will serve as a lesson for next year. For this year, I can only renew my intentions from the past years. From the end of August 1934 until now, how many unexpected changes have taken place! I am in Turkey. What am I missing here in opportunity and in grace to make me holy?... How much work there is here! I bless God who fills me with the consolations of this sacred ministry. I must be resolute, however, in giving more calmness and order to everything I do.

Roncalli reflected on the Turkish law that required everyone, even clergy, to use civilian dress in public places — a distasteful norm for many. "All my clergy overcame even the trial of secular dress. K, however, must always set an example of dignity and edification. May the Heart of Jesus inflame and sustain me, and increase in me his own spirit. Amen."[17]

That first year ended with the painful news of his father's death on July 28. Roncalli's responsibilities did not allow him to return to Sotto il Monte, as would be the case when his mother died four years later. In a letter to Mother Ignazia Radici, superior of the community of the Daughters of the Sacred Heart in Milan, he described his great loss.

> The wound the Lord willed by taking from me my old, much venerated, and greatly loved father, penetrated my heart and found me very sensitive and more like a child than I had thought. The situation here did not permit me to run and gather his last breath. And my sisters? They did run, poor things. But they had just arrived home and were going upstairs when the dear old man died. Eternal peace and joy to his beautiful soul that was permeated by faith and by the fear and love of God. In life, in death, and after death, for having raised his children and for having given one to the altar, he enjoyed satisfactions and honors that many great people of the world would have envied.[18]

Roncalli's letters to his family show the deep love they had for one another; despite the distance that separated them, they seemed to be together in moments of suffering or parting.[19]

Greece: In the Land of Orthodoxy

As apostolic delegate to Turkey and Greece, Bishop Roncalli had to deal with two extremely different and mutually hostile countries. While he was apostolic administrator for the Latin Rite Catholics of Constantinople, Greece experienced a very difficult period in every respect: recurrent political and institutional crises, the tragic aftermath of World War I, the historical conflict with Turkey, World War II and the occupation. For Roncalli, the political-religious context of Mustafa Kemal's Turkey represented a difficult proving ground, but the Greek situation was even more challenging. He wrote: "My ministry in Greece is most bitter for me"; and again, "Greece, wherein lies the most painful part of my ministry."

Complex historical factors contributed to the circumstances in Greece.

The situation of the Catholic Church was perhaps worse in Greece [than in Turkey]. The Turkish government professed to take a neutral stand toward religious affairs. But the Athenian government openly identified its cause as supporting Orthodoxy, claiming that the government was to be both its guardian and its secular arm.... Moreover, in Greece, Catholics were considered foreigners. Although Greek Catholicism had many Greek members besides the various national communities, the Greeks almost always associate Catholics with the Italians. When Mussolini invaded Greece, the few Catholics scattered throughout the country [35,000] went through one of the most difficult moments of their history.[20]

His contacts with the political world of Greece proved very trying for Roncalli, who was forced to travel with a tourist visa for the entire first year of his ministry there. The following year, however, the situation changed after Pope Pius XI sent a congratulatory letter to George II on his election to the throne. As the bearer of the pope's letter, Roncalli was received kindly by the monarch and, therefore, by the Ministry of Foreign Affairs, the office that finally resolved the issue of his passport. The following September, Roncalli was received by Prime Minister Metaxas, who recommended that he draw up a list of points for a possible agreement with the Holy See. But the changing political situation prevented further developments.

If Roncalli's dealings with political authorities were difficult, those with the Orthodox authorities were thornier. He had been in Istanbul for only a year when Patriarch Fozio died on December 29. The election of his successor, Patriarch Benjamin I, on December 6, 1936, was influenced by the Greek and Turkish governments that ruled in a climate of "marked decline."[21]

He described his state of anticipation to his relatives: "With the Turks, you know how things are, but with the Greeks, the difficulties are greater. Those good people give me beautiful words, but when it comes to action, you know how much the Orthodox fear the pope. So I need a lot of patience. In this regard it is better to be tolerant; a single outburst can jeopardize everything."[22]

In the meantime, he continued visiting the small, scattered communities of Catholics, even in the isolated Aegean islands. On one of his trips, while aboard a ship headed for Patrasso, he met the leader of the Greek Orthodox Church, His Beatitude Giovanni Crisostomo Papadopulos, the archbishop of Athens. Roncalli wrote of their brief encounter: "Contrary to my initial intention to remain unnoticed, the circumstances suggested that I have a conversation with him, which lasted forty-five minutes. I thank the Lord and St. Joseph for this meeting, which I hope will bear good fruit in due time."[23]

The opportunity for a public meeting with the Patriarch of Constantinople presented itself with the death of Pius XI and the election of his successor Pius XII. As the apostolic delegate, Roncalli organized a number of ceremonies with the intention of making contact with the patriarch. He dubbed the initiative "Project Roncalli."[24] A large crowd of distinguished civil and religious authorities gathered in the Cathedral of the Holy Spirit for the funeral ceremonies.

The election of Pius XII was announced with a solemn *Te Deum* on his coronation day, again in the presence of government and church officials. The encounter marked the first time since the great schism that the Orthodox Church had been advised of the election of a new pontiff. At the end of the ceremony, Roncalli met with Bishops Maximos and Costantinidis who expressed the wishes of Patriarch Benjamin I that the new pope enjoy a long and happy pontificate. Visibly moved, Roncalli promised to send the message to Pius XII as soon as possible.

After four years in Istanbul, Roncalli was finally able to make an official visit as apostolic delegate to Fanar.

> This morning, May 27, 1939, I offered the Holy Mass — the most important act of the day. At 11:00, I was in Fanar with Collaro, Guillois, Filippucci, and Testa, each wearing a simple garment that indicated his rank in the pontifical court. Patriarch Benjamin received us very well: two metropolitans and archdeacons, six monks, four or five deacons, the interpreter Costantinidis — fifteen people in all. I expressed myself in a lively yet discreet manner, and the patriarch responded with sincerity and warmth. We did not touch on the question of unity to avoid any obstacle. Yet, we did not lack topics for an animated and interesting conversation during our very pleasant exchange: the work for peace on the part of all the religious leaders, Byzantine studies, my research on St. Charles, the two popes named Pius, and the centenary of St. Vladimir.[25]

The following years of war brought with them great hardships, especially for the population in Greece that was suffering from a famine. Roncalli was authorized by Rome to meet the Metropolitan Damaskinos Georges in Athens to organize relief efforts. In his report Roncalli described the Metropolitan: "Tall, unassuming, with a straightforward manner of doing things; he speaks as an upright man of convictions." "He said to me," Roncalli wrote, "that at his coronation he promised to concern himself with the sufferings of his people.... The conversation naturally touched on the war, but without either of us taking sides. Toward the end we discussed the beauty of a new order of rapport and contact between the Catholic and Orthodox clergy. He was profoundly convinced that this was now opportune, and for his part, he would promote it from that moment on."[26]

The meetings with the Patriarch at Fanar and with the Greek Metropolitans were brief and not the proper moments for open and dispassionate discussion on the divisions among the Christian churches and the need for renewed unity. An atmosphere of distrust prevailed that the passage of centuries could not seem to erase.

The War and Diplomatic Activities

Roncalli began 1939, the year World War II broke out, by issuing a severe condemnation of the evils that would mark the coming years with blood: Italy's racial laws, Germany's Nazi regime, and Spain's practice of racial discrimination and persecution. In his strong and candid discourse, Roncalli denounced all of these as contradictory with the Gospel. His address had widespread impact and one local Jewish newspaper gave it special coverage.

> Yesterday, in the Catholic cathedral of Pancaldi, on the feast of the Epiphany, Bishop Roncalli preached on a topic of burning interest today: faith in God and racism. In a language that everyone could understand, and with the energy of ardent persuasion, the eminent clergyman stated that the Church disregards all racial divisions. He recalled for the faithful that the relics of the Magi are found in Cologne, in the country that proclaims, "We no longer want Christ; we no longer want Christianity."' He declared that in the end humanity would be reconciled to the idea of charity and equality among people.[27]

Roncalli was surprised by the attention his words had gained. In writing to the Bishop of Smyrna, he emphasized that he had not intended to refer to specific events, but only to confirm the Church's position on important general topics. Of course, the rise of anti-Semitism in Europe made it understandable for the Jewish paper to give particular importance to his words in their report.

On August 2, Roncalli met with the new German ambassador to Ankara, Franz von Papen. Always able to see the good side in everyone,
Roncalli had to appreciate the faith of the ambassador's family and the
devotion of his wife who placed a bouquet of flowers in the chapel of the
delegation. The topic of their conversation seemed so important that
Roncalli wanted to go to Rome immediately to speak with the Secretary
of State, Cardinal Maglione.

His trip to Italy provided an opportunity to visit Sotto il Monte and to
pay a son's homage at his mother's tomb. On his return to Turkey, he
stopped at Gorizia to visit his predecessor, Bishop Carlo Margotti, and
they visited the war memorial at Redipuglia. He wrote to his family on
September 20 that while he contemplated the gravesites of the tens of
thousands killed in World War I, he could not help feeling dismayed that
"there are those who still want a war that would cut down the finest flowers of Europe's youth. Let us pray to the Lord to preserve us."[28] Perhaps
he was referring here to Italy after the German invasion of Poland in
September. Roncalli organized assistance and relief for the Polish people,
an act of solidarity with the victims of the conflict — the first of many
acts that sealed his commitment to works of charity during the war years.

Although Turkey was a neutral country and an island of peace, the
events in Europe greatly disturbed Roncalli. Writing to Mother Cecilia
Kosternarova in Bulgaria, he confessed:

> The world is going insane, my good Cecilia. One even hears of
> priests and religious who are calling down the fire of heaven to ex-
> terminate one race or another, as if the world were divided among
> the innocent and the sinners, and as if the triumph of the three
> concupiscences [the devil, the flesh, and the world] would not be
> terrible for all of us without distinction. It is always the prince of
> this world who rages.[29]

In mid-August 1940 Roncalli had another important conversation
with von Papen at his request. Having just returned from Germany, von
Papen wanted to give Roncalli a detailed report of the situation in Europe,
where he met with Hitler whom he found to be "calm and reflective."
What he had to say, therefore, was especially important, or so he implied.

According to von Papen, England was responsible for the escalation
of the events of the preceding months. Hitler, on his part, fulfilled his
duty as a reasonable statesman warding off the "contempt" heaped on

him by his enemies. Von Papen not only evaluated those events, but also spoke of the future. Doing his utmost to cajole the apostolic delegate, the ambassador said that if German Catholics proved themselves faithful patriots of the Reich, they would have a more prominent role in the country than Protestants. Von Papen attempted to flatter the Italian patriot in Roncalli when he claimed that the future Italy would play a major role and gain more territory at the expense of France.

While Roncalli met with von Papen, Roncalli's new secretary, Monsignor Righi, was speaking with Baron von Lersner from the German embassy. To give a more precise idea of what the German diplomats "were confiding" to the papal diplomats, I cite the following from a report sent by Roncalli to the Vatican:

> Germany will absorb Alsace, Lorraine, and Luxembourg; Belgium and Holland will have their independence restored, but will be demilitarized. The same is said of the new Poland and the Protectorates of Bohemia and Moravia. Finally, the burden of the war expenses for the two Axis powers will be placed on the colonies of Belgium and Holland, which will contribute raw materials. France will cede to Italy the border territory up to and including Nice, along with Corsica. Furthermore, France will return those colonies that had belonged to Germany and will pay all war costs. Both von Papen and von Lersner foresee that the war will be over by the end of the autumn [1940].[30]

The office of the secretary of state delivered a rather severe assessment of Roncalli's actions. He seemed not to know how to keep his distance and to evaluate von Papen's words critically — yet another addition to the legend of the roncallian "naïveté."

Despite the misfortunes of that meeting, a second one followed in early 1941. This time the German diplomat assured Roncalli that the new pact with the Soviet Union, the Ribbentrop-Molotov accord, would hold "100 percent." Six months later, the Germans attacked the Soviet Union.

For his part, Baron von Lersner continued to have a critical attitude toward Hitler's regime. He said, however, that Germany would not be backed against a wall. Only one man, he concluded, had the moral influence to persuade the political leaders to work toward concrete peace proposals: Pius XII.

Obviously, the German diplomats tried to use Roncalli and, through his contacts with the Holy See, inform the Allied forces of dynamics and possible developments of the conflict. Roncalli scrupulously transmitted to the Vatican the information he received in its smallest details, although the reports were sometimes puzzling to those receiving them in Rome.

On April 23, 1942, von Papen met with Roncalli again. While their previous encounters had taken place under a diplomatic umbrella, this meeting took place as Germany's military power was in rapid decline.

According to Don Pierre Blet,[31] the German ambassador "showed his preoccupation for peace and Germany's future. Together with his friend, Baron von Lersner, von Papen proposed that Pius XII make some kind of discreet inquiry among the Allies." Roncalli wrote to Bishop Montini, "I listened with polite interest, but nothing more."[32]

Roncalli was willing to help Baron von Lersner by fulfilling his request for appropriate introductions for contacts within Vatican circles. In a memo written on April 24, Roncalli stated, "I prepared a confidential letter to Montini to introduce Baron von Lersner to the Vatican. I have a good impression of this Protestant man, and I believe he is upright and sincere. But I do not know what those in Rome will think of the man or my gesture — which is also upright and sincere. I have great faith in a forthcoming peace, and I hope that it will truly be a just peace."[33] When von Lersner did go to Rome for his "mission," he accomplished nothing.

Meetings between von Papen and the apostolic delegate were infrequent. Roncalli's report to Montini, dated July 8, 1943, mentioned one in particular.

> In six months, I have seen him only once and that was briefly (March 4, 1943), during my Easter visit to Ankara. Everyone was talking about the Katyn massacre [the Soviet massacre of several thousand Polish officials], which von Papen said should have made the Poles realize it would have been to their advantage to turn to the Germans. I replied sadly that first of all the Poles would have had to forget the millions of Jews killed or forced out of Poland, and that in any case, this was a good opportunity for the Reich to change its treatment of the Poles.

Capovilla rightly noted, "An explicit accusation such as this is not found easily in diplomatic documents. It does honor to Roncalli and perhaps even to von Papen, who did not respond. Perhaps in his heart he agreed."[34]

Their last meeting, which von Papen described many years later, was quite poignant: "When I had to leave, having been recalled to Berlin [August 1944], he came to say goodbye to me at the first station out of the terminal. For ten minutes we walked up and down like old friends.

Finally, I knelt and asked his blessing. I had a clear sense that we would never see each other again because the Allies would surely hang me. Then the apostolic delegate placed a letter in my hands, which is now in the American archives. A brother could not possibly have written with more warm-heartedness."[35] After the war von Papen's memoirs state that even if Roncalli had not seen alternatives to Germany's defeat, he still transmitted the ambassador's pleas to the Vatican, "so that the Allies would take into account the difference between Hitler's regime and the German people."[36] On this occasion perhaps von Papen recovered the sincerity that, as a diplomat, he did not know or could not possess.

Journeys for Ministry and Charity

Among Roncalli's photographs is one that was taken in Istanbul in 1941. On the back he wrote, "Monsignor Roncalli at sixty. It is the best age: good health, greater wisdom, a more joyful disposition to see clearly, with gentleness and confident optimism." This is how Roncalli saw himself while he lived on the Turkish Golden Horn.

Roncalli never lacked intimations of the condition of his health and age. Indeed, his well-being had endured a rigorous test during the years in Turkey. The Vatican Delegation to Istanbul had become the intermediary for contacts with many diplomatic offices of the Holy See. "Being here I handle all the correspondence that passes from the Vatican to Syria, Palestine, Egypt, Mesopotamia, Persia, India, and all of Africa."[37] But the tasks that weighed on him most were those associated with his diplomatic and pastoral offices. He had to keep direct contact with government representatives and the Catholic communities, requiring frequent travel, which the war made even more strenuous.

In speaking of the war, it would be easy to forget the "logistic side" of the apostolic delegate's life. Yet, in reviewing the list of his journeys, it is amazing how Roncalli carried out so many heavy responsibilities at his age.

In May 1935, he completed his first trip to Greece as delegate and remained there for about ten days, visiting a few of the islands. Another trip followed in September. The next year he was in Greece for part of April and May and visited Corinth, Nauplia, Micene, Epidaurus, Dhelfoi, and Thebes — finding some time for archaeological excursions. In May, he traveled to Mount Athos, and at the beginning of September returned to Greece. He made his retreat in mid-October near Bergamo.

The year 1937 was exceptionally grueling. He traveled to Greece three times, the last visit in the exhausting heat of August. He visited the islands of Tinos and Delos, Syra, Corfu, Patras, Aghia Laura, and several others. In May 1938 he went to Crete, and in November he visited Volos, Meteore, Thebes, and Chalcis.

The year the war began, 1939, was intense as no other before. He was in Greece in May, and from there he went to Beirut to participate in the Eucharistic Congress. He left for Palestine from Beirut and then visited Jerusalem, Jaffa, and Syria (Palmyra, Homs, Aleppo) — the trip to Palestine and Syria had to be made in only four days. In August, he went to Gazzaniga, near Bergamo, where he participated in the local Eucharistic Congress. The following September he was in Rome, where he was received by Pius XII.

The following is Roncalli's own vivid account of his trips, written in a letter to his sisters.

I have a very heavy workload, so do not grow impatient if I do not write often. I am enjoying excellent health and spiritual peace, but the inconveniences of traveling still bother me. This time, for example, Monsignor Testa accompanied me to Istanbul. We left on Saturday the 7th, and after three hours on a German plane, arrived in Sofia. But from there we could not get a connecting flight to Athens. Patience. When Princess Eudossia came to visit me at the delegation, I requested a favor: to ask her brother, the king, for a car to travel to Thessalonica. He immediately loaned us a Mercedes along with a chauffeur. We arrived in Thessalonica after eight hours, traveling the same road along the Struma River that the German army had used last year. We stopped to eat in the village of Delcevo, where we found three Eucharistine nuns. Just think of the consolation for them and for us. I rested a few hours in Thessalonica and on the morning of Tuesday, the tenth, I was again in a car — this time one offered by the Italian military command. At noon, we stopped at Larissa, where General Ruggiero, commander of the Forlì Division, offered us lunch and every other courtesy. At 10:00 P.M. we arrived in Athens, after fifteen hours of continuous travel. From Sofia to Athens is twenty-three hours by car, whereas by plane it would have taken less than an hour and a half, and without all the trouble. I hope to leave on the 26th, flying from Athens to Sofia, and then again by air on the 27th from Sofia to Istanbul. I feel some fear every time I fly, but since I am not doing my will but the Lord's, and I am not traveling for pleasure but to fulfill the responsibilities of my apostolic ministry and charity, I remain in peace, ready for anything.[38]

In a letter of July 30, he confided to his brother Giovanni:

The day after tomorrow, August 1, I leave for Istanbul. I will fly from Athens to Sofia, and then take the train from Sofia into Istanbul now that the railway has been restored. I want to spend even more than a month and a half here in Greece before the end of the year. Will I succeed? I cannot say. Will I succeed in getting a little rest in Sotto il Monte during this time? I want to, but I cannot be sure.[39]

In January 1943 he wrote to his sisters about his December travels.

My return trip from Athens to Istanbul turned out well. St. Joseph is protecting me. Just think, in Athens we could not take the plane to Thessalonica and Sofia because of bad weather. We took off for Belgrade. But just when I thought we were halfway to Belgrade, we landed. Where? In Sofia. Ah, St. Joseph! I always call upon him and he always helps me. From Sofia I went to Istanbul by train, arriving just in time to celebrate Christmas. We had wonderful festivities that were a lot of work for me, but the pastoral consolation was even greater.[40]

While it may seem that Roncalli spent all of his time in fatiguing journeys, he also enjoyed moments of tranquillity and rest. In a letter to his brother Giuseppe, he described one of those occasions.

After Monsignor Testa left, I came here to the villa of Prinkipo that our sisters know so well. The house is older now and needs repairs, but all in all it is an earthly paradise. So here I am, all by myself and absorbed in my writing day and night. There are three nuns cooking for me and they do the cleaning.... Twice a week I return to the city for meetings and functions. There are always some important people who visit me out of courtesy or for official business. I will be here until September 30. When I return to the city, I will prepare for another visit to Greece where still more work awaits me.[41]

Refugees Flee for Their Lives

During World War II, Roncalli was tireless in his efforts to alleviate the terrible suffering around him and give help to the countless number of people who approached him for assistance. The matters relating to the Jewish tragedy are certainly among the most important and worth mentioning.

The turmoil of war made Turkey, a neutral country, one of the preferred escape routes for the many refugees who were fleeing the ever
tightening net the Nazis stretched over Europe. The Jewish communities
from countries that drifted toward the Balkans viewed Turkey as the
natural road to safety in Palestine and beyond. This was especially true
for the communities in Bulgaria, Romania, and Hungary.

The events of the February 1942 sinking of the *Struma,* a ship carrying 750 refugees, deeply affected Roncalli. He responded to a request
made by a nun to search for a friend's daughter:

> Providence helped me find a rather speedy response to Mrs.
> Mayer's anxieties. But what a response. The first statement in Feb-
> ruary contained the truth about the *Struma.* The unfortunate ship
> sank and only one man survived. My source of information was
> certain of this. Most Reverend Mother, we are faced with one of the
> greatest mysteries in the history of humanity. Poor children of Is-
> rael! Every day I hear their groans all around me. I mourn with
> them and do my best to help them. They are the relatives and coun-
> trymen of Jesus. May the Divine Savior come to their aid.[42]

What could the papal delegate do for all these people? Only one
thing: act as a link between the requests of the Jewish organizations, the
Holy See, and by means of the latter, the representatives of countries
and international organizations.

His calendar contained many references to contacts and meetings
with representatives from Jewish organizations. On January 20, 1943,
for example, Roncalli met with Chaim Barlas, the leader of the representatives of Palestinian Zionists in Istanbul. Barlas gave Roncalli a
memorandum that asked the Holy See to verify whether neutral countries could admit Jewish refugees to their territories, even temporarily,
and to communicate to the German government that the Jewish Agency
had arranged for five thousand certificates of immigration to Palestine.
Finally, he asked that Vatican Radio announce that the Church considered any help given to the persecuted Jews as a "work of mercy."[43]

It was not always possible for the Vatican delegation to respond adequately to every request or recommendation. For various reasons, therefore, its actions are not always evaluated objectively today. Roncalli,
however, never failed to provide whatever assistance was possible. Perhaps the Holy See felt uneasy about helping Jews migrate to Palestine
because of a conflict with the Zionist movement concerning the role of
Catholicism in a Jewish Palestine. Roncalli's activity, nevertheless, dem-

onstrated a fraternity that transcended political and historical circumstances. It came as no surprise then, when he became occupied with the Jews escaping from Slovakia into Palestine — a stance that earned him the gratitude of the Zionist emissary.

The same diplomatic report that records the words of gratitude offered by Chaim Barlas also contains the tragic fate of other Jews.

> Istanbul. May 22, 1943. To Cardinal Maglione. I had a visit from the Chief Rabbi Dr. Markus of the Askenazim community of Istanbul. I sympathized with him and urged him to write down his thoughts. I am now transmitting his letter and the list of the poor unfortunate people who are fleeing amid such grave danger. As much as I emphasize how difficult it is for the Holy Father in his intervention on behalf of the Jews, the people do not cease to plead, comforted to know that this intervention is often efficacious, always positive, and constant.[44]

A document that is often cited is the 1943 letter Roncalli wrote to King Boris III of Bulgaria asking for help and support for Bulgarian Jews and refugees.

> As Your Majesty well knows, the Holy See, faithful to its tradition, continues to multiply the forms of charitable assistance to those who are suffering the effects of war — people of every language and nation, without excluding the children of Israel, so as not to do wrong to the universal message of Christ. I humbly seek to work in his footsteps...and it is precisely this exercise of charity, extended to the Jews, that provides me with the occasion to appeal to Your Majesty's heart. I am aware — based on what I read from Bulgarian sources — that some sons of Judah are not faultless. Along with the guilty, however, there are also many innocent persons. Some sign of clemency, besides the great honor it would bring to the dignity of a Christian sovereign, would become before the God of mercy a promise of blessings during these times of trial.[45]

At the foot of this document, Roncalli later appended a note that tells us King Boris did heed his appeal.

Roncalli intervened in another situation when Jewish refugees were trapped in the region of Trans-Dniestria in 1944. In one of his notes he wrote: "February 23. Many visits today. The most important was that of the Chief Rabbi Isaac Herzog of Jerusalem...accompanied by Dr. Chaim Barlas.... The Rabbi felt compelled to offer official thanks to the Holy Father and his collaborators for the help given to the Jews, and to ask me to intervene for those who were in danger on the other side of the Dnieper where the Germans were retreating. He also wanted to convey his special thanks to Bishop Cassulo, nuncio of Bucharest. A warm, affable person, that Chief Rabbi."

The next day Roncalli returned the visit. "The Chief Rabbi received me at Pera Palace. His son and Dr. Barlas were also there. We related some episodes regarding the rapport between Jews and Catholic prelates."[46]

Upon leaving Istanbul on February 28, Rabbi Herzog wished to offer a final tribute to the apostolic delegate for all his efforts:

> Before leaving this evening, God willing, I would like to express to you my profound gratitude for your continued and energetic activity on behalf of our unfortunate people, who are innocent victims of the incredible horrors inflicted by a cruel power that totally ignores the principles of religion that are the foundation of humanity. You place yourself within the profound humanitarian tradition of the Holy See and follow the noble sentiments of your heart. The people of Israel will never forget the help you brought to its suffering brothers and sisters from the Holy See and from its highest representatives in this very painful period of our history. I also beg you to give my sincere thanks to your esteemed secretary [Thomas Ryan] who is truly a worthy representative of the Irish people, to whom I will always remain closely tied [Herzog had been Chief Rabbi in Ireland]. May God bless you with the blessing of Zion and of Jerusalem.[47]

In a letter to Chaim Barlas dated March 23, Roncalli assured him of the concern of the Holy See over the current problems. He concluded with: "May God be with you and may he bring you grace and prosperity. Ever at your service and at the service of all the brothers of Israel."[48]

At times Roncalli worked in an intricate web of secret or outright interventions, and was able to obtain help from Franz von Papen. Although limited, the German ambassador's participation in the humanitarian activities of the apostolic delegate — who gave him due recognition in a deposition — was enough to save his life in the Allied courts after the war. How many episodes could be recounted!

Roncalli's earnest activity and constant accessibility were legendary. There are stories of "baptismal certificates" which Roncalli supposedly falsified in order to save entire bands of Jews. Ira Hirshman, of the American Office for War Refugees, noted this in his memoirs. In reality, these were not baptismal certificates but certificates of immigration that the apostolic delegate issued for the benefit of the Jews of Hungary and Romania. Roncalli himself clarified this in a letter to the nuncio of Budapest, "Since the 'certificates of immigration' that I sent to you in May have contributed to saving the lives of Jews — indeed their very purpose — I accepted from the Hebrew Agency of Palestine three new packages. I beg Your Excellency to have them reach the person to whom they are addressed."[49]

His good rapport with the Jews continued throughout the years, fortunately under very different circumstances. Roncalli's compassionate pursuits as apostolic delegate would always remain impressed on the minds of the representatives of the Jewish people. When a large delegation of American Jews went to the Vatican in October 1960, their leader, Rabbi Herbert Driedman, reminded Roncalli of his interventions while he was delegate in Turkey and Greece. In responding, the Pope recalled the story of Joseph, *"I* am your brother. Of course," he continued, "there is a considerable difference between those who acknowledge only the Old Testament and those who add to it the New as their law and supreme guide. But this distinction does not suppress the brotherhood that derives from the same origin. We are all children of the same Father.... We come from the Father, we must return to the Father."[50]

Good Must Be Done Well

In the autumn of 1940, the Italians invaded Greece. The war that Roncalli had followed from his peaceful See of Istanbul now concerned him personally. The presence of soldiers from his native land (even from Bergamo) reawakened Roncalli's genuine sense of patriotism. He had always clearly distinguished nationalism, which he abhorred, from patriotism, which he considered a positive sentiment. For him the word *"patria"* (native land) kindled feelings of attachment to one's own country and ancestors. As delegate, he had frequent contact with the Italian troops from simple soldiers to commanding officers. Although they maintained their area of competency, there was collaboration — as with the German command — though in a more formal manner. Being Catholic and Italian placed the delegate in a very delicate position with the Greeks.

Throughout the war, Roncalli had the task of searching for missing persons and prisoners. The delegate received many requests and often took a personal interest in the uncertain fate of so many unfortunate people. To obtain news of Italian prisoners held by the Soviets, he went directly to the Soviet embassy in Ankara, but with no results.

These were years of intense suffering for Greece. The occupation by foreign armies, the war effort, and the breakdown of political structures made life more unbearable every day. The greatest losses were among civilians. "Among a population of 7,300,000, about 23,000 soldiers were lost, while civilian deaths numbered almost 400,000. About 60,000 men were allegedly shot by the Bulgarians [an occupying force], as well as by the Germans and Italians. Living conditions have deteriorated rapidly, causing such widespread poverty that in three years approximately 200,000 people died from starvation."[51]

Roncalli could offer only limited assistance. One of the major preoccupations for the Greeks were the shipments of grain already en route to their ports. A British blockade stopped the shipments for fear that they would also benefit the occupying troops. Unfortunately, it also prevented the Greeks from receiving much-needed supplies. The situation forced the Greeks to turn to Rome and the Holy Father through his delegate. The circumstances called for a meeting, which was held on September 10, 1941, between Roncalli and the top religious authority of Athens, Metropolitan Damaskinos.

After their cordial encounter, Roncalli traveled to Rome, but not even the Holy See could secure the help everyone hoped for. Conditions worsened. By the time Roncalli returned to Athens in November, the situation was desperate.

November 17: The laments of the suffering and dying continue. Oh! What a great pity! I do not wish to exaggerate, but misery is certainly widespread.

November 18: Demetriadis...asks a little meat and milk for his son who has tuberculosis.

November 19: With eagerness, I have resumed the work of receiving people; everyone asks for help and for my recommendations.

November 22: How many miseries have passed under my eyes this morning!

November 28: Starving men and women. Oh! What sorrow not to be able to give them everything I would like to!

December 1: Hunger and misery are all around me. I cannot get to everyone, and even for those few I can get to, it is so little. This is a great cross.... Encounters without end and all painful, ending with many alms and homemade bread.

December 4: Severe cold in these days, then rain. In the homes, moans and sighs as hunger claims its victims. They calculate up to 1,500 [?] deaths every day. It is better to verify; perhaps it is too many. Regardless of the number, deaths are increasing. It is painful for me not to be able to give anything except some bread and money. But what is the money worth, the drachmas, in this hellish abyss of the black market?[52]

The following is taken from a letter written at the beginning of 1942.

Ah, Greece is a field of despair. I told you some things the last time I was home. The situation has worsened. Let us pray to the Lord and have the young boys pray to be spared the post-war horrors like the ones that the Greeks are suffering today. War is ugly and so is disease, but hunger is something horrible to speak of and to endure. I repeat for our boys what I said last time: we must deny ourselves and pray to the Lord for the many old people and children who are sick and dying from weakness. I foresee a spring that will be even more painful for the poor people who are already suffering so greatly. Together with Monsignor Testa I have organized several works for assistance. The Holy Father has sent me half a million lire to begin with. But we will need the gift of miracles. Enough.[53]

Roncalli and his collaborators initiated what they called "Hearths of Providence" to help the starving. He then did something which in the historical context of the conflict between the Greeks and Turks was rather shocking. A Christmas collection was taken up in Turkey for the starving children of Greece. The Holy See contributed a sizable sum and initiated diplomatic action to secure provisions, placing itself at the disposition of other international organizations such as the Red Cross. All of this came about because of the intervention and concerned interest of Roncalli.

During that time, he wrote: "Thanks be to God. During that period of national calamity in Greece, we can say that the Catholic Church, through its representatives and its coordinated activity, was equal to the task, in its best tradition. I enjoy confirming all this while repeating before the Lord and before the Holy Father who inspires, helps, and directs us, the *servi inutiles sumus* [useless servants we are, Lk 17:10]."[54] In all of this Roncalli followed to the letter the rule of love that his beloved bishop and mentor, Radini Tedeschi, had taught him: "good must be done well."

Spiritual Exercises During Disruptive Years

His spiritual exercises were of utmost importance to Roncalli.[55] In the silence of his retreat, he could look into his heart and renew the strength of his spirit. How much need he must have felt for this during those turbulent years of war that were filled with so much misery. The stress of diplomacy and the strategies of politics required a heart ever more open to a secure and serene perspective of faith. With this in mind, the retreat notes from his *Journal of a Soul* are worth exploring. In 1939, the exercises were given by Elia Châd at the Jesuit house in Ankara.

> Finally the retreat that I desired: closed away, without contact with the outside world, and conducted with a method. Don Elia Châd, the Jesuit superior, gives us points for meditation according to the method of St. Ignatius, and he does well. He gives more than the points, however; instead of a quarter of an hour he takes half an hour. Then we continue our reflections in our room. I help myself by reading the Ignatian text — the Latin translation annotated by Don Rootham. I note, however, that — even for us priests and bishops — giving the material bit by bit, just to be faithful to the method, then leaving the rest to each one, is not practical. We are all somewhat like children who need to be guided by the living voice of one who presents the beautiful doctrine already prepared. Therefore, the method of St. Ignatius, but adapted to modern life....

Retreat was also a time for Roncalli to reflect on his own life:

> In a few days I will have completed 58 years. Having assisted Bishop Radini in his death at the age of 57, every year I live beyond that age seems as if it were an extra gift. Lord, I thank you. I still feel young and healthy, but I do not pretend anything. Whenever you want me, here I am, ready. Even in dying, and above all in dying, *fiat voluntas tua* [your will be done, Mt 6:10].... The confessor tells me that the Lord is pleased with my service. Pleased? Really? Oh, if only he were! I am only partly content with it. The "election" of my state has been made for quite a while. Even regarding the details of my life and activity, everything is quite clear and fixed by the *impendam et superimpendar pro animabus* [to spend and be spent for souls, 2 Cor 12:15]. I do not really neglect my episcopal duties, but — oh, my! — how many shortcomings in fulfilling them! Above all I am tormented by the disproportion between what I do and what remains to be done, and what I would like to do but cannot manage to do. The fault must be partly my own.

Notice his comparison of the Golden Horn fishermen to the challenge of faith.

Every evening from the window of my room here at the Jesuit house, I watch the gathering of boats on the Bosporus. They come in tens and hundreds from the Golden Horn, gathering in a prearranged place. Then they are illuminated, some more brilliantly than others, forming a spectacular array of colors and lights.... These lights stay on all night, and one can hear the cheerful voices of the fishermen. The scene moves me. The other night around one o'clock it was pouring rain, but the fishermen were there, undaunted by their hard labor. Oh, what an example for me, for us priests, *piscatores hominum* [fishers of men, Mt 4:19]! Passing from the image to the lesson, oh, what a vision of work, of zeal, of apostolic activity proposed to us! Very little of the kingdom of Jesus Christ remains here, only remnants and seeds. But how many souls to win for Christ.

In 1940, Roncalli made his retreat in Terapia at the house of the Sisters of Our Lady of Zion. The exercises lasted one week (November 25– December 1) and focused on an extended reflection of Psalm 51:3–21 — fitting for a time of war. Though he was engulfed in the peaceful atmosphere, Roncalli could not forget the war that still raged. On November 25, he wrote: "Yesterday the Holy Father Pius XII invited the whole world to join with him to sing, mourn, and pray the litanies of the saints and the *Miserere*. All of us from West to East united with him in his prayer."

On Tuesday, November 26, Roncalli's meditation turned to the lament of the nations over the war. Following the indication given by the retreat master, he reflected on the hypocrisy of nations — how they cause wars, but in times of misery and misfortune complain and expect God to spare their country.

Then the following days were spent in reflections centered on the theme of mercy, a topic Roncalli seemed quite comfortable with: "Not just any mercy will do. The weight of social and personal iniquities is so heavy that a gesture of ordinary charity is not enough to pardon them. Therefore we call upon the great mercy, which is proportionate to God's greatness, *secundum magnitudinem ipsius, sic et misericordia illius* [for equal to his majesty is his mercy, Sir 2:18]. It is well said that our miseries are the throne of divine mercy."

Roncalli did not simply focus on generalities during his spiritual exercises. Rather he concentrated on personal holiness.

The ideal of holiness, smiling among tribulations and the cross, is always with me. Interior calm founded on the words and promises of Christ produces an imperturbable serenity that is reflected in one's face, words, and character — the exercise of all-winning charity. We feel renewed energies, both physical and spiritual: *dulcedo animae sanitas ossium* (sweetness to the soul and health to the body, Prov 16:24). To live in peace with the Lord, to feel pardoned and in turn to pardon others....

Roncalli felt compelled to reflect on holiness because of his sixtieth birthday. This was an incentive for him to make progress along the path of holiness.

I have chosen to make my retreat now because this is the beginning of my sixtieth year. I am entering a time when one begins to be considered old. Oh, at least in my old age may I attain that perfection which, as a bishop, I should have already achieved, but which I still lack so much! To sanctify the beginnings of this year with prayer and meditation, in a spirit of penance, is already a start; certainly, thanks to the Lord, it is a plea for mercy.

Because he had been delayed in Greece, Roncalli was unable to make his spiritual exercises in 1941. In 1942, he wanted to make his retreat at the Jesuit house again, but for the sake of caution, he was advised to remain at his own residence. Roncalli did not find this agreeable, but he adapted himself to the circumstances. His retreat notes that year contain a passage of timeless value — one worth considering here.

The two great evils poisoning the world today are secularism and nationalism. The first is characterized by government leaders and by the laity, while the second is found even in ecclesiastics.... The Holy Church, which I represent, is the mother of nations, of all nations. All the people with whom I come into contact must find in the papal representative a deep respect for the nationality of everyone, augmented by courtesy and compassionate judgment, which encourages universal trust. This requires great prudence, respectful silence, and cordiality in every circumstance. It would be wise to insist on this line of conduct from staff members and associates both at home and outside. All of us are infected with nationalism to some degree. The apostolic delegate must remain untainted by this plague and show that he is free from this contagion. *Sic Deus me adiuvet* [May God help me].

At the height of the war, Roncalli identified secularism and nationalism as two poisons at the root of such great destruction. It became clear to him that in order to move forward in his mission he had to go beyond diplomacy; he had to progress toward a form of pastoral care. In the future, this would actually become the characteristic mark of his ministry in his new assignment — France.

CHAPTER 12

APOSTOLIC NUNCIO IN FRANCE
1944–1953

Unexpected Telegram

On December 6, 1944, Roncalli received a telegram from the Vatican notifying him of his new assignment as nuncio to France.[1] Given his respectable though hardly exceptional résumé, it was an unexpected promotion for the 63-year-old Roncalli. It surprised him. The French nunciature was among the most prestigious in the world, and the position required a leading diplomatic figure capable of dealing with the sensitive relationship between France and the Holy See. Another unforeseen stage was about to begin in the "incredible itinerary of Roncalli."[2]

When the telegram arrived, Roncalli was at his residence in Istanbul. According to one biographer, Roncalli immediately looked for his secretary, Monsignor Thomas Ryan; either he could not decipher the message or he thought it must be some mistake. This is what he wrote in his diary:

> Late this evening, like a clap of thunder, the telegram from Tardini arrived communicating my nomination as papal nuncio to France. I was surprised and astonished. I went to the chapel to ask myself, before Jesus, if I should withdraw from the weight of the cross or accept it as it is, without hesitation. I remained absorbed in my thoughts, but calmly decided to accept and *non recuso laborem* [not refuse the work]. So I spent the night with St. Nicholas and St. Ambrose, both called to be bishops, which made them saints and sanctifiers.[3]

The day after he shared the news with his relatives.

My dear sisters, brothers, and everyone in the family.... Last night I received a telegram from Vatican City telling me that the Holy Father has appointed me papal nuncio to France. I could not believe it since I never thought myself worthy of such a great honor and heavy responsibility. Now they are awaiting approval from the French government; then I am to leave at once to arrive in Paris by the first of the year. I cannot tell you how I feel. There is a deep distrust and fear of myself and of my strength to bear such a heavy burden, and at the same time a great confidence in the Lord. He will surely help me because I have never desired or even dreamed of this position. The Holy Father could have chosen from so many more mature, learned, and holy prelates. But he looked for me here, where I have felt so much at ease and willing to remain for a long time. As long as we are without pretense, God uses humble creatures to work out the design of his glory. Now I have a much greater need to grow in holiness, and your prayers will be a big help! Perhaps Paris will be my Calvary, so that a poor man like me might be consumed in sacrifice and in service of the Holy See during such a difficult and uncertain time for religious renewal.... I cannot express the sorrow I feel in having to leave these children and brothers of mine here in Istanbul, where for ten years I have been father and pastor to them. Now, in Paris, there will be no pastoral ministry, something I enjoyed so much and for which I became a priest. I will only be handling religious affairs and these often touch politics, which is not good. I must tell you that I am not moving to Paris except to work and sacrifice myself. For this mission, I should be ten years younger. I will do my best and endure as long as my good health continues.[4]

Upon accepting the "obedience for Paris," Roncalli prepared for a quick departure from Turkey. He had to cancel the spiritual exercises "already prepared and scheduled for the end of 1944," which "Léveque from the Lazarists was going to preach."[5]

Motives for the Appointment

Why did the pope suddenly replace Bishop Valerio Valeri? Why was Roncalli chosen, and why did he have to be in Paris by January 1? Perhaps answers to these questions can be found in the long conflict between Charles de Gaulle and Pius XII.

General de Gaulle met Pope Pius XII on June 30, 1944,[6] after Allied forces landed in Normandy. He had asked Rome to replace the nuncio,

Bishop Valeri, because de Gaulle thought he had been too close to the Vichy regime of Marshal Pétain. General de Gaulle also asked for the removal of some thirty bishops also believed to have collaborated with the Pétain government.[7] These requests were made after the liberation of Paris, Pétain's ousting, and de Gaulle's triumphal entry into the Cathedral of Notre-Dame (August 26) to offer thanks. The archbishop of Paris, Cardinal Emmanuel Suhard, was not at the ceremony because he too was accused of being a "collaborator" and was being held "prisoner" in his residence.

Pius XII had tried in vain to convince de Gaulle to put an end to his demands. He argued that papal nuncios are appointed to a country, not a government. He also reminded the general that Valeri had gone to France in 1936 while the Popular Front was in power. De Gaulle responded by sending a delegation to Rome to repeat the request for a new nuncio; he received a negative answer. Georges Bidault, former president of the National Committee of the Resistance and the leader of the Christian Democratic Party, pressed for the nuncio's removal and insisted that the bishops who had "collaborated" with the previous government also be removed.

While de Gaulle persisted, the pope held fast to his refusal in hopes that the time gained would perhaps see a change in the transitional government. But the passing of time only seemed to support the new regime. When the Vichy ambassador to the Holy See resigned, he was temporarily replaced by de Gaulle's envoy, Hubert Guérin, but the Holy See refused to recognize the interim government. In fact, the Soviets were the first to recognize de Gaulle's government and to confirm its ambassadors. For this reason in particular, the pope could no longer postpone acting. Traditionally the senior ambassador in the diplomatic corps, usually the papal nuncio, delivered the New Year greetings. But in the absence of a papal nuncio, the oldest ambassador would give the speech and, in Paris at the time, this meant the Soviet ambassador. At all costs this had to be avoided to save both de Gaulle and Pius XII from embarrassment. The situation had reached a head. Pius XII was forced to concede and Roncalli had to depart quickly for Paris.

As Fouilloux later summarized: "A note by Tardini dated October 14, 1944, confirmed that Pius XII, although displeased over the hostility toward Bishop Valeri, quickly resigned himself to the withdrawal. The Vatican was satisfied with supporting its position by confirming the irregularity of the situation and the unavailability of substitutes."[8] Vinatier was probably correct in stating that although the Vatican had given in to de Gaulle's demands, the pope realized France needed a sincere Catholic committed to work for national peace. "Please do whatever is possible to safeguard the rights of the Holy See regarding the bishops in question. On the other hand, however, do all you can to maintain the best rapport with General de Gaulle," the pope enjoined Roncalli.[9]

Valeri's letter of reassignment arrived on November 29. On December 4 during a farewell audience, Valeri received the Great Cross of the Legion of Honor from de Gaulle himself, veiling the actual reasons for his departure. So the "compromised" nuncio returned home decorated with the highest of honors bestowed by the interim government.

Pius XII's Choice

The pope's first choice for the new nuncio to France was the papal delegate in Argentina, Bishop Giuseppe Fietta. When Fietta refused for reasons of health, Pope Pacelli immediately turned to Roncalli. According to what Tardini told Ambassador Hubert Guérin, the pope chose Roncalli because of "his experience and his big heart." These qualities would make him "particularly suited to deal effectively with the French authorities regarding present and future problems, especially those related to the bishops."[10]

Authors such as Roquette and Alberigo assume less plausible interpretations. They suggest that the pope specifically chose Roncalli in response to de Gaulle's affront to the Holy See. Rather than choosing a high profile candidate, the pope nominated a little-known, secondary diplomatic figure to that prestigious post.[11] (In fact, until his nomination as nuncio, Roncalli was not even a member of the diplomatic corps.) This hypothesis suggests that Pius XII was being irresponsible. Whatever the reason, the fact remains: Valeri's successor was not chosen "from among second class nuncios...nor even from the internuncios, but from among the papal delegates." Hence France's nunciature seemed to be "downgraded to second class."[12] Aside from the various immediate reactions, however, the French government's approval for the new appointment arrived on December 19. On December 12, 1944, Roncalli informed the French diplomat in Ankara, Mr. Jacques Tarbé de Saint Hardouin, who sent this comment to Paris: "Even if I have mild reservations regarding his impartiality, I must pay homage to his pleasant character, his undeniable willpower, and his good outlook toward France. He is straightforward and prudent."[13] The new nuncio was probably found from among the few men of the Holy See whose reputation could be bared to the victorious Allies. After all, not many diplomats during the war had labored so much for the Jewish people or for the Germans against Hitler. During the war, Roncalli had also been especially cautious about the political situation in France. While he had maintained good relations with Pétain's representatives, he had also established relations with de Gaulle's representative, Gérard Jouve, in November 1942, before the fall of Stalingrad. Asking his complete discretion, Roncalli spoke to Jouve of his admiration for de Gaulle and added that the Vatican had its own "de Gaulle," in the person of Cardinal Tisserant, who received the nickname from Curia personnel.[14]

Leaving other conjectures aside, what is clear is that Pius XII personally chose Roncalli and sent him as his representative to the country once called "the eldest daughter of the Church." Roncalli's diary and several letters document this. When the newly appointed nuncio stopped in Rome on his way from Ankara to Paris, Pius XII told him in a brief audience: "First, I really want to tell you: about this appointment to Paris, you are not indebted to anyone. I myself thought, prayed, and decided. So be assured that God's will for you could not be more clear and encouraging."[15] In a letter to his sisters on December 29, 1944, Roncalli wrote: "[The pope] told me that my appointment to this important post is due only to himself personally."[16] In another letter to Giovanni Rossi, Roncalli said of his new role: "It was completely a personal idea of the Holy Father."[17]

Farewell to Turkey

On December 23, Roncalli addressed the clergy gathered for the farewell banquet at his residence in Istanbul. Paolo Kirejian, the Armenian Catholic archbishop, and Dionigi Varouchas, the Greek Catholic bishop, were there for the occasion.

Roncalli took the train for Ankara at the Haydar-Pasa station, where many other important clergymen and laity were waiting for him. "The thought of what awaits me," he noted in his diary, "does not diminish the sacrifice of what I am leaving behind, something I will always carry in my heart."[18]

An entry in his diary reveals a personal desire that he had set aside for the sake of prudence: "Before leaving Turkey, I would have been happy to greet the head of state, Inönü. I realized this might seem pretentious, and I do not like that — discretion and humility until the end. To know how to wait is the best way to win."[19] Roncalli spent his last Christmas in Turkey greeting the different religious and civil authorities and the diplomats from various countries. On December 27, he boarded an old airplane with four Turks and an American journalist and flew to Cairo via Beirut. While in Egypt, he stayed with the apostolic delegate in Zamalek, and the next day he flew on to Rome, via Benghazi and Naples. Upon arriving in Rome at 3:00 P.M., he headed straight for the Vatican.

> At the Vatican I found Tardini waiting for me, and he told me that the only one who thought of appointing me was the pope himself, trusting in the *vigor lenitatis* [the strength of gentleness]. I had a few words with Montini. I feel sorry seeing these faithful and astute servants of the Holy See so busy, as if they were condemned to hard labor. About the situation in France, I can get very little information. The Lord will help me.[20]

Roncalli was in the Vatican again on December 29, for an audience with Pius XII. "The Holy Father received me and confirmed what Tardini had said. He was the one who thought of my poor name and who wanted me in Paris. He believes that with my temperament I will accomplish more than those who are more forceful. He added such encouraging words and instructions that my weary heart felt renewed."[21] Later he spoke with Valeri who provided him with "some valuable practical information."[22] After visiting the Congregation for the Oriental Churches where he met Bishop Arata and Cardinal Tisserant, he paid a visit to Cardinal Rossi. That evening he had dinner at the French embassy with Guérin.

The First Days in Paris

Roncalli finally left for Paris on December 30 and after a four hour flight, took a taxi to the nunciature at 10 Wilson Avenue where he was welcomed by the auditor, Alfredo Pacini, and the secretary, Carmine Rocco. That same evening he went "with Bishop Pacini to the Quai d'Orsay for his first visit to Mr. Bidault, the Minister of Foreign Affairs, who was extremely courteous."[23] The next evening, Roncalli met with Cardinal Suhard, the archbishop of Paris, to whom Montini had sent a letter of introduction.[24] Roncalli noted: "He welcomed me warmly and left an excellent impression on me."[25] According to the bishop's auxil-

iary, Jean Vinatier, this was the first of forty-five encounters (not counting the telephone calls!) that Roncalli would have with Suhard in four
and a half years — too many for a relationship described as "stormy."

When January 1, 1945 arrived — the date for the first public appearance of the new nuncio — Roncalli presented his credentials to de Gaulle
at the Elysium; then he conveyed formal greetings for the New Year from
the diplomatic corp. He confessed in his diary that he only read the
"simple, plain, innocuous" text his predecessor had prepared in Rome.

> Mister President.... Thanks to your political foresight and your en-
> ergy, this beloved country has effectively recovered its freedom and
> faith in its destiny. We have no doubt that the coming year will wit-
> ness new progress and advances. France is reclaiming its traditional
> physiognomy and the place it deserves among the nations. With
> your enthusiasm for work, your love for freedom, your spiritual
> magnetism...you will show us the path that — in the unity of hearts
> and in justice — will lead our society to tranquil times and lasting
> peace.[26]

In substance, these words resemble those de Gaulle used a few hours
later in his New Year's radio message to the French people. A deeper
analysis of Roncalli's words reveals a full recognition of the interim
government, while hinting at expectations for a just *normalization.*

At Roncalli's side was the Russian ambassador, Alexander Bogomilov, who would have delivered the greetings if Roncalli had not arrived.... The nuncio greeted Bogomilov at that first encounter that
would be followed by many more formal meetings. As the senior member of the diplomatic corps, Roncalli had occasion to meet Churchill,
Eisenhower, Pandit Nehru, and other great figures of twentieth-century
history.[27]

That same day Roncalli met the Turkish ambassador, Numan
Menemencioglu, who commended him for his work there. He later commented to George Bidault: "You will see why the pope came to Turkey
to search for a new nuncio for Paris. Bishop Roncalli lived among us for
ten years and we did everything we could to thwart him, but we never
succeeded. Not only that; after following his actions closely, we had to
admit that he is a prelate who understands us and is worthy of our esteem and appreciation, which we always tried to show him."[28] According to Peter Hebblethwaite, "Roncalli's first public appearance in France
was a miniature triumph. He calmed de Gaulle and showed consideration for the Russian ambassador."[29] The New Year inaugural speech

would become a regular event in Roncalli's diplomatic career, and something he would take great pains to prepare.

Roncalli's mission in France was primarily diplomatic, but carried out with great pastoral sensitivity. As nuncio, he had to deal with the French government, which maintained a clear separation of Church and State. Conscious of his episcopal office, however, he insisted that the State should guarantee Catholics their legal rights. On January 6, 1945, the feast of Epiphany, Roncalli sent his first letter to the French bishops, which, generally speaking, was welcomed by all, especially by those bishops who stood accused of being "collaborators" of the previous government. The letter made it clear that Roncalli was ready to work with them without reservation.

On January 21, Roncalli celebrated Mass for a large congregation at St. Joseph des Carmes, the church of the Catholic Institute, and added a few words to Don Louis Bouyer's homily.[30] At the end of the month he wrote to his friend Don Fortunato Benzoni: "I already feel part of a family, as if my previous poor life, including my twenty years in the East, were only a preparation for this mission." He wrote to Montini: "I believe I started off well."[31]

The "temptation to preach" and "the temptation to travel" were constantly with him. On February 20, 1945, he wrote to Don Giovanni Birolini, pastor of his home parish: "I have also started to preach here and there, continuing the practice I began in Istanbul. The people here like it, though I cannot match Bossuet or Massillon. They consider my speaking in French a sign of great respect and affection, and they readily forgive the lack of precision and the uncertainty in expressing myself. As long as Christ is preached, we can be satisfied."[32]

He also wrote his relatives his first letter from France. With his usual reassuring tones he mentioned something about the situation: "In Paris I sleep better than in Istanbul. A little sleep is enough for me, but that little is quite peaceful. There are important issues to deal with; the good of the Catholic Church in France depends on them. I do my best...."[33] A month later, he wrote to Cardinal Alfredo Ildefonso Schuster: "These first three months of my work in Paris have been good. I work the best I can, with a peaceful heart." But he also mentioned that he felt like he was "walking on burning coals."[34] What were these "burning coals"?

Searching his *Journal of a Soul* for that period, there is no clear answer. He made his first retreat in France at the Benedictines in Solesmes during Holy Week, from March 26 to April 2, under the direction of Abbot Germain Cozien. In the entries of that retreat, he still considered the events of the previous months. "What has happened in my poor life these past three months continues to amaze and confound me.... I went from Istanbul to Paris.... Here I overcame — successfully, I believe — the initial difficulties. Once again the *oboedientia et pax* has brought its blessing...." He wrote of the cardinal virtue of prudence: "This is the characteristic virtue of the diplomat. I should cultivate it with particular care." And he also wrote of the passing of time: "This is the season of maturity: I should then do more and better, especially considering the possibility that the time still given me to live is brief...."[35]

Although the facts in his "spiritual diary" are rather vague, Roncalli's daily agenda is more specific. His entry for April 11, 1945 reads: "May the Lord sustain me until the end of this confrontation, which has been caused only by the government's fear of the extremist parties. Certain that I stand on solid ground, I also tremble for these poor bishops I want to save."

Replacement of Bishops

One of the burning issues Roncalli had to face surfaced in his first meeting with French Foreign Minister Georges Bidault. The question of the bishops believed to be "collaborators" in Pétain's regime came up immediately. Extensive negotiations took place with de Gaulle's government, first with the Ministry of Internal Affairs and later with the Ministry of Foreign Affairs. The testimony of André Latreille,[36] the liaison for religous groups for the Ministry of Internal Affairs (July 1944 to August 1945), gives us useful information in this matter. A list of the accused prelates had been prepared as early as July 26, 1944. The twenty-five names it contained included Cardinals Suhard (Paris), Gerlier (Lyons), and Liénart (Lille); Bishops Beaussart (auxiliary of Paris), Courbe (the Director of Catholic Action), Maurice Feltin (Bordeaux), Marmottin (Reims), Delay (Marseilles), and Caillot (Grenoble). The government prepared another list with the names of bishops they believed worthy of elevation to the rank of archbishop and the names of more than twenty priests considered by them to be suitable "bishop-material."

Once heated feelings had cooled by January 1945, the list of bishops was reduced to twelve names. Although de Gaulle would have been satisfied with replacing four to five prelates, Bidault was more demanding and pressed Latreille to hold fast to their demands. But Latreille had to face the objections of the Holy See, which Roncalli firmly upheld. Rome asked for clear evidence of the bishops' involvement in the past events in question and reaffirmed its position that the nomination of bishops is the exclusive prerogative of the Holy See.

Latreille's account of his first meeting with Roncalli on February 17, 1945 is quite interesting:

> Very cordial and welcoming, a lively conversationalist, good-natured, stout, talkative.... He expressed his desire to be well informed. He tells me the way the Vatican is likely to interpret the events: that the bishops have committed no fault, and though they might have made some mistakes, they have become the victims of a handful of angry people. It is hard to express clearly....
>
> I explained to him not so much the attitude of the government as that of the Catholics in the Resistance Movement. The bishops bore a heavy responsibility. The silence of the majority and the statements made by some gave the impression that they had failed to apply the principles and policies of the Holy See to the present time. It truly caused a serious conflict of conscience for the French, especially for those who had worked in the Resistance. Today, there is a natural reaction, which is not as hostile to the Church. However, it cannot be ignored without exposing the Church to serious internal divisions, a revival of anti-clericalism, and a disdainful indifference on the part of the people.
>
> I made myself understood. The nuncio agreed that the public peace must be safeguarded and that *odium plebis* [being hated by the people] could be an argument against the offending prelates. He said, however, that it is necessary to specify exactly what we want and we must produce documentation...and not expect the new nuncio to be the Torquemada of the French bishops.[37]

Latreille's statement agrees exactly with the deposition of another political leader, Léon Noël, who testified in the investigation for Roncalli's beatification. He says that Roncalli responded repeatedly to the French government's demands that the Holy See had no reason to reproach the bishops. He persistently requested specific documentation, which was never delivered.[38]

The crisis ended at the end of July 1945, as seven prelates were discreetly "dismissed" without a public statement. Actually, they were leaving because of health-related issues or because they had resigned. The prelates involved were Archbishop Dubois de la Villerabel (Aix-en-Provence); Bishops Dutoit (Arras), Auvity (Mende), and Beaussart (auxiliary of Paris, later chosen by Roncalli as his confessor); and Apostolic Vicars Vielle (Rabat), Pissan (Saint-Pierre-et-Miquelon), and Grimaud (Dakar).

Who was the ultimate victor in the conflict? The historian Alberigo finds the question difficult to answer because of the complex roles played by Roncalli, the French government, the French Ambassador to the Holy See, Jacques Maritain, and the Holy See itself. Official documentation reveals that Maritain, the philosopher and ambassador, was instrumental in resolving the issue. Chosen for the position of ambassador because he was a Catholic and a supporter of de Gaulle, Maritain had been in direct contact with Bishops Tardini and Montini, and acted as intermediary with de Gaulle and Bidault. He had firsthand information on the viewpoints of some bishops and many priests, which included a confidential statement written by De Lubac.[39]

On the other hand, Roncalli had frequent meetings with members of the French government, from de Gaulle and Bidault to Latreille and Paleski, etc. In addition, Roncalli's personal notes and his reports to Tardini confirm the key role he played in settling the matter. Excerpts from his diary show Roncalli's determined efforts at working toward a resolution.

April 11, 1945: In the afternoon, a meeting with Minister Bidault at the Quai d'Orsay about the question of the unwelcome bishops. More than an hour of biting remarks. I was able to speak calmly and precisely, while he was excited and disorganized.

April 18, 1945: Not a file or a list from the Ministry of Foreign Affairs.

April 27, 1945: In the afternoon, Prof. Latreille.... I still linger over the question concerning the bishops.

May 1, 1945: Meeting with Mr. Paleski, the closest person to President de Gaulle, regarding the matter of the unwelcome bishops.

May 11, 1945: I went to Paleski, at President de Gaulle's. At last, I saw the blacklist. I believe I succeeded in excluding Bishop Feltin. Many important things said. Then I saw His Eminence Cardinal Suhard and, as soon as I was back in my office, I worked all night to prepare the report for the Vatican.

May 13, 1945: In Notre-Dame at 11:00 A.M....for a great disappointment. Threatening voices of the Communists. De Gaulle did not show up.

May 14, 1945: Sorrow in my heart because I cannot accomplish everything.

May 15, 1945: My visit to Minister of Information Teitge. A good man, upright and eager. I will have helpful new contacts. He keeps returning to the same theme: to reach out to the people, to put aside outdated ways, to be understanding and compassionate — the only way to prevent the environment from being contaminated and destroyed by communism."

May 18, 1945: In the evening, dinner at President de Gaulle's residence. I was with Pacini. Good conversation, calm regarding the bishops and other matters. Always cordial and well intentioned.

June 12, 1945: In the afternoon, I went to the Ministry of Foreign Affairs with S. Hardouin, to petition for the definitive elimination of the list.

June 19, 1945: Concern over my speech in Lyons caused some painful anxiety. More serious in talking with Beaussart, and then with all the bishops and the cardinals attending the meeting, whom I wanted to update regarding the question of the unwelcome bishops.

July 9, 1945: Hard work to prepare the note about the unwelcome bishops. Efforts to achieve objectivity and moderation require time and reflection.

July 20, 1945: At home. I reviewed the question of the unwelcome bishops after the resignation of Bishop Dutoit.

July 21, 1945: Among other visits...Prof. Latreille and Compte François De la Noe about the resignation of the bishops. This fussing over Beaussard is a bit annoying — reveals some pettiness.

July 22, 1945: The news about Bishop Dutoit's resignation comforts me, because it represents the end of a long suffering. But the form of suffering will change now. Yet, the situation is getting better day by day.[40]

A solution was being worked out. The ministry reports indirectly acknowledge the nuncio's victory: "Because of the nunciature's strong opposition, the number had been reduced." Again: "If the nuncio seems satisfied with his success, he cannot ignore the agitation and disappointment among Catholics."[41]

Years later, Roncalli made this entry in his diary: "No greater honor for the nuncio than having avoided or greatly reduced the 'purging' of the bishops" (May 10, 1948). And he wrote to Suhard regarding the same: "What a grace, what a motive for most humble gratitude! This sentiment stayed with me all day. My interior joy could not have received a better confirmation than to have Feltin nominated as new archbishop of Paris. His name had been one of the five remaining in the black book. I remember telling de Gaulle I would put my name and my nuncio's zucchetto over Feltin's name; de Gaulle replied: 'Well, we will let it go for the sake of the nuncio.' From that to having Feltin made an archbishop is the greatest of graces, one that increases humility and patience" (August 10, 1949).

Promotions and Episcopal Nominations

The struggle with the French government did not only concern the substitution of bishops, but also new appointments to the cardinalate and the episcopate. The government, virtually beaten in the first round, pursued a more unyielding strategy in the second.

The choice of three new cardinals — Bishops Petit de Julleville (Rouen), Rocques (Rennes), and Saliège (archbishop of Toulouse) — met the full agreement of the Holy See, the nunciature, and the government. In a diary entry for October 8, 1945 Roncalli wrote: "In the morning, visit to the Vatican for an audience with the Holy Father, whom I found healthy, confident, fatherly. He asked my opinion regarding the cardinals to nominate in France. I indicated Rocques and Petit de Julleville." Roncalli had reservations regarding Saliège because of his poor health. Two and a half months later, on Christmas Eve, Roncalli noted: "The news of last night is confirmed. The pope announced thirty-two cardinals, among which are Saliège, Rocques, and Petit de Julleville. I was not expecting the first one because of his health, but I am happy about it. Everyone is pleased."[42]

Instead, the new episcopal nominations did not prove satisfying to everyone. The entry for October 8, 1945 in Roncalli's diary states that Pius XII was satisfied with "the resolution of the bishops' question" and the "nominations in progress." On March 31, 1946, Roncalli wrote to

Bishop Calavassy: "Then the nominations of about ten bishops arrived.... The government was perfectly satisfied. This gives the nuncio a reason for peace and satisfaction."[43] However, the reports of some government officials contradict Roncalli's assessment. The general comments about the new bishops from the Quai d'Orsay were negative. A report dated November 29, 1945 reads: "The recent nominations of bishops and coadjutors submitted to the government reflect the nunciature's concern to choose candidates whose mediocrity is a guarantee of their total obedience to the Holy See." Another report delivered a similar statement: "In 1945, mediocre personalities were appointed as bishops and coadjutors, and it seems as if the Holy See has refused to give the miter to those clerics who showed their valor in the Resistance."[44]

Indeed, the Holy See did not select its bishops according to Bidault's criteria of "outstanding behavior during the Resistance." The French embassy applied pressure to the Holy See, going so far as to propose that the Holy See begin *ad limina* visits "in order to put the problem of the episcopal nominations in the right perspective, and to compare the false and illusory impressions from the insufficient and biased documentation reaching the pope through his representative in Paris and through some French bishops, as well as through some lay visitors."[45] Fouilloux fixes the end of the crisis sometime in the spring of 1947 under the following agreement: "The nuncio will express his proposals to the councilor of the Quai d'Orsay who, within ten days, will present the names to the government and meanwhile provide his suggestions to the nuncio; then the Quai d'Orsay will inform the nuncio of the government's judgment regarding his proposals. The private nature of the negotiations avoids any diplomatic incident."[46] This Roncalli did as his diary attests: "I went to the Quai d'Orsay where I spoke with Chauvel and showed him the list of the four new bishops *sub secreto* [under secret]."[47]

For Roncalli, the real problem was finding "good and holy bishops, dedicated completely to the sanctification of souls, beyond any political concern." That was his desire and the pope's; it was consistent with how Roncalli interpreted his role as nuncio in particular and his pastoral ministry in general.[48]

Roncalli was clearly an *out-of-the-ordinary* diplomat. "I leave to everyone else the surplus of cunning and so-called diplomatic skills, while I am satisfied with my good nature and simplicity of feeling, word, and manner. The end result always favors those who are faithful to the teaching and the examples of the Lord."[49]

The Nuncio's Travels

Roncalli's pastoral spirit became even more evident in his many trips throughout France, primarily between 1946 and 1949. He visited the various dioceses, cities, and towns, shrines, sanctuaries, abbeys, and convents. He could be seen at exhibits of sacred art, cultural centers, and popular centers of devotion, from Lisieux to Lourdes, from Paray-le-Monial to Solesmes. His frequent contacts with religious congregations in France showed his concern and respect for their works. Little by little he came to know all of Catholic France. He attended Eucharistic and Marian Congresses, social weeks, and celebrations of religious anniversaries. He was adept in taking advantage of every opportunity to defend wonderfully the Church's freedom as an indispensable condition for carrying out its mission. He was present at cultural events, such as the week for Catholic writers at the Catholic Institute, the inauguration of the academic year at the Sorbonne, and conferences at the French Academy. Roncalli liked to browse through the shops along the Seine, always searching for books, his most frequent "distraction." Among his friends in Paris, he counted simple, unknown people as well as famous intellectuals. Roncalli's letters are filled with warmth and affection when describing events and persons. "We must get to know one another better. The nuncio must be the heart, the eye, and the helping hand of the pope. He should approach people without prejudice, speak without allusions, converse without arrogance."

As nuncio, Roncalli met people of every social, professional, and ideological sphere: writers, artists, politicians, workers, farmers, etc. He celebrated solemn liturgies in the ancient cathedrals that had witnessed great achievements; he visited the French Academy and went into the streets of Paris to meet the poor and the homeless.

> His was...diplomacy in the open air, a continuous pastoral visit lasting eight years. He would go from a Lenten homily to a charity benefit, from a nursing home to a convent for an investiture ceremony, from a Pontifical Mass to the blessing of a ship. After baptizing the child of a prince he would go down into a coal mine.... He would attend official banquets among socialist ministers and fashionable women, and then applaud the performance of an orphanage's little theater.... He would visit museums.... His was a diplomacy on the road.[50]

His pastoral excursions gave him great spiritual satisfaction in their "abundant contact" with the "uncountable crowd"[51] of faithful from the eighty-seven French dioceses. They also became the cause of great sorrow. The French government did not appreciate his frequent trips,[52] nor did the pontiff. In Roncalli's way of reasoning, any and all the honors he received in France were always directed to the pope: "Direct contact with people will make the pope and the Holy See, which I represent, better loved. This is the mission of good Vatican diplomacy, of a good servant of Peter."[53]

Pius XII did not seem to share this point of view. Perhaps he was influenced by those who spoke about the nuncio's "absenteeism," but he called Roncalli to Rome. During a private audience, the pope expressed his displeasure with Roncalli's unconventional diplomatic style. Roncalli wrote in his diary: "I accepted everything with serenity and humility, grateful to God that he humbles me this way, and that he humbles me so little. I gave some respectful explanations, but without insisting on my own defense."[54] Years later, Capovilla would hear John XXIII recount the explanation he had given to Pius XII.

> Your Holiness, your confrere Monsignor Francesco Marmaggi told me: "Roncalli, now they are sending you on a papal mission. Do not wear out your elbows on your desk; they are not going to read everything you write in Rome anyway! Remember that above all you should be the eye of the pope that sees, the ear that listens, the word that speaks, the heart that blesses. You have to act in a way that will honor the pope." Your Holiness, I am doing my best to hold to this fundamental standard. Moved by these words, Pius XII replied: "I know, Monsignor. I read it in your reports."[55]

A few months later as Roncalli re-examined the incident he wrote: "Mine is a unique situation. To go out on pastoral visits pleases the bishops, priests, and lay people; they invite me. The service I give to the Holy Father in this way is evident; but His Holiness does not prefer it this way. I would rather shed my blood and abandon everything than offend the Holy Father."[56]

The deposition given at Roncalli's beatification process by Paolo Marella echoes Roncalli's difficult position: "The first thing my superiors told me [as successor to Roncalli] was to remain in the nunciature as much as possible. I must say, however, that the French bishops did not like this approach, so the same superiors told me to accept the invitations. I believe it is necessary to state that, in France, the presence of the nuncio also required the presence of the civil authority. In conclusion, Roncalli was right in his way of thinking."[57]

Not only did Roncalli have his own ideas about Vatican diplomacy, which differed from those of his colleagues and collaborators,[58] but he also wanted direct knowledge of his host country and to grow to love it. A journal entry at the end of 1947 reveals some of Roncalli's deeper sentiments.

> I am finishing my third year as a nuncio…. My prolonged stay in France gives me reason to admire this country and grow in my sincere affection for these *nobilissimam Gallorum Gentem* [noble French people]. However, in my conscience I feel a contrast, which at times is a source of scruples. On the one hand, I too like to praise these valiant French Catholics, while on the other, I feel I cannot ignore their deficiencies and simply pay compliments for fear of displeasing them. In fact, the real state of the "eldest daughter of the Church" reveals several problems I am concerned about: the unsolved question of the schools, the lack of priests, the spread of secularization and communism. On these issues, my duty clearly is a matter of form and measure. Otherwise, the nuncio is no longer worthy of being considered the ear and the eye of the Holy See if he only praises and extols what is really painful and serious.[59]

Actions on Behalf of Prisoners of War

Post-war France had many open wounds and Roncalli exercised many works of mercy. According to Höfer, the German Director of Catholic Aid, Roncalli's concern for the German prisoners of war went beyond his duty as papal nuncio.[60] In conformity with the Vatican and the French episcopacy, he continually intervened for the prisoners of war who, by 1947, numbered over 260,000. He pressed for the liberation and improved treatment of prisoners, some of whom were seminarians and professors. Thanks to the help of Don Franz Stock — who knocked at the nunciature's door many times — it was possible to organize theology courses within the prison camps. The "mini-seminary" was established near Chartres and opened in September 1945. Roncalli visited it several times; often accompanied by Monsignor Harscouët, cofounder of Le Meur Abbey, and military and religious authorities. After the long ceremonies of Holy Saturday, Roncalli wrote to his relatives:

> Yesterday I went to Chartres…to a camp for German prisoners where more than 500 young seminarians are being held. During the Mass, I ordained two of them. What a moving sight! Now it seems they will be allowed to return to their country; this is what I have

worked for. So you see what beautiful occasions I have here to do good and to extend the Holy Father's charity, which reaches out to everyone.[61]

Roncalli also worked for the repatriation of the French and Italian soldiers, cooperating with the Committee for War Prisoners and the Italian ambassador to France, Giuseppe Saragat. "Mr. Saragat presents himself well and lets us hope for the best. By reading his articles and interviews, I noticed he has exceptional capabilities, but his theories are definitely socialistic. However, he is proud of his devout wife and his children who are enrolled in the French Catholic Action." Later, Roncalli described him as "a very interesting and friendly socialist, with whom it is easy to find points of agreement."[62]

The issue of the prisoners of war distressed Roncalli so greatly that he referred to it in his official and private letters and in the pages of his personal diary. On September 18, 1945 he wrote: "Today, along with Bishop Vagnozzi and Abbot Rodhain, I visited the prison camp in Chartres and was warmly welcomed by the French officers and by the 15,000 Germans. What a sorrowful effect, all this slavery. The conditions of forty undernourished, walking skeletons broke my heart!" On February 22, 1946 he wrote: "With Bishop Vagnozzi and Abbot Rodhain I visited some German prisoners at a camp near Noisy, and then some Austrian prisoners who will soon be leaving. A good reception from the French officers. But why don't they let them go free?"

In these pages of his diary, often written *currenti calamo* (with a rapid pen) at night, Roncalli mentions meetings with Abbot Stock. On May 16, 1946 he noted: "I received the warmest welcome at the seminary for the German prisoners, meeting with all the seminarians who presented a beautiful program of songs and readings. Abbot Franz Stock spoke in French and Latin." April 19, 1947: "Audiences: Abbot Stock, from the seminary of the prisoners in Chartres, and Ferretti. One tells me that support for de Gaulle is growing, the other that the prisoners' release is still delayed. The prevailing spirit does not understand the Gospel precept, 'Do unto others, etc.' This lack of understanding is threatening to ruin France, which has so many reasons to survive." This same issue comes up again in 1948: "Visit to prisoners in Douai...a mixture of touching yet sad impressions. I said and did whatever I could." The following is underlined: "The prolonged presence of these prisoners in France is unjust and sorrowful. I left Libercourt with a heavy heart."[63]

According to Denise Aimé-Azam,[64] Roncalli's efforts to free the prisoners were supported by Bishop Rhodain, Abbot Desgranges, and Abbot Le Meur of Catholic Relief. Roncalli's efforts were supported by his awareness that the future would bring about a reconciliation of France and Germany — an insight not inspired by political suppositions. For Roncalli the goal of reconciliation was its transcendent, supernatural value; it was the only goal of his so-called *political actions*. And it has always been very difficult to apply any well-defined political labels to Roncalli — especially when considering his encounters without barriers or connections with either left or right. Naturally, the nuncio had to take an interest in the political situation in France and in the different policies of candidates, particularly when these related to the tasks assigned him by the pope. Nonetheless, Roncalli's public and private behavior was transparent and punctuated by a sense of discipline. No political party, no paper, or periodical, not even the Catholic journal *La Croix,* could claim to have been pressured by the nunciature in any way.[65]

When the Popular Republican Movement (the anticommunist party formed in the spring of 1946) won the national election, Roncalli wrote in his diary: *"Dies albo signanda lapillo* [This is a favorable day.] In yesterday's referendum good sense triumphed and this encouraged the people not to be afraid, but to continue to march forward against communism. For this I praise and thank the Lord. My holy Masses devoted to this intention were useful, then." A few months later, just before another election, he remarked: "Today the elections are the most important thing. Naturally, the bishops play a major part, perhaps too much. The other side feels disappointment and worry."[66] Roncalli later noted in his daily agenda: "It is painful to see the passion that 'ecclesiastics' put into business they should not be interested in. This explains certain serious mistakes and miseries in French history." And finally: "Total absenteeism of the nuncio; about the ecclesiastical candidates — the Holy See opposes them in theory, but in practice it allows the bishops to judge individual cases. The nuncio does not desire disputes among Catholics, but the unity of all on the fundamental points such as schools, freedom, etc."[67]

The Debate over Free Schools

During the entire time Roncalli was in France, an intense debate was underway regarding *les écoles libres* or the Catholic schools that received insufficient state funds. The nuncio discreetly intervened in order to maintain "peaceful relations between the Church and the State," which was "the principal goal of the nunciature."[68] Roncalli's diary reveals his thoughts on the matter.

> **May 18, 1945:** The question of the school is not going well. To be satisfied one would only have to think of the former conditions under the Vichy regime. Between two forms of protest, aggressive and moderate, I prefer the second.

On March 23, 1944, he addressed the issue with some "evening visitors":

> Count Vladimir D'Ormesson and the former senator, Count De Blais (Blosius), who interests me because of the education question. This is a serious matter; one that reveals the wounds of France, and of teachers educated to atheism.

By the end of the year, the dispute had grown stronger:

> Distressing observations about the danger of battles and persecutions against the free schools. This is the dreadful problem of tomorrow and the day after tomorrow. May the Lord help us and protect the freedom of his children.[69]

The endless debate ended, though not definitively, in the summer of 1951, when the government adopted laws that provided funding for private schools. Roncalli postponed his vacation, indicating: "To stay here is my duty. Even the offering of my good will and prayers supports the cause of the free schools."[70] A few days later, on September 6, it appears the issue was finally resolved: "In the meantime, fairly good news from the Parliament. There will be no winners and no losers, but the cause for scholastic freedom and State aid for poor schools is gained. We have to be satisfied with little and to proceed gradually as best we can, never forgetting that we belong to the Church militant, not the Church triumphant."[71]

That day Roncalli informed the bishop of Bergamo who was awaiting his arrival:

> These good people are debating a central issue, the most important among the concerns of the Church in France. How could I leave before seeing it resolved? Now I believe it is settled. Until last night, we were only one step away from a crisis. Just imagine what trouble. In a democratic environment, what counts is the vote: the half plus one is enough. Finding these votes guarantees success for a good cause.[72]

September 7, 1951: A busy day, especially in preparing the third report for the debate in Parliament over the free schools. At midnight, I heard on the radio the news of the favorable vote for the Barangè plan. *Laus Deo* [Praise God]. Now I can leave.

Two weeks later when he was finally on vacation in the quiet of Sotto il Monte, he wrote: "At midnight it was announced over the radio that the long-debated school question in France ended today with the success of the Berangè proposal. *Deo gratias* [thanks be to God]."[73]

Worker Priests

Roncalli faced another serious question in the movement of the "worker priests"; as nuncio he had to communicate his concerns to the Holy See. Denise Aimè-Azam writes: "I do not believe I am mistaken in affirming that at the basis of this were some discreet warnings given to Rome, and even if he detached himself personally, he did not detach himself from the substance of the matter."[74]

Much has been written about the movement that began at the end of 1943 with the Paris Mission, when many priests worked side by side with factory workers. The movement, pride of the Church in France, was also a source of tension and contradiction. For some time the media focused on the new frontiers the movement could open, but beyond the significance of priests in the workplace, it posed many problems. Among them was the relationship between particular experiences *in partibus infidelium* (among infidels) and those of the entire Church in class-related issues in the world of labor.[75]

What were Roncalli's thoughts on this new pastoral experiment? We can summarize them by saying that in the beginning he held a moderate view. After meeting with the superior of the Paris Mission, Jacques Hollande, he wrote: "Twelve priests became bona fide workers in order to enter the workers' environment; I admire, encourage, and bless them."[76] In 1953, however, he supported Rome's directives when the Vatican halted the experiment. "The 'worker priests' appear more than ever to be in contrast with the priestly spirit. Now the Holy See is providing the necessary rules. I do not believe they will be able to conform."[77] It was up to Marella, Roncalli's successor, to implement the directives, and Roncalli supported the nuncio's outlook: "The worker priests are sources of scandal. The young cleric is in danger. If this continues, it will be harmful for the Church. The communist influence on the worker priests is clearly manifested."[78]

On February 23, 1954 Roncalli wrote to Morella:

Your Excellency,

Enclosed is some paperwork that Your Excellency will need to deal with as soon as possible, I suppose with the help of the consulate. I assure you of my vigorous and affectionate support for that bit of anxiety in your heart during these weeks of turmoil, and of my spiritual solidarity regarding the matter of the worker priests. I say "that bit of anxiety" because I too know the background — outside of any reaction from the nunciature — of what is now happening, which in my times was only an experiment. It is very easy to assign blame for what happened. How many similar events took place in France in modern times! There is no Consalvi, or Caprara, or Lambruschini, or Ferrata to prevent them. The apostolic nuncio is like the figure of St. John the Evangelist on the tapestries of the Apocalypse at Angers: he is present, he is a witness, and, when the time comes, he writes, informs, and executes. The real tragedy is that the lessons of the past are not considered. The storm will pass and the truth will find its way; everybody will take responsibility for his part. It will be known then that the nuncio was — among other things — a gentleman, intelligent, good-hearted, and honest, as he always has been and still is. But after a short time, at the first occasion, the bad habit will begin again, and the Holy See and its representatives will renew its patience, goodness, and maternal care — correcting, bearing with, warning, and then entrusting all to Providence: *Nihil sub sole novum* [There is nothing new under the sun]. I beg your pardon, Your Excellency, if, finding myself with pen in hand, I wrote more than I had intended. I want to reassure you that I understand and offer you my solidarity, affection, and prayer....

Yours,
Angelo Giuseppe Cardinal Roncalli[79]

For the future John XXIII, the dispute over the worker priests was not only a matter of avoiding Marxist influence. "Between Karl Marx and Jesus Christ, an agreement is impossible" (Diary, October 28, 1947). Nor was it simply a matter of following a decree (July 1949) from the Holy Office reiterating the penalty of excommunication for communist Catholics.[80] As the 1937 encyclical *Divini Redemptoris* stated: "Communism is intrinsically evil, and no collaboration with it can be allowed." Roncalli viewed this issue as a more traditional or conservative interpretation of the priesthood.

In his study of Roncalli's sermons, Maurilio Guasco suggests: "Those who may want to confront one of the most disturbing texts on the problem of priests in the world of the workers and the de-Christianized — i.e., *Itinéraire de Henri Perrin, prêtre-ouvrier* [Paris 1958] — with the various writings concerning Roncalli's priesthood, will discover quite a different approach and very different problems."[81] Roncalli was a son of his own culture, his own life-journey, and his own spiritual character, summarized in his episcopal motto: obedience and peace.

This also helps to explain his relationship with Cardinal Suhard, with whom Roncalli did not agree on the issue of the worker priests. However, he still appreciated Suhard's famous pastoral letters *(Essor ou déclin de l'Eglise?,* 1947; *Le sens de Dieu,* 1948; *Le prêtre dans la cité,* 1949) and shared his missionary concern.[82]

Perhaps this explains Roncalli's approach to the *nouvelle théologie* which attempted to harmonize theology and science through dialogue with the modern world, and his reaction to Pius XII's sanctions in *Humani Generis* (1950) on the false opinions threatening the foundations of Catholic doctrine. Roncalli's support of the pope and his attention to "purity of doctrine" can also be gleaned from his diary: "Professor Lenz Medoc also repeats some French and German lamentations over the encyclical *Humani Generis.* What ridiculous boldness those little boys of science have, who still have milk in their mouths yet allow themselves to judge without any criteria or method."[83]

Reading his agenda, one finds very interesting, brief notes about famous people of the time from Gide to Abbot Pierre, from de Gaulle to Massignon, etc. His daily notes are an echo of important historical events, such as the "shameful end inflicted on Mussolini and Clare Petacci by the Partisans — the so-called patriots"; or "the imprisonment of Cardinal Mindszenty, primate of Hungary." *Journal of a Soul* instead offers abundant information on the nuncio's thoughts and actions.

Personal Holiness in Public Life

The surest way to my personal sanctification and successful service to the Holy See is the constant effort to reduce everything — principles, objectives, position, business — to the utmost simplicity and tranquillity; to always prune my vineyard of useless leaves and tendrils and concentrate on truth, justice, and charity, but above all charity. Every other way of acting is pretension and a search for personal affirmation, which soon reveals itself as absurd and burdensome. Oh, the simplicity of the Gospel, of the *Imitation of Christ,* of *The Little Flowers of St. Francis,* of the most exquisite passages from St. Gregory in the *Moralia: deridetur iusti simplicitas* [the simplicity of the just is mocked] and what follows. How I enjoy these pages more and more, and how often I go back to them with interior pleasure! All the wise men of this world, all the wily ones of the earth, even Vatican diplomats...make such a bad impression when seen in the light of the simplicity and grace emanating from this great and fundamental teaching of Jesus and his saints!

He continues in his retreat notes from November 23–27, 1948:

My character is inclined toward compliance and to readily seeing the good side of people and things rather than to criticize and judge harshly. This, along with the considerable age difference — which gives me more experience and a deeper insight into the human heart — often cause me interior distress because of those around me. Any type of ill treatment or distrust shown toward anyone, but especially toward the humble, the poor, the lowly; every harsh and thoughtless judgment causes me pain and great suffering. I remain quiet, but my heart bleeds. My colleagues are good ecclesiastics; I appreciate their excellent qualities; I am very fond of them and they deserve every good. But I suffer much in relation to them. On some days and in some circumstances I am tempted to react strongly. But I prefer silence, believing it to be a more eloquent and effective instruction. Could this be a weakness of mine? I must, I want to keep bearing the weight of this light cross in peace, together with the already mortifying sense of my littleness....[84]

I must have great understanding and respect for the French people. My prolonged stay among them helps me appreciate their fine spiritual qualities and the fervor of Catholics of every type, but at the same time, it has enabled me to see their flaws and excesses. So I must be very careful when I speak. I am free to form a judgment, but I must guard against any criticism, trivial or pleasant, which might offend them. Oh! Do not say or do to others what you do not want to be said or done to you....

Continuing with this entry during his retreat on Holy Saturday 1952 he wrote: "See to the most important work more quickly, especially in what concerns the bishops' nominations, relations with the Holy See, and important and timely information. Do not hurry, but avoid delay. I will make this particular point the object of my daily exam."[85]

A few days earlier, he had written a passage entitled, *"Defections among the young clerics,"* in another notebook where he remarked: "Perhaps it is a matter of tens or even of hundreds. This clearly shows a flaw in the seminaries; they fail to apply the sound principles of ecclesiastical discipline. I am going to begin an investigation which I foresee will be very painful and surprising in regard to the Church in France."[86]

This period of Roncalli's career raised questions. Was he a diplomat or pastor? Was he the representative of the Holy See or one of the leaders of the Church in France? The records kept in the archives of the Quai d'Orsay do not mention Roncalli very often. In 1951, D'Ormesson, Maritain's successor, wrote: "The nunciature does not inform the Vatican secretary of state about the life of the Church in France as well as it should. Thus, Feltin sensed that Tardini was somewhat irritated with Roncalli."[87] The evaluations from the audiences between Tardini and the pope were often positive. His diary confirms this:

> **October 3, 1947:** I went to the Vatican. Tardini welcomed me into his home with great familiarity and mutual satisfaction, about one and a half-hours of pleasant conversation on important matters.
>
> **September 13, 1949:** Tardini, for an hour and a half. All is clear. He only wants me to write more substantial reports. This I will do.
>
> **September 16, 1949:** At Castelgandolfo. Day of joy and gratitude. The Holy Father spoke with me for a long time, more than three-quarters of an hour, on serious questions, and always in a very amiable way. I could not desire anything better. No reproof, great unity in everything, and much encouragement. His health, though, seemed a little weak. *Dominus conservet eum* [May the Lord preserve him].
>
> **October 12, 1951:** The Holy Father, always very amiable, treated me with great confidentiality, more like a brother to me than a father.

Surely, and especially in the Vatican, it was impossible to deny Roncalli's respect for the human person, cultures, and civilizations, and at the same time his adherence to the teachings of Christ. It was on these principles that he based his *diplomatic approach* to peace, a theme he reiterated in official speeches and personal conversations regardless of the Cold War atmosphere. On various occasions he spoke of the need to establish agreements that would build peace and justice in the world. He also spoke at UNESCO, an institution in which he said he had great faith, and that nominated him a Vatican observer on June 4, 1952. He spoke of peace in the French dioceses and in Algiers, where in March 1950 he opened up his heart "to the multitude of Arabs and the countless African people of different races and languages," to the "sons of Israel," "in the mutual spirit of human brotherhood."[88]

Roncalli wrote to his relatives and friends about his memorable trip to French Africa, which was made more sensitive by the increasing violence of national liberation movements and the consequent French repression. He considered the trip to be "a true triumph of many people's devotion to the Holy Father and the Church." It was a significant experience: "Paris, Ars, Lyons, Valencia, Marseilles, then across the sea to Algiers, Tunis, Constantine, Algiers again, then Oran.... From March 19 to April 10, a succession of incomparable displays of religious devotion. Then, April 10...in a private capacity to Morocco...an earthly paradise in spring. There I visited all the Islamic holy cities, the places were the Moors once kept Christians as slaves: Fez, Marrakech, Merkez, Casablanca, Rabat, etc.; then Tangiers, Tetouan, Ceuta. From there to Gibraltar and Spain...and then, the French border...."[89]

Meanwhile, unknown to Roncalli, his time in France was nearing its conclusion. On November 10, 1952, Substitute Secretary of State Montini sent Roncalli a confidential letter[90] on behalf of the pope, asking if he could be available to succeed the patriarch of Venice, Carlo Agostini, who was quite ill. They did not have to wait long for his reply.

> I received your confidential letter of the tenth of this month. I took enough time to confide in the Lord and reflect on it, but I did not need much time. In what Your Excellency proposes to me there is really nothing of my own will. So I repeat my episcopal motto, the one of Caesar Baronius, the well-loved disciple of St. Philip Neri who every day would kiss the foot of St. Peter and say: *"Oboedientia et pax."* The Holy Father may use me with perfect freedom of spirit. May Your Excellency be pleased to assure His Holiness that I have little regard for myself; for me everything is more than I deserve. Having renounced my personal preferences for so long makes everything easier and more serene for me, and it assures me of great peace. With all my heart I wish that the Lord might heal the Patriarch of Venice and give him a long life. But if I happen to succeed him, may the Lord make me worthy of meriting the ancient praise of St. Mark, disciple and interpreter of Peter.[91]

Roncalli read of Cardinal Agostini's death in the Italian journal, *Le Figaro,* of December 29. His own life was about to take a new turn.[92] In the afternoon of the last day of the year, Roncalli delivered the customary New Year's speech to President Vincent Auriol at the Elysium. That evening, while Paris celebrated New Year's Eve, Roncalli prayed at the sanctuary of the Sacred Heart in Montmartre. Then, seated at his desk, he continued to reflect on what the new month and the new consistory would bring.

"The humble papal nuncio will be satisfied to simply have a few rooms of the Elysium, in the presence of very few people. But the honor granted him on that occasion will remain one of his fondest memories of France..." he told Cardinal Pierre Gerlier. "May Your Eminence remember me on January 15 when I will be granted the same honor in a beautiful hall at the Elysium. Since the cardinalate is neither a sacrament nor a sacramental, I will leave with a position similar to yours. The Holy Father is always the one who acts. The nuncio or the president of the Republic are only delegated by him," so he wrote to Cardinal Jules-Gérard Saliège. And he reminded Cardinal Achille Liénart, "Becoming a cardinal is not a sacrament, perhaps not even a sacramental; however, it involves holy and formidable responsibilities, which require special graces that only prayer can obtain."[93]

Departure from Paris

On January 2, 1953, Pius XII announced in his second and last secret consistory the elevation of Cardinal Roncalli to the Patriarchal See of Venice. Another twenty-four cardinals (ten Italians among them) were created. Three days later President Vincent Auriol of the French Republic exercised the privilege traditionally allowed to some Heads of State: he presented Roncalli with the red biretta in the pope's name. In his words of thanks, the new cardinal said: "It will be enough for me if all the French, in remembering my humble name and my stay among you, could say: he was always a faithful priest, tranquil, a trustworthy and sincere friend of France in all circumstances."[94] President Auriol bestowed the medal of the Legion of Honor on Roncalli and gave a short speech. In his biography, Hebblethwaite highlights a key sentence in the president's speech. Auriol stated that Roncalli's experiences "allowed you to appreciate French action in the world and predisposed you, for a long time, to understand the great traditions of tolerance and justice which have always been the honor of our nation, and which should unite, after the solemn exhortation of Leo XIII, all the French spiritual families around the Republic."[95]

Roncalli's thoughts were now turned to the city of the Laguna and his staff in Venice. On February 3, Don Loris Capovilla arrived at the nunciature in Paris together with Macacek, the chief Vicar of Venice. Roncalli first met Capovilla in April 1950 during his visit to Venice for the second anniversary of the death of Pietro Manug Mechitar, founder of the Mechitarists. The new patriarch of Venice asked Capovilla if he would be available to join his staff. Capovilla accepted. He would accompany Roncalli until his death.

Then the farewell meetings began. On February 5, a farewell dinner was held at the nunciature and Roncalli met the French Prime Minister René Mayer and his predecessors of the past eight years. In Montreuil he greeted the Italian mission and the Redemptorists of Rue Montparnasse. On February 19, General Georges Vanier, Canadian ambassador and senior member of the diplomatic corps, offered Roncalli the gift of the cardinal's robes on behalf of himself and his fifty-nine colleagues. On February 20, President Auriol met the nuncio for a final visit.

Roncalli was still in Paris when he began signing his papers with the title of Patriarch of Venice. In a letter to Donna Cecilia Costova, O.S.B., he wrote: "Only a word while I am leaving France to arrive in Venice by March 15. It says it all: salutations, blessings, and an invitation to pray for me. Angelo Giuseppe Cardinal Roncalli, Patriarch of Venice."[96]

He also wrote to De Gasperi expressing his approval:

A cordial and reverent greeting while I am leaving for Venice. I am planning to visit you when I return to Rome to receive the cardinal's hat. This simple touch right before your ceremony at taking the oath of office is enough by now to tell you all the faithfulness of my spirit: respect, admiration, sharing of concerns, invocation of heavenly graces for you and for all you represent for the Holy Church and our beloved country in its internal order and international relations. May the Lord help us in the service he asks each of us.[97]

When the time came to leave Paris, Roncalli wrote these words in his diary: "Final departure from France. Awoke at 4:30 after a good night.

Sorrow in leaving, but delight in union with God, peace of mind and *goodness, which has become love.* Mass at 6:00. Farewell at 7:30, silent, moved, even some tears here and there.... I bless the Lord and give him thanks *pro universis beneficiis suis* [for all his goodness toward me]."[98]

PART III

PASTORAL MINISTRY
1953–1963

Goffredo Zanchi

CHAPTER 13

PATRIARCH OF VENICE
1953–1958

Appointment and Arrival

The exact reasons for Roncalli's appointment to the Patriarchal See of Venice cannot be known. Whether a change of nuncios was the chief concern or whether it was the assurance of a swift succession is uncertain, but Monsignor Montini's letter indicated that the pope desired not to leave the See of Venice vacant for too long.[1] Roncalli's advancing age and easygoing temperament suggest that the choice was intended as a means to reestablish a more relaxed atmosphere in the diocese after the very rigid government of Archbishop Carlo Agostini (1949–1952). Roncalli seemed aware of this when, writing to Bishop Bernareggi of Bergamo on February 11, 1953, he hinted that some malicious voices in Venice had described him as the long-awaited "calm after the storm." Roncalli quickly added, "This will be tested," as if to say that his more placid style did not signify inactivity.[2]

In any case, the proposal was not so disagreeable to Roncalli. He had always given precedence to whatever was pastoral, even when carrying out assignments that were essentially diplomatic. True, he was no longer young, but he still felt enough energy to do something useful for souls, especially since the prestigious See he had been called to serve was not excessively large and would therefore be manageable. In 1953, the See of Venice comprised 360,000 persons, 94 parishes, 241 diocesan priests, 301 religious, and about 30 seminarians.[3] This was a rather pleasant homecoming to what constituted the heart of his priestly vocation from the start. Soon after his installation he wrote:

> It is interesting that Providence has brought me back to where my priestly vocation took its first steps — that is, to pastoral service. Now I find myself in full, direct ministry to souls. Truthfully, I have always held that for an ecclesiastic, diplomacy — properly so called — should be permeated with a pastoral spirit; otherwise, a holy mission counts for nothing and borders on the ridiculous. Now I am confronted by the true interests of people and of the Church, according to her purpose, which is to save souls — to guide them to heaven.[4]

On November 29, two weeks after Roncalli's appointment, news arrived that in a few days he would be raised to the cardinalate, a worthy crowning achievement for a diplomatic career that had brought him to the prestigious nunciature of Paris. A telegram of congratulations from Monsignor Montini also arrived.[5] Word of this elevation did not stun Roncalli; he was content not to boast or exalt himself; rather, he sought to abandon himself to the will of the Lord with trust. Nor did he have much time to celebrate his prestigious appointment, because after the death of Archbishop Agostini on December 28, 1952, Pius XII insisted that he go to Venice as soon as possible.

Roncalli's arrival in Venice was set for Sunday, March 15. Leaving Paris on February 23, he reached Rome by train two days later. He had numerous meetings with members of the Vatican dicasteries and the secretary of state, and took the oath at the Quirinal in the hands of President Luigi Einaudi. From Friday, March 6, until Sunday, March 8, he spent three days in Bergamo, where civil and religious authorities royally welcomed him.

The trip to Venice was punctuated with carefully chosen stops of historical interest and significance for his personal devotions. From March 10 to 14, he spent some days of retreat in the Benedictine Abbey of Praglia whose abbot, Aurelio Mutti, would later become the patriarch of Venice. On March 14, Roncalli arrived in Padua as the guest of Bishop Bortignon. The next morning he celebrated Mass in the cathedral at the altar of Blessed Gregorio Barbarigo (1626–1697), a great Venetian bishop he particularly admired — second only to St. Charles — and whom he himself would canonize.

The next afternoon he traveled on to Venice where he was taken by motorboat to St. Mark's Square in the midst of a cortege of gondoliers and crowds, who greeted their new patriarch from the shore and the bridges.

In the basilica he gave his first official discourse, presenting himself as a man, as a priest, and finally, as a shepherd. With a warm and friendly tone, he revealed himself to the Venetians as a fellow human being who did not intend to hide anything or keep secrets. The charming recollections of his humble origins and his rich accumulation of experiences showed how eager he was to communicate and to establish a trusting, fraternal relationship with his faithful. He exhorted his listeners to look only for the priest in him and to expect from him only the good that pertained to his ministry. In the third part of his discourse, dedicated to the pastoral style with which he wanted to exercise his ministry, he continued to present the strong, spiritual characteristics of his mission. Calling to mind the sublime model of Christ, as treated in John 10, his speech seemed to be an anticipation of those he would give after becoming pope: "Therefore, do not look at your patriarch as a politician, as a diplomat; look for the priest, the shepherd of souls, who exercises his office among you in the name of the Lord."[6]

The Beginnings of the Venetian Ministry

Roncalli's commitment to be wholly a shepherd is confirmed in notes jotted down during the spiritual exercises he made in the villa of the Fietta Seminary (May 15–21). It also showed itself in his direct encounters with a variety of the faithful.[7] Here the sincerity of his agreeable and communicative temperament was fully manifested. His character contributed immediately and decisively to the creation of an atmosphere of trust and understanding.

Two days after his arrival, he visited the sick in the city hospital. On May 27, he met with the workers of Porto Marghera. He made plans to personally administer the Sacrament of Confirmation in the parishes during May and June. He wanted to keep in direct contact with his priests, to remember their personal anniversaries, to be informed of their situations and sometimes invite them to dine with him at the patriarchate. Particular attention was given to the various lay associations, especially to groups of Catholic Action and to the ACLI.

He familiarized himself with the city by visiting institutions, churches, and the sick. Accompanied by his new secretary, Loris Capovilla,

Roncalli often walked here and there through the small squares of the city and took the public steamer instead of using a personal motorboat. Gondoliers, restaurant owners, and shopkeepers all began to know and greet him, and he willingly stopped for spontaneous conversation.

Contrary to the practice of many bishops of the time, Roncalli loved to give habitually short homilies while presiding at liturgical celebrations in St. Mark's Basilica.

At the solemn afternoon Vespers of his first Easter in Venice, while visiting the Nicopeia (an ancient icon regarded as the protectress of the city), he was involved in an episode that he would later remember with great emotion. According to the testimony of Monsignor Capovilla:

> At the conclusion of the celebrations on Easter Sunday…after the singing of evening Vespers and Eucharistic benediction, the patriarch did not expect anything to follow the Divine Praises. Instead, the choir of seminarians began to sing the litany with the charming rhythm of patriarchine modulation…. The patriarch turned to the assistant on his left, Canon Francesco Silvestrini, and gestured to ask: "What is this?" The old priest answered, "Your Eminence, they are going to the altar of the Nicopeia to rejoice with the Lady Mother, because her Son is risen!" This pious custom, followed by the faithful with such fervor, moved him to the point of tears.[8]

On April 24, he published his first pastoral letter in which he expressed a desire to be in continual contact with his children through brief and frequent letters. Thus, he linked himself to the example of his noted predecessor, Cardinal Pietro La Fontaine (1915–1935). The approaching feast of St. Mark led him to reflect on the holy protector whose image could not remain merely an object of historical remembrance. It had to be an inspiration so that his teaching and example would be applied to modern times.[9] The new patriarch introduced the concept of tradition as an important source of pastoral planning. This strict connection between history and pastoral choices constituted a prominent component of the roncallian personality. Revisiting the past in light of the present, he found the basis for many of the decisions he would make during his Venetian episcopate and later during his pontificate. If the influence of history is clearly perceptible in Roncalli's pastoral style, it is likewise evident that the historical research he had carried out was in turn conditioned by his pastoral passion. For this reason, most of his studies have contributed to pastoral history.

In his letter of April 24, the main texts of Mark the Evangelist were connected to the Gospel message and to Mark's fidelity to Peter as his interpreter and disciple (cf. 1 Pet 5:13). The Venetians were encouraged to deepen their understanding of Gospel teaching and to develop a more felt devotion to the Church and to the pope.[10] Special attention was also given to Pius X, who had been one of Roncalli's predecessors in Venice (1894–1903). His memory would punctuate Roncalli's whole Venetian period, starting with his opening discourse on March 15 and the moving recollection of his personal meeting with the pope in St. Peter's Basilica as a young priest after his first Mass.[11] The anniversaries and the canonization of Pope Sarto in 1954 were occasions for numerous initiatives and pilgrimages, such as the climbing of Mount Grappa on August 4, 1953, the fiftieth anniversary of Giuseppe Sarto's election to the papacy. In the pastoral letter of the bishops of Triveneto in July of 1953, Roncalli expressed his sincere admiration for this illustrious predecessor — his sanctity, his work in reforming the Church, and his battle against modernism.[12]

Roncalli's particular ecumenical sensitivity showed itself at the first Octave of Prayer for Christian Unity in January 1954. In the years that followed, the patriarch conferred great importance on the Octave with a special letter that called both clergy and faithful to work together for the diffusion of Christian thought and brotherhood. Liturgical and cultural functions were scheduled, as well as conferences. At least three such occasions were led by the patriarch himself.[13]

The innovations of the first months, springing chiefly from Roncalli's character, which was more communicative and affable than that of his predecessor, did not break the substantial continuity of government. For many reasons, he had determined to continue the more significant initiatives of his predecessors, even as a sign of deference. Thus, he decided to begin his pastoral visitations exactly where Archbishop Agostini had left off. He inaugurated the Catholic University of Pius X at the former Church of St. Basso and had the construction of the minor seminary at Fietta completed. Regarding the latter, he would eventually change his mind because of the strong disadvantage of having a seminary outside the diocese. Instead, he would bring the seminary back to Venice and place it in the renovated area that was near the Church of Our Lady of Health.

During his first year as patriarch, Roncalli completed the selection of his closest collaborators. As soon as he had arrived in Venice, he wrote a letter to Cardinal Piazza asking for an auxiliary. Within two months his request was granted in the person of Bishop Gianfranceschi.[14] Cardinal Roncalli was somewhat surprised by this appointment since the man chosen was not among those he had proposed. Nevertheless, he declared in his response to Cardinal Piazza that he was content to apply a principle from the *Imitation of Christ* that he had always found beneficial: "To do the will of another rather than my own."[15]

While the relations between Roncalli and his auxiliary were always proper, they were not always easy because of differences in temperament.

Bishop Gianfranceschi was assigned the office of pro-vicar, while the elderly Monsignor Ermino Macacek was reconfirmed as vicar general and Monsignor Vecchi continued his position as rector of the seminary. Don Gino Spavento, who had served Archbishop Agostini as secretary, continued to exercise that office until October when he was named rector of the minor seminary at Fietta. Only Don Loris Capovilla remained as secretary. Roncalli had invited him to join the "family" at their first meeting on February 3 in the Paris nunciature. (Capovilla had accompanied Vicar General Macacek in a visit to the new patriarch.)[16]

After Monsignor Gianfranceschi was named bishop of Cesena at the beginning of 1957, it became possible to restructure the higher positions in the diocese in a way that was perhaps more agreeable to the patriarch's desires. A new auxiliary was chosen, Joseph Olivotti, who was also given the position of vicar general. Monsignor Alessandro Gottardi was chosen as pro-vicar, with effective authority in the diocesan curia. The elderly Monsignor Macacek remained vicar general emeritus and delegate for religious.

Concerning organizational matters, the patriarch indicated two particular sufferings in the notes he wrote during the spiritual exercises at the end of May 1953. The first was due to a poverty that was described as "somewhat humiliating and embarrassing," because the episcopal meals were so meager. The second was a direct consequence — the inability to provide for the multitude of poor and to grant requests for help in various needs. Since Roncalli did not lack the strict necessities, however, he was disposed to accept discomforts with serenity, even if they did not contribute to a fruitful ministry.[17]

A Tridentine Tradition Updated

After the "novitiate" of the first year, Roncalli enlivened his pastoral work by carrying out the typical tasks of a bishop, including pastoral visits. There was no need for him to undergo a long training. As he often declared, he had always lived his diplomatic experience with a pastoral attitude, even when the two aspects were not directly united, as at Constantinople where he had guided a small Catholic community. The patriarch had been strongly influenced by his historical studies, which had familiarized him with two exceptional figures of the Tridentine reform: St. Charles Borromeo and St. Gregory Barbarigo. To those great men could be attributed the restructuring of the Lombardo-Venetian Church in the modern age. The effects of their activities and influence were still visible in the twentieth-century bishops of the region who were committed to inserting the Church into a society in the midst of profound transformation. For almost ten years as a young priest, Roncalli had been close to the great Radini Tedeschi. He had profoundly assimilated his thought and he related this in his moving biography.[18] Radini Tedeschi's outlook became Roncalli's standard, yet he also allowed his personality and many experiences to color his updating of Trent.

If he inherited Radini Tedeschi's ability to see beyond the immediate and embrace larger perspectives, Roncalli insisted that he was not sufficiently predisposed for planning detailed programs, nor did he have the iron control so indispensable for their accomplishment. Roncalli's way of implementing initiatives was not so much to follow pre-established guidelines, but "the spontaneity of natural development." Thus, he valued all useful opportunities and those people with the strength and willingness to pursue the appointed goal. He trusted his collaborators and normally gave them commendable amount of liberty in their work, which led some people to feel he absented himself from an effective government of the diocese. The concession to greater freedom of action for those working under Roncalli complemented his personal understanding and benevolent character that burned with a desire to be a shepherd and father. This did not at all signify an absence of resoluteness in decisive moments or an abdication of his responsibilities.[19]

Roncalli established his episcopate on the foundations of being shepherd and father, and with a reaffirmation of his total dedication to his most friendly style.

I do not desire, I do not think of anything else but to live and to die for the souls that have been entrusted to me…. For the few years that remain of my life, *I want to be a holy shepherd* in the full meaning of the word, like my predecessor, Blessed Pius X, like the Venerable Cardinal Ferrari, like my bishop, Radini Tedeschi…. But I will continue on my own road and with my own temperament. Humility, simplicity, adherence to the Gospel in word and works, with courage, meekness, impregnable patience, paternal and insatiable zeal for the good of souls.[20]

All of his actions unfolded in an atmosphere of wholesome and balanced optimism, which was the fruit of his historical wisdom and great faith in Providence. In the pastoral letter of Lent 1955, he declared himself the enemy of a nostalgic return to the past. He preferred "the time that *is* to the time that *was,*" and characterized those who so easily yielded to pessimism as "timid and incompetent" people who doubted their Redeemer's help.[21]

Roncalli's pastoral vision may explain the clash between him and one of the most influential personalities of the immediate postwar period: the Jesuit priest, Riccardo Lombardi (1908–1979), founder of the movement, "For a Better World." The ideas of this zealous Jesuit included a reform program encompassing the highest and lowest levels of Church membership and would call for new forms of apostolate. Lombardi's ideas were widely diffused throughout Italy. His promoters worked tirelessly, speaking at crowded meetings in public squares and, above all, the well-attended formative courses for diocesan religious priests, bishops, and laity in the city of Mondragone, near Rome — the center of the movement. Because Pope Pius XII had personally approved Don Lombardi's ideas and methods, the Italian bishops took legitimate interest in the initiative, "For a Better World," and sent their priests to the formative courses.

Before Roncalli's appointment, the coldness of the bishops of Triveneto toward Lombardi's initiative had reached the ears of Pius XII. Informed by Monsignor Dell'Acqua of the pope's displeasure, Roncalli thought it appropriate to invite Don Lombardi to be the retreat master at the annual spiritual exercises of the Venetian bishops held at Torreglia Alta.

Lombardi accepted and somewhat imprudently made use of the occasion to outline the plan of his movement, which only resulted in disturbing his listeners even further. Roncalli continued to show deference for Lombardi and went to him for confession that same day. He hoped to use the opportunity to hint at the preacher's excesses, but the patriarch found himself confronted with statements and judgments about the present times that did not correspond to his own sensibilities. He wrote: "Regarding appreciation for the historical order and of a one-sided view of today's world...a single form of perception and expression; he is perhaps too simplistic in his thought, too pessimistic and aggressive in tone."

Roncalli's honesty, however, enabled him to appreciate the preacher's enthusiasm and religious zeal. Since Lombardi's program enjoyed the pope's approval, Roncalli proposed a renewal of pastoral commitment: "I sincerely admire him and I want to make an effort to turn my energies and those of others to this movement of conquest."

The passionate preacher had convinced Roncalli to make a serious examination of conscience on his more calm and accommodating pastoral style.

> But I agonize over the thought of not being able to see everything, and further, of not achieving everything, of the temptation to indulge my easy-going temperament, which makes me prefer living quietly to risking myself in uncertain positions. Doesn't Cardinal Gusmini's principle: "One does not issue an episcopal decree unless it is sure to be followed," make it easy to fear that reactions will stir up more trouble than solutions to the evils we are trying to correct?[22]

It could be said that this encounter compelled Roncalli to make a serious discernment regarding his own pastoral style. He did not doubt the efficacy of his "watchful, patient, and long-suffering goodness" that "achieves more results with more speed than harshness and the whip," but he may have questioned his reluctance to intervene more often and authoritatively.

Subsequent contacts with Lombardi only reaffirmed for Roncalli the goodness of his own choices. In October, he invited Lombardi to return to Venice for an extraordinary series of conferences at St. Mark's. As they shared a meal at the patriarchate, Roncalli commented on Lombardi's opinion of the Church as decadent, of the clergy and bishops as lacking commitment, and on the necessity of a radical reform imposed by a reformer pope. Don Lombardi reacted vehemently to Roncalli's observations, and the unpleasant incident was smoothed over only by Roncalli's patience and humility.

A more complete and conclusive opinion about the Jesuit's work may be seen in a letter drafted by Roncalli in the name of the bishops of

Triveneto and mailed to Monsignor Dell'Acqua on November 6, 1955. Roncalli's uncertainties were directed toward "For a Better World," inasmuch as Lombardi demanded that his project be exclusive and that it transcend the competence of already existing bodies in various sectors of Church life. In fact, Lombardi wanted "For a Better World" to be directly under the pope, and to have the power to direct the whole life of the Church. This would result in a new order that was contrary to the canonical legislation in force and would distort the structure of the government of the Church. Roncalli's letter was delivered to the pope who expressed his appreciation and found the observations useful.[23]

The diverse views of Roncalli and Lombardi persisted over the years — until the pontificate of John XXIII. While the desire for reform was mutual, Roncalli preferred to speak of it as "updating," and their ways of going about it were different. Lombardi believed that intervention from the top was needed in order to shake up an incompetent episcopate. Roncalli, having a greater awareness of the value of tradition, believed that an authentic reform could not avoid a proper recognition of authority and involve the decisive participation of the bishops who possessed legitimate apostolic authority. His defense of the dignity and role of the bishops, clearly derived from Trent, was one of the principal points of conflict.

Roncalli's appreciation of the role of the episcopacy is revealed in a letter to Lombardi. In it, Roncalli excuses his absence from the inauguration of the international center of "For a Better World," with the reason that he was engaged in the pastoral visit to the parish of St. Cancian in Venice. In a position to have to choose, Roncalli gave priority to the fulfillment of his duties as bishop: "There is nothing else to consider. In the hierarchy of the bishop's duties this has held priority from when the Council of Trent imposed this very solemn and meaningful act."[24] His episcopal government was clearly indebted to the Tridentine tradition of pastoral visits, synods, particular attention to the priests and seminary, catechesis, popular missions, and veneration of the saints.

The Acts of His Episcopal Ministry

In a short letter to the clergy and faithful dated February 2, 1954, Roncalli announced the opening of his pastoral visits scheduled to begin on February 28 at the Basilica of St. Mark. He would start with the twenty-four parishes that his predecessor had been unable to visit because of illness. With respect to customs, nothing substantially new was announced; the novelty lay in the patriarch's attitude as he prepared to carry out his duty. He wanted to be a shepherd and father, terms that pointed to and defined each other. As a shepherd, he wanted to know, call, and defend his sheep; as a father, he wanted to correct, but above all to encourage and console.[25] These concepts were confirmed at the Basilica of St. Mark in the opening discourse: "Your patriarch will come to you with neither whip nor scourge; he will come with affection, with respect, in a fatherly way to discover what can cause you harm, what is deficient, and especially to recall and comfort you."[26]

These principles found practical verification in the way Roncalli conducted the visit, especially in the tone of the decrees issued for the individual parishes. His visits differed from those of his predecessors. He departed from the former juridical character and precepts in order to assume a more affable and personal tone, which included expressions of satisfaction as well as warm invitations to persevere in doing good and making progress.

It took three years to complete the visits and then, according to an accepted practice, the patriarch called for a diocesan synod. As the thirty-first synod in the religious history of Venice, it was celebrated exactly thirty-one years after the last, held in 1926. Because of its collegial character, Roncalli linked this important moment for the diocesan Church to the process of updating, just as he would do later in the conciliar experience. The parallelism cannot fail to make an impression: "Haven't you heard the word *aggiornamento* [updating] repeated many times? Here is our Church, always young and ready to follow the different changes in the circumstances of life, with the intention of adapting, correcting, improving, and arousing enthusiasm. In summary, this is the nature of the synod: this is its purpose."[27]

After a preparatory meeting with his chief collaborators, the patriarch proceeded to issue the official communication and to constitute four commissions that were entrusted with formulating proposals about the Church's members, teaching authority, worship, and goods. So that every priest could become familiar with the proposed drafts, the commissions' work had to be completed by the end of July. In September, a daylong meeting of priests was held at the vicariate level for group discussions and the presentation of proposals for improving the drafts.

The synod itself was carried out in the Basilica of St. Mark on November 25–27, 1957. Some 510 constitutions were promulgated and Roncalli wrote five discourses, three of which were particularly significant because they concerned the patriarch, the clergy, and the faithful. Together, these outlined his thought and the principles that guided his pastoral activity.

The first discourse constituted one of the richest expressions of Roncalli's concept of the bishop's mission and its concrete exercise. His chief sources were Scripture and the liturgy which, meditated and translated into practice, had intimately shaped his personality from his time as delegate to Turkey.

For Roncalli, the episcopal mission could be summed up in fatherhood under the aspects of total gift, daily renunciation, and service to one's brothers and sisters. The preference for the spiritual over the juridical dimension rested on the mystery of Divine love: the love of the Father who gives the Son, the Church as the family of God's children, and the hierarchy as a sign of the Divine fatherhood.

Through this lens, Roncalli recalled the serious tasks associated with the exercise of his authority and the duty to avoid the dangers of authoritarianism and paternalism. He offered a precise and fitting description of these dangers:

> Authoritarianism truly suffocates life and leads to rigid, exterior discipline, to complicated and bothersome organization. It halts legitimate initiatives; it does not know how to listen; it confuses harshness with firmness, inflexibility with dignity. Paternalism is actually a counterfeit of fatherhood. It keeps people under guardianship to maintain superiority in the exercise of government. One may be generous to someone yet dispense oneself from respecting the rights of subordinates. One speaks with a protective tone and does not accept collaboration.
>
> The exercise of authority must include a correct relationship with people and a respect for their rights. If this is valid as a general principle, it is much more necessary for the Church, instituted by its Founder as a family in which primacy is given to love. For this reason, the bishop should have recourse to the instruments of his power from the perspective of love and only in case of real need. The submission and obedience of the clergy are consequences of participation in the same apostolic mission.

It is striking how little space is given in this discourse to the bishop's rights as compared with the ample treatment of the risks of the degeneration of his authority, bearing witness to Roncalli's unequivocal respect for people and his preference for convincing rather than constraining.

On the solemn occasion of the synod, Roncalli outlined his episcopal style and manifested his feelings with great simplicity and without any pretense. His aim was to create a climate of greater trust and familiarity with his clergy.[28] The statement of his principles made it easier the following day for Roncalli to recall some particularly urgent points of ecclesiastical discipline that he reasonably expected would meet a certain amount of resistance.

Practical suggestions for renewal followed in the discourse to the clergy. The priestly ministry was summarized in terms of the two symbols of missal and chalice. In the period preceding the liturgical reform, the missal contained the yearly cycle of the biblical Mass readings and, therefore, represented the Bible, the deposit of sacred doctrine with which the priest was to nourish the Christian people. The chalice recalled the "second function of the priestly ministry — that is, the ministry of the distribution of grace, for which the priest has been called by the Lord."[29] This theme constituted the dominant motif of Roncalli's Venetian episcopate.

The general plan coming out of the synod corresponded more closely to the pastoral innovations Roncalli desired than did the individual constitutions. These were divided into two books, devoted to persons and to pastoral activity, which were in turn divided into doctrinal and liturgical activity, with direct references to the missal-chalice symbols. In this way, the subdivisions ignored the canon law of that period, which would have called for three books dedicated to general norms, goods, and persons.

The constitutions maintained a generally traditional character with the exception of some more innovative points regarding the laity. The activity of the common faithful was an object of major consideration, and Catholic Action was viewed as an apostolate and witness of faith in the midst of society. Secular institutes that had recently been approved by Pius XII, though not always well accepted, were the subjects of attentive consideration. The juridical-disciplinary character inherited from the traditional synod was not disregarded, but it is evident that an effort had been made to bend it to pastoral requirements. Such efforts would be made with greater success in the Roman synod that John XXIII would celebrate three years later.

The immediate effects of the Venetian synod included a redistribution of the offices of the curia, carried out in great part by the pro-vicar, Monsignor Gottardi. Offices were instituted to deal with the clergy, churches, parish activities, ecclesiastical archives, libraries, the liturgy, and Eucharistic activities. The diocesan office "Amate" was instituted to assist priests who were sick or in need of other help. A new system of city and suburban vicariates was established proportionate to the growing number of parishes to facilitate meetings with the clergy. Traditional assemblies of clergy were replaced by priests' days: a retreat and cultural congress with a teacher from the seminary participating. Behind many of these initiatives was the inspiration of the pro-vicar. Roncalli, according to his style of authority, left his collaborators free to be creative as long as their initiatives were in accord with the good of the diocese.[30]

The city mission (March 20–April 3, 1955) was another event reminiscent of pastoral traditions, though the method had been entirely revised. The patriarch was able to take advantage of his long-standing friendship with Don Giovanni Rossi, founder of *Pro Civitate Christiana,* and entrusted this initiative to him. In the Lenten pastoral letter of that year, the city mission was presented as the summit of the spiritual renewal that the entire Christian people were urged to carry out as a fruit of their adhesion to Christ. It was impossible to remain inert at a time when Roncalli was grappling with the problems and risks facing Christianity and striving to avoid the pitfall of pessimism. He arranged to meet the faithful on March 20 at the Church of the Pietà where they would process to the Basilica of St. Mark. The patriarch led them, carrying a cross. Missionaries, clerics, and the people of Venice followed him.[31]

The year 1956 marked the solemn celebrations for the fifth centenary of the death of St. Lawrence Justinian, first patriarch of Venice. The remembrance of this great figure of the past was joined with a preoccupation to derive stimuli and useful teachings for the present. The celebrations opened with the solemn pontifical liturgy of January 8 celebrated at the Basilica of St. Mark by Cardinal Piazza. Cardinals Lercaro, Siri, and Feltin, Archbishop of Paris, were invited to the diocese. Giovanni Battista Montini, now the Archbishop of Milan, was invited for the closing ceremony. Roncalli treated Montini with particular deference.

In addition to the festive ceremonies, pontifical liturgies, and the *laurentian* pilgrimage when the saint's body was transported to various parts of the city, historical readings were presented. It was at this time that Roncalli began a fruitful relationship with Don Giuseppe De Luca, the famous spiritual historian interested in the study of thirteenth- and fourteenth-century Venetian spirituality. This cultured and learned priest had dampened Roncalli's enthusiasm when the patriarch had mistakenly believed he had discovered a precious, unpublished writing of Justinian, "Commentary on the Davidic Psalms," preserved at the Ambrosian University of Milan.[32] Roncalli intended to publish the complete works of the first patriarch, part of which had been translated into Italian, but in the end nothing came of it. De Luca concluded the *laurentian* celebrations by giving a conference in honor of St. Justinian at the Church of St. George the Great.

The most important initiative of that year was Roncalli's pastoral letter for Lent. The letter's theme, "Scripture and St. Lawrence Justinian," was chosen to remind the faithful of the centrality of the Scriptures and to foster the growth of their appreciation of them. A pastoral project was developing in Roncalli's mind that was certainly avant-garde and nurtured by a twofold consideration. The first was directed to the present and recognized the Christian people's need of a formation drawn directly from the sources of Christian life. The second recalled the faithful to the experience of the Fathers of the Church and authors such as Lawrence Justinian, whose wealth of theological and spiritual thought had grown out of their daily familiarity with the Bible.

In this, Roncalli professed himself a habitual reader of the Scriptures. He affirmed with certainty: "All that immense patristic doctrine takes substance and light chiefly from Sacred Scripture."[33] He intuited that a more widespread understanding of the Bible would produce a general renewal of the Christian life. The remarkable connection established between Sacred Scripture and the Sacrament of the Eucharist, through the binomial "missal-chalice" symbols, anticipated ideas that were to acquire a familiar sound only at Vatican II.

> To teach Sacred Scripture, particularly the Gospel, to the people; to familiarize these children of the Church committed to our care with the sacred Book is like the "alpha" of the activity of a bishop and his priests. The "omega" is represented by the blessed chalice at our daily altars. In the Book, the voice of Christ always resonates in our hearts; in the chalice, the blood of Christ is presented for grace, for atonement, for the well-being of each of us, of the holy Church, and of the world.[34]

Toward the end of the year the exhortation of the pastoral letter was followed by the publication in the diocesan bulletin of "Practical norms for the reading and study of the Holy Book."

Among other initiatives for the *laurentian* year was a new professorship, called the *Laurentianum,* in the school of theology at the seminary; the institution of a library for priests at the seminary (which would actually be little used); and the transfer of the minor seminary near the major seminary at Our Lady of Health.

One project never saw completion. The patriarch wanted to acquire the island of St. George in Alga, then in ruins, where St. Lawrence Justinian had established a community of secular canons and had lived as both local superior and superior general. Roncalli's aim was to construct a college for oriental students and thus to give the island renewed worth by transforming it into a meeting place between the East and West.[35]

In addition to the conclusion of the pastoral visit and the synod, Roncalli issued an "Easter Letter" on Holy Thursday, April 18.[36]

After briefly weighing the initiatives of the preceding year, the patriarch treated some liturgical problems. With displeasure, Roncalli had noticed that in many parishes the Sunday noontime Mass was often celebrated with negligence, coldness, and little fervor. He heartily recommended attention to liturgical song and the involvement of the faithful in order to eliminate the reticence that made too many celebrations cold.

The next section of the letter was dedicated to the erection of churches. Because of the great demographic development, the churches most urgently needed were to be built on the mainland. Although the effort he put forth during his administration permitted the construction of sixteen new parishes and ten rectories, another twenty-eight churches with adjacent parish centers still needed to be built, and some parishes needed furnishings.

Roncalli then began to consider the liturgical functionality of the Basilica of St. Mark. The question he raised in June–July 1955 regarding the marble panels of the *iconostasis* in the basilica became a national issue. As Roncalli noted in 1955, from the day of his arrival in Venice he had seen that the *iconostasis* was a serious obstacle that prevented most of the faithful from viewing the liturgical rites taking place in the sanctuary. This problem had existed from the time of Patriarchs Pyrker (1821–1827) and Monico (1827–1851), when St. Mark's had been chosen as the cathedral church.

Roncalli suggested two possibilities. The more extensive would be to remove the marble panels without eliminating the *iconostasis*. The other consisted in either reducing the size of the marble panels or placing them on small swivels so that they could be rotated. This would allow the faithful in the main basilica to view the liturgical rites at least on the most solemn feasts. The proposal was formulated in such a way that both sides of the question found it agreeable. Supporters of the inviolability of the artwork and the responsible ecclesiastics concerned with liturgical needs and with preventing the church from becoming a kind of museum were pleased. The precise technical proposal, which could be carried out easily, decreased the risk of any alteration to the *iconostasis*.

Despite these assurances, a violent media campaign was initiated by the major daily newspapers and national periodicals against the alleged "surprise attack" launched by the patriarch of Venice. Cultural institutions like the Academy of Fine Arts in Venice, the Venetian Atheneum, and other competent public organizations such as the High Council of Fine Art expressed their negative views. Honorable Scaglia, the undersecretary, suggested the project be postponed until things quieted down. The following year, Roncalli resumed his negotiations by involving the leadership of the Pontifical Commission for Sacred Art in Italy in the persons of Monsignor Giovanni Costantini and Monsignor Giovanni Fallini, whose agreement of the proposed changes he obtained. His last interaction with the Italian authorities began on April 11, 1958, through a letter to the President of the Council, Aldo Moro, whose understanding he sought.

Roncalli's election to the papacy did not allow him to bring the project to completion personally, but it did assist in gaining prompt permission at the beginning of 1959.[37] What he had been denied as the patriarch could not be refused to him as the pope.

Openness to the World

Roncalli's attitude of reaching out to those realities and environments that were traditionally distant or estranged from the Church manifested itself again during the Venetian period. He instinctively narrowed any kind of distance with his ability to initiate contact with anyone. The wealth of sympathy that emanated from his person facilitated the establishment of cordial relationships and, very often, of true friendships which favored the defeat of misunderstanding and extreme prejudice, and created the grounds for a constructive dialogue. This attitude has been authoritatively defined as Roncalli's "diplomacy of the heart." The incredible results he obtained were based on his authentic goodness and dictated by no other motive. Roncalli also showed sincere esteem for the alienated; he was completely willing to listen and to accept whatever portion of truth their arguments contained. He had a great trust in Divine activity at work in the intimacy of the human conscience, which inexorably dissolves differences, modifies the most rigid positions with time, and prepares new opportunities for encounter.

The year after his arrival in Venice, Roncalli had to confront the problem of the "Biennial of Modern Art," an exhibition his predecessors had always condemned. The clergy had been forbidden to attend the exhibition because of the moral quality of the art. For the exhibition of 1954, Cardinal Roncalli renewed the prohibition, but with a more nuanced and less confrontational tone. But by 1956 and 1958, he had made some important changes. On June 18, 1956, the patriarch opened the doors of his official residence for a solemn reception of all the foreign and Italian delegations meeting in Venice to inaugurate the exhibition. Roncalli conversed amiably with his guests and demonstrated an understanding of contemporary themes in art. At the next day's opening ceremony of the exhibition, a member of the curia officially represented the diocese, and his presence was noted with positive results. Although he took some precautions, the patriarch went to visit the display on October 19.[38] Two years later, on July 24, 1958, he visited the exhibit in the company of Professor Apollonio. The advent of abstract art certainly facilitated this development, but there is no doubt that the patriarch's attitude represented a change which showed that the Church was taking a more lively interest in modern art.[39]

Roncalli manifested a similar attitude of greater availability to dialogue concerning motion pictures and the prestigious Venetian Film Festival.[40]

Openness to the Political Left

Patriarch Roncalli's balance, farsightedness, and greatness of soul were manifested during the delicate stage of political life in Italy during the 1950s. Following the 1953 elections, the Christian Democrats initiated attempts to open government activities to the Socialist Party's involvement. The Socialists were at that time detaching themselves from the iron pact, which had bound them to the Communist Party.

Naturally, this could not occur immediately on a national level; preparations and trials were necessary at the level of local administration. The commune and province of Venice became one of the first workshops for this new political stage.

In his solemn discourse at the Basilica of St. Mark on February 11, 1954, on the twenty-fifth anniversary of the signing of the Concordat, the patriarch showed that his extraordinary human sensitivity transcended political ranks. This was one of the many miracles of balance accomplished by the future Pope John. When a topic was controversial, he managed to find a point on which everyone could share. With great tact, he called for mutual understanding and pardon, and acknowledged the historical merits of Mussolini for signing the Lateran Treaty.

> This man whom Providence introduced to the Holy Father, Pius XI, later caused the Italian people great sadness. However, he was human and Christian. Do not challenge at least the title of honor that remains to him in the midst of his great tragedy — that is, his valid and decisive cooperation in the preparation and execution of the Lateran Treaty. Let us entrust this humiliated soul to the mystery of the mercy of the Lord.... My brothers and sisters, I know that you understand what I am trying to say. Let us respect even the pieces of this broken vessel and make use of the teachings it provides for us.[41]

These words received widespread approval, especially in ecclesiastical circles.

Certainly the matter was made more complex by the fact that some of the major proponents resided in Venice. The inspirer behind the cause was Vladimir Dorigo, a young intellectual who had belonged to the leading group of *Giac* in Rome. Upon his return to Venice, Dorigo was entrusted with the direction of *Popolo Veneto,* a weekly regional newspaper of the Venetian Christian Democrats. In this periodical, he set forth views favorable to opening the political scene to the Socialists. This was a minority position in the Catholic world, one that was strongly opposed by Vatican leadership and the Venetian episcopate.

The Triveneto Episcopal Conference, which met in Torreglia from October 18–21, 1955 under Roncalli's presidency, decided to publish an official letter on the subject. Bortignon, Bishop of Padua, and other bishops wanted the letter to be published before the Venetian Christian Democratic Congress, scheduled for November 20. Roncalli, instead, chose to postpone its publication. Thus he was able to discuss the matter with members of the Roman dicasteries and with the bishops who gathered at Pompeii from November 9–11 for an Episcopal Conference. At this meeting, as Roncalli later wrote to Bishop Bortignon on November 10, there was unanimous agreement to oppose openness to the left.[42]

Following the example of Lecaro, Montini, and other prelates, and after a broad consultation with the Venetian episcopate, Roncalli set about drafting a pastoral letter. The letter, dated December 14, was read in all the churches of Venice on December 18. The document was incontestable in its clarity:

> The time has finally come to put an end to this pastime of useless words, of relaxation, of openness, of compromises with persons who are known to be, or openly profess themselves to be, friends of those who are intent on the destruction of the Christian social order and tend with open eyes toward the exaltation and practical realization of other doctrines — who practice and tolerate in a shameless and terrible way the violence and terror for which much blood and many tears of the oppressed afflict the earth.[43]

The strong tone of the letter showed the patriarch's unreserved adherence to the official position of the bishops. The entire document, which Roncalli had rewritten to tone down the uncompromising style of the Venetian bishops, reveals his personal method of imposing prohibitions on the faithful. He strove to keep his intervention within the limits of the necessary precision of doctrine without allowing himself to be dragged into chiefly political polemics. The paternal and concerned tone in his warnings, the absence of language as a form of psychological and moral pressure, and his care to avoid every incitement of militant confrontation manifested Roncalli's willingness to listen. He sincerely regretted that objective conditions did not make other actions possible, and his avoidance of offensive expressions that could generate useless resentment was obvious.[44] Political developments confirm this impression.

At the beginning of January 1956, as a follow-up to complaints concerning the situation in Venice, Cardinal Roncalli received a letter from Cardinal Pizzardo of the Holy Office. Pizzardo requested information about the Dorigo case and Roncalli's opinion of what measures should be taken. The patriarch answered a few days later. He made it clear that *Popolo Veneto,* the periodical in question and the object of Pizzardo's preoccupation, did not belong to the diocese but to the Christian Democrats of Venice, and was therefore independent of Roncalli's authority. He delineated the condition of the Venetian party and indicated that the political group favored collaboration with the Socialists and endeavored to imprint a decidedly reform image on the Catholic party. Finally, he submitted his observation that, following the publication of the letter from the Triveneto episcopate in December, the periodical had not featured any articles by Dorigo. Cardinal Pizzardo, who had no knowledge of the official document Roncalli mentioned, thought it best not to take any steps and was more satisfied with the patriarch's clarifications than with the published declarations of the episcopate.[45]

The situation seemed to be returning to normal until the administrative elections of May 27 approached. Roncalli again had to intervene because there were elements of the Christian Democratic left among the candidates, including Dorigo. In a letter to Pizzardo, Roncalli explained that while he had not vetoed the name, he had made his disapproval known — a decision that was a sign of the patriarch's respect for political autonomy.[46] Roncalli issued two public messages at the beginning of May, one to the clergy and one to the faithful, as reminders of their obligation not to vote for candidates who "represent a complete and decided opposition to Christian teaching...by which is meant especially all who are Communists or belong to that sector of the Socialists who are well qualified to be their accomplices."[47]

The election results were not satisfactory. Both in the province and in the city of Venice, a council was formed of Christian Democrats and Social Democrats who had the external support of the Socialists. The example of the major city was followed in some of the smaller towns of the province.

Once more Roncalli sent an explanation to the Roman authorities. In his letter of July 26 to Cardinal Ottaviani, he presented the new political formula that had arisen out of the need to avoid a situation where no government — or worse, a Socialist-Communist government — would have been formed. The reappointment of two Christian Democrats as mayor and president of the province offered the best guarantee that the city would not yield to the Communists.

> The appointment of the mayor and of the president of the provincial administration, and of the two councils, occurred at the first session on June 9 and 10 respectively. Negotiations were difficult. After repeated meetings with the central committee, it seemed to the provincial secretary and members of Parliament that acceptance of external support from the Socialist Party (which the media had already been preoccupied with) would provide the combination of numbers that the Christian Democrats needed to avoid...the victory of the Socialist candidate, who would have been elected mayor on the fourth ballot with the votes of the Socialist Party, the Communist Party, and

the Social Democratic Party.... In conclusion, this game was provoked, here as elsewhere, by those who wanted to open up to the
left at all costs with the illusion of broadening their political base for
the sake of the elections of 1958. Roberto Tognazzi, the mayor, and
Giovanni Favoretto-Fisca, president of the provincial administration, were reconfirmed in office. They are perfectly balanced and
resolve not to consent to any compromises with the Communist
Party and its satellites.[48]

Still, the fear that a Socialist-Communist council would be elected
was well founded. After the fall of the Christian Democratic council on
September 8, 1958, a council from the left would indeed be elected to
power, although it remained only briefly.[49]

Roncalli's assurances did not weaken the firm opposition to openness of the supreme authority of the Church toward the political left.
Pius XII went to battle on July 22, 1956, during an audience with thousands of Christian Democratic administrators. The pope declared the
impossibility of political collaboration with those who continued to be
enemies of the Church. The discourse was carefully noted by Roncalli,
who relayed the message in a letter to the clergy on August 1.[50] After
such a stand at the highest level of the Vatican, an authoritative declaration became necessary at the local level. This was especially true since
Amintore Fanfani, the national secretary of the Christian Democrats,
had decided to intervene against the party's left wing. On August 9, the
Vatican learned that the controversial Dorigo had quit his post as director of *Popolo Veneto*.[51]

In agreement with the bishops of Triveneto and, as it were, to forestall
any possible direct intervention from the Vatican, Roncalli published a
letter to his "beloved sons of the clergy and the laity." The August 12 letter
stated that openness to the left was unequivocally condemned as a grave
doctrinal error and a clear violation of Catholic discipline.

It is an error to...be in league with an ideology, Marxism, which is
a denial of Christianity and whose applications cannot mesh with
the premises of the Gospel of Christ.... The violation of discipline
consists in placing oneself in direct and explicit opposition to the
living and active Church, as if in this serious matter the Church did
not have the authority and competence to guard against approaches
and compromises that have been judged dangerous.
Either we are with the Church and follow her directives and
merit the name Catholic, or we prefer to follow our own ideas —

promoting and favoring divisions — and have to take the responsibility. Then the name Catholic is no longer appropriate.[52]

The present circumstances were not the only motivating factor. The
patriarch was truly convinced of the impossibility of collaborating with
Marxism because of the great disparity between Catholic and Marxist
philosophical and political principles. Furthermore, he was determined
that ecclesial discipline should be observed and not ruptured; dissent
was termed non-Catholic. From his words, Roncalli's preoccupation can
be detected. The Catholic world would expose itself to grave danger in
the case of a rupture at this very delicate moment. His personal judgment of the Council of Venice might have been more hopeful than what
he expressed to Rome, but he respected the decisions of his superiors,
which were certainly well motivated, and promptly aligned himself ac-
cordingly. The Italian Socialists continued their close connection with
the Communist party that committed terrible acts of repression wherever it had gained power.[53] This would be confirmed a few months later
with the dramatic suppression of the Hungarian revolt by Soviet troops.

Yet, Roncalli used formulas of sincere respect for the adversaries
whom he always viewed as brothers to be esteemed and loved in trusting
expectation of better times. He avoided breaking with them completely.

> All this involves respect for those who fight for other parties — re-
> spect for the free will of others, which our blessed Lord respects in
> all people created and redeemed by him. It is clear that this leniency
> cannot mean indifference toward the errors of the various ideolo-
> gies or political practices that so greatly distance people from
> Christianity that they suppress the inalienable rights of the human
> person and his or her immeasurable value in autonomy from the
> Divine law and Christian sociology.[54]

With these specific statements, the patriarch felt that he had accomplished his duty to illuminate consciences, but he would not risk aggra-
vating the situation further.

Roncalli's document was well accepted at the national level. However, probably feeling that the patriarch's letter was too soft, the other
bishops of the Venetian province decided to intervene with their own
document. It contained an explicit condemnation of *Popolo Veneto* and
counseled against reading and diffusing the periodical in view of the
norms of the sacred canons. This document was published in the diocesan bulletin of Venice on August 21, but without the patriarch's signa-

ture. Roncalli probably wanted everyone to express themselves according to their own views and styles; for his part, Roncalli tried to avoid explicit condemnation.[55]

A few months later, another episode directed the public's attention to the patriarch of Venice. In February 1957, the National Congress of the Socialist Party was to be held in Venice. In anticipation of the occasion, the patriarch sent a text to the faithful that created a stir:

> Representatives of all the regions of the peninsula will hold another convention, the Congress of the Italian Socialist Party, these days in Venice. As a good Venetian who greatly honors hospitality and agrees with the Pauline precept that the bishop is to be "welcoming and good," I am permitting myself to make some respectful and calm remarks. You will understand, therefore, that I appreciate the exceptional importance of this event. It is a highlight in the current history of our region. Certainly it is inspired by the effort to successfully build a system of mutual understanding regarding what is more valuable, in the sense of improving living conditions and social prosperity. Such efforts can be approved of for their sincere good will, for their right and generous intentions.
>
> Always with some pain — at times very intense pain — a shepherd of souls has to observe that although honest intellects focus on heaven, where religious truths always shine, these truths remain dimmed, ignored, and neglected. The light of evangelical doctrine has given life to twenty centuries of history, science, and art, which were the glory of European nations, the glory of the world. Yet, it is believed possible to reconstruct the modern socioeconomic order on foundations other than Christ.
>
> Having spoken frankly of spiritual positions, as may be done among friends, I add my heartfelt wish that my Venetian sons and daughters would be welcoming and friendly, as is their custom. May they contribute to making worthwhile this gathering of so many brothers from different regions of Italy for a common elevation toward the ideals of truth, goodness, justice, and peace. And to this wish I add an invitation to those who believe, hope, and love, especially during this week, that heartfelt and pure prayers may be raised up to Almighty God for the benefit, consolation, and encouragement of all, so that they may understand, desire, and do what is good.[56]

What seemed a greeting to the Socialists was in reality an exhortation to the faithful on what attitude to assume in the face of this political event. In its straightforward style, the text was aimed at pastoral goals, and Roncalli limited himself simply to showing the faithful the importance of a congress that would certainly have repercussions throughout the country. Naturally, the patriarch expressed his best wishes for its positive results and indicated the conditions for such. The supporters of materialistic systems needed to draw closer to a largely spiritual vision, and to seriously consider the Christian tradition that they had ignored or directly combated. This exhortation was one of the strongest examples of Roncalli's unique ability to express points of dissension with extreme tact and yet without culpable omissions, while simultaneously arousing sympathy for the alienated. And those who felt alienated would recognize in the words Roncalli addressed to them a sincere invitation to trusting dialogue and mutual respect.

Roncalli had a gift for finding the opportune moment and the right action to remove the sting from hearts that had already been alienated by fierce and longstanding controversies. He could overcome barriers of prejudice and misunderstandings in order to create a more constructive atmosphere for an encounter between the Church and the many sons and daughters who had abandoned it. Without the slightest concern for political strategy, Roncalli's ways were motivated by the logic of the well-being of souls. He wanted to approach the alienated and felt convinced that this would be possible if the Church moderated its excessive rigidity.

Within the context of a greater respect and good will as a possible foundation for future dialogue, the patriarch's choice of words acquired political significance. People of the opposing side wanted to read concrete political objectives into Roncalli's pastoral exhortation. This exploitation prompted a broadcast by Vatican Radio and an article in *L'Osservatore Romano* that could have been understood as retractions. Capovilla informed Roncalli of the many northern Italian bishops who were displeased. "In the evening Monsignor Loris returned from Padua and told me about the uncertainty…among the Council of Bishops of Upper Italy regarding the suitability of my letter of February 1. This was a source of pain to me, but not of humiliation. I am ready for everything. The moment for the 'science of humility' has arrived."[57]

On the other hand, Count Giuseppe Della Torre, the director of *L'Osservatore Romano,* wrote a personal letter of praise to the patriarch. He welcomed the constructive spirit and skill with which Roncalli had propelled the Italian Socialists into an attitude of greater respect toward the Church, as was indeed the case.[58]

Roncalli referred to the fact in a letter to a priest-journalist, Don Fausto Vallainc, whom he thanked for correctly interpreting his intervention. Roncalli had observed that for the most part his text was seldom quoted in its entirety, and that this opened the way to distorted interpretations. He discussed the principle that inspired his conduct:

> I see that you understand me very well. With time and patience, everything will be straightened out. If judged in its integral and complete text, and not on the basis of its principal sentences and those maimed by the malicious scissors of interested adversaries, my original communication would have contributed to more sincerity and a good exercise of courtesy. In fact, here in Venice the reserved behavior of the patriarch — and I know this from honest and reliable sources — has restrained people from talking too much...and has led many to reflect and be respectful. "To speak the truth with love" is still a good doctrine of St. Paul and gives honor to all.[59]

In Treviso on February 19, Roncalli remembered Monsignor Mantiero on the first anniversary of his death and spoke of the principle behind his actions. His thoughts supply the key to Roncalli's originality; indeed the patriarch of Venice distinguished himself from other prelates of his time. For Roncalli, the pastoral action of the Church presented a twofold obligation: the defense of the truth with the practice of charity. Roncalli seemed to be saying that the duty of charity was not always properly considered though there were new avenues for exploration and new possibilities for speaking the truth. He had chosen a field of action that was agreeable to him but unknown to most, and he intended to plumb it to its depths. He would pursue this with even greater determination as pope.

"Next to purity of doctrine, of which the Roman pontiff is the most reliable and respected interpreter, the fields and horizons of charity open up to us — the charity of giving, of sacrifice; the charity that begins as that respect and courtesy with which human living is adorned and which ascends vigorously to great and heroic outpourings of pastoral service."[60] It was in this light that he invited his initiatives to be read and interpreted. Roncalli's spirit of accommodation was neither artificial nor did it conceal weakness of character; it sprang, instead, from a profound wisdom of life.

While maintaining great propriety, the patriarch did not exempt himself from becoming involved in public protests against decisions which threatened the religious or civil interests of the city.[61] One example of this would be a protest he initiated on April 5, 1957, against transferring the winter location of the sports stadium from the Lido to the neighborhood of St. Mark's Square — the religious and civic heart of the city. Although the intervention was protracted, the desired result was eventually obtained.

Venetian Period

Roncalli's entire Venetian period was characterized by an intense activity that was sometimes exercised in significant ways beyond the confines of his diocese. His efforts were sustained by good health despite his advancing age. The precise chronology recorded by Monsignor Capovilla, though terse, illustrates this clearly.[62] The patriarch made several trips abroad to discharge official duties. From October 19–25, 1954, he went to Beirut, Lebanon, as the pontifical legate to the First National Marian Congress. At the invitation of the Bishop of Leira the following year (May 9–15) he went to Fatima to preside at the celebration of the thirty-ninth anniversary of the first apparition. He read his homily in Portuguese before a half-million faithful.[63] From March 23–26, 1958 he was at Lourdes, another great Marian sanctuary, for the consecration of the new lower basilica dedicated to St. Pius X.

There are still two more episodes of particular importance to mention. Following the death of Cardinal Adeodato Piazza, secretary of the consistory on November 30, 1957, Roncalli was offered this important Vatican position. As secretary of the consistory he would oversee the election of bishops. For the first time in his life, Roncalli gave a gentle yet firm refusal. He did add his promise to submit fully if the assignment were imposed on him as an act of obedience. In his letter of December 6, 1957, he offered three reasons for his refusal. The first was his age. He had just completed his seventy-sixth year, and he felt that this new assignment required fresh energies and an ability to bear the heavy preoccupations inherent in such a delicate assignment. The second reason was his lack of competence in both legal and curial procedures. His most serious reservation, however, was the third. He had no good reason to leave Venice, where he felt completely fulfilled in his pastoral activity. The sudden change from a pastoral to a predominantly bureaucratic duty would cost him greatly.

On December 6, he wrote to Monsignor Dell'Acqua:

This afternoon I received your note of yesterday. I took the time to reflect calmly and to speak and consult humbly with the Lord. Afterward I had my lunch and an hour of calm rest. When the bells of St. Mark's tolled the agony of Jesus at exactly 3:00 ᴘ.ᴍ., I wrote this reply to your inquiry. My spirit is ready for any sacrifice that is imposed on me by obedience, for whatever defeat, even the most mortifying and perilous, "but my flesh is weak" — not because of a lack of physical energies, since my health is good even in this seventy-seventh year I've just begun, but because of that faithful and admonishing "know thyself." The sum total of the preoccupations that such a duty would entail is far superior to my powers of endurance and to the just and judicious balance needed between the serious duty to be accomplished at any cost, and the "truth, gentleness and justice toward everyone that has to be sought and practiced without favoritism." Also, I do not feel well trained in either canon or civil law, nor am I expert in the affairs of the Curia.

Your Excellency, since you care about me, have pity on me before the Holy Father. The Lord is filling my lowly pastoral life here at Venice with consolations and blessings. In almost five years of governing this diocese, which by now has become quite vast and open to an apostolate that is always more alive and promising, the grace of the Lord has encouraged me to behold an old age that is still fervent and fruitful in the midst of these faithful priests of mine who give me much peace through their correspondence of obedience and love. I remember how much the late-lamented Cardinal Piazza suffered his detachment from Venice, which for him was truly drastic. I tried my best to console and cheer him with the attentions of his devoted successor and admirer.

Oh! Excellency, help me, so "that this chalice may pass me by." How can I resist the clear and obvious will of the Lord that the Holy Father wants to place upon me? But as long as I am free to express my feelings, I cannot do so in other words. This concerns the resolution of a more serious problem, the true problem of my life and eternal happiness or unhappiness.

Excellency...I unite myself to the Holy Father with all my heart, so that the Lord will assist him in choosing a new secretary of the consistory who will be a blessing and joy for the whole Church.[64]

Pius XII thought it best to leave Roncalli in Venice. The office was given to the cardinal of Naples instead.

Another significant episode occurred at the end of Roncalli's Venetian episcopate. He completed the fifth and final volume of the *Acts of the*

Apostolic Visit of St. Charles Borromeo at Bergamo (1575). At last, the fear that this monumental undertaking would remain incomplete vanished forever. He had begun the work in 1906 and had to prolong it over the course of fifty years. Roncalli's work was a fundamental contribution to the understanding of his beloved home diocese and an incentive for historiography to consider the acts of pastoral visits (until then quite neglected), as essential sources for understanding religious and social history.[65] But perhaps the most outstanding benefits of this endless undertaking were reaped by the author himself, who had entered a historical period of exceptional importance. He had been able to admire both from on high and from the perspective of the most humble parishes the development of a systematic design for reform, originated by the Council of Trent, and of a renewed pastoral style. His remarkable experience had a decisive influence on the choices he would make as the future Pope John. He did not discover and study ancient records to satisfy his intellectual curiosity; rather, for him such study was a "warning and invitation to do well, to do better" — a source of inspiration for the present day.[66]

Roncalli's entire Venetian episcopate showed the relevance of the Tridentine tradition reread and updated according to new needs. So many factors might lead one to believe that his had been a merely routine episcopate: advanced age, a prestigious See viewed as an honorable conclusion to a dignified ecclesiastical career, his good-natured personality that disliked being in the limelight. Instead, Roncalli's return to pastoral life and to the leadership of a diocese had fulfilled the most profound aspiration of his whole life. He had dedicated himself to it with youthful enthusiasm and an enviable wealth of experience that allowed him — even concerning traditional pastoral practice — to live a relevant present-day experience that was original. Roncalli's originality sprang from his pastoral style, the priority he gave to goodness, his capacity to base collaboration on the principles of delegating and encouraging initiatives, from his discretion that limited his interventions to only what was strictly necessary. He took inspiration from an often-cited standard: "See everything, overlook much, correct little." In the midst of the traditional shepherding that Roncalli had taken up with commitment and generous dedication, new attitudes flourished through his keen perception of new needs. All of these elements prevent us from associating Roncalli's episcopal experience with anything routine or predictable.

CHAPTER 14

POPE JOHN XXIII:
THE FIRST ONE HUNDRED DAYS

"We Have a Pope"

On the third day of the conclave, at 5:08 P.M. on Tuesday, October 28, the long-awaited white smoke signaled the election of a new pope. Almost an hour later, at 6:05 P.M., Cardinal Canali officially proclaimed the *gaudium magnum* (great joy). At 6:20, the successor of Pius XII presented himself to the packed crowd in St. Peter's Square to impart his first blessing "to the city and to the world."

From that first moment, John XXIII made a very different impression than his predecessor. A well-known Vatican reporter wrote about his first appearance:

> Angelo Giuseppe Roncalli, a man without fame. When Cardinal Canali pronounced the name from the balcony of blessing, the crowd in the square remained momentarily stunned. They could not put a face to the name. Then came the applause, but not so much for the man as for the new name he had chosen. It was a name completely unforeseen and very dear to the Romans.... For the election of Eugenio Pacelli, it was enough for the faithful to hear "Eugenio" and the piazza had been filled with applause.

Then he noted the different tone of the new pope: "The anguish that vibrated in the voice of Pacelli...almost ethereal, was unknown to Ron-

275

calli. The voice of the new pope descended on the crowd in blessing — warm, very human, melodious, in truth quite beautiful. It was a friendly and paternal voice."[1]

In contrast with the election of Pacelli, and later with Montini, Roncalli's election had been unexpected. This was an ecclesiastic relatively unknown to the great crowd of the faithful. Nonetheless, from the choice of his name, his paternal gesture, and his inviting tone of voice, the new pontiff showed unmistakable signs of a strong personality that would certainly not be hidden by the great figure of his predecessor. Already in their first contact with the new pope, the crowd glimpsed in the agreeable figure someone surprisingly pleasant. They would soon discover the man in all his richness.

The cardinals who elected him were also destined to experience surprise at the man who was startlingly different from their expectations. Indeed, Roncalli shattered the rather mediocre pontificate they envisioned with the incredible change of direction he would give to the life of the Church.

The Conclave

The election to the highest position in the Catholic Church was a prospect Roncalli never considered seriously, not even toward the end of Pius XII's life. When Pius XII died on October 9, 1958, Roncalli presided over the ritual ceremonies in memory of the late pontiff in the Basilica of St. Mark, greeted the citizens of Venice, and left for Rome by train on October 12.

As noted in his calendar, the days immediately preceding the conclave were full of discussions with cardinals and members of the Curia either on an individual level or in general congregations of cardinals that were held in the Consistory hall.[2] It was during these meetings that the candidates developed and support for them was organized. Roncalli met with Cardinals Elia Dalla Costa of Florence and Fossati of Turin and other important members of the Curia, including Ottaviani, Pizzardo, Cicognani, Ciriaci, Masella, and Tardini who was not yet a cardinal but exercised an enormous influence as pro-secretary of state. There was no want of contacts with notable foreign prelates, such as the archbishop of Paris, Cardinal Feltin.

The elderly patriarch from Venice must have felt some inkling of the course the electors would take. It was certain that they did not want a long pontificate that would simply be a continuation of Pacelli's, and electing Cardinal Siri, archbishop of Genoa, would certainly guarantee this would happen. At the same time, undoing the strongly centralized system developed by Pius XII was too great a risk and would not be entirely acceptable to the Vatican Curia. In the absence of a clear direction, the electors were well disposed to allow a waiting period that would permit a clarification of the still undefined traits of the Church's situation. Thus, it appeared that the best route to take would be a brief, transitional pontificate with a routinely rigid government to assure no substantial changes. Possible candidates were the elderly Roman cardinal, Aloysius Marella, who would ensure a brief government that would be in conformity with Roman tradition, and the other suitable candidates were Cardinals Pietro Agagianian and Angelo Roncalli.

Agagianian had the support of Cardinal Celso Costantini, pro-prefect of the Propagation of the Faith. Agagianian's Armenian origins offered the possibility of freeing the Holy See from the claim that it was too Italian, and would also open a door to Eastern Christianity and the missions. His background and education were a secure guarantee of *romanità*.

At best, Roncalli was seen as the candidate who would ensure a balance in the government. He would help the Church to return to normal after the strong personal imprint of Pius XII. Well known for his good-natured character and love of tradition, Roncalli seemed perfectly suited for a peaceful, transitional pontificate.

It was during this prelude to the conclave that Roncalli became aware of a significant number of cardinals supporting his election. He now realized that there was a concrete possibility that he could be elected pope. His letters of October 23 and 24 to the bishop of Bergamo, Giuseppe Piazzi, and to his friend Giuseppe Battaglia, bishop of Faenza, testify to this. In its discreet and typical roncallian style, the letter to Battaglia eloquently expresses the anguish Roncalli was experiencing at having to confront this entirely unexpected possibility. The patriarch was honest and wise enough not to be deceived by the prestige of his call and office, which carried a tremendous weight of responsibilities. As usual, he lived this delicate moment in the light of the Divine will and expressed this through the psalms proposed by the liturgy of the day. These prayers of petition helped him pour out his sentiments and placed him within the Divine Word. He felt profoundly his own unworthiness and littleness, but united this to a deep sense of the power and goodness of God who never fails to come to the aid of those who hope in him.

To Bishop Battaglia he wrote: "I am experiencing some preoccupation. I ask you to read with me Psalms 77 and 86 from today's Compline. There you will find the throbbing of my spirit." He recommended that his nephew, Don Battista, who was ministering in the diocese of Faenza, not be allowed to come to Rome without his approval. This was to prevent further gossip in an atmosphere already roiling with it. He continued:

> When you hear that I had to surrender to the will of the Holy Spirit, expressed by the common desire, let Don Battista come to Rome.... As for me, I wish heaven would let this chalice pass me by! For this reason, do me the charity of praying for me and with me. At this point, if it were said of me: "You have been weighed in the balance and found lacking" [cf. Dan 5:27], I would rejoice with my whole being and would bless the Lord for it. Of course, these are all just words.[3]

Embracing these sentiments, Cardinal Roncalli entered the conclave the afternoon of October 25. Fifty-one cardinals were present and of these, eighteen were Italian. The required majority would be thirty-five votes.

Although Roncalli's name began to appear on the ballots from the beginning, his election was not taken for granted. Without the official documents, which at present are inaccessible, historians have attempted to reconstruct the progress of the conclave based on official news and has more or less reliable rumors.[4] The direct testimony of some of the major protagonists has also been used here.

The first testimony is from John XXIII himself when he spoke on February 1, 1959 at the Armenian College. When Roncalli greeted Cardinal Agagianian, he confided to the students, "Did you know that your cardinal and I were paired in the conclave of last October? Our names kept going up and down like chick-peas in boiling water."[5]

Cardinal Fossati of Turin, one of Roncalli's supporters, comments on the conclave in his preface to the first edition of a biography of Algisi. As Roncalli's election became imminent, Fossati tried to give some encouragement to his friend:

> Everyone knows that our rooms were assigned by drawing lots. Cardinal Roncalli was given number 15 in the apartment of the Noble Guards and I was given 16. We were, therefore, close. I do not believe we are obliged to secrecy, and in any case I am certain of being absolved by the great and indulgent goodness of the Holy Father, if I say that there came a moment when a friend felt the need to enter his friend's room to encourage him.[6]

The ninth and tenth ballots on the morning of October 28 were decidedly inclined toward Roncalli, almost to the point of a definitive election. Roncalli's secretary, Monsignor Loris Capovilla, recalls that toward noon the sentiments spreading among the patriarch's staff were those typical when people feel they are drawing near a great event. And Roncalli's demeanor only confirmed these sentiments. When the patriarch went up to his room, Capovilla's inquiring gaze saw a peculiar, although not despondent, expression on his face.

The patriarch did not go down to the dining room with the other cardinals for lunch, but ate a frugal meal with Capovilla. The two exchanged only a few words; a knot seemed to be lodged in their throats. After a brief rest, the future pope wrote some notes on three pieces of paper and put them in his pocket. The bell that tolled for the final voting reverberated in the hearts of both the cardinal and his secretary. Capovilla accompanied the patriarch as far as the entrance of the Sistine Chapel, and he knew that from then on everything would be radically different.[7]

The eleventh ballot was almost predictable, though it surpassed the required quorum only slightly.[8] The outcome of the vote was announced and Cardinal Tisserant asked Roncalli if he would accept. After a brief moment of reflection, the newly elected pontiff replied affirmatively. He called himself John, an unusual choice considering that the last pope by that name lived in the fifteenth century.[9] Already, Roncalli seemed to be indicating that he would continue being himself even on the chair of Peter and not allow the figure of his immediate predecessor to determine his choice. The name "John" was full of familiar memories and of ecclesiastical echoes for Roncalli. It was the name of the parish church where he had been baptized, and St. John Lateran was the pope's cathedral. Spiritually, it recalled John the Baptist and John the Evangelist, two saints who were very close to the Savior. Peter's new successor would link his mission to the Evangelist's witness and charity and to the Baptist's example of preparing for the Lord a people well disposed.

Perhaps it appeared to many that his choice stemmed from the immediate situation, or that it could be attributed to his historical erudition. Rather, his choice was well meditated in spite of the accompanying circumstances. It was a personal summons to charity and the necessary reform of the People of God. His name summed up the goals and long-range plans that John XXIII would develop during his pontificate.[10]

After the announcement of *gaudium magnum* and the blessing to the crowds, the first hours of Roncalli's pontificate were intense. That evening, the vacant apartment of the secretary of state was put at the pope's disposal. Ignoring the clamor of excitement rising from St. Peter's Square, he recollected himself in prayer and completed his recitation of the breviary. Then he began to prepare for the first acts of his pontificate. He sent three messages: to the Venetians, to the people of Bergamo, and to his relatives. Then his first duty of importance was the preparation of a radio message for the next day. This he did with the help of the substitute secretary of state, Monsignor Dell'Acqua, and the Latinist, Monsignor Giuseppe Del Toni. Following a quick supper and the recitation of the rosary, he asked Monsignor Capovilla to call for the pro-secretary of state, Monsignor Tardini. A few hours after his election, Roncalli made a swift and strategic choice that would form part of a larger project to normalize the structure of the Curia, where vacancies had multiplied during the final years of Pius XII's pontificate.

Normalization of the Curia

A reorganization of the Curia, which would please the majority of the cardinals who elected John XXIII, began on the evening of his election with the appointment of the secretary of state — a position that had been vacant for some fourteen years. According to Capovilla, around 10:00 P.M. the pope met with Tardini, the man who had once been Roncalli's rigid superior when he served as a diplomat of the Holy See. The new pope prevailed upon Tardini to accept the burdensome position of secretary of state.

Perhaps the pope saw this as a necessary move, or perhaps the more influential cardinals — Ottaviani, Pinzerdo, Aloisi, and Morella, to name a few — had made the appointment a topic of conversation at the conclave. In any case, the choice of Tardini for the office clearly had its advantages. First, the appointment would reassure the Curia, which would view the choice of one of their most prestigious members as a reconfirmation of their system of government. They would feel impelled to adopt an attitude of collaboration with the new pontificate. Secondly, having spent most of his priesthood in the Vatican made Tardini an "expert" who could introduce the pope into the workings of the Holy See. He would be helpful in directing the Curia and the government of the Church. Tardini was endowed with an intense religious piety, was a sound theologian and possessed good judgment — although he was not entirely impartial concerning curial positions. Known for his rather independent character, Tardini would not become the pope's man. John XXIII knew how much they differed, but he trusted that a loyal collaboration would ultimately benefit them both. In fact, Roncalli would later confide to a friend: "He's a bit academic.... Tardini has had a unique experience in the affairs of the Church, but he has never left the Vatican; he lacks the contacts that I have had."[11]

Anticipating what the new pope was about to propose, Tardini began immediately to ward off the possibility of a nomination by presenting his poor health as a valid motive for not accepting the position. After Roncalli's assurances that his nomination was not purely for show, that he would be kept informed on the most important decisions, and that his opinion would be heeded, Tardini accepted the assignment imposed in obedience. Tardini was officially instated the following November 17, during an audience for the employees of the Secretariat of State.[12]

The pope's expansion of the College of Cardinals helped the Curia to come out of a state of emergency to resume its normal functioning. In an address to the consistory (December 15), the pope invited the cardinals who held two curial positions to relinquish one. For most of the prelates, this was a welcome invitation, but some resented it. In any case, Pizzardo, head of the Congregation of the Seminary and of the Holy Office, was the first to cede a position. Cardinal Gaetano Cicognani left the Apostolic Signature, and Tisserant renounced his position in the Oriental Congregation in favor of the Library and Vatican Archives.

The papal household began to take shape as well: Monsignor Capovilla was confirmed as secretary, and Monsignor Alfredo Cavagna, originally from Bergamo, was chosen as the pope's confessor. Then the maggiordomo was appointed, the first palatine prelates, the master of the chamber, and the prelates of the antechamber. The revival of these traditional positions would restore normalcy to the Apostolic Palace and break with the customs that made access to the pope difficult. On October 30, the pope reinstated the *tabella,* audiences granted on fixed dates to the heads and secretaries of dicasteries to discuss administrative problems.

The College of Cardinals

After the appointment of the secretary of state, the most urgent problem was the full reinstatement of the College of Cardinals. Since the last consistory of Pius XII in 1953, there were a number of vacancies. John XXIII created twenty-three new cardinals, surpassing the total of seventy fixed by Pope Sixtus V (1585–1590). Pope John later recalled that he and the secretary of state hesitated only briefly before exceeding the number as he realized how profoundly the times and circumstances had changed.

As a testimony to his esteem and affection for Archbishop Montini, and almost a foreshadowing of a not-so-distant future, John XXIII placed him first on the list. The other names were listed in order of seniority according to episcopal consecration. The pope placed Tardini in the nineteenth position.

> Thursday…I began to address the most important matters and to make provisions for the future. Before all else came the consistory and the appointment of new cardinals. I said the names beginning with Monsignor Montini, Archbishop of Milan, and Monsignor Tardini. With these, we began our litany and we found ourselves in perfect agreement. Arriving at the number seventy, among old and new, we stopped a moment. Then, noting that at the time of Sixtus V the Catholic Church occupied only a third of its present territory, we continued on and reached the number of twenty-three new appointments.[13]

There were personalities of distinction among the new cardinals. They included Urbani, Roncalli's successor in Venice, as well as Confalonieri, Cicognani, König, and Döpfner. Eight more cardinals would be created on December 14 of the following year. The creation of ten more cardinals on March 28, 1960, was particularly significant because for the first time a Japanese, a Filipino, and an African bishop were chosen. Two other consistories would follow later, one on January 16, 1961, with four new cardinals, and one on March 19, 1962, with ten. In all, the prelates elevated by John XXIII numbered forty-five.

The criteria for selecting the cardinals were extremely objective, but there was a preoccupation with making the Sacred College more international by appointing representatives from the emerging churches of the Third World. Some of the pope's personal friends also appeared on the list, among them Gustavo Testa of Bergamo, but this was not unusual. Nor did it produce the sense that certain ecclesiastics were followers of the pope and thus had his confidence and inserted themselves into the central government of the Church.

The pope did more than simply increase the number of cardinals. He found ways to adapt the Sacred College to the changing needs of the Church. Since the increased duties of the Roman Congregations made it impossible for cardinals to provide attentive pastoral care, the suburban dioceses were entrusted to the care of their proper bishops.

The abandonment of ancient tasks identified with the needs of the local church, and the direct association with the pope in the government of the Universal Church, rendered anachronistic the traditional distinctions between cardinal bishops, cardinal priests, and cardinal deacons. Because cardinal deacons were not bishops, this placed them in a position of objective inferiority with respect to the tasks they were called to perform. John XXIII decided to grant all the members of the Sacred College an equal episcopal dignity. On Holy Thursday (April 19, 1962), in the Basilica of St. John Lateran, Roncalli consecrated as bishops twelve cardinal deacons. Among the new bishops were Ottaviani and Bea, and this act reflected the pope's particular care in nurturing the prelates of the Oriental Churches. The fact that Eastern bishops, and especially patriarchs, were lower in order of precedence than priests had been an intolerable situation.[14] While Pope John's measure eased that issue, the Melchite Patriarch Maximos IV would still voice his protest that Oriental patriarchs were treated as inferiors in their seat assignments at the Council.

A Pastoral Pope

The pope's first acts and decisions revealed a personality neither hesitant nor uncertain. He already showed his decisiveness in quickly resolving problematic situations that had existed for years despite a sufficient understanding of what direction to take. Again, the choice of his name indicated two themes very dear to Pope John: fraternal charity as a basic value of Christian existence, and clear pastoral action on behalf of the entire Christian people. The official acts of his coronation and taking possession of the Basilica of St. John Lateran would give him the opportunity to clarify and develop these themes.

In his radio message of October 29, he sent warm greetings to the whole Church and explicitly mentioned the unjust persecution Christian communities suffered behind the Iron Curtain. His message did not conclude with harsh tones or condemnation, but with the hope that these sufferings would finally end through the conversion of governments. Alongside this theme — which was an unavoidable one during the years of the Cold War — the pope touched on the topic of ecumenism. He declared that he wanted to open his heart and his arms to his separated brothers — to bring about the unity desired by Jesus himself: "That all may be one." He deplored the terrible waste of the world's enormous resources for the construction of destructive weapons rather than using them for the progress of peoples, particularly the poor.[15]

The discourse delivered at his solemn coronation on November 4 was a more thorough presentation of the points Roncalli had treated during the preceding days. The points converged in a pope who would inspire action. Pope John vigorously reaffirmed the eminently pastoral character of his ministry so that no ambiguity and misunderstandings could threaten to alter its image. The call to a pastoral spirit, so roncallian in content and style, was Pope John's most relevant contribution to the life of the Church. That theological principle inspired the convocation of the Second Vatican Council and was indelibly stamped on all its activity.

In the ceremonial of the solemn coronation of a pope, the new pope usually did not address the people. But John XXIII did, and some of his words remain justifiably memorable.

> There are those who expect the pontiff to be a statesman, a diplomat, a scientist, a social organizer, or rather someone who has opened his spirit to all norms of modern progress without exception. All of these ideas are off track, because they have shaped a concept of the supreme pontiff not entirely conformed to the true ideal. Through the course of life's events, the new pope is like the son of Jacob who, when he met his unfortunate brothers, laid bare to them the tenderness of his heart, and bursting into tears, exclaimed: "It is I...your brother Joseph" (Gn 45:4). Above all, the new pontiff wants to realize in himself the splendid image of the Good Shepherd.[16]

One discerns in his words the presence of a personal project that had accompanied him throughout his life and to which he had remained faithful, even during the difficult decades of diplomatic service. Roncalli's personal style had not always met with acceptance, but his superiors must have appreciated it because he was entrusted with increasingly important assignments. His election to the chair of Peter was like a definitive confirmation of the validity of his principles. This time he would apply them in an official way for the benefit of the whole Church.

Roncalli's vision of the ideal of the Good Shepherd was more a matter of the heart than of the intellect. The Good Shepherd was intimately connected to a profound sense of brotherhood, and while Pope John was the highest authority in the Church, he was first of all a brother. Relationships within the Church had to take inspiration from the model of the family; it was sustained by the most profound affections that originate in the heart. Being together and recognizing each other as members of the same family was the most authentic experience of Church. Pope John expressed this idea again in a meeting with journalists two days later: "I am also your brother, even if before God I am the first among brothers, and as shepherd have the duty of guiding my brothers."[17]

The second essential point of reference for John XXIII was the sweet and gentle example of Christ as the source and model of every pastoral action. Total dedication to the good of souls, as well as the virtues of meekness and humility, held a privileged place in this Divine model. The pope believed that these virtues were essential for him to achieve his aspiration of being a good shepherd. Pope John addressed this message to the faithful of the whole world so that everyone would ask God to grant these virtues to their pontiff.

The last part of his speech hinted at future decisions. The source of Pope John's pastoral doctrine, after the Gospels, was Church history. His choice to celebrate his coronation on November 4, the feast of St. Charles Borromeo, was his way of recalling the great saint's pastoral example. Borromeo had manifested his pastoral spirit at a time when the Church was not experiencing happy circumstances, but he successfully promoted a vigorous reform by implementing the decrees of the Council of Trent. Pastoral spirit, reform, and council are three distinctly important points that emerged in Roncalli's inaugural speech and would mark his pontificate.

The highly explosive content of his words could not be fully understood or appreciated in that context. The incongruity of his statement of principles and the solemn and magnificent five-hour-long ceremony would not escape us today. Pope John wore the papal tiara that symbolized the spiritual and earthly power of the papacy. Personally, Pope John felt very distant from this vision. Burning straw while uttering the wise admonition, "So passes the glory of the world" was more harmonious to his emphasis on humility.

Bishop of Rome

Roncalli rooted his insistence on the pastoral nature of Peter's ministry in the well-defined plans that he would soon realize. The pope intended to exercise his role as Bishop of Rome fully and not merely symbolically. A praxis and theology that focused only on the universal dimension of the Holy See's activity with little sensitivity to the local church of Rome was unacceptable. In conformity with tradition, John XXIII inverted the relationship by insisting that the episcopal service of Peter's successor had primacy. The duty of guiding the Universal Church follows and stems from the pope's position as Bishop of Rome. Pope John said as much to Tardini on the evening of his election: "I propose to emphasize the first service to which the Lord has called me. In fact, I am pope insofar as I am Bishop of Rome."[18]

His conviction had put down roots in his cultural history and contacts with the Eastern Churches. Indeed, the Oriental Churches had a greater appreciation of the value of the local church, and this approach renders the Petrine primacy more understandable. From this viewpoint, the episcopal ministry of the Bishop of Rome acquired greater importance, and Pope John wished to honor it with the highest commitment. He would restore normal pastoral practice according to the traditional Tridentine model of a good bishop. He knew this tradition well. Not only had his experiences in his native diocese helped to bring his understanding to maturity, but he also exercised in Venice what he had learned from his wide-ranging historical studies.

The first hundred days of Pope John's pontificate are testimony to his episcopal commitment. As Bishop of Rome, he took possession of his Basilica of St. John Lateran, visited the Roman Seminary, inaugurated the academic year at the Pontifical Lateran Atheneum, met with pastors, visited the sick and imprisoned at Christmas, and announced the diocesan synod.

His predecessors had given relative importance to taking possession of St. John Lateran, "mother and head of every church in the city and in the world." Pope John saw the act as exercising part of his universal ministry. In the ceremony, which took place on Sunday, November 23, the new pope officially left the Vatican for the first time after his election. The public seemed to understand that he desired to establish a relationship with his city. People lined up along the route he traveled by car, displaying their affection and appreciation for a pope who was not isolated in Vatican palaces but closer to his faithful.

In his homily after the Gospel, he proposed the theme of the book and the chalice to the faithful of Rome. It was a theme very dear to Roncalli and one he had already used amply in Venice to sum up his episcopal ministry. The missal, which included the biblical readings, symbolized the commitment of announcing the Divine Word, "communicating the great doctrine of the two testaments and making it penetrate into souls and into life." The chalice represented the Eucharist, culmination of the encounter between God and humanity and of Christian perfection. Therefore, the pope invited the faithful to "always look on the altar for the bishop and the priest, in the act of distributing the Body and Blood of Christ."[19]

Contented, the pope wrote in his journal that evening:

> Sunday, November 23. One of the most beautiful days of my life. I took possession of my Cathedral of St. John Lateran. Everything was beautiful and solemn.... The return from the Lateran to the Vatican, simply triumphant.... The homage to their new bishop and pope of the Roman people along the way, touching and unexpected, and for this reason much more dear. Going and returning, I was accompanied by Cardinals Tisserant and Pizzardo. They could do nothing more than weep with emotion. I could only hold myself in humiliation, as a sacrificial offering for my people, but in great and joyful simplicity.[20]

And on the same occasion he offered his first ecumenical gesture by stopping at St. Clement's Church to venerate Saints Cyril and Methodius. On the following Thursday, November 27, he returned to the Lateran for a second visit, which he considered his "first act of episcopal paternity." The object of this visit was the seminary, "pupil of the eye and the core of every bishop's heart."[21] Instead of giving an official address, he engaged a spontaneous conversation with the seminarians on the topics of friendship and confidence. He spoke of his own formation in the Roman Seminary years before, remembering the exemplary superiors and professors toward whom he still nurtured tremendous gratitude for all the good he had received.

He did not hesitate to confide how awkward he felt in adjusting to his new role and how disconcerting it was to be called *Your Holiness*.

> When I hear people around me speaking of the pope directly or indirectly — for example: "The pope should be told; he needs to tell the pope; he needs to bring this up with the pope," etc., I still always think of the Holy Father Pius XII of revered memory, whom I so venerated and loved. I often forget that the person in question is really I, I who have chosen to be called John.... Every time they use the title "Holiness" or "Most Blessed Father" with me, you do not know how this confuses me and makes me reflect. Oh, my sons! At least you are my friends! Pray to the Lord, that he may grant me the grace of holiness that is attributed to me.[22]

Pope John was not afraid to show himself a brother to the young seminarians and to share his uncertainties with them, yet he never lost sight of having been vested with a high dignity. The figure of the Vicar of Christ underwent a kind of demythologization. Pope John presented himself as more human and fatherly, growing in gentleness and affection. In this way, his exhortations found a more direct route to the hearts of his listeners.

Roncalli delivered an official discourse at the solemn opening of the academic year of the Lateran Atheneum, the pope's university among the numerous theological faculties of Rome. The official character of the visit did not stop him from sharing a personal reminiscence. At the same university, Cardinal Pompili had asked him to occupy the chair of patrology, only to have to renounce it soon afterward because of his appointment as apostolic visitor to Bulgaria.[23]

On Monday, December 22, in the Consistorial Hall of the Vatican, he received all the pastors of Rome in audience for the first time. The vicar, Cardinal Micara, accompanied them. The conversation was very cordial. After reminiscing about the two periods of time he had spent in Rome, the pope did not miss his opportunity. He shared some practical pastoral reflections with the men carrying out their ministry in the city of Rome, a very different Rome from the one he had known. He made some preliminary observations, which became the principles and nuclei of a pastoral program yet to be developed. Taking note of the state of the parishes, he said he would very much like to visit them — a desire he would begin to realize at the beginning of Lent.

Bearing in mind the theme of the book and the chalice, he offered general criteria for pastoral practice that included fidelity to traditional teachings. This had to be united to an ability "to accept promptly and in an orderly way whatever the new times suggest that has greater breadth and practicality, yet with that unity of direction that supports edification, not confusion."[24]

His final observation concerned preaching. He invited preachers to give up pompous tones and excessive argumentation and to adopt a more simple, understandable, and respectful manner. He would speak more completely on this topic in the future.

At the conclusion of the audience, he told a secret that received lively approval: he intended to make some visits to Roman hospitals and prisons during the upcoming Christmas celebrations. The pope added that he could thus celebrate the feast of Christmas by practicing the works of mercy which occupied an important place in the teaching of John XXIII. Many statements and recommendations testify to this. The works of mercy derive naturally from the theological and cardinal virtues, and their exercise identifies them with the constant and faithful practice of Christianity: "They therefore merit to be appreciated with words and example."[25] The virtues cannot be neglected in any way by the bishop; he is like a master of the Christian life or like a father who cannot forget his most needy and suffering children.[26]

His visits to the hospitals of the Holy Spirit and the Infant Jesus on Christmas Day, and to the prison of *Regina Coeli* the next day, moved the hearts of the people. The spontaneity of the pope's appearance and its symbolic value stirred the emotion of the crowd, which rippled out beyond Rome thanks also to the media. News reports spread this unusual papal figure by stressing Roncalli's fatherly aspect rather than his superiority and authority to command. On Christmas Day 1958, Pope John showed the faithful and the entire world the image of a shepherd — certainly not a new image, but one that had become somewhat tarnished over time. He renewed the image by using the treasures of tradition to give it new vitality. Satisfied, and feeling a touch of wonder, he wrote on the evening of December 27: "Everything focuses on the festive charity of Christmas. Not only the Italian press, but also the whole world continues to marvel at my gesture of visiting the prisons yesterday. It was such a simple and natural thing for me."[27]

In the first two months of his pontificate, Pope John had accomplished the amazing feat of helping the papacy to shoulder its way into the center of world attention. Once more, the world was interested in the Church because it was fascinated with the person at its head. While Pope John was true to himself and to the spiritual tradition in which he had been formed, he exercised the mission as Peter's successor in a new and most appealing way.

It has been extremely important to recall the first months of this pontificate, not only for biographical purposes, but also to illustrate the context in which Vatican Council II occurred, so closely connected and in perfect harmony with the pope's actions. From the very first months of his pontificate, Roncalli anticipated themes, programs, and directives that would be treated in greater detail at the conciliar assembly. He had not shown the slightest hesitation to interpret the exalted position to which he had been called in a new way. He followed the needs and dictates of his unique and strong personality.

Throughout the course of his life that was rich in contacts and experiences, he became always more aware that he witnessed to an aspect of Christian tradition that had been relegated to second place. During the first half of the twentieth century, the Church had favored discipline and doctrine and thus placed itself opposite a world that was becoming progressively more secularized. John XXIII believed it was necessary to understand that arguments alone do not adequately define the face of the Church. People had to see the Church's maternal features, which were derived from Christ. The Church had to proclaim herself the good shepherd, and this conviction of Roncalli's directed all of his actions, personal bearing, public activities, and pastoral initiatives.

The transformation extended to the pope's words. Rooted firmly in doctrine, Pope John spoke with an amiable, brotherly eloquence that was meant to encourage a building up and unity rather than disagreement and criticizing. Roncalli's desire to communicate with people directly immediately fashioned the content of his words. From the very first, Pope John singled out the themes that would become the objects of his constant interest: ecumenism, peace, and freedom among peoples. He explicitly set forth the guiding principle of his whole pontificate: fidelity to tradition united to the ability to grasp, in a prompt and orderly manner, what the new times were suggesting. He accomplished his mission with spontaneity and without fatigue, as he affirmed in his personal notes. His spirit remained calm and serene, and he felt consoled by the public's acceptance and the general approval of his way of proceeding.[28]

His renewal of the papacy undoubtedly facilitated his decision to convoke an Ecumenical Council. After all, the unique style of any pope is not confined to his personal surroundings; it also affects and enters the life of the Church or it risks being viewed as eccentricity. Therefore, the whole ecclesial community had to be on the same wavelength. Given Pope John's reluctance and impossibility of imposing reforms from on high, he chose to ask the Church, and especially the episcopate about the validity and relevance of the questions raised by his style of pontificate. Besides, Pope John was not a professional theologian, but a man of action who, guided by his pastoral instinct, translated ideas that still lacked complete theoretical formulation or existed chiefly on the level of pure intuition into activity. Entirely aware of his limitations, Pope John desired to convoke those responsible with him to stimulate a collective reflection on the renewal of the Church and her mission in the world. This author holds, therefore, the necessity of reaching an agreement between the life of the Church and Pope John's own pastoral style in determining the serene and spontaneous character, all things considered, of the decision to convoke a Council.[29]

The Decision for the Council

> Another grace: ideas that were not complex in themselves, actually very simple, but vast in their effects and full of responsibilities regarding the future. I was immediately successful — one must be able "to accept the good inspirations of the Lord with simplicity and trust" (cf. Prov 10:9). Without having thought of it before, I put forth the idea of the Ecumenical Council, the diocesan synod, and the revision of the Code of Canon Law in an early conversation with my secretary of state on January 20, 1959. Contrary to all my suppositions or imaginings on this point, I was the first to be surprised by my proposal, which no one suggested to me. Everything seemed to follow so naturally in its immediate and continued development.[30]

Thus reads the celebrated text from the *Journal of a Soul,* written by Pope John on September 9, 1962, exactly one month before the opening of Vatican II. A similar text was presented during an audience granted to the Venetians on May 8, 1962.[31] From these two testimonies it seems that the idea for a Council first came to the pope at the time of his meeting with Tardini.

Pope John made a partial correction to this in his journal notes the day after his meeting with Tardini. The pope says explicitly that the idea of a Council had come to him earlier. And from a number of reliable testimonies, we know that John XXIII began to speak of a Council on the day after his election.[32] Monsignor Capovilla affirms that the pope brought the subject up in a conversation about problems described by the cardinal electors. The pope proposed a Council, and Capovilla quickly tried to discourage him, counseling the pope to undertake less demanding initiatives and to trust above all in his paternal charisma.[33] At this point a Council was still a hypothesis, but one that Pope John was moving toward. In a note written by the pope on his agenda about a meeting of November 2, 1958, we find documented confirmation of this fact. The topics discussed with Cardinal Ruffini included "the Council."[34]

That same month, Pope John spoke about the Council with Cardinal Urbani, his successor in Venice; Monsignor Bortignon, Bishop of Padua;[35] and his confessor, Monsignor Cavagna. As the month progressed, the project seemed to become more solidified. On November 28, the pope noted: "I have in mind a program of work that is not strenuous but definite."[36] There is no risk of error in seeing these words as a reference to the Council, which had become a settled point in his mind and an inevitable decision.[37]

Daniel Feltin, who accompanied Cardinal Agagianian to a private audience with the pope on December 12, 1958, gives further confirmation of this direction. Agagianian requested the promulgation of the fifth part of the Code for the Eastern Churches. John XXIII's response was that this would be done "after the Council." Then, to add to their bewilderment, the pope told Agagianian how he had dreamed of a Council since his days in Istanbul. Its realization — that is, its announcement, to be kept secret for the moment — would be made at St. Paul Outside the Walls on the following January 25.

Some of the details provided by Feltin arouse doubt concerning the reliability of his testimony, but considering the space of some fourteen to eighteen years, the substance of his testimony as a whole seems acceptable.[38]

Don Giovanni Rossi, founder of *Pro Civitate Christiana* and Roncalli's longtime friend, testifies that the decision was effectively made by the beginning of January. In his diary Rossi refers to an audience with the pope on January 9, 1959, and adds this marginal note: "He told me, 'Tonight I have a great idea: the Vatican Council.'"

Rossi's note seems too artificial, and its familiar tone quite out of context, especially the mention of the Council's name. Rossi places his meeting at the beginning of January, but Pope John would not decide on a name for the Council until the next summer. In any case, the core of the note is substantially true, as shown by an article in *La Rocca* on January 15, 1959. In it Rossi wrote that the pope had said "many beautiful things, but above all he confided one of them to me as a great secret. May the Lord give him the joy of accomplishing what will be one of the most glorious and memorable events of the Church in our times and of his pontificate."

Evidently he is alluding to the Council and to the fact that a decision had already been made.[39]

The pope informed Monsignor Angelo Dell'Acqua, a longtime friend and substitute for the secretary of state, about the conciliar project.[40] Dell'Acqua proposed uniting the Roman synod to the Council. The list of people in whom the pope had confided is certainly incomplete. But the evidence cited is clear; the prospect of a Council existed from the beginning of Roncalli's pontificate and matured over the first three months. However, it remained on the level of a simple exchange of ideas and informal consultations to help in making the decision definite.

Before an official announcement, it was first necessary to communicate with Secretary of State Cardinal Tardini and to obtain at least his general approval. Indeed, Pope John knew that he could not take Tardini for granted because of the frank and independent character of his principle collaborator. Therefore, on the morning of January 20, Roncalli was apprehensive when he began their meeting.

> In my conversation with Secretary of State Tardini, I wanted to see his reaction to the idea that had come to me: to propose to the members of the Sacred College who would convene at St. Paul's on January 25…the project of an Ecumenical Council to be assembled, all things considered, at the proper time with the participation of all the Catholic bishops of every rite and region. I felt rather hesitant and uncertain. His immediate response was the most exultant surprise I could ever have expected. "Oh! This is an idea — an enlightened and holy idea! This really comes from heaven, Holy Father. You need to cultivate, develop, and diffuse it. It will be a great blessing for the whole world."
>
> I needed nothing more. I was happy and thanked the Lord that this plan of mine had received the first sign that I could have expected here below in anticipation of a heavenly one, which humbly I did not lack. Hail Mary, hope of the world! Hail, gentle and holy! A bright day — a precious gem. I have to say that my spirit rejoiced in God. Everything was clear and simple in my spirit and I did not believe it necessary to add words. It was as if the idea of a Council had sprung from my heart with the naturalness of a spontaneous and very sure reflection. Truly it is the Lord who has done this, and we find it marvelous to behold.[41]

The pope's words leave no doubt about the importance of Tardini's consent. He represented the Roman Curia in an eminent way and his support would not only guarantee their collaboration, it would also minimize hostility. The conversation of January 20 had been the project's test by fire; now that it had overcome, it could enter the next phase.

The secretary of state confirmed his agreement in a personal note dated the same day:

Important audience. Yesterday afternoon His Holiness reflected and meditated on the program of his pontificate. He conceived three ideas: a Roman synod, an Ecumenical Council, and the updating of the Code of Canon Law. He wants to announce these three points to the cardinals next Sunday, after the ceremony at St. Paul's. When the Holy Father asked me about this, I said: "For my part, I like what is new and good. Now, these three projects are excellent, and the method of announcing them to the cardinals beforehand, though connected with ancient papal traditions, is appropriate and novel."

Tardini was not a man to have reservations about expressing his judgment to the pope — and he had judged positively. Some qualifications concerning the pope's report of the meeting with Tardini are justifiable, since Roncalli would be inclined to accentuate Tardini's enthusiastic approval. The fact remains, however, that their meeting was largely positive and the pope considered it a confirmation that the idea of a Council had come from God.

The multiplicity and, to some extent, the diversity of accounts seem to suggest that Pope John emphasized the divinely inspired character of the project by making it appear proximate and by dramatizing the circumstances. The pope was profoundly convinced of the Council's Divine origin and he reaffirmed this many times. Therefore, it would not be out of place to think that Pope John had more or less consciously found efficacious ways of supporting his convictions. He was more preoccupied with the great significance of the event rather than the concrete circumstances of its origin.

This contributed to the safeguarding of the specific character of Vatican II at a crucial moment in its course — the year it opened, 1962. The most relevant peculiarity of the Council would be its pastoral character, something that was not well understood by a large portion of the episcopate in the central offices of the Curia. Members of the Curia thought that the Council should be doctrinal, after the models projected by Pius XI at the beginning of his pontificate, and by Pius XII's in the 1950s to complete Vatican I. The risk of a fatal misunderstanding was not unreal, as many of the drafts prepared by the pre-conciliar commissions indicate. A reductive interpretation of the term "pastoral" could redimension the Council itself, in the case that it should refrain from the definition of new truths or the condemnation of errors. With the stress on the newness and the Divine inspiration of the Council, John XXIII defended the dignity and foundational rationale for convoking it.

The Announcement

The pope waited in a spirit of prayer and recollection for the day of the Council's announcement.[42] He added the finishing touches to the discourse he would deliver to the cardinals. On January 25, he awoke at dawn. After celebrating Mass and assisting at Capovilla's, he went to the Basilica of St. Paul Outside the Walls in silence and recollection. At the conclusion of the solemn commemoration of the Conversion of St. Paul, the final day of the week of prayer for Christian unity, the pope entered the chapter room of the nearby Benedictine Abbey accompanied by seventeen cardinals. Everyone else was asked to leave.

The discourse, "This Festive Anniversary," marked the official beginning of the great conciliar adventure and a milestone in Roncalli's pontificate. Pope John did not propose a Council, he communicated the decision he had made in virtue of his authority and upheld by his secretary of state. His first concern was to present the cardinals with adequate reasons for his decision. These were basically three: his personal conversations with members of the Roman Curia, the good of souls, and the urgency he felt that his pontificate correspond to the needs of the present times. These motives suggested the necessity of initiating extraordinary new activities in the normal exercise of the pope's pastoral activity, both as Bishop of Rome and Shepherd of the Universal Church.

With respect to the capital of Christianity, Rome had undergone profound changes from immigration and the consequent urban development. The face of the city had changed radically and thus the natural development of civic and religious life was made more difficult. While he expressed profound sadness at not being able to offer an adequate response to these dramatic needs, Pope John stressed the urgency of making an extraordinary effort toward this. The Church faced problems of great importance worldwide. Without euphemisms, he denounced the strained situation of the Church of silence within Communist countries that had become the object of a systematic persecution aimed at its destruction. Concurrently, in the so-called free world the search for well-being carried with it the danger of a general weakening of the spiritual dimension, which could cause grave harm to the life of the Church. The pope's prophecy was not motivated by nostalgia for the past; as a skilled historian, Pope John was a critical admirer of the past. He knew that the Church had faced many perilous hours over the centuries and had stood up to them with "ancient forms of doctrinal declarations and wise disciplinary regulations." The contemporary situation required the discovery of new means that would yield the same effective results. Therefore, "certainly trembling somewhat with emotion, but with humble resolve," he announced the double celebration of a diocesan synod for the city of Rome and a general Council for the Universal Church.

The text of the pope's declaration would be communicated to all the cardinals, because the pope hoped to receive suggestions and expressions of availability from the whole College of Cardinals. Secretary of State Tardini personally informed the heads of a few dicasteries: Pizzardo, Ottaviani, and Ciriaci. Pope John also invited "the faithful of the separated Churches to participate with us in this banquet of grace."[43] His respectful words acknowledged the true ecclesial quality of the communities of separated brethren and clarified the ecumenical goal of the new Council.

The cardinals received the pope's address and his invitation to respond. Between January 26 and April 14, only twenty-five Cardinals replied, and most of their comments were largely awkward expressions of great concern over the projected Council. The general reaction to the announcement was silence. This deeply troubled John XXIII. Later he would recall their unresponsiveness. "Humanly speaking, after having heard the address one would believe that the cardinals would gather around us to express approval and congratulations. Instead, there was an impressive, formal silence." But as always, the pope was inclined to interpret even this in a kindly manner, especially when the cardinals began to make amends in various ways. "This [silence] would only be explained during the following days, when the cardinals, coming for an audience, would tell us individually that their emotion had been so intense and their joy so profound...that they could not find adequate words to express their joy and limitless obedience."[44]

Even those who were considered more open, such as Archbishop Montini of Milan, felt alarmed. When he heard the news on the radio, Montini quickly telephoned his good friend Bevilacqua. "Have you heard, Father?" he asked. "What a hornet's nest! What a hornet's nest!"[45]

Notwithstanding the prevailing silence, January 25 was a most happy day for Pope John, who commented in a personal note: "All has gone well. I maintained my continual communication with God. On my return, the celebration of the Romans from St. Paul's to St. Peter's was unforgettable. It was like my return from the Lateran on November 23. Praise be to God. Praise be to God!"[46]

With his announcement, Pope John was convinced that he had accomplished a duty imposed on him by his mission and had corresponded to the will of God — the horizons within which he loved to move, and his fountain of peace. On the way back to the Vatican, Capovilla asked the pope if he felt content. He replied, "It is not a matter of myself or of my personal feelings. We have exercised the will of God fully. Now I need silence, recollection. I feel detached from everything and from everyone, just as the first psalm for the preparation for Mass says: 'It is beautiful to rest in your tabernacles, O Lord'" (cf. Ps 84:5).[47]

The History of the Decision

Roncalli's decision was strictly a personal one. Detailed research of available sources indicates that the relative proximity of the idea of a Council had been circulating within the Catholic world during Roncalli's adult years. Nevertheless, the idea for "his" Council matured independently.

The most significant precedents for Vatican II were the tentative steps taken by Pius XI and Pius XII. In 1922, Pius XI set up a small commission of theologians to evaluate Vatican I. What had the Council accomplished and what had it not been able to accomplish for lack of time? This was followed by an extensive, secret consultation of the bishops. Many favored convoking a Council, and they proposed concrete topics. But the project was quickly abandoned because of the diverse and opposing viewpoints that emerged: some prelates expected a reinforcement of the condemnation of modernism, while others expected a relaxation of this. Since the Roman question had yet to be settled, the Holy See could not be guaranteed sufficient security. From Monsignor Capovilla we know that Pope John had not participated in that episcopal consultation which took place before his episcopal consecration on March 19, 1925. However, John XXIII later discovered all of the paperwork relating to the project in the private papal library — certainly after January 25, 1959.[48]

When the Roman question was resolved in 1929, renewed interest in a Council increased. The movement culminated in a project developed by Monsignor Celso Costantini, Secretary of the Propagation of the Faith, at the conclave of 1939. No longer was there a plan to continue Vatican I; under certain aspects Costantini's project was already oriented toward a "Vatican II." By the spring of 1959, John XXIII knew of Costantini's proposal to revitalize the role of the bishops and to begin using the vernacular in the liturgy.[49]

Pius XII had made a similar attempt. Besieged by the hostile forces of Communism, the Church was put on the defensive and found it necessary to present a united front through stronger disciplinary and doctrinal union. Prelates like Ruffini and Ottaviani, councilors of the Holy Office, were trying to halt the infiltration of theological and philosophical errors. In 1948, the pope set up a commission, which was attached to the Holy Office, to prepare a program for a Council. A central commission was established with Monsignor Bogongini Duca as its chairman. Pius XII appointed members of the preparatory commission and things began to move along rapidly, but the restriction on the number of participants at the Council caused dissatisfaction. Differences of opinion regarding the direction and procedures of the Council led to a suspension of the project in January 1951. Logistical difficulties, economic restrictions, and the advanced age of the pope also contributed to the project's termination.

Pope John's conception of the Council was undoubtedly an entirely different reality, and in some respects one unknown in the history of the Church. Pius XII's initiative certainly anticipated the climate of Vatican II, and the active involvement of Cardinals Ottaviani, Parente, Browne, Bea, and others gave continuity to the two proposed Councils.[50]

Aside from its originality, Pope John's decision was the fruit of a conviction that had matured slowly with the encouragement of others. He did not seek counsel or give the impression that the matter was open for discussion. As chief shepherd of the Church, Pope John assumed full responsibility for its convocation. He declared this explicitly in the *Journal of a Soul:* "The conduct of the servant of the servants of God in regard to the celebration of the Ecumenical Council is completely his initiative and under his jurisdiction as the head."[51]

The unexpected announcement also contributed to the Council's uniqueness. Historically speaking, conciliar convocations were preceded by lengthy negotiations and were often imposed on the pope who was forced to accept. Councils were frequently called in order to deal with grave errors that had surfaced, which required a firm response to clarify or maintain orthodoxy. No such circumstance gave rise to Vatican II. The doors to this unanticipated Council were opened by the solitary decision of a venerable old man whose election was supposed to guarantee a peaceful, transitional administration through a passing phase of the history of the Church. But at the helm of that "peaceful, transitional administration" was a man who became the undisputed protagonist of a momentous turning point in the life of the Church.

The pope's initiative appears more courageous in light of the prevailing ecclesiastical mentality. The definition of papal infallibility and papal primacy of jurisdiction by Vatican I seemed to render Ecumenical Councils unnecessary.[52] Roncalli had the advantage of being able to admire past Councils from the perspective of an historian. He called the Church's attention to the Ecumenical Council as a very important instrument of her tradition. And he did so because he foresaw the beneficial experience it would be for the contemporary Church. From the moment of the first announcement, and based on suggestions offered, he was convinced that the Council would be the greatest manifestation of the Church's vitality and that the Holy Spirit would make his presence felt most completely through it. The work of the Holy Spirit would continue far beyond the Council. The Spirit, who is always present in the Church, would guide the Council throughout the realization of its work and in the many generous pastoral initiatives that would contribute to the renewal of the Church. The Council would be a fixed point that the Church could refer to constantly in order to be faithful the apostolic model. Pope John often turned to the example of the first apostolic Council of Jerusalem as the prototype and model of every successive Council.

John XXIII was a great admirer of the conciliar tradition, but his was a renewed sense of the value of its importance, and he wished to recover its rich ecclesiastical meaning at a moment when it had become blurred. By bringing the entire episcopate together and offering ample possibilities for exercising the supreme authority of the Church, Pope John was indeed acting contrary to the secular tendency toward increasing centralization.

Lengthy investigations and the painstaking research have been undertaken to clarify the motives that inspired John XXIII. Those who hold the opinion that the decision was made superficially, with little or no awareness of its importance or consequences, are not convincing. The elderly pope understood that the needs of the times required new responses from the Church. It was not a Council for a Christian society as was Lateran Council IV (1215); nor a Council for union with separated Churches as the Council of Florence (1439); nor a defensive Council as that of Trent (1545–1563); nor a Council of resistance and opposition to the world as was Vatican I (1869–1870). Pope John's Council would usher the Church into a phase of epochal transition from its post-Tridentine state into one of witness and proclamation. This Council would recover the strong and permanent elements of tradition

and act as a guarantee of evangelical fidelity even during very demanding times.[53]

As conditions for a more effective announcement of the Gospel, the
renewal of the Church and the revision of how to present Christian doctrine constituted the pope's greatest concern. He confided to Capovilla
the evening before the Council's announcement:

> The world is starving for peace. If the Church responds to her
> Founder and more truly rediscovers her identity, the world will ben-
> efit. I have never had doubts about the faith. But something has left
> me dismayed. For 2,000 years Christ has remained on the cross
> with his arms outstretched. Where are we with the proclamation of
> the Good News? How can we present authentic doctrine to the
> people of our time?[54]

In itself the announcement of a Council of "light, edification, and
joy for all the Christian people" and of "a loving and renewed invitation
to the separated Churches to participate with us in this meeting of grace
and brotherhood" unleashed great ferment. The pope truly perceived the
basic needs of the Church, yet his words indicated that all the goals were
not clearly defined in his mind. He wanted to be a docile instrument of
the Holy Spirit and so he avoided imposing a rigid program. The clarification of the character and goals of the Council would be undertaken
gradually over the years and would be enriched by discussions that
would interest wider areas of the Catholic world.

The Precedents: Continuity or Rupture?

As Pope John's distinctive projects took shape, people began to
wonder if his pontificate was developing naturally from his experiences
as the man who had been a papal nuncio and Venetian patriarch, or if it
departed radically from his past. In the course of his long life, Pope
John's appearance of simplicity and goodness were manifestations of a
human sensitivity and an ability to recognize the needs of the times in
rather exceptional ways. His many experiences were filtered through
and fortified by a continual comparison with the texts of Scripture,
Christian tradition, the liturgy, the Fathers of the Church, and the *Imitation of Christ*. These all converged to form a dimension of genuine wisdom within him. From this wisdom he derived his principles of behavior
and criteria for judgments.[55] His wisdom helped him to see the past (the
object of his continual interest) as more than a means for satisfying in-

tellectual curiosity. It taught him not to lock the past within an uncritical and nostalgic admiration that isolates it from the present. For Roncalli the historian the past was dynamic, and he always tried to glean from it lessons for the present, for life, for human and Christian wisdom. History furnished criteria for comparisons that were neither hasty nor banal. He so often loved to say that the Church is not a museum to be preserved but a garden to be cultivated. The Deposit of Faith was not merely a precious treasure to be protected, and tradition did not equal immobility. Pope John had lived through critical historical events and knew the dynamism that had characterized each period.

Roncalli's first experiences as a young priest gave him firsthand knowledge of the pastoral action of the Church in Bergamo, guided by the firm hand of Bishop Radini Tedeschi. The activities in his home diocese, expressed in Catholic movements, taught Roncalli that pastoral action had to be adapted to changing historical conditions. He had learned to move forward by maintaining a just balance between an inflexible nostalgia for the past and a frenzied and imprudent flight into the future. His obvious passion for historical studies, which he had taken up in Bergamo and cultivated throughout his life, was particularly centered on the reform of St. Charles Borromeo. In Borromeo he encountered a genuine model of adaptation who benefited the Church in many ways.

Roncalli often referred to the Tridentine reform as an exemplary response of the Church to the religious crisis of the 1500s. Vatican II had to make the Church capable of responding to modern times in the same way. His study of history had taught him to appreciate the usefulness of the conciliar institution in delicate moments in the life of the Church, as he stated explicitly in his discourse of January 25.

Roncalli's life as a priest and a bishop contributed immensely to the pastoral character of the future Council. He often repeated that the pastoral spirit is characterized by the concern to proclaim the Gospel before all else and to remain in the properly religious sphere so that its effectiveness is not compromised by involvement in openly political activities.

Pope John's temperament played no small part in his formation as a shepherd of souls. He had been graced with a frank, understanding, and lovable character that was refined by ascetical practices and his adherence to the spirituality of the saint of mildness, St. Francis de Sales. As a nuncio he had lived in a pastoral rather than a rigid, diplomatic spirit. His assignments brought him into milieus that were already de-Christianized (France), non-Catholic (Bulgaria), and non-Christian (Turkey).

The First World War had opened his eyes and heart to a worldwide dimension and had shown him the urgency of establishing peace between peoples. As a diplomat, he personally experienced that the Roman Curia, as the center of Church government, did not always perceive the situation of many of the local churches correctly and did not listen to them enough. As nuncio, he suffered the rejection of some of his proposals by Vatican offices. His many experiences had placed him in touch with a variety of situations that were more or less distant from the Church often because of misunderstandings and prejudices. Sometimes his personal manner had effected reconciliation.

Pope John's lively desire to initiate a dialogue with the people of his time translated into a sincere respect for their dignity, an effort to understand their ideas, and an admission of the faults and errors committed by the Church. Therefore, he was convinced of the necessity of a great collective effort to design anew the lifestyle and doctrinal heritage of the Church so that it might draw closer to contemporary humanity.

CHAPTER 15

BISHOP OF ROME

The Synod Announced

In his discourse of January 25 at St. Paul's Outside the Walls, John XXIII had stressed his ministry as bishop and his duties as shepherd of the diocese of Rome and of the Universal Church. He had learned of the many pastoral activities in progress from conversations with his vicar, Cardinal Micara. But he considered these insufficient for meeting the present needs that continued to grow at a dizzying rate with the swelling population. In convoking the diocesan synod, the pope put the diocese of Rome on a par with any other, which required the direct involvement of its bishop. Why should Rome be denied the experience of one of the highest moments of diocesan life? Indeed, with the exception of the provincial synod called by Benedict XIII in 1725, Rome's last diocesan synod had been held in 1461 under Pius II.[1]

Pope John's idea was not actually original. He confided: "During prayer the Lord made the idea of an Ecumenical Council blossom in the intimate simplicity of my heart. When afterward I spoke of it quietly, an enthusiastic voice suggested: 'Holy Father! The idea of an Ecumenical Council is excellent, but why not think first of a diocesan synod for the center of Christianity which in half a century, according to the latest statistics, has grown from 400,000 inhabitants in 1900 to over two million today?'"[2]

The authoritative testimony of Monsignor Capovilla has identified that "enthusiastic voice" as Monsignor Angelo Dell'Acqua's, substitute for the secretary of state. Roncalli had known Dell'Acqua from the time he was the secretary to Cardinal Eugenio Tosi of Milan. In 1935 at the delegation in Istanbul, they had collaborated for seven months.[3]

The pope's project was meant to help the church in Rome to be aware of its diocesan character through the restoration and normal functioning of its diocesan structures, beginning with the vicariate, which was presided over by an elderly and ailing Cardinal Clemente Micara.

Immediately following the Second World War, the vicariate's direction of the diocese of Rome had often been subordinate to the projects of Pius XII, which were aimed at mobilizing the entire diocese through trusted individuals and groups that worked directly under him. These initiatives — the Crusade of Goodness of 1949, the Holy Year of 1950, the Marian Year of 1954, the campaigns of Catholic Action under the guidance of the Civic Committees of Luigi Gedda — were all intended to make Christian Rome truly "the Holy City." By the end of Pius XII's pontificate, a widespread fatigue was evident in the clergy from having pursued what had become an obviously inadequate pastoral strategy.

John XXIII recognized the need for normalcy in the diocese, and to accomplish this he made a general reorganization the objective. The diocese suffered from other serious problems. The abundant presence of religious institutes in the parishes and territory made the coordination of their pastoral action and its diocesan character problematic; the religious were often more sensitive to the expectations of their various institutes than of the diocese. The various dicasteries of the Roman Curia professed exemption from the authority of the vicariate, and there were more than forty seminaries, colleges, and other institutions directly linked to the Vatican dicasteries. This whole complex of realities led some to conclude that an authentic diocesan life in Rome was impossible, and thus to consider a synod was superfluous. In a public letter written a few days after his announcement, Pope John mentioned that not everyone agreed a synod was appropriate for the diocese.[4]

The pope, having noted the opposition to the project even on the part of Cardinal Micara, quickly assumed full responsibility for the synod and its direction as Bishop of Rome. He began with the appointment of honorary and executive commissions and various sub-commissions.[5] He found capable and convinced collaborators in the vice-director, Monsi-

gnor Traglia, and the secretary, Maccari, who both agreed that the diocesan and parochial structures should be properly utilized in Rome.

The Work of the Synod

The official *iter* (program) of the First Roman Synod opened on
February 18, 1959, with the pontifical document *Ut huius almae,* which
appointed a preparatory commission consisting of fourteen members
who were installed by Pope John on February 23. On March 17, a meeting of all the members of the preparatory and sub-commissions was
held. During this preliminary phase, decisive measures were put in place
to facilitate the good outcome of the synod.

Traglia was put in charge of the project. The first great problem he
faced was the choice of the members for the central commission. The
pope wanted the commission to represent the different ecclesial entities
of the diocese of Rome. In the end, the diocesan clergy was the least
represented, with only two representatives out of the fourteen.

Most of the commission's members were highly specialized and
qualified to draft constitutions. This specialization, however, did not
qualify them for a pastoral appraisal of the city and thus, seven sub-
commissions were created: persons, the magisterium, divine worship
and sacramentals, the sacraments, apostolic action, the education of
youth, and objects. Through the express will of John XXIII communicated at the meeting of March 17, another sub-commission for aid and
beneficence was added.[6]

The pope followed the work of the commissions with interest and
granted relatively frequent audiences to Traglia, who brought him up-to-
date on the thorniest problems. Pope John wanted the diocese to be entirely
involved in the synod so he held two meetings with the pastors, one with
the vice-pastors, and another with the religious. A questionnaire was distributed to all the pastors, although fewer than half responded.

To stimulate the work, John XXIII asked to meet with the members
of the sub-commissions on June 18. After praising the commitment and
competence with which the preparations were being carried out, the pope
confronted a point of strong disagreement within the sub-commissions:
the problem of Catholic Action. He declared that he wanted a change:
Catholic Action had to return to its original tasks of apostolate and formation, and avoid all forms of political action. Moreover, it was to be
placed under the control of the Italian Episcopal Conference and not the

secretary of state or the pope. It would exist *within* the structure of the Church, not *alongside* it. This change signified an empowerment of the diocesan offices and a rejection of the administration of Luigi Gedda.[7]

Toward the end of July, the initial part of the preparatory phase concluded with the drafting of 973 articles.

The successive phases, including the revision of texts, had to be prolonged because the Holy Father decided to broaden the consultation on the texts to various ecclesiastics, and to involve those who had opposed the synod. In an audience of September 22, the pope asked that the texts be sent to a commission of ten pastors and twenty-five consulters of the synod, as well as cardinals, secretaries of the Vatican congregations, provincials of religious orders, and seminary rectors. In the midst of these preparations, the pope wrote to Traglia on October 25 to communicate his decision to open the synod on January 25 — exactly three months away. Perhaps John XXIII hoped that in fixing a date he would help to speed up the work that had already dragged on longer than necessary.[8]

Little by little, the commission released the articles. Pope John read them personally and corrected them in Italian and/or in the later Latin translation. The texts of the amended articles were then delivered to the vicariate with surprising regularity.[9]

At his first meeting with the central commission, the Holy Father described his attitude toward the preparatory phase, saying he had always liked the motto: "Know how to do it, allow it to be done, and have it done." He refrained from imposing any precise directives and limited himself to some general objectives that would be interpreted by the commissions instituted to compare the different positions and identify the most concrete ways of carrying out their mandate. All sides, therefore, had the possibility of expressing themselves and challenging one another, with an evident enrichment from the debates that were neither academic nor predetermined.

As the work progressed there were heated discussions among the commissions' members, and this was a true mirror of the ecclesial reality of Rome. A major difficulty involved the diocesan and religious clergy: on one side stood the secular clergy who upheld their diocesan rights; and on the other, the religious clergy who jealously guarded their autonomy and refused complete insertion into the diocesan structure. The same could also be said of Catholic Action. Since the end of the war, it had been under the central offices and the pope; was it now to be placed under the diocesan offices? It was certainly no surprise that the sharpest differences of opinion concerned these very issues.

After all opinions were expressed, the pope intervened. He attempted to blur the sharp lines of contrast and to bring the opposing positions closer together, to eliminate the obstacles that could block the project, to correct dispositions, and to make choices between alternative courses of action. He did all of this with calm and the greatest sense of respect and moderation. Just as Pope John had intervened in the affairs of Catholic Action, bringing it into fuller submission to the authority of the bishops, he now intervened with the religious. At Traglia's urging, he wrote to them to ask for greater conformity to diocesan regulations.[10]

The Celebration of the Roman Synod

As the entries of his journal testify, the pope felt that his most personal and meaningful contribution as Bishop of Rome was the discourses he delivered at the synod. The thought of the synod had so occupied him that when he was unable to sleep, he carried on an intense and trusting dialogue with Jesus.

> As soon as I had gone to bed, the thought of yesterday evening took over, stopped me from sleeping and invited me to get up from 11:00 P.M. to 2:00 A.M. It provided me with ideas and images for composing the first discourse that I intended to prepare for January 25 at St. John Lateran for the opening of the synod. This nocturnal conversation at my kneeler with Jesus crucified...initiated my spiritual elevation toward the event that the whole Church awaited as an introduction to the more distant celebration of Vatican Council II. May the Lord accept my good will to serve him. The fervor of that night accompanied me during the entire recitation of the breviary and the Mass of St. Stephen.[11]

Officially convoked with the pontifical document *Sancti Spiritus,* the Roman Synod opened on the afternoon of Sunday, January 24, 1960, in the Lateran Basilica. During his discourse to the representatives of the city, cardinals of the Curia, bishops, laity, and the community council, the pope seemed preoccupied with making understood the timeliness of the diocesan synod in a local church that had not celebrated such an event since 1461. He proposed to update the Church and adapt disciplinary laws to the changing needs that were evident in a city undergoing a significant transformation. The expressions the pope used were characteristic of his approach to ecclesiastical legislation, necessary but mutable.[12]

Besides the changeless truth of God, which endures forever, there are things that change in their outward forms. They are always to be respected but are capable of being diminished or vitally strengthened. This is what happens in the holy Church. She is the depository and interpreter of the doctrine of Jesus and continues to impart his teaching, which is unchanging. With regard to discipline and outward and secondary forms, however, some modifications are allowed according to time and circumstance.

The opening ceremony was followed by the three main sessions of the synod, which took place over the next few days in the Hall of Blessings at the Vatican. Each session lasted an entire morning, from 8:00 to 12:00, and included the Eucharistic celebration, the pope's discourse, and the public reading of a portion of the articles of the constitutions — all in Latin. The pope had chosen a unifying theme: the priest. It was treated under the following: the priest, a sacred person, holiness of life; the priest's head, heart, and speech; priest and shepherd.

The selection and treatment of the theme was aimed at adequately motivating the clergy to a theological and spiritual consideration of their high dignity and of their duties. The pope was well aware of the inadequacy of rules — even when wisely updated — for achieving an authentic renewal. He did not pretend to be teaching new things. Instead, he spoke of the fundamentals of the personal holiness of priests according to Tridentine teaching, the priest's intimate union with Christ in the Eucharistic celebration, and his power to remit sins. By having recourse to these truths, the pope recalled their consequences on the spiritual and ascetic life of every individual priest. In a word, it was a call to the duty of holiness.

On the second day, Pope John's starting point was the chapter *De reformatione* of the twenty-second session of the Council of Trent. He approached the practical topic of personal conduct through the three aspects of the head, the heart, and the tongue — that is, intellectual and affective formation and the moderate and charitable use of words. Regarding the heart, John XXIII confirmed the validity of ecclesiastical celibacy and lamented that "in order to save some shred of lost dignity, some can daydream that the Catholic Church would be willing or would find it convenient to renounce what, for century after century, has been and remains one of the noblest and purest glories of her priesthood."[13]

Rather than a theological-spiritual treatment, the third discourse concentrated on applying pastoral principles to the concrete situation of

Rome. Clearly, the pope had at heart a concrete issue so very familiar to him from his personal experience. The problem was a preoccupation with careerism, leading many priests to have greater esteem for assignments in curial offices than for those in parishes. The most negative aspect of this attitude was its wide diffusion among the clergy and its general acceptance. Pope John re-established priorities and emphasized the essentially pastoral character of the ministerial priesthood that must also be the inspiration for bureaucratic activity.

The synod officially closed on the afternoon of Sunday, January 31, in the Basilica of St. Peter, in the presence of the cardinals, the commissions, and many of the clergy and laity. The pope expressed his satisfaction with the impressive work that had been accomplished and which testified to the vitality of the Church in Rome. He had witnessed the participation of all the groups in the church, which he had not found elsewhere. He spoke of the three theological virtues as a true synthesis of the Christian life — firm faith, indomitable hope, effusive charity — and indicated that the most authentic goals and results of the synod would consist in the practice of these virtues. Finally, the pope touched on the upcoming opening of Vatican Council II, which would constitute the background in which the work of the Roman Synod could be situated. For the diocese of Rome, the synodal work had been the most suitable preparation for the Council — a sort of anticipation of it, an introductory experience in the method of collegial work that would be refined.

The documents of the synod were officially promulgated with the apostolic constitution *Sollicitudo* of June 29, 1960. The official ceremony took place on the afternoon of the following day in St. Peter's Basilica. The vicar, Cardinal Micara, was given the official text, now reduced in its final wording to 755 articles. The pope thanked the elderly cardinal for having retreated so humbly into the background to allow the Bishop of Rome to exercise his ordinary powers. Forestalling more or less justifiable criticisms, John XXIII offered his unreserved praise for the work of the synod, again assuming complete responsibility — even for what might not have been completely satisfactory.

The temporary and perfectible character of the synodal norms emerged in the discourse given to the secular and religious Roman clergy at their audience of November 24 (the occasion on which the synodal decrees took effect). "From the initial meeting of January 24 in our holy Lateran Basilica, to the more solemn one of June 29 at the tomb of St. Peter, we have been able, with the help of the Lord, to celebrate what was certainly a good work, even if in some respects it was not perfect."[14] In this discourse, John XXIII indicated what he held essential: the greatness of the priestly mission and the virtues that ought to characterize it — spotless conduct, fraternal love, care not to fall into slander or backbiting, renunciation of the world in order to follow Christ completely, and avoidance of the pitfall of excessive activism. He identified the most urgent need as the effort for renewed motivation in mission. It was the indispensable premise of authentic renewal. The pope drew almost exclusively from classic and traditional sources — the Bible and the Fathers — as if indicating the perspective from which to evaluate the synodal legislation.

According to Pope John, this clarified the content of an updated diocesan pastoral action that was not to be a feverish search for the new. Rather, priority had to be given to an integral recovery of tradition, implying that the recovery of the living tradition of the Church would make possible the discovery of the most suitable means for renewal.

Weighing everything together, the objectives indicated by Pope John were only partially realized. In the synod's 755 canons, a juridical and disciplinary character prevailed over a pastoral one. This is particularly evident concerning priestly activity.

To someone who felt moved to point out defects, whether real or presumed, in the synodal texts, the pope answered, "Nothing is perfect in this world. If there are shortcomings or repetitions, my successor will improve the texts when celebrating the second Roman synod. The first was celebrated by poor Pope John."[15]

Many authors point out the synod's meager immediate effects. Nevertheless, these effects, small as they were, certainly reflected the capacity of the diocese in Rome at that moment in history. It should also be stressed that this was an initial moment in a process of reorganization that was destined to yield greater fruit some ten years later under Pope Paul VI.[16]

Visits to the Parishes

Unlike his predecessors who rarely left the Vatican, Pope John left its confines at least 152 times. John considered his excursions an obligation if he hoped to establish a direct relationship with the people of Rome, and they, impressed with the novelty of having a pope among them, quickly nicknamed him "John outside the walls."

The pope made twenty-five visits to the Roman parishes over a period of five Lenten seasons — from the spring of 1959 to that of 1963. Added to these, the pope made four appearances, beginning in 1960, at the Ash Wednesday penitential processions at Santa Sabina on the Aventine Hill.

Monsignor Capovilla testifies that the idea for these Lenten visits originated with John XXIII. Quite familiar with the traditions of the Roman church, and inspired by his personal love for the liturgy, the pope decided to combine his Lenten visits with the Stations of the Cross.[17]

The pastoral visits had two stages. The first stage was liturgical and included a procession and Eucharistic benediction with a bishop of the vicariate officiating. The second was the pope's encounter with the parish, delivering a discourse — with the help of loudspeakers — to the throng of faithful in and outside the church. As the pope's visits continued, there was an observable growth from the first encounter in the number of participants. This was a unique phenomenon of such occasions.

The visits began on February 22, 1959, the second Sunday of Lent, in the Church of St. Maria in Dominica at Celio. On the following Sunday, the pope visited the Basilica of St. Lawrence. His third and last visit of 1959 was to the Church of St. Prisca on the Aventine, which had been his titular church as a cardinal.

After the first year, John XXIII began to make Lenten visits to the more heavily populated outlying parishes where, for the most part, the people were less anchored in their religious traditions. The people greatly appreciated the pope's visits and participation steadily increased so that the attendance rose from 100,000 to 200,000 — not counting the thousands who showed their homage to Pope John along the route he traveled going or coming.

Although his Lenten visits necessarily lost something of their penitential character, they were stronger moments of joy. This did not mean that the pope renounced his duty as shepherd to preach prayer, fasting, and almsgiving, but his spontaneous conversations, with great simplicity and skill, allowed him to find ways of communicating the religious meaning of the circumstances and surroundings. He never failed to recall the traditional values of Lent as a time of prayer and penitence.

His visits to the outlying parishes were suspended during the Lent of 1962, when preparation for the Council was imminent.

In the spring of 1963, the last months of his life, he again began visiting the outer parishes. At this point, the pope knew he did not have long to live, and his closest collaborators were so preoccupied with his health they pleaded with him to slow down and take better care of himself. He responded kindly but firmly, "Leave me alone, I've thought it over. Do not put obstacles in my way." On one occasion, Monsignor Capovilla warned the pope to be careful because he feared the pope was in danger of hemorrhaging. Pope John responded, "Well, what would be so bad about that? Many Christians die in the streets. Why should it be so bad for a pope to die that way?"[18]

Five Sundays of festive encounters took place in the suburban parishes southwest of Rome and at Ostia. Perhaps the familiarity between John and the Romans reached its culmination on March 31, in one of the most problematic regions at the parish of St. Basil. To this neighborhood, a stronghold of openly radical political elements, Pope John presented some moral themes of St. Gregory the Great that concerned the Christian use of earthly goods and their just distribution. He concluded his talk hinting at the possible and proximate end of his life and his hope of entering eternal happiness.[19]

The crowd's enthusiasm prompted the pope to prolong his calendar of visits to include Palm Sunday. He visited the parish of St. Tarcisius at Quarto Miglio in a small town on the Appian Way. A particular episode that took place there demonstrates the climate created by Pope John's personality. Upcoming elections slated for the spring of 1963 had led to intense political promotion of parties, and the whole neighborhood was plastered with posters and large banners for one side or another. At the pastor's request, all parties agreed to remove these signs of political confrontation, which had been particularly bitter that year. Photos taken during the pope's visit to Quarto Miglio show houses sporting banners praising the pope; one that hung on the facade of the church exclaimed: "Long live the good Pope!"[20]

Pope John's natural manner made him welcome even where people felt somehow alienated by the clergy and had perhaps grown hostile. He believed that this precise group of people, those who felt alienated, constituted the privileged part of his flock; they were the ones in greater need of their bishop's attention. Indeed, he was the good shepherd.

> Anyone who wants to take the simplest application from the Gospel will immediately see the Good Shepherd in search of his sheep. Undoubtedly, even in the center of the city they need a Father's care. But the sheep that best show the color of the flock, so to speak,

of our Lord Jesus Christ are found in the countryside that is becoming, or rather has already become, a city.[21]

He was strongly convinced that he had identified a valid means for staying in touch with his faithful — a familiar practice in tradition, but one that had been out of use in Rome for at least a century. Later, in the final moments of his illness, Pope John confided that if the Lord permitted him to live longer, he would continue his pastoral visits to the parishes after the Council in order to explain its message.[22]

Preaching and the New Site of the Vicariate

Pope John was very interested in preaching. His most meaningful discourses were given at the traditional yearly meeting with preachers at the beginning of Lent. Here also, Pope John's personality left its imprint. He held a purely conversational encounter on December 22, 1958, with 170 pastors who had been invited to meet the new pope after his election. At that gathering, he touched upon some themes with regard to preaching that he would develop later.

For the first three years of his pontificate, Pope John held an official encounter with pastors and preachers at the beginning of each Lent. A fourth encounter followed in 1962, but it can be considered extraordinary in nature in comparison with the others. (No encounter took place in 1963.) His principal recommendations on preaching are seen in his first discourse of February 10, 1959. He concentrated on the three qualities of wisdom, simplicity, and charity.

Wisdom was exercised by the preacher in a careful choice of themes that helped the simple faithful form a complete knowledge of the principal truths of Christianity. In the preaching he had heard addressed to the people of Rome he had noted "a certain discontinuity of planning, leaving aside one or another aspect of doctrine, so as to express, on various points, little adherence to the general plan to teach all the revealed truths." He recommended a moderate use of edifying stories and anecdotes, because the people were asking for the substantial bread of truth. He proposed a series of alternative themes to treat during Lent: "the notion of guilt and punishment, giving to each his own due, private and public worship, the sanctification of feast days, the sacred duties of marriage, the education of children, and respect for the human person." He warned against superficiality and directed similar criticism toward scholarly preaching that did not meet the needs and sensibilities of the actual people and times. "There can be a temptation to prepare poetry and literature on the most pleasing topics; or else to specialize in apologetics, perhaps lingering on ancient forms without recognizing the sometimes tremendous necessities of the present times and the progress of pastoral experience."[23]

The priest should aim at touching the hearts of the faithful with simplicity and thus arouse in them a profound change of life. The pope stressed that preaching was by no means an easy art or the fruit of improvisation. Rather:

> It requires a serious preparation of prayer and study and an exact calculation of time and words. Simplicity is the precise aiming of one's thought toward the goal one wants to reach. It is the measure of the time available — however much is needed for the instruction of the faithful and not for the pleasure of listening to oneself.... Remember the words of St. Bernard, who says that he preferred to listen to the voice of a preacher who does not applaud himself, but moves persons to repentance (cf. sermon 59 on the *Song of Songs*).[24]

Besides the simplicity that touches the heart (the pope gave some memorable examples of this), charity had an important place. The pope's impassioned words, which he repeated, are the emblem of his style and the reason for his effectiveness. "Nothing is a more sure and more excellent praise in a sacred orator than that his listeners are led to think: he is really the image of the good Jesus; he is Jesus' disciple, worthy of veneration, meek and humble of heart."[25] The pope's many recommendations to preachers, which he never tired of repeating, were derived from these words: avoid polemical and excessively offensive tones, whether addressing individuals or the whole of society.

> Words that are rude, gloomy, or polemically biting are not appropriate on the lips of priests. Neither should one insist on describing and detailing evil. The weak like to dwell on this. Just a touch, nothing more. One word and not two.... Under the cloak of zeal and fervor, some people go to excess and let themselves be agitated by a spirit of indignation and rage.... This is a mistake.[26]

Here we find John XXIII's pastoral style expressed completely. In his opening discourse at the Council, with the authority of the successor of Peter, he would indicate this as a task for the Universal Church.

Looking at Pope John's sources and models, there is an apparent lack of contemporary works and authors. The pope always recommended the Fathers of the Church, St. Bernardine of Siena, St. Lawrence Justinian, St. Antoninus of Florence, Bossuet,[27] and naturally the Bible, the liturgy, the breviary, and the directives of the magisterium, which he mentioned explicitly in his third discourse on February 13, 1961.[28] These authors and works defined the spiritual and cultural physiognomy of Pope John XXIII as a man of tradition. His sensibilities made tradition the object of his criteria. Earlier centuries had a surfeit of exhortations that tended toward severity and public denunciation. In John's magisterium there are no traces of stern warnings or those elements that made up the "pastoral approach of fear." Yet, he had grown up with this common method practiced in Bergamo toward the end of the nineteenth century and the beginning of the twentieth.

The pope made another important decision concerning the transfer of the vicariate of Rome. Since 1906, the vicariate had been located in the Marescotti-Maffei Palace at the Piazza della Pigna. The palace was an admirable edifice, but far too small by this time to meet the increased needs of the city. In addition, access to the building was difficult because of the narrow alleys leading to it and its distance from the other diocesan institutions, including the Roman Seminary and the Lateran University. The inadequacy of the location had already been discussed ten years earlier by the vicar, Cardinal Micara, who proposed that the vicariate be transferred to the Lateran. However, financial difficulties made it impossible for Pius XII to approve.

The issue remained unsettled until 1962 when a decision was made — probably without Pope John's direct knowledge — to transfer the vicariate offices to the more spacious surroundings at St. Callistus in Trastevere. When Pope John learned that the process for relocation was already underway, he formulated a plan for transferring the vicariate to the Lateran. Apparently the idea came to the pope as he prepared his discourse for the feast of the Nativity of John the Baptist.[29] On the evening of the feast, June 24, the pope made the announcement in the Lateran Basilica.[30] "At the end of my brief discourse I expressed the desire that all the offices of the vicariate be transferred definitively to the great pontifical palace at St. John's, since no other location could be more worthy of the government of the diocese of Rome."[31]

This desire quickly became a decision with the encouragement of the new secretary of state, Amleto Cicognani, who had succeeded Tardini. On July 12, the pope sent a letter to Cicognani to inform him that he had constituted a commission to study and cooperate in the matter. The commission was composed of eleven members — six of whom were cardinals — with the secretary of state acting as chairperson.[32]

After an initial meeting in July at Castelgandolfo, the pope went "very secretly" to the Lateran Palace on the afternoon of Sunday, September 16, to personally observe the situation. Realizing the extent and time involved in the work, he consented to the temporary transfer of the offices of the vicariate to St. Callistus. The interim move was to take place at the end of 1963, while the definitive transfer would occur in 1967 under Pope Paul VI.

John XXIII gave great importance to this decision, because with it the Church of Rome recovered its ancient center of life and pastoral activity and its authentic and prestigious exterior image. He was so certain of the value of this move that in his last testament he expressed his desire to be buried there.[33] This bears witness to his dynamic episcopal consciousness fully identified with the Church, for which he was responsible as guide.

Without depreciating Pope John's many initiatives, one might say that his most outstanding merit lay in his new perspectives — as well as in his short- and long-term lines of action — rather than in immediate and efficacious solutions. In fact, it would be impossible to expect such. Under certain aspects, Pope John's initiatives were quite pioneering, but he lacked sufficient time to bring them to full realization.

CHAPTER 16

GOVERNING THE CHURCH

One Heartbeat

In the personal pages of his journal, John XXIII wrote in August 1961, the vigil of his eightieth birthday, his recollections on being elected to the papacy. Being given the title "Vicar of Christ" troubled him immensely, though he accepted it on a predominantly spiritual level. He understood the title as an invitation to an intimate and personal relationship with Jesus, after the example of Peter who was called to make a triple profession of his love by the Risen One at the Lake of Tiberias. Pope John wrote that between Jesus and Peter there was only love, the source and reason for the conferral of the mission of vicar and, therefore, of his obligation to be totally dedicated to souls.

As successor of Peter, Pope John made every effort to live this bond intensely — a bond strengthened by the pope's contemplation of the crucifix. Jesus' arms extended as if to embrace the whole world and the shedding of his blood were images of a love spending itself for the salvation of the entire human race.

The mystery of the cross was central to the spirituality of Pope John. Through contemplation, he felt that he was not only an object of God's infinite, divine mercy, but that he was also called to perpetuate God's mercy in human history by sharing it. He accepted this bond of love as absolute and exclusive. He worked out his life as Christ's Vicar within this relationship.

Thus and always more so must the life remaining to me here below be animated: at the foot of the cross of Jesus Crucified, watered by his most precious blood and by the tears of the Sorrowful Virgin, Jesus' Mother and my own. In these days, this interior impulse has taken me by surprise. *I feel it in my heart* as a new pulse and a new spirit; it is a voice that infuses in me generosity and great fervor.[1]

Pope John often expressed his desire to be totally united with the Lord: "Clasp me tightly to your Heart — in one heartbeat with mine. I love to feel indissolubly bound to you...."[2] He expressed the centrality of this relationship through attitudes which permeated him entirely as pope: detachment from everything and from every reason to be proud; awareness of his personal limitations and shortcomings; exclusive pursuit of God's glory; commitment to total charity toward his neighbor; and total availability to accept all sufferings sent by the Lord, with profound trust in the help that Christ never fails to assure his Vicar.

This intimate relationship with Christ made holiness an obligation. It called for an effort to strive toward an always more perfect similarity to Christ, in order to diffuse the divine glory destined to shine brightly in the holy Church. "The most sacred duty of the poor pope is to conform all his intentions to this light of glory and to live in such a harmony of doctrine and grace as to merit the greatest honor of resembling Christ in perfection, as his Vicar."[3] Pope John's unique assimilation gave ordinary elements of meditation new emphasis. In Christ, his model, he chose to focus on the presence of love, humility, and meekness as specified by the Good Shepherd, who is meek and humble of heart (cf. Mt 11:29). Pope John always sought to live that attractive simplicity which lies farthest from every sort of affectation that "knows of mystery or cautious fear."[4] It is not difficult to find evidence of this typical roncallian style that could exercise such a fascination on others.

Although he was now at the apex of the Church, his motto, "obedience and peace," which had inspired his choices and assured his tranquillity of spirit, was as operative as ever. Now, having no higher superior, his obedience revolved directly around the person of Christ, who never failed to communicate to his Vicar projects for the good of the Church. This communication presupposed an attitude of humility on the part of the pope and the complete awareness of his own nothingness. This meant being unconcerned about the world's appreciation, being indifferent to fame, and being a docile instrument in the hands of God while trusting in his help and presence in the Church and in human history. Matured by a lifetime of commitment, these attitudes had become stable elements at the foundation of Pope John's personality and the spontaneous reference points for his conduct. The gravest news or the most demanding tasks no longer threw him into a state of anxiety or paralyzing uncertainty; they did not hinder him from an attentive and realistic appraisal of the difficulties involved and their related problems. With a personality built on an enviable sense of balance, where wisdom and human virtue were wedded to a serene optimism based on faith, Pope John confronted the problems relating to his role as Vicar of Christ.

During his spiritual exercises, the pope humbly acknowledged the gifts he possessed and described them in his notes at the beginning of December 1959:

> Above all, I thank the Lord for the temperament he has given me, which preserves me from anxiety and the fatigue of discouragement. I feel that I am obeying in everything. My awareness of being so sustained, in great things and small, confers on my insignificance a power of bold simplicity. Since it is completely evangelical, this power calls for and obtains general respect and edifies many.[5]

Underlying all of Pope John's decisions was a perfect integrity of spirit, total uprightness, and constant availability to comply with Divine plans. His choices were not founded on calculated interests; they were acts of obedience to the inspirations suggested by the Lord. His sole duty was to comply. The Vicar knew what Christ wanted of him; there was certainly no need for him to advise Christ or to impose his own projects. A fundamental rule of the pope's conduct was to be satisfied with his *present* state and not to puzzle out the *future*, which he awaited from the Lord without counting on plans or taking human precautions. He judged that the initiatives of the first year of his pontificate were acts of obedience.

> Of the various pastoral initiatives that have adorned this sample year of papal apostolic commitment, everything originated from the absolute, peaceful, lovable — and I would also say silent — inspiration of the Lord to this poor servant of his who, without any merit of his own other than the simplicity of not objecting, merely complied and obeyed, thus becoming an instrument to honor Jesus and edify many souls.[6]

In the spiritual exercises for his eightieth year, he renewed his commitment to the main points of his life of prayer. Prompt rising in the early hours of the morning allowed him to live an intense moment of prayer. He recited the first hours of the breviary, celebrated holy Mass, and then prayed the hours of Sext and None and the joyful mysteries of the rosary. He continued his prayer after lunch with a brief visit to the chapel. Afterward he rested — not lying down, but sitting on a simple seat or deck chair. Then he prayed Vespers, Compline, and the sorrowful mysteries. The last moments of prayer took place in the evening at 7:30. With the papal household he prayed the glorious mysteries of the rosary and made a second visit to chapel to recommend the hours of the night to the Lord.[7]

Through his devout practices, the pope aimed at living in constant intimacy with Jesus.

> The breviary keeps my spirit constantly elevated; the holy Mass immerses it in the *Name,* in the *Heart*, and in the *Blood of Christ.* Oh! What tenderness and delight this morning Mass of mine contains! The rosary, which I have obliged myself to say devoutly in its entirety since 1958, has become an exercise of continual meditation and tranquil and daily contemplation. It keeps my spirit open to the vastest field of my magisterium and ministry as Chief Shepherd of the Church and of Universal Father of souls.[8]

We know that Pope John loved to attach particular intentions to each of the fifteen mysteries of the rosary; for example, the nativity of Jesus was dedicated to all the children born during that day. The rosary occasioned the meditation on the mysteries of salvation and, at the same time, prayer that their benefits might spread throughout the whole world. The reflection on his personal experience is clearly traced in the encyclical *Grata Recordatio* (Grateful Memory), published on September 26, 1959. Sowing seeds in the furrows plowed by Leo XIII, he exhorted the faithful to recite the rosary. On one hand, this prayer opens the horizons of contemplation on the highest mysteries of the faith as if in a set of paintings; on the other, it gives private prayer a universal scope. The pope proposed the intention of the difficulties of the missions and of justice and peace among peoples.[9]

Another important aspect of Pope John's spirituality was his practice of poverty. On the vigil of his election to the papacy, he jotted down the extent of his savings: "my deposit with the Works of Religious: 2,045,000 lire [today approximately $920 in U.S. dollars], in addition to 100 francs." This was the extent of his personal funds shortly after becoming pope — after thirty years of service to the Holy See, and six in the episcopate of Venice.[10] Later, when Capovilla had to inform Pope John of his imminent death, he chose to leave the little money in his account to the office of the secretary of state. He said, "I want the Lord to find me as I am in reality: poor and with nothing."[11] He used this phrase in a letter he sent to his brother Xavier on December 3, 1961, when he responded to certain voices that criticized him for leaving his brothers to their modest living. Pope John wrote that among the pope's duties, that of enriching or ennobling his family with prestigious titles was not included. He was ready to help his relatives if they were ever in need and according to their individual conditions. He was certain that his restraint would be one of the greatest honors of Pope John and the Roncalli family.[12] Later, on the advice of his confessor, Monsignor Cavagna, he consented to leave a small pension for his brothers after his death.

The Encyclicals

In the course of his brief pontificate, John XXIII published eight encyclicals. In chronological order they are: *Ad Petri Cathedram* (From the Chair of Peter), June 29, 1959; *Sacerdotii Nostri Primordia* (From the Beginning of Our Priesthood), August 1, 1959; *Grata Recordatio* (Grateful Memory), September 26, 1959; *Princeps Pastorum* (Prince of Shepherds), November 28, 1959; *Mater et Magistra* (Christianity and Social Progress), May 15, 1961; *Aeterna Dei Sapientia* (The Eternal Divine Wisdom), November 11, 1961; *Paenitentiam Agere* (To Do Penance), July 1, 1962; *Pacem in Terris* (Peace on Earth), April 11, 1963. We will present a brief commentary on the lesser known four, which are not mentioned, further on.

From the Chair of Peter is the programmatic encyclical of John's pontificate. The pope sets forth themes that he identifies as the most urgent of his apostolic commitment: truth, unity, and peace — goods to be achieved and promoted according to the spirit of Christian charity. These themes had already appeared among the objectives of the Council, and they effectively constituted the environment within which unfolded the work of John XXIII.

The theme of truth has not yet been treated in view of its specifically roncallian features. Pope John developed this theme in his encyclical in a completely traditional way and used uncharacteristically sharp words in referring to those who denied God's revealed truth and opposed it through falsehood or the promotion of an attitude of indifference. The prevailing tone is one of condemnation: "Those...who declare that the human mind can grasp no truth with complete certainty and who reject the truths revealed by God, which are essential for our eternal salvation, are beyond all doubt wandering miserably far from the teaching of Christ."[13]

The document lacks the nuances found later in the opening discourse of the Council when the pope stressed the need for a better understanding of Christian doctrine in order to present it in a manner more suited to contemporary humanity.

His marked insistence on maintaining peace reveals a strong preoccupation with the possibility of war in a world dangerously divided. However, he was also aware of the role he could play as head of the Catholic Church in view of his neutral and non-partisan leadership. The pope seemed to have selected the area wherein to maneuver, and it allowed some distance from a markedly pro-Western stance.[14] He would insist on the already obvious arguments to bring opposing sides together: the absurdity of war with the imminent possibility of employing atomic weapons and not concentrating on "the things which cause men to be separated from each other, but rather...those by which they can be united in a fair and mutual esteem."[15] These premises gave birth to his impassioned appeal for all governments to strive for mutual understanding.[16]

The introduction to the theme of unity within the Church and among the Churches reveals the pope's desire to make known the topic he was particularly fond of: "Let us now speak of that unity which we especially desire and with which the pastoral office committed to us by God is most closely linked."[17] The discourse takes on a decisively ecumenical tone, manifesting a sincere respect toward other Christian confessions. It confirms the necessary adhesion to the doctrinal patrimony defined by the magisterium, but, referring to John Henry Newman, it recalls the right to free theological debate on whatever has not yet been defined. This reference is obviously an invitation to those theologians who considered themselves the most qualified custodians of orthodoxy to respect their colleagues and to establish a climate of greater trust within the Church: "In essentials, unity; in doubtful matters, liberty; in all, charity."[18] Regarding our separated brothers and sisters, John XXIII expressed sentiments of authentic fraternity and esteem long cultivated in his soul and now vested with the authority of the Vicar of Christ: "Indulge this gentle longing we have to address you as brothers and sons.... We lovingly invite you to the unity of the Church. We are inviting you

Roncalli at St Peter's on the day of his coronation, November 4, 1958.

Pope John XXIII with Dominico Tardini, his secretary of state.

The Holy Father during his visit to Loreto
where he prayed to the Virgin Mary for graces for the Council.

John XXIII at the Basilica of St. Paul Outside the Walls where,
on January 25, 1959, he announced the celebration
of the Second Vatican Council to the College of Cardinals.

John XXIII with Cardinal Giovanni Battista Montini,
his future successor who would take the name of Paul VI.

John XXIII at Assisi to invoke
the Virgin Mary's protection over the Council.

John XXIII opens the Second Ecumenical Vatican Council
on October 11, 1962, with the words, "Exalt Mother Church."

Delivering his Easter message on April 22, 1962.

Pope John XXIII imparts his *Urbi et Orbi* blessing from St. Peter's.

Taking a break from a busy schedule.

Pope John XXIII's final greeting to the faithful and to all people, May 22, 1963.

Pope John XXIII lies in state in St. Peter's Basilica.

The tomb of Pope John XXIII in the crypt of St. Peter's Basilica.

not to the home of a stranger, but to your own home, to the Father's house which belongs to all."[19] Contrary to the widely held theological opinions of the time, the pope recognized an authentic ecclesial character in the non-Catholic Christian communities: "All those, therefore, who are separated from us, we address as brothers, using the words of St. Augustine: 'Whether they like it or not, they are our brethren. They will cease to be our brethren only if they cease to say Our Father.'"[20]

The pope wrote the next encyclical, *From the Beginning of Our Priesthood*, for the centenary of the death of the Curé of Ars, St. John Marie Baptiste Vianney. Pope John had been at the beatification ceremony of the Curé of Ars on January 8, 1905, and he was now perfectly at ease with seeing this humble and heroic French priest as the model of the modern pastor.[21] Pope John loved to linger over the exposition of the spiritual and pastoral elements that constituted the person of the priest. He experienced an intimate joy when speaking of this reality, now so dear to him and perfectly assimilated. The encyclical moves in a traditional theological-pastoral context, yet the model he proposed is spiritually intense and an impetus to confront contemporary problems.

Prince of Shepherds is also a commemorative work. On the fortieth anniversary of *Maximum Illud* (November 30, 1919), the pope declared it the great missionary encyclical of the century. This document reiterates the directives of John's predecessors regarding the constitution of local churches and adds some new points. Pope John confirmed the necessity of creating local hierarchies and of fostering indigenous clergy. Due appreciation should be shown them by the conferral of appropriate, and not merely secondary, duties.[22] Among other things, the document expresses the desire that seminarians in Asia and Africa be formed by their fellow countrymen, and that indigenous clergy rapidly assume the direction of their local dioceses. The document gives particular attention to the laity, because of the necessary Christian presence in the many countries that had just gained, or were in the process of gaining, independence. The serious problems of initiating autonomous political activity and of developing workable socioeconomic projects are stressed.

The encyclical *The Eternal Divine Wisdom* commemorated the fifteenth centenary of the death of Leo the Great. It is a testimony to Pope John's passion for and knowledge of the Fathers, which had given him an opportunity to acquire new, though not systematic, perspectives in theology compared with the teachings in conventional texts. A theology drawn from the Fathers also had an ecumenical thrust — with the authoritative expression of traditional thought that dated back to a time without divisions.

Leo the Great is presented as a herald and defender of the Church's unity concerning both doctrine and discipline.[23] In addition to recalling Leo's contribution to the solemn Christological definition of the Council of Chalcedon in 451, Pope John refers to his doctrine about the transmission of the Roman primacy from Peter to his successors. Citing Theodoret of Cyrrhus, one of the most important Eastern Fathers of the fifth century, and St. Irenaeus of Lyons from the second century, Pope John affirms that in the East this primacy was also recognized.[24]

Notwithstanding the respectful and friendly tone of this encyclical, the reference to the controversial Canon 28 of Chalcedon, which gave the Church of Constantinople primacy over all the Eastern Churches, triggered an ecumenical incident. John XXIII recalled that Leo the Great opposed the canon because it contradicted earlier traditions that favored the more ancient Churches of Alexandria and Antioch. In a sense, the canon placed ecclesiastical and civil structures on the same level.[25] Various leaders of the Eastern Churches were somewhat irritated by this reference to the canonical controversy and judged it an obstacle to ecumenical dialogue. Nevertheless, it was only a small incident along the way, which compromised neither the dialogue already begun nor the future participation of Orthodox observers at Vatican II.[26]

Ordinary Government and Some Thorny Questions

In his discourse on the afternoon of June 5, 1960, the feast of Pentecost, Pope John presented the preparation phases and development of Vatican II. He reaffirmed that the competent congregations of the Curia, under the guidance of the pope, had been entrusted with the ordinary government of the Church. However, preparations for the Council would be carried out in a completely autonomous manner. If members of the Curia were made part of the organizations of preparation, it would be because of their personal competence.[27]

Thus, in contrast to his predecessors, Pope John did not interfere with the Roman congregations' traditional activity. Perhaps Pope John did not insert trusted friends into the curial structure — with the exception of Cardinal Gustavo Testa — because he foresaw his brief pontificate.[28] Instead, he preferred to avail himself of the collaboration of people he considered suited to specific tasks. For example, he chose Cavagna as his personal confessor and counselor; Verardo was assigned to the Holy Office and Pavan worked with social problems. For cultural matters, he had thought of Giuseppe de Luca, but the priest's premature death prevented that collaboration. Eventually, Pope John established harmonious relations with some of the cardinals through whom he would succeed in giving Vatican II the direction he desired. These included Cardinal Bea for ecumenism, and Suenens and Léger for the direction of the conciliar work.[29]

The pope's papers mention a sarcastic remark circulating in the Vatican which reflected the opinion that John XXIII was substantially absent from active government and had been replaced by collaborators and powerful men of the Curia: "Angelo (Dell'Acqua) reigns; Carlo (Confalonieri) informs; Alfredo (Ottaviani) supervises; Domenico (Tardini) governs; and John blesses." The pope commented: "Strong words, cutting deed."[30] Though it was true that he exercised his role with great discretion — carefully avoiding heated conflicts — John XXIII followed the events of the Church closely and never failed to give direction or to intervene authoritatively.

A matter of interest, although of secondary importance, occurred during the first year of his pontificate. In his typically friendly manner, the pope made some direct and casual contacts with the various Vatican employees. He discovered that the employees' earnings were entangled in a veritable remunerative jungle. The pope quickly set up a commission to examine the matter, and upon his suggestion, a substantial increase was established. The lowest level of remuneration jumped from 51,500 to 70,000 lire — a 36 percent increase — while the highest stipends underwent a modest 12 percent increase. Additionally, a consistent system for family allowances and pension benefits was introduced.[31]

As for the appointment of bishops, the pope's approval of the movement for independence in the Third World countries facilitated the progressive passage from a missionary Church governed by European clergy to an indigenous Church governed by local clergy. The episcopal appointments during his pontificate numbered a good 1,076. The appointments were marked by an increased attention to the continents outside Europe, a selection of candidates from the local clergy, and a decrease in the median age of the new bishops. The number of bishops grew from 2,480 in 1958 to 2,809 in 1963. The number of residential Sees grew from 1,638 to 1,916.[32] Significantly, the interventions of the

Holy Office were becoming fewer — a sign of an overall change of climate in the new pontificate.

The first intervention of the Holy Office to provoke controversy was the *monitum* (warning) issued in December 1958 against the book entitled *Pastoral Experiences,* written by Lorenzo Milani, a Florentine priest. On October 1 of that year (only a few days before his election), Cardinal Roncalli had written a letter to Monsignor Piazzi, bishop of Bergamo, in which he had expressed a decidedly negative judgment of the book. When Ottaviani brought the new pope the prepared text of the official reproof, the pontiff wanted to make sure that it censured only the *work* and not the *author.*[33] The book was removed from circulation.

Another priest, Primo Mazzolari, had often been censured by the Roman Curia as an alleged supporter of socialism and was still not entirely free of suspicion. The pope took a different attitude toward John Mazzolari, and this contributed to his rehabilitation. Roncalli had known Mazzolari in Venice and the two had enjoyed a good relationship. On February 5, 1959, John XXIII greeted him in an audience with great warmth: "Here is the trumpet of the Holy Spirit from the lowlands of the Po [Valley]!" This gesture filled Mazzolari with joy. Less then two months later, he passed away suddenly.[34]

The extremely complicated matter of the question of worker priests became very troubling for John's pontificate. The innovative experiment of the Church in France early after the Second World War had been drastically curtailed by the Holy Office in 1954. Notwithstanding Vatican prohibitions, a reflection on the problem of how to evangelize the working classes continued. With Pope John's election, there were hopes that Rome would take on a more lenient attitude toward the movement. Instead, the Holy Office prepared a new and still more restrictive document in which the experiment was judged incompatible with the traditional meaning of priesthood, and it called for the gradual and prudent conclusion of this activity. While institutions of laity and priests would replace the worker priests, they would be limited to carrying out the role of chaplain — confining their activities outside the workplace. Although the document bore the official date of July 3, 1959, Cardinal Feltin, archbishop of Paris, had been informed of it by June 11. Received in audience by Pope John, the cardinal failed to obtain any modifications to the document. Cardinal Liénart, the elderly bishop of Lille, wrote to the author of the precautions, Cardinal Pizzardo. Liénart expressed his bitterness over a decision that deprived episcopal authority of its power and created conflicts of conscience in the clergy and militant Catholics. The greatest reserve had been exercised in the matter, including the dispatch of the decree. On September 15, the French newspaper *Le Monde* published the decree and a tremendous uproar ensued. Then Pope John intervened. In a personal letter to the archbishop of Paris, he still supported "what is here believed to be *suggested in the Lord,*" but he made an effort to clear the atmosphere. He recalled his ties of profound friendship with the cardinal, whom he had known since his years at the nunciature in Paris, and repeated his esteem for the numerous proofs of his apostolic zeal. He presented the decision of the Holy Office as an inevitable moment of reflection on a very delicate topic "which, closely touching the pure substance of the Catholic priesthood in its highest and most sacred aspects, deeply concerns the daily ministry of truly winning souls, governing them well, and sanctifying them."[35]

John XXIII strongly adhered to a completely traditional concept of the priesthood, according to the model he had outlined in his recent encyclical, *From the Beginning of Our Priesthood*. Nevertheless, he regarded the above-mentioned decision as provisional and in a sense suspended the problem while he waited for the situation to clarify itself in light of the discussions at the Council. Receiving a delegation of French worker priests in February of 1960, Pope John said: "I am not against your institution.... Patience! Patience! The Council and my successor will decide."[36] The climate of openness at the Council would indeed enable Paul VI to grant permission for a new phase in this evangelization effort.[37] Pope John did not want to change the precedents of his predecessors; however, he laid the groundwork for overturning them by introducing new ideas, especially concerning the Council as an instrument for the complete evaluation of the Church's life.

The Council would also end the heated dispute over the use of the historical-critical method in biblical studies. Those who were following the method could boast the support of Pius XII's encyclical, *Divino Afflante Spiritu*. From the time of its publication, the new approach had been imposed on the institutes of research, faculties, and seminaries that composed the Pontifical Biblical Institute or the *Biblicum*. The approach alarmed traditionalists who were especially active in Rome and in some groups in the United States. They felt that the Church ran the risk of destroying the historical value of both the Old and New Testaments with the new methods. If under Pius XII the conflict was to some extent contained, under Pope John it exploded. In August 1960, Alonso Schökel published an article in *Civiltà Cattolica* in which he defended some authoritative professors at the Pontifical Biblical Institute. He showed that their teachings were consistent with the directions of *Divino Afflante Spiritu*, which had marked a turning point in exegetical studies, although some "abuses of freedom and some errors" were acknowledged in the application of the new methods.[38]

The reaction was immediate. Monsignor Romeo, professor at the Pontifical Lateran University, responded in a long article that attacked the new methods. He charged that they were inspired by rationalism and were plainly in contradiction to the traditional and magisterial interpretation of the Bible. He launched into *Biblicum* Professors Alonso Schökel, Zerwick, Lyonnet, and Levie. His aggressive and coarse tone is verified by the following quote attributed by Romeo to one of the collaborators: "We have removed the Old Testament from the battle: now there remains only to accomplish the same with regard to the New Testament; the fight will be longer and more difficult, but we will succeed."[39]

In turn, the Biblical Institute immediately published an article in its defense and received expressions of solidarity. A withdrawal of both articles was ordered and the question was apparently referred to the Holy Office. On June 23, the Holy Office issued a warning against the exegetes for endangering the historicity of Scripture, especially the New Testament, and for not taking into account the doctrine of the Fathers and of the magisterium. On September 1, Zerwick and Lyonnet were suspended from teaching at the *Biblicum*. One of the goals of the campaign had been achieved.

Pope John's viewpoint on all of this is not very clear. We know with certainty that he disapproved of Monsignor Romeo's article and that he esteemed the *Biblicum*. In fact, he immediately appointed its rector, Vogt, to the theological commission. However, even within the circle of his collaborators, there was some perplexity over certain aspects and results of modern exegesis. This may explain Pope John's hesitancy to become further involved. It is also possible that the control exercised by the offices of the Curia created difficulties.

What is certain is that the great absentee from the fray was the Biblical Commission. Pope John had expected it to take an authoritative stance because of its expertise. To arouse it from its culpable laxity, the pope wrote a letter to its president, Cardinal Tisserant, during the first half of 1962. In a tone that was unusually harsh and threatening for the pope, John XXIII wrote:

Either the Biblical Commission will decide to stir itself, work, and take action, making suggestions to the Holy Father that are suited to the needs of the present day, or it would be worthwhile that it be dissolved so that higher authority can provide *in the Lord* for a reconstitution of this organization. As for the uncertainties that are circulating here and there, doing no one justice, it is necessary to eliminate the alarmist impression that well-defined positions must be taken with regard to the trends of individuals and schools.... It would be a source of great consolation if, in the preparation of the Ecumenical Council, a biblical commission of such depth and dignity emerged as to become a point of reference and esteem for all our separated brethren who, when they abandoned the Catholic Church, took refuge as an escape and salvation in the shadow of the Sacred Book, differently read and interpreted.

The pope followed up his threats by taking precautions. Between July 14 and 21, 1962, he assigned some outstanding and open-minded exegetes to the commission, including Schnackenburg, Spicq, Rigaux, and Léon-Dufour.

As in the case of the worker priests, the intervention of the Roman congregations, counterbalanced by some of Pope John's decisions, would have only short-term effects. All the questions concerning biblical exegesis would be taken up in depth at the Council.[40]

John XXIII and the Italian Church

In the process of enhancing the role of the episcopate, John XXIII gave greater responsibilities to the Italian Episcopal Conference (CEI). Refining the initiatives already begun by Pius XII, he had a new statute enacted in September 1959. In October of the same year, he appointed as the new president Cardinal Siri of Genoa. The latter interpreted the decisions of the pope thus: "Some changes...have the significance of giving the Italian episcopate a collective responsibility in the general affairs of making and executing programs concerning Italy." This was no small advantage for a Church that seemed enveloped within the structure of the Roman congregations and had until then received its directives principally from the pope. The roncallian style was different. In Pope John's first meeting with the representatives of the CEI on December 14, 1958, he manifested some of his concerns without giving authoritative indications for action.[41]

However, the bishops' freedom to express themselves autonomously gave rise to a somewhat different direction than Pope John intended. In fact, the Church in Italy continued to use the governing style of Pope Pacelli by re-proposing its central direction. This was shown on March 25, 1960, with the publication of the pastoral letter treating the theme of *laicism*. This set off an alarm, not entirely unjustified, about the growing progress of secularization that had been infiltrating Italian society at the end of the 1950s. This letter of the CEI differed considerably in its approach to modern society than would be taken by the two major social encyclicals of Pope John.[42] The complex social phenomenon of modern life was analyzed in a summary manner under the comprehensive category of *laicism*. Misgivings were expressed about the new theological current characterized as "neo-modernism." The letter expressed a preoccupation with safeguarding the traditional hierarchical model within the Church in order to exercise strict control over the laity involved in politics — concretely, over the decisions made by the Christian Democrats. Here could be detected the residue of that mentality which expected to maintain the Church's influence over public life.

The divergent idea of the CEI and Pope John was not slow in showing itself, right from the beginning of 1960 when the CEI vetoed dialogue between the Christian Democrats and the Socialists. This contrasted with the more open and detached attitude of John XXIII. In the face of these difficulties, the leaders of the Christian Democrats did not hesitate to go to the pope directly, shoving aside the CEI which had been entrusted with the administration of Italian concerns. This provoked protests from Cardinal Siri, a prelate who had been very close to Pius XII and who correctly interpreted the will of Pope John regarding the CEI's responsibility.[43]

The freedom and examples offered by Pope John stimulated and encouraged the emergence of a variety of positions, represented especially by Cardinal Montini and Cardinal Lercaro, the archbishop of Bologna. These two outstanding Italian prelates believed a new phase in Church-state relations was possible. They became the most articulate and least intransigent spokespersons of a position that was still in the minority, but that would eventually receive great acceptance and a following at the Council.

CHAPTER 17

THE POLITICS OF THE POPE

Principles of Conduct:
The Role of the Pope and the Bishops

Pope John prepared for his eightieth birthday by making a spiritual retreat; he chose as his guide an anthology of the ascetic and spiritual texts entitled *Christian Perfection* by Antonio Rosmini. The work contained a letter that Rosmini had written to a Monsignor Samuelli, bishop of Montepulciano, on November 23, 1848. Samuelli had asked Rosmini's advice on how to comport himself during that extremely turbulent and dramatic period for the Church. The priest offered a response that was outstanding in its precision. Rosmini drew a clear distinction between the political and religious spheres, and he stressed the necessity of safeguarding the latter from contamination. Pope John found the content of this letter pertinent and so close to his own way of thinking that he copied the text in its entirety. He did not even distinguish the text from his own brief considerations, which he incorporated into his copy of the original.

Above all, *Christian Perfection* affirmed that the mission of the pope and of the bishops was to preach the Gospel. Through their teaching, the truth of the Gospel must shine, not be obscured by political exploitation. Unlike the inconstancy of political currents, the Gospel asserts its unchangeable truth. From this stems the pastors' duty to prudently distance themselves from political questions and to avoid making partisan choices that could disorient the faithful. Pope John expressed his personal convictions about the nature of pastoral ministry:

The pope reads the Gospel and comments on it with the bishops, the one and the other, not as participants in anyone's worldly concerns, but as *citizens of that tranquil and happy city of peace* from which descends the divine law that can rightly direct the earthly city and the whole world. In fact, this and nothing else is what wise men expect from the Church.

In his examination of conscience on his whole life, Pope John noted with contentment that he had always been attentive to this norm: "My good conscience regarding my conduct during these three years as a new pope puts me at peace, and I ask the Lord to help me always to stay faithful to this good beginning." This verification further calmed the pope, who a few lines earlier had stated that as head of the Church he was to be an example for the whole episcopate. He continued to stress his duty and responsibility to caution the bishops whenever they ran the risk of unduly interfering in political affairs.

The shepherd must be a man *above factions* so that he can pour out the Gospel's riches on everyone without distinction. In Rosmini's text,[1] Pope John found that many points converged with his own pastoral style of gentleness, tact, mercy, and goodness.

> *Preach to all equally and generically justice, charity, humility, gentleness, kindness, and the other evangelical virtues, tactfully defending the rights of the Church where they would be violated or compromised. Always, but especially in these times, the bishop is advised to spread the perfumed oil of mildness on the wounds of humanity. He has to beware of every rash judgment, every harmful word about anyone, all flattery given out of fear, every connivance with evil suggested by the hope of helping someone. He is to preserve a serious, restrained, and solid content in his speech, being especially careful to conduct conversations that are pleasant and affectionate toward all, and — with the aid of sacred doctrine, but without any vehemence — capable of distinguishing the good from the evil.* Every study and intrigue of human origin is worth very little in these affairs of worldly interest.

Coming face-to-face with the elevated nature of episcopal ministry placed the wiles and skills that those involved in worldly interests prided themselves on in perspective. Given the context, we can perceive an allusion or veiled reproof of ecclesiastics who too easily interfered in worldly matters and were proud of their successes and abilities in what did not pertain to their mission. Yet, noninterference did not imply a lack of interest in politics or a renunciation of the influence of the Church upon it. Rosmini's words gave the pope a way of intervening that, without undue interference, could assure real help for political activity: the sanctification and instruction of the faithful.

> *Rather, diligently and with more assiduous and intense prayer pro-mote among the faithful divine worship and exercises of piety, the frequenting of sacraments well received and administered,* and especially religious instruction. This will also contribute to the resolution of problems of the temporal order much better than other human shrewdness, which cannot succeed. *This will draw the divine blessings down on the people, preserving them from many evils, and calling back to proper sentiments those minds that have strayed. Help will descend from on high, and the heavenly lights will scatter the darkness.*

The pope added instruction to the means Rosmini suggested. His reason is found in the social doctrine of the Church in which the popes had offered guidelines for interpreting social phenomena and principles of action. Except for this and a few other small additions, Pope John's thoughts harmonized with those of Rosmini not only regarding the Church's attitude and political action, but also regarding significant elements of pastoral style. Therefore, he concluded his written reflection of Sunday, October 13, 1961 — calling it *The Exercise of Prudence by the Pope and the Bishops* — with these words: "This thought and pastoral concern of mine must last for today and all time."[2] This was not a completely new beginning for Pope John. Rather, it only reaffirmed an attitude he had acquired during one of the most pivotal and delicate moments of postwar politics in Italy.

The Wider Tiber

At the beginning of 1960 the political system of *centrism* — the alliance of the Christian Democratic Party with the minor parties of Liberals, Republicans, and Social Democrats — entered a definitive crisis with a slim parliamentary majority. The resignation of the Segni government in February initiated an extremely ambiguous political phase.

Segni had attempted to create a new government of Republicans and Social Democrats, with a possibility of non-involvement on the part of the Socialists. This attempt failed because of unspecified "Vatican interference."[3] President Gronchi then entrusted the responsibility to Tambroni, who obtained a majority in the Chamber of Deputies with the help of votes from the far right. The strong reaction this provoked, however, caused his withdrawal. A third attempt followed. Fanfani tried to repeat Segni's formula of a government of Republicans and Social Democrats with the external approval of the Socialist Party. His failure was largely due to strong reservations on the part of Christian Democratic party members in Parliament.

Immediately following World War II, the Socialist and Communist parties constituted what was known as the Popular Front. Their political "pact" of collaboration was not broken until 1956 after the Russian invasion of Hungary. In 1959, the Socialist Party officially extended an invitation to the Christian Democrats to form a political alliance and create a program of reform.

The Christian Democrats stood to gain much by collaborating with the Socialists. It would enlarge the parliamentary majority of Christian Democrats, and the Communist Party, once deprived of its precious ally, would be politically isolated. However, this also posed serious problems in the Catholic world that considered the Socialist Party ideologically bound to Marxism and under the dominion of the Communist Party. The Church's repeated condemnations of Communist and of Marxist ideologies led many to believe that collaboration with a political party linked with Marxism would be contrary to the directives of the ecclesiastical magisterium.

Fanfani's resignation on April 22 brought Tambroni back to the fore. In his second attempt, he succeeded in forming a government with the help of votes from the far right. The repercussions on the life of the country were immediate. At the beginning of July serious incidents of mob violence erupted in some cities as police and leftist demonstrators clashed, leaving many dead or wounded. On July 17, Tambroni was forced to resign.

Since it appeared impossible to form a government sustained in some way by the extreme right, it was inevitable that one oriented toward the left would be instituted. With the abstention of Republicans, Social Democrats, and Socialists, Fanfani successfully launched a one-party Christian Democratic government.

At the congress at Naples in January 1962, there was a solid consensus around a proposal of the Christian Democratic secretary, Aldo Moro, to initiate collaboration with the Socialists. Amid this struggle, Pope

John defined his political course, which he called "the wider Tiber." He would work gradually to decrease direct hierarchical interference in the decisions of the Christian Democratic Party and to recognize the autonomy of Catholics involved in politics. The first hints of this shift appeared in the difficult spring of 1960. The failure of Segni and Fanfani to form governments was due to opposition from deputies who were being pressured by the episcopate and members of Catholic Action. The pastoral letter of the Italian Episcopal Conference, "Catholic Action and Politics," made the claim that the hierarchy had the right to express itself even in the "secular sphere," and it deplored the devious tendencies of Catholics who evaded ecclesiastical directives.

As president of the Italian republic and a Catholic, Gronchi sent the pope some "confidential remarks" on the theme of "Catholic Action and Politics." He questioned "the legitimacy of interference, whether manifest or concealed, direct or indirect, carried out by members of Catholic Action, laity, or ecclesiastics...in regard not only to the institutes or institutions of the Italian State, but also to political parties...considering that such interference has been directed...to influence the formation of the government, invading the area that the Constitution expressly reserves to the Head of State."

After consulting with the secretary of state, John XXIII responded in a letter that integrated some of Tardini's observations without diminishing his own original content. The pope maintained that the accusations of undue interference could not be made against the "authority guaranteed to the Church," guardian of the fundamental principles regarding Church-State relations. He was aware that persons in positions of authority had inquired about the political orientation of various prelates, but that their responses had not provoked a crisis of conscience. The pope confirmed that he himself kept a respectful attitude toward the institutions of the Italian State. If there had been a lack of moderation, he felt equally concerned to correct it.[4] He assured President Gronchi that on his part he wanted to preserve correct behavior and to respect the political decisions of the Christian Democratic leaders.

The ecclesiastics in Italy were not yet ready to share the pope's positions and anguished over the possibility of having a Marxist Party in the government. On May 18, an article entitled "Firm Points," attributed variously to Ottaviani or Siri, appeared in *L'Osservatore Romano*. The article emphasized the Church's right to express its judgment on the

moral lawfulness of the political choices of the faithful and to exact obedience from them. Emphasis was given to the incompatibility of Marxist
and Christian ideologies and on the impossibility of collaboration. The
article prompted the secretary of the Christian Democrats, Aldo Moro,
to sound out the Holy Father. The response was encouraging. Later,
when Moro was asked how the pope accepted his observations, he responded: "I have reason to believe they were well taken."

The incident created a division between the pope and the great ranks
of the Holy Office, as well as a good part of the Italian Episcopal Conference, including its president, Cardinal Siri. The attacks against Moro
continued for an entire year and finally culminated in a letter from Cardinal Siri dated February 18, 1961. Writing in the name of the CEI, Siri
warned Moro not to persist in his plans to reach an agreement with the
Socialists.

Moro decided to go directly to the pope. He met Monsignor Spada,
the director of the *Echo of Bergamo* and friend of Pope John XXIII.
Spada suggested that Moro send a confidential note explaining the reasons behind the decision that the leaders of the Christian Democrats had
made. Spada hastened to alert the Holy Father of the communiqué and
expressed his full approval of the party's leaders. He assured the pope
that those involved deserved trust and that they should be spared the unjust attacks that discredited them.

The pope's reply reached Moro on April 11, 1961, during an official
visit to the Vatican of the president of the council, Amintore Fanfani. In
his welcoming speech, Pope John spoke of the centenary of Italian unification and his shared sentiment of joy and gratitude to Providence,
which, even through bitter conflicts, had led Italy to occupy a prominent
position among nations. He recalled the struggles surrounding the Roman question, happily resolved with the Lateran Treaty that was directed toward mutual agreement and respect between the Church and
State and the avoidance of future conflicts. The pope's friendly words
were a veiled reproof of anyone imprudent enough to attempt to compromise the good relations that had been achieved. No need to create
conflicts between the Rome of the Vatican and the Rome of the Quirinal,
history was already full of them. Church and State should each remain
on their own turf. This last recommendation, equivalent to a program,
was intentionally placed at the beginning of the pope's statement and its
importance was seen at once.

The unique situation of the Catholic Church and Italian State... presupposes a distinction between them and a relationship that is restrained, although courteous and respectful. This renders much more pleasant the occasions, from time to time, when their highest representatives meet one another, even to share joys and edifying encouragement in the search for the good things that are most precious for the life of society.[5]

As always, Pope John expressed his deepest sentiments in his diary during retreat in August 1961. In light of the events in Italy, the pope's observations acquire a particular fullness of meaning:

The bishops find themselves more exposed to the temptation to interfere beyond good measure. They have a greater need to be asked by the pope to refrain from taking part in anything political and controversial, and from declaring themselves in favor of one or another fraction or faction.

The pope's stance, while it could not be ignored, did not succeed in quieting the uproar. The leadership of the Italian Episcopal Conference met in Rome in November and issued a compromise. In a published decree, they restated the perennial validity of the social doctrine of the Church and its incompatibility with doctrine contrary to Christianity. The document could be interpreted in restrictive ways by ecclesiastics and laity who might present this as the sole, binding truth.

The sensitivity of the moment and the approaching Christian Democratic Congress in Naples prompted Moro to send Pope John another "confidential memo" dated January 20, 1962. He summarized Italy's critical political situation, which did not allow for an alliance with the extreme right. He emphasized that the Party's attempt to incorporate the Socialists into the ruling majority was the political, not religious, decision *par excellence* and therefore had to be evaluated according to political advantages and risks. The leaders of the Christian Democrats believed the benefits far outweighed the dangers.[6]

In his report of January 27 to the Congress at Naples, Moro once more insisted on the distinction between political and religious decisions, and he stressed the necessity of autonomy for lay persons committed to politics — hence, the autonomy of a party of Christian inspiration, like the Christian Democrats, from the Church.

Although Moro's view won the approval of the vast majority, arguments continued. For this reason John XXIII appointed a group of theologians to examine the speeches made by the two principal government leaders, Moro and Fanfani, to discover if there were any points that strayed from Divine Revelation and the social doctrine of the Church. The pope received a very detailed and positive report. The theologians found that the discourses were in line with both Divine Revelation and the social documents of the magisterium, and they concluded that the disagreement between the Catholic hierarchy and the Christian Democrats could be detrimental for Italy. Therefore, they suggested that it would be wise for the Italian bishops, especially those with greater responsibilities, to end their opposition to the direction of the Moro-Fanfani government.[7]

On February 3, Moro sent a personal letter of gratitude to the pope "for the direct fatherly interest, understanding, and great benevolence with which Your Holiness has kindly encouraged the endeavors of Catholics engaged in public life at this difficult time."[8] This confirms that the pope's attitude of restrained respect made possible the change that took place at Naples, which represented a significant shift in handling relations between the hierarchy and laity, and in the very concept of political life.

However, the controversy continued. On February 15, Cardinal Ottaviani addressed a federation of small and medium-sized businesses and spoke harshly against the center-left. He described the leaders of the Christian Democrats as "ignorant Christians" and accused them of shamefully bartering their convictions for personal gain.

That day, the pope cancelled a meeting with Ottaviani that had been scheduled for the following day. "A sad morning. I had to dispense myself, with reasonable excuses, from the audience with Cardinal Ottaviani, whom I greatly esteem and love in the Lord, but who is a source of painful uncertainty to me." Obviously, some very difficult decisions were unavoidable. Somehow, Roncalli had to ensure that eminent Vatican prelates would abide by the policy of restraint that he had adopted.

The next Monday the pope met Ottaviani at the funeral Mass for Cardinal Muench. Inspired by his desire to eliminate any feelings of resentment or misunderstanding, he took advantage of the opportunity and murmured a few respectful and sympathetic words to Cardinal Ottaviani.

> Cardinal Ottaviani was near me. Good words afterward in the chapel of St. Leo the Great. "Your Eminence, my heart is always the same. There are differences to be looked at concerning some

matters. Let us both stay well united, as two men who pray *together*. Then at the audience of February 25, we will see. And courage." I feel a bit distressed, but the meeting was good.[9]

The pope's emphasis of the word "together" could only mean that their reconciliation would have to be rooted in common prayer.

On March 2, Fanfani presented Parliament with plans for a center-left government and a substantial program that included the nationalization of electrical power plants. The program, perceived as based on Marxist principles, immediately provoked renewed and bitter debates in Catholic circles. Was this step toward the nationalization of power plants simply a forerunner to similar programs? Would it endanger the principle of private ownership? This time, Cardinal Siri sent the pope a communiqué in which he declared the proposed system immoral. He accused the leadership of the Christian Democrats of abandoning economic collaboration between classes by espousing programs that would only favor a few.

Again, in order to study the question objectively, the pope turned to some trusted men: Augustine Ferrari Toniolo and Monsignor Pavan, a professor of Christian social doctrine at the Pontifical Lateran University. In their report, they supported the pope's orientation of non-interference in the Italian government. When President Antonio Segni paid an official visit to the pope on July 3, Roncalli reconfirmed his position. Pope John said that the city of Rome had "many mansions" with different areas of competence, though they were illuminated from above by the rays of the same Divine light which inspired their actions.[10]

The pope received another request to meet with Furio Cicogna, president of an industrial firm supplying electrical energy in Italy, and his vice-president, Angelo Costa — individuals who were certainly interested in the outcome of this latest conflict. They were heads of the independent electrical plant, Confindustria, and granting an audience to them would be a definite risk for the pope to take. Undoubtedly an audience with them would be seen as proof that the Vatican disapproved of the proposed nationalization of electrical energy. However, the pope agreed because of his concern over Catholics forming opposing ranks. He was a Father to all people, and he had no wish to alter his "hands-off" policy, as he wrote on July 9 to Capovilla.

In the four years since Pope John began carrying out these responsibilities, he has never had nor taken nor profited by one single occasion or encounter with persons of government or of corporations...to abandon his position of restraint. I follow the ancient example of the patriarch Jacob in the midst of his sons who, when they were taking sides, contented himself to watch, to suffer, and to keep silence: "The father kept silent and pondered the matter" (cf. Gn 37:11).[11]

This verifies Pope John's consistent conduct from which he had no intention of deviating. It also helps to clarify his motives. He was preoccupied with avoiding any exploitation of the truth of the Gospel and of the Church's mission through a partisanship detached from religious principles. Any intimation of this now could seriously harm the Church's credibility and its social teaching.

Throughout this serious political crisis, Pope John — as all the popes of the twentieth century — showed how very dear the social doctrine of the Church was to him. And the pope intended to navigate carefully within the perimeters of these social teachings. In this, John followed the example of Pius XI in his *Quadragesimo Anno,* on the seventieth anniversary of Leo XIII's *Rerum Novarum.* Pope John embarked on the necessary updating of the Church's social teaching with the encyclical *Mater et Magistra.* (Significantly, the document, dated May 15, 1961, was published on July 14, the anniversary of *Rerum Novarum.*) John XXIII defined the Church's social doctrine as a teaching "that clearly points out the sure way to reconstruct social relationships according to universal criteria which correspond to the nature and various environments of the temporal order and to the characteristics of contemporary society, therefore making them acceptable to all."[12] While the document did state the importance of rigorously safeguarding the universal value of Catholic social doctrine, it also called for the recognition of possible variations in concrete applications. In such instances, it was the duty of Catholics to search for the greatest convergence through respectful discussions. "Among upright and sincere Catholics, some divergence can arise in making such applications. When this occurs, it should not diminish mutual consideration, reciprocal respect, and the good will to identify points of convergence in view of timely and effective action."[13] These words are reminiscent of an earlier exhortation of Pope John for "his sons" to respect one another even in their diversity of opinions in political and economic affairs.

The encyclical treats socialization, a theme of unquestionable importance. Pope John analyzes the origins of socialization, its breadth, and its effect on society as an historical phenomenon connected to the growing interference of public authorities in the most delicate areas of life. The pope nurtured trust in the positive implications of greater socialization and did not condemn the extension of the powers of the State. He explicitly allowed public ownership of the means of production, "especially when they carry such economic weight that they cannot be left in the hands of private citizens without endangering the common good."[14] Perhaps this was a reference to the case of nationalizing electrical energy, although public intervention was linked with the more basic principle of subsidiarity. The encyclical certainly did not ignore the problems that had surfaced in the difficult years of 1960–1962.

A final example may serve to complete the picture of the pope's major inspirations for his actions: the collaboration of Catholics with a political party associated with an ideology incompatible with Christianity. This is merely touched on in *Mater et Magistra*. "Catholics engaged in social-economic activities find themselves with others who do not have the same vision of life. In such relationships our sons must be careful...but at the same time they must be...disposed to collaborate sincerely in the realization of objectives that are of their nature good or at least reducible to good."[15] The matter would be addressed in a more suitable and timely way in *Pacem in Terris* (1963), which makes clear the distinction between false philosophical doctrines and social-political movements. "Doctrines that have been developed and defined remain always the same; instead, the aforesaid movements, having developed in historical situations, are constantly evolving. They cannot escape external influences and are therefore subjected to changes — even profound changes."[16]

John XXIII offered a decisive contribution to an anguished and difficult moment in Italian politics. He initiated a new stage in the relationship between the hierarchy and laity in Italy through the recognition of the autonomy of the political sphere and supported by solid, basic doctrine. This would become a precious addition to the future Council.

Peace

During his spiritual exercises at the Vatican (November 29–December 5, 1959), Pope John wrote down a few simple sentences that expressed his profound sense of universal belonging.

> From when the Lord called me, miserable as I am, to this great service, I have no longer felt that I belong to something particular in life — family, region, nation or particular directions in regard to

study and projects, even if good. Now, more than ever, I see myself as the unworthy and poor "servant of God and servant of the servants of God." The whole world is my family. This sense of universal belonging has to give style and energy to my mind, to my heart, to my actions.[17]

This resolve explains Pope John's effort to be attentive to everyone without distinction and to include even those who stood aloof from or enemies of religion. To such people he wished to address a sincere appeal for brotherhood and mutual respect in order to insure the supreme good of peace. He understood perfectly that a convinced word spoken from the heart could meet with unexpected echoes in every human soul, for peace is a universal good desired by all people. Therefore, this theme was given notable importance from the first acts of his pontificate. Above all, the pope was concerned with averting new conflicts, a proximate possibility in a Cold War climate. John XXIII did not hesitate to recall the horrors he had personally experienced in two world wars and to stress the inevitable catastrophe of a general conflict because of the power of atomic weapons.

In Pope John's first radio message of October 29, 1959, he asked:

Why are the resources of a gifted humanity and the riches of peoples often channeled into the production of arms — harmful instruments of death and destruction — which do not foster the welfare of all classes of citizens, particularly of the poor? Turn your gaze toward the people entrusted to you and listen to their voices. What are they asking? What are they begging of you? They are not asking for those monstrous war devices discovered in our time that can bring about fratricidal slaughter and universal massacre. Rather, they are asking for peace — that peace through which the human family can freely live, flourish, and prosper.[18]

Pope John's message was a rational and insistent reminder of the absurdity of war. His first encyclical, *Near the Chair of Peter* (June 29, 1959), had reflected on the horrors of the First and Second World Wars and the tremendous grief they had caused, attested to by the innumerable military cemeteries. He invited human beings to be sensible and "justly deplore a situation that is so uncertain that we could either launch out toward a solid and true peace or run with extreme blindness to a new and frightening war. With extreme blindness we have said: such is the power of the monstrous weapons of our time, that there would be nothing for anyone other than an immense massacre and universal ruin."[19]

Pope John's plea for rationality was accompanied by a strong reminder of the reasons for unity and the brotherhood that indissolubly binds the human race. The basic principle of his ecumenical attitude, the insistence on unity rather than division, also applied to relations between peoples and nations in pursuit of peace. The message was enriched by the pervading evangelical inspiration that rendered it appealing and fruitful. Pope John did not aim so much at formulating an organic doctrinal system on the problems of peace and war. Rather, he attempted to emphasize the value of harmony and brotherhood within the universal perspective of the Gospel. He was less concerned with organization than with pointing to the evangelical dynamism that illumined the historical situations that had arisen. He emphasized the plea for peace issuing from the hearts of people.[20] Wherever the elaboration of doctrine could be the cause of divisions and misunderstandings, John XXIII's charismatic approach rendered typically Christian motives and absolute moral principles unifying in their universal breadth — for believers and nonbelievers alike.

One example is found in his common expression: "men of good will." Derived of course from the Gospels and the Christian tradition of Christmas, from Pope John's mouth the words became a pressing and fraternal appeal to all people, without distinction of faith or ideology, who worked for peace. The words retained their Christian reference, for example, during the Christmas radio message of 1959 when the pope said: "It is necessary to repeat first of all that persons of good will are needed — those righteous ones to whom the angels of Bethlehem announced peace: 'Peace on earth to men of good will'" (cf. Lk 2:14). In fact, only these people can bring about the necessary conditions for peace as defined by St. Thomas: "the ordered harmony of citizens."[21]

Pope John's ability to speak a universal language did not diminish his identity as a Christian shepherd whose universal fatherhood stood out clearly. The pope's credibility was rooted in his capacity to be a man *above factions,* one who did not have preferences but listened and respected everyone equally.[22] This contributed to a climate of trust and, in particular, a trust in the person of Pope John himself. He established a cycle of virtue — the leaders of the great powers were compelled to renounce some measure of their political calculations and to share the pope's evangelical and humanitarian concerns. This explains the success of Pope John's appeals for peaceful solutions to dangerous international crises.

Pope John supported the process of de-colonization in Africa during the early 1960s. In his radio message to the Catholics of Africa (June 5, 1960), the pope expressed his "great satisfaction in seeing the progressive realization of admittance to sovereignty: the Church rejoices in it and places trust in the decision of these young States to take the place that is rightfully theirs in the symphony of nations." He recommended that the new States profit by their independence by promoting a "healthy development in their countries, being wisely aware of the real potential, and especially respecting the true values, which are the very soul of a people."[23]

The pope understood that the new independent countries would need concrete and active help from more economically advanced nations. In *Mater et Magistra,* the problems of hunger and underdevelopment in Third World countries were listed as among the most critical problems that Christians and all responsible human beings could not remain indifferent to. Peace depended on the resolution of economic imbalance. "Given the always greater interdependence among peoples, it is not possible that a lasting and fruitful peace can reign among them when there is too great an imbalance in their social-economic conditions."[24] The pope urged rich nations to fulfill their duty of solidarity with underdeveloped nations not only during times of emergency but also with scientific, technical, and financial cooperation. He warned those who "influence the political situations of communities undergoing economic development in order to carry out plans for domination" and condemned this new form of colonialism.[25] Pope John introduced new topics of concern, which would also demand the attention of his successors.

Interventions for Peace

The pope accompanied his teachings with prudent, decisive, and valued deeds on behalf of peace at critical moments in international politics. We limit ourselves to mentioning some episodes.

On April 24, 1961, Pope John sent a message of support to Archbishop Duval of Algiers, praising his sensible and effective pastoral action for peace. North Africa's bloody struggle for independence gave birth to a dramatic moment in the revolt of occupying French forces against the government of Paris. The pope's position was unmistakable. In opposition to those who would deny Algeria's independence, he wished the Algerian people "the realization of their legitimate aspirations of justice and liberty."[26]

In August of the same year, the existing problems in Germany intensified with the construction of the Berlin Wall, which blocked direct communication between the inhabitants of the divided city. The Soviet Union threatened to restrict all air traffic to and from Berlin as well, and, as if that were not enough, Khrushchev announced that the Soviet Union would resume nuclear testing. The United States responded with a similar decision to continue nuclear testing, though President Kennedy specified that the experiments would be conducted in an underground laboratory. Representatives of the non-aligned nations who were gathered for a conference in Belgrade expressed their deep concern, and they appealed to the superpowers to back down.

John XXIII carried that burden and those of all responsible people in his heart. After celebrating Mass at a special convention of prayer for peace, in the presence of thousands of faithful at Castelgandolfo, the pope urged all governments to remember their absolute obligation to promote peace. Pope John carefully refrained from taking sides while clarifying the solely humanitarian nature of the Church's intervention. The Church could not be removed in the face of such serious issues for all of humanity. He invited world leaders to place themselves before their own consciences and the judgment of God and of all peoples who, shattered by the ordeal of two terrible world wars, only wanted peace. He emphasized the terrible harm wrought by war — the devastating material damage left in the wake of modern weapons and the spiritual damages because "every military conflict throws individuals, peoples, and regions into confusion and causes them to lose their own characteristics."[27]

Nikita Khrushchev's response to the pope's message was published in official Soviet newspapers.

> The concern for peace shown by the pope proves that those on the outside understand always better that madness and the spirit of adventure in world politics do not lead to anything good.... John XXIII is reasonable when he puts governments on guard against a general catastrophe and exhorts them to give an accounting for the immense responsibility they have before history. His appeal is a good sign.[28]

The tone and content of Khrushchev's message gave credibility to Pope John's activities on behalf of peace even among the governments notoriously hostile to the Holy See in the Communist bloc.

Pope John's stance toward the countries of Eastern Europe, intended to build up trust in the good will of those in government, became one of the principal reasons for the successful mediation of the Holy See in the Cuban crisis of October 1962.

Not since the end of World War II had world peace been so endangered as during the Cuban missile crisis. The Soviet deployment of military installations and missile launch sites in Cuba strained an already taut relationship with the United States. When incontrovertible proof of Soviet activity in Cuba was obtained, President Kennedy reported this in a national speech that was broadcast on October 22. He also announced the U.S. countermeasure of a naval blockade of Cuba. A test of strength ensued, both sides solidly determined to hold to their positions. The situation seemed to be escalating into a war.

During this time, a group of Soviet and American academics and journalists were meeting at Andover, Massachusetts for the third in a series of discussions on East-West relations. After the crisis was announced, the group decided to continue their work. Moreover, they endeavored to provide a positive outlet. Felix Morlion, a Dominican priest and former rector of the University *Pro Deo* in Rome, attended the meeting as an observer. Members of both delegations urged Morlion to telephone the Vatican secretary of state on their behalf. Cicognani expressed the Holy See's concern to Morlion and said the Vatican was willing to intervene in the crisis, but only on the condition that a solution be found that was agreeable to both countries. In particular, Cicognani asked if a halt to the U.S.S.R. shipment of war materials to Cuba would end the United States' naval blockade.

Norman Cousins, head of the U.S. delegation at Andover, was informed that President Kennedy would value a papal intervention and confirmed his willingness to lift the naval blockade on the condition that the U.S.S.R. end its military build-up and dismantle its missile sites. Cousins transmitted this to the Vatican.

In the meantime, a member of the Soviet delegation contacted the Kremlin. He later reported that Khrushchev was ready to accept the pope's proposal to end the shipment of military arms to Cuba on the condition that the United States lift its naval blockade.

When Pope John was assured that his involvement was welcome and that a sufficient basis for beginning negotiations existed, he decided to intervene. In his discourse to pilgrims from Portugal on the morning of October 24, Pope John added a note praising all statesmen who sought to avoid war through negotiations.[29] The pope had worked on the message the night before with Dell'Acqua and Cardinale; he left his desk occasionally and went to the chapel to pray. The message was consigned to the American and Soviet embassies in Rome before its official broadcast by Vatican Radio on October 25.

> The Church has nothing more at heart than peace and brotherhood among men, and she will work tirelessly to establish it. In this regard, we remember the serious duties of those who carry the responsibility of power. And we add: With a hand on their conscience, may these listen to the cry of anguish that goes up to heaven from people in all the corners of the earth — from innocent children to old people, from individuals to communities — "peace! peace!" We renew today this solemn invitation. We implore all leaders not to be deaf to this cry of humanity. May they do all in their power to safeguard peace. Thus, they will preserve the world from the horrors of a war whose terrible consequences cannot possibly be foreseen. May they continue to negotiate, for this sincere and open attitude has great witness-value for the individual conscience and before history. To promote, to foster, to agree to meet on all levels and at every moment is a rule of wisdom and prudence that draws blessings from heaven and earth.[30]

On October 26, *Pravda,* the official newspaper of the Soviet Communist Party, dedicated an article to the pope's gesture. Unquestionably, this signified Khrushchev's approval of John XXIII's message. The way was open and negotiations began immediately that same day, October 26, with a personal letter from the Soviet leader to President Kennedy. Though the tension remained high throughout November, the crisis was resolved with a compromise: withdrawal of Russian missiles from Cuba and a guarantee of Cuban independence on the part of the United States.[31]

Pope John's intervention established him as a trustworthy point of reference for all people of good will who desired to work concretely for peace. He had fostered an initial dialogue between the superpowers and contributed to the eventual reduction of Cold War hostility. The Church seemed no longer to follow a markedly Western, partisan line — an obstruction to its mission as universal mother and teacher, a point of encounter among peoples. One of Pope John's greatest merits was his recognition and support of the still fragile yet very real changes in the world situation.

The Beginning of Dialogue

The positive epilogue of the Cuban missile crisis was renewed relations between the Church and the Soviet Union. From the beginning, Pope John's tone with Communist countries had been deliberately standard, without harshness or condemnation, even if he did not forget the shadow that saddened the Church. Russia viewed the Vatican with interest. Khrushchev sent the pope a personal congratulatory message for his eightieth birthday. Perhaps the Kremlin hoped to broaden relations with the West; for some time it had been making overtures to the Vatican, albeit without results. With the coming of John XXIII, Russian leaders sensed the situation might change. The secretary of the Italian Communist Party, Palmiro Togliatti, and Don Giuseppe De Luca, a close friend of the Communist leader, acted as intermediaries.[32]

When Vatican Secretary of State Cicognani asked the pope about the propriety of responding to Khrushchev's message, John XXIII replied without hesitation: "Yes, let's respond. This thread comes from Providence. We do not have the right to break it. A caress is better than a slap."

John XXIII replied personally to Khrushchev: "His Holiness, Pope John XXIII, thanks you for your greetings and on his part expresses, also to all the Russian people, cordial wishes for the growth and consolidation of universal peace, through happy agreements of human brotherhood. For this I offer fervent prayers."[33]

The pope's response implied his intention to end a phase of hostility and mutual opposition. He wished to initiate a new one, even if for the moment it had to remain almost exclusively on the level of human relations and his personal prestige. Norman Cousins would later write that Pope John did not hesitate to use all possible channels.

Cardinal Ottaviani monitored the measure with anxious preoccupation and Cicognani with scant enthusiasm. Instead, Pope John hoped to reestablish relations with that vast area of the world and thus alleviate the sufferings of Christians, renew contacts with the Catholic communities of the East, and have their bishops participate in the Council.

This last motive was a prime objective. The pro-nuncio to Turkey, Bishop Ladrone, maintained direct contact with Pope John and was one of his closest collaborators. When Ladrone conveyed his impression that positive things were happening on the Soviet side, the pope summoned him to Rome. Ladrone was then given the task of sounding out the Eastern European bishops to see if they thought their governments would allow them to participate in the Council. Ladrone promptly set about his work, but the final results hardly fulfilled his expectations. Communist-controlled countries issued few visas for bishops to travel to Rome, and yet the fact that at least some prelates from the East did in fact attend the Council was significant.

A problem that weighed on John XXIII was the imprisonment of Bishop Slipyi, Metropolitan of the Uniate Church of Eastern Ukraine, an Eastern Rite Church united to Rome. In 1946, the Uniates had been forced into integration with the Russian Orthodox Church. Its hierarchy had been dispersed and the Church had been deprived of all its buildings, including the Cathedral of Lvov. Almost no information could be obtained about the whereabouts or condition of Slipyi, whom John XXIII named a cardinal in 1960.

Problems with the Communist State were united to that of the Russian Orthodox Church, which was traditionally against the Uniate Church. The pope tried different channels to make some progress toward improved relations. Through Cardinal Gustavo Testa, Pope John was able to involve two observers of the Russian Orthodox Church at Vatican II. On their return to Russia, the observers presented their report on the work of the Council and the Vatican's request for Slipyi's liberation.

The pope used another very personal but most effective channel: Norman Cousins, a friend of Soviet Premier Khrushchev. Cousins had planned a trip to Moscow to increase his contacts there and to foster détente. Cousins had offered to act on behalf of the Holy See and stopped in Rome on his way to Moscow. He was received by Cardinal Bea, who entrusted him with presenting the pope's desire for Slipyi's liberation and the possibility of introducing religious publications for various categories of believers in the Soviet Union.[34]

Cousins met with Khrushchev on December 13, 1962, and they spoke for three hours. The tone of their conversation was very cordial, and it was evident that the Soviet leader felt great esteem and appreciation for the work of Pope John. Cousins did not hesitate to assure Khrushchev that Slipyi's liberation would not become a pretext for anti-Soviet propaganda.[35] Cousins returned to Rome on December 19, and was received by the pope. After giving a brief summary of what had transpired, which seemed hopeful, Cousins delivered a greeting card from the Soviet leader: "In the holy days of Christmas I send the wishes and greetings of a man who wishes you good health and vigor for your continued efforts on behalf of peace, happiness, and well-being for all humanity."[36]

Pope John was touched by the gesture and responded on December 21 with reciprocal warmth:

> Many thanks for your courteous message of greetings. I exchange them from the heart with the same words that came to us from on high: Peace on earth to men of good will. We bring to your attention two Christmas documents of this year calling for the consolidation of justice and peace among peoples. May the good God listen to us and respond to the ardor and sincerity of our efforts and of our prayers.... Joyful greetings of prosperity to the Russian people and to all the people of the world. [37]

He sent this communication with the texts of his Christmas radio messages and greetings to the diplomatic corps.

In a short space of time, a string of signs of attention and warmth arrived from an area of the world that had been totally closed off and hostile. It was entirely unexpected and filled the pope's heart with joy. Notwithstanding these positive signs, it was still necessary to exercise great prudence in the midst of an undecipherable phenomenon; conclusions could not be drawn hastily. Nevertheless, the signs were undeniably a glimpse into what had been, only a short time before, unimaginable horizons.

On December 22, Cousins' written account of his mission reached the pope, accompanied by a summary letter with Khrushchev's expressed desire to appeal to the spiritual power of the pope to open a new, private channel of communication. Russia recognized that the pope was working for the happiness and well-being of all peoples; moderate Communists were seeking an alliance to help strengthen peace; and they recognized the need for greater religious freedom. Cousins' report undoubtedly inspired John XXIII to insert the following words into his Christmas radio message:

> Unquestionable signs of high-level understanding assure us that words regarding the Cuban crisis were not spoken to the wind but have touched minds and hearts and have opened new perspectives of fraternal trust and the gleam of tranquil horizons, of true social and international peace.[38]

On December 27, another extraordinary event occurred: *Pravda* published a lengthy excerpt of the pope's Christmas message with a commentary. These were truly unforgettable days for the pope. The joy of the liturgical season mingled with his happiness over the first signs of an opening in the Soviet Union to recognize the Church and its activity — from a part of the world believed to be insensible to any religious interest.

Cousins' report was definitely surprising, and some of Khrushchev's statements made a positive impression on the pope. According to the Soviet leader, religious persecution in the U.S.S.R. had risen out of the strict alliance between the Church and the former Czarist rule. Now that the religious role of the Christian Churches had been clarified, it seemed feasible to begin allowing a certain amount of religious freedom. Were such undreamed-of possibilities suddenly becoming real? The seemingly infinite succession of suffering and persecution that the Church of silence had to endure might be reduced.

The intense emotion the pope experienced made it difficult for him to rest even at night. In the quiet of the darkness, he would evaluate the importance of the events in which Providence had directly involved him during the last days of his life. He wanted to thank God, but he also felt called to make greater efforts so that the process, fragile in its early beginnings, would be strengthened and eventually produce the hoped-for fruits. On the night between December 26 and 27, during a period of ardent prayer before his crucifix, Pope John offered his life for the people of Russia.

> Peaceful St. Stephen. The liturgy makes the greatest impression on me. It prolongs in my spirit my concern about what the Lord is mysteriously working out. This Khrushchev — is he not perhaps preparing a surprise for us? Tonight, after meditating much and reading the introduction to the *Grammar of the Russian Language* by Hector Lo Gatto, which Monsignor Capovilla bought for me yesterday for the feast of Christmas, I got up from bed. Kneeling down before my crucifix, I consecrated my life to Christ with the final sacrifice of my whole being for what he wants of me in this great task of the conversion of Russia. I will repeat this in Masses celebrated in this spirit.

The next morning Pope John had a meeting with the Prefect for the Propagation of the Faith. Cardinal Agagianian, the Armenian prelate whose opinion Pope John greatly esteemed, agreed with the pope's appraisal of Khrushchev's communication and his hopes — not too long in being realized.[39]

On the evening of January 25, 1963, the Soviet ambassador to Rome consigned a note from Khrushchev to Amintore Fanfani. In recognition of the role he had played in relaxing relations between Russia and the Vatican, Fanfani had been chosen as the channel of this information to the pope.[40] The message was immediately communicated, and Pope John read the note that announced the liberation of Metropolitan Slipyi. This was, as Khrushchev stated, entirely an act of good will on the part of the Soviet government, especially since, in the reconsideration of the case, there emerged no motives for acquittal of guilt for which Slipyi had been convicted.

Cardinal Willebrands, a collaborator with Cardinal Bea in the Secretariat for Unity, who had just been to Moscow to invite Russian observers to the Council, was now given the task of bringing the Ukrainian primate to Italy with the greatest discretion. Willebrands arrived in Moscow on January 31 and was able to meet Slipyi on February 2. It took Willebrands two days to convince the primate to accompany him to Rome; Slipyi agreed after the Soviet government refused his request to return to the Ukraine at least for a visit with his faithful. Meanwhile, the former prisoner, accustomed to acting under crisis situations, decided to clandestinely consecrate a bishop in order to assure the continuity of the Uniate Church. He summoned from Leopoli a Redemptorist priest named Velytchkovsky, whom he consecrated before leaving for Rome.[41]

Slipyi did not want to fly, and so the journey to Rome had to be made by train. On the evening of February 9 Willebrands and Slipyi arrived at the train station of Orte in Italy. They were welcomed with the greatest care by Capovilla and Archbishop Igino Cardinale. The prelate was taken to the monastery of Grottaferrata for the night. The next day Slipyi was taken to the Vatican. Slipyi prostrated himself at the feet of the pope who quickly raised him up and warmly embraced him. Together they went to the chapel to pray the *Magnificat* in thanksgiving. They conversed for over an hour and then Slipyi presented the pope with a map of the U.S.S.R. that showed the location of the concentration camps where those persecuted for their faith were being held. The pope would keep this map with him until his death. In the margins he wrote: "Prayer runs in search of those who have greatest need of feeling understood and loved." To his prayer, Pope John had added a courageous and active interest that ultimately brought about the liberation of one of those persecuted believers: Slipyi. This would be the preamble to similar gestures.

In an audience with Cardinal Montini and the alumni of the Seminary of Lombardy shortly before meeting Slipyi, John XXIII said:

> Last evening I received a touching consolation from Eastern Europe and I humbly thank the Lord. It is something that, in the Divine secrets, can prepare for the holy Church and upright souls a new impetus of sincere faith and of peaceful and beneficial apostolate. Let us not disturb the design in which God calls everyone to cooperate, weaving the threads of a fabric that will be completed with his grace and with the ready service of innocent, meek, and generous souls.[42]

Chapter 18
Preparation for the Council

The Pre-Preparatory Phase

On Pentecost, May 5, 1959, four months after announcing the Council, John XXIII made public the establishment of a pre-preparatory commission. The principal aim of the commission would be to collect material for the launch of the actual preparatory phase. The ten members and Cardinal Tardini, who was entrusted with the role of president, were chosen from the Curia — all secretaries of their respective congregations. Because of Tardini's role in the commission, the pope was able to directly involve the Curia in conciliar initiatives while still allowing the commission a more flexible direction and conformity to his expectations. Right from his first meetings with the commission, Tardini provided precise directions in the name of the pope, which were therefore understood as matters not open for discussion. At the commission's meeting on May 26, 1959, Latin was declared the official language of the Council.

The assembly was not merely a continuation of Vatican I. On June 30, the pope clarified that the Council — a subject of more or less well-founded conjectures since its announcement — would have an ecumenical purpose. Above all, the Council was meant to renew the Catholic Church. Unlike the Council of Florence (1439), which had brought about a temporary reconciliation with the East, this would not be a Council of union. The renewal fostered by the new Council would facilitate relations with the brethren of other Churches.[1] On July 3, in a meeting with the presidents of the theological faculties, Pope John emphasized the "pastoral" rather than "dogmatic" character of the upcoming Council.

Naturally, the pre-preparatory commission was limited to noting these desires. The only topic actually discussed was the global consultation of the episcopate to avoid restricting the Council as happened at Vatican I. In the meeting of May 26, the commission members discussed possible outlines for a preliminary letter to all the bishops. This letter would be followed by a questionnaire to help the bishops to be focused in their responses. The definitive text of the letter was presented during the meeting of June 30, but it was not accompanied by a questionnaire. Instead, the pope had decided to give Tardini precise directives for composing a new text, so that the letter emphasized that it was the pope, and not the commission, who was addressing the bishops. The bishops were given the greatest liberty to state whatever topics they considered most relevant for discussion at the future conciliar assembly. The commission did not meet again until April 8 of the following year. During the intervening period, it mailed, collected, and sorted all of the bishops' written proposals.[2]

Around the beginning of July 1959, John XXIII chose a name for the Council. On July 4, as the pope entered the Vatican gardens, he had a sudden inspiration: "The Ecumenical Council under preparation ought to be called the *Second Vatican Council,* since the last one, celebrated in 1870 by Pope Pius IX, was named Vatican Council I."[3] This was communicated to Tardini ten days later and he made it official at a meeting with the presidents of Ecclesiastical Faculties.

From July 1959 until the summer of 1960, thousands of replies returned from those who had been consulted: universities, superiors general, and especially bishops. A rather significant number of bishops — 77 percent — had replied. Yet despite the number of replies, the obvious convergence of proposals indicated their mediocre quality and relevance. The bishops were more accustomed to acting rather than proposing. They had been shaped by a theological formation that tended toward polemics. Only a few bishops from northeastern Europe, around the French-German region, showed a greater awareness of the new needs and the limitations of a traditional pastoral approach. The secretariat of the commission prepared a thematic analysis of the bishops' proposals, synthesized by category, and then a final synthesis.

When the first phase of categorizing was completed, the commission made a partial synthesis of the proposals of each bishop. In this way, they hoped to gain a more precise vision of the needs of the local churches and make it easier to access the boundless material that Pope John had requested and now anxiously awaited. The communication between Bishop Pericle Felici, the secretary of the commission, and Capovilla was simplified so that the completed syntheses could reach the pope in a timely fashion. About 300 typewritten pages were prepared, and John XXIII spent about a month and a half reading them. From these the pope was able to view the response of the entire Catholic episcopate.[4]

Some contemporary historians view the contribution of the Italian bishops as distinctly conservative with little openness to other ideas.[5] The most prevalent issues included canonical questions pertaining to ecclesiastical discipline and the bishop's authority within the diocese. There were persistent requests for new condemnations and for Marian definitions. There were also signs of agitation and uncertainty that were not always well expressed.[6] But John XXIII heaved a deep sigh of relief when he read the final document. Evidently he saw in it sufficient elements for launching the work of the Council which, except for his basic directions, had appeared an empty container waiting to be filled. He felt that these initial steps were "a first and happy brightening of the horizon that well prepared the spirit for the work that will be unfolding day by day."[7] His satisfaction was particularly keen with regard to the pastoral area as one of the principal thrusts of the future Council. Determined requests surfaced for the introduction of the vernacular into the liturgy and to address problems relating to pastoral ministry. "I have read the first comments made by the bishops of Italy, reflecting the desire of the clergy and the people regarding the liturgy and pastoral ministry to be brought up at the Council. These points are serious and worthy of respect."[8]

While we do not have the actual syntheses presented to the pope, we do know that the majority of the responses from the French bishops must have favored a peaceful and moderate reform,[9] because Pope John noted the divergence from the responses of the Italian episcopate. "In short, they combine with those of the Italian bishops and show a happy disposition to agree on principal points that correspond to the needs of the present circumstances."[10]

The pope's attitude might seem surprising, but it becomes more understandable in light of his situation and personality. The principal objective of this consultative phase was to feel the pulse of the episcopate
and by doing so to gain a clearer vision of the real situation of the
Church in the contemporary world. This would help to identify the most
urgent topics to be treated in the conciliar assembly. For the Council to
work with conviction and bear fruitful results, the bishops needed to introduce the topics they deemed indispensable. For the moment, the distinction between "conservatives" and "progressives" seemed less relevant. The precise characteristics of these groups would become clearer
when the Council began. The pope's concern was to gather the meaningful points of convergence from which to begin a discussion about the
renewal of the Church. The actual *content* of that renewal had yet to be
decided.

Pope John's character always tended to focus on the reasons for
unity rather than division; thus, he easily singled out the points of convergence. Perhaps it may appear that he did so with extreme simplicity,
but the fact that certain requests presented by the bishops — such as the
definition of new dogmas — were absolutely excluded right from the
start indicates his observant care.

In reading the syntheses, John XXIII had every reason to feel profound satisfaction and to trust that the Council would have positive results. He expected that journey would be easy enough, or so he implied
in a diary entry dated March 24, 1960:

> I would like to thank the Lord, because we are already at a good
> point. The thoughts of many of the bishops about the various issues
> of doctrine and discipline have been disclosed in an orderly and ap-
> pealing way. Who knows? The Council might come to a conclusion
> between 1961 and 1962.[11]

On April 7, the pope read the eighteen-page "Final synthesis of the
advice and suggestions of the bishops and prelates of the whole world
for the future Ecumenical Council." This concluded the most intense task
and first phase of the commission's work. At the commission's final meeting on April 18, 1960, Tardini announced the pope's intention of reserving to himself the selection of topics to be submitted to the preparatory
commissions. These topics would become the basis for the drafting of
documents to be discussed at the Council; the pope would present the project to a central commission that would coordinate the preparatory work.

The Preparatory Phase

The preparatory phase was launched with the motu proprio *Superno Dei Nutu* (By the will of the most high God) on June 5, 1960, which established a central commission and ten preparatory commissions. Nine of these commissions corresponded to the offices of the Curia, while the tenth was similar to the permanent board for the lay apostolate congresses. There were two secretariats: that of the mass media and that for Christian unity. The latter was a true novelty even if for the moment its activity was limited to establishing contacts with separated brethren. The purpose of the central commission — personally presided over by the pope — was to monitor and coordinate the work of the preparatory commissions. Each commission consisted of a cardinal-president, a secretary, active members, and consultants — all named by the pope. The presidents and secretaries were members of the central commission by right.

On June 6, the names of the presidents of the commissions became public — they were all the cardinal prefects of the corresponding congregations of the Curia. The pope, however, did not permit the presidents to bring their own secretaries to the commission meetings. Rather, the secretaries were appointed from outside the Curia. This reflected an implementation of two principles set forth by Pope John. In his discourse of Pentecost, June 5, 1960, he spoke of the distinction between the ordinary government of the Church under the Curia and the Ecumenical Council, which required the broadest collaboration of the whole of Catholicism.

> Regarding this conciliar work, two points worthy of emphasis need to be singled out. First, the Ecumenical Council has its own structure and organization, which cannot be confused with the ordinary and characteristic functioning of the various dicasteries or congregations that constitute the Roman Curia. Even during the Council, these will follow the ordinary course of their customary assignments in the general administration of Holy Church.... Second, the Ecumenical Council will result from the presence and participation of bishops and prelates who will be the living representation of the Catholic Church spread throughout the world. A precious contribution will be given to the preparation of the Council by listening to educated and very competent persons from every land and of every tongue.[12]

The central commission did indeed fulfill the criterion of universality with its large representation of presidents of episcopal conferences (where such had already been constituted), and of bishops from every region of the world. Of the 842 persons called on to be part of the commissions, almost two-thirds were strangers to Rome — recruited from the whole Catholic world, and especially the regions of Europe.[13] John XXIII felt that he had respected the universal physiognomy of the Church and had restrained, within acceptable limits, the Curia's pressure. In an audience with the director of *Civiltà Cattolica* (June 7, 1960), the pope spoke at length about the preparations for the Council. He expressed his desire to enlist the energies of all valid collaborators, even from outside Rome, so that the world would not see the Council as primarily a "Roman" matter. As for the criticism by members of the press that the pope had yielded to pressure from the Curia, John XXIII responded by saying he could not act without their support; after all, they were the men who worked at his side and aided him in governing the Church.

John XXIII gave the preparatory commissions remarkable freedom to act within the sphere of their work. And the results reflected the natural predisposition that existed based on the composition of members and the strong relationships among the various constituents. Most of the drafts produced during this preparatory phase were later rejected by the Council Fathers and completely rewritten. The drafts did not correspond to the broad vision that the pope had proposed for the Council. The texts of the theological commission, presided over by Cardinal Ottaviani, were conceived as a response to contemporary threats against the purity and integrity of the deposit of Revelation. Those who worked on the pastoral texts limited themselves to making adjustments in the prevailing system. The reworking of the "pastoral" concept was weak and reduced to the level of the purely technical application of dogmatic principles. Only the liturgical commission and the Secretariat for Christian Unity really seemed to reach the level the pope had envisioned. They continued to set their sights on the high purpose of the Council as John XXIII described in official and occasional papal discourses, which anticipated the themes he would propose in the opening discourse of Vatican II.

The discourse of November 14, 1960, which launched the work of the preparatory commissions, and the Bull of Indiction *Humanae Salutis* of December 25, 1961 are especially noteworthy.[14] In both talks Pope John looked at past Councils and placed the new conciliar event in its own historical context. The pope's analysis of the contemporary situation was innovative. Pope John knew that profound changes were occurring in society, which greatly interfered with a direction toward religious values. However, he did not denounce these social changes with an apocalyptic tone that seemed dear to certain Catholic traditions. At the same time, he stressed the possibility that society would lose a sense of the spiritual at a point in history when humanity's moral progress failed to keep pace with its material progress and people often tried to ignore the Creator completely.[15] The interaction of the pope's profound vision of faith with this judgment was strikingly original. Faith prevented him from yielding to a temptation to condemn and become pessimistic. Instead, he maintained a positive, hopeful perspective. The Church had to trust the promise of its Divine Founder, who guaranteed his lasting presence and the assistance of his Spirit.[16] With the certainty of one who is divinely assisted and guided, Pope John could not abandon himself to a lack of trust, but felt called to discover the many possibilities for good in the modern era. The pope recognized that there was now a greater openness to spiritual values and a commitment towards the integration of individuals, social classes, and nations.

In Pope John's eyes, the Church was anything but afraid and inert. Clergy and laity were manifesting a remarkable vitality in their apostolates and in their prayer. The urgency of this turning point, this crucial moment in history, justified a general gathering of the whole Church "called to confront tasks of immense gravity and breadth, as in the most tragic periods of her history."[17] The Council's objective could not be restricted to specifying particular points of discipline or Church doctrine, as happened in the past. The goal of this Council was more vast and demanding. In a sense, the Church was entering a new chapter in its history, and for this precise reason it was more difficult to grasp the full meaning of the Council. A complete renewal of Christian life was needed, eliminating what had become obsolete and counterproductive so that Christians might bear credible witness to the Gospel.[18]

Through the provocation of history, God was calling for a *Universal Church, restored and renewed.*[19] The Council would hold the key to this renewal of direction during the decision-making period and the period of realization that would follow. Appealing to history and to his faith as a believer, Pope John summed up his hopes thus:

New horizons will open up in the near future with the celebration of the Ecumenical Council. History teaches that every Council is followed by an era of extraordinary spiritual fruitfulness, in which the breath of the Holy Spirit raises up generous and heroic vocations and gives the Church persons who are needed and suitable. May this vision of faith and hope kindle foresight and expectation in our hearts.[20]

Was the pope being consistent with his ideals? Evidently he had allowed the extensive pre-preparatory work to proceed along a direction that was often opposed to what he desired. The argument that the work of the commission fully reflected the pope's intentions seems implausible, even if supported by notes of approval which Pope John jotted in the margins of drafts.

Important doctrinal texts came out of these drafts, including: "On the Sources of Revelation," "On the Moral Order," "On the Deposit of Faith," and "On the Sacred Liturgy." It is only fair to note that the pope had only three days (July 10–13, 1962) to read and approve the drafts.[21] His praise of the work was accompanied by his explicit reservations regarding the harsh and negative tone which some of the drafts contained. In an audience on July 27, the pope told the director of *Civiltà Cattolica* of his dissatisfaction with some of the drafts he had been reviewing and annotating. He mentioned one in particular, which was simply a list of errors nearly two pages long. The pope was probably alluding to the document "On the Moral Order." Later, when Pope John spoke with Cardinal Suenens during an audience at Castelgandolfo, he also lamented the inadequacy of the drafts.[22]

The suggestion made by some scholars is that the pope's apparent inconsistencies were a case of "institutional solitude." They propose that Pope John's power was limited in an ambient so foreign to his own sensibilities. There was little left for him to do but wait for the conciliar event to overturn the situation.[23] Given the pope's pastoral heart and active involvement, this hypothesis seems rather farfetched.

The pope's position was certainly complex. From the outset, he had envisioned the Council as an arena of open discussion, with no preestablished conclusion — not even his own. Although he was sensitive to the need for change, he was also searching for an adequate response. He limited himself to assigning a theme; its development would be the task of the entire episcopate. This explains why he allowed the preparatory commission such freedom in the work. No measures were taken to restrain the Roman Curia's dominant position within the commissions. Curial members were free to express their own views, which the pope did not immediately reject. Rather, he was disposed to carefully evaluate each position and to find noteworthy points in all of them. Perhaps this happened often because his theological formation bore a similar traditional imprint.

Pope John's greatest preoccupation was making understood the requests at the root of the conciliar convocation, and to render it possible to listen to those voices which had been almost suffocated. For this reason, he wanted a universal consultation that was not restricted to the episcopate. With great care he instituted the Secretariat for Christian Unity in the spring of 1960 to carry forward his ecumenical desires, which had not received sufficient attention in curial circles. Enjoying the pope's constant trust and support, this body was transformed, notwithstanding Cardinal Ottaviani's opposition, from a simple technical instrument into a valid preparatory commission with the right to present documents for discussion.

In whatever way possible, the pope wanted to launch an authentic Council that would respond to the great faith placed in it as an instrument of Church life. By means of its open examination of the Church's reality, and sustained by the assistance of the Holy Spirit, it would not fail to find suitable solutions. Pope John's conduct during this phase was inspired by the criteria of his being the impartial guarantor and the one responsible for the orderly development of the Council's program of work. The growing criticism that the work lacked coordination led him to create a sub-commission for miscellaneous matters. After the completion of the pre-preparatory commission's work, he would attempt to give the sub-commission an organic character.[24]

The pope's preoccupation with defending the Council's freedom to make decisions and also to assure the public of its autonomy were the basis for his stand regarding Don Riccardo Lombardi's book, *The Council — For a Reform of Charity*. Lombardi, founder of "For a Better World," maintained the necessity of taking decisive steps toward the renewal of the structures of the Church. In particular, Lombardi took aim at the Roman Curia. He insisted that a simplification of curial structures had to begin from the top down.

Lombardi presented a copy of his book to the pope at the conclusion of an audience on December 23, 1961. A press campaign, initiated at the beginning of January, used the occasion to suggest that Lombardi's work had the pope's approval. Lombardi's strong criticism of the Curia made this a rather embarrassing situation, and members of the Curia were quite disturbed. The publicity did not appear entirely without basis because of the author's prestige and the fact that he had once enjoyed the friendship and esteem of Pope Pacelli.

Some clarification was inevitable. It took the form of a firm stance by *L'Osservatore Romano* in an article published on January 11. The article emphasized that the author's ideas had advanced not through their own merit, but because of his personal associations. It described "certain judgments that the author ventures to make against the clergy and the Roman Curia" as "rash and unjust."[25]

The Council's autonomy became more defined with the publication of the apostolic constitution *Veterum Sapientia* (February 22, 1962), a confusing collection of conflicting positions. Its one connecting thread was the reaffirmation of Latin as the language of the Church, following the rigid norms established for teaching Latin in ecclesiastical studies and using it to impart the sacred disciplines and perform the sacred rites. The document seemed to end all discussion of the translation of the liturgy into the vernacular — a question hotly debated by the liturgical commission at exactly that time. Criticism was leveled against interpreting the document as closing the issue, and many participants sought assurances with respect to the freedom of the Council. In the end, the question of using the vernacular would remain on the Council's agenda.[26] Except for the work of the commissions and in the debates held in the Council hall, however, Latin would be the official language of the Council. This would prove a serious obstacle to many participants who did not understand the language.

The pope's Easter letter of 1962 confirmed his intention of convoking the bishops for a true exercise of co-responsibility. At last he interrupted the reserve shrouding the preparatory work by stating that the bishops would evaluate the drafts of the preparatory commissions in a complete and collegial manner.[27] They would not be allowed a mere passive acceptance. The same points were confirmed in the motu proprio *Appropinquante Concilio* (The Upcoming Council) of August 2, which approved the Council's rules of procedure.[28]

During this phase of the work, Pope John made his most decisive intervention. Tardini's prediction in October of 1959 that it would take a period of no less than three years before the Council could convene proved true. In the Bull of Indiction of December 25, 1961, the pope announced the opening of the Council for the following year, but without specifying an exact date. In February of 1960, the date was fixed for October 11, notwithstanding the many requests he received to postpone the opening for a year because the preparations were behind schedule.

The comments Pope John jotted down on the bishops' proposals are evidence that he believed the Council would progress quickly. It became clearer as the conclusion of the pre-preparatory work drew near that this would not be the case. Such an enormous amount of valuable and diverse material had been accumulated, which only accented the sharp contrast between two lines of thought. On April 8 the pope suggested the idea of holding two sessions. He repeated this on many occasions, up to the day the Council convened. In any case, nothing was actually decided, since the duration of the Council depended on how the bishops accepted the documents they examined.[29]

At the conclusion of the preparatory phase, the question of the Council's agenda became pressing. The members of the central commission made no secret of the poor quality and excessive length of many of the drafts. Meeting with the pope in March 1962, Cardinal Suenens of Brussels — one of the more authoritative members of the central commission — became the mouthpiece for these complaints. The pope gave him the task of sorting through the already prepared material. In a brief memo, Suenens affirmed that 80 percent of the texts did not constitute suitable material for a Council. He proposed that a special commission be created to prepare an agenda for the Council that would be restricted to the more important matters corresponding to the pope's desire for pastoral renewal. John XXIII approved the memo and asked Suenens to further develop the proposal.[30]

Others shared the concerns expressed by Suenens; among them was Cardinal Frings. At a meeting of the central commission on May 5, Frings proposed that a special commission be established to select the questions on which to base a coherent program for the Council, which met with widespread approval. Meanwhile, Suenens sent his more detailed plan to the pope as requested. In it, Suenens suggested that the conciliar work begin with the draft, "On the Church: Mystery of Christ," to provide some organic unity. This would be followed by several drafts dealing with the Church *ad intra* (in itself): its ministries of evangelization, catechesis, sanctification, and worship. Finally, the Council would look at the Church *ad extra* (looking outward), in order to respond to the world's hopes concerning social problems. Suenens also reiterated the need for a special commission to draw up the Council's agenda. John XXIII agreed with this proposal and suggested that it be submitted to cardinals whom he would name. Secretary of State Cicognani hastened to carry this out three days later.

Pope John's first documented response to these proposals uncovers the "original sin" of the preparatory phase. In a directive sent through Cicognani on May 20, the pope assured the bishops that they would have enough time to review the drafts which would reach them by July or August. This was meant to guarantee better participation, but also to dissipate the conclusions being drawn about the content of the conciliar drafts because of the secrecy that had been maintained.[31] During May and June the pope seemed preoccupied with establishing direct contact with the bishops to avert dangerous misinterpretations that could compromise the good outcome of the Council. All the members of the central commission were therefore invited to send any of their suggestions or observations.[32]

The step of sending out the drafts called for immediate decisions. For the moment, the programs suggested by Suenens and Frings were set aside. Instead, the work of existing commissions would be used. In a memorandum to the pope dated May 27, the secretary, Bishop Felici, sent word that the sub-commission for amendments had already modified six drafts according to observations that had emerged from members of the central commission. After the pope's approval, the following texts would be sent to the bishops in July: "On the sources of revelation," "On safeguarding the deposit of faith," "On the moral order," "On chastity, virginity, marriage, and family," "On the sacred liturgy," and "On the media of social communication."

Felici's report was not entirely accurate — corrections were still being inserted into the drafts. Nevertheless, on July 10 he was able to present the pope with the six documents he had promised, and added a seventh on ecumenism, "On the unity of the Church," which had been prepared by the commission for the Eastern Churches.[33]

Meanwhile, the earlier proposal of Cardinal Suenens, now refined, had gained wider approval. Suenens' letter of July 4 informed the pope of a meeting he had with Cardinals Döpfner, Montini, Siri, and Liénart at the Belgian College in Rome. They had discussed the expediency of the Council having an organic program and of beginning the first session with the doctrinal section, which in its turn would be introduced with a study of "On the Church: Mystery of Christ." Suenens had been asked to insert the drafts that had already been prepared into the general framework of his program, which he accomplished easily enough. The Belgian cardinal sent the pope a copy of his broader program.[34]

Döpfner, Montini, Siri, Liénart, and Suenens had also recommended that the drafts not be sent to the bishops in a helter-skelter manner. In fact, this was already being done, and the process was too far underway to be reversed. In any case, among the documents being sent to the bishops were drafts on doctrinal fundamentals, about which it was possible to hold serious discussions, as would happen. "On the Church" did not appear among the documents, however, because it was not yet ready. Pope Roncalli treasured these precious contributions, which he would use in a radio message on September 11 as he presented the Council to the whole world.

During the first week of the Council, the pope met with Suenens and informed him that his program was being kept safely in the pope's desk, but that he would not fail to use it at the proper moment.[35]

CHAPTER 19

ECUMENISM

Cardinal Bea and the Secretariat for Christian Unity

The ecumenical purpose of Vatican II emerged in the very first discourse of January 25, 1959, with the invitation "to the faithful of the
separated Churches to participate...at this banquet of grace." Because of
the obvious impossibility of overcoming centuries of separation and
prejudice, the Council would not even attempt to negotiate for unity
among the Christian Churches. Nevertheless, it was not exempt from an
obligation to promote mutual advances in unity. John XXIII had carried
this desire in his heart from his time in Bulgaria. But in Rome he had not
found a climate prepared to welcome and share his projects.

The development of an ecumenical movement transcending the traditional concept of the return of separated brethren to the Catholic Church
was still a peripheral phenomenon. Its first significant expression was
found in the activity of a few associations, most important of which was
the Catholic Conference on Ecumenical Questions, founded in 1952 principally as the initiative of Jan Willebrands of the Netherlands.[1]

The appointment of the Jesuit, Augustine Bea, to the cardinalate on
November 16, 1959 made possible the encounter between two great personalities whose collaboration would be decisive for the destiny of
ecumenism and for Vatican II itself.

Bea had been the personal confessor of Pius XII, rector of the Pontifical Biblical Institute, and consultor of the Holy Office. Bea spoke di-

rectly to John XXIII about the ecumenical problem after he received a request from Bishop Jaeger of Paderborn, who hoped the Vatican would establish a commission for ecumenical activities.

His first audience with the pope took place on January 9, 1960, and upon leaving he commented, "We understood each other perfectly."[2] Bea's brief remark fully expressed what had happened. At that encounter he discovered a perfect harmony of ideas and plans and a great mutual esteem and understanding. After their first meeting, Pope John would confide to his secretary: "This Cardinal Bea is a man and a religious of great worth. Only to look at him inspires trust: so learned and humble, ascetic and studious, capable of descending from his professor's chair to teach simple catechism: the stuff of which a shepherd is made. I felt inspired to open myself to him in confidentiality, and I did so. He will be very useful to me."[3]

As Capovilla recalls, the cardinal became part of the pope's group of *friends of the soul:* "Their long conversations brought comfort to the Supreme Pontiff, who, sustained by the like-mindedness of a man of such stature, felt stimulated to make further efforts in his apostolic commitment.... He felt at ease with him. He had the feeling of having always walked with him."[4] Pope John had found the right man to support his deepest intuitions, as he himself recognized: "Cardinal Bea accomplishes what I carry in my heart."[5]

The pope's admiration was reciprocated by a man who knew how to read the depths of John's soul. Bea grasped the whole spiritual depth of Pope John, his simple and solid faith and his limitless trust in God's protection over his Church and his humble servants. Bea understood that the pope's courage, so extraordinary for a man of about eighty, was rooted in God. Bea was fascinated by this.

> My personal contacts with Pope John were always a spiritual feast for me. He allowed me to penetrate his profound religious life and observe how his judgments and activity welled up from this hidden spring.... I never left an audience that had been granted to me without having been profoundly impressed by his character. He had such breadth of vision. He was so tolerant and indulgent, yet so strong and inflexible in his principles and plans.... It has been well said by a writer who knew the situation that the Council was first an act of faith on the part of Pope John and the fruit of his trust in God. No other explanation corresponds to the facts. He succeeded in inspiring others with his faith and courage.[6]

And such admiration was not without its effects. According to his friends, after Bea's assignment to the ecumenical commission, his contacts with the pope seemed to change him for the better.[7]

The firmness of their relationship explains the swiftness with which the Secretariat for Christian Unity was instituted and the important role it assumed in the preparatory phase and the progress of Vatican II. Very soon after the audience of January 9, 1960, Bea set about developing an outline, which he submitted to Bishop Jaeger, for the creation of a pontifical commission to coordinate and promote ecumenical activity. The project was presented to John XXIII on March 11, 1960, as an initiative of the Johan Adam Möhler Institute of Paderborn. A letter from Bea accompanied the project. In it he supported the appropriateness of "a central and official body to watch over all Catholic ecumenical activity and impart the necessary directives and instructions in a timely manner." Such an undertaking would be especially urgent for the continuation of the Council's thrust. It seems the pope agreed; that Sunday, the pope met with the cardinal immediately and communicated his complete concurrence. Bea was made the president of the pontifical commission, although for the moment the pope preferred to consider it a conciliar commission rather than a stable body within the Roman Curia — a step that would be taken later.

Pope John has left testimony about his decision. In his own hand he wrote on the letter Bea sent to him:

> Consulted the Card. secretary of state and Card. Bea (March 12–13). It will be done as suggested. Card. Bea will be the president of the proposed pontifical commission. He will respond to and maintain contact with the bishop of Paderborn. He will prepare everything. But as for official release of the news, we will wait until after Easter, placing this body in the line-up of commissions that will be named according to the various themes of the Council.... So be it. March 14, 1960. Jo. XXIII.[8]

To adapt the secretariat to the new criteria, Bea revised the statutes expressing the end and purpose that were to constantly inspire its activity. The strictly normative section of the statutes was not approved by the pope because he wanted to insert the secretariat into the institutional framework of the Council's preparatory phase. Only later would it acquire a central role within the Curia and relieve the Holy Office, which had been handling ecumenical affairs.

The pope preferred to distinguish the new body from the other commissions by giving it the title "secretariat," and it was listed this way in the motu proprio *Superno Dei Nuto* of June 5, 1960. From the start, this decision gave rise to lively disputes. As a secretariat it was given minimal importance within curial circles, because it was considered a purely technical instrument for improving the quality of information about the separated Churches. Instead, by using the less restrictive title, John XXIII gave this body greater liberty than it would have had as a preparatory commission. The pope informed Bea of this privately. Then, on May 30, he did so publicly in his library when he announced to the cardinals the imminent formation of the preparatory commissions.[9]

The existence of the secretariat initiated more intense and official contacts with other Christian confessions and made possible a series of promising visits by their representatives to the pope, whose openness they admired and whom they wished to know personally.

The first request for an audience came from the Anglican primate, Dr. Geoffrey Fisher. Unfortunately, the event revealed the central administration's lack of preparedness for welcoming those making "courtesy visits." On December 2, 1960, *L'Osservatore Romano* used its smallest typographical characters to publicize Dr. Fisher's visit. Exterior preparations were reduced to the minimum because of various concerns, among them the fear that the visit would imply that the Anglican episcopal consecration was considered legitimate — Holy Orders being a major disagreement between Catholics and Anglicans.

The press was completely excluded from the meeting between Pope John and Dr. Fisher. It was a friendly visit and afterward, Pope John confided to Tucci that even in the absence of favorable conditions for complete union it was still possible to intensify a unity of spirit based on what was already held in common. He added that these steps were not a cause for fear because they were steps *toward* one another — and this was real progress. As for the Curia, he said, "Not everyone here understands these things: they want perfection or nothing."[10]

The encounter immediately brought about the appointment of permanent representatives, one from the Anglican Communion to the Vatican the following February, and one to the Council from the Evangelical Churches of Germany the following year.[11] The road was now clear for direct encounters between the leaders of Christian Churches, which John XXIII noted a few days before his death while contemplating the intense development of ecumenical relationships.[12]

The harmony of thought that existed between Bea and Pope John was expressed in the ideas developed within the Secretariat and presented — not without ample debate with the Curia — as contributions to the ecumenical aim of the Council. In contrast to the excessively juridical concept of the Church that inspired a strong reserve in meetings with other Christians, Bea kept in mind a motto very dear to Pope John — to distinguish between errors and the persons involved. The proclamation of the truth could not be separated from the exercise of charity and, therefore, from an evaluation of the situation and the hopes of the separated brethren. Bea often quoted the phrase from the letter to the Ephesians, "Speak the truth in love" (cf. 4:15), and the pope repeated it in his discourse of Pentecost (1960) when he explained the recently released, *Superno Dei Nutu*. Indeed, the pope declared that Paul's words "well deserved to appear on the doors to the Ecumenical Council."[13]

Such awareness fostered the recognition of the real communion existing among all Christians and therefore of their membership in the Church, although not in its fullness but based on what is common to all and unites all. The root of this communion lies in Baptism and its effects, which are also valid outside of Catholicism. Bea upheld such positions and referred to Pope John's various official declarations, especially the programmatic encyclical, *Near the Chair of Peter* (1959), in which the pope speaks of other Christians as sons and daughters:

> Indulge this gentle longing we have to address you as brothers and sons.... All those who are separated from us, we address as brothers, using the words of St. Augustine: Whether they like it or not, they are our brethren. They will cease to be our brethren only if they cease to say the "Our Father."[14]

Bea met strong opposition from Cardinal Ottaviani, president of the theological commission, and Tromp, the secretary. Ottaviani and Tromp discussed the matter with Bishop Parente of the Holy Office and decided to exercise extreme caution since it was common knowledge that Bea's positions mirrored those of Pope John.[15]

In order for the Secretariat for Christian Unity to carry out the work for which it had been instituted, the pope's favor sufficed in some circumstances, but in others his intervention became necessary. From the beginning the Secretariat enjoyed great liberty, and it was the only body among the commissions that had the courage not to deal simply with decisions based on the bishops' proposals but also with the demands of the outside world, Catholic theology engaged at the forefront of ecumenism, and representatives of the separated communities. It treated those problems proper to ecumenism but also began to reconsider various theological themes of particular interest to ecumenical dialogue. Among these themes were ecclesiology and the restoration of the centrality of Scripture, from both a pastoral and theological perspective, to rectify the choice of the post-Tridentine Church giving pride of place to the sacraments.

Visser't Hoof, secretary of the World Council of Churches, asked Cardinal Willebrands to consider the question of religious liberty as an essential presupposition for any collaboration of the World Council with the Catholic Church. A necessary change of attitude would be that the Catholic religion was the one, true faith that tolerated others only to avoid graver evils. By now outdated, this idea totally disregarded human rights. However, some convinced supporters still existed within the Theological Commission, which claimed the right to control every document of a theological nature. Foreseeing the commission's defeat of the document "On Religious Liberty," which had been drafted by the secretariat, Bea had recourse to the pope. On February 1, 1962, Pope John arranged for the new text to be presented directly to the central commission "with the interference of no other commission." The texts that had been drafted by the Theological Commission and the secretariat were submitted to the central commission simultaneously and compared closely. Since the commission could not reconcile the opposing elements, it decided to refer the matter to the pope. Pope John appointed a diverse commission composed of Ottaviani, Tromp, Bea, and Willebrands, who could not reach an agreement.[16]

The very important decision of other Christian Churches to send observers to the Council would radically transform relations among Christians. It has been said that this marked the end of the counter-reformation. In January of 1959 Pope John extended this "friendly invitation to the faithful of the separated Churches to participate with us in this banquet of grace and brotherhood." If his intention and desire were clear, how such participation would take place remained vague. In the course of that year, the pope would return often to the topic. In April he stated that the future Council would not be one of union in the traditional sense of the term, but one that represented an invitation to unity.[17] In a discourse given at Castelgandolfo in August 1959 the pope spoke more precisely on the issue and added his hope for the direct participation of non-

Catholics in the Council. The separated communities expressed their desire to send representatives to the Council. Faced with this fact, the pope stated that the Church "must welcome them since the Church is always their home from which they have become distant in the course of the changing situations of history."

The ice had been broken. While attendance was dependent on explicit requests of non-Catholics, the possibility of a direct invitation had been authorized by the pontiff.[18] The secretariat presented the central commission with a project for the invitation of representatives of the other separated Churches as observers with the possibility of following the Council's work even outside the public sessions. In choosing representatives, theologians were preferred over bishops. The proposal was presented to the central commission in its session of November 1961, where it gained the majority of votes.

John XXIII was very satisfied with the commission's decision and could now make the participation of separated communities official. The pope's task was also made more pleasant because the decision freed him from having to impose it on the decision-making body of the Council. In the Bull of Indiction of the Council of December 25, 1961, all Christians of the separated Churches were invited to unite in a chorus of prayer for the Council's good outcome.

> And we know that the announcement of the Council has not only been welcomed by them with joy, but also not a few have already promised to offer their prayers for its good outcome and hope to send representatives from their communities to follow its work from close at hand. All of this constitutes for us a source of great comfort and hope. It was precisely in order to facilitate such contacts that already, some time ago, we established a secretariat with this specific purpose.[19]

Pope John also entrusted the secretariat with realizing the work pertaining to relations with the Eastern Churches. Negotiations with the Eastern Churches constituted a most demanding test. The secretariat experienced failures, above all due to the rivalry between Constantinople and Moscow. While Patriarch Athenagoras wished to send observers, he was prevented from doing so; on the other hand, two observers arrived from Moscow on October 12, the day after the Council opened.

The moment had finally come when the efforts of Bea and the secretariat — and the ecumenical hopes Pope John had cultivated for decades — were actualized. On one of the first days of the Council, an emotional and solemn meeting took place between the pope and forty observers, representing almost all of the great federations of Christian confessions during the Reformation, and a good number of Eastern Churches. The pope did not sit on the papal throne, but instead took his seat on a simple armchair that was raised on a dais slightly higher. The observers sat on either side of the pope, their seats forming an oval. The onlookers understood that they were witnessing an historical event which marked the end of an era. After four centuries, Christians of almost every confession were gathered in a fraternal atmosphere seeking to respond to the Gospel's call to be one. "It's a miracle, a true miracle," commented Cardinal Bea as he witnessed the event, which only a short time before had seemed utterly impossible.[20]

Without minimizing the Holy Spirit's role, it is fair to say that the aged pope, threatened with a serious illness and nearing death, was the chief architect of this miracle. Indeed, very few had been able to refuse his invitation to attend the Council as observers; their presence honored not only his person, but also his style of fraternity and goodness that were the distinguishing mark of his activity and had directed his course toward the separated communities for decades. In his discourse during this meeting, Pope John did not touch on theological problems, but offered as a testimony of his relationship with the separated communities the motivations that had inspired him and the values he had sought.

With his characteristic openness, he invited his hearers to read his heart to find the inspiration for his ecumenical commitment that, above all else, was an expression of his fraternal charity. Outside of his strictly diplomatic assignments as a representative of the Holy See, this charity inspired his association with numerous representatives of the various Churches. He had forged profound friendships on a mutual esteem and respect. The pope's recollections unfolded with the intensity of personal ties.

> There were twenty years of very happy and serene friendships with persons of venerable age and generous youth whom I regarded with love, even though my assignment of representing the Holy See in the Near East was not explicitly directed to this. Then also in Paris, one of the crossroads of the world…I had frequent encounters with Christians of various denominations. It never happened that in some circumstances there was a confusion of principles among us. Nor was there any disagreement on the level of charity in our common work — imposed on us by circumstance — of aiding the suffering. We did not negotiate; we conversed. We did not wrangle; we wished one another well.

Pope John's ecumenical sensitivity had not matured only in his later life; he had committed himself to it during the most important years of his episcopal ministry, and he also intended to commit his remaining days to the cause of unity — still in its initial phase — and to offer his life for it.

> Your welcome presence here and the anxiety that pulses in my priestly heart…the anxiety of my beloved collaborators — and yours, too, I am sure — inspire me to tell you of the resolve burning in my soul to work and suffer so that the hour will come when the prayer of Jesus at the Last Supper will be accomplished.[21]

No one applauded at the end of the discourse. Then the pope, after consulting briefly with Bea on the appropriateness of the gesture, rose and imparted his blessing. The Orthodox made the sign of the cross, the Anglicans knelt, and the others bowed deeply. When he gave the final greeting, everyone applauded and no one was dry-eyed. They had lived an unforgettable day.[22]

The sequel to this first encounter, which ended happily and nourished hopes, was the real possibility that observers would be able to follow the Council's work and express their observations, even during the discussion of conciliar decrees.[23]

The surprising results in such a brief period only confirmed the pope's excellent decision to create the Secretariat for Christian Unity and to appoint Cardinal Bea as its president. The secretariat's work was recognized as indispensable for the continuation of ecumenical projects, and it began to be seen as more than a commission oriented toward the Council. It was a structure with a particular and exclusive connection to the pope. Pope John had respected the competence of the Curia during the preparatory phase and did not interfere with the preparation of conciliar drafts. But he maintained his own space and liberty of action, exemplified in the creation of the secretariat to which he had given all the powers it needed to exercise an effective influence on the work of the Council. Rather than being a simple technical instrument, as it might have appeared in *Superno Dei Nutu,* the secretariat was recognized as a true and proper commission authorized to present drafts to the central commission.

Still, the secretariat's overall situation was not secure, as would become more evident at the opening of the Council. In fact, the conciliar rules of procedure placed the Secretariat for Christian Unity among the external secretariats and not among the commissions. This signified such a serious redimensioning of its structure that almost any influence the secretariat could have exerted on the work of the Council would have been blocked. As soon as the work began, Bea went directly to the pope asking that the secretariat be placed on the same level as the other commissions. Bea was also concerned with preventing members of the secretariat from being elected to serve on other commissions. The pope granted Bea's request, and a four-point communiqué was composed to avoid any misunderstanding.[24] Once the secretariat was on the same level as the other commissions, it was in a position to exert a decisive influence on the work of the Council and ensure that more attention would be given to ecumenical concerns.[25]

Catholic-Jewish Relations

Pope John had also entrusted the secretariat with work at another frontier: the delicate matter of the relationship between the Church and the Jewish people. The great tragedy of the Holocaust demanded a radical clarification and careful review of nearly two millennia in this regard.

This topic had not been part of the initial objectives assigned to the Council, but was included by the force of some of the pope's actions — the fruit of his pastoral instinct — and their consequences, which drew the attention of sensitive souls like Dr. Jules Isaac.

The pope had made a first step toward the Jewish world at the time of his election when, notwithstanding the absence of official diplomatic relations between Israel and the Vatican, he had the news communicated to the State of Israel. The initiative pleased some of the Israeli authorities, and the great Israeli rabbi, Dr. Isaac Herzog, telegraphed his "sincere blessings" to the pope.

A second step taken by the pope was found in a note, perhaps written on March 15, 1959:

> For some time we have been concerned about the *"pro perfidis Judaeis"* that occurs in the Good Friday liturgy. We have sure testimony that our predecessor Pius XII, of holy memory, personally removed that adjective from the prayer, saying simply: "Let us also pray for the Jews." Since this is our own thought as well, we dispose that on the next Good Friday the twofold supplication be shortened in this way.[26]

Thus, on Good Friday, March 27, 1959, in the universal prayer of the solemn afternoon liturgy, the presiding cardinal avoided the expression *"perfidis"* in the presence of the pope. It is true that the term *perfidis* was originally understood to mean "non-believing"; however, with time and the evolution of language, it acquired a far more negative meaning. Sensitive Catholics felt a strong aversion to using such a harsh and disrespectful tone in the prayer. Subsequently, the pope had the offensive phrase eliminated from all liturgical books.[27] His initiative was noticed.

A French Jew by the name of Jules Isaac (1877–1963) immediately noted Pope John's extraordinary move. Dr. Isaac was a professor of history who had held important political positions in France. Tragically, during the Second World War both his wife and daughter died in Nazi concentration camps. After the war, Isaac dedicated himself to the cause of establishing a relationship of mutual esteem between Jews and Christians. Confronted with the millennia-long tragedies suffered by his people, he grew always more convinced of the strong anti-Semitic impact of some ideas diffused by Christianity through catechesis. One example is the accusation leveled against the Jews of having committed deicide, and the consequent curse of the Jewish people. As a historian, Isaac well understood that largely all anti-Semitic legislation derived from such ideas, which in turn fostered great hatred for the Jews and, ultimately, lay at the basis of Nazi crimes.

For Dr. Isaac, Pope John's gesture announced that an important transformation was beginning to take place in Catholicism. The moment had arrived for him to engage the highest authority of the Catholic Church in the question of the Christian/Jewish relationship.

Dr. Isaac obtained permission for an audience that was scheduled for June 13, 1960. He prepared himself for a careful explanation and advancement of his project for the revision of Christian teaching concerning the Jewish people. In the brief time available to him, Dr. Isaac spoke to the pope about the history of the dramatic relationships between Christianity and Judaism. The pope showed great interest. Dr. Isaac submitted that serious acts of discrimination had originated from the excessive insistence on the theme of deicide and the divine curse that weighed upon Judaism — justified neither biblically nor historically. Dr. Isaac called for a radical change to abolish the prejudices that held such a commanding position because they could be traced back to the fourth-century Church Fathers. He also referred to recent surveys that showed how Catholic opinion was wavering and uncertain, awaiting an authoritative posture that would state the truth and give positive direction to consciences.

During his time in Istanbul, John XXIII had witnessed firsthand the tragedy of the persecution of Jews by the Nazis, and he immediately agreed on the importance of the question. When Dr. Isaac asked whether he might have grounds on which to place his hope for the fulfillment of his request, the pope replied, "You have the right to more than hope!" Then he added, smiling, "I am the 'boss,' but I must also consult my collaborators. If problems come up, a study is made by the offices to solve it. We don't have an absolute monarchy here." The encounter concluded with a cordial and strong handclasp. Then the pope introduced Dr. Isaac to Cardinal Bea as a man "whom you can trust and in whom you can confide."

The pope became absorbed by the Jewish question, and from that very day it took its rightful place among the topics for the future Council. The Church had to show that it did not stand aloof from the suffering of the Jews or defend only baptized Jews, as Isaac seemed to imply. Once and for all the Church had to proclaim that Christians had no right to interpret the words, "let his blood be upon us," as a definitive condemnation of the Jews. For this radical review of the Church's past conduct, which would meet with many obstacles, the pope turned once more to the trusty Bea and officially handed him the task on September 18, 1960.[28]

Further proof of Pope John's particular sensitivity toward the Jewish question was given at an audience with about 130 members of the United Jewish Appeal, under the leadership of Rabbi Herbert Friedmann. The pope conducted the audience in his inimitable style of spontaneous affability that created an atmosphere of reciprocal, fraternal respect. The visitors already respected the pope for his commendable efforts in Turkey to save Jews from Nazi persecution. Dr. Friedmann recalled those events, and he thanked the pope for the concrete aid he had been able to give during that terrible time.

In his turn, John XXIII recalled one episode that clearly left a profound impression on his soul. Through his personal intervention as the apostolic delegate, Roncalli had succeeded in having a ship that carried thousands of Jewish children rerouted to a friendly port. For this, the Grand Rabbi of Jerusalem traveled to Istanbul in order to convey his gratitude personally. In their conversation, Roncalli observed that despite the religious and cultural distance between their two worlds, it was possible for them to draw nearer on the basis "of love, which itself is the unconquerable law of life and of human brotherhood." Christians and Jews firmly root their love in their faith in one God and Father, a solid, indisputable foundation.

As he spoke with the members of the United Jewish Appeal, Pope John again concentrated on what united rather than what divided, and he emphasized this in a unique way. He recalled the story of Joseph. "At first, innocently but astutely, Joseph hid himself from their sight." But he could not contain the impulse of his heart and, after shedding tears in secret, he exclaimed: *I am Joseph, your brother.* [29]

The pope's singular attitude toward the Jews, which was an example for the whole Church, is reflected in the summary notes he jotted in his calendar. "A group of 140 Jews from America, whom I welcomed with the remembrance of Joseph recognized by his brothers, and with best wishes for the harmony of the Old and New Testaments in the spirit of universal love and brotherhood among peoples."[30]

Another event, perhaps perceived in the opinion of the Jewish people as the most important, took place in Rome on March 17, 1962. On that day John XXIII was traveling along the Lungotevere when the car passed in front of the Synagogue of Rome at the precise moment when people were exiting the building. The pope had the car stopped and he blessed them. Rabbi Toaff, an eyewitness of the event, wrote how "after a moment of understandable bewilderment, the Jews encircled him and applauded enthusiastically. This was the first time in history that a pope had blessed Jews, and perhaps this was the first true gesture of reconciliation."[31] A year later, the same Rabbi Toaff entered St. Peter's Square with a group of Jewish faithful to pray and keep vigil during Pope John's last moments of life, as if to give silent but effective testimony to the greatness of that soul who opened himself to all people without distinction, and especially to his Jewish brothers and sisters.

The pope continued to follow Bea's work with interest. When the draft on Judaism was ready, John XXIII allowed Bea to present it along with the draft on religious freedom directly to the central commission. This simplified the process that the two documents had to go through in order to be discussed at the Council. Thus an unpleasant and perhaps perilous journey had been avoided.[32] The doctrinal commission, and Ottaviani who presided over it, would surely have created difficulties for these texts which presented a great departure from tradition. Indeed, the draft on religious freedom provoked a bitter clash between Bea and

Ottaviani; and the one on Judaism was withdrawn from discussion by the central commission because of the "politically inappropriate timing." The specific events referred to involved the World Jewish Congress, which had announced, without consulting the secretariat, its designation of Dr. Wardi as its special representative to Vatican Council II. As a citizen of Israel, Dr. Wardi's appointment had political implications, particularly when the Israeli Ministries of Foreign Affairs and Religious Affairs gave their official approval. The Arab world raised a series of protests that constrained the Vatican Secretariat of State, with Bea's agreement, to take the unusual step of canceling the discussion of the draft in the central commission, thus excluding it from the topics on the Council's agenda.

As he communicated the decision, Secretary of State Cicognani used expressions that were not completely in accord with the intentions of John XXIII. The reasons Cicognani offered were that the topic did not pertain to the purpose of the Council and that there was no need for clarifications regarding the Jewish people.[33] Obviously, the particular political difficulty responsible for the setback was only a sign of the struggle the document would have encountered before any conciliar approval.

Cardinal Bea never considered the decision definitive and insisted that at the proper moment the document would be presented again. Hardly had the first session of the Council closed in December 1962, when he returned to his task and set forth for the pope the whole question of the Jewish people. A few days later on December 13, in confirmation of his enduring and profound sensitivity to this topic, the pope responded:

> I have attentively read this report of Cardinal Bea. I agree entirely that this interest of ours is serious and that we have a grave responsibility. "His blood be upon us and upon our children" (cf. Mt 27:25) does not dispense any believer in Christ from becoming involved in the problem and apostolate for the salvation of all the children of Abraham on an equal basis with everyone else living on earth. "Therefore, we beseech you to help your servants, whom you have redeemed with your precious blood" *(Te Deum).*[34]

CHAPTER 20

THE FIRST SESSION OF VATICAN II

Prayer Vigil

During Pope John's retreat at the Vatican, made from November 26 to December 2, 1961, he noted: "A great part of my daily concerns is absorbed in expectation of the Second Vatican Ecumenical Council. A desire is emerging in my spirit to surround my daily prayer with the prayers of all the Catholic clergy, both diocesan and religious, and of the congregations of women religious in an official and universal manner. I am waiting for some happy inspiration to invite them...."[1]

The inspiration became concrete on the feast of the Epiphany, 1962, with the publication *Sacrae Laudis,* a letter addressed to the clergy of the entire world that invited them to pray the breviary for the intention of the Council. The pope declared that this prayer would be their first form of cooperation because of the inherent liturgical nature of the conciliar event. In this new Pentecost, as the Council had often been defined, the Holy Spirit would be the absolute protagonist.

Pope John evoked other analogies for the Council. In some circumstances, he preferred to perceive it as the renewal of the Epiphany. The Council was to be an act of worship that the bishops, like the three magi, would perform before the Savior and Divine Founder of the Church. "Can we not say that before it will be a new and majestic Pentecost, the Ecumenical Council will be a genuine and new Epiphany, one of the many manifestations that have renewed it throughout the course of history — one of the most solemn?"[2] Therefore, as the mysterious but real encounter between Christ and his Church, it had to arrive adequately prepared in order to derive the greatest benefit from it.

With this logic, on July 1, 1962, Pope John released the encyclical *Poenitentiam Agere* (Do penance), in which he stressed the necessity of prayer and penance based on the twofold recommendation of Scripture and Tradition.[3] Since 1959 the pope had recommended the recitation of a prayer he had composed for the Council. He now asked that every parish celebrate a novena in honor of the Holy Spirit and that every diocese have a penitential service.

On July 2, 1962, he addressed women religious in particular. Besides recommending prayer, he also invited them to reconsider "with renewed fervor the obligations of their vocation," and to prepare themselves to welcome the dispositions of the Council.[4] Pope John desired that the whole Church feel itself united with the Council in a communion of prayer and of spirit, so as to participate intensely and enthusiastically in the event he considered decisive for the future of Catholicism.

He chose to prepare himself with a week of retreat (from Monday, September 10, to Saturday, September 15) in complete isolation in the Tower of St. John, only recently restored and made suitable for retreats within the Vatican. Through his meditations on the theological and cardinal virtues, Pope John reached an intense union with the Lord, which left him with "an increase of fervor in regard to the substance of my ministry and apostolic mandate. Lord Jesus, fill up my deficiencies. Lord, you know everything — you know that I love you (cf. John 21:17)."[5]

Pope John's awareness of his personal limitations moved him to make a serious examination on the uprightness of his decision concerning the convocation of the Council. He asked himself if, at the origins of the Council, some human self-interest could have entered to cloud the supernatural, or if his decision had been too imprudent or hasty. On the eve before the opening of the Council, such questions might have caused anguish to an aged pope who had made a binding decision amid such skepticism and opposition. But John XXIII did not discern any shadows in the way he had proceeded; rather, the presence of Divine action appeared most clear and he had docilely complied. When he considered his election as supreme pontiff, he was absolutely certain that he had done nothing to encourage or seek the office. He had accepted "the honor and burden of the papacy with simplicity."[6] Among the great graces of his life he considered this foremost.

Regarding his decision to convoke the Council, John XXIII was thoroughly convinced of the Divine origin of his inspiration that had taken him by surprise and to which he had submitted in obedience. As already noted, the suddenness of this intuition has become somewhat exaggerated. We know with certainty that he had begun to think of a Council within the first days after his election. His vast personal experience and conversations with cardinals on the eve of the conclave about the most pressing problems of the Church directed him toward an Ecumenical Council as the highest of ecclesial events. The successor of Peter felt the need to gather around himself his brothers in the episcopate for a fraternal discussion on the principle problems of the Church and especially those connected with evangelization.

Vatican II owed its being to the personality of a pope who had "little esteem for himself but received good inspirations and followed them in humility and trust."[7] His low self-esteem made him more docile to Divine action but also to human collaboration. His immense trust in God and in the unfailing support of Christ allowed him to launch a demanding project without losing his tranquillity.[8]

His serenity never diminished during the three laborious years of preparation. Now he had joyfully reached the "sacred mountain,"[9] an expression alluding to the Exodus and that testifies to the roncallian vision of the Council as the place of encounter and manifestation of God to his Church.

Part of Pope John's spiritual preparation was a pilgrimage to Loreto and Assisi on October 4. With great simplicity John XXIII confessed that he decided to make the trip, so unusual for a pope of that time. It was actually the first time since 1870 that a pope had officially traveled outside of Rome.

The trip began at 6:30 A.M. from the Vatican station where Pope John boarded the presidential train, which had been placed at his disposal by the nation of Italy. At the first stop, a civic delegation led by the head of the government, Amintore Fanfani, joined him. Upon his arrival in Loreto, he was greeted by President Segni, who had traveled ahead by plane. Along the route, and especially at the major stations, the pope became the object of enthusiastic public gatherings.

He explained why he chose Loreto as his destination during his discourse there. First, he desired to revive the traditional meaning of the word, "pilgrimage." During times of particular difficulty throughout the centuries, the shrine of Loreto had been the favored destination of popes and leaders in the Church. Following his predecessors, John XXIII desired to perform an act of supplication that would be the culmination and seal of the prayers that the faithful worldwide had been raising to God for the propitious outcome of the Council.

The second motive for his pilgrimage was its symbolic meaning of the Church's journey to reach the peoples of the entire world and, in the name of Christ, light of the nations, to establish "a kingdom at the service of brotherly love, a sign of peace, orderly and universal progress."[10] Moreover, the mystery of the Incarnation evoked by the holy house of Loreto, which tradition identifies as the site of the Annunciation, alluded to the task entrusted to the Council. The objective of the Council would be the worldwide diffusion of salvation's benefits — a renewal which had its beginning in the union between heaven and earth accomplished by the Incarnate Word. The pope expected Vatican II to make a contribution that would extend to all earthly realities — the object of the one redemption of Christ. It was certainly not by chance that the discourse at Loreto treated two realities so close to humanity as work and family life.

The supplication to the Mother of God concluded with the traditional ceremony of crowning the statue of the Virgin and Infant. John XXIII blessed and placed the crowns on their heads.

In the next stage of Pope John's pilgrimage, he offered the life of St. Francis as a model for renewal according to the Gospel. The saint of Assisi was a reminder of some of the most necessary attitudes for any authentic reform: the simplicity of children in order to enter a knowledge of the Divine mysteries before which "human wisdom, secular wealth, uncontested domination — whatever the world feeds on under the names of fortune, greatness, politics, power, and prestige — are blocked and shattered."[11] The pope's discourse in Assisi concluded with a warm exhortation for peace among peoples and a Franciscan call to the spirit of poverty that must inspire a just division of the many goods given to humanity by God. Notwithstanding the clamorous enthusiasm of the crowds, the pope spent the day in quiet joy and serenity of spirit. He called it "one of the most holy and noteworthy days of my pontificate."[12]

Pope John's spiritual preparation concluded with a solemn procession from the Basilica of St. Mary Major to the Basilica of St. John Lateran. He dedicated the procession to prayer for reconciliation and the invocation of the Holy Spirit as the Church's perennial Life-Giver and Supreme Guide.[13]

While the pope was in the midst of his spiritual preparation, he received some disturbing news. The stomach pains he had been suffering from were becoming more intense and the pope underwent a thorough physical examination. On September 23, he was informed that he had cancer. Capovilla, who was with the pope, wrote: "The pope seemed calm as he asked for explanations of the x-rays and the gastric pains that were bothering him."[14] John XXIII now knew he had little time left to live and, as he had repeatedly written, he was ready for anything.[15] He would face the remaining time left to him by proceeding as normal. Just a few months before, in the summer of 1962, Pope John had received Cardinal Suenens in an audience where he confided: "I know that my contribution to the Council will be that of suffering."[16] It is possible that he was referring to the difficulties that he expected were awaiting him at the Council, or perhaps he had some presentiment of the seriousness of his illness from the symptoms that had already been a kind of warning to him. In any case, after the doctors communicated their diagnosis, these words took on a more touching and concrete meaning. While the threat of death made the realization of his projects more urgent, the pope did not force the schedule of the Council. Rather, he assured its regular progress with more freedom — the freedom of one who no longer has anything to lose.[17]

Immediate Preparation

As the opening of the Council drew near, logistical deadlines had to be met. When, in July, Pope John was presented with the Council's *regolamento* (rules of procedure), he introduced some modification, which included increasing the membership of the Council of Presidents (presiders) from seven to ten for a larger representation. But this also meant that the Council's labors could become more difficult. The pope instituted the Secretariat for Extraordinary Affairs to screen the proposals presented by the Council Fathers. The majority required for all conciliar votes, except for the election of persons, was raised from 60 percent to two-thirds. The pope's praiseworthy intention to secure greater majorities for documents of considerable importance would nevertheless cause inconveniences even during the first session. In any case, John XXIII considered the rules of procedure to be somewhat experimental and knew he could intervene to adjust them according to the needs of the assembly.

The rules were promulgated on August 2 with the motu proprio *Appropinquante Concilio* (The Approaching Council), and published in *L'Osservatore Romano* a month later.

With an apostolic brief issued on September 4, the names of the members of the directive bodies of the Council were made public. The composition of the group was balanced with the presence of open personalities such as Cardinals Liénart, Frings, and Alfrink among the presiders; and Montini, Suenens, and Döpfner in the new secretariat. The Curia would not have the same influence it had during the preparatory phase. Furthermore, the pope reserved to himself the appointment of theologians, canonists, and others as conciliar "experts." On September 28, the pope appointed 224 persons; another one hundred would be added during the month of November. It is conceivable that the pope wanted to guarantee an adequate representation of the new currents of theological renewal.[18]

Pope John's most exacting task during the vigil before the Council was the radio message he would deliver on September 11, which contained one of his most authoritative reflections on the Council.

In his vision, the conciliar event found its reason for being in the very heart of the mystery of the Church, which owes its vitality to the indissoluble relationship with its Founder who continually enlivens and renews it. This regeneration cannot be limited to the ecclesial community, but must be extended to the whole of humanity. Therefore, illumined by Christ, the Church diffuses its light throughout the world, as indicated by the expressions used by the pope: "light of Christ," " light of the Church," "light of nations." These key words would also be used later by the Council. The Council represented a particularly intense moment in the ongoing relationship of the Church with Christ. The Lord regenerates his Church in view of the salvation of the world:

> In fact, what is an ecumenical Council if not the renewal of this encounter with the face of the risen Christ, glorious and immortal king, shining radiantly on the whole Church, for the well-being, joy, and splendor of humanity?[19]

The Council was to renew evangelization, and to this end the pope indicated two principal phases. First, the Church had to redefine itself concerning structure and faith — a necessary introduction for a fruitful evangelizing activity directed to the entire world. From this emerges the intuition that the Church does not exist for itself, but for the world for which it must radiate the light of Christ.

In relation to these points, the pope used Cardinal Suenens' suggestion to proceed in two phases — first treating the Church *ad intra,* and
then the Church *ad extra*. These would be two closely linked and essential stages. The Church must interest and concern itself with the problems facing humanity which constitute part of its evangelizing mission;
the Church must shoulder the difficulties and struggles of humanity in
the present historical circumstances.

Aside from the topic of peace — still very fragile in a Cold War climate — John XXIII listed a number of themes for the upcoming Council
to focus on. These included: "the basic equality of all peoples, exercising
their rights and duties among the entire family of nations; a strong defense of the nature of marriage, which demands understanding and generous love on the part of the spouses; the religious and moral aspects of
the procreation of children which arises from marriage."[20] To this he
added a completely new point: "Another beacon. Confronted by the underdeveloped nations, the Church must present itself as it is and wants to
be — the Church of everyone, especially the Church of the poor."[21]

In his radio message there emerged primarily a treatment of the outward dimension of the Church. A balance would be struck when Pope
John delivered his opening discourse and more time would be given to
aspects of the internal life of the Church.

The content of the pope's radio message plainly contrasted with
most of the drafts written by the various commissions during the preparatory phase, which were weighed down by an ecclesiology that was
apologetic in nature. The drafts lacked the intuition of a Church at the
service of the world, and thus scarcely paid attention to the world's problems. Instead, with his message the pope opened new perspectives that
kindled outstanding initiatives among the Council Fathers and paved —
not without difficulty — the way that would lead to *Gaudium et Spes*.

The Solemn Opening

In the days immediately before the opening of the Council, about
2,500 bishops arrived in Rome. The Council would be a great novelty
for all of them, because of the event's extraordinary nature and the outstanding role that they would be called to exercise.

The pope desired and expected the bishops' active and responsible
participation, but many of the conciliar members felt quite differently.
They had come to Rome because the pope had called them and they
were disposed to agree with the decisions he would present to them.

This was how they had always lived their relationship with Rome. They awaited directives to be carried out and submitted weightier matters to Rome believing that from the Vatican, as from the center, a more exact evaluation of their situations could always be made.

Some bishops would try to lock the conciliar dynamism into a traditional perspective. They feared that the unfolding of a free dialectic would risk divisions and opposing positions which could disorient the great majority of the faithful who needed simple and sure directives.

On the morning of October 11, a long procession of bishops descended the stairs of the Apostolic Palace and filed into St. Peter's Basilica, where a gallery of 2,905 seats had been erected for the Council Fathers, experts, and observers.[22] Amid acclamations from the faithful, John XXIII crossed St. Peter's Square in the *sedia gestatoria.* He entered the basilica, descended from the chair, walked down the nave, and knelt before the altar where he intoned the *Veni Creator*.

At the Eucharist celebrated by Cardinal Tisserant, the Gospel was proclaimed in Latin and Greek. Afterward the Gospel was enthroned — an act that would occur with every conciliar assembly — as a much-appreciated reminder of Christ's sovereignty over the gathering.

The cardinals, patriarchs, and representatives of the bishops carried out the rite of obedience to the pope, recited the Profession of Faith, and proclaimed the oath. The Sistine Chapel Choir sang the Creed while the bishops remained silent. Despite the restlessness of some liturgists with the lengthy rite, which illustrated the very inconsistencies they hoped to eliminate through an appropriate liturgical reform, the spectacle of the impressive gathering of bishops left an indelible impression on those present.[23]

After nearly three hours of ceremonies, the time came for the pope's discourse — the most awaited moment for many of the bishops who hoped that some light would finally be shed on what they were expected to do. The discourse did not disappoint them. This was one of the culminating moments of Pope John's pontificate. The bishops would only gradually learn to fully understand and appreciate his innovative thrust and to make it their point of reference in the most crucial moments of the Council.

The pope had written the entire text of the discourse, *Gaudet Mater Ecclesia* (Mother Church Rejoices). This discourse, which he said was simply a little "flour from his sack," could be defined as the fulfillment of wisdom matured through a rich accumulation of lifelong experiences which were reread in the light of the Gospel. His talk contained no program or precise directives, but it offered an official indication of the course the Council Fathers should take. While his talk contained few innovations, since the various topics had already been treated in other discourses, in that opening presentation they acquired an expression so undeniably complete that they became unforgettable.

The definition of the place of the Church, situated between Christ and the world, allowed it to clarify its nature and mission. Illumined and animated by Christ, who stands at the center of human history, the Church had received the mandate to announce him and to bring the blessings of salvation to all humanity. The pope stressed the privileged character of every Council as a realization of that bond: Christ-Church.

> Ecumenical Councils, which gather every so often, are solemn celebrations of the union between Christ and his Church. Therefore, they lead to the universal radiation of truth; to right direction for personal, domestic, and social life; to strengthening of spiritual energies, perennially directed toward the true and eternal goods.[24]

Pope John adequately justified the convocation of the Council by emphasizing its theological dimension and centrality in the life of the Church. He did not hesitate to acknowledge his responsibility for a decision that had been entirely his and was being carried out in virtue of the authority conferred on him through his succession to the Chair of Peter.

An age in profound transformation demanded new responses to the needs of humanity. It was imperative that the Church re-examine its activity and adopt suitable updating. The pope was absolutely convinced that this would only come about through an ecumenical assembly because of the extraordinary riches of grace and Divine assistance that would be released.

> The Church, we firmly trust, will grow in spiritual wealth and, drawing strength from new energies, will courageously look to the future. In fact, with suitable updating and the wise organization of mutual collaboration, the Church will help persons, families, and peoples truly to orient their spirits toward heavenly matters.[25]

John XXIII found a further motive for trust in the "happy circumstances" in which this delicate work of revision would be carried out. The Church's activity would not be subject to the interference and restrictions of political powers as in the past — an advantage that proved it was possible to find positive elements in modern times even while acknowledging aspects of concern. John XXIII exhorted his listeners to overcome paralyzing forms of pessimism by turning to the wisdom of history and the considerations suggested by faith. History, the great teacher of life, instructs us not to idealize the past to the detriment of the present. Some people could only see the decadence of the present times, but faith in Providence leads people to await the fulfillment of God's designs with trust and patience. The Lord's plans, however hidden they may seem, are for the good of the Church.

> In the present state of affairs, the goodness of Providence is leading us toward a new order of human relationships, which, through human activity and for the most part beyond people's expectations, will bring us to the accomplishment of still higher and undreamed of plans. Even human opposition works toward the greater good of the Church.[26]

Only an attitude of openness and the strength of sincere understanding would allow the Church to begin a dialogue and offer constructive proposals. Pope John's words attested to the urgency of a profound change in the style that the magisterium had assumed toward the modern world. An overly critical and pessimistic attitude merely accentuated the reasons for not understanding modern society and for standing aloof. Motives of balance and objectivity, as well as trust in Providence, prompted the pope's stern appeal:

> Sometimes our ears are wounded by the insinuations of those who, while burning with zeal, do not have a strong sense of judgment or balance. They see the modern world as nothing but deceit and ruin…. We feel that we must disagree with these prophets of misfortune who are always forecasting calamity, as if the world were about to end.[27]

A condemnation of nostalgia for the past equaled the renunciation of any plan to restore the former Christian era. It demanded an awareness of the true purpose of Christianity and a willingness to serenely and confidently entrust it to the times as prepared by Providence.

Having laid down these premises, the pope brought into consideration the aspect of doctrine. He wanted to show that the saving work of Christ extended to the whole of human existence. In the course of developing his thought, Pope John introduced a new and important concept: the task of the Church is not only to guard intact the Deposit of Faith, but also to teach it in a more effective way by looking "at the present, at the new conditions and ways of living introduced into the modern world."[28]

This attention to modern life lay at the root of the pastoral character of the Council, whose task it would be to present the unchangeable doctrinal heritage of Catholicism in new formulas more suited to contemporary humanity. The problem could not be reduced to a question of formulas, as Pope John's distinction between the substance and formulation of doctrine might lead one to believe. Rather, he was calling for a new look and a deeper understanding of doctrine. It would be misleading, therefore, to think that the Council had been summoned in order to define some further point of doctrine.

> The main point of this Council, therefore, will not be to discuss one or another article of basic Church doctrine that has repeatedly been taught by ancient and modern fathers and theologians.... A Council is not needed for this.[29]

It was not the time for new definitions, but for a redefinition of Christianity in faithfulness to the tradition.

> [B]ut starting from renewed, serene, and tranquil adhesion to the whole teaching of the Church in its entirety and detail...the Christians and Catholics of apostolic spirit throughout the world await a leap forward in doctrinal penetration and the education of consciences, especially in ever greater fidelity to authentic doctrine. Even doctrine, however, is to be studied and expounded in the light of contemporary methods of inquiry and the language of modern thought. The substance of the ancient doctrine of the deposit of faith is one thing, and its formulation is another. The latter must be taken into greater account. Patience is needed. Everything has to be measured in the forms and proportions appropriate for a chiefly pastoral teaching.[30]

Undoubtedly this was the greatest intuition of John XXIII and the most difficult task awaiting Vatican II. Aside from his general affirmation, the pope did not have nor wish to offer the ingredients for a solution. Yet, his pastoral instinct suggested a course of action tightly connected to the hoped-for doctrinal renewal. From that moment forward, the Church would have to give priority to "the medicine of mercy rather than that of severity," and choose the road of conviction, "showing the validity of her doctrine, rather than issuing condemnations."[31] In place of the severe image of inflexible power, which the pope judged counterproductive, John XXIII preferred the image of a motherly and loving Church that did not seek secondary goals, but interested itself solely in proclaiming the Gospel for the good of all peoples and according to the purest apostolic model.

> The Church…wants to show herself as a loving mother to all — kind, patient, full of mercy and goodness, even toward the children who are separated from her. To the human race, oppressed by so many difficulties, she says, as did St. Peter to the poor man who asked for alms: "I have neither gold nor silver, but what I have I give: in the name of Jesus Christ the Nazarene, arise and walk."[32]

The expanse of the Church's activity was to be universal, oriented to the attainment of "a total and strong unity of souls, to which is linked true peace and eternal well-being." But even before the attainment of this final goal, in its deeds the Church was already a force of reconciliation and mutual understanding between the Catholic Church, the separated Churches, and the rest of humanity. This effort could be perceived in the prayer of Christians and in their desire to reestablish the unity that had been lost; among other people, it could be seen in their growing esteem for the Catholic Church.

The discourse concluded with a profession of trusting hope for the new times reserved by the Lord for his children and now ushered in by the Council.

The pope was aware of the importance of his statements and of the perplexity they would provoke. That same day, he confided to Capovilla, "Every once in a while I glanced at the friend to my right [Ottaviani]." His attention to Ottaviani's reaction was not at all casual — the pope had placed in question many of the orientations and ideas very dear to the prefect of the Holy Office.[33]

It is not possible to overvalue *Gaudet Mater Ecclesia;* its historical significance has certainly been considerable, and its consequences, both for the activity of the magisterium and for theological reflection, have become clearer with the passage of time. John XXIII stood at the dawn of a turning point. Not only did he convoke a new Council and by his authority prevent it from merely reproposing traditional teaching, but he also introduced a new image and understanding of its role. The Council's function could not be reduced to defining doctrine by building one upon another. This was the idea of the magisterium John XXIII had alluded to when he stated that there was no need for a Council to formulate new dogmas. Instead, the Council's role was to be understood as the retranslation of perennial, ancient dogmas into the vocabulary of modern culture in order to assure comprehension without altering their meaning or significance.

The Council carried out this change of course, but the merit for pointing out the new direction and setting down the conditions for its effective realization belongs to Pope John.

By his own admission, the origin of his intuition cannot be identified with any particular theological competence of his. Rather, it would be found at a deeper level, in a more spiritual dimension.[34] John XXIII was convinced that an authentic experience of faith places people in the position of finding the proper language and new ways of living that render the faith communicable and attractive. In fact, an intimate and joyous experience of the truth allows one to grasp its universal communicability as an intrinsic characteristic. Thus, the idea of dialogue is not a factor of some recent research to be added eventually to an already known truth. Dialogue is a requirement of the Christian quality of the truth and universal significance of Jesus Christ. This explains Pope John's inexhaustible optimism that was not theological or pastoral, but spiritual.

The historic importance of *Gaudet Mater Ecclesia* is one reason that the text underwent undesirable changes in its official Latin version. Some of the more demanding statements were weakened if not completely annulled. The passage regarding the distinction between "the substance of the ancient doctrine of the deposit of faith" and "its formulation" is a typical example. The Latin text added the expression *seu veritates* (or the truths) after *depositum,* practically annulling the importance of the distinction between substance and formulation by linking the former with the plural form "truths." But more importantly, the introduction of a particular formula from Vatican I which reads: "retaining, however, the same sense and meaning" rendered the text inconsistent. In fact, if "same sense" corresponds to "substance" (the substance of a statement is its sense), it is difficult to understand how one can hold the possibility of a *different* formulation that maintains the *same* expression and meaning. John XXIII did not protest the changes officially, but afterward, when delivering public discourses, he quoted the original text as he had conceived and written it.[35]

The opening day of the Council ended with an unforgettable evening. St. Peter's Square became the stage for a great rally. An immense crowd, which police estimated at about 200,000, included young people of Catholic Action and of the ACLI. In memory of the torchlight procession of the Council of Ephesus in 431, they carried torches and formed a huge flaming cross.

No one expected the Holy Father to appear at the event, but Capovilla's gentle request prompted Pope John to bless the crowd and give a spontaneous talk that remains the most famous and best known of his addresses to the general public.

On this occasion, the uncommon ability of Pope John XXIII to establish an immediate rapport with a crowd was intensified by the profound and indelible impressions he had experienced during that day. Through the simple words he addressed to the throng, the pope revealed his state of soul and invited them to share in it. In the pope's eyes, the conciliar assembly of bishops from all parts of the world constituted an exceptional manifestation of universal brotherhood, which inspired him to hope for the strengthening of harmony within the Church to be radiated into the world. "We are concluding a great day of peace — yes, of peace. Glory to God and peace on earth to people of good will!" exclaimed the pope. He recalled the basic principles of a life authentically inspired by charity. He had repeated these words many times, but when he articulated them that night, they assumed the confidential tone of fraternal advice and at the same time rang with the authority of a papal pronouncement.

Pope John shared with the crowd in St. Peter's Square a principle that had guided him since his youth: attribute all merit to God and give little consideration to self.[36] He wove into this motif the fraternal dimension at the foundation of the hierarchy. He put it in its true light by recalling the Divine fatherhood from which it was derived and to which it was completely related. Very simply, he corrected an ecclesio-centric tendency, typical of post-Tridentine Catholicism, which did not adequately recognize the primacy of God.

The final motif of Pope John's address might be defined as the golden rule upon which he based his relationships: the primacy of unity over division.

> My person counts for nothing. It is your brother who speaks to you, a brother who has become your father by the will of our Lord. But all of this — fatherhood, brotherhood — is a grace of God. Everything, everything! Let us therefore continue to love one another, to love one another like this. Let us go ahead, making use of what unites us, leaving aside whatever could place us in some difficulty, if there be any. We are brothers![37]

He confided in the faithful without fear of revealing his expectations for the Council. Not having given the Council a precise program but merely orientations, the pope did not conceal that he, too, was awaiting the future events that would herald benefits for the Church as the fruit of Divine grace. His trust transcended fear of the inevitable difficulties that would be hard to overcome and, as he already foresaw, would make a second session necessary.

> Today…we are entering upon a year that will bring outstanding graces. The Council has begun and we do not know when it will end. If it cannot conclude by Christmas because, perhaps, we will not be able to say everything, to treat all the topics by then, another day will be necessary…. And so, may these days go well: we await them with great joy.

In these moments, speaking as a Shepherd with his faithful, Pope John found the words to touch hearts and to convey perfectly the intensity of his affection as a father and brother:

> When you return home to your children, give them a caress and say, "This caress is from the pope." Perhaps you will find some tears to dry. Comfort those who are suffering. Let them know that the pope is with his children, especially in their times of sadness and bitterness.[38]

At the end of that historic and emotional day, John XXIII jotted a few notes in his diary that confirmed his intention to remain a docile instrument of the Divine will without asking anything for himself — not even the grace of seeing the conclusion of the Council. He was ready to accept any circumstance.

> I was disposed to renounce even the joy of this beginning. With the same calm I repeat: May your will be done in respect to my remaining in this primary position of service for whatever time and circumstances are left of my poor life, and to feel that death may approach at any moment, because the pledge to proceed, continue, and finish [the work] will be passed on to my successor.[39]

The Difficult Beginning

Don Tucci, the director of *Civiltà Cattolica,* recalled the words confided to him by the pope during an audience on February 9, 1963.

The Council only truly and fully entered its work during its concluding weeks, when it began to understand the implications of the
September message and the opening discourse of October 11. In the
first session, [the pope] preferred not to intervene in the debates in
order to leave the Fathers the freedom to discuss, and the possibility
to find the right way on their own. In any case, since he did not have
the necessary competence in various matters, some of his interventions might have done more harm than good. The bishops had to
learn for themselves, and that they have done.[40]

The pope's judgment faithfully reflected the course and dynamics
that had characterized the first two months of conciliar work. The bishops
were given the broadest freedom of expression and decision-making
power. The pope called them to Rome in view of an authentic collaboration. By being true protagonists, they would have greater awareness of
their responsibility as shepherds of the Universal Church at the side of
Peter's successor. The discourses of September 11 and October 11 constituted Pope John's clearest directives, and they were a far cry from rigid
restrictions or obstacles to the free exercise of personal responsibility.
The pope truly placed the destiny and outcome of the Council in the
hands of the Fathers.

The difficulties that emerged grew out of an episcopate that, as a
whole, had lost the awareness of together forming the College of Cardinals. They were accustomed to simply executing the decisions made by
those with central responsibilities in the Holy See. The inability to overcome this mentality hindered the pursuit of the renewal envisioned by
the pontiff. Yet, it was no great secret that those who sought the approval
of the theological documents drafted during the preparatory phase actually welcomed such hindrances.

Pope John assumed a role of animating the beginnings of an effective examination without any direct intervention lest he influence the
debate. He participated in the Council from his study linked to the basilica by closed-circuit television — an eloquent testimony of his respect
for the bishops' liberty. Any direct interventions he did make were to
eliminate procedural obstacles through the modification of the rules. He
also used his authority when the assembly reached an impasse. In both
cases, the pope's interventions were advantageous for regulated discussions. He remained faithful to these tasks and his resolution to leave the
bishops free to do their work. Meanwhile, an appeal arose from eminent
persons urging the pope to be more concerned with the fact that there

was no organic program to follow, which was aggravated by the great jumble of paperwork and the inadequacy of the prepared drafts. Improvisation seemed to be the great mark of the Council's beginning.

Cardinal Montini expressed his concern in a letter to the pope dated October 18. He enclosed suggestions — reminiscent of Suenens' plan — together with a proposal to coordinate the material already prepared and eventually to integrate it around the theme of "Church." Montini lamented the lack of some organic direction to attain the goals indicated by the pope, and he expressed his hope for some intervention from "above" to free the initial work from uncertainty and chance.

Yet, even the appeals of an admired cardinal did not change John XXIII's personal course of restraining from interference. He preferred that the Council find its own way, convinced as he was that projects, ideas, and experiences existed among the bishops which would emerge through their free discussion with significant results.[41]

The fundamental differences between supporters and adversaries of a truly decision-making Council became evident at the first general assembly (October 13), with the election of members of the commissions. The agenda had provided for one morning to be dedicated to voting for the members, which was facilitated by lists with the names of those who had belonged to the preparatory commissions. In fact, the nearly 2,500 Council Fathers, who still did not know one another, would prefer to vote for the names on the lists. The danger of this maneuver was averted by some French prelates who pressed Cardinal Liénart, a member of the Council of Presidents, to intervene. Despite Cardinal Tisserant's opposition, Liénart read a brief motion containing a request to postpone the voting for several days. This would allow the Fathers to get to know one another and give the Episcopal Conferences time to draw up their own lists. This intervention, seconded by Cardinals Döpfner and König, received prolonged applause of approval — an obvious sign that there had indeed been widespread dissatisfaction. Shortly thereafter, the Council of Presidents postponed the elections.

In this first decisive act of the assembly, the majority distanced themselves from previously established procedures. This put into motions the institutions that would favor the active participation of the Fathers, such as the Episcopal Conferences. The pope met with Liénart at his request and granted the Council three days for consultations. The cardinal later said that John XXIII had told him, "You've done well to speak your mind; it's for this that I called the bishops to the Council."[42]

The pope brought the intervention to completion on October 20, when he communicated that the members who had received an absolute majority as well as those with a relative majority would be admitted to the commissions. This was the first departure from the rules of procedure in order to simplify the very long and complicated electoral process. With this decision, Pope John showed that he was prepared to support the legitimate choices made by the Council, a line of action which he would faithfully maintain.

There were new faces among the elected members — a significant 43 percent. The pope named a third of the membership that, at the last moment, had been increased in number from eight to nine per commission for a total of ninety persons. It is hard to identify Pope John's criteria. Only 30 percent had participated in the pre-conciliar work. The more favored Italians and Spaniards, known for being tendentiously conservative, were balanced by the pope who assured the representation of episcopates that received little or no recognition.

The Council Comes to Life

From October 22 to November 13, the draft on the liturgy was debated. It became a useful proving ground for putting the Council's method of work into focus, and the tendencies of the Fathers emerged in the setting of a discussion of one of the few drafts that called for renewal. One of the major points of conflict was the question of replacing Latin in the Mass and Breviary with the vernacular — a point raised particularly by the missionary bishops.

The pope seemed moderately in favor of the introduction of the vernacular. His diary notes reveal a pastor rich in experience and reasonably attached to Latin, as he believed it should remain the official language of the Church.

> Without a doubt, the question of Latin divides those who have never left home or Italy from those of other nations, especially mission lands, or from those Italians who live and sacrifice themselves in distant regions. On this point of Latin in the liturgy, it will be necessary to proceed slowly and by degrees.[43]

During the discussion of the draft on the liturgy, the pope made two direct interventions. The first pertained to a revision of the rules of procedure to restrict the debates within acceptable time limits, given the tendency of the Fathers to multiply similar interventions. On November 6, John XXIII gave the Council presidents the power to propose to the assembly the suspension of a discussion by proceeding with votes once a topic had been sufficiently treated and nothing new could be added. The assembly exercised this possibility at once when it voted to end the discussion of the first chapter of the draft on the liturgy. Then the passage of the successive chapters occurred with obvious acceleration.

The next intervention by the pope reflected one of his personal devotions. On November 13, the secretary of state declared the Holy Father's decision — based on a petition signed by thirty cardinals and 436 bishops the preceding spring — to introduce St. Joseph's name into the canon of the Mass immediately after the name of Mary. In the midst of heated discussions on far more demanding matters, this completely unexpected decision seemed out of place. Although it received diverse criticism, it was ultimately recognized as a secondary issue that certainly did not need to be discussed at the Council.[44]

On November 14, the draft on the liturgy obtained the approval of an overwhelming majority. Only forty-six of the Fathers, or 3 percent, voted against it. The assembly of bishops was beginning to develop a defined physiognomy favorable to moderate renewal. Still, they were not dealing with a decisive turning point yet.

That turning point would come during the discussion of the document, "The Sources of Revelation," drawn up by the Theological Commission. Evidently the members of the commission, whose ideas had prevailed in the drafting of the document, were supporters of a traditional theology characterized by strong arguments against every attempted reformulation of the Christian message and hostile to any ecumenical efforts. It was not by chance that the document confirmed the principle of Trent and Vatican I that Revelation had two sources, understood reductively as a single body of truth. The emphasis on the Magisterium of the Church obscured the primacy of the Word of God. For all practical purposes, the approval of this draft would have meant the end of the Council's proposals for reform and would have seriously compromised ecumenical dialogue. The pope realized that the stakes were high, and in his diary emphasized the stubbornness of those responsible for the draft — they had not given sufficient attention to his directions.

The beginning of the discussion of the sources of Revelation was interesting. Some conflict is predictable. On the one hand, the draft's proposal has not taken into account some precise directives given by the pope in his official discourses; on the other, the support of at least eight cardinals miserably discredits the principle point of the proposal. May the Lord assist and reunite us.[45]

Two elements determined the document's defeat. The first was the opening discourse, *Gaudet Mater Ecclesia,* whose innovative aspects were beginning to be assimilated. The second was the formation of a theological consensus in keeping with the thoughts expressed by theologians such as Rahner, Schillebeeckx, and others, which won widespread agreement among the Council Fathers. The theologians had the advantage of being able to show the discrepancy between the directions offered by the pope in *Gaudet Mater Ecclesia* and the argumentative tone of the draft. At least twenty-two interventions referred explicitly to *Gaudet Mater Ecclesia* and its central points, and eleven implicitly re-proposed its content. Even the six interventions made by traditionalists appealed to the papal discourse, including the presenter and inspirer of the document, Cardinal Ottaviani. He maintained that the pastoral orientation the pope hoped for consisted in precision and clarity of doctrine, not in pastoral applications which should be developed by others rather than a Council.[46] One direct intervention, made in the name of the Secretariat for Christian Unity by the Belgian bishop, DeSmedt, pointed out the serious ecumenical deficiencies of the text. This made a tremendous impression on the assembly.

After a series of substantial interventions, the Council of Presidents decided to suggest a vote on November 19. The question was formulated according to a proposal by Ruffini: "whether or not the discussion should be interrupted." The next day Felici announced the proposal in the Council hall and moments of confusion followed; the bishops did not completely grasp the meaning. Ruffini clarified the proposal by stating that a suspension of the discussion would result in the withdrawal and rewriting of the draft. The subsequent vote created a puzzling situation — 1,368 members voted in favor of an interruption, and 822 for a continuation. According to the existing rules of procedure, a two-thirds majority was required for a proposal to pass, but the proposal was dismissed despite the sizable majority in its favor.

In this difficult case, the pope acted as a true moderator for the assembly. Pope John's decision was influenced by Cardinals Leger and Bea. Leger had communicated his opinion to the pope through Cicognani, and it was fortified by the approval of Cardinals Frings and Liénart.[47] Bea, instead, spoke directly with the pope at the conclusion of an audience with the Canadian bishops. He suggested that the draft be withdrawn and rewritten by a commission created to redraft documents during the phase between sessions. The idea obviously pleased the pope,[48] because that is what he decided the next day. In answer to Cicognani's perplexity, Pope John replied, "Your Eminence, let us communicate this suggestion by all means. I have prayed much and thought about it all night. Let's do it calmly."[49]

In the pope's message, read by the Secretary of the Council, Cardinal Felici, John XXIII explained why a withdrawal of the text would be appropriate. The text would be rewritten by a commission made up of some members from the Theological Commission and some from the Secretariat for Christian Unity. This decision freed the Council from the burden, and the rejection of "The Sources of Revelation" marked a theological turning point of incalculable importance. It implied the abandonment of forms of expression dating back to a season of theology that had already passed, and put the Council on the road to renewal.[50]

The Conclusion of the First Phase

After the pivotal events of November 20, the assembly dealt with two topics that required little contribution. On November 23, the examination of the draft on the means of social communication began. It was approved, although with the request for serious modifications. The examination of the draft on ecumenism prepared by the Commission for the Oriental Churches began on November 27. The text was rejected, but with a suggestion that it be combined with two related texts prepared by the Theological Commission and the Secretariat for Christian Unity.

More important than either of these two drafts was the one on the Church given to the Fathers on November 23. It became the major object of discussion from December 1 to 7. The experience with the document on Revelation liberated the Council Fathers from reticence in facing members of the central bodies. It had also convinced many members of the inadequacy of the traditionally theological drafts, and of the relevance of the critiques advanced by proponents of new theological currents. In the light of this evolution, the defeat of the draft on the Church seemed inevitable — but no one thought of taking a vote.

Following the suggestion made by the pope on November 21, the presiders decided to devote the remaining days of the Council's first session to examining drafts under general aspects. In this way, the views expressed by the bishops could be considered in the revisions to be made before the second phase. During the debate on the document concerning the Church, seventy-seven Fathers intervened; they were divided along the same lines of thought as with "The Sources of Revelation."

However, new factors had a decisive influence on the Council's outcome. The closing of the first session (December 8) was imminent and the need for an evaluation was urgent. Equally urgent was the formulation of a precise plan that would clearly indicate goals and objectives. Cardinal Suenens felt that the moment had finally come for him to officially present the plan he had drafted the preceding spring. However, a serious difficulty arose. Toward the end of November, the pope's health began to decline rapidly and he could not receive visitors. The work of the Council threatened to come to a halt. On December 2, Suenens sent the pope a letter of good wishes and enclosed a copy of the intervention he planned to make soon at the Council. To his great surprise, he was called to the Vatican by Bishop Dell'Acqua early the next morning. Dell'Acqua informed Suenens that the pope had read the project and had added his observations in the margins. Suenens had these carefully translated to avoid any misunderstandings. Comforted by the pope's support, he presented his ideas on December 4, with a favorable outcome.

In his talk, Suenens repeated his view that the central theme of the Council should be the Church, considered *ad intra* and then *ad extra*. He suggested instituting a secretariat, similar to the one established for ecumenism, to look at the problems of the contemporary world and analogously, how these were related to economic issues.[51] Suenens' proposal was supported by Cardinal Montini, whose words carried a great deal of weight since, in the eyes of the Council Fathers, the Archbishop of Milan was the prelate most likely to succeed the pope. Had the pope encouraged Montini's intervention? Perhaps. But whether or not this was the case, the assembly interpreted Montini's words as having originated with Pope John.[52]

On December 6, the Council received information on some important decisions made by the pope the preceding day. With the end of the first session, plans began for the work of the second session. The pope established that the commissions would reexamine the drafts in light of the suggestions made by the Council Fathers. Citing at length from *Gaudet Mater Ecclesia,* he reaffirmed the aims that he had given to

Vatican II, which would later have value as inspirational guidelines for the Council. There would be no new dogmatic definitions, but a renewed presentation of the deposit of faith with preference given to mercy and understanding over severity. Thus the pope put his mark on both the beginning and the end of the work with his opening discourse, and eliminated uncertainties about his intentions.

The most important undertaking would be the establishment of a commission to coordinate and direct the Council's work. Made up of cardinals and bishops from the Council's secretariat, and under the presidency of the secretary of state, this commission's task would be to shorten drafts, coordinate the work of the various commissions, and verify whether everything corresponded to the purpose of the Council. Reedited drafts were to be submitted to the pope and, after receiving his general approval, would be sent to the bishops through their episcopal conferences. Positive and negative observations would be collected and sent to the commissions as quickly as possible. The commissions would then make the necessary changes so that the texts could be submitted to the Council by September 8 — the date for the opening of the second session. Thus the activity of the Council was not really suspended. It would continue according to an organic and well-constructed plan that permitted the assembly's prompt resumption of work — now more aware of its role and directly involved in preparing the drafts.[53]

Before the official closing of the first session, the members voted on the introduction and first chapter of the draft on the liturgy that had been corrected according to the observations made during the Council's first weeks. Of the 2,118 votes, those in favor numbered 1,992 — a large majority that assured a solid base for the fundamental principles of the liturgical renewal.[54]

Meanwhile, the pope had recovered from the medical crisis he suffered at the end of November. He was able to participate in the closing ceremony at St. Peter's Basilica on December 8. In homage to the new liturgical spirit, the assembly of bishops personally chanted the Mass of the Angels. Afterward, the pope delivered a discourse that included a general evaluation of the activity of the past two months and an outline of the future program of work — again, with his proposed objectives.

Though the Council Fathers were returning home with empty hands — there were no definitively approved texts — John XXIII seemed satisfied. The delays and uncertainties of the beginning were perfectly understandable considering the number of bishops participating and the fact that they came from every part of the world with such varied experiences and different mindsets. A period of adjustment had been necessary.

> It was necessary that these brothers, coming from afar to unite around the same hearth, should reestablish contacts with greater reciprocal knowledge. Eyes had to meet so that hearts could beat fraternally. Individual experiences had to be shared for a meditated and fruitful exchange of pastoral contributions.

The vote on the liturgical draft recorded a significant convergence. From the number of observations on the other five drafts, it seemed that the period of adjustment was already past and the season for reaping a harvest from the fatiguing preparatory work was approaching. The pope invited the bishops to collaborate generously and in a timely manner through the study and correction of the texts that would be sent to them. Trusting in the positive outcome of Vatican II, and perhaps foreseeing the inevitable resistances, John XXIII invited them all to accept its conclusions with docility. He called for the full collaboration of the whole Church in view of the desired new Pentecost.[55]

The Council continued to be Pope John's principal concern. After Christmas, he realized he should send a personal letter to each bishop to recommend that the Council remain a priority for the renewal of the Church, and her mission in the world depended on it.

The pope mentioned the principal follow-up directives being carried out. He announced the constitution of the Coordinating Commission and named its members: Cardinals Cigognani, Liénart, Spellman, Suenens, Döpfner, Confalonieri, and Urbani. The erection of this body concretized the distinction between the ordinary government of the Church and the Council's call for the creation of distinct and autonomous bodies. The pope's emphasis on the supreme authority of the new commission also affirmed that the others were subordinate, including the general secretariat of the Council, established to guarantee the necessary collaboration "in the exercise of its proper executive functions."

The pope insisted that the bishops remember that they were to guarantee their collaboration in governing the Universal Church. The ecclesiological model to which John XXIII called them provided for a constant and continual collaboration between the pope and bishops as a normal way of exercising their episcopal authority. Consequently, if the successor of Peter had the role of giving general directives to the Council and conferring the force of law on its conclusions, then it was the task "of the Council Fathers to propose, discuss, and prepare the sacred deliberations in due form and to sign them together with the chief Shepherd."

Pope John was calling them back to the normative model of the apostolic Church, which he often evoked as a biblical justification for episcopal authority and its greatest application: the Council itself. In fact, the apostles joined Peter in the Council of Jerusalem to discuss and deliberate collegially, thus offering "the perfect model of a Council. From that time the authority of the bishops and their serious task has been manifested in every Ecumenical Council from that of Jerusalem to today's Vatican II."[56]

This statement was followed by a warm recommendation to be as available as possible to study and correct the texts they would be sent. There can be no doubt that through these exhortations and requests for active collaboration, Pope John was teaching and directing the entire episcopate toward the recovery of collegiality.

He reminded the bishops of their obligation not to disappoint the expectations of the world concerning the Council. In the pope's eyes, the bishops' responsibility had a global dimension in accord with an ecclesiological vision of openness to the world and its problems as an integral part of the mission of the Church.

The pope's letter — rightfully called his conciliar testament — attests to his total involvement in the conciliar adventure.

In the few months of his life that remained, Pope John attentively followed the work of the various commissions. He began with the Coordinating Commission, which had for the most part succeeded in expressing the proposals for renewal that were to serve as guidelines for the reexamination of the surviving texts. (At the end of the first session, the number of drafts was reduced from seventy-two to twenty and later to seventeen.)

After the first meeting of the commission, the pope received the members in audience on January 28, 1963. In writing about the encounter, Pope John noted how he had gradually reached a decision to become more active in the direction of the work than he had during the first session. As the true head of the Church, he had to assure the unity of direction in the assembly. Naturally, this would have to be carried out with the necessary discretion: "I confess that this has been weighing on my conscience. Contrary to what happened in the first two months, from

October 11 to December 8, the pope should take his position and discreetly make his authority felt, as a true president according to his full right as head of the Catholic Church."[57]

Two months later, on March 28, the pope visited the commission again, as it was in the midst of its second meeting. He was able to participate in a discussion over Cicognani's request to reassign the topic of ecumenical relationships with the Orthodox. Rather than having it fall under the Secretariat for Christian Unity, Cicognani suggested that it belonged more appropriately under the Commission for the Eastern Catholic Churches, of which he was president. Notwithstanding the opposition expressed by several members, the proposal seemed to have passed. The next day, however, Cicognani made a radical about-face by expressing his disposition to allow the topic to remain in the draft "On Ecumenism," prepared by the Secretariat for Christian Unity. Without the availability of formal evidence, it is difficult to know the exact reasons for this unexpected change. According to Jan Grootaers, it is very likely that John XXIII, having been present at the discussion, intervened directly with his secretary of state — and for no small reason. The Secretariat for Christian Unity, which favored a more open ecumenism, would thus be directly responsible for the dialogue with the Orthodox Church.[58]

On April 22, John XXIII approved twelve of the seventeen texts that had been submitted for redrafting. He directed that they be sent immediately to all the bishops for their comments. Despite his repeated urgings, several weeks dragged on before Felici sent the first six. The texts were examined during the summer. As the pope's letter of January 6 had allowed, the bishops called on experts to help them and kept in constant contact with each other, either directly or by mail. Never before in the history of the Church had such a circulation of ideas taken place on a worldwide scale.

CHAPTER 21

THE FINAL MONTHS

Public Recognition

In the last months of Pope John's life, his popularity reached its zenith. The whole world had come to know him and to appreciate his exceptional human gifts and wisdom. His involvement in international politics and the convocation of the Council had increased his prestige. Far from young, he had shown a fresh, youthful courage and capacity to launch projects of considerable importance.

At the end of 1962, *Time* Magazine named John XXIII "man of the year" and dedicated the cover to a portrait of him by Bernard Safran. The article was gratifying: "Pope John has given the entire world what neither diplomacy nor science could give it: a sense of the unity of the human family."[1] Robert Piser, a journalist with *Time,* was in Rome during the first session of the Council. He sang the pope's praises in a book written to help make him better known to the American public.

On February 22, 1963, Capovilla opened a letter from Piser that contained an unusual proposal. The pope was invited to New York for a gathering of famous personalities who had also been featured on the cover of *Time,* including Kennedy, de Gaulle, Adenauer, Khrushchev, Monnet, Hallstein, Barth, Niebuhr, Hotchins, and Picasso. When Piser spoke with Cardinal Bea about the matter, he raised a series of objections as to the timeliness of the event, while he acknowledged its usefulness.

When John XXIII read the letter, he did not exclude the possibility of accepting the opportunity. He preferred to remain open to what Providence disposed. He did recognize, however, that the conditions were not yet ripe. Therefore, he wrote at the bottom of his letter to Piser, dated February 24: "Nothing opposes a project that one day or another might be acceptable. But many other circumstances are needed for it to mature."[2]

The second act of recognition was the conferral of the Balzan prize on John XXIII. In a private audience on the morning of March 7, the pope received Senator Giovanni Gronchi, president of the general prize committee of the International Balzan Foundation. Gronchi and other representatives of the foundation officially informed the pope of the award. They related that at the committee's plenary session of March 1 in Zurich, the members from various nations had unanimously decided to award the prize to His Holiness, Pope John XXIII.

Afterward, in the presence of journalists from many nations, Senator Gronchi read an official statement giving the reasons for awarding the prize to the pope. The cause of world peace, supported by Pope John in countless ways, had been manifested on three levels. First, he contributed to the maintenance of international peace, especially in 1962, "both through peaceful appeals to the good will of persons and through his recent diplomatic initiatives" — a clear reference to the Cuban missile crisis. Secondly, he began the initiative to establish better relationships between Christians of various Churches, as testified to by the participation of non-Catholic observers at the Council. Finally, he persistently worked to create an attitude of mutual understanding both in and outside the religious sphere.

Pope John, addressing those present in French, said that he regarded this choice as recognition of the Church's activity and teaching in favor of peace in the pontificates of modern times. The loss of its temporal power allowed the Church and its head to enjoy neutrality above national interests, and yet did not reduce it to an attitude of passivity. The liberation from immediate political concerns permitted the Holy See to witness to peace by launching a vast program of initiatives that covered a wide area including doctrinal, diplomatic, and pedagogical issues. The latter were directed toward human formation — that persons "might have peaceful thoughts, hearts, and hands."[3]

Among the many congratulatory messages the pope received was one from Soviet Union Premier Nikita Khrushchev:

I sincerely congratulate you for having been awarded the prize for peace and humanitarianism by the committee of the Balzan foundation in recognition of your efforts for the noble cause of maintaining peace. I wish you good health and the strength to carry out further fruitful activities on behalf of peace. N. Khrushchev.[4]

The actual conferral of the prize would take place on May 10 at a solemn ceremony. At first St. Peter's Basilica was considered for the location, but John XXIII did not want that building, consecrated to the memory of the first apostle, to be used as the setting for his personal glorification. He decided, instead, to receive the award privately in the papal State Room and follow this with a rite in St. Peter's to thank the most high and all-powerful God.

At 11:00 A.M. on May 10, President Antonio Segni of Italy conferred the award, consisting in 100,000,000 lire, which the pope allocated to a perpetual fund for peace.

To set a proper tone to the whole ceremony, Pope John opened with an invocation of praise and thanksgiving to God. He then recalled that the State Room they occupied was no longer used exclusively for the great ones of the earth who had come to honor the successor of Peter. Since 1891, at the time of the promulgation of the document, *Rerum Novarum,* many faithful from the working class had gathered in it. The pope discerned in that fact an especially striking aspiration for peace.

After the ceremony, a solemn procession formed that accompanied the pope into St. Peter's Basilica, where he was welcomed by a great crowd milling about the stands reserved for the Council Fathers. Slipyi stood out in the midst of the cardinals and bishops in his first public appearance. Not far from him stood Sergei Romanowski, the first representative of the Soviet Union to be present at an official ceremony in the basilica.

Senator Gronchi presented the Holy Father with the emblems of the prize: a garland, a large medal, and a parchment. Then the Holy Father gave an eloquent discourse with moving passages because of his sincerity in opening his heart to his listeners. He repeated that the honor he was receiving belonged to his predecessors, who had contributed to the elevation the influence of the papacy. As for himself, Pope John was full of gratitude to God, who had given him a great serenity that kept him from exalting or debasing himself, and allowed him to pursue his work in the service of humanity.[5]

The great crowd gathered around him for the celebration was a source of encouragement, prepared by the Divine goodness so that he might continue his ministry. He intended to continue to fulfill this ministry in a spirit of humble service and fidelity to the teaching of the Gospel, without either harshness or permissive weakness, which are both harmful to souls.

In no other words of the pope can we discern a hint of the violent accusations that were assailing him during the month of May. He was being accused of weakness, and many felt his recent actions, including the publication of the encyclical, *Pacem in Terris,* had facilitated the Communist Party's success in the Italian elections of April 28. Pope John suffered terribly from this situation, although his awareness of having acted rightly was a source of serenity. Now especially he willingly accepted the encouragement of the joyous gathering of eminent personalities and the great crowd.

The pope made other references to the contested encyclical. He was convinced that he had given the best of himself and had remained within the magisterial sphere and not crossed over into politics. He cited a passage of the encyclical in which he had listed the four principles of order upon which peace is based: "order founded on truth, built according to justice, enlivened and integrated by love, and activated by liberty."[6] Defending the document's sublimity against all the attempted distortions of adversaries, he added: "We are convinced that in years to come, in the light of past experience and through an objective and serene appreciation of ecclesial language, the doctrine the Church offers the world will exert influence by its very clarity."[7]

The next day the pope and other winners of the Balzan prize were received with all honors by President Antonio Segni at a reception in the Quirinal Palace. This event had much greater historical significance than the celebration of an award. In fact, it marked the first time since the occupation of Rome in 1870 that a pope paid an official visit to a head of the Italian State. Conscious of the exceptional nature of this event, Pope John spent two hours on his knees in prayer. Capovilla saw him on his knees and urged the pope not to weary himself, especially when he was experiencing such intense physical pain. Pope John replied, "An exceptional event is going to take place; it is necessary to pray."

The pope left the Vatican for the Quirinal Palace at 5:10 P.M. During the drive, he said he was about to make "an act of deference" toward his country, to which he owed much, and "not only to Bergamo, but to the whole land of Italy."

At one point along the route of Glauco Della Porta, the mayor of Rome greeted the pope with a salute. At the Quirinal Palace, President Segni welcomed him and — as established by protocol — accompanied him into the palace chapel for a brief prayer. The reception in the Hall of Celebrations was attended by high-ranking civil authorities, diplomatic corps, many cardinals, and other eminent persons. Among the individuals who shared the honor of the Balzan prize were the Russian mathematician, Andrej Kolmogorov; the biologist, Karl von Frisch; the historian, Samuel Eliot Morrison; and the musician, Paul Hindemith.

In his brief response to the president's welcome address, Pope John thanked him for his great courtesy and stressed the work for peace undertaken by his predecessors. He added that he "relied on our Lord Jesus Christ, whom — unworthily, but with a generous and submissive effort at imitation — we have been called to represent on earth."[8] The ceremony concluded with an emotional embrace of the Holy Father and President Segni.

On the way home, the pope realized he had reached the limit of his strength. He returned to the Vatican at 7:30, received the secretary of state, and watched a replay of the ceremonies on television. Before going to his room, he remarked, "A few hours ago, compliments and acclamations; now here I am with my pain. And this is appropriate, for the pope's first task is to pray and to suffer."

He spent some time writing about the events of the past two days — days that were historical in his own life and in his service to the Holy See and Italy. He concluded:

> Thinking about this, even though I am a bit cool toward such matters, I do not know how to restrain my emotion and my gratitude to the Lord, "who has looked on the humility of his servant…he who is powerful has made me great." Who would ever have thought of describing my weakness with these mysterious words that are suffused with such grace?[9]

A Visit to the Vatican

After Cardinal Slipyi's liberation, another gesture on the part of the pope enhanced the growing dialogue with the U.S.S.R. through Nikita Khrushchev.

Khrushchev's daughter Rada and his son-in-law Alexis Adzhubei visited Italy in February. Adzhubei was a member of the Soviet Central Committee and director of *Izvestia,* the government newspaper of the Soviet Union. He had hardly reached Rome when he requested an audience with the pope in order to deliver a message from Khrushchev.

Although John XXIII had already decided to respond positively to the request, he knew the matter demanded caution. Accepting the request could have unforeseeable consequences because of the almost half-century of opposition between Catholicism and Communist Russia. The pope consulted some trusted officials.

When Pope John spoke with Cardinal Ottaviani, the cardinal expressed his misgivings about the audience. He stressed the possible risk of political manipulation connected to the meeting. A positive response on the part of the Vatican could harm Catholics in the Eastern bloc; they might be so shaken by the initiative as to renounce their faith. In the West, the political left could use the event to their own advantage by saying that an agreement between Catholicism and Marxism was possible. Everywhere, but especially in Italy, this could increase votes for the Communist Party. Yet, Ottaviani would not shut the door entirely to the possibility. He agreed that a "courtesy visit" of Adzhubei to Cardinal Testa or Cardinal Bea might be a feasible compromise.

Capovilla manifested his deep concern to Bea and insisted, "Don't say that there *won't* be an audience, but don't say that there *will* be one, either!"[10]

Despite the sensitivity of the issue, John XXIII had been convinced from the outset that, while exercising the necessary prudence, it would be opportune to grant such an audience and that the advantages would far outweigh the risks. He wrote on March 1:

> I have asked the advice of the secretary of state, and through him of Cardinal Ottaviani, regarding the *manner,* not the *fact,* of conducting the audience. They have responded that to refuse would be prejudicial and to accept could cause shock. Considering everything carefully, it is good to grant the audience, and in the customary way, not secretly…. I would condemn all my previous conduct if I refused to see a man who courteously, and without any pretext, has asked to greet me and give me a gift. It must be remembered that without any move on our part, the Russians have extended gestures of courtesy toward the pope three times already: on his eightieth birthday, on Christmas 1962, and on his designation as recipient

of the Balzan prize. The information received through Cousins deserved careful evaluation. It led me to assume a state of soul that would not brusquely reject a budding relationship of the proper kind. We must recall that at Christmas 1962 I received a communication that Slipyi was to be released (as happened at the beginning of February) without any conditions — only to please the pope and manifest good will.[11]

Pope John glimpsed the possibility of initiating relations that could, appropriately and without dangerous compromises, improve the conditions of the persecuted Churches of the East, establish ecumenical relationships with the Orthodox Church, and ease international tensions. At the same time, the Church could be freed from a vision that concentrated on the West. The sincerity of Russia's intentions could be tested without renouncing such firm tenets as the incompatibility of a totalitarian and atheistic ideology with the request for freedom of worship for the Christians of the East.

On Russia's part, there was certainly no outstanding intention to revise religious policies. Regularizing relations with the Vatican could become part of an overall plan for improving East-West relations, as Khrushchev's policies were already pointing to. That Khrushchev had already chosen Italy as a bridge to the West must have motivated his plan to visit Rome. But it was first necessary to ascertain the Vatican's attitude: would the pope protest or ignore him? Would he grant an audience? This would please the Soviet leader. Norman Cousins had already advised John XXIII of Khrushchev's intent to pursue a policy of détente. If that policy should fail, a door would be left wide open for the Kremlin's hard-line factions.

Pope John knew how to take advantage of the opportunity to begin a policy more consonant with the protection of religious interests. It would also allow him to demonstrate the Church's autonomy from political concerns and ensure its nature as an institution above factions. This would have undeniable advantages for the work of the Church on behalf of peace.[12]

Adzhubei was granted an audience, and Pope John's relationship with Communist countries made a quality leap forward. If this relationship was carried out secretly and through intermediaries before, it was now public and involved him personally. However, the pope maintained a prudent reserve. As a journalist, Adzhubei had been invited to attend the ceremony for the official announcement of the conferral of the Balzan prize on the pope. A private meeting with Adzhubei was scheduled for the end of this audience.

On the eve of the audience, a number of declarations, negative comments, and expressions of serious reservations concerning the meeting and the risks it involved arose from the traditional hierarchical ranks.

On the morning of March 7, Adzhubei and his wife Rada were assailed by cameramen and photographers in St. Peter's Square. When they had made their way through the square and had entered the bronze door, they still had to contend with the watchful gaze of journalists who did not miss a single gesture. The couple took their assigned place in the second row of armchairs in the State Room. After the ceremony, the pope received them in his private library.

Pope John immediately made his guests feel at home and entertained them in a kindly fashion, explaining the various paintings and tapestries hanging in the library. He reminisced about his first contacts with Slavic culture, which he had made in Bulgaria. In every way, the pope tried to create a cordial atmosphere to help put the couple at ease.

Adzhubei conveyed to John XXIII Khrushchev's greetings and appreciation for the pope's work on behalf of peace. Then Adzhubei proposed that diplomatic relations between the Holy See and the U.S.S.R. should begin in order to facilitate the resolution of problems, including the liberation of prelates. Not at all surprised by this move, John XXIII tested the proposal to see whether it represented a wisely calculated political project or an adventuristic move. He spoke convincingly and with great discretion.

> You are a journalist. Surely, then, you know the Bible. There one reads that God took six days to create the heavens and the earth…. On the first day, the creative words were, "Let there be light." Today the light of my eyes shines in yours! Already, this means a great deal. If it be according to the designs of the Almighty, we will take other steps, inspired by the principle of prudence, which is the first of the cardinal virtues. I must also hear the relevant opinions of my closest collaborators. God took six days to create the world. We who are less powerful than God need to learn a lesson and proceed by stages, without haste, preparing public opinion for these respectful contacts. Actually, right now such a step would be misunderstood. In the meantime, let us continue to work for the reconciliation of all peoples with discretion and trust.

Alexander Koulic, S.J., who acted as interpreter at the meeting, and Capovilla were present. Neither Koulic nor Capovilla mention any conversation during the audience that touched on political matters.[13] In an interview released in 1989, however, Adzhubei revealed that he had obtained the pope's assurance that he would probably meet with Khrushchev if he were to visit Italy. Adzhubei quotes the Holy Father as saying, "I hope that if Mr. Khrushchev visits Rome, both of us will find time for a meeting. I'm sure he will not be afraid to converse...."

The pope also announced the will of the Holy See to establish contact with religious Russia: "The Vatican has two hands...and we want to shake the two hands of the U.S.S.R., that of the State and that of all the members of the Russian Church."[14] This testifies to the presence, at least in the pope's mind, of a sufficiently worked out plan for a global overture to the Communist countries to be realized with gradual efforts.

The audience had been dominated by the pope's desire "to find words that were common and very, very affectionate," as Rada Khrushchevska recalls.[15] In this, Pope John again proved himself a master diplomat of incredible understanding. The pope mentioned the three sons of the illustrious couple: "Madam, I know you have three sons. I have been told their names, but I would love to hear you say them, for on a mother's lips the names of her children acquire an inexpressible sweetness." In a faint voice, Rada replied, "Nikita, Alexis, and Ivan." Pope John responded warmly: "Nikita — for the grandfather. In Venice, people venerate the body of Niceta, a holy Eastern monk. Alexis is a common name throughout East and West. And Ivan is like me — John. When you return home, give Ivan a hug first. The other two will not mind."

Departing from custom in such circumstances, the pope gave the lady a rosary, telling her that he prayed it with special devotion every day and that one decade was always for the children born within the past twenty-four hours. He added, "Looking at it, remember that once there was a mother who was perfect in love — Mary."[16]

At the conclusion of the audience, the pope entrusted Adzhubei with a personal message for Khrushchev, thanking him for the recognition expressed on the conferral of the Balzan prize.

> Thanks to the Almighty and to all those who have cooperated in such a meaningful recognition of the activity on behalf of peace that has been carried out by the Catholic Church. We wish prosperity and well-being to the entire Russian people, who are most dear

to us. We want to assure them that we will continue to engage all our efforts for the attainment, in justice and love, of true brotherhood among peoples, and peace for the whole world.[17]

The two guests left the audience visibly moved. "It was perhaps the strongest experience of emotion I have ever felt in my life," Rada later stated in an interview with Enzo Biagi.[18]

But the atmosphere outside was immensely different. The controversy that was already intense on the eve of the audience now raged, especially in Italy, and beyond Italy, it was clear that people were struggling to grasp an adequate understanding of the significance of the event.

Koulic had written a detailed account of the meeting and the pope asked for it to be published at once. But his request was ignored. The head division of the Secretariat of State, which treated both extraordinary and foreign affairs, was reluctant to comply with the pope's wishes.

On March 20, with some bitterness the pope wrote:

> The absolute clarity of my language, first in public and then in my private library, deserves to be revealed and not glossed over. There is no need to defend the pope. I said and I repeated to Dell'Aqua and Samore that Koulic's notes, the sole witness of the audience granted to Rada and Alexis Adzhubei, were to be published. The head division does not listen to my urging, and I am displeased…a desire of the *pope*…. When I was nuncio or patriarch…. When they know what *I* said, and what *he* said, I believe that the name of Pope John will be blessed. Everything must be written down with diligence. I deplore and pity all of those who have, during these days, given themselves over to unspeakable schemes. *I overlook and forget.*[19]

Criticism of the pope did not seem to abate. On March 17, he responded to it directly in a discourse given to the cardinals gathered to extend their best wishes for his name day: the feast of St. Joseph. He recalled the foster father of Jesus, chosen as the protector of the Council and often considered by the pope as the model diplomat.

He used the occasion to reassure the thirty cardinals who were present about the source of his serenity. It was not born of inexperience or an ignorance of history — never a deficiency in Rocalli's life — but from solid faith in Divine Providence.

> The serenity of our spirit as the poor servant of the Lord does not have its origin in a lack of knowledge of human beings or history and does not close its eyes to reality. It is a serenity that comes from

God, the most wise fashioner of order in human vicissitudes, whether with regard to the Council or in the ordinary and serious service of the universal government of the Church.

This faith induced him to believe that grace works mysteriously in all hearts without exception. The pope's purpose was clear: to avoid demonizing communism because Divine action was being exercised even upon communists, and as shepherds of souls they had the task of discerning and complying with Providence. Finally, his serenity was confirmed by the promise of Christ concerning his indefectible presence in the Church.

These were the principal inspirations for his conduct as a Christian shepherd that guaranteed humility, balance, indifference to the judgments of the world, and a courageous availability to comply with the often unforeseen Divine designs. Pope John thus justified his openness to the light of a dynamic historical vision abounding in God's action — a light that called the Church to surmount all forms of rigidity and inertia.[20]

The criticism in Italy became more severe after the elections of April 28, when the Communist Party gained a significant increase in votes. Without hesitation, the pope's policies were considered as a possible cause. He was guilty of having cracked the traditional boundary of uncompromising firmness against the Soviet Union. But as he had told the cardinals, trust in God gave him "a Christian indifference in the face of the judgments of the world," and this helped him to continue his dialogue with Eastern Europe. It should be remembered that the principal request made by the Holy See to the Soviet Union was religious liberty for Catholics, especially the Uniates and the Orthodox. Adzhubei felt particularly impressed with a phrase he had heard from a Vatican official in Rome: "Give the people the possibility of praying as they wish."[21]

Pope John's effort broadened the possibilities for initiating overtures toward other Eastern bloc countries — something that would have been unimaginable without the prior consent of the Russian government.

On April 18, Cardinal König of Vienna traveled to Budapest to visit Cardinal Mindszenty in the American embassy where he had taken refuge during the Hungarian Revolution of 1956. König communicated the pope's personal invitation for Mindszenty to leave Hungary for Rome, where he would live as a guest. The cardinal refused. He would leave only if the legal process of 1949 was annulled and he was completely rehabilitated by the Hungarian government.

On May 3, Cardinal Casaroli traveled to Budapest. Six days later, he was in Prague where he opened contacts with the Hungarian government. This would eventually lead to an agreement in September of 1964 for the ordination of new bishops — the first in fourteen years — and some relief for the Hungarian Church. In 1963, Bishop Beran would obtain amnesty from the Communist government of Czechoslovakia and, in 1965, would receive permission to leave — an exile in Rome.

When Casaroli returned from his first mission in Eastern Europe, the pope was eager to hear the results. Then he observed, "It's not necessary to rush, nor to have illusions, but we must trust in God."[22]

The policies regarding Eastern Europe would continue under Pope Paul VI, and the always more credible results would testify to the soundness of Pope John's intuitions, pursued with great prudence and caution so as not to compromise their success.

Well aware of his illness, John XXIII told Tucci on February 9, "Dear Father, I already know that I have very little time left. Therefore, I must be more careful than ever to weigh every move. Otherwise, the conclave that will take place after my death may be a conclave *against me* and make a choice that would destroy what I've begun to build."[23]

Although he proceeded carefully, Pope John perceived that changes were coming that would transform a reality which from the outside appeared as solid as granite and according to many could only be confronted with determination, inflexibility, and strength. Instead, the moment had arrived for gentler tactics.

The Encyclical *Pacem in Terris*

Capovilla traces the pope's inspiration for the document, *Pacem in Terris,* to October 25, 1962. On that day, John XXIII wrote his appeal for negotiations during the Cuban missile crisis.[24] That grave moment had further convinced the pope of the need for a document to present completely and systematically the magisterial teachings on peace in light of changing cultural conditions and the new framework of international politics. It was urgent that war be prevented. The possible use of nuclear weapons in a full-scale war would constitute a colossal, perhaps final, tragedy. Moreover, a progressive disarmament would free economic resources that could be used for the realization of social justice in accord with the directives of *Mater et Magistra*.

Pope John took advantage of the common willingness of the superpowers to maintain peace — and their greater willingness to listen to him. He quickly issued an appeal for peaceful negotiations — a matter he kept particularly at heart. He confided this to Bishop Pietro Pavan, professor of social doctrine at the Pontifical Lateran University, who became one of the principal editors of *Pacem in Terris*. Other collaborators and editors from various fields were also involved, which makes it more difficult to identify the pope's personal contribution to the document.[25]

The very purpose of the encyclical explains the first and most obvious innovation it contained: the adoption of a language and style that did not appeal to reason or rely exclusively on revealed data. At the official signing on April 19, 1963, the pope emphasized that the encyclical was addressed to all humanity.

> On the face of the encyclical shines the light of Divine Revelation, which gives living substance to the thought. But the teachings arise from nothing other than the intimate needs of human nature and, for the most part, belong to the realm of natural law. This explains an innovation of this document. It is addressed not only to the episcopate of the Universal Church, but also to all persons of good will.[26]

By now, Pope John's openness and universality had become the hallmark of his most significant initiatives, and this conferred a prestige upon his pontificate that reached its culmination toward its end. His typical roncallian style is fully applied in the encyclical: trust in humanity through a positive assessment of modern transformations and sincere sympathy and fraternal understanding of humanity's sufferings. The pope was particularly attentive to stress the bonds of unity that existed among human beings, such as the dignity of the person and the value of peace as an object of universal desire. On this basis, it is possible to overcome divisions and to establish relationships that are more fraternal. The fascination of the document is increased by the authentic touches of a prophetic tone that grasps new perspectives and offers motives for hope. This made a deep impression on the public.

The encyclical is divided into five parts: relationships between individuals; relationships between individuals and public authority; relationships between political communities; relationships of individuals and States with the world community; and finally, pastoral norms.[27]

At the foundation of the order that must prevail among human beings, the pope places the human person as the subject of "universal, inviolable, and inalienable" rights and duties, which he then summarizes. For the first time, a magisterial document recognized the right to a correct conscience and to religious freedom. The right to religious freedom, however, was still expressed rather generically and thus variously interpreted.[28] In any case, it became the prelude to *Dignitatis Humanae,* Vatican II's declaration on religious freedom, which reiterated and clarified Pope John's statement. In this way, the pope attuned himself with the modern logic of human rights while avoiding the risk of going adrift in the current of individualism, in the cult of the subject released from every social relationship and religious reference. Rights and duties, instead, are described by the pope as indissolubly linked because "every natural right in a person involves a respective duty in all other persons."[29]

Another innovation of the encyclical is a dynamic vision of human rights that, in the course of time, have been increasingly specified and clarified in the human conscience, impressing new goals to better life within society.

Though in a rather sketchy form, the phrase "signs of the times" made its first appearance in *Pacem in Terris*. It was a phrase destined for success because of its invitation to scrutinize new social changes in view of the development of the human spirit's awareness of its proper dignity. Three particular phenomena were cited as signs of the times: the economic and social progress of the working class; women entering the working world and facing the challenge of recognition as persons in domestic as well as public life; and the sociopolitical transformation of humanity with its efforts to overcome colonialism, racial discrimination, and the superiority of one people over another.[30]

Global disarmament was another extremely relevant subject that was directed in a special way to all people of good will. Emphasizing the absurdity of building peace on a foundation of a balance of terror, the pope asked in the name of justice, wisdom, and humanity:

> [T]hat the arms race should cease; that stockpiles which exist in various countries should be reduced equally and simultaneously by the parties concerned; that nuclear weapons should be banned; and finally, that all come to an agreement on a fitting program of employing mutual and effective controls.[31]

Further on in the document, the principle of the impracticability of war in an atomic age was formulated, which put into question the principle of a just war: "It is completely irrational to think that, in an atomic age, war can be used as an instrument of justice."[32] Pope John was a skilled enough diplomat not to expect unilateral disarmament, but using the leverage of good will, he exhorted the superpowers to find some point of convergence to begin concretely to take a stand opposite the one that had been taken.[33]

The pastoral section of *Pacem in Terris* contains some interesting points. Guidelines were given for the conduct of Catholics who might be working with people of other faiths and perhaps opposed to Christianity. The pope believed even in this circumstance, possible forms of cooperation existed as long as human reason found the objective good. In the context of collaboration with non-believers, the pope stressed the importance of remembering the distinction between the *error* and the *erring*, and that respect should be shown at all times to preserve the dignity of the human person.

A second distinction between false philosophical doctrines and sociopolitical movements made possible some forms of collaboration that were not opportune before.

> While the teaching, once it has been clearly set forth, is no longer subject to change, the movements, precisely because they take place in the midst of changing conditions, even profound ones, are readily susceptible to change.[34]

The responsibility for collaboration was left to the competence of lay persons involved in politics. Such persons were urged to act with prudence, which directs the virtues that regulate the moral life, and to harmonize their decisions with the natural law and the social doctrine of the Church. The appeal to the directives of Church authority constituted a precaution that did not weaken the innovations presented in the encyclical. Pope John broke down the boundaries of the Catholic world to encompass wider collaboration with political and cultural movements of diverse origins in view of building a more peaceful world.[35]

Pacem in Terris was the first solemn document of the pontifical magisterium that dealt with dimensions of such breadth. The Church stepped outside a strictly Catholic sphere to propose the building up of peace through a grand alliance among people of good will.

In general, the text was more welcome and struck a deeper chord than had been foreseen. "In no moment since the age of the Reform, perhaps even the age of the separation of the Churches of East and West, has a Bishop of Rome addressed such a vast and receptive audience," commented the *New York Herald Tribune*. The *Washington Post* said: "This is not only the voice of an elderly priest, or only that of an ancient Church. This is the voice of the world's conscience."[36]

For the first time the contents of a papal encyclical were published inside the Eastern bloc: the Soviet news agency *Tass* circulated a long summary. The document was also well received by the Russian Orthodox Church. The man responsible for the international relations of the Patriarchate of Moscow (1960–1972), Metropolitan Nikodim, wished to support the pope's action and thought, and decided to dedicate his doctoral thesis to "John XXIII, Roman Pope."[37]

Amid the international praise and approval, however, criticism was never lacking, especially from the more traditional elements, which viewed the encyclical as abandoning a staunch anticommunist stand. One daily paper in Rome ironically dubbed the encyclical *"Falcem in Terris"* (sickle on earth).

After the elections of April 28, the criticism grew more severe in Italy. Capovilla remembered this as one of the few times the pope showed amazement. John XXIII was deeply saddened by remarks that claimed that the fifth part of the encyclical had helped the left to achieve its victory. When the pope was asked if it might not have been better to avoid the audience with Adzhubei and to wait until after the elections to publish the encyclical, he emphasized the exclusively pastoral character of the document and the evangelical reasons that had inspired it.

> The doctrine set forth in the encyclical is without doubt perfectly derived from the testament of the Lord and in harmony with the pontifical magisterium of the past seventy years. The meeting with Adzhubei was coherent with the direction my service has taken. After all, I have said and repeated that the text of the conversation with the director of *Izvestia* can be published with tranquillity.[38]

Physical Decline and Death

Pope John's condition became noticeably worse in the spring. The intense Holy Week ceremonies were occasions of prolonged sufferings and exhaustion for him. On Good Friday, April 12, the pope went to St. Peter's for the solemn adoration of the cross, while his doctors and those close to him held their breath throughout the service, fearing that Pope John might collapse at any moment. On April 15, the pope wrote:

I came through Easter contented, but actually in very bad shape....
Holy Mass peacefully at home, then abandonment in God. Yesterday St. Peter's Square was simply triumphal, as in the most rare of
circumstances. In solidarity, the packed crowd expressed greetings
and well wishes to the pope on the balcony.... Continual pain
makes me think seriously about my personal affairs.[39]

Capovilla's notes concerning the pope's condition during these days
constantly mention the sudden onset of acute pain that was only interrupted by brief moments of relief. This was the case on May 2, for example, when Pope John managed to spend the day reading the conciliar
texts that were ready for the bishops.[40] During the ceremonies when he
received the Balzan prize and visited the Quirinal, he was suffering very
much, but for the most part managed to hide it.

On May 15, Pope John went to St. Peter's for a public audience. It
would be the last time. Although he was very pale, he seemed joyful and
animated. The day was significant. It was the anniversary of the publication of *Rerum Novarum* and *Mater et Magistra* — documents which updated the Church's social teachings. To these, Pope John had added
Pacem in Terris. He remembered the warm and universal welcome the
encyclical received and he invited his listeners to rejoice over the renewed splendor truth was radiating across the earth. Pope John's face
appeared thinner and at the same time luminous with the pallor of his
illness. Pope John suddenly exclaimed, "We are not here around the
tomb of the Apostle for a funeral! But certainly even funerals are not a
sorrow, but a joy. Oh, the *Hail Mary*, the *Hail Mary!* The first *Hail Mary*
of the infant, the final *Hail Mary* of the dying!"[41]

On May 17, the pope celebrated his last Mass. From then on, he
could only participate in Capovilla's Mass, which took place every
morning in the study next to his bedroom, near the window of the *Angelus*. He received Communion in bed.

On Sunday, May 19, he went to the window for the afternoon
Regina Coeli. His voice was still strong and resonant; his gestures of
welcome were particularly affectionate and prolonged. He brought his
hand to his lips several times and blew a fatherly kiss to the faithful.

The next day he had his final audience. Cardinal Wyszynski and four
bishops came to visit the pope before departing for Poland. To their
"Goodbye until September" for the resumption of the Council, the pope
replied with a smile, "In September you will find either me or another

pope. You are well aware that within a month everything can be done — the funeral of the one and the election of the other."

That same day the pope showed signs of a persistent hemorrhage, although not extreme. The next day his condition showed such a dramatically increased intensity that Dr. Mazzoni, assisted by Dr. Valdoni and Dr. Gasbarrini, resorted to anticoagulants, transfusions, and intravenous feeding.[42] The pope obeyed when the doctor asked him, in the name of "obedience and peace," to forego his general audience. He did go to the window from which he usually gave a brief discourse to the thousands of pilgrims gathered in the square. Wishing them a good feast of the Ascension on the following day, he added, "In the joy of the Mount of Olives, from which the Savior returned to the Father, let us run behind the Divine Master as he ascends. Since we are not able to follow him at once and have to remain on earth, let us imitate the apostles who gathered in the cenacle around Mary, invoking the Holy Spirit." Returning to his bed the pope remarked that he was ready to die and that he had intentionally said, "let us run behind the Divine Master...."[43]

The next day he went to the window to recite the *Regina Coeli* and give his blessing to the crowd for the last time. Their applause prevented him from speaking, and this moved him profoundly. On Friday, May 24, he felt weaker and he continued to receive aggressive medical treatments. He felt it was time to give his last recommendations, to leave a final testament containing the profound convictions that had inspired his actions — the philosophy of his pontificate. To his closest collaborators, Cardinal Cicognani and Bishop Dell'Aqua, who visited him every morning, he confided:

> For the benefit of the whole world we deal with matters of the greatest importance, taking our inspiration from the Lord's will. Now more than ever, and certainly more than in centuries past, we intend to serve man as he is, not just Catholics; to defend above all and everywhere the rights of all human beings, not only those of the Catholic Church. Contemporary circumstances, the needs of the last fifty years, doctrinal deepening, have placed a new reality before our eyes. As I said in my discourse at the opening of the Council, it is not the Gospel that has changed, it is we who begin to understand it better. One who has lived longer, who was alive at the beginning of the century faced with the new demands of social action that empowers every man; one who has been, as I was, in the East for twenty years and in France for eight, and was able to compare di-

verse cultures and traditions, knows that the moment has arrived to recognize the signs of the times, to seize the opportunities, and to look far beyond.[44]

The following Sunday, the doctors forbade him to get out of bed to go to the window. A medical bulletin was released, which stated that the stomach ailment had caused an anemic condition "controlled through appropriate treatment." Therefore, the patient was ordered to have complete rest and to limit all physical activity as much as possible.

The lack of appearances by the pope provoked a justifiable alarm throughout the world. Telegrams began to arrive. Even in this, John XXIII was able to perceive a positive sign of the times: "At the beginning of this century, official Rome ignored the death agony of Leo XIII. I remember that when I was a young seminarian, as I walked to the Vatican to learn some news of the ailing pope, I would hear disrespectful, insolent expressions in the streets and villages…. Times have certainly changed for the better!"

To the messages and prayers said for him, Pope John dictated responses that were published in *L'Osservatore Romano*. He stated that he was ready to offer his life for the Church, the Council, and all humanity. But if the Lord decided to allow him to live a little longer, he hoped that the prayers offered for him would help both his collaborators and himself to become holy for the expansion of the kingdom of God. Finally, he hoped that such interest and concern were signs of greater fervor in the Christian life and adherence to Gospel values.[45]

Pope John spent part of the day absorbed in prayer. He asked that the *Imitation of Christ* be read to him as well as pages of *Fire of Love* by Thomas of Bergamo (1563–1631), an illiterate Capuchin friar who had reached mystical heights.

The medical bulletin of May 30 gave reason to hope for some improvement, so Dr. Gasbarrini returned to Bologna. But the final crisis was imminent. At 11:30 P.M., the pope complained of intense pain. Dr. Mazzoni suspected that he had suffered a perforation of the stomach — and the consequences were inevitable.

Capovilla realized that the moment had come for him to fulfill a duty the pope had given him during the first year of his service. In the morning, Capovilla went to the pope's room immediately as usual. He drew near the suffering pope and, in a voice racked with emotion, told him that the Lord was calling him. When Capovilla confirmed for the pope that this was the doctors' verdict, Pope John asked that his final hours of life be spent according to the directives of the *Caeremoniale Episcoporum* (ceremonial of bishops), for the edification of the clergy and the faithful. He added, "Help me to die as a bishop, as a pope should."

At 11:00 A.M., he received Viaticum from the hands of Bishop Cavagna, his confessor. He spent some quiet moments with the Blessed Sacrament. Then he gave his final discourse — about fifteen minutes long — in the presence of Cardinals Cicognani, Dell'Aqua, and Samore. After reaffirming his desire to offer his life for the Church, the Council, world peace, and Christian unity, he said that the secret of his entire priesthood was found in the crucifix. Directing their attention to the one hanging on the wall in front of his bed, the pope said,

> He looks at me and I speak to him. In our long and frequent conversations during the night, the thought of the redemption of the world has appeared more urgent to me than ever: "I have other sheep that are not of this fold." These arms proclaim that he died for everyone — for everyone. No one is rejected from his love, from his forgiveness. But it is the words "that they may be one" that Christ has especially left as a testament to his Church. The sanctification of the clergy and of the people, the catechesis of Christians, and the preaching of the Gospel to the nations are therefore the principal task of the pope and bishops.

He recalled his humble origins and expressed his gratitude for the Christian education he had received in his family and from the priests he had known: his pastor Don Rebuzzini, Bishop Radini Tedeschi, and Cardinal Ferrari. Then he continued, "For my part, I do not recall having offended anyone, but if I have done so I ask pardon…. At this last hour I feel tranquil and I am certain that my Lord, in his mercy, will not reject me." His next words were almost an expression of his greatest desire: "That they may be one, that they may be one."[46]

After a few moments of silence, he received the Anointing of the Sick from Bishop Van Lierde who, in the emotion of the moment, forgot the order in which he should anoint the senses. The pope had to direct him. Then, after personally greeting each person standing around him, he murmured a word about his successor; without hesitation, he predicted that it would be Cardinal Montini.

At 4:00 P.M., the cardinals in Rome came to see the pope. Despite his grave condition and the intense day it had been for him, John XXIII exercised remarkable self-control.

Evening brought more visitors: his brothers with other relatives, Cardinal Montini, and the bishops of Bergamo and Venice. From all over the world inquiries and good wishes arrived from private individuals and public authorities — including Soviet Premier Khrushchev. The world followed the progress of the pope's illness hour by hour via the radio. His condition worsened steadily. He often dozed off; when he awakened, he joined in the prayers of those around him. To his nephew Xavier who stood at the foot of his bed, the pope said clearly, "Please move over, you are hiding the crucifix from me."

At 5:00 P.M. on June 3, the Monday after Pentecost, an impressive crowd had gathered for a Mass that Cardinal Traglia was about to celebrate for the dying pope. Many people in the crowd were not believers or not practicing their faith, but their shared sorrow and affection brought them to St. Peter's Basilica. Near the pope's bedside stood his relatives, Capovilla, and members of the papal household. Cavagna recited the prayers for the dying. At 7:40 A.M. the next morning — about the same time that the Mass was concluding with the liturgical dismissal, "Go, the Mass is ended" — John XXIII seemed to give a start, then a barely audible gasp. There was nothing more.

When the doctors confirmed his death, those standing around his bed prayed, "May the angels lead you into paradise," the *Magnificat*, and the *Te Deum*. The crowd outside either heard the news over Vatican Radio or understood when they saw a light suddenly illuminating the *Angelus* window. The sculptor, Manzu, was hastily called to take an impression of the pope's face and right hand.[47]

The next day, contrary to custom, the body of John XXIII was carried through St. Peter's Square into the basilica where thousands offered their homage and prayers. Mourners filed by uninterruptedly until 6:00 P.M. on June 6, the day of the funeral and entombment in the Vatican. The funeral was televised. Regardless of personal beliefs, people all over the world were moved by the ceremony. It seemed that one of the pope's last prayers, "That all may be one," was truly realized that day in a unique way. In a sense, the whole world was gathered around the deceased pope in a universal affirmation, never before experienced in the history of the papacy, of their respect and love for Pope John XXIII. It was worthy testimony to the reality that Pope John's message, which he endeavored to spread through his many activities, had not only been understood and welcomed, but had also entered people's hearts. The fruit this message had borne was evident in this act of homage and in sharing the ideals that had sustained his life. Could the pope have foreseen this public display of affection? In a conversation with Capovilla during his last days the pope had said: "This interest in the pope, who humbly represents the Lord, indicates new fervor in prayer; thoughts and proposals of peace; certain and clear convictions that what matters in life is contained in the Gospel: humility, gentleness, love."[48]

Yves Congar, one of the most attentive observers of John XXIII's pontificate, commented on the tremendous impact Pope John's life continued to have even after his death: "An extraordinary kind of humanity has been created." And it was clear to the theologian that it was not Pope John's "ideas, but his heart [that] constituted the decisive factor."[49] Congar's prominence at the Council might lead one to expect him to praise Pope John's thoughts, words, and projects. Instead, what Congar found most genuine about Pope John was his emphasis on goodness.

Congar's words are an echo of what Cardinal Roncalli once confided to a group of seminary teachers in Bergamo. He had been a guest at the seminary in August 1958, only a few months before he was elected pope. He told the teachers about an audience he had with Pius XII. The pope had asked Roncalli for his opinion about the virtue most necessary for governing the world. Roncalli promptly replied, "Goodness, Holy Father!" When Pius XII protested that he found justice more suitable, Rocalli repeated that as far as he was concerned, goodness should take first place. Goodness was the absolute guiding principle of all his pastoral activity right up to the very chair of Peter.

Surely John XXIII's goodness, supported by a joyful character, had conquered the world. But his goodness was not merely being good-natured. It was a phenomenon very rich in its simplicity and an object of general admiration. Pope John's goodness was the theological virtue of charity. His charity had matured in the rugged school of the Gospel, which demands self-renunciation, a death to self. His goodness was in perfect harmony with wisdom and that became a coherent lifestyle giving credible and convincing witness of his way. His was an enlightened goodness that sought the collaboration of intelligence, as expressed in a complete program of reform for the Church culminating in the convocation of Vatican II. Ultimately Pope John XXIII lived a farsighted, prophetic charity that knew how to courageously "recognize the signs of the times, seize opportunities, and look far ahead."

BIBLIOGRAPHY

Writings of Angelo Roncalli / John XXIII

Works

"Il Cardinale Cesare Baronio" (Cardinal Caesar Baronius). In *La Scuola Cattolica* 26 (1908), s. IV, v. 12, 129. Reprint, Rome, 1961.

Il Santuario di S. Maria della Castagna: Note storiche (The shrine of our Lady of Castagna: Historical notes). Bergamo, 1910.

La Misericordia Maggiore di Bergamo e le altre Istituzioni di beneficenza amministrate dalla Congregazione di Carità (The *Misericordia Maggiore* of Bergamo and other Institutions of charitable works administered by the Congregation of Charity). Bergamo, 1912.

Gli inizi del seminario di Bergamo e S. Carlo Borromeo (The beginnings of the seminary of Bergamo and St. Charles Borromeo). Bergamo, 1939.

Gli Atti della Visita Apostolica di S. Carlo Borromeo a Bergamo (1875) (The acts of the Apostolic Visit of St. Charles Borromeo to Bergamo). 2 vols. in five books. Florence, 1936–1958 (in reality, 1959).

Collected Writings and Discourses

Souvenirs d'un nonce. Cahiers de France (1944–1953). Rome, 1963.

Scritti e discorsi (Writings and discourses) 1953–1958. 4 vols. Rome, 1959–1962.

Discorsi Messaggi Colloqui di S. S. Giovanni XXIII (Discourses, Messages, Talks of Pope John XXIII). 5 vols., and a 1 vol. index. Vatican City, 1960–1967.

La predicazione a Istanbul. Omelie, discorsi e note pastorali (Preaching in Istanbul: Homilies, discourses, and pastoral notes). Edited by A. Melloni. Florence, 1993.

Bollettino del segretario del clero 1904–1908 (Bulletin of the secretariat for the clergy).

La Vita Diocesana (Diocesan Life), (Bergamo) 1–6 (1909–1914).[*]

L'Eco di Bergamo (The Echo of Bergamo), (Bergamo) 25–120 (1906–1981).

La Propagazione della fede nel mondo (The propagation of the faith in the world), (Rome) 1–5 (1921–1925).[**]

L'Osservatore Romano, (Vatican City) 62–126 (1932–1986).

---

[*] The diocesan newspaper of Bergamo was edited chiefly by Roncalli. A list of his articles, published in 1963, can now be found in the introduction to *Il Pastore,* 20–25, disagreeing in part with the list derived from copies on which Pope John XXIII initialed his own articles.

[**] The articles by Roncalli are collected in a volume with the same title. Rome, 1958.

Vita Cattolica (Catholic life), Istanbul.
Bollettino diocesano del Patriarcato di Venezia (Diocesan bulletin of the Patriarch of Venice), (Venice) 44–49 (1953–1958).
La voce di S. Marco (The voice of St. Mark), (Venice).
Acta Apostolicae Sedis, (Acts of the Apostolic See), (Vatican City) 50–55 (1958–1963).
Bollettino del Clero Romano (Bulletin of the Roman Clergy), (Rome) 39–40 (1958–1959).
Rivista Diocesana di Roma (Review of the Diocese of Rome), (Rome) 1–4 (1960–1963).

Correspondence

Lettere ai familiari (Letters to relatives and friends). Edited by L. F. Capovilla. 2 vols. Rome, 1968.
Il Pastore: Corrispondenza dal 1911 al 1963 con i preti del Sacro Cuore di Bergamo (The pastor: Correspondence from 1911 to 1963 with the priests of the Sacred Heart of Bergamo). Edited by G. Busetti. Padua, 1982.
Papa Giovanni prete romano (Pope John, priest of Rome). Rome, 1982.
Giovanni e Paolo, due papi: Saggio di corrispondenza 1925–1962 (John and Paul, two popes: Wisdom from their correspondence 1925–1962). Edited by L. F. Capovilla. Brescia, 1982.
Lettere dall'Oriente (Letters from the East). Edited by C. Valenziano. Bergamo, 1973.
Lettere alla famiglia (Letters to the family). Edited by E. and M. Roncalli. Milan, 1988.
Gli autografi di A. G. Roncalli all'arciprete di Fusignano (The writings of A. G. Roncalli, to the archpriest of Fusignano). Faenza, 1963. Rev. ed., 1984.
Lettere 1958–1963. Edited by L. F. Capovilla. Rome, 1978.
Ottima e reverenda madre: Lettere di papa Giovanni alle suore (Excellent and reverend mother: Letters of pope John to religious women). Edited by G. Busetti. Bologna, 1990.
Lettere familiari (Letters to friends). Edited by G. Farnedi. Casale Monferrato, 1993.
Fiducia e obbedienza: Lettere ai rettori del seminario romano 1901–1959 (Trust and obedience: Letters to the rectors of the Roman seminary). Edited by G. Badalà. Milan: Cinisello Balsamo, 1997.

Personal Diaries

Pensieri dal Diario (Thoughts from the Diary). Venice, 1963. First published in L'Osservatore Romano, 4–8, 10–11, 13, 16 June 1963.
Memorie e appunti 1919 (Memories and notes, 1919). Humanitas 28, (1973/6), 419–473.
Il Giornale delle'Anima (Journal of a Soul). Edited by L. F. Capovilla. Rev. ed., Rome, 1964.
Questo è il mistero della mia vita (This is the mystery of my life). Edited by L. F. Capovilla. 3 vols., and one illustrated vol. by A. Allegretti. Bergamo, 1989.

Documentary Appendices

Algisi, L. *Giovanni XXIII.* Turin, 1959. 4th ed., edited by L. F. Capovilla, 1981.
Battelli, G.; S. Trinchese; G. Alberigo; A. Melloni. *Fede tradizione profezia: Studi su Giovanni XXIII e sul Vaticano II* (Faith, tradition, prophecy: Studies on John XXIII and Vatican II). Brescia, 1984.

Blet, P.; A. Martini, R.; A. Graham; B. Schneider; eds. *Actes et documents du Saint Siège relatifs à la seconde guerre mondiale* (Acts and documents of the Holy See relating to World War II). Vols. 4–11. Vatican City, 1967–1981.

Battaglia, G. *Il papa buono nei miei ricordi di discepolo, di collega, di amico* (The good pope in my memories as disciple, colleague, friend). Faenza, 1973.

Capovilla, L. F., *Quindici letture* (Fifteen letters). Rome, 1970.

———. *Il Maestro inatteso* (The unexpected Teacher), s.l. 1972.

———. *Papa Giovanni XXIII Gran Sacerdote, come lo ricordo* (Pope John XXIII: How I remember a great priest). Rome, 1977.

Biographies

Algisi, L. *Giovanni XXIII.* Turin, 1981.

Hebblethwaite, P. *Giovanni XXIII: Il papa del Concilio* (John XXIII: Pope of the Council). Milan, 1989.

Roncalli, M. *Giovanni XXIII nel ricordo del Segretario L. F. Capovilla.* (John XXIII in the memories of his Secretary L. F. Capovilla). Milan: Cinisello Balsamo, 1994.

For a useful chronology of John XXIII's life, see *Appunti per una cronologia completa di Giovanni XXIII,* in L. F. Capovilla, *Giovanni XXIII. Quindici letture.* Rome, 1970, pp. 513–765.

Besides the cited works, a great deal of biographical material can be found in the publications by Capovilla, especially volumes 6 and 7 of *Pubblicazioni commemorative* (Commemorative publications). It is difficult to select the most significant aspects of this material.

General Works

An important conference was held in Bergamo from 3–7 June 1986. Its proceedings were collected in three volumes:

Papa Giovanni. Edited by G. Alberigo. Bari, 1987.

Giovanni XXIII: Transizione del Papato e della Chiesa (John XXIII: Transition of the papacy and of the Church). Edited by G. Alberigo. Rome, 1988.

L'età di Roncalli (The age of Roncalli). In *Cristianesimo nella Storia,* 8 (1987), pp. 1–217.

Alberigo, A.; Alberigo, G. *Profezia nella fedeltà.* Brescia, 1978.

Alberigo, G. *La miséricorde chez Jean XXIII.* In *La Vie Spirituelle,* 72 (1992), pp. 201–215.

———. *Jean XXIII: Itinéraire spirituel.* In *La Vie Spirituelle,* 69 (1989), pp. 391–413.

L'eredità spirituale di Papa Roncalli. In *Servitium,* 22 (1988), 59–60, pp. 1–140.

Zizola, G. *Giovanni XXIII: La fede e la politica.* Bari, 1988.

———. *L'utopia di papa Giovanni.* Assisi, 1973.

Bergamo (1881–1921)

Battelli, G. *La formazione spirituale del giovane Angelo Giuseppe Roncalli. Il rapporto col redentorista Francesco Pitocchi.* In *Fede, Tradizione, Profezia: Studi su Giovanni XXIII e sul Vaticano II.* Brescia, 1984, pp. 13–103.

———. *Un pastore fra fede e ideologia: Giacomo M. Radini Tedeschi.* Genoa, 1988.

Benigni, M. *Papa Giovanni XXIII, chierico e sacerdote a Bergamo 1892–1921.* Bergamo-Milan, 1998.

Aa. Vv. *Cultura e spiritualità a Bergamo nel tempo di Papa Giovanni XXIII.* Conference at Bergamo, 19–22 November 1981. Bergamo, 1983.

Melloni, A. *Carlo Borromeo nell'esperienza e negli studi di A. G. Roncalli / Giovanni XXIII.* In *Rivista di Storia e Letteratura religiosa,* 23 (1987), pp. 68–114.

———. *Formazione e sviluppo della cultura di Roncalli.* In *Papa Giovanni,* pp. 3–34.

Propaganda Fide

Trinchese, S. *L'accentramento a Roma dell'Opera della Propagazione della Fede: La missione Roncalli–Drehmans.* In *Fede, Tradizione, Profezia.*

Trinchese, S. *L'esperienza di A. G. Roncalli alla presidenza dell'Opera della Propagazione della Fede in Italia (1921–1925).* In *Giovanni XXIII: Transizione del Papato e della Chiesa,* pp. 8–29.

———. *Roncalli e le missioni.* Brescia, 1989.

Sophia—Istanbul—Paris

Della Salda, F. *Obbedienza e pace: Il vescovo A. Roncalli tra Sofia e Roma (1925–1934)* (Obedience and peace: Bishop A. G. Roncalli in Sofia and Rome). Genoa, 1988.

Fouilloux, E. *Straordinario ambasciatore? Parigi 1944–1953* (Extraordinary ambassador? Paris 1944–1953). In *Papa Giovanni,* pp. 67–95.

Melloni, A. *Fra Istanbul, Atene e la Guerra: La missione di A. G. Roncalli 1935–1944* (Between Istanbul and Athens in the War: The mission of A. G. Roncalli). Genoa, 1992.

Venice

Aa. Vv. *Angelo Giuseppe Roncalli. Dal Patriarcato di Venezia alla Cattedra di Pietro.* Edited by V. Branca and S. Rosso–Mazzinchi. Florence, 1984.

Alberigo, G. *Stili di governo episcopale: Angelo Giuseppe Roncalli.* In *I cattolici nel mondo contemporaneo (1922–1958).* Milan: Cinisello Balsamo, 1991, pp. 237–254.

De Rosa, G. *L'esperienza di A. Roncalli a Venezia.* In *Papa Giovanni,* pp. 97–111.

Dossetti, G. *Prefazione a "Genesi."* Official version edited by the community of Monteveglio. Turin, 1986, pp. vii–xvi.

Ferrari, S. *I Sinodi di Angelo G. Roncalli.* In *Cristianesimo nella Storia,* 9 (1988), pp. 120–135.

Niero, A. *Il cardinale Roncalli e l'arte sacra.* In *Cultura e spiritualità in Bergamo nel tempo di Papa Giovanni,* pp. 383–413.

Tramontin, S. *Il cardinale Roncalli patriarca di Venezia.* In *Le Chiese di Pio XII.* Edited by A. Riccardi. Bari, 1986, pp. 227–255.

———. *Il primo esperimento di apertura a sinistra; la formula di Venezia.* In *Storia della Democrazia Cristiana.* Edited by F. Malgeri. Rome, 1988, pp. 371–396.

———. *Venezianità del cardinale Roncalli.* In *Cultura e spiritualità in Bergamo,* pp. 351–371.

Zizola, G. *Il microfono di Dio.* Milan, 1990.

Pontificate of John XXIII

Alberigo, G. *Il pontificato di Giovanni XXIII.* In *La Chiesa del Vaticano II (1958–1978),* I. Milan: Cinisello Balsamo, 1994, pp. 15–51.

Casula, C. F. *Il cardinale Domenico Tardini.* In *Le deuxième Concile du Vatican (1959–1965).* Rome, 1989, pp. 207–227.

Guasco, M. *La predicazione di Roncalli* (The preaching of Roncalli). In *Papa Giovanni,* pp. 113–134.

Manzo, M. *Papa Giovanni vescovo a Roma* (Pope John, bishop of Rome). Milan: Cinisello Balsamo, 1991.

Miccoli, G. *Sul ruolo di Roncalli nella Chiesa italiana* (The role of Roncalli in the Italian Church). In *Papa Giovanni,* pp. 175–209.

Nicolini, G. *Il cardinale Domenico Tardini.* Padua, 1980.

Riccardi, A. *Dalla Chiesa di Pio XII alla Chiesa giovannea* (From the Church of Pius XII to the Church of John). In *Papa Giovanni,* pp. 135–173.

———. *Il potere del papa: Da Pio XII a Giovanni Paolo II* (The power of the pope: From Pius XII to John Paul II). Bari, 1993, pp. 154–219.

———. *Il Vaticano e Mosca* (The Vatican and Moscow). Bari, 1992.

Ruggieri, G. *Appunti per una teologia in papa Roncalli.* In *Papa Giovanni,* pp. 245–271.

Schmidt, S. *Agostino Bea: Il cardinale dell'unità* (Agustine Bea: The cardinal of unity). Rome, 1987.

Toschi, M. *Giovanni XXIII e la pace* (John XXIII and peace). In *Giovanni XXIII: Transizione del papato e della chiesa,* pp. 151–173.

Velati, M. *Una difficile transizione: Il cattolicesimo tra universalismo ed ecumenismo (1952–1964)* (A difficult transition: Catholicism amid universalism and ecumenism). Bologna, 1996.

The Second Vatican Council

Sources:

Acta et documenta concilio oecumenico Vaticano II apparando, series I (ante-praeparatoria). Vatican Polyglot Press, 1960–1961; series II (praeparatoria). Vatican Polyglot Press, 1964–1995.

Studies:

Aa. Vv. *A la veille du concile Vatican II. Vota et reactions en Europe et dans le catholicisme oriental.* Edited by M. Lamberigts and C. Soetens. Leuven, 1992.

Aa. Vv. *Il Vaticano II fra attese e celebrazione.* Edited by G. Alberigo. Bologna, 1995.

Aa. Vv. *La Chiesa del Vaticano II (1958–1978),* I. Milan: Cinisello Balsamo, 1994.

Aa. Vv. *Le deuxième concile du Vatican (1959–1965).* Rome, 1989.

Aa. Vv. *Verso il Concilio Vaticano II (1960–1962)*. Edited by G. Alberigo and A. Melloni. Genoa, 1993.

Alberigo, G. *Giovanni XXIII e il Vaticano II*. In *Papa Giovanni*, pp. 211–243.

———. *L'ispirazione di un concilio ecumenico: le esperienze del cardinale Roncalli*. In *Le deuxième concile du Vatican*, pp. 81–99.

Alberigo, G. and A. Melloni. *L'allocuzione "Gaudet Mater Ecclesia" di Giovanni XXIII (ottobre 1962)*. In *Fede, Tradizione, Profezia*, pp. 185–283.

Capovilla, L. F. *Il Concilio Ecumenico Vaticano II: La decisione di Giovanni XXIII. Precedenti storici e motivazioni personali*. In *Come si 'e giunti al Concilio Vaticano II*. Edited by G. Galeazzi. Milan, 1988, pp. 15–60.

Caprile, G. *Il concilio Vaticano II*. 5 vols. Rome, 1966–1968.

Melloni, A. *"Questa festiva ricorrenza."* Prodromi e preparazione del Discorso di annuncio del Vatican II. In *Rivista di Storia e Letteratura Religiosa*, XXVIII (1992), 3, pp. 607–643.

Storia del Concilio Vaticano II. General editor G. Alberigo. Vol. *I, Il cattolicesimo verso una nuova stagione: L'annuncio e la preparazione*. Bologna, 1995. Vol. II, *La formazione della coscienza conciliare: Ottobre 1962–Settembre 1963*. Bologna, 1996.

Suenens, L. J. *Ricordi e speranze*. Milan: Cinisello Balsamo, 1993.

Abbreviations used in Notes

AACB   *Archivio Azione Cattolica di Bergamo*
(Archives of Catholic Action of Bergamo)

AAS   *Acta Apostolicae Sedis*
(Acts of the Apostolic See)

AC   *Archivio comunale*
(Municipal archives)

ACCB   *Archivio del Capitolo della Cattedrale di Bergamo*
(Archives of the Cathedral Chapter of Bergamo)

ACVB   *Archivio della Curia vescovile di Bergamo*
(Archives of the episcopal curia of Bergamo)

ADSS   *Actes et documents du Saint-Siège relatifs à la seconde guerre mondiale*
(Acts and documents of the Holy See relating to the second world war)

AP   *Archivio parrocchiale*
(Parish Archives)

AR   *Archivio Roncalli*
(Roncalli Archives)

ARB   Personal archives of Msgr. Roncalli Battista at Sotto il Monte

ASFSC   Archives of the motherhouse of the Daughters of the Sacred Heart of Bergamo

ASRM   Archives of the major Roman Seminary

ASVB   Archives of the Episcopal Seminary of Bergamo

ASVR   Historical Archives of the Roman Vicariate

DMC   *Discorsi, Messaggi, Colloqui di S. S. Giovanni XXIII*
(Discourses, Messages, Talks of Pope John XXIII)

Eco   *L'Eco di Bergamo*
(The Echo of Bergamo)

FdO   A. G. Roncalli, *Fiducia e obbedienza: Lettere ai rettori del seminario romano, 1901–1959*
(Trust and obedience: Letters to the rectors of the Roman Seminary, 1901–1959)

FFSA   Archives of the Daughters of St. Angela Merici at Bergamo

GdA   John XXIII, *Il Giornale dell'Anima e altri scritti di pieta*
(Journal of a Soul and other pious writings)

GMRT   A. G. Roncalli, *In memoria di Msgr. Giacomo M. Radini Tedeschi, vescovo di Bergamo*
(In memory of Bishop Giacomo M. Radini Tedeschi, bishop of Bergamo)

Lettere   John XXIII, *Lettere 1958–1963*
(Letters 1958–1963)

Lf   John XXIII, *Lettere ai familiari*
(Letters to family and friends)

LV   Letters to the Bishops of Bergamo

Positio   Congregation for the Causes of Saints: *Beatificationis et canonizationis servi Dei Ioannis Papae XXIII, summi pontificis (1881-1963). Positio super vita, virtutibus et fama sanctitatis,* vol. IV, 2, Romae 1996

SD   *Scritti e discorsi 1953–1958*
(Letters and discourses)

SdN   *Souvenirs d'un nonce: Cahiers de France (1944–1953)*

UDC   Minutes of the Catholic Women's Union from 1910 to 1923

VD   *La Vita Diocesana*
(Diocesan Life)

NOTES

Foreword by Loris Francesco Capovilla

1. GdA, n. 969.
2. GdA, p. 538 (n. 898).
3. Milan, 1964.
4. F. Mauriac, *Le nouveau Bloc-notes 1961–1964,* p. 296.
5. Ibid.
6. John XXIII, *Pacem in Terris,* 168.
7. F. Mauriac, ibid., p. 293.
8. *Papa Giovanni nella mente,* p. 106.
9. Morcelliana, *Ultimi scritti politici* (Brescia, 1964), p. 335.
10. M. Delbrêl, *Noi, delle strade* (Gribaudi, 1969).
11. DMC, V, 109–110.
12. GdA, p. 507 (847).

PART I

BERGAMO
1881–1921

CHAPTER 1

The Roncalli Family

1. GdA, p. 662 (1096).
2. C. Fumagalli, *"Dello stemma di Papa Giovanni XXIII: La genealogia dei Roncalli, Ronco e Roncaglia,"* in *Atti dell'ateneo di scienze, lettere ed arti di Bergamo, XXXIV* (1968–1969), pp. 11–22.
3. AR, G. Petró, *Camaitino di Sotto Il Monte,* 1995.

4. AR, VI 707, letter to G. Birolini, 12 May 1929.

5. AR, VII 261, letter to G. Birolini, 18 May 1933.

6. Gaetano Camillo Guindani (1834–1904) was the bishop of Bergamo from 1879 until his death. He had been the vicar general of Cremona, his home diocese, from 1872–1879; he was bishop of Borgo San Donnino (today Fidenza). For more on him, see F. Vistalli, *Msgr. Guindani nei suoi tempi e nella sua opera,* vol. 1, Bergamo 1943; vol. 2, unedited manuscript in ACVB, *Fondo Vistalli.*

7. ACVB, *Visite Pastorali,* G. C. Guindani, vol. 134, Sotto il Monte.

8. Francesco Rebuzzini (1825–1898) was born in Pizzino in Val Taleggio. He was ordained in 1849 and became a chaplain and teacher at St. Anthony Abbandonato until 1855. He was parish priest at Camerata Cornello from 1855 until 1872 when he was transferred to Sotto il Monte. In 1878, he became a member of the *Collegio Apostolico,* an association of diocesan priests founded in 1700.

9. GdA, p. 664 (1099).

10. ACVB, *Fondo Vescovi Diocesani,* Speranza, directory of priests.

11. Giovanni Morlani (1870–1939), ordained a diocesan priest for Bergamo in 1893, he became a canon at the cathedral in 1894 and the prior of St. Mary Major from 1909. He was a member of the family that owned the land that the Roncallis cultivated.

12. G. Della Valentina, *"Note e ipotesi intorno al decollo industriale,"* in *Il movimento operaio e contadino bergamasco dall'unita al secondo dopoguerra,* ed. A. Bendotti (Bergamo, 1981), pp. 25–37.

13. N. Rezzara, *Il movimento cattolico nella diocesi di Bergamo: Primo saggio di statistica* (Bergamo, 1895).

14. AP, Sotto il Monte, registry of the Federated Society of Mutual Help of the group of St. John the Baptist in Sotto il Monte, 1884.

15. AC, Sotto il Monte, birth registry for 1881, n. 41.

16. GdA, p. 249 (416).

17. AR, letter to his family, 29 July 1935; see also Lf, vol. 1, pp. 353–356.

18. AR, VIII 149, letter to Sister Maria of St. Joseph, 9 December 1935.

19. AR, letter to his family, 21 February 1939; see also Lf, vol. 1, pp. 459–462.

20. AP, Sotto il Monte, marriage registry, 1877, n. 5.

21. AC, Sotto il Monte, marriage registry, 1877, n. 10.

22. AP, Sotto il Monte, *Stato d'anime* 1873, p. 118, Zaverio Roncalli.

23. AP, Sotto il Monte, Chronicle, 31 July 1935.

24. GdA, pp. 664 ff (1100).

25. DMC, vol. 4, p. 23, *Omelia in anniversario coronationis* (Homily on the anniversary of his coronation), 4 November 1961.

26. Oral testimony given by John XXIII to L. F. Capovilla; now in GdA, p. 85n.

27. GdA, p. 665 (1101).

28. Ibid.

29. DMC, vol. 5, p. 444. See also A. Fredi, *Giovanni XXIII fanciullo dalla nascita fino ai dodici anni* (John XXIII the boy from his birth to twelve years) (Bergamo, 1963), p. 29.

30. *Il rosario con papa Giovanni* (The rosary with Pope John), ed. L. F. Capovilla (Rome, 1979), p. 16.

31. SD, vol. 2, p. 422, *Omelia a Fatima il 13 maggio 1956* (Homily at Fatima, 13 May 1956).

32. AR, IV 2, Diary 1919, 11 May; see also *Humanitas* 28, (1973), p. 446.

33. AR, XI 139, letter to G. B. Montini, 26 August 1960; now in *Giovanni e Paolo due papi. Saggio di corrispondenza 1925–1962* (John and Paul, two popes: correspondence from 1925–1962), ed. L. F. Capovilla (Brescia, 1982), pp. 120–122.

34. SD, vol. 3, pp. 620–621, *Preghiera durante la cerimonia delta incoronazione delta statua delta Madonna il 24 agosto 1958.*

35. *Eco,* 28 March 1993, brief account of a pilgrimage, ed. L. F. Capovilla.

36. On the Federal Feast, begun on 11 September 1888 at Sarnico, and celebrated annually in the most important centers of the diocese until 1913, see G. Belotti, *Nicolò Rezzar* (Bergamo, 1982), pp. 115–124.

37. *XV anniversario della morte di papa Giovanni. Giugno 1963–1978* (The fifteenth anniversary of the death of Pope John), 3 June, 1963–1978, ed. L. F. Capovilla (Rome, 1978), p. 11.

38. AR, IV 2, Diary 1919, 7 September.

39. AR, VII 261, letter to G. Birolini, 18 May 1933.

40. AR, recollections of his uncle's death.

41. ARB, *Memorie storiche del martirio e del culto dei SS. Martiri Solutore, Avventore ed Ottavio protettori della citui di Torino, raccolte da un Sacerdote torinese* (Turin, 1866); ARB, autographed copy.

42. AR, VIII 425, letter to G. Birolini, 24 June 1937.

43. Letter to V. Bugarini, August 19, 1922; now also in FdO, p. 228.

44. AR, VIII 573, letter to B. Bianchi, 17 July 1938.

45. Letter to P. Donizetti, 8 March 1933 in D. Cugini, *Papa Giovanni nei suoi primi passi a Sotto il Monte* (Bergamo, 1965), p. 70.

46. AR, letter to his family, 20 December 1932; now in Lf, vol. 1, pp. 282–284.

47. GdA, p. 613 (1039).

48. D. Cugini, *Papa Giovanni nei suoi primi passi a Sotto il Monte* (Bergamo, 1965), pp. 36–37.

49. GdA, p. 613 (1039).

50. F. Bettini, *I programmi di studio per le scuole elementary dal 1860 al 1945* (The programs of study for elementary school, 1860–1945) (Brescia, 1961), *passim.*

51. GdA, p. 666 (1103).

52. Ibid.

53. AP, Sotto il Monte, documents of the association, 2–9 October 1881.

54. GdA, p. 666 (1102).

55. AR, VIII 681, letter to G. Birolini, 29 January 1939.

56. GdA, p. 250 (417).

57. *Alle radici del clero bergamasco 1854–1879* (The roots of the clergy of Bergamo 1854–1879), *Studie e Memorie,* 8 (Bergamo, 1981), pp. 233–240.

58. GdA, p. 667 (1104).

59. John XXIII, *Questo é il mistero della mia vita* (This is the mystery of my life), ed. L. F. Capovilla (Bergamo, 1989), vol. 1, p. 64.

60. Francesco Benedetti (1848–1914) was born in Caprino and ordained in 1870. When he was 27 years old, he was named rector of Celana, a position he held until his death. For more on him see the Episcopal College School of Celana: *Nel XXV anniversario del rettorato del sacerdote don Francesco Benedetti 1875–1900,* Bergamo, 1900; (E. Alemanni), *In memoria di mons. Francesco Benedetti,* Bergamo, 1915.

61. A. Belotti, *Il Collegio convitto vescovile di Celana, Memorie storiche* (Bergamo, 1898).

62. Andrea Castelli (1876–1970), born in Villasola, was ordained a priest on 21 December 1901. From the year 1919, he was associated with the same College of Celana, as a master organist from 1907, and as chaplain 1915–1919. Later he was an assistant at St. Lucy's parish in the city, near Loreto, then the first pastor of St. Thomas in Calvi. For more on him see: A. Paiocchi, *Don Benigno: La verita con il cuore. Msgr. Benigno Carrara vescovo di Imola 1888–1974* (Don Benigno: The truth with love. Msgr. Benigno Carrara, Bishop of Imola 1888–1974) (Bergamo, 1998), pp. 35–37.

63. AR, testimony of A. Castelli.

64. AR, VI 507, letter to G. B. Merisio, 24 June 1928.

65. GdA, p. 667 (1104).

Chapter 2

The Seminary

1. ASVB, Inscription Registry from 1881–1882; 1905–1906.

2. A. G. Roncalli, *Gli inizi del seminario di Bergamo e san Carlo Borromeo* (The beginning of the seminary of Bergamo and St. Charles Borromeo) (Bergamo, 1939), p. 83.

3. E. Agazzi, *Gli edifici dal medioevo al 1962* (Buildings from the Middle Ages to 1962), in Aa.vv., *Il colle di San Giovanni. Storia e arte* (The hill of St. John. History and art) (Bergamo, 1996), pp. 13–175; see also A. Roncalli, *Il seminario di Bergamo* (The seminary of Bergamo), in *VI Congresso Eucaristico Nazionale* (The sixth national Eucharistic congress) vol. I (Bergamo, 1912), pp. 42–45.

4. ACVB, *Fondo seminario,* the rector's reports to the bishop, manuscript in 25 folios, 25 October 1902.

5. Oral testimony of Msgr. L. F. Capovilla places the date on Thursday, 3 November, based on John XXIII's own recollection.

6. GdA, p. 667 (1105).

7. *Regole prescritte ai chierico del seminario di Bergamo cavate dagli atti di san Carlo Borromeo d'ordine di Msgr. vescovo Luigi Ruzini rinnovate e confermate dai vescovi successori e ultimamente da Msgr. illustrissimo vescovo Gaetano Camillo Guindani* (The rule prescribed for the clerics of the seminary of Bergamo as found in the instructions of St. Charles Borromeo to Bishop Luigi Ruzini and confirmed by successive bishops including Bishop G. C. Guindani) (Bergamo, 1892).

8. A. G. Roncalli, *Gli inizi del seminario,* p. 67.

9. ASVB, General Catalog, reg., a 51, a 66, a 68, a 79, a 85; envelope 12: reg. 3; envelope 12, reg. 4–12; registry of payments and debts, envelope 11: reg. 3, 10–13; scholastic registry c 335–340, 316. The curriculum could be put in today's terminology as follows: 1892/1893 third gymnasium; 1893/1894 fourth gymnasium; 1894/1895 fifth gymnasium; 1895/1896 first year of secondary school; 1896/1897 second year of secondary school; 1897/1898 third year of secondary school; 1898/1899 first theology; 1899/1900 second theology.

10. GdA, p. 250 (44).

11. ASVB, *Fondo Roncalli,* letters to F. Rebuzzini from G. Dentella, June 12, 1895; now in *Cultura e spiritualità in Bergamo nel tempo di Papa Giovanni XXIII* in *Studie e Memorie,* 9 (Bergamo, 1983), p. 250 ff.

12. ASVB, registries already cited.

13. GdA, p. 668 (1105); ASVB, registry of Holy Orders, 28 June 1895, n. 33.

14. GdA, p. 250 (417).

15. AR, letter to G. Testa, 3 May 1907.

16. AR, testimony of A. Castelli.

17. AP, St. Gregory, *Libro cassa, ad diem.*

18. GdA, p. 250 (417).

19. Sacred Congregation for the Causes of Saints, *Positio super virtutibus servi Dei Andreae Caroli Ferrari* (The heroic virtues of the Servant of God Andrea Charles Ferrari) (Rome, 1974), p. 392; deposition of Cardinal Roncalli, 14 December 1952.

20. ACVB, *Fondo Vescovi Diocesani,* Radini Tedeschi, on the Thirteenth Eucharistic Congress, Milan, 1895.

21. GdA, p. 668 (1105).

22. GdA, pp. 47–53 (1–9).

23. R. Amadei, *Manuale del maestro de'novizi: notizia di un manoscritto* (Manual for the master of novices) in *Cultura e spiritualità,* pp. 229–250; see also GdA, p. 56 ff.

24. GdA, pp. 53–55 (10–13).

25. GdA, p. 131 (166).

26. GdA, pp. 74–76 (45–47).

27. Confided by John XXIII to his secretary L. F. Capovilla, now in GdA, p. 9.

28. C. Castelletti, *Vita del Servo di Dio Luigi Maria Palazzolo e memorie storiche intorno agli istituti di carità da lui fondati* (Life of the Servant of God Luigi Maria Palazzolo, and historical remembrances of the Institute of Charity which he founded) (Bergamo, 1894).

29. Letters of the postulator to Pius XI for the cause of canonization of Don Luigi Palazzolo, 13 May 1927; now in *Ottima e reverenda madre: Lettere di papa Giovanni alle suore* (Excellent and reverend mother: Letters of pope John to religious women), ed. G. Busetti (Bologna, 1990), p. 391.

30. ASVB, Registry of Third Order Franciscans, n. 43.

31. DMC, vol. 1, pp. 249–256, 16 April 1959, *Discorso per il 750th anniversario dell'approvazione pontificia alla Regola francescana* (Discourse for the 750th anniversary of the pontifical approval of the Franciscan rule); also the cit. on pp. 254–255.

32. GdA, p. 77 (48).

33. GdA, p. 128 (163).

34. GdA, p. 80 (55).

35. GdA, p. 78 (49), 80 (54).

36. GdA, pp. 81–83 (56–59).

37. GdA, p. 83 (59).

38. GdA, p. 88 (66–67).

39. Cf. GdA, pp. 90–93 (70–75).

40. GdA, p. 93 (76).

41. GdA, pp. 94–121 (77–144).

42. GdA, p. 115 (131).

43. GdA, p. 108 (111).

44. ACVB, *Lettere pastorali* (Pastoral letters), G. C. Guindani, 29 May 1898, pp. 11–13.

45. Cf. for example AP, Sotto il Monte, *Decreto del generate regio commissario straordinario Bava in data 26 Maggio 1898* (Decree of the extraordinary royal general commissary Bava).

46. AP, Sotto il Monte, registry of the Federal Society of St. John the Baptist, official record of dissolution.

47. GdA, p. 114 (129).

48. ASVB, *Fondo Roncalli,* report of the rector during the vacation of 1898.

49. In ARB, copies of the work with a firm autograph.

50. GdA, p. 117 (137).

51. Ibid., pp. 117f. (138–139).

52. Ibid., p. 121 (145).

53. Ibid., pp. 672–674 (1111–1112).

54. Ibid., p. 119 (141).

55. Ibid., p. 71 (38).

56. Ibid., p. 128 (162).

57. Ibid.

58. AR, I, 2, *Maria nel cenacolo: Ai cheirici. Esercizio di eloquenza 1899,* 29 pages.

59. GdA, p. 128 (161).

60. ASVB, registry of ordination, 25 June 1899, n. 15.

61. Luigi Battaglia (1852–1917), ordained in 1877. He was the assistant of Brusaporto, and later in the parish of Pezzolo until 1883.

62. AR, III 54, *In morte di don Luigi Battaglia,* necrology.

63. AR, 22 May 1899, manuscript; now in GdA, p. 134 (173).

64. Alessandro Locatelli (1850–1918) from Sotto il Monte; student of the college of St. Alexander up to his ordination. He became the assistant pastor at Roncola San Bernardo, and at Bonate Sopra for more than 30 years. Radini Tedeschi assigned him as the steward of the bishop's residence and, in 1910, the canon of the cathedral. A. Roncalli, *La morte del canonico Locatelli,* in *Eco,* 2 August 1918.

65. GdA, p. 668 (1106).

66. GdA, p. 144 (195).

67. GdA, p. 149 (205).

68. GdA, pp. 155–156 (222–223).

69. GdA, p. 158 (227).

70. ACVB, *Pastoral Letters,* Guindani, 25 November 1899.

71. *La Gazzetta Provinciale di Bergamo,* 29, n. 205, 27–27 August 1900, p. 1: *Rivista della stampa.*

72. AR, XI 187, letter to C. Valsecchi, 14 February 1961; now in Lettere, pp. 286–287.

73. L. F. Capovilla, *Quel treno che non arrivava mai a Roma,* in *Eco,* 28 March 1993.

74. GMRT, p. 27.

75. R. Angeli, *Cronistoria dell'Anno Santo* (Tipografia Vaticana, 1912), 3 vols.

76. GdA, p. 668 (1106).

77. ARB, original diploma, 18 September 1900.

78. DMC, vol. 4, p. 557, 4 October 1962, *Allocuzione nel santuario di Loreto.*

Chapter 3

The Roman Seminary

1. Regarding the noble ecclesiastic Flaminio Cerasola (more commonly, Cerasoli) and the College, see *Il Collegio Cerasoli: Commemorazioni centenarie 1735–1935* (Rome). Regarding the Archconfraternity, see the recent *L'Arciconfraternita dei Bergamaschi: 450 anni di vita: aspetti storico-artistici di una sodalitas romana,* A. Capriotti, D. Frascarelli, L. Testa (Bergamo, 1989).

2. Archive of the College of St. Alexander, *Incartamenti ufficiali della pratica,* 26, V.

3. GdA, pp. 669–670 (1107).

4. Archive of the Archconfraternity, manuscripts now published in *Arciconfraternita dei bergamaschi in Roma: Papa Giovanni prete romano* (Rome, 1982), pp. 150–158.

5. Archive of the Cavagnis-Caldera and Serina families (Bergamo), letter of 11 December 1900; now in FdO, p. 63, n. 3.

6. ASRM, letter of V. Cavadini to V. Bugarini (1 January 1901). Vincenzo Cavadini (1873 –1949) from Calcinate, received his degree in theology and *utroque iure* in Rome. Ordained a priest in 1895, he was soon made a professor in the seminary of Bergamo, where he would become vice-rector in 1907 until 1920. After a short period of rest in the parish of Colognola from 1920 to 1924, he served as rector until 1935. Vincenzo Bugarini (1852 –1924) was a Roman priest, professor of Oriental Languages and rector of the Roman Seminary, 1893 –1910. He was a guest of Roncalli beginning in 1921 and until his death on 24 January 1924.

7. ASVR, *Positiones Ordinandorum,* fasc. b.16: *Pro memoria per le sacre ordinazioni,* authographed by Roncalli, 8 January 1904; now in *Papa Giovanni prete romano,* cit. p. 159.

8. ASRM, entrance registration, 1824 –1912, n. 1567.

9. F. Iozzelli, *Roma religiosa all'inizio del Novecento* (Religious in Rome at the beginning of the 1900s) (Rome, 1985), p. 112.

10. AR, letter to his family, 12 January 1901; now in Lf, vol. 1, pp. 3 –5.

11. See FdO, p. 21.

12. G. Moioli, *Un parroco modello: Don Giuseppe Mojoli, prevosto di Trescore Balneario, Bergamo* (Rome, 1948), p. 21.

13. AR, letter to his parents, 19 July 1901; now in Lf, vol. 1, p. 11.

14. AR, Holy picture with the sentence in Roncalli's own writing, dated 2 June 1903.

15. AR, letters to G. Testa, 19 May 1910 and 2 June 1903.

16. AR, VIII 487, letter to T. Trocchi, November 8, 1937. Tito Trocchi (1864 –1947) ordained a priest since 1887, was professor of Italian in the Roman Seminary's secondary school for more than twenty-five years, and vice-rector from 1893 to 1902. He was made titular bishop of Lacedemonia in 1915 and sent to Cuba, Puerto Rico, Bolivia, and Peru. When he returned to Rome in 1926, he was general auditor of the Apostolic Chamber and vice-treasurer of the Holy See.

17. Achille Ballini (1880 –1922) was ordained on July 25, 1903. Afterward he was made coadjutor at Lurano in Ponte San' Pietro, at Santa Maria Imacolata delle Grazie in Bergamo, at Borgo Santa Caterina, and director of the Work Office. He died soon after being nominated parish priest of *Santa Grata inter vites,* in Borgo Canale in Città Alta.

18. Guglielmo Carozzi (1880 –1970) was ordained on 25 July 1903. He earned a degree in philosophy, theology, and both civil and ecclesiastical law, and was treasurer of the seminary of Bergamo. He was professor of dogmatics 1909 –1919, when he was nominated Arch-priest of Seriate, where he remained until his death. He was honored with the title of Msgr. in 1927, and in 1931 nominated the bishop's delegate for the administrative sector.

19. AR, letter to his parents, 27 January 1901; now in Lf, vol. 1, pp. 5– 8.

20. GdA, p. 164 (232).

21. AR, letter to Sister M. Angiola, 21 January 1948; now in *Ottima e reverenda madre,* p. 274.

22. AR, letter to his family, 16 February 1901; now in Lf, vol. 1, p. 9.

23. GdA, p. 176 (258).

24. *Tornata solenne tenuta in Arcadia il 21 aprile 1901 per la promozione alla porpora degli E.mi e R.mi Cardinali Luigi Tripepi e Felice Cavagnis* (Rome, 1901).

25. AR, *Ricordi di Papa Giovanni,* G. Littarru, cit., 5.

26. ARB, original document.

27. John XXIII, *Discorso al Pontificio Seminario Romano Maggiore, il 27 novembre 1958;* now in FdO, cit., pp. 322–329; the quotation on p. 325.

28. AR, the textbooks used by Roncalli that bear his signature.

29. Letter to V. Bugarini, 19 August, and 4 November 1901; now in FdO, pp. 3, 7.

30. AR, G. Littarru, *Ricordi di Papa Giovanni,* cit., *passim.*

31. ASRM, letter of D. Re to V. Bugarini, 14 July 1901; AR, letter of G. Masoni to A. Roncalli, 18 October 1901.

32. AR, personal documents, n. 8/4.

33. Letter to V. Bugarini, 23–28 December 1901; now in FdO, pp. 9–10.

34. GdA, p. 195 (299). ASVB, book records of *Biblioteca Leoniana, sub voce "Chierici,"* 1902.

35. Letter to V. Bugarini, 29 June–6 July 1902; now in FdO, pp. 15–17.

36. FdO, p. 15; cf. GdA, p. 195 (300).

37. Letter to V. Bugarini, 26 October 1902; now in FdO, pp. 20–21.

38. Letter to V. Bugarini, November 19, 1902; now in FdO, pp. 22–23. The Latin quotations are taken from Ex 15:1; Song 2:11; *Introit* to Easter Mass; and Ps 138:18.

39. GdA, pp. 167–179 (236–265); Mt 1:12.

40. Luigi Oreste Borgia (1840–1914) remained in the seminary after his ordination in 1863. He was a tutor until 1867, and then spiritual director until his death.

41. GdA, p. 179 (266); the invocation to the Sacred Heart was a common short prayer at that time.

42. Francesco Pitocchi (1852–1922) was a priest of the diocese of Alatri and parish priest of Vico in Lazio, his hometown. He entered the Congregation of the Most Holy Redeemer, was a confessor and auxiliary spiritual director in the Roman Seminary with Canon Borgia from the summer 1899 (or 1898) until a few years before his death.

43. A. G. Roncalli, *In memoria del padre Francesco Pitocchi,* in *"Sursum Corda,"* 5 (November 1922), art. 11, pp. 39–47, republished in Giovanni XXIII, *Il giornale dell'Anima e altri scritti di pietà* (Rome, 1964), pp. 467–476; *Testimonianza di don Angelo Roncalli a P. Francesco Pitocchi, Rapallo 14 dicembre 1922,* from which the quotations are taken. On the relationship Roncalli-Pitocchi, see also G. Battelli, *La formazione del giovane Angelo G. Roncalli. Il rapporto col redentorista Francesco Pitocchi,* in *Fede tradizione profezia. Studi su Giovanni XXIII e sul Vaticano II* (Brescia, 1984), pp. 13–103.

44. GdA, p. 181 (271).

45. GdA, p. 183 (278).

46. *Discorso al Pontificio Seminario Romano,* cit. p. 324.

47. *Testimonianza (...) a P. Francesco Pitocchi,* cit. p. 468.

48. Ibid., p. 470.

49. Ibid., p. 472.

50. Ibid., p. 469.

51. GdA, p. 187 (285).

52. GdA, p. 197 (303).

53. GdA, p. 190 (290).

54. GdA, p. 193 (296).

55. GdA, pp. 194–195 (299).

56. AR, VI 849, letter to A. Coari, 14 December 1929; now partly in L. Algisi, *Papa Giovanni XXIII* (Rome, 1988), pp. 366–367.

57. AR, X 234, letter to N. Turchi, 14 August 1954; now in L. Algisi, *op. cit.* p. 367.

58. Letter of N. Turchi to Roncalli, 26 August 1954; now in L. Algisi, *op. cit.* p. 368.

59. GdA, p. 193 (296), in Terentius' *Andria,* I, I, 34.

60. GdA, p. 193 (297).

61. Ibid. The quotation is from *Imitation of Christ,* Book I, Chapter III.

62. Ibid. The quotation is from *Imitation of Christ,* Book I, Chapter II.

63. *Testimonianza (...), P. Francesco Pitocchi,* cit., pp. 471–472.

64. ASVR, *Positiones Ordinandorum,* file b. 16 contains all the documents relative to the subdiaconate, diaconate, and priesthood of Don Angelo Roncalli.

65. GdA, p. 222 (360–361); cf. Ps 84:1–2.

66. AR, personal documents, n. 46.

67. AR, VI 410, homily in the church of St. Joseph in Sofia, on 12 February 1928, in *Nel VI anniversario dell'incoronazione di Pio* X (On the sixth anniversary of the coronation of Pius X); now in F. Della Salda, *Obbedienza e pace: Il vescovo A. G. Roncalli tra Sofia e Roma 1925–1934* (Genoa, 1989), pp. 178–183.

68. GdA, p. 244 (407).

69. GdA, p. 671 (1109).

70. GdA, p. 671 (1109).

71. Giuseppe Ceppetelli (1846–1917) vice-regent from 1899 to 1917, and Latin Patriarch of Constantinople from 1903 to his death.

72. GdA, p. 263 (440).

73. GdA, p. 264 (441).

74. Domenico Spolverini (1871–1939) was made vice-rector of the seminary in Rome in 1902 and rector in 1910. Regarding the ordination day, however, L. F. Capovilla corrects what he believes is a *lapsus* (error) of the future pontiff (cf. GdA, p. 442), stating:

> Actually, Spolverini missed his train and therefore did not arrive in time for the ordination. As a result, Ernesto Bonaiuti, acting as the assistant to Turchi, helped Roncalli. Spolverini accompanied Roncalli, leaving the Celio the day after, August 11.

75. GdA, p. 264 (442).

76. GdA, p. 264 (442).

77. ACVB, *Fondo Roncalli,* letter to A. Bernareggi, 10 August 1940; now in LV, p. 75.

78. GdA, p. 265 (443).

79. Ibid.

80. Letters to D. Spolverini, 11 August 1916, and 4 August 1929; now in FdO, pp. 141, 227.

CHAPTER 4

Radini Tedeschi: Bishop of Bergamo

1. AR, VI 816, letter to G. B. Floridi, 19 October 1929; see also AR, VIII 954, letter to L. Drago, 23 February 1941.

2. *Atti del Congresso mariano mondiale tenuto in Roma l'anno 1904, compilati per cura di Msgr. Giacomo Maria Radini Tedeschi vescovo di Bergamo, segretario della commissione cardinalizia, e del p. maestro Pellegrino Maria Stagi, priore generale dell'Ordine dei Servi di Maria, segretario generale del Congresso* (Rome, 1905); see also GMRT, p. 28.

3. SD, vol. 1, pp. 320–321, *Al venerando clero e ai diletti figli del Patriarcato, per l'incoronazione dell'Immacolata della basilica vaticana* (To the venerable clergy and to the beloved sons of the Patriarchate, on the occasion of the coronation of the Immaculate of the vatican basilica), 4 October 1954.

4. John XXIII, *Sacerdotii nostri primordia,* 1 August 1959, in AAS 51 (1959), 11, p. 546.

5. Giacomo Maria Radini Tedeschi (1857–1914), of the diocese of Piacenza, in Rome from 1890, where he had offered his services to the Congregation for Public Affairs and had followed the Catholic Union and the *Opera dei Congressi* from 1896 to its dissolution in 1904. From 1883, he was involved in the organization of the pilgrimages of the Italian National Committee for Palestine and Lourdes, which he had founded. For more on Radini Tedeschi, see GMRT, and the more recent work of G. Battelli, *Un pastore tra fede e ideologia, Giacomo M. Radini Tedeschi 1857–1914* (Genoa, 1988).

6. Stanislao Medolago Albani (1852–1921) was an active promoter of the Catholic movement, and he directed the second section of the *Opera dei Congressi* until its dissolution in 1904, after which he became president of the Socio-Economic Union. Later Pius X called him to lead the Popular Union, together with Giuseppe Toniolo and Paolo Pericoli. For more on Albani, see G. Belotti, *Nicoló Rezzara,* cit., *passim;* R. Amadei, *Appunti sul modernismo bergamasco* (Notes on Bergamasque modernism), in *"Rivista di storia della Chiesa in Italia,"* XXXII (1978), 2, pp. 381–414, in particular p. 385, n.10; G. Battelli, *Un pastore tra fede e ideologia,* cit., p. 386 and *passim;* for documentation see ACVB, *Fondo Rezzara;* for the correspondence with G. M. Radini Tedeschi see A. Bedolago Albani, *Alcune lettere di Msgr. Radini Tedeschi riguardanti Bergamo* (Some letters by Msgr. Radini Tedeschi regarding Bergamo), in *"Bergomum,"* 80 (1985), 1, pp. 3–137.

7. ACVB, *Fondo Vescovi Diocesani,* G. M. Radini Tedeschi, VI 1, letter by A. Roncalli to G. Signor, 11 January 1905; now in part in G. Battelli, *Giacomo Maria Radini Tedeschi and Angelo Roncalli (1905–1914),* in *Papa Giovanni,* ed. G. Alberigo (Bari, 1987), p. 37.

8. Giovanni Battista Scalabrini (1839–1905), born in Fino Mornasco, ordained in 1863, was a teacher and then rector of the minor seminary of Como until 1870. Appointed pastor of St. Bartholomew in Como until his consecration in 1876 as bishop of Piacenza, where he remained until his death. His name is also linked to the founding of the Missionaries approved in 1887, and of the Missionaries for the Emigrants with Mother Francesca Cabrini in 1900. For more information, see M. Francesconi, *Giovanni Battista Scalabrini vescovo di Piacenza e degli emigrati* (Rome, 1985).

9. GMRT, pp. 37–38; see also *L'Osservatore Romano,* 30 January 1905.

10. SC, vol. 4, pp. 166–175, *Msgr. Luigi Fadini, perla del clero lodigiano,* cit. on p. 171; see also letter to G. Piazzi, 22 March 1958; now in LV, pp. 172–173.

11. ACVB, *Fondo Vescovi Diocesani,* G. M. Radini Tedeschi; letter to G. M. Radini Tedeschi, 5 February 1905.

12. AR, testimony of G. Carozzi.

13. GMRT, p. 37; see also letter to A. Bernareggi, 18 June 1936; now in LV, pp. 56–57.

14. SD, vol. IV, pp. 166–175, Msgr. Luigi Fadini, cit., pp. 171–172; Mt 24:25.

15. GMRT, p. 39.

16. GdA, p. 307 (514–414); see also letter to D. Spolverini, 7 February 1906; now in FdO, p. 51.

17. GdA, p. 308 (517).

18. Letter to V. Bugarini, 9 May 1905; now in FdO, pp. 35–36.

19. GMRT, pp. 9–10.

20. Letter to V. Bugarini, 9 May 1905; now in FdO, pp. 35–36.

21. GMRT, pp. 449–459, *passim.*

22. Letter by G. Fachinetti to Roncalli, 7 June 1905; now in *Il Pastore,* pp. 80–81.

23. Letter to V. Bugarini, 1 September 1905; now in FdO, pp. 38–39.

24. Letter to V. Bugarini, 3 November 1905; now in FdO, pp. 42–43.

25. Letter to D. Spolverini, 3 November 1905; the biblical citation is from Ps 40:10.

26. A. Roncalli, *I Preti del Sacro Cuore di Bergamo: Appunti per la storia* (The priests of the Sacred Heart of Bergamo: Notes for its history), published then in *VD* (1909), pp. 362–367, and in *I Preti del Sacro Cuore,* cit., pp. 1–22.

27. *VD* 1 (1909), p. 367.

28. Letter to V. Bugarini, 14 December 1905; now in FdO, p. 47.

29. AR, II 2/4, Diary 1905–1906, *ad diem.*

30. Letter to V. Bugarini, 7 February 1906; now in FdO, p. 51; see Lettere, p. 563 for the episode.

31. GMRT, p. 41; for the pastoral visit, see ACVB, *Fondo Vescovi Diocesani,* G. M. Radini Tedeschi, schedules of the visit.

32. Letter to V. Bugarini, 2 April 1906; now in FdO, p. 55.

33. Letter to V. Bugarini, 7 June 1906; now in FdO, p. 57.

34. Letter to D. Spolverini, 7 February 1906, cit.

35. *Eco,* 3–4 October; 10–11 October; 15–16 October; 23–24 October; 24–25 October 1906; now in A. Roncalli, *1906: Viaggio in Terra Santa* (Milan, 1993); also in GdA, pp. 278–304 (463–511).

36. *"Pro Familia,"* supplement n. 52/1906.

37. GdA, pp. 285–286 (477–578).

38. GdA, p. 288 (482).

39. GdA, pp. 290–291 (486).

40. GdA, p. 293 (490).

41. GdA, p. 297 (497–499).

42. GdA, pp. 298–299 (500–502).

43. GdA, p. 303 (509).

Chapter 5

Professor of Church History

1. AR, letter of G. M. Radini Tedeschi to Roncalli, 1 November 1906; now in part in G. Battelli, *Un pastore tra fede e ideologia* (A pastor between faith and obedience), cit., pp. 321–322 ff.

2. AR, letters of A. Pedrinelli to Roncalli, 7 February and 12 November 1906.

3. A. Roncalli, *Il Cardinal Cesare Baronio,* cit., pp. 39–40.

4. AR, testimonies, Giuseppe Vavassori.

5. AR, II. 23, *Celebrandosi nella prepositurale di Sant'Andrea una funzione solenne per le nozze d'oro sacerdotali di Sua Santità Pio X ed il cinquantesimo dell'apparizione della Beata Vergine Immacolata di Lourdes, 25 marzo 1908* (In celebrating in the provostal church of St. Andrew a solemn function for the golden anniversary of the priesthood of His Holiness Pius X and the fiftieth anniversary of the appearance of the Blessed Immaculate Virgin at Lourdes), written in his own hand.

6. ACVB, *Fondo Vescovi Diocesani;* G. M. Radini Tedeschi, *Diario particolare 1907;* AR, Diary 1907, from 1 January to 23 February 1907.

7. GdA, p. 308 (517).

8. AR, letter to G. Testa, 6 June 1909.

9. AR, letter of A. Pedrinelli to Roncalli, 24 April 1907.

10. AR, letter to the same, 6 June 1909.

11. AC, Dalmine; letter to Mayor F. Damiani, 14 August 1907.

12. AR, personal documents; Military District Command of Bergamo, dispensation from the draft per instructions, 17 August 1907.

13. *"Comunità Santa Maria,"* parish bulletin n. 34, September 1995.

14. AR, IV 2, Diary 1919, 17 August; now in *Humanitas* 28 (1973), p. 456.

15. AR, II 4, expense register; AP, Sforzatica Santa Maria, baptismal register.

16. AR, II 15, letter to Duke F. Borgoncini, 2 October 1907; now in *XII anniversario della morte di Papa Giovanni 1963–3 giugno 1975* (Twelfth anniversary of the death of Pope John XXIII 1963–3 June 1975), ed. L. F. Capovilla, (Rome, 1975), p. 42; see also AR, expense register, cit. 19 July and 22 August 1907.

17. AAS 40 (1907), 596 ff., Pope Pius X, *On the Doctrines of the Modernists.*

18. AR, II 15, letter to Duke F. Borgoncini, 2 October 1907, cit.

19. Ibid.; Ovid, *Epistulae ex Ponto,* 2, 7, 40.

20. C. Patelli, *Uomini e vicende del seminario di Bergamo dal 1567 to 1921* (Men and events of the seminary of Bergamo from 1567 to 1921) in *Studi e memorie,* 1, 1972, p. 110.

21. Ibid.

22. G. Battaglia, *Il Papa buono nel decennio della sua morte nei miei ricordi di discepolo, di collega, di amico* (The good pope in the decade since his death in my memories as a disciple, as a colleague, as a friend) (Faenza, 1973), p. 18.

23. AR, testimonies, G. Carozzi.

24. AR, letter to Duke F. Borgoncini, 2 October 1907, cit.

25. A. Roncalli, *Il Cardinale Baronio,* p. 46.

26. G. Calenzo. *La vita e gli scritti del Cardinale Cesare Baronio della Congregazione dell'Oratorio, bibliotecario di Santa Romana Chiesa* (The life and works of Cardinal Caesar Baronius of the Congregazione dell'Oratorio, librarian of the Holy Roman Church) (Rome, 1907); in AR copy with autograph.

27. *Eco,* 5 December 1907.

28. A. Roncalli, *Il Cardinale Cesare Baronio. Nel terzo centenario della sua morte* (Cardinal Caesar Baronius. On the third centenary of his death) in *La Scuola Cattolica,* 36 (1908), pp. 3–29.

29. Ibid., (Monza, 1908); a third edition was edited in 1961 by G. De Luca for the *Edizioni di Storia e Letteratura di Roma.*

30. AR, letter of A. Ferrari to Roncalli, 7 March 1908.

31. A. Roncalli, *Il Cardinale Baronio,* cit., p. 34.

32. Ibid., p. 46.

33. AR, letter to G. Testa, 10 January 1907.

34. A. Roncalli. *Il Cardinale Baronio,* cit., p. 46.

35. Ibid., pp. 43–44.

36. Ibid., p. 44.

37. AFCB, letter to E. Congiorni, 6 February 1908; now in A. Gappani, *Paolo Guerrini,* in *Memorie storiche della diocesi di Brescia,* p. 63.

38. *Bolletino del Segretariato del Clero,* 2 (1907), 10, pp. 78–80; 2 (1907), 11, p. 88.

39. *Bolletino del Segretariato del Clero,* 3 (1908), 1, pp. 102–105; 3 (1908), 2, pp. 115–118; 3 (1908), 4, pp. 136–139; 3 (1908), 5, pp. 148–150; 3 (1908), 6, pp. 160–163.

40. *VD* 1 (1909), p. 3, 34.

41. Letter to G. Oazzi, 25 August 1961; now in LV, cit., p. 190.

42. AR, XI 121, *Nota informativa sulla Vita Diocesana di Bergamo,* 11 May 1960; now in Lettere, p. 497.

43. *VD* 1 (1909), pp. 48–49.

44. AR, III 52, letter to A. Agliardi, s.l., s.d., but 1911; now in AR, the articles initialed with an "R" by Roncalli himself gathered into 6 vols., ed. L. F. Capovilla.

45. G. M. Radini Tedeschi, *Alla egregia Commissione per il Centenario di San Charles* (To the esteemed committee for the centenary of St. Charles), 16 April 1909, in *VD* 1 (1909), p. 139.

46. Id., *Lettera pastorale per il Terzo Centenario della Canonizzazione di San Charles Borromeo* (Pastoral letter for the third centenary of the canonization of St. Charles Borromeo), 28 November 1909, in *VD* 1 (1909), pp. 328–352.

47. *VD* 2 (1910), pp. 72–73.

48. A. G. Roncalli, *Gli Atti della visita pastorale apostolica di San Charles Borromeo a Bergamo 1575* (The acts of the apostolic pastoral visit of St. Charles Borromeo to Bergamo), vol. 1, part 1 (Florence, 1936), pp. 29–30.

49. AR, letter of A. Ferrari to Roncalli, 17 (?) April 1909.

50. AR, II 31–35, letter to A. Ratti, 16 April, 4 and 6 May 1909; AR, II 42–43, letter of A. Ratti to Roncalli, 3 May 1909; letter to A. Ratti, 28 and 31 March 1910.

51. AR, letter to L. Manzini, 6 February 1910; now in L. F. Capovilla, *Papa Giovanni XXIII gran sacerdote, come lo ricordo* (Pope John XXIII great priest, as I remember him) (Rome, 1977), pp. 130–131; see also ADCB, letter to P. Guerrini, 18 May 1910; now in A. Fappani, *Paolo Guerrini,* cit., p. 64.

52. AR, letter of D. Spolverini to Roncalli, 9 November 1909.

53. ACCB, letter to Venerando Capitolo, 30 June 1909; letter to G. B. Floridi, 7 July 1909.

54. A. G. Roncalli, *Gli Atti della visita,* cit., p. 31.

55. ACCB, letter to G. B. Floridi; cit., AR, 32, letter to A. Agliardi, (June) 1909.

56. AR, personal documents, nn. 52, 52b; diploma, July 4, 1909 and accompanying letter, 23 July 1909, of the Lombardy Historical Society.

57. AR, letter to G. Testa, 6 June 1909.

58. A. G. Roncalli. *Gli Atti della visita,* cit., pp. 37–41, *passim.*

59. *VD* 1 (1909), pp. 317–320; see also *VD* 2 (1910), pp. 253–261, 311–313.

60. A. Roncalli, *Rilievi di storia bergamasca nella vita di San Charles Borromeo. Appunti storici* (Importance of Bergamasque history in the life of St. Charles Borromeo), in *Eco,* 23–24 June 1910, pp. 1–2.

61. Id., *San Carlo Borromeo e la Chiesa di Bergamo* (St. Charles Borromeo and the church of Bergamo), in *"San Charles Borromeo nel terzo centario della canonizzazione,"* (Milan, 1909–1910).

62. *"La Schola Cattolica,"* 38 (1910), pp. 320–323.

63. AR, letters to G. Testa, 25 December 1910 and 30 January 1911.

64. *VD* 2 (1910), pp. 212–213, *San Charles Borromeo: Pastor Bonus.*

65. *VD* 2 (1910), pp. 441–447, *Le feste centenarie di San Carlo Borromeo in Bergamo, 4 dicembre 1910.*

66. C. Arvisenet, *Memoriale vitae sacerdotalis* (Turin, 1892).

67. AR, letter to G. Testa, 16 March 1910.

68. *VD* 1 (1909), pp. 317–320, *San Borromeo e il Clero nelle prossime fest centenarie* (St. Borromeo and the clergy in the upcoming centenary festivities), the cit. of p. 318; the cit. in Latin is from Fedro, 4, 2, 6.

69. *VD* 2 (1910), pp. 457–495.

70. *"Humilitas. Miscellanea storica dei seminari milanesi."* n. 25 and final (1938), pp. 988–1014.

71. *Gli inizi del seminario di Bergamo e san Carlo Borromeo. Note storiche con una introduzione sul concilio di Trento e la fondazione dei primi seminari* (The origins of the seminary at Bergamo and St. Charles Borromeo. Historical notes with an introduction on the Council of Trent and the founding of the first seminaries) (Bergamo, 1930); most recently published in *Il colle di San Giovanni, Omaggio a Papa Giovanni* (The hill of San Giovanni, homage to Pope John), ed. *Centro Studi Giovanni XXIII-Fondazione,* L. F. Capovilla, inaugural edition, (Bergamo, 1997), pp. 19–44.

72. *VD* 1 (1909), pp. 207–220; *VD* 2 (1910), pp. 91–92; 95–96; 100–101; 119.

73. *VD* 1 (1909), p. 228.

74. CD 2 (1910), pp. 146–151, 196–203; see also GMRT, pp. 106–113.

75. *VD* 2 (1910), p. 148.

76. *VD* 2 (1910), p. 150; 1 Jn 5:4.

77. *VD* 2 (1910), p. 203; 2 Tm 4:7.

78. *Bergomensis Ecclesiae Synodus XXXIII. A reverendissimo domino Jaboco Baria Radini Tedeschi episcopo habita,* (Bergamo, 1910).

79. AR, letter to G. Testa, 19 May 1910.

Chapter 6

Assistant to the Union of Catholic Women

1. *VD* 2, (1910), p. 198.

2. *VD* 2, (1910), pp. 207–208.

3. Nicolò Rezzara (1848–1915) of Chiuppano in the province of Vicenza. After his first experiences in the Catholic associations in his city of origin, he moved to Bergamo in 1878, where he began the intense activity that, with operative methods and visions of reality sometimes a bit distant from the other mainstays of Catholic Action of Bergamo, was often intertwined with Count Medolago Albani. There is a vast bibliography on him, which is easily available: G. Belotti, *Nicolò Rezzara nella storia del movimento sociale cattolico in Italia* (Nicolò Rezzara in the history of the Catholic social movement in Italy) (Bergamo, 1956 and published again in 1980). P. A. Gios, *Nicolò Rezzara e il movimento cattolico in Italia* (Nicolò Rezzara and the Catholic movement in Italy) (Rome, 1990). An ample unpublished documentation in ACVB, *Fonda Rezzara.*

4. AR, personal documents, n. 53, notification of appointment, 22 January 1910.

5. *VD* 3, (1912), pp. 155–159.

6. AACB, book of minutes of the Catholic Women's Union from 1910 to 1923, pp. 8, 11.

7. UDC, 18 May 1910, p. 25.

8. UDC, 18 May 1910, p. 27.

9. UDC, 16 July 1911, p. 67.

10. UDC, 22 July 1910, p. 33.

11. UDC, Ibid.

12. AR, letter to G. Testa, 2 February 1912.

13. *VD* 3, pp. 29–30, letter to the prefect of Bergamo, 14 January 1911; Angelo Roncalli is among the signers.

14. *VD* 2, (1910), pp. 308–310.

15. ACVB, board minutes for Catholic Action, VI 19, 30, 38.

16. AR, letter to G. Testa, 29 December 1910.

17. AR, letter to G. Testa, 4 March 1913.

18. Letter to V. Bugarini, 23 February 1910; now in FdO, pp. 82–83.

19. Letter to his father, 3 March 1910; now in Lf, vol. 1, p. 28.

20. Letter to V. Bugarini, 27 June 1910; now in FdO, p. 86.

21. R. Amadei, *Appunti sul modernismo bergamasco* (Notes on the modernism of Bergamo), cit., pp. 382–414.

22. ACVB, sourcebook of diocesan bishops, G. M. Radini Tedeschi, personal agendas, 1909.

23. Letter to V. Bugarini, 15 September 1910; now in FdO, pp. 88–91.

24. AR, letter to G. Testa, 27 June 1910.

25. Letter to V. Bugarini, 15 September 1910, cit.

26. GdA, pp. 314–315 (257–529).

27. L. Algisi, *Papa Giovanni,* cit., pp. 36–37.

28. *VD* 3, (1911), p. 311; *VD* 5, (1913), p. 263; *VD* 6, (1914), p. 276.

29. AR, letter of appointment signed by G. M. Radini Tedeschi, 7 August 1912; see also *VD* 4, (1912), p. 171; letter to P. Guerrini, 18 April 1913; now in A. Fappini, *Paolo Guerrini,* cit., p. 66.

30. *VD* 5, (1913), p. 51; *VD* 6, (1914), p. 105.

31. AR, letter to G. Testa, 5 August 1910.

32. AR, letter to G. Testa, 25 December 1910.

33. AR, letter to G. Testa, 7 March 1912.

34. Ibid.

35. Ibid., 16 March 1910.

36. *VD* 4, (1912), p. 31.

37. AR, letter to A. Pedrinelli, 14 April 1911.

38. AR, letter to G. Testa, 18 June 1912.

39. Ibid., 14 April 1913.

40. Ibid., 29 December 1907.

41. Ibid., 10 January 1907.

42. Ibid., 5 August 1910.

43. Ibid., 10 January 1907.

44. Ibid., 29 December 1910.

45. Ibid., 7 March 1912.

46. *VD* 4, (1912), pp. 299–334.

47. AR, II 71.

48. ASVB, *Fondo Roncalli,* handwritten pages of the first draft of the document.

49. *Atti collettivi e deliberazioni dell'Episcopato Lombardo nelle annuali conferenze* (Collective acts and deliberations of the Lombard episcopate from the annual conferences) (Milan, 1911). For the event, cf. G. Rumi, *La Rerum novarum e il movimento cattolico italiano* (Rerum novarum and the Italian Catholic movement) (Brescia, 1995), p. 193.

50. G. M. Radini Tedeschi, *Il problema scolastico odierno ossia pensieri sulla libertà e sulla religione nella scuola* (Bergamo, 1912); see GMRT, pp. 116–123.

51. Lettere, p. 548. In particular, he reviewed *Il giovane studente istruito nella dottrina cristiana* (The young student educated in Christian doctrine); *Misteri cristiani* (Christian mysteries); *Seguiamo la ragione* (Let us follow reason); *Questioni morali e sociali del giorno* (Moral and social issues of the day).

52. *La libertà della Chiesa e l'insegnamento religioso* (Freedom of the Church and religious teaching) (Rome: *Società Editrice Romana,* 1912).

53. G. Gallina, *Il problema religioso nel risorgimento e il pensiero di Geremia Bonomelli* (Rome, 1974), p. 379.

54. Lettere, p. 548.

55. *VD* 4, (1912), p. 301.

56. Ibid., p. 334.

57. Ibid., p. 307.

58. Ibid., p. 314.

59. Ibid., p. 324.

60. A. Roncalli, *La Misericordia Maggiore di Bergamo e le altre istituzioni di beneficenza amministrate dalla Congregazione di Carità* (Bergamo, 1912).

61. AR, letter to G. Testa, 22 December 1912.

62. Ibid., 2 February; 4 March; 5, 10, and 18 April 1913; 25 April 1914; and 10 May 1914.

63. *I primi sette anni dell'Università Popolare di Bergamo* (The first seven years of the Popular University of Bergamo), cit., pp. 19, 33.

64. *Eco,* 22 January 1914.

65. *VD* 5, (1913), p. 180.

66. AR, letter to G. Testa, 18 June 1912.

67. Letter to D. Spolverini, 12 April 1914; now in FdO, p. 117.

68. AR, letter to G. Testa, 4 November 1912.

69. AR, personal documents, n. 54b, 70; see in *Il Pastore* (The pastor), photographic insert, pp. 80–81; for the names cited, see *I Preti del Sacro Cuore* (The Priests of the Sacred Heart), cit., pp. 215–290.

70. GdA, p. 331 (559).

71. Letter to D. Spolverini, 4 November 1913; now in FdO, pp. 112–113.

72. GdA, p. 331 (558).

73. AR, letter to G. Testa, 10 January 1914.

74. GdA, p. 330 (557).

75. GdA, p. 329 (555).

76. AR, letter to G. Testa, 15 December 1913.

77. GdA, p. 335 (566).

78. AR, II 86, letter to G. De Lai, 2 June 1914.

79. AR, Mass register, 6–9 June 1913: "*in cubiculo infirmi episcopi*—in the room of the sick bishop."

80. GMRT, pp. 193–194.

81. L. Duchesne, *Histoire ancienne de l'Église,* (Paris, 1906).

82. AR, letter by G. De Lai, 12 June 1914.

83. Letter by G. De Lai, 12 June 1914; now in *X Anniversario,* cit., pp. 65–66.

84. Letter to G. De Lai, 2 June 1914; now in *X Anniversario,* cit., pp. 63–64.

85. Letter by G. De Lai, 12 June 1914, cit.

86. Letter of G. M. Radini Tedeschi to Mattiussi, 18 June 1914; now in G. Battelli, *Un pastore tra fede e ideologia* (A pastor between faith and ideology), cit., pp. 441f.

87. A. Fogazzaro, *Il Santo* (Rome, 1905); the novel was placed on the *Index of Prohibited Books* on 4 April 1906.

88. Letter to G. De Lai, 27 June 1914; now in *X Anniversario,* cit., pp. 67–68.

89. Letter by G. De Lai, 29 June 1914; now in *X Anniversario,* cit., p. 70.

90. Letter to D. Spolverini, 29 July 1914; now in FdO, cit., pp. 121–123.

CHAPTER 7

The Death of Bishop Radini Tedeschi

1. Letter to his parents, 28 July 1914; now in *Giovanni XXIII,* Lf 152 inediti dal 1911 al 1952, ed. G. Farnedi (Casale Monferrato, 1993), pp. 21–22.

2. Letter to D. Spolverini, 27 July 1914, cit.

3. GMRT, pp. 199–200; see also GdA, pp. 333–336 (561–567).

4. Ibid., pp. 200–201.

5. Ibid., p. 204.

6. Ibid., p. 206.

7. Ibid., p. 217.

8. Ibid., pp. 219–220.

9. Ibid., p. 220.

10. Letter to G. Viganò, 20 June 1951; now in *Il Pastore,* pp. 328–329.

11. Letter to A. Grossi Gondi, 12 November 1914, cit.

12. Letter to L. Drago, 5 February 1915; now in *Il Pastore,* p. 84.

13. To V. Bugarini, 13 September and "second half of September" 1914; now in FdO, pp. 129, 130.

14. GdA, p. 336 (569).

15. ACVB, minutes from Catholic Action from 18 February to 10 March and 4 May 1915.

16. UDC, p. 177.

17. *VD* 7 (1915), p. 98.

18. GMRT, pp. 237–425, *Discorsi e commemorazioni, Testimonianze.*

19. Letters to D. Spolverini, 20 January, 6 March 1916, 2 August 1917; now in FdO, pp. 133–134, 135–136, 155–156.

20. Gerolamo Volpi (1869–1929) of Bergamo, Major Medic of the Reserves; in AR, photo in remembrance of his death.

21. AR, VIII 4, personal military service file.

22. *VD* 9 (1917), report on the life of the seminary in the first years of the war, pp. 80–85.

23. AR, III 14, letter to Colonel D. Zanchi, 28 June 1915.

24. *VD* 8 (1916), pp. 195–197, 240–243.

25. *VD* 6 (1914), pp. 343–347, 364–372.

26. GMRT, p. 3; in ACVB, *Fondo Roncalli,* manuscript and print proofs of the pamphlet.

27. Letter to D. Spolverini, 20 January 1916; now in FdO, pp. 133–134.

28. Letter to D. Spolverini, 11 August 1916; now in FdO, p. 141.

29. *VD* 9 (1917), pp. 80–85, report to the rector, David Re.

30. ACVB, *Fondo Seminario,* administrative report, 8 October 1917.

31. Letter to D. Spolverini, 22 March 1917; now in FdO, pp. 150–151.

32. AR, S. Bottani (1895–1980), *L'insegnamento del prof. Roncalli in seminario di Bergamo,* typewritten s.d., pp. 4–5.

33. Letter to D. Spolverini, 6 March 1916; now in FdO, pp. 135–136. The garrison infirmary was in the barracks at Piazza d'Armi, in the zone of Borgo Santa Caterina.

34. Letter to D. Spolverini, 20 January 1916; now in FdO, pp. 133–134.

35. AR, LIV 222, A. Roncalli, *Discorso al VI Congresso Eucaristico Nazionale,* 9 September 1920; now in *Il rosario con papa Giovanni,* ed. L. F. Capovilla (Camerino, 1979), pp. 119–131, cit., pp. 126–127.

36. AR, LIV 74, *I nostri preti-soldati,* November 1917, manuscript.

37. UDC, pp. 183–195.

38. *VD* 7 (1915), pp. 192, 309.

39. *VD* 7 (1915), pp. 224–253, 311; see also *Relazione morale e finanziaria al 31 Dicembre 1917,* eds. Comitato della Mobilitazione civile (Bergamo, 1918).

40. GMRT.

41. Ibid., p. 4.

42. Letter to his brother Zaverio, 12 December 1916; now in Lf, cit., vol. 1, p. 42.

43. Letter to the same, 17 September 1916; now in Lf op. cit., ibid.

44. Diary, 30 January–19 March 1917; on 6 February; Ps 27:1b.

45. AR, III 1, Speech on the Sacred Heart, 11 June 1915, handwritten.

46. Letter to V. Burgarini, 4 April 1918; now in FdO, pp. 162–163.

47. AR, III 26, *Appunti nella festa della Madonna di Lourdes,* 11 February 1917, handwritten; Jn 2:16, where it is written: *"concupiscenza della carne, concupiscienza degli occhi, superbia[!] della vita"* ("concupiscence of the flesh, concupiscence of the eyes, pride of life").

48. ASFSC, *Chronicon,* cit., 6 July 1916, summary of a homily to the nuns.

49. Letter to his brother Zaverio, 6 May 1917; now in Lf, vol. 1, p. 48.

50. Letter to his brother Giuseppe, 5 December 1917; now in Lf, vol. 1, p. 61.

51. Letter to D. Spolverini, 26 April 1917, cit.

52. *VD* 9 (1917), p. 47; see also Diary 1917, 1 January 1917.

53. Letter to his brother Zaverio, 6 May 1917; now in Lf, vol. 1, p. 48.

54. Diary 1917, 30 January.

55. Ibid., 7 March; Ps 68:29.

56. Letter to his father, 23 June 1917; now in Lf, vol. 1, p. 52.

57. *Discorso al VI Congresso Eucaristico Nazionale,* cit., p. 15.

58. Letter to G. Bosis Crippa, 27 April 1916; now in *Prof. Gilda Crippa ved. Bosis. La fondatrice dell'Associazione vedove e dell'Opera Salus,* cit., pp. 25–26.

59. AR, III 34, *Triduo di preparazione alla festa di S. Ignazio di Loyola, 28–30 luglio 1916,* handwritten 30 July.

60. Letter to G. Bosis Crippa, 23 January 1917; now in *Prof. Gilda Crippa ved. Bosis. La fondatrice dell'Associazione vedove e dell'Opera Salus,* cit., pp. 28–29.

61. Diary 1917, 19 March.

62. Ibid., 2 Cor 7:4; 5:14.

63. Ibid., 30 January; the Latin cit. often used by St. John Bosco, from Gn 14:21.

64. Diary 1918, 15 May.

65. Ibid., 24 March.

66. Ibid., 9 July.

67. Ibid., 31 March.

68. Ibid., 17 August.

69. Ibid., 22 April; see also Ibid., 15 July; 29 May; 1 and 17 June; 20 August; 5 October; 5 and 25 December.

70. Ibid., 29 May. Alludes to the letter to the rural vicars and pastors of the diocese in *Indirizzi pratici di ministero pastorale, VD* 10 (1918), pp. 87–88.

71. Diary 1918, 17 September.

72. Ibid., 5 November.

73. Ibid., 10 November.

74. Ibid., 11 February; Mt 5:5.

75. Ibid., 15 May.

76. Ibid., 10 July.

77. Ibid., 29 July.

78. Letter to D. Spolverini, 2 (or 4?) August 1918; now in FdO, pp. 164–165.

79. Diary 1918, 9 October.

80. Ibid., 31 December; Rev 22:20.

81. AR, Diary 1919, 19 January.

82. GdA, p. 359 (596).

83. Diary 1918, 27 February.

84. Ibid., 15 March; Acts 2:11.

85. Letter to D. Spolverini, 24–25 December 1918; now in FdO, pp. 166–168.

86. AR, III 77, *L'Opera Sant'Alessandro in Bergamo per l'educazione e l'assistenza della gioventù studiosa. Note illustrative,* 10 signed folios.

87. Ibid., 20 September; now also in M. Benigni, *Angelo Roncalli e il collegio Sant' Alessandro* in *Chiesa e società a Bergamo nell'Ottocento* (Milan, 1998), pp. 430–431.

CHAPTER 8

The Association for Young Catholic Women

1. Diary 1917, 1 March.

2. Enrico Mauri (1882–1967), ordained a diocesan priest of Milan in 1908, was the secretary of Msgr. Marelli first at Bobbio and then at Bergamo, until 1916. Once he returned to the diocese, he joined the Oblates of St. Charles. Coadjutor of the parish of St. Gregory in Milan, in 1916 he conceived an association for girls, an idea that was developed by the Servant of God Armida Barelli and led to the constitution of the Association for Young Catholic Women, of which Don Mauri was National Assistant from 1918 to 1922. Mauri participated in the foundation of the *Centre d'Apostolato ascetico Madonna del Grappa* that he directed until his death, of the secular institute "Oblates of Christ the King." He was also national director of the Pontifical Work of St. Peter the Apostle of the local clergy.

3. C. Dau Novelli, *Società, Chiesa e associazionismo femminile. L'unione fra le donne cattoliche d'Italia (1902–1919)* (Rome, 1988).

4. Dairy 1918, 10 February; see also DMC, vol. 4, pp. 316–322; Speech to the delegation of the Association for Young Catholic Women of Milan, 1 June 1962, the allusion on p. 317.

5. UDC, p. 248; on the beginning of the Association for Young Catholic Women in Bergamo, see B. Curtarelli, *L'Azione Cattolica Femminile a Bergamo dal 1918 al 1940,* dissertation for a degree at the University of Studies of Milan, 1994.

6. Dairy 1919, 6 February.

7. AR, VI 738, letter to G. Boni, 4 July 1929.

8. Diary 1919, 13 January.

9. Regione Lombardia, *Bibliografia dei periodici femminili lombardi 1786–1945* (Milan, 1993), pp. 159–161.

10. *Eco,* March 18, 1919: *Attività cattolica femminile: Una conferenza della professoressa Magnocavallo; Eco,* March 1919: *Per l'attivitá femminile: La conferenza Magnocavallo.*

11. Ps 92:13.

12. Diary 1919, 9 November; see also UDC, p. 262.

13. Ibid., on 9 June.

14. Letter to D. Spolverini, 24 September 1919; now in FdO, p. 179.

15. UDC, p. 261.

16. Letter to G. Boni, 26 May 1919, cit.

17. Diary 1919, 3 November.

18. Report to Benedict XV, 5 November 1919; now in *Il Pastore,* pp. 85–87, and in *Humanitas,* 6 (1973), cit., pp. 475–477.

19. Letter to P. Gasparri, 14 November 1919; now in *Il Pastore,* pp. 87–88, and in *Humanitas,* cit., pp. 478–479.

20. Diary 1920, 12 April.

21. ASVB, *Fondo Roncalli,* letter to P. Merati, 20 October 1921.

22. Ibid., letter to the same, 8 October 1923.

23. ASFSC, *Chronicon,* cit.

24. *"Arma contro Arma." Lo Congresso interdiocesano della Buona Stampa, Bergamo 26–27 ottobre 1919* (only issue).

25. Diary 1920, *ad diem.*

26. AR, *La Madonna della Fiducia. Nella chiusura delle feste;* Rome, 10–12 May 1920, autographed text of the speech.

27. Diary 1920, *ad diem;* see also letter to A. Bernareggi, 10 August 1940; now in LV, pp. 75–77.

28. AR, IV 38, *Esercizi Spirituali tenuti a San Vittore di Bologna,* 18–22 September 1920, handwritten.

29. ASVB, *Fondo Roncalli,* autographed notes of the speech.

30. AR, Personal documents nn. 59 and 59b, nomination and diploma.

31. Diary 1919, 23 August.

32. Letter to D. Spolverini, 2 September 1920; now in FdO, p. 189.

33. Diary 1920, 22 September.

34. R. Amadei, *Le vicende dell'Ufficio del Lavoro (1919–1921),* in *Il movimento operaio e contadino bergamasco dall'unitá al secondo dopoguerra,* ed. A. Bendotti (Bergamo, 1981), pp. 81–92.

35. *VD* 11 (1919), p. 134.

36. G. Laterza, *Il Partito Popolare a Bergamo,* in *"Archivio Storico Bergamasco,"* 5 (1983), pp. 295–343.

37. Diary 1919, 20 February.

38. Diary 1919, 16 November.

39. Ibid., on 17 November.

40. CD 12 (1920), pp. 32, 35.

41. Simone Pietro Grassi (1856–1934) of Schilpario; ordained a priest in 1878 and immediately proved himself an excellent preacher and writer. In 1895, he was named parish priest of Verdello, his adopted country; from his boyhood, he had been a guest of his uncle Don Davide Pizio, then titular vicar of that parish. In 1911, he declined the nomination to the two episcopal sees in Melfi and Rapolla. In 1914, he was made bishop of Tortona, where he remained until his death.

42. AR, IV 37, *Discorso tenuto al Congresso eucaristico nazionale a Bergamo, il 9 settembre 1920,* typewritten; published in *VI Congresso Eucaristico Nazionale,* cit., pp. 251–257; now also in *Il Rosario con papa Giovanni,* cit., pp. 119–131, from which we cited.

43. Ibid., p. 131.

44. Ibid., p. 129.

45. Ibid., pp. 129–130.

46. Diary 1920, 3 December.

47. Guglielmo van Rossum (1954–1932), prefect of Propaganda Fide 1918–1932. From 1913, he was also Cardinal Protector of the Daughters of the Sacred Heart of Bergamo. On him, see J. Metzler, *Präfekten un Sekretäre der Kongregation in der Neuesten Missionsära 1918–1972,* in *S. C. de Propaganada Fide Memoria Rerum, III–2,* (Roma-Friburg-Wien 1972), pp. 303–314.

48. Diary 1920, *ad diem.*

49. AR, IV 47, letter to P. Giobbe, 21 December 1920; now in L. Algisi, *Papa Giovanni,* cit., p. 419.

50. AR, IV 45, letter to L. Marelli, 14 December 1920.

51. Letter from A. Ferrari, 17 December 1920; now in L. Algisi, *Papa Giovanni,* cit., p. 416.

52. Diary 1920, 19 December.

53. Letter to P. Giobbe, 21 December 1920, cit.

54. Paolo Giobbe (1880–1972), Roncalli's roommate, ordained in 1904; rector of the Collegio di Propaganda Fide; titular archbishop and Apostolic Nuncio in Colombia from 1925–1936, then in Holland from 1936–1958; created cardinal by John XXIII in 1958.

55. AR, letter to A. Guerinoni, 20 December 1920.

56. Letter to P. Giobbe, 21 December 1920, cit.

57. *I Preti del Sacro Cuore,* cit., pp. 97–99.

58. *VD* 11 (1919), pp. 91, 116, 139, 151.

59. Diary 1919, 23 November.

60. *"La vita missionaria, Giornaletto mensile, organo dell'unione missionaria del clero di Bergamo,"* (Missionary life, monthly journal of the missionary union of the clergy of Bergamo), ed. Priests of the Sacred Heart in Bergamo, 1921.

61. *VD* 12 (1920), pp. 77, 181.

62. *"La vita missionaria,"* I (July, 1921).

63. SD, vol. III, pp. 39–55; 17 February 1957, *Commemorazione del Servo di Dio Guido Maria Conforti nel XXV della morte.*

64. Diary 1921, 9 January.

65. Ibid., 14 January.

66. Letter to D. Spolverini, 21 January 1921; now in FdO, cit., p. 205; Acts 20:22 and Ps 27:1.

67. AR, V 5, letter to G. van Rossum, 14 January 1921; Acts 11:24.

68. Diary 1921, 19–31 March.

69. Letter to D. Spolverini, 26 June 1921; now in FdO, p. 209.

70. *VD* 13 (1921), p. 70.

71. *Archivio capitolare,* minutes of 10 March 1921; the text is repeated in AR; letter from L. M. Marelli dated 15 March 1921.

72. AR, V 13, letter to L. M. Marelli, 16 March 1921.

73. AR, letter, 5 June 1921.

74. *"Vita missionaria,"* cit.

75. *Eco,* 6 June 1921.

76. *Archivio capitolare,* letter to G. B. Floridi, 17 March 1921.

77. Diary 1920, 3 December; Rom 14:8.

78. AR, IV 45, letter to L. M. Marelli, 14 December 1920; now in *Natale 1970,* p.12 and in L. Algisi, *op. cit.,* p. 414.

79. GdA, pp. 577–578 (969).

80. GdA, p. 334 (563).

81. Diary 1917, 30 January; Phil 1:18.

82. Letter to G. Moioli, cit.

83. Letter to D. Spolverini, 29 December 1919; now in FdO, pp. 182–183.

PART II

IN THE SERVICE OF THE HOLY SEE
1921–1953

CHAPTER 9

At the Office for the Propagation of the Faith
1921–1925

1. From a discourse commemorating Msgr. Ramazzotti, 3 March 1958; it was actually seventeen years after his ordination.

2. To D. Spolverini, 14 January 1921.

3. Diary, 11 May and letter to his parents and brothers, 3 May 1921.

4. From the commemoration on 17 February 1957; now in S. Beltrami, 116.

5. To C. Bortolotti, 23 January 1921.

6. Paolo Manna to Tragella, 20 April 1921.

7. Costantino Aiuti to Roncalli, 23 February 1921.

8. To G. van Rossum, 30 January 1921.

9. To G. Testa, 9 January 1922.

10. Report to G. van Rossum, 14 February 1922; to G. Testa, 21 April 1922.

11. To his family, 10 January 1922; Lk 2:32.

12. FFSA, notebook, VI, 3-B, p. 246: *"Pontificale Msgr. Roncalli, Easter of 1925, Bergamo."*

13. A. Kozaroff, 12 April 1925, to D. Theelen.

14. AAS, 8 June 1922, p. 406.

15. To G. Testa, 21 April 1922.

16. S. Beltrami, 416.

17. Discourse, September 1957, in S. Beltrami, 104 f.

18. To P. Merati, 30 June 1922.

19. To V. Teani, 10 August 1922.

20. Discourse, 13 September 1957, cit.
21. To V. Bugarini, 9 August 1922.
22. Ibid.
23. To V. Bugarini, 24 August 1922.
24. To V. Bugarini, 7 November 1922.
25. To his family, 25 May 1923.
26. To V. Bugarini, 22 May 1923.
27. To V. Bugarini, 29 May 1923.
28. To V. Bugarini, 11 November 1923.
29. To G. Testa, 30 December 1923.
30. To G. Testa, 25 March 1924.
31. Diary, 11 January 1924.
32. To Marchetti Selvaggiani, 25 December 1924.
33. Diary, 8 February 1924.
34. Diary, 10 August 1924.
35. GdA, p. 381 (629).
36. To B. Pompili, 25 November 1924; to G. Serafini, 29 November 1924.
37. AAS L (1958), p. 1009; now in Galluzzi, 114 f.
38. Diary, 24 December 1924.
39. Circular, 6 January 1925.
40. L. Drago to Roncalli, 17 January 1925; Conforti, 632 f.
41. To E. Piatti, 8 March 1925.
42. Diary, 17 February 1925.
43. To G. Birolini, 2 March 1925.
44. Galluzzi, 115.
45. S. Beltrami, 429.
46. GdA, p. 379 (624).
47. Ibid.

Chapter 10

Apostolic Visitor and Delegate in Bulgaria

1925–1934

1. GdA, p. 385 (632).
2. To G. van Rossum, 23 February 1925.
3. Diary, 17 February 1925.
4. To G. Birolini, 2 March 1925.
5. To his family, 19 February 1925.
6. GdA, p. 387 (637).
7. Ibid.
8. To G. Birolini, cit.
9. To G. van Rossum, cit.
10. GdA, p. 388 (638).

11. GdA, p. 412 (689).
12. Diary, 19 March 1928.
13. To V. Cavadini, 30 December 1927.
14. FFSA, notebook, n. 13 f., 246.
15. To his sisters, 25 April 1925.
16. To his parents, after 25 April 1925.
17. Report, 19 May 1925.
18. To G. Testa, 29 April 1925.
19. To G. Tacci, 4 May 1925.
20. To G. Tacci, 19 May 1925.
21. To G. Testa, 29 May 1925.
22. To G. Tacci, 8 June 1925.
23. To L. Sincero, 18 August 1927.
24. Ibid.
25. To G. Tacci, 8 June 1925.
26. To his sisters, 29 May 1925.
27. To G. Tacci, cit.
28. Ibid.
29. To P. Giobbe, 4 July 1925.
30. Report to G. Tacci, October–November 1925.
31. To G. Testa, 2 July 1925.
32. Ibid, 29 August 1925.
33. To G. Testa, 19 November 1925.
34. To I. Papadopoulos, 1 September 1925.
35. To S. C. Kertev, 1 November 1925.
36. To B. Pompili, 20 October 1925.
37. To P. Giobbe, 6 November 1925.
38. To G. Testa, 13 November 1925.
39. Ibid, 5 December 1925.
40. To D. Theelen, 8 December 1925.
41. To Maria, 20 December 1925.
42. To G. Birolini, 25 December 1925.
43. To G. Testa, 15 March 1926.
44. To P. Giobbe, 29 March 1926.
45. Istina, 10 February 1926.
46. To G. Birolini, 20 June 1927.
47. Report, 7 March 1926.
48. Report, 9 March 1926.
49. Report, 10 March 1926.
50. Ibid.
51. To D. Spolverini, 3 August 1926.
52. To G. Testa, 27 February 1926.
53. To G. Dieci, 20 June 1926.
54. To S. R., 22 August 1926.
55. Marcocchi, 29 f.
56. GdA, p. 392 (641).
57. To G. Dieci, 16 March 1926.

58. To G. Crippa, 31 July 1926.
59. To L. Drago, 6 January 1926.
60. To his family, 13 April 1927.
61. To Sister Eugenie, 15 August 1926.
62. To P. Giobbe, 19 August 1926.
63. To G. Testa, 31 May 1926.
64. To D. Spolverini, 3 January 1927.
65. To G. Testa, 31 January 1927.
66. To L. Sincero, 2 March 1927.
67. To F. Paris, 2 May 1927.
68. To Sister Maria, 21 February 1927.
69. To G. Birolini, 19 February 1927.
70. Ibid, 21 March 1927.
71. To L. Sincero, 28 April 1927.
72. To L. Sincero, 21 July 1927.
73. To the Plenary Council, 23 December 1927.
74. To E. Viganò, 11 May 1927.
75. To L. Sincero, 21 July 1927.
76. To M. D'Herbigny, 20 July 1927.
77. To L. Sincero, 29 June 1927.
78. Ibid, s.d.
79. Ibid, 11 August 1927.
80. Report, 19 October 1927.
81. To L. Sincero, 18 August 1927.
82. To G. B. Floridi, 24 January 1928.
83. To L. Sincero, 18 August 1927.
84. To G. Carminati, 10 August 1927.
85. To Sister Cecilia, 21 June 1927.
86. Ibid.
87. To L. Bugada, 11 December 1927.
88. To Sister Maddalena, 9 July 1927.
89. To P. Carrara, after 11 February 1929.
90. To P. Forno, 18 February 1929.
91. To G. Clandestini, 23 November 1927.
92. To L. Papadopulos, 29 December 1927.
93. To L. Sincero, 16 June 1929.
94. G. M. Radini Tedeschi, 15 December 1929.
95. P. Forno, 18 December 1929.
96. G. Rotta, 25 January 1930.
97. L. Sincero, 20 January 1930.
98. GdA, p. 409 (684).
99. L. Sincero, 1 February 1930.
100. L. Sincero, 12 February 1930.
101. Don Pietro (?), 28 February 1930.
102. Marelli, 15 April 1930.
103. Testa, 2 February 1930.
104. G. Rotta, 22 February 1930.

105. GdA, pp. 410–413 (686–691).

106. Ibid, 692, p. 413.

107. G. M. Radini Tedeschi, 31 May 1930.

108. G. Birolini, 24 June 1930.

109. L. Sincero, 27 May 1930.

110. Mother, 28 January 1931.

111. Interview, 5 October 1931.

112. L. Sincero, 28 February 1931.

113. D. Theelen, 27 December 1930.

114. GdA, p. 412 (690).

115. Mother, 28 January 1931.

116. D. Theelen, 20 March 1931.

117. Viganò, 5 February 1931.

118. Diary, 25 November 1930.

119. Sister Metodia, 20 April 1931.

120. C. Perico, January 15, 1931.

121. L. Sincero, 14 November 1931.

122. Cattaneo, 22 November 1931.

123. Diary, 25 November 1931.

124. L. Sincero, 23 April 1932.

125. L. Sincero, 6 February 1932.

126. L. Sincero, 28 April 1932.

127. L. Drago, 11 January 1933.

128. Nasalli Rocca, 17 March 1932.

129. G. Birolini, 21 May 1932.

130. Ibid.

131. G. Testa, 3 March 1932.

132. S. C. Kertev, July 1932.

133. Mother Maria, 2 July 1932.

134. N. Fressati, 2 April 1933.

135. Rosella, 17 January 1933.

136. L. Drago, 11 January 1933.

137. F. Brignoli, 29 January 1933.

138. E. Pacelli, 9 February 1933.

139. E. Pacelli, 10 May 1935.

140. M. Di Trinità, 14 February 1933.

141. N. Flessati, 2 April 1933.

142. Ibid.

143. Msgr. L. F. Capovilla, who inherited the cross from John XXIII, gives his written testimony. He in turn gave the cross to the convent at Assisi where, after her death at the beginning of the year 2000, Queen Giovanna was buried.

144. Cited in the letter from Msgr. L. F. Capovilla to Giulio Berrettoni, guardian of the Holy Convent of Assisi on 1 March 2000. The Queen kept her promise by paying a visit to Pope John on 8 November 1958, twenty days after his election.

145. Reported in F. Della Salda, *op. cit.,* p. 259.

146. F. Della Salda, *op. cit.,* p. 140.

147. Letter to Christo Morcefki on 27 July 1926.

148. In F. Della Salda, *op. cit.,* p. 261.

CHAPTER 11

Apostolic Delegate to Turkey and Greece
1934–1944

1. P. Hebblethwaite, *Giovanni XXIII: Il papa del Concilio* (John XXIII: pope of the Council), Italian edition ed. Marco Roncalli (Milan, 1989), p. 199.

2. Letter to G. Testa on 27 October 1934.

3. Letter to G. Testa on 6 November 1934.

4. In the audience, Roncalli carefully avoided the topic of the transfer to Istanbul, a detail that impressed the Pope.

5. Letter to G. Testa, 17 November 1934.

6. Letter to G. Testa 25 November 1934.

7. Ibid.

8. Ibid.

9. A. Melloni, *Fra Istanbul, Atene e la guerra. La missione di A. G. Roncalli 1935–1944,* (Between Istanbul and Athens and the war. The mission of A. G. Roncalli 1935–1944) (Genoa, 1992), p. 147.

10. A. Melloni, *op. cit.,* p. 149.

11. P. Hebblethwaite, *op. cit.,* p. 212.

12. Ibid.

13. R. Morozzo della Rocca, *Roncalli diplomatico in Turchia e Grecia 1935–1944,* (Roncalli, diplomat in Turkey and Greece 1935–1944), in *"Cristianesimo nella storia,"* 8 (1987), pp. 33–72.

14. L. Algisi, *Giovanni XXIII* (Turin, 1961), p. 124.

15. R. Morozzo della Rocca, *op. cit.,* p. 44.

16. R. Morozzo della Rocca, *op. cit.,* p. 45.

17. GdA, pp. 436 ff. (727).

18. G. Busetti, ed. *Ottima e reverenda madre. Lettere di papa Giovanni alle suore* (Bologna, 1990), p. 84.

19. F. Della Salda, *Obbedienca e pace. Il vescovo A. G. Roncalli tra Sofia e Roma 1925–1934,* (Obedience and peace. Bishop A. G. Roncalli in Sofia and Rome 1925–1934) (Genoa, 1989), pp. 128 ff.

20. R. Morozzo della Rocca, *op. cit.,* p. 70.

21. Ibid.

22. Lf, I, p. 408.

23. *Positio,* p. 875.

24. *Positio,* p. 575 ff.

25. *Positio,* p. 1020.

26. V. U. Righi, *Papa Giovanni sulle rive del Bosforo,* (Pope John on the shores of the Bosporus) who sites ADSS, V, pp. 211 ff. (Padua, 1971), p. 209.

27. *Positio,* pp. 574 ff.

28. Lf, I, p. 479.

29. G. Busetti, *op. cit.,* p. 223.

30. ADSS, IV, pp. 105 ff.

31. P. Blet, *Pio XII e la seconda guerra mondiale negli archivi vaticani,* (Pius XII and the second world war from the vatican archives) (Milan: Cinisello Balsamo, 1999), p. 176.

32. A. Melloni, *op. cit.,* p. 257.

33. *Positio,* p. 1259.

34. L. F. Capovilla, *Giovanni XXIII nel ricordo del segretario Loris F. Capovilla,* (John XXIII in the memories of his secretary Loris F. Capovilla), interview by Marco Roncalli with unpublished documents (Milan: Cinisello Balsamo, 1994), p. 38 f.

35. P. Hebblethwaite, *op. cit.,* p. 277.

36. P. Hebblethwaite, *op. cit.,* p. 271.

37. Lf, I, p. 581.

38. Lf, I. pp. 571 f.

39. Lf, I, p. 590.

40. Lf, I, p. 608.

41. Lf, I, p. 596.

42. G. Busetti, *op. cit.,* 257.

43. P. Hebblethwaite, *op. cit.,* p. 265, who cites ADSS.

44. ADSS, IX, p. 306.

45. ADSS, IX, p. 371.

46. For both citations, cf. *Positio,* pp. 1407 ff.

47. ADSS, 10, p. 161.

48. Ibid., p. 189.

49. Ibid., p. 391.

50. V. U. Righi, *op. cit.,* p. 197.

51. R. Ristelhueber, *Storia dei paesi balcanici* (Florence, 1959), p. 585.

52. The citations are taken from *Positio,* pp. 1222 ff.

53. Lf, I, p. 568.

54. L. Algisi, *op. cit.,* 190.

55. The citations relative to the spiritual exercises are taken from GdA, pp. 444–481 (735–809).

CHAPTER 12

Apostolic Nuncio in Paris

1945–1953

1. Cf. *Actes et documents du Saint-Siège relatifs à la Seconde Guerre Mondiale* (Vatican City, 1981), vol. 11, pp. 633, 637, 639.

2. Angelina and Giuseppe Alberigo, *Giovanni XXIII: Profezia nella fedeltà* (Brescia, 1978), p. 18.

3. Diary, 6 December 1944; the quotations are largely unedited.

4. Cf. Lf, vol. 1, pp. 654–655.

5. Cf. GdA, p. 484 (812).

6. Cf. Charles de Gaulle, *Mémoires de Guerre,* vol. 2 (Paris: Plon, 1954), pp. 233–234.

7. Cf. André Latreille, *De Gaulle: la Libération et l'Eglise catholique* (Paris, 1978).

8. Cf. Etienne Fouilloux, *Straordinario ambasciatore? Parigi 1944–1953,* in *Papa Giovanni,* ed. G. Alberigo (Rome-Bari, 1987).

9. Jean Vinatier, *I rapporti del nunzio Roncalli con il card. Sahard* (The relation of the Nuncio Roncalli with Cardinal Suhard), in *Giovanni XXIII, transizione del Papato e della Chiesa* (John XXIII, transition of the papacy and of the Church), ed. G. Alberigo (Rome, 1988), p. 54.

10. Archive of Quai d'Orsay, Europe/Holy See 1949–1955, II, 14 December 1944; the confirmation of Mr. d'Ormesson (always through Tardini) in *"La nouvelle revue des deux mondes"* (New review of two worlds), July 1973, pp. 126–127, quoted by E. Fouilloux, p. 92.

11. Cf. Robert Roquette, *Le mistère Roncalli* (The mystery of Roncalli), in *La fin d'une Chrètientè* (The end of a Christianity) (Paris), pp. 307–322; Giovanni Alberigo, *Giovanni XXIII*, cit., p. 18.

12. Archive of Quai d'Orsay, Europe/Holy See 1944–1949, 2, with the notes of 2 and 26 January 1946, Louis Canet; quoted by E. Fouilloux, p. 76.

13. Archive of Quai d'Orsay: Europe/Holy See 1944–1949, II, note of 12 December 1944. Quoted by E. Fouilloux, p. 93. Less enthusiastic was the comment of the government according to J. Chauvel, *Commentaire: D'Alger à Berne* (1944–1952) (Paris, 1972), p. 17.

14. Giuseppe Alberigo, *Jean XXIII, devant l'histoire* (Paris, 1989), p. 36; cf. also Jean Neuvecelle, *Giovanni XXIII, una vita* (Milan, 1970), p. 17.

15. Letter to Giacomo Testa, dated 7 February 1945, published by L. F. Capovilla in his commemorative booklet: *Nono anniversario della morte* (Rome, 1974).

16. Lf, ed. G. Farnedi, Casale Monferrato, 1993, p. 305.

17. L. F. Capovilla, *Papa Giovanni: Gran sacerdote come lo ricordo* (Rome, 1972), p. 170.

18. Diary, 23 December 1944.

19. Diary, 24 December 1944.

20. Diary, 28 December 1944.

21. Diary, 29 December 1944.

22. Diary, 29 December 1944.

23. Diary, 30 December 1944.

24. Cf. A. G. Roncalli, SdN, p. 4; in the letter Montini stated he was sure "that you will feel a great satisfaction, just knowing the reputation of the good qualities of the new representative of the Holy See in France, who already distinguished himself in his previous functions in Turkey and in Greece, as well as in the ministry of souls."

25. Diary, 31 December 1944.

26. A. G. Roncalli, SdN, cit. p. 5–6; biographies of John XXIII have stated that the neo-nuncio borrowed the text of the speech from Russian Ambassador Bogomilov.

27. GianCarlo Zizola, in his book, *Giovanni XXIII: La politica e la fede* (John XXIII: politics and faith) adds Molotov's name to the list. However, in his diary, on 30 April 1946, Roncalli wrote: "I saw Molotov, but I had no contacts with him."

28. Diary, 5 January 1945.

29. Cf. P. Hebblethwaite, *Giovanni XXIII: Il papa del Concilio* (John XXIII: pope of the Council), Italian edition ed. by Marco Roncalli (Milan, 1989).

30. Cf. SdN, cit., p. 53.

31. The letter to Fortunato Benzoni, dated 27 January 1945, and the one to G. B. Montini, dated 30 January 1945, in the Capovilla archives.

32. Cf. SdN, cit., p. 53.

33. Cf. Lf.

34. Cf. the letter dated 24 March 1945 in *Shuster-Roncalli: Nel nome della santità. Lettere,* ed. Elio Guerriero and Marco Roncalli (Milan: Cinisello Balsamo, 1996).

35. Cf. GdA, pp. 813–816.

36. André Latreille, *De Gaulle, la libération et l'Eglise catholique,* cit. See also: Herbert Lottman, *L'Epuration* 1943–1945 (Paris, 1986), pp. 343–346.

37. Ibid., p. 60. Passage quoted from P. Hebblethwaite, *Giovanni XXIII. Il Papa del Concilio,* cit., translation by Marco Roncalli.

38. Congregation for the Causes of Saints, *Positio super vita, virtutibus et fama sanctitatis,* vol. 2a (Rome, 1997), p. 791.

39. The memorial was published in February 1992 in the *Revue des deux mondes* thanks to Jean-Luc Barré; see also *Ambassadeur de France au Vatican,* L. Gothelf and Jacques Maritain (Paris, 1984).

40. The passages are quoted from the Diary, under the respective dates.

41. Archive of the Quai d'Orsay, Europe/Holy See 1944–1949, II, 29 November 1945; quoted by E. Fouilloux, p. 77.

42. Diary, 24 December 1945. Other opinions regarding Saliège's promotion are found in other entries of the diary that same year. On 31 July 1945, while in Toulouse, the Nuncio wrote: "Great compliments and continuous allusions by Bertaux to the red hat for Msgr. Saliège. Everyone considers only a part of the reality that is under their eyes, and they are not concerned about the whole reality." On 3 August 1945: "Toulouse...I leave with Giulio for a visit to Commissary Berteaux where again I find new allusions to the hat for Saliège, and hard and vindictive reports on the Italians held in concentration camps."

43. L. F. Capovilla, *XV Anniversario della morte di papa Giovanni* (Rome, 1978), p. 89.

44. Archive of the Quai d'Orsay, Europe/Holy See 1944–1949. Quoted by E. Fouilloux, p. 78.

45. Ibid., dispatch by Maritain dated 1 March 1947; quoted by E. Fouilloux, p. 79.

46. Cf. E. Fouilloux, cit., p. 79.

47. Diary, 17 September 1945.

48. Cf. SdN cit., p. 144. Notations on this topic can be found in the diary. For example, on 20 February 1952, Roncalli writes: "The Holy Father always worries about finding good bishops. In fact, as a fruit of patience they are always better and better. These last two, for example, Bayeux and S. Flour, are excellent. A credit to me? The Lord knows the simplicity of his servant."

49. Cf. GdA, p. 824.

50. Cf. G. C. Zizola, *L'utopia di papa Giovanni* (Assisi, 1974), p. 126; see also Luis Marín de San Martín, *Juan XXIII, Retrato eclesiológico* (Barcelona, 1998), pp. 128–132.

51. Cf. the letter dated 15 April 1945 to Angelo Pedrinelli, in L. F. Capovilla, *Papa Giovanni: Gran Sacerdote come lo ricordo* (Rome, 1972), p. 169.

52. Cf. E. Fouilloux, cit., p. 74, who quotes from a letter in the Quai d'Orsay, written by François Mejan, director of the office for religious affairs and associations, dated 16 August 1949. It reads: "These trips are becoming more and more frequent both for private and religious reasons. The papal Nuncio, contrary to the practice of his predecessors since 1921, seems willing to lead all the important religious ceremonies celebrated in our country."

53. Cf. Michel De Kerdreux, *Jean XXIII* (Paris, 1966), p. 158.

54. Diary, 27 September 1946.

55. Cf. Marco Roncalli, *Giovanni XXIII nel ricordo del segretario L. F. Capovilla* (Milan: Cinisello Balsamo, 1996), p. 206.

56. Diary, 17 January 1947.

57. *Positio* 2a, cit., p. 161.

58. In his years in Paris these were: A. Pacini and C. Rocco (1945); A. Pacini and E. Vagnozzi (1946); E. Vagnozzi and S. Oddi (1947); S. Oddi, R. Forni, and B. Heim (1948–1949); R. Forni, B. Heim, and E. Righi-Lambertini (1950); G. Testa, E. Righi, and B. Heim (1951); G. Testa, E. Righi-Lambertini, and B. Ladisladz (1952), who were joined by A. Pedroni in 1953.

59. Cf. GdA, pp. 817–825.

60. Cf. Michel De Kerdreux, *Jean XXIII,* cit., p. 164.

61. Lf, 6 April 1947.

62. Quotations are from the Diary, 20 April and 13 July 1945, respectively.

63. Diary, 21 January 1948.

64. Denise Aimé Azam, *L'extraordinaire ambassadeur* (Paris, 1967).

65. Cf. the article by Francesco Margiotta Broglio, *De Gaulle fra Pacelli e Roncalli,* in *"La nuova antologia,"* 1978, pp. 267–268.

66. Diary, 3 November 1946.

67. Diary, 19 November 1948; 27 April 1951.

68. Cf. SdN cit., p. 42.

69. Diary, 30 December 1945; the previous quotations are also from the diary.

70. Diary, 4 September 1951.

71. Diary, 6 September 1951.

72. Letter to Msgr. Bernareggi, 6 September 1951; LV (1931–1961) (Bergamo, 1973); (A definitive edition by A. Pesenti is in preparation).

73. Diary, 21 September 1951.

74. Denise Aimé-Azam, *L'extraordinaire ambassadeur,* cit., p. 137.

75. Cf. Emile Poulat, *Rome et les prêtes-ouvriers, in Une eglise émbranlée* (Tournai, 1980), pp. 119–148; see also *Naissance des prêtes-ouvriers* (Paris, 1965).

76. Denise Aimé-Azam, *L'extraordinaire ambassadeur,* cit., p. 137.

77. Diary, 11 April 1946.

78. Jean Vinatier, *Les prêtres ouvriers, le cardinal Liénart et Rome* (Paris, 1985), pp. 72–73.

79. Cf. Marco Roncalli in his recent volume: *Giovanni XXIII: La mia Venezia,* with introduction by M. Cè and foreword by L. F. Capovilla (Venice, 2000), p. 53. It should be noted that Cardinal Pizzardo's letter to the Cardinal of Paris, Feltin, in 1959—which seemed to put an end to the question—was approved by Pope John, who wrote to Feltin to accept the decision with docility. Cf. *Lettere,* pp. 1169–171.

80. In the diary entry of 14 July 1949, when the decree was published, Roncalli wrote:

> I read in the newspapers about the decree excommunicating those Catholics who profess communism. By a coincidence, soon afterward I met the Russian ambassador Bogomilov, who perhaps was not yet aware of it. I attended the July 14 parade for the great national holiday with him. At 11:45, I again saw President Auriol, who also was not aware of the news. Once I told him, he expressed his greatest satisfaction. Now one must be ready for the unexpected. *"Dominus illuminatio mea et salus mea, quem timebo?"* (The Lord is my light and my salvation; whom should I fear? Ps 27:1.)

81. Cf. Maurilio Guasco, *La predicazione di Roncalli* (The preaching of Roncalli), in *Papa Giovanni,* ed. G. Alberigo, cit., p. 129.

82. Cf. J. Vinatier, *I rapporti del nunzio Roncalli,* cit., p. 66. In a letter of thanksgiving to Msgr. Brot, Cardinal Suhard's personal secretary, who, fulfilling Roncalli's desire for a memento of the late cardinal, sent him a beautiful surplice. The nuncio wrote:

Almost five years of spiritual contact between us sealed a bond of fraternity which was not spoiled by even the slightest shadow. I understood him completely, and he understood me. To honor this gift, I wanted to wear it for the ordination of forty-nine priests, which—after an invitation from the head vicar, S. E. Msgr. Beaussart—I had the great honor and the unforgettable joy to celebrate in Notre-Dame for the solemnity of Saints Peter and Paul, on June 29. This seemed to me the best way to express the symbol of the rituals. The humble Elisha took the place and, temporarily, the role of Elijah. He wore the same pallium, becoming the one to transmit the same spirit to those vigorous blossoms, grown and matured during eight years of his holy and glorious episcopate, which prepared them for the episcopate and their battles of the future.

83. Diary, 20 December 1950.

84. Cf. GdA, pp. 828 and 830.

85. Cf. GdA, pp. 848–849.

86. The passage, dated 24 March 1952, is in *Giovanni XXIII, Scritti spirituali,* ed. Marco Roncalli (Milan: Cinisello Balsamo, 2000).

87. The note of 15 November 1951 is quoted in E. Fouilloux. See also the informative note of Ambassador D'Ormesson in the Archive of the Quai d'Orsay 1949–1955; 5 and 8 March 1954.

His Excellency might be a little surprised to know that, in this group of papabili, there is the serious possibility of including His Eminence Cardinal Roncalli.... I will only say that his affability, and that uncomparable mixture of qualities, which made him successful with certain personalities and environments in Paris, near and far from the Church can be the same virtues, which could obtain the votes of the Sacred College. He would be good for the integralists, and reassuring for the undecided or the conciliatory; he can represent the "middle of the road" and from various sources, I am told that his "star" is rising.

88. Cf. *Souvenir d'un nonce,* cit., p. 94.

89. Cf. Lf, cit., pp. 216–217.

90. *Giovanni e Paolo: due papi. Saggio di corrispondenza: 1925–1962,* ed. L. F. Capovilla (Brescia, 1982). The substitute secretary of state wrote:

Most Reverend Excellency: Surely you do not know the sorrowful news, kept rather private, about the serious health condition of the Most Excellent Msgr. Carlo Agostini, Patriarch of Venice. Even though it is not possible to foresee the course of his illness, we have reason to believe it will not be very long.... Since such an important See should not remain vacant for long, especially in these times, His Holiness, in this morning's audience, gave me the honorable task of asking your Most Reverend Excellency, under strict secrecy, if you are available for that patriarchal See, in the sorrowful event of His Excellency Msgr. Agostini's death. I am waiting for a first response from you, and I pray that God will assist you with his light. I add my own personal impression that this proposal should be for Your Excellency a new, great proof of the benevolence of the Holy Father and the trust he has in you....

Also cf. L. F. Capovilla, *Christmas 1975–New Year 1976* (Rome, 1975), p. 45. On 13 October 1962, John XXIII recalled this episode in a conversation with the delegates from Christian Churches and communities separated from Rome:

In 1952, Pope Pius XII, in a sudden and surprising act, asked me to become patriarch of Venice. I told him that I did not need any time to think about accepting it. In fact, in the proposal, I did not consider my will, for I had no desire to be sent to one place or another, for one ministry or office rather than another. My episcopal motto was enough for my reply: *Oboedientia et pax....*

91. Ibid., p. 57.

92. On this topic, see the paragraph "The reason for the nomination" in Marco Roncalli, *Giovanni XXIII: La mia Venezia,* cit., pp. 39–41.

93. The three letters, to P. Gerlier, J. G. Saliège, and A. Liénart, published in *Pasqua di Risurrezione* 1969, ed. L. F. Capovilla (Rome, 1969), pp. 52–53.

94. Cf. SdN cit., p. 43.

95. Cf. P. Hebblethwaite, *Giovanni XXIII. Il papa del Concilio,* cit., who quotes SdN cit., p. 45.

96. Cf. *Ottima e reverenda madre: lettere alle suore,* ed. G. Busetti (Bologna, 1989), p. 377.

97. Cf. *De Gasperi scrive. Lettere di De Gasperi o scritte a lui,* ed. M. Romana De Gasperi (Brescia, 1974). In the first week of August De Gasperi, unaware of his serious health condition, received his last letter from Patriarch Roncalli, with an invitation to Venice. The text ends as follows: "Are we not all working for the same shining ideal of the social good and peace?" Cf. also the words of the patriarch on the death of the president, on 19 August 1954, in *XIII Anniversario,* L. F. Capovilla (Rome, 1976), pp. 76–77.

98. Diary, 23 February 1953.

PART III

PASTORAL MINISTRY
1953–1963

CHAPTER 13

Patriarch of Venice
1953–1958

1. G. Alberigo, *Stili di governo episcopale: Angelo Giuseppe Roncalli,* in *I cattolici nel mondo contemporaneo 1922–1958* (Catholics in the modern world) (Milan: Cinisello Balsamo, 1991), p. 237.

2. LV 1931–1961 (Bergamo, 1973), p. 153.

3. G. Alberigo, *Stili di governo,* p. 237, n. 2.

4. GdA, pp. 513–514 (854).

5. *Giovanni e Paolo,* pp. 57–58.

6. SD, p. 19.

7. GdA, pp. 513–516 (853–859).

8. L. F. Capovilla, *L'ite missa est di papa Giovanni* (The "ite missa est" of Pope John) (Bergamo, 1983), pp. 94–95.

9. SD, I, pp. 23–24.

10. Ibid., pp. 25–26.

11. Ibid., pp. 20–21.

12. Ibid., pp. 51–59. S. Tramontin, *Venezianità del cardinale Roncalli* (The Venetian aspect of Cardinal Roncalli), in *Cultura e spiritualità in Bergamo al tempo di papa Giovanni XXIII* (Culture and spirituality in Bergamo in the time of Pope John XXIII) (Bergamo, 1983), pp. 356–359.

13. G. Alberigo, *Stili di governo* (Rome, 1978), p. 80.

14. SD, IV, pp. 138–139.

15. L. F. Capovilla, *Pasqua di resurrezione* (Rome, 1978), p. 80.

16. GdA, p. 515 (858).

17. Ibid., p. 515 (857).

18. G. De Rosa, *Angelo Roncalli e Giuseppe De Luca,* in *Angelo G. Roncalli: Dal Patriarcato di Venezia alla cattedra di San Pietro* (The Patriarchate of Venice and the chair of St. Peter) (Florence, 1984), pp. 93–96.

19. G. Battelli, *G. M. Radini Tedeschi e Angelo Roncalli 1905–1914,* in *Papa Giovanni,* ed. G. Alberigo (Bari, 1987), pp. 50–54.

20. GdA, pp. 514–515 (854–855, 858).

21. SD, II, pp. 30, 32–33.

22. GdA, pp. 533–534 (889).

23. *Lettere,* pp. 142–145.

24. G. Zizola, *Il microfono di Dio* (The microphone of God) (Milan, 1990), pp. 410–416.

25. SD, I, pp. 156–157.

26. Ibid., p. 179.

27. SD, III, p. 264.

28. Ibid., pp. 317–326.

29. Ibid., p. 344.

30. S. Tramontin, *Il cardinal Roncalli patriarca di Venezia* (Cardinal Roncalli, Patriarch of Venice) in *Le Chiese di Pio XII* (The Church of Pius XII), ed. A. Riccardi (Bari, 1986), pp. 240–241; 246.

31. SD, II, pp. 28–40.

32. G. De Rosa, *L'esperienza di A. Roncalli* (The experience of A. Roncalli), in *Papa Giovanni,* pp. 100–103.

33. SD, II, p. 341.

34. Ibid., p. 337.

35. S. Tramontin, *Il cardinal Roncalli,* pp. 231–232.

36. SD, III, pp. 81–104.

37. A. Niero, *Il cardinal Roncalli e l'arte sacra* (Cardinal Roncalli and sacred art), in *Cultura e spiritualità in Bergamo,* pp. 383–413.

38. A. Niero, *Un fermo dialogo con il mondo dell'arte contemporaneo* in *L'Osservatore Romano,* 2 August 1995.

39. A. Niero, *Il cardinal Roncalli,* pp. 377–380.

40. SD, II, pp. 185–187; 471–474.

41. SD, I, p. 167.

42. Letter to Msgr. Bortignon, 10 November 1955, in the Capovilla archives.

43. SD, II, p. 265.

44. G. De Rosa, *L'esperienza di Roncalli a Venezia,* p.105.

45. G. Zizola, *L'utopia di papa Giovanni,* pp. 291–295.

46. Letter to Cardinal Pizzardo, 25 May 1956, in the Capovilla archives.

47. SD, II, pp. 420–421.

48. Letter to Cardinal Ottaviani, 26 July 1956, in the Capovilla archives.

49. S. Tramontin, *Il primo esperimento di apertura a sinistra; la formula di Venezia* (The first experiment in opening to the left; the formula of Venice) in *Storia della democrazia Cristiana* (History of the Christian democrats), ed. F. Malgeri (Rome, 1988), pp. 371–396.

50. SD, II, p. 448.

51. G. Zizola, *Giovanni XXIII. La fede e la politica* (Faith and politics), pp. 79–81.

52. SD, II, pp. 456–457.

53. Ibid., p. 460.

54. Ibid., p. 461.

55. S. Tramontin, *Il cardinal Roncalli,* p. 237.

56. Original manuscript in the Capovilla archives.

57. Diary, 26 February 1957.

58. G. Zizola, *L'utopia di papa Giovanni,* p. 304.

59. Ibid., p. 305.

60. SD, III, p. 58.

61. Ibid., pp. 78–80.

62. L. F. Capovilla, *Giovanni XXIII. Quindici letture* (John XXIII: Fifteen lectures), pp. 642–746.

63. SD, II, pp. 422–432.

64. Letter to Msgr. Dell'Acqua, 6 December 1957, in the Capovilla archives.

65. G. De Rosa, *Angelo Roncalli e Giuseppe De Luca,* pp. 83–86.

66. SD, IV, p. 604.

CHAPTER 14

Pope John XXIII: The First One Hundred Days

1. B. Lay, *Vaticano aperto* (The open Vatican) (Milan, 1968), pp. 13–14.

2. L. F. Capovilla, *Vent'anni dalla elezione di Giovanni XXIII* (Twenty years since the election of John XXIII) (Rome, 1978), pp. 38–42.

3. Ibid., pp. 48–49.

4. P. Hebblethwaite, *op. cit.,* pp. 398–402; G. Zizola, *Giovanni XXIII. La fede e la politica* (Rome, 1988), pp. 94–98; A. Riccardi, *Il potere del papa. Da Pio XII a Giovanni Paolo II* (The power of the pope. From Pius XII to John Paul II) (Rome, 1993), pp. 154–159.

5. L. F. Capovilla, *Vent'anni dalla elezione,* p. 25.

6. L. Algisi, *Giovanni XXIII*, Casale M., 1959, pp. 6–7.

7. L. F. Capovilla, *Vent'anni dalla elezione*, pp. 7–8.

8. G. Zizola (*op. cit.*, p. 99) and P. Hebblethwaite (*op. cit.*, p. 314) speak of 38 votes. Cardinal Tisserant, in a work published posthumously, spoke of only 36 votes.

9. The last pontiff with the name of John was Baldassare Cossa (1410–1415), an anti-pope during the great schism of the West who was deposed by the Council of Constance.

10. DMC, I, pp. 3–5; G. Alberigo, *Il pontificato di Giovanni XXIII* (The pontificate of John XXIII) in *La Chiesa del Vaticano II (1958–1978)* (Milan, 1994), pp. 19–20. Cf. also L. F. Capovilla, *Vent'anni dopo*, pp. 27–28.

11. A. Riccardi, *Il potere*, p. 169.

12. *Lettere*, pp. 57–60. The personal secretary of the pope places the acceptance of Tardini's name the same evening of 28 October. Giulio Nicolini speaks only of a preliminary colloquy with Tardini the evening of the 28, while reserving the following days for the confirmation of the acceptance of the appointment. G. Nicolini, *Il cardinale Domenica Tardini* (Padua, 1980), pp. 176–178; cf. also C. F. Casula, *Il cardinale Domenica Tardini*, in *Le deuxième concile du Vatican 1959–1965* (The Second Vatican Council 1959–1965) (Rome, 1989), pp. 207–227.

13. L. F. Capovilla, *Vent'anni dalla elezione*, p. 44.

14. DMC, IV, pp. 213–217, pp. 192–194. L. Algisi, *Papa Giovanni XXIII* (Genoa 1981), p. 252.

15. DMC, I, pp. 6–9.

16. DMC, I, pp. 10–14.

17. P. Hebblethwaite, *Giovanni XXIII*, p. 420.

18. M. Manzo, *Papa Giovanni: vescovo a Roma* (Pope John: Bishop of Rome) (Milan, 1991), p. 37.

19. DMC, I, pp. 39, 41.

20. L. F. Capovilla, *Vent'anni dalla elezione*, p. 37.

21. *Lettere*, p. 85.

22. Ibid., p. 87.

23. DMC, I, pp. 52–57.

24. DMC, I, pp. 539–542.

25. DMC, I, p. 542.

26. G. Ruggieri, *Appunti per una teologia in papa Roncalli*, in *Papa Giovanni*, ed. G. Alberigo (Bari, 1987), pp. 268–269.

27. L. F. Capovilla, *Vent'anni dalla elezione*, p. 46.

28. Ibid., p. 46.

29. GdA, pp. 614–616 (1041–1043).

30. Ibid., pp. 763–764.

31. DMC, II, pp. 258–259.

32. L. F. Capovilla, *Concilio Ecumenico Vaticano II: La decisione di Giovanni XXIII. Precedenti storici e motivazioni personali* in *Come si è giunti al Concilio Vaticano II*, ed. G. Galeazzi (Milan, 1988), p. 39.

33. Ibid., pp. 35–36.

34. A. Melloni, *"Questa festiva ricorrenza: Prodromi e preparazione del discorso di annuncio del Vaticano II"* in *Rivista di Storia e Letteratura religiosa* (Journal of history and religious literature), XXVII (1992), p. 617.

35. G. Caprile, *Il Concilio Vaticano II* (Vatican Council II), I (Rome, 1966), p. 40.

36. *XIV Anniversario della morte* (Fourteenth anniversary of death), ed. L. F. Capovilla (Rome, 1972), p. 37.

37. G. Alberigo, *Il pontificato di Giovanni XXIII* (The pontificate of John XXIII), p. 21.

38. So judges A. Melloni, *"Questa festiva ricorrenza,"* p. 617.

39. Ibid., pp. 618–619.

40. M. Manzo, *Papa Giovanni vescovo a Roma,* pp. 48–49.

41. L. F. Capovilla, *Il Concilio Ecumenico Vaticano II,* p. 39.

42. Ibid., pp. 39–40.

43. A. Melloni, *"Questa festiva ricorrenza,"* pp. 642–643. The author has reconstructed the various phases of the drawing up of the text. The official edition in DMC, I, pp. 129–133, presents some relevant variations concerning the manuscript.

44. DMC, IV, p. 259.

45. Fappani-Molinari, *Gianbattista Montini giovane* (The young Gianbattista Montini), Turin, 1979, p. 171.

46. L. F. Capovilla, *Il Concilio Ecumenico Vaticano II,* p. 43.

47. L. F. Capovilla, *Giovanni XXIII: Quindici Letture,* p. 268.

48. F. C. Uginet, *Les projets de concile general sous Pie XI et Pie XII* (The project of the general Council under Pius XI and Pius XII), in *Le deuxième Concile* (Rome, 1989), pp. 69–75; cf. also G. Caprile, *Il Concilio Vaticano II,* pp. 3–14.

49. F. C. Uginet, *Les projets,* pp. 75–76; E. Fouilloux, *La fase antepraeparatoria (1959–1960),* in *Storia del Concilio Vaticano II* (History of Vatican II), directed by G. Alberigo, I (Bologna, 1995), pp. 79–80.

50. G. Caprile, *Il Concilio Vaticano II,* pp. 15–35; F. C. Uginet, *Les projets,* pp. 75–78.

51. GdA, p. 610 (1033).

52. J. Forget, s.v., *Conciles* (Councils), in *Dictionnaire de théologie catholique,* III, I, col. 669.

53. G. Alberigo, *L'annuncio del Concilio. Dalle sicurezze dell'arroccamento al fascino della ricerca* (The announcement of the Council. From the security of the fortress to the fascination with inquiry), in *Storia del Concilio Vaticano II,* I, p. 58.

54. G. Zizola, *L'utopia di papa Giovanni* (Assisi, 1974), pp. 323–324.

55. G. Alberigo, *L'annuncio del Concilio,* pp. 28–29.

Chapter 15

Bishop of Rome

1. M. Manzo, *Papa Giovanni,* p. 51.

2. DMC, II, p. 128.

3. M. Manzo, p. 49.

4. Lettere, 2 February 1959, p. 58.

5. Ibid., letter to Cardinal Micara, 1 February 1959, p. 96.

6. *Adunanza della Commissione e delle Sottocommissioni per il Sinodo di Roma alla presenza del S. Padra* (The calling of the committees and subcommittees for the Synod of Rome in the presence of the Holy Father), 17 March 1959, in M. Manzo, p. 296.

7. *Verbale dell'udienza papale del 6 giugno 1959* (Text of the papal audience of 18 June 1959), in M. Manzo, pp. 305–306.

8. Lettere, to Msgr. Luigi Traglia, 25 October 1959, p. 179.

9. C. Maccari, *Straordinaria affermazione di vitalità religiosa* (An extraordinary affirmation of religious vitality), in *L'Osservatore Romano,* 26 April 1985.

10. M. Manzo, pp. 159–160.

11. L. F. Capovilla, *Natale* (Rome, 1969), pp. 11–12.

12. DMC, II, pp. 137–138.

13. Ibid., p. 153.

14. DMC, III, p. 38.

15. Lettere, p. 183.

16. M. Manzo, pp. 214–215, 278–279; J. O. Beozzo, *Il clima esterno,* in *Storia del Concilio Vaticano II,* vol. I, pp. 408–410; G. Alberigo, *Il Pontificato di Giovanni XXIII,* p. 25.

17. M. Manzo, p. 28.

18. DMC, VI, p. XVIII.

19. DMC, V, pp. 405–412.

20. M. Manzo, p. 235.

21. DMC, II, p. 602.

22. L. F. Capovilla, *Quindici letture,* p. 472.

23. DMC, I, pp. 139–140.

24. DMC, I, p. 141.

25. Ibid.

26. DMC, II, pp. 220–221.

27. M. Guasco, *La predicazione di Roncalli,* in *Papa Giovanni,* ed. G. Alberigo, p. 116.

28. DMC, III, pp. 150–156.

29. Lettere, p. 409.

30. DMC, IV, pp. 405–406.

31. L. F. Capovilla, *XIV anniversario* (Rome, 1977), p. 41.

32. Lettere, p. 466.

33. M. Manzo, pp. 268–269.

Chapter 16

Governing the Church

1. GdA, p. 572 (956–957; italics added).

2. Ibid., p. 577 (968).

3. Ibid., p. 576 (966).

4. Ibid., p. 574 (962).

5. Ibid., p. 559 (933).

6. Ibid., p. 597 (971–972; italics added).

7. Ibid., pp. 582–583 (980).

8. Ibid., pp. 581–582 (978; italics added).

9. *Enchiridion delle encicliche* (Collection of encyclicals), vol. VIII, *Giovanni XXIII — Paolo VI* (Bologna 1994), pp. 128–137.

10. L. F. Capovilla, *Vent'anni,* p. 106.

11. L. F. Capovilla, *Quindici letture* (Rome, 1970), p. 483.

12. Ibid., p. 503.

13. *Enchiridion delle encicliche,* p. 15.

14. Ibid., p. 21.

15. Ibid., p. 23.

16. Ibid., p. 25.

17. Ibid., p. 33.

18. Ibid., pp. 37–39.

19. Ibid., p. 41.

20. Ibid., p. 41.

21. Ibid., p. 69.

22. Ibid., p. 155.

23. Ibid., p. 329.

24. Ibid., pp. 347–349.

25. Ibid., pp. 331–333.

26. M. Velati, *Una difficile transizione: Il cattolicesimo tra unionismo ed ecumenismo* (A difficult transition: Catholicism between unionism and ecumenism) (Bologna, 1996), pp. 307–308.

27. DMC, II, pp. 393–394.

28. Lettere, pp. 412–413.

29. G. Alberigo, *Il Pontificato di Giovanni XXIII,* p. 27.

30. Lettere, p. 518.

31. A. Riccardi, *Dalla Chiesa di Pio XII alla Chiesa giovannea* (From the Church of Pius XII to the Church of John), in *Papa Giovanni,* ed. G. Alberigo, pp. 146–147.

32. G. Alberigo, *Il Pontificato di Giovanni XXIII,* pp. 29–30.

33. LV, to Msgr. Giuseppe Piazzi, 1 October 1958 (Bergamo, 1973), pp. 175–176.

34. G. Zizola, *Giovanni XXIII,* pp. 113–114.

35. Lettere, pp. 169–171.

36. A. Riccardi, *Il potere del papa* (The power of the pope), pp. 173–176.

37. E. Poulat, *Les prêtres ouvriers* (The worker priests) (Paris, 1999), pp. 566–568.

38. L. Alonso Schökel, *"Dove va l'esegesi cattolica?"* (Where is Catholic exegesis going?), in *La Civiltà Cattolica,* III (1960), pp. 1–12.

39. A. Romeo, *L'enciclica "Divino Afflante Spiritu" e le opinions novae* in *Divinitas,* 4, (1960), pp. 387–456.

40. M. Pesce, *"Il rinnovamento biblico"* (The biblical renewal), in *La Chiesa del Vatican II (1958–1978),* II (Milan, 1994, pp. 168–186); J. Komonchak, *"La lotta per il Concilio durante la preparazione"* in *Storia del Concilio Vaticano II,* directed by G. Alberigo, I (Bologna, 1995), pp. 297–301; G. Alberigo, *Il Pontificato di Giovanni XXIII,* p. 28.

41. DMC, I, pp. 531–533.

42. *Enchiridion della Conferenza Episcopale Italiana* (Collected works of the Italian Episcopal Conference), I, 1954–1972 (Bologna, 1985), pp. 76–95.

43. A. Riccardi, *Vescovi d'Italia* (Milan: Cinisello Balsamo, 2000), pp. 41–42.

Chapter 17

The Politics of the Pope

1. The words in italic are the text of Rosmini, between which John XXIII's added notes appear in Roman type.

2. GdA, pp. 573–574 (958–961).

3. P. Scoppola, *La Repubblica dei partiti* (The Republic of the parties), Bologna, 1991, p. 337.

4. G. Zizola, *Giovanni XXIII,* pp. 267–271.

5. DMC, III, pp. 204–205.

6. G. Zizola, *Giovanni XXIII,* pp. 272–274.

7. Ibid., pp. 275–278.

8. Ibid., p. 279.

9. *Agenda,* 16 and 18 February 1962.

10. DMC, IV, p. 419.

11. Lettere, pp. 403–405.

12. *Enchiridion delle encicliche* (Collection of encyclicals), vol. VII, *Giovanni XXIII—Paolo VI* (Bologna 1994), pp. 299–301.

13. Ibid., p. 307.

14. Ibid., p. 249.

15. Ibid., p. 307.

16. Ibid., p. 441.

17. GdA, p. 559 (931).

18. DMC, I, pp. 8–9.

19. *Enchiridion,* p. 23.

20. M. Toschi, *Giovanni XXIII e la pace* (John XXIII and peace), in *Giovanni XXIII. Tradizione del papato e della Chiesa* (Traditions of the papacy and the Church), ed. G. Alberigo (Rome, 1988), pp. 171–172.

21. DMC, II, p. 88; V, pp. 44–45.

22. M. Toschi, *Giovanni XXIII e la pace,* p. 172.

23. DMC, II, p. 387.

24. *Enchiridion,* p. 273.

25. Ibid., p. 279.

26. Lettere, pp. 302–303.

27. DMC, III, p. 410.

28. G. Zizola, *L'utopia,* pp. 169–170.

29. DMC, IV, pp. 860–861.

30. DMC, IV, pp. 614–615.

31. G. Zizola, *L'utopia,* pp. 17–25; G. Fogarty, *L'avvio dell'assemblea* (The beginning of the assembly), in *Storia del Concilio Vaticano II,* II (Bologna, 1996), pp. 114–121.

32. A. Riccardi, *Il Vaticano e Mosca* (The Vatican and Moscow) (Bari, 1992), p. 224.

33. G. Zizola, *Giovanni XXIII,* p. 181; John XXIII, Lettere, pp. 336–340.

34. S. Schmidt, *Agostino Bea: Il cardinale dell'unità* (Augustine Bea: The cardinal of unity) (Rome, 1987), pp. 672–673.

35. G. Zizola, *Giovanni XXIII,* pp. 281–293.

36. Ibid., p. 191.

37. Lettere, pp. 438–439.

38. DMC, V, p. 45.

39. G. Zizola, *L'utopia,* p. 199.

40. A. Riccardi, *Il Vaticano e Mosca,* p. 242.

41. Ibid., pp. 243–244.

42. DMC, 5, p. 123.

CHAPTER 18

Preparation for the Council

1. DMC, I, p. 690.

2. G. Alberigo, *Passaggi cruciali della fase antepraeparatoria,* in *Verso il Concilio Vaticano II 1960–1962,* ed. G. Alberigo and A. Melloni (Genoa, 1933), pp. 21–24.

3. G. Alberigo, *L'annuncio del Concilio,* p. 66.

4. E. Fouilloux, *La fase antepraeparatoria 1959–1960,* in *Storia del Concilio Vaticano II,* pp. 152–156.

5. Ibid., pp. 156–160.

6. R. Morozzo Della Rocca, *I "vota" dei vescovi italiani per il Concilio* (The "votes" of the Italian bishops through the Council), in *Le deuxième concile du Vatican 1959–1965,* pp. 119–137.

7. Fondo Roncalli, *Agenda Note Concilio Vaticano II, 1958–1962* (The agenda of Vatican Council II), 19 February 1960, pp. 15–17.

8. Ibid., 11 February 1960, p. 47.

9. Ibid., 3 March 1960, p. 18.

10. Ibid., 24 March 1960, p. 29.

11. DMC, II, pp. 393–394.

12. A. Indelicato, *Formazione e composizione delle commissioni preparatorie* (Formation and composition of the preparatory committees), in *Verso il Concilio Vaticano II 1960–1962,* pp. 43–69.

13. G. Caprile, *Il Concilio Vaticano II,* I, 1, p. 181, n. 18.

14. DMC, III, pp. 15–26 (Rome, 1965), pp. 17–21.

15. DMC, III, p. 18; IV, pp. 867–869.

16. DMC, IV, p. 868; III, pp. 18–19.

17. DMC, IV, pp. 867–868.

18. DMC, III, pp. 19–24.

19. DMC, IV, p. 163.

20. DMC, IV, p. 92.

21. J. Komonchak, *La lotta per il Concilio durante la preparazione* (The struggle for the Council during the preparations), in *Storia del Concilio Vaticano II,* I, p. 370.

22. G. Caprile, *Il Concilio Vaticano II* (The second Vatican Council), I, 2, p. 279, no. 6; L. J. Suenens, *Ricordi e speranze* (Memories and hopes) (Milan: Cinisello Balsamo, 1993), p. 108.

23. G. Lercaro, *Linee per una ricerca storica* (Rome, 1965), pp. 17–21.

24. J. Komonchak, *La lotta per il Concilio,* p. 376.

25. G. Zizola, *Il microfono di Dio,* pp. 443–464.

26. J. Komonchak, *La lotta per il Concilio,* pp. 237–240.

27. Lettere, to all the bishops in the world, 15 April 1962, p. 377.

28. *Acta et documenta concilio ecumenico Vaticano II apparando* (Acts and documents of the Second Vatican Council), IV, 1, pp. 253–280.

29. J. Komonchak, *La lotta per il Concilio,* pp. 338–362.

30. L. J. Suenens, *"Aux origines du Concile Vatican II"* (The origins of Vatican II) in *Nouvelle Revue Théologique,* 105 (1985), 1, pp. 3–21; ID, *Ricordi e speranze,* pp. 76–96.

31. Lettere, pp. 535–536.

32. DMC, IV, p. 386.

33. J. Komonchak, *La lotta per il Concilio,* pp. 367–368.

34. L. J. Suenens, *Aux origins,* pp. 9–10; J. Komonchak, *La Battaglia,* p. 369.

35. L. J. Suenens, *Ricordi e speranze,* p. 97.

Chapter 19

Ecumenism

1. M. Velati, c. *Il cattolicesimo tra universalismo ed ecumenismo 1952–1964* (Bologna, 1996), pp. 44–47.

2. S. Schmidt, *Agostino Bea: Il cardinale dell'unità,* p. 342.

3. Ibid., p. 868.

4. Ibid., p. 878.

5. S. Schmidt, *Agostino Bea: Cardinale dell'ecumenismo e del dialogo* (Milan: Cinisello Balsamo, 1996), p. 7.

6. S. Schmidt, *Agostino Bea. Il cardinale dell'unità,* pp. 879–880.

7. Ibid., p. 878.

8. Ibid., pp. 344–346; M. Velati, *Una difficile transizione,* pp. 185–190.

9. M. Velati, *Una difficile transizione,* pp. 197–199; S. Schmidt, *Agostino Bea,* pp. 348–349.

10. G. Caprile, *Il Concilio Vaticano II,* II, 1, pp. 303–304; S. Schmidt, *Agostino Bea,* pp. 366–367.

11. M. Velati, *Una difficile transizione,* pp. 209–210.

12. L. F. Capovilla, *Giovanni XXIII nel ricordo,* op. cit., pp. 77–78.

13. DMC, II, pp. 396–397.

14. S. Schmidt, *Agostino Bea,* pp. 434–435.

15. J. Komonchak, *La lotta durante la preparazione,* p. 311.

16. Ibid., pp. 318–320; S. Schmidt, *Agostino Bea,* pp. 397–399.

17. DMC, I, p. 288.

18. M. Velati, *Una difficile transizione,* pp. 280–281.

19. Ibid., p. 267; S. Schmidt, *Agostino Bea,* pp. 378–380.

20. S. Schmidt, *Agostino Bea,* pp. 496–497.

21. DMC, IV, pp. 609–610.
22. G. Zizola, *Giovanni XXIII: La fede e la politica*, p. 237.
23. M. Velati, *Una difficile transizione*, pp. 326–329.
24. G. Caprile, *Il Concilio Vaticano II*, II, p. 56.
25. M. Velati, *Una difficile transizione*, pp. 321–323.
26. Lettere, p. 484.
27. J. O. Beozzo, *"Il clima esterno,"* in *Storia del Concilio Vaticano II*, pp. 417–418.
28. S. Schmidt, *Agostino Bea*, pp. 351–355.
29. DMC, II, p. 698.
30. Agenda, 17 October 1940.
31. E. Toaff, *Perfidi guide—fratelli maggiori* (Milan, 1987), pp. 219–220.
32. S. Schmidt, *Agostino Bea*, p. 374.
33. Ibid., p. 400; J. O. Beozzo, *Il clima esterno*, p. 421.
34. Lettere, pp. 561–562.

Chapter 20

The First Session of Vatican II

1. GdA, p. 608 (1030).
2. Lettere, p. 352.
3. *Enchiridion delle encicliche*, p. 519.
4. AAS, LI, p. 832.
5. Lettere, p. 393.
6. GdA, p. 614 (1040).
7. Ibid., p. 615 (1042).
8. Ibid., p. 614 (1042).
9. Ibid., p. 615 (1043).
10. Ibid., p. 616 (1043).
11. DMC, IV, p. 557.
12. Ibid., p. 564.
13. Agenda, 4 October 1962.
14. K. Wittstadt, *Alla vigilia del Concilio* (On the eve of the Council), in *Storia del Concilio Vaticano II*, p. 465.
15. P. Hebblethwaite, *Giovanni XXIII*, p. 599.
16. GdA, p. 607 (1028).
17. L. J. Suenens, *Ricordi e speranze*, p. 109.
18. P. Hebblethwaite, *Giovanni XXIII*, p. 599.
19. K. Wittstadt, *Alla vigilia*, pp. 467 ff.
20. DMC, IV, p. 521.
21. Ibid., p. 523.
22. Ibid., p. 524.
23. K. Wittstadt, *Alla vigilia*, pp. 500 ff.

24. A. Riccardi, *La tumultuosa apertura dei lavori* in *Storia del Concilio Vaticano II,* II, pp. 30–34.

25. A. Melloni, *Sinossi critica dell'allocuzione di apertura del Concilio Vaticano II, "Gaudet Mater Ecclesia," di Giovanni XXIII* (Critical synopsis of the allocution opening Vatican II, "Gaudet Mater Ecclesia," of John XXIII), in *Fede, Tradizione, Profezia* (Faith, Tradition, Prophecy) (Brescia, 1984), pp. 246–247.

26. A. Melloni, *Sinossi,* p. 251.

27. Ibid., pp. 255–256.

28. Ibid., pp. 253–255.

29. Ibid., p. 264.

30. Ibid., pp. 267–269.

31. Ibid., p. 271.

32. Iaüt., pp. 272–273.

33. A. Melloni, *Giovanni XXIII e il Vaticano II* (John XXIII and Vatican II), in *Vatican II commence* (Vatican II begins), p. 75.

34. A. Bertuletti, *Il Magistero pastorale di Giovanni XXIII* (The pastoral magisterium of John XXIII), in *Echi di papa Giovanni,* 20 (1999), 1, p. 22.

35. Discourse, 4 November 1962; DMC, V, p. 13; discourse, 23 December 1962: DMC, 5, pp. 55–56.

36. G. Alberigo, *L'itinerario spirituale di papa Giovanni* (The spiritual journey of Pope John), in *Servitium,* 22 (1988), 59–60, pp. 43–45; G. Battelli, *Angelo Giuseppe Roncalli e Francesco Pitocchi* in *Fede, Tradizione, Profezia,* pp. 39 ff.

37. DMC, IV, p. 592.

38. Ibid., p. 593.

39. Agenda, 11 October 1962.

40. G. Alberigo, *"Imparare da sé." L'esperienza conciliare* ("To learn from itself." The conciliar experience) in *Storia del Concilio Vaticano II,* pp. 621–622.

41. A. Riccardi, *La tumultuosa apertura,* pp. 85–86.

42. R. Aubert, *Lo svolgimento del Concilio* (The unfolding of the Council), in *La Chiesa del Vaticano II: Storia della Chiesa* (The Church of Vatican II: The history of the Church), XXV/1 (Milan, 1994), p. 229.

43. A. Riccardi, *La tumultuosa apertura,* p. 69.

44. M. Lamberigts, *Il dibattito sulla liturgia* (The debate on the liturgy), in *Storia del Concilio Vaticano II,* II, pp. 172–173; R. Aubert, *Lo svolgimento del Concilio,* p. 235.

45. G. Ruggieri, *Il primo conflitto dottrinale* (The first doctrinal conflict) in *Storia del Concilio Vaticano II,* II, pp. 282–283.

46. Ibid., pp. 276–282.

47. S. Schmidt, *Agostino Bea,* p. 458.

48. Lettere, pp. 434–435.

49. S. Schmidt, *Agostino Bea,* p. 458.

50. G. Ruggieri, *Il primo conflitto dottrinale,* pp. 289–293.

51. L. J. Suenens, *Ricordi e speranze,* p. 84.

52. R. Aubert, *Lo svolgimento del Concilio,* p. 243.

53. G. Ruggieri, *Il difficile abbandono della teologia controversista* (The difficult abandoning of theological controversy), in *Storia del Concilio Vaticano II,* II, p. 372.

54. M. Lamberigts, *Il dibattito sulla liturgia,* p. 192.

55. DMC, V, pp. 24–31.

56. Lettere, pp. 440–450.

57. G. Alberigo, *"Imparare da sé,"* p. 621.

58. J. Grootaers, *Il concilio si gioca nell'intervalla. La seconda preparazione e i suoi avversari* (The council shifts course. The second preparation and its adversaries) in *Storia del Concilio Vaticano II,* II, pp. 506–507.

CHAPTER 21

The Final Months

1. P. Hebblethwaite, *Giovanni XXIII,* p. 660.

2. Lettere, pp. 569–570.

3. DMC, V, pp. 148–151.

4. Lettere, p. 456.

5. G. Zizola, *L'utopia,* pp. 159–161; L. F. Capovilla, *Giovanni XXIII,* pp. 457–463.

6. *Enchiridion delle encicliche,* p. 467.

7. DMC, V, p. 247.

8. Ibid., pp. 251–253.

9. L. F. Capovilla, *Giovanni XXIII,* pp. 464–465.

10. G. Zizola, *Giovanni XXIII,* p. 199.

11. Ibid., pp. 199–200.

12. A. Riccardi, *Il Vaticano e Mosca,* pp. 252–255.

13. Lettere, pp. 454–456; G. Zizola, *L'utopia,* pp. 216–219.

14. A. Riccardi, *Il Vaticano e Mosca,* pp. 253–256.

15. Ibid., p. 257.

16. Lettere, pp. 455–456.

17. Ibid., p. 454.

18. G. Zizola, *Giovanni XXIII,* p. 202.

19. Ibid., p. 207.

20. DMC, V, pp. 163–164.

21. A. Riccardi, *Il Vaticano e Mosca,* p. 236.

22. Ibid., pp. 258–259.

23. G. Zizola, *L'utopia,* p. 247.

24. L. F. Capovilla, *Ite missa est* (Padua, 1983), p. 180.

25. G. Zizola, *Giovanni XXIII,* pp. 238–239; G. Alberigo, *Il pontificato di Giovanni XXIII* (The pontificate of John XXIII), p. 42.

26. DMC, V, pp. 192–193.

27. Ibid., p. 193.

28. *Enchiridion delle encicliche,* p. 387; G. Martina, *La chiesa nell'età del liberalismo* (The Church in the age of liberalism) (Brescia, 1995), p. 272, n. 6.

29. *Enchiridion,* p. 387.

30. Ibid., pp. 399–403.

31. Ibid., p. 437.

32. Ibid., p. 443.

33. Ibid., p. 439.

34. Ibid., p. 461.

35. Ibid., p. 463.

36. G. Zizola, *Giovanni XXIII*, p. 243.

37. A. Riccardi, *Il Vaticano e Mosca*, pp. 260–261.

38. L. F. Capovilla, *Giovanni XXIII*, p. 461.

39. Ibid., p. 453.

40. Ibid., pp. 453–458.

41. G. Zizola, *L'utopia*, p. 453.

42. L. F. Capovilla, *Giovanni XXIII*, pp. 471–472.

43. Ibid., pp. 473–474.

44. Ibid., p. 475.

45. Ibid., pp. 478–481.

46. Ibid., pp. 482–485.

47. Ibid., pp. 493–494.

48. Ibid., p. 481.

49. Cited by J. Grootaers, *Il concilio si gioca nell'intervalla: La seconda preparazione e i suoiavversari,* in *Storia del Concilio Vaticano II,* II, p. 534, n. 350.

BOOKS & MEDIA

The Daughters of St. Paul operate book and media centers at the following addresses. Visit, call or write the one nearest you today, or find us on the World Wide Web, www.pauline.org

CALIFORNIA
3908 Sepulveda Blvd, Culver City, CA 90230   310-397-8676
5945 Balboa Avenue, San Diego, CA 92111   858-565-9181
46 Geary Street, San Francisco, CA 94108   415-781-5180

FLORIDA
145 S.W. 107th Avenue, Miami, FL 33174   305-559-6715

HAWAII
1143 Bishop Street, Honolulu, HI 96813   808-521-2731
Neighbor Islands call: 800-259-8463

ILLINOIS
172 North Michigan Avenue, Chicago, IL 60601   312-346-4228

LOUISIANA
4403 Veterans Memorial Blvd, Metairie, LA 70006   504-887-7631

MASSACHUSETTS
Rte. 1, 885 Providence Hwy, Dedham, MA 02026   781-326-5385

MISSOURI
9804 Watson Road, St. Louis, MO 63126   314-965-3512

NEW JERSEY
561 U.S. Route 1, Wick Plaza, Edison, NJ 08817   732-572-1200

NEW YORK
150 East 52nd Street, New York, NY 10022   212-754-1110
78 Fort Place, Staten Island, NY 10301   718-447-5071

OHIO
2105 Ontario Street (at Prospect Avenue), Cleveland, OH 44115
  216-621-9427

PENNSYLVANIA
9171-A Roosevelt Blvd, Philadelphia, PA 19114   215-676-9494

SOUTH CAROLINA
243 King Street, Charleston, SC 29401   843-577-0175

TENNESSEE
4811 Poplar Avenue, Memphis, TN 38117   901-761-2987

TEXAS
114 Main Plaza, San Antonio, TX 78205   210-224-8101

VIRGINIA
1025 King Street, Alexandria, VA 22314   703-549-3806

CANADA
3022 Dufferin Street, Toronto, Ontario, Canada M6B 3T5
  416-781-9131
1155 Yonge Street, Toronto, Ontario, Canada M4T 1W2
  416-934-3440

¡También somos su fuente para libros, videos y música en español!